Tax policy in the real world

This volume collects articles from the Symposium series of the *National Tax Journal* from 1993 to 1998. Leading economists and other scholars discuss and debate current tax policy issues in nontechnical language and illustrate how the principles of tax analysis can be applied to real-world issues. Among the topics addressed are the practical feasibility of consumption tax alternatives to the current income tax, the rationale and implications of devolution of fiscal responsibilities to state and local governments, the effect of tax policy on economic growth, and the value of local tax incentives designed to attract and retain business.

Joel Slemrod is the Paul W. McCracken Collegiate Professor of Business Economics and Public Policy at the University of Michigan Business School, and Professor of Economics in the Department of Economics. He also serves as Director of the Office of Tax Policy Research, an interdisciplinary research center housed at the Business School, where he has taught since 1987. Previously Professor Slemrod was a national Fellow at the Hoover Institution and in 1984–85 was the senior staff economist for tax policy at the President's Council of Economic Advisers. Professor Slemrod is currently editor of the *National Tax Journal,* the leading academic journal devoted to the theory and practice of taxation. He has been a consultant to the U.S. Department of the Treasury, the Canadian Department of Finance, the New Zealand Department of Treasury, the World Bank, and the OECD; coordinator of the National Bureau of Economic Research project in international taxation; and has testified before the Congress on domestic and international taxation issues. He is the author of numerous academic articles and editor of the books *Do Taxes Matter?: The Impact of the Tax Reform Act of 1986, Taxation in the Global Economy, Why People Pay Taxes: Tax Compliance and Enforcement, Studies in International Taxation, Tax Progressivity and Income Inequality,* and *The Taxation of Multinational Corporations.* He is co-author, with Jon Bakija, of *Taxing Ourselves: A Citizen's Guide to the Great Debate over Tax Reform.*

Tax policy in the real world

Edited by
JOEL SLEMROD
University of Michigan

PUBLISHED BY THE PRESS SYNDICATE OF THE UNIVERSITY OF CAMBRIDGE
The Pitt Building, Trumpington Street, Cambridge, United Kingdom

CAMBRIDGE UNIVERSITY PRESS
The Edinburgh Building, Cambridge CB2 2RU, UK   http://www.cup.cam.ac.uk
40 West 20th Street, New York, NY 10011-4211, USA   http://www.cup.org
10 Stamford Road, Oakleigh, Melbourne 3166, Australia

First published 1999

Printed in the United States of America

Typeset in Times, Desktop Publishing

A catalog record for this book is available from the British Library.

Library of Congress Cataloging-in-Publication Data

Tax policy in the real world / edited by Joel Slemrod.
      p.   cm.
   Includes index.
   ISBN 0-521-64137-3. — ISBN 0-521-64644-8 (pbk.)
   1. Taxation. 2. Fiscal policy. I. Slemrod, Joel.
HJ2305.T179   1998
336.2—dc21   98-31981
                                                 CIP

ISBN 0 521 64137 3 hardback
ISBN 0 521 64644 8 paperback

Contents

Contents

Public finance and public choice
James M. Poterba

Contributors

Jonas Agell
Uppsala University

James Alm
University of Colorado at Boulder

Alan J. Auerbach
University of California, Berkeley

Timothy J. Bartik
W. E. Upjohn Institute for Employment Research

Richard M. Bird
University of Toronto

Paul N. Courant
University of Michigan

Eric Engen
Federal Reserve Board of Governors

Peter Englund
Uppsala University

Alan L. Feld
Boston University

William G. Gale
The Brookings Institution

Martin D. Ginsburg
Georgetown University Law Center

Steven D. Gold
The Urban Institute

Edward N. Gramlich
Federal Reserve Board of Governors

Jane G. Gravelle
Congressional Research Service

Harry Grubert
Office of Tax Analysis

Walter Hettich
California State University

Randall G. Holcombe
Florida State University

R. Glenn Hubbard
Columbia University

Louis Kaplow
Harvard Law School

Michael Keen
University of Essex

Helen F. Ladd
Duke University

John L. Mikesell
Indiana University

Matthew N. Murray
University of Tennessee

T. Scott Newlon
Office of Tax Analysis

William H. Oakland
Tulane University

Wallace E. Oates
University of Maryland

James M. Poterba
Massachusetts Institute of Technology

John M. Quigley
University of California, Berkeley

Andrew Reschovsky
University of Wisconsin

Daniel L. Rubinfeld
University of California, Berkeley

Jonathan Skinner
Dartmouth College

Joel Slemrod
University of Michigan

Jan Södersten
Uppsala University

Peter Birch Sørensen
Copenhagen Business School

Stanley Winer
Carleton University

John Yinger
Syracuse University

CHAPTER 1

THE REAL WORLD OF TAX POLICY

JOEL SLEMROD[*]

THE REAL WORLD

Over the past half century, the academic analysis of taxation has become more technical, increasingly involving sophisticated mathematics and statistics.[1] For this reason, its language and reasoning have become less and less accessible to those outside academia. Academics hoping to influence the policy process have to think carefully about how to "translate" what they know into what can be convincing and useful for policy. Even those who think carefully about this translation have, I suspect, often been greeted by a dismissive reply that begins, "Yes, but in the real world . . ."

What is it about the real world, or about the modern analysis of taxation, that reduces the potential contribution of academics to the policy process? I can think of four problems.

(1) The real world is more complicated than highly stylized economic models allow.

(2) The models are too complicated to be of use in the real world.

(3) A real-world tax system needs to be administered and enforced, and some tax systems that look

promising on paper fail on these practical grounds.

(4) The tax system is forged within a political process that constrains what can be accomplished.

The purpose of the Symposium section of the *National Tax Journal*, which debuted in the June 1993 issue, is to bridge the gap between academics and those who live in the trenches of the real world. For each Symposium, experts—both scholars and practitioners—were commissioned to write nontechnical papers on the leading policy issues of the day, or to reflect on what first principles should inform the policy process. Most of the Symposium pieces have been collected in this volume; only a few papers about particular policy proposals have been deleted.[2]

The papers have been organized into three sections. The following section deals with reforms of the federal tax system; next is a set of papers on federalism and subfederal taxes. The final section contains essays on tax principles and how those principles get translated into practice.

REFORM OF THE FEDERAL TAX SYSTEM

That real-world perceptions of how the tax system works often differ markedly

*Office of Tax Policy Research, University of Michigan Business School, Ann Arbor, MI 48109-1234

from the perceptions of tax "experts" is well illustrated by the corporation income tax: it remains popular among taxpayers, but generally gets low marks from academics. For many reasons,[3] its importance as a revenue raiser has declined markedly over the last few decades; in 1950, it raised 6.0 percent of GDP; by 1994, that share had fallen to 2.5 percent.

The June 1995 Symposium addressed the problems and promise of the corporation income tax. First, Jane Gravelle reviews the modern debate about it, addressing (1) who pays the corporate tax—capital, labor, or consumers—and whether it plays a role in a progressive federal tax system; (2) how significant are the economic distortions it causes, and (3) are there feasible, sensible revisions? She concludes that most extensions and alternatives to the now-classic model of Harberger (1962) share its conclusion that the burden of the corporate income tax falls largely on capital, which supports some role for the tax in maintaining the progressivity of the tax system. However, because the tax appears to produce large distortions relative to its yield, there is certainly a payoff to fundamental reform. She advocates a gradual movement in the direction of what the U.S. Treasury dubbed the Comprehensive Business Income Tax (CBIT). Under CBIT, all business income—both from debt and equity—would be taxed at the firm level; firms would not be able to deduct interest, but this interest would not be taxed to the recipient, nor would dividends.

While the U.S. debate on its classical corporate tax plods on, most European countries have already enacted measures to alleviate the double taxation of corporate-source income, e.g., by granting a credit for the underlying corporate tax against the personal tax of dividends and/or by offering favorable personal tax treatment of capital gains on shares. European economists have also been at the frontier of new ways of thinking about the impact of the corporate income tax. In the companion paper of the June 1995 Symposium, Peter Sørensen reviews these new models. He discusses three new developments: Sinn's (1991) dynamic "nucleus" theory of the firm, in which the double taxation of dividends increases the cost of capital during the growth phase (when the firm does not pay dividends), whereas the dividend tax will be neutral for mature firms (when dividends are paid); the theories of Kannainen and Södersten (1994), which highlight the importance of accounting conventions, which constrain the amount of dividends distributed; and models that stress the importance of cross-country capital mobility. Sørenson concludes that, although the new theories lead to rather different predictions about the influence of tax policy on the cost of corporate capital, there is broad agreement that the policy of double taxation of dividends hampers the growth of young and expanding firms and that, for analysis, it is critical to distinguish between taxes on saving and taxes on investment when analyzing the impact of different components of the corporate tax system in the open economy.

The March 1997 and December 1995 Symposia looked in detail at proposals to replace the income tax entirely with various versions of a consumption tax: the Hall–Rabushka flat tax, a personal expenditure tax called the unlimited savings allowance (USA) tax, and a national retail sales tax (NRST). In contrast to the first two kinds of tax systems, the United States has a lot of experience with the retail sales tax, albeit at the state and local level. Because no country operates either of the first two, one must speculate about what problems would arise; in the case of a retail sales tax, we can do better than that, by examining the real-world experiences of the states.

In their Symposium papers, neither John Mikesell nor Matthew Murray is sanguine about the prospect of a NRST replacing the federal income tax. Mikesell argues that, while the sales taxes are impressive revenue producers for state and local governments, they are poorly designed as consumption taxes: they tax too few household services, they exempt too many household purchases of goods, and they tax too many business inputs, especially capital asset purchases. Currently, state and local sales tax rates are relatively low, so compliance appears not to be a major problem, and economic distortions, while real, have not been very costly. However, as Mikesell points out, the much higher rates needed to replace the federal income tax—arguably over 30 percent—would create many more problems.

Moreover, Mikesell concludes that attempting to levy a national tax as a supplement to state sales taxes would be folly, because there is too little uniformity in what states tax and what they exclude to allow a linked federal tax to be fair and efficient. On the other hand, a separate NRST would complicate the work of state tax collection, increase the problems that businesses face in complying with multiple tax bases, and tax on a base not equal to household consumption. He concludes that other countries probably have it right when they use the value-added taxes to raise considerable revenue at the national level, because, in practice, such taxes using the credit-invoice method more fully exclude business purchases from tax, more completely tax household purchases than do retail sales taxes, and leave a better trail for enforcement.

Murray focuses on the avenues for avoidance and evasion under an NRST and discusses the implications for the underground economy. He argues that, although an NRST would benefit from relatively positive taxpayer attitudes toward compliance that prevail in the United States, incentives and opportunities for both tax avoidance and tax evasion will be sustained, although the specific avenues for reducing one's tax liability may change. Moreover, administrative enforcement will be hampered by the high costs associated with observing taxable transactions (especially in the context of services), not unlike the current system of income taxation.

Murray acknowledges that there are certain features of the proposals for an NRST that may constrain abuse, including one proposal's requirement of tax (and subsequent provision of tax credits) on dual-use inputs and another proposal's use of rebatable input taxes and formal filings with the tax administration. But there will be ample avoidance opportunities, including de minimis provisions for international purchases and casual sales, and potentially serious evasion problems associated with the concentration of revenue at the retail stage and input credit fraud.

The real world contains an army of professionals who look for inconsistencies or "loopholes" in the income tax, in order to benefit their clients. That some, but not all, taxpayers exploit these loopholes causes inequities; moreover, the loopholes cost the government revenue, which in turn requires higher tax rates than otherwise on the narrower base. Some of these problems arise because of ill-advised intentions of the legislators, but, as Bradford (1986) has eloquently argued, others are inevitable in any income tax, given the inherent conceptual difficulties of measuring real capital income. It is these inescapable difficulties that have led many tax experts to advocate a consumption tax base.

However, given the complexity of most corporations and many individuals' financial situations, it may be that any equitable tax system would be riven with complexity. At a minimum, we should take a hard look at tax systems that exist only in blueprint in order to be sure that they would work well in the complex real world.

The December 1995 Symposium subjected two leading consumption tax proposals to the sharp pencils of tax lawyers, to foresee what problems might arise in the real world. Martin Ginsburg examined the USA tax system, which combines a broad-based graduated personal consumption tax with a subtraction-method value-added tax on business entities. Ginsburg concluded that the USA tax was riddled with inconsistencies, producing a world "in which municipal bonds pay interest in even years only, executive compensation and the yield on at least one class of each corporation's stock is paid only in odd years, and the rich with borrowed money buy new land or works of art they admire but may not expect to keep forever" (p. 585). Ginsburg does not, though, condemn the cash-flow personal consumption tax model out of hand, arguing that such a tax, which includes borrowed amounts in the tax base but does not hold the recovery of pre-enactment basis hostage to taxpayers' postenactment conduct, will perform better than the USA plan.

Nevertheless, it is sobering that a serious attempt to move the personal consumption tax beyond the blueprint stage to the real world, including addressing the difficult issues of transition, falls short of Ginsburg's standards for a successful tax system.

In the companion paper, Alan Feld takes a look at what life would be like under the Hall–Rabushka flat tax. Feld accepts that the tax would eliminate at least four features of the current income tax system that create complexity—bracket arbitrage, recovery of investment over different time periods, the capital gains–ordinary income distinction, and arbitrage between different accounting systems. He argues, though, that other causes of complexity in the present income tax would remain and that new distinctions created under a flat tax would require new statutory solutions. Feld concludes that, in addressing these concerns, "something will give way in their resolution: the revenue yield, the simplicity of the tax, or the simplicity of the business transactions that will take place" (p. 615). Although Feld cautions that a real-world flat tax would not be as simple as its proponents might proclaim, there is wide agreement that it would certainly be simpler than the current income tax, at least in terms of lower administrative and compliance costs.

Harry Grubert and Scott Newlon's paper reminds us that international considerations can significantly affect the projected effects of replacing the U.S. income tax with a consumption tax. They argue, contrary to the general view, that such a shift could either decrease or increase the U.S. capital stock, because, although equity capital would flow into the United States, debt capital might flow out. The authors also cast doubt on whether such a shift would be welfare-improving. The likely net return of U.S. capital exports would be a plus, but the United States would give up some tax revenue from foreign equity investment in the country. Grubert and Newlon accept that a consumption tax would permit substantial simplification of existing international tax rules, but note that it would raise some new administrative and compliance issues. They also compare destination basis taxes, in which there are adjustments at the border, with origin basis taxes in regard to their effect on trade, the location of investment and consumption, transition incidence, and compliance problems.

FISCAL FEDERALISM AND DECENTRALIZATION

Throughout the world, there is no more controversial economic issue than the appropriate division of fiscal (and other) responsibility between the national government and subnational jurisdictions, and between national and supranational entities. The U.S. debate on this subject has recently led to a devolution of responsibility, from the federal to state governments, for the country's principal income maintenance program, Aid to Families with Dependent Children, or welfare. Two separate *National Tax Journal* Symposia have dealt with federalism and fiscal decentralization. In the debut Symposium in the June 1993 issue, three of the most insightful academics working on these topics— Richard Bird, Edward Gramlich, and Wallace Oates—addressed these issues.

Richard Bird discusses the meaning and rationale for fiscal decentralization, arguing that the objectives and context are critical to evaluating any component of the process. He takes as his starting point that the primary objective is to improve efficiency. From this perspec-

tive, he argues that local revenues should be as clearly benefit-related as possible—user charges are best, local property taxes have some attractions, but local income taxes may be even better. Bird also argues that intergovernmental transfers are invariably necessary if local governments are responsible for significant expenditures, but that a good case can be made for tax capacity equalization conditioned on local expenditure performance. He concludes with cautions that policy recommendations in specific instances can be decided only on the basis of close study of the local terrain, and specific institutional knowledge is essential.

Gramlich also addresses decentralization strategies, but from the perspective of Musgrave's (1959) three branches of government—allocation, distribution, and macroeconomic stabilization. He sides with Bird that the provision of public services should be done at the lowest level possible and that user fees and local income and property taxes are valuable forms of local finance; matching grants are the best way to deal both with benefit spillovers and disparate abilities to finance human capital distributional programs. Gramlich, though, breaks with Bird and most public finance economists by arguing that distributional programs should be a mixed responsibility of the national and local governments, and that regional business cycles can be counteracted by subnational governments running rainy day funds or borrowing from designated trust funds.

Oates' contribution to the fiscal decentralization Symposium addresses a more focused question—the relationship between decentralization and economic development, and what to make of the empirical observation that developed countries, on average, have more decentralized fiscal systems. Oates argues that whether the theoretical case for decentralization—that local outputs can be differentiated according to local tastes and outputs—applies in the real world depends on several factors, including whether local governments are less corruptible than national governments. Oates also argues that local governments must raise a significant portion of their funds from their own revenue sources, in order to preserve local fiscal independence and preserve the incentives for responsible local decisions. Second, local governments often do not have the administrative capacity to implement appropriate benefit taxes such as a property tax. Oates concludes that the potential of decentralized finances to promote economic development depends on the proper structure of local institutions.

The June 1996 Symposium revisited fiscal federalism in light of recent U.S. initiatives to "devolve" certain previously federal responsibilities to the states—the so-called "devolution revolution." John Quigley and Daniel Rubinfeld view these trends with some trepidation. They recognize that devolution does provide a significant opportunity to reduce the central government budget, but question whether devolution is supported by federalist principles. Moreover, they argue that there is no systematic evidence suggesting a better management capacity by local governments. They argue that a switch from open-ended matching grants to block grants of fixed size will, because of moderate price elasticities of response, reduce the aggregate size of these programs. Much of the budgetary savings comes from the elimination of federally imposed rules for program eligibility and participation; it is the elimination of the entitlement aspects of the programs that

permits them to be devolved to the states.

Steven Gold's contribution to the Symposium stresses the implications of the devolution developments for public finance research and is concerned with two related questions: how can research be improved so that it is better able to explain the policy choices that state and local governments are making, and what can be done to make research more useful to state policymakers? Gold cautions that researchers should avoid the pitfall of placing too much emphasis on policies adopted in the one or two years after devolution goes into effect. He stresses the importance of using appropriate data and lays out the strengths and weaknesses of the data provided by the Census Bureau, as well as by the states themselves and the national organizations of state governments. Finally, he emphasizes the importance of disaggregation, both by state and by type of spending program, because the nature and responsiveness of these programs will not be monolithic.

The March 1994 Symposium addressed one of the most controversial aspects of intergovernmental relations—the attempts by state governments at "fiscal equalization" in the financing of public education. Andrew Reschovsky reviews states' experience with fiscal equalization and concludes that the most compelling goal is one that requires state governments to guarantee that all children are provided with an adequate education without placing an unreasonably high property tax burden on residents. He argues that attention paid to taxpayer equity, instead of student-based equity, is misguided. The student-based equity goal can be achieved by using a cost-adjusted foundation formula, with the foundation spending level adjusted by a cost index reflecting the costs of providing education services that are beyond the control of local school officials, and where each school district is required to levy a minimum tax rate.

Helen Ladd and John Yinger agree that it is important to be clear on the precise equity objective to be achieved by a state equalization program. In their paper, they show that many different categorical equity objectives can be attained with an appropriately designed equalizing aid program. They draw out the similarities and differences among formulas in a common framework, show how to incorporate cost considerations into the various aid formulas, and highlight the role of capitalization of property taxes in the objective of equalizing real incomes. They agree with Reschovsky that the appropriate approach for elementary and secondary education is a cost-adjusted foundation plan with a minimum tax rate and a relatively high minimum service level.

In the closing essay of this Symposium, William Oakland takes issue with the general approval of appropriately designed equalization plans expressed by both Reschovsky and Ladd–Yinger. He argues that, as a means of addressing inequalities, such plans are poorly targeted and often seem based on a dubious primacy of public goods and services. Moreover, as a means of equalizing regional disparities in resource endowments, they may give rise to both inequities and inefficiencies. Finally, Oakland opposes extension of equalization to cover cost disparities in the provision of public services, advocated by the authors of both of the other contributions to this Symposium, and argues that direct targets of aid to the poor by the federal government is a superior policy.

One perennial issue for subfederal governments is how generous to be with "economic development" programs—programs that assist individual businesses with tax or financial subsidies, or special public services. These programs aim to increase local jobs or improve local business "competitiveness," somehow defined. Although increasingly popular in the real world, they have been widely criticized by economists and others, often because they generally feature a high revenue cost per job "created" and because the local governments ignore any costs imposed on the residents of the places from which the businesses are attracted.

The fact that in the previous paragraph so many phrases are surrounded by quotation marks suggests that semantics—or to be precise, the prominence of loosely defined buzzwords—is a problem in this area. The objective of the December 1994 Symposium was to clarify what lessons economic theory can offer to state and local governments contemplating economic development programs. In his paper, Paul Courant urges that attention be directed away from job creation and directed toward the ultimate welfare of citizens. His review of the issues leads him to conclude that governments interested in increasing local economic welfare should focus on efficiently providing local public services and on taxing mobile factors according to the benefit principle. He argues that neither of these principles justifies fiscal incentives to industrial location, except insofar as pre-existing taxes exceed benefit taxes. Courant also considers why economists and local politicians (the academy versus the real world?) hold such divergent views about jobs, and speculates that it is because people place a high value on insuring a way of life in a place of one's choice. However, providing effective insurance of this kind—especially if it means shoring up increasingly unproductive activities—is very expensive.

Timothy Bartik is somewhat more sanguine about the value of research on the costs and effectiveness of economic development programs in creating jobs and enhancing productivity. We know some useful things, he asserts: that tax incentives for economic development are not self-financing, but have significant costs per job created, and that some programs that promote productivity appear to be effective. He recommends that state and local policymakers target subsidies more carefully, in particular to high unemployment areas, and that policies place more emphasis on improving business productivity, such as worker training. Furthermore, metropolitan cooperation is essential, to prevent competition for jobs within a labor market.

PRINCIPLES, POLITICS, AND THE PROFESSORS

As every public finance textbook repeats, tax policy should be judged by the criteria of equity, efficiency, and simplicity. Going much beyond that statement immediately involves difficult issues of values, measurement, and economics, and also involves trading off these uncontroversial objectives. The last set of Symposia addresses how one should evaluate how well a tax system is meeting these criteria and whether we should add a fourth criterion of political sustainability. One article concerns what policies tax experts themselves favor, and how their views differ from politicians, whose views presumably reflect that of the taxpayers themselves. Who is right depends, in part, on how well the experts understand how the real world works.

Who wins and loses from proposed tax changes is always highly contentious, and the debates over this issue offer a fascinating window into what happens when academic economics meets the policy process. The December 1993 Symposium gave a platform to two prominent academics who had just served a stint in Washington: Alan Auerbach as Deputy Chief of Staff of the Joint Committee on Taxation, and R. Glenn Hubbard as Deputy Assistant Secretary (Tax Policy) at the U.S. Treasury.

Both Auerbach and Hubbard address the potential contribution of careful economic reasoning to informed policymaking. Auerbach recommends four steps that would help policymakers confront the weaknesses and inconsistencies of the current methods of assessing the distributional and revenue implications of proposed tax changes:

(1) the provision of more complete information about the long-run and distributional effects of tax proposals;
(2) the rejection of meaningless measures of fiscal responsibility;
(3) the insistence that information on the revenue and distributional impact of proposals meets the most basic tests of economic consistency; and
(4) the refusal to provide information when such information does not exist and an indication of the quality of information that is being provided.

As an example of his third point, Auerbach stresses the inadequacy of the change in taxes paid as a measure of an individual's burden from a tax change, rejecting it because it leads to "the ridiculous implication that, should a tax be so distortionary that reducing it actually increases revenue, the burden of taxation *increases* (p. 525, emphasis added).

Hubbard agrees that economists should resist providing "information when such information does not exist" and focuses on the use of "distributional tables," which purport to show exactly which groups of individuals gain or lose from particular tax changes and by how much. He proposes resisting the policymakers' demand for such tables, in favor of an educational process on what can and cannot be learned from these tables, and accompanying what tables must be produced with specific statements qualifying the (incorrect) appearance of exactitude.

The question of how much can tax systems contribute to, or hinder, economic growth has come to dominate policy discussions in the United States since about 1980, when "supply-side economics" burst onto the scene. In the December 1996 Symposium, Eric Engen and Jonathan Skinner address this issue, using three distinct kinds of evidence— the U.S. historical record; cross-country data; and microlevel studies of labor supply, investment demand, and productivity growth. They argue that the weight of the evidence supports the view that "beneficial" changes in tax policy can have modest effects on output growth, and that these growth effects can have an important long-term impact on living standards. They also conclude that the composition of the tax system is probably as important for economic growth as is the absolute level of taxation, and that countries that are able to mobilize resources through broad-based structures with efficient administration and enforcement will be likely to enjoy faster growth rates than countries with lower overall tax collections assessed inefficiently.

In order to assess the growth effects of tax systems, Engen and Skinner bring to bear a wide variety of evidence. An alternative approach is to study in depth one tax reform, as Auerbach and Slemrod (1997) have done with regard to the U.S. Tax Reform Act of 1986 (TRA 86). In the companion piece of the December 1996 Symposium, Jonas Agell, Peter Englund, and Jan Södersten discuss another fascinating recent episode: the 1991 Swedish "tax reform of the century"(henceforth, TR 91), which slashed income tax rates in concert with broadening of the income and value-added tax bases, and which introduced a new system of taxing capital income on a separate, proportional basis.

In contrast to the TRA 86, which was enacted during a relatively tranquil period of the U.S. business cycle, the implementation of the TR 91 was accompanied by the most severe economic downturn in Sweden since the 1930s, greatly complicating the ability to make causal inferences about its impact. Nevertheless, Agell, Englund, and Södersten argue that the pattern of economic impact mirrored that observed in the United States. Specifically, many financial activities were quite responsive to changes in their tax treatment, but neither labor supply nor saving appeared to be very sensitive to the tax changes, at least in the short run. The authors conclude, though, that from a starting point of the very high marginal tax rates pre–TR 91 of Sweden—70 percent or more—even small behavioral elasticities can be consistent with substantial efficiency gains from tax reforms. In the Swedish case, they argue, these likely long-term benefits were accompanied by large short-term costs due to the rapid implementation, which helped trigger the macroeconomic collapse.

In his comment on the Engen–Skinner and Agell–England–Södersten papers, Alan Auerbach ponders why questions about the effects of tax reforms are so difficult to answer. He catalogues a number of problems, including the fact that large-scale tax reforms are complex packages of provisions; that tax policy is endogenous to economic conditions; that it is impossible to parse out confounding influences on behavior; and, finally, that some of the potentially important effects of a tax reform are difficult to observe and measure. In light of these problems, Auerbach offers some useful principles to apply to the analysis of tax reforms, including the importance of clearly distinguishing between assumptions and evidence; the need to reconcile micro- and macro-effects; and, perhaps the most difficult of all, the capacity to be appropriately humble in qualifying one's conclusions. Auerbach concludes that even radical tax reform is unlikely to be a panacea for economic problems, and our uncertainty about its impact should temper our willingness to experience the significant transition problems associated with the shift to a major new tax system.

In the March 1996 Symposium, James Alm and Louis Kaplow address the policy implications of the reality that a tax system needs to be enforced and thereby generates both administrative and compliance costs. Alm considers how these issues will affect the standard optimal taxation rules. He argues *against* taking simplicity as an explicit, separate criterion for a good tax system, but rather is for assessing the equity, efficiency, and revenue-yield impacts of complexity and enforcement. He speculates that a full analysis of these factors would lead to modification of the standard optimal tax rules, pointing to commodity tax rules that are largely proportional, broad-based income taxes, with minimal use of special tax incentives at consistent marginal tax rates, and with generous exempt levels of income, and a mix of direct and indirect taxes. Alm cautions, though, that the optimal tax system is certain to differ country by country, so that the search for a universal optimal tax scheme is futile.

Kaplow also aims to provide a general conceptual framework for addressing problems involving complexity, compliance costs, and enforcement difficulties. Like Alm, he argues that no new analytical tools are needed. The appropriate framework is still the constrained maximization of a social welfare function, which embodies judgments about the society's distributive preferences, the same judgments from which the tax base and rate structure were devised. He counsels against bringing to bear any criterion of "horizontal equity" independent of the social welfare function when assessing costly measures to improve the accuracy of the process that determines tax liability.

One obvious but important aspect of the real world of taxation is the political system, which has been blamed for the tax system's complexity and inefficiency and which many suspect would eventually undermine any radically simplifying tax reform. The June 1998 Symposium featured three essays addressing how people who offer tax policy advice need to account for the political system. Strikingly, the authors agree on very little except that accounting for politics and political institutions is important. Randall Holcombe argues that, to minimize political costs, tax systems should be part of a stable fiscal constitution, with generally agreed-upon rules. He speculates that uniform and broad-based retail sales taxes could be more efficient than a set of excise taxes intended to conform to the rules from a Ramsey-style optimal commodity tax formula, because, when different rates can be legislated for different goods, this invites rent-seeking and an escalation of political costs; furthermore, because of political pressures, the resulting rules are unlikely to conform to the Ramsey rule anyway. He speculates further that uniform and broad-based retail sales taxes could entail lower political costs than income taxes, but that a more definitive conclusion requires careful analysis of the relative political costs involved. Holcombe also cautions against using the tax system as a redistributive mechanism, because it favors those with political power rather than those who are in need.

Stanley Winer and Walter Hettich take a different tack on this issue, stressing that a tax system is part of a broad set of equilibrium policy outcomes and that tax measures cannot be evaluated in isolation from related policies. They argue that consideration of political equilibrium undermines traditional arguments for broadly based taxes, because, in a competitive political system, governments create special provisions as a way of taking differing economic and political responses to taxation into account, while economizing on administration costs. This, they argue, suggests that special provisions should be preserved rather than eliminated, apparently in stark contrast to the spirit of Holcombe's essay. They concede, though, that there may be political market failures that justify limitations on the power to open and close special provisions, but believe that these must be identified in a normative analysis that acknowledges the existence of collective choice.

In his comment on the Holcombe and Winer–Hettich papers, James Poterba acknowledges that political factors play a key role in the determination of tax policy, but argues that, for two reasons, economic analysis can have an impact on the tax-writing process. First, well-crafted economic analysis can quantify the net burdens of current policies and alert policymakers to unintended consequences of actual or prospective policies. Second, in the hands of "political entrepreneurs," who are prepared to argue for efficiency–based reform of the tax system, analyses that uncover aspects of the tax code that are inefficient can influence policy outcomes; Poterba cites the TRA 86 as an encouraging example of this possibility.

Armed with assessments of how well alternative tax policies meet the criteria of equity, efficiency, and (possibly as a separate criterion) simplicity, we can begin to choose our favorites. The March 1995 Symposium examines what policies are preferred by people in the tax business—academics, policymakers, and practitioners. The paper I wrote for this Symposium reports the results of a survey of National Tax Association (NTA) members conducted in 1994, and compares the responses to the responses to a similar set of questions posed to senior professors 60 years earlier, and also to the responses of current politicians. The survey reveals that tax "experts" are not inclined to replace the graduated income tax as the backbone of the federal tax system nor do they favor abandoning the property tax and sales tax as important features of the local and state revenue systems. However, on average, they do favor some significant reforms of the federal tax system, such as integration of the corporate and individual income tax, comprehensive inflation indexing, and elimination of the mortgage interest deduction. With regard to state and local taxes, a majority favor extending the sales tax to services, increasing reliance on user fees, and eliminating homestead exemptions from the property tax.

This paper compares the NTA members' responses to those of delegates to the 1992 Republican and Democratic National conventions, as reported by Fuller, Alston, and Vaughn (undated). In general, the NTA respondents' opinions resemble the Democrats more than the Republicans, seeing redistribution as a legitimate role for government and mixed on whether lower capital gains taxes encourage investment and on whether government expenditure should be reduced. However, they resemble the Republicans in taking more seriously the probability that lower marginal income tax rates increase work effort.

The last Symposium reprinted in this volume is the one that appeared in the *National Tax Journal's* 50th anniversary issue of December 1997. For that special issue, the *National Tax Journal* and the British journal *Fiscal Studies* jointly commissioned two articles on the lessons that the United States could learn from the U.K. tax system, and vice versa; William Gale took on the first challenge, and Michael Keen the second.

Gale is struck by the much simpler structure and administration of the British income tax, and speculates as to whether the "no-return" nature of the remittance process constrains the system's complexity. In any event, the British system shows that the U.S. system could be much simpler, if only Americans were willing to reduce the extent to which the income tax attempted to tax all income or tried to administer social policy through the tax code. It is notable that the British parliament, in which the party in control has much more power than the majority party in Congress, has yet managed to keep their tax system remarkably free of tax breaks for favored constituencies. Finally, Gale concludes from the British experience that value-added taxes (VATs) are neither as simple, nor as much of an elixir for growth, as is sometimes claimed.

Michael Keen argues that careful study of the U.S. tax system is especially important now for Europeans, both because the Labour government is apparently strongly influenced by it and because of its lessons for the European federalism debate. Keen addresses five features of the American tax system that seem, from a British and European perspective, to be both especially peculiar and potentially instructive. These are the remarkably low level of taxation; the absence of a VAT (or any other major general national tax on consumption); the absence of any explicit interstate equalization; the marginal subsidization of low earnings under the earned income tax credit; and the fragmentation of power in policymaking.

A recurring theme of these Symposia is that, although—indeed, because—the real world is messy, policy needs to be infused with consistent principles and sound economic reasoning. Platitudes and special interest pleading can produce bad tax policy, and good economics can help to drive these policies out. Alas, often, the economics itself is abstract, complicated, and unintuitive. Nevertheless, a continued dialogue between those who do tax policy and deal with its principles and those who think about policy and its principles can only be helpful, and the papers in this volume are offered in the spirit of continuing that dialogue.

ENDNOTES

[1] Goode (1997) documents the changes over its half-century history in the papers published in the *National Tax Journal*; Rosen (1997) addresses the same trend in the textbooks of the period.

[2] Because of their topical nature, the June 1994, June 1997, and March 1998 Symposia have not been reprinted here. The first contained a paper on the Clinton administration health care reform proposal by Henry Aaron, a paper on welfare reform by Robert Haveman and John Karl Scholz, and a paper on tax policy implications of NAFTA by Roger Gordon and Eduardo Ley. The second featured pieces on the Clinton administration higher education tax assistance plans by Thomas J. Kane and C. Eugene Steuerle. The last contained critical essays on the Taxpayer Relief Act of 1997 by Bruce Bartlett and Robert Reischauer. (Also not reproduced here are short comments on the March 1995 Symposium by Gerard Brannon and George Break.) These papers can, of course, be obtained in the *National Tax Journal*.

[3] See Auerbach and Poterba (1987).

REFERENCES

Auerbach, Alan J., and James Poterba. "Why Have Corporate Tax Revenues Declined?" In *Tax Policy and the Economy* 1, edited by Lawrence Summers, 1–28. Cambridge, MA: MIT Press, 1987.

Auerbach, Alan J., and Joel Slemrod. "The Economic Effects of the Tax Reform Act of 1986." *Journal of Economic Literature* 35 No. 2 (June, 1997): 589–632.

Bradford, David F. *Untangling the Income Tax.* Cambridge, MA: Harvard University Press, 1986.

Fuller, Dan A., Richard M. Alston, and Michael B. Vaughn. "Political Economy: Views of Economists and Politicians." Manuscript. Weber State University, Ogden, UT, Undated.

Goode, Richard. "The *National Tax Journal* in 1948–50 and 1994–96." *National Tax Journal* 50 No. 4 (December, 1997): 707–18.

Harberger, Arnold. "The Incidence of the Corporation Income Tax." *Journal of Political Economy* 70 No. 3 (June, 1962): 215–40.

Kannainen, Vesa, and Jan Södersten. "Costs of Monitoring and Corporate Taxation." *Journal of Public Economics* 55 No. 2 (October, 1994): 307–22.

Musgrave, Richard A. *The Theory of Public Finance.* New York: McGraw-Hill Book Company, 1959.

Rosen, Harvey S. "The Way We Were (and Are): Changes in Public Finance and its Textbooks." *National Tax Journal* 50 No. 4 (December, 1997): 719–30.

Sinn, Hans-Werner. "Taxation and the Cost of Capital: The 'Old' View, the 'New' View and Another View." In *Tax Policy and the Economy* 5, edited by David F. Bradford, 25–54. Cambridge, MA: MIT Press, 1991.

CHAPTER 2

THE CORPORATE INCOME TAX: ECONOMIC ISSUES AND POLICY OPTIONS

JANE G. GRAVELLE*

The United States still relies, although less heavily than it did in the past, on revenues from the corporate income tax. While the tax is currently a distant third in share of federal revenues, trailing both the individual income tax and the payroll tax, it was much more important in the past. The corporate tax's decline as a share of federal revenues results from both the growth of other revenue sources and the decline of the corporate tax as a percent of GNP. This latter effect, in turn, arises from both a decline in corporate profits as a share of output and a decline in effective corporate tax burdens.

A separate corporate tax has been justified at various times by the special privileges the corporation receives (in terms of limited liability), the independent economic power obtained by large corporations, and the need to tax corporations in order to prevent the sheltering of income by high-income individuals given the complexities of partnership taxation. The corporation is a popular target for raising revenue, since it is not very visible. Finally, if one expects the tax to be paid by owners of capital, the tax may

*Congressional Research Service, LM-325 Library of Congress, Washington, D.C. 20540–7430.

contribute to a more progressive overall federal tax system, an outcome that is desirable in some quarters.

Many of these arguments for retaining the separate corporate tax would be viewed with skepticism by most economists. Indeed, it has been primarily economists who have been the most critical of the corporate income tax, citing its creation of a variety of distortions. For example, economists would view the availability of limited liability as an efficient way to organize the raising of large amounts of capital and allocating risk. To tax corporations simply detracts from the economic efficiency that benefits us all.

The argument that the corporate tax prevents the sheltering of income in corporations does not seem to justify both corporate-level and individual-level taxes when the top corporate rate (35 percent) is almost as high as the top individual rate (39.6 percent). Approaches to relief of double taxation such as dividend deductions or personal-level exclusions of the tax are straightforward, and partial forms of integration have been practiced successfully in other countries.

Although corporate taxes have declined,

explorations aimed at fundamental reform—pursued most recently under the Carter, Reagan, and Bush administrations—have generally not progressed very far. This state of affairs may be in part because proposals for corporate tax integration have received little or no support from corporations themselves, who may fear the pressure to distribute dividends, or feel that they have little to gain from the revision compared to other types of tax reductions.

The modern debate about the corporate tax seems to rest on three issues. First, who pays the corporate tax—capital, labor, or consumers—and does it play a role in a progressive federal tax system? Second, how significant are the distortions caused by the excess corporate tax? Third, how can the revenue from the tax be replaced? And, finally, are there feasible revisions? The next section considers the first two of these questions; a discussion of policy options follows.

WHO PAYS THE CORPORATE TAX AND HOW DOES IT CAUSE DISTORTIONS?

Economists begin by distinguishing between the short run and the long run. Presumably, the tax falls on shareholders in the short run, when the firm cannot change the amount of capital employed. One can imagine, however, some circumstances in which the tax could be shifted to prices in the short run (*e.g.*, firms may attempt to mark up the price immediately). In the long run, the amount of capital employed in the firm can be altered, so that other prices and incomes in the economy may change and affect the burden of tax.

The question of who pays the corporate tax is relevant to issues of distribution and progressivity. Capital income tends to be more concentrated among higher income individuals, and the corporate tax contributes to tax progressivity if it falls on capital. If it falls on labor or consumption, however, it does not tend to contribute to a progressive tax structure.

Government agencies that provide official tax distribution numbers have differed in their incidence assumptions—the Treasury's Office of Tax Analysis assigns the tax to all capital, the Joint Committee on Taxation has assigned it to shareholders, and the Congressional Budget Office has allocated half the tax to labor and half to capital in the past.

The Harberger Model

Harberger's (1962) landmark study shows how the reactions of investors to lower after-tax returns, following the imposition of the tax, spread the tax to others. His model depicts two industries, one corporate and one noncorporate, reacting to a tax imposed only on capital used in one of them. As the return falls in the taxed sector, investors shift their investments to the untaxed sector and its (initially) higher rates of return. This shift sets in motion a series of adjustments in prices, wages, rates of return, output, and factor allocations.

In equilibrium, the corporate sector becomes smaller, with higher relative prices, and with lower ratios of capital to labor than it had before, while the noncorporate sector becomes larger, with lower relative prices and higher ratios of capital to labor than it had before. (The overall price level can be thought of as constant so that the real consequences of the tax on the ability to purchase goods can be assessed.) The pretax rate of return in the corporate sector rises, while the pretax return in the untaxed noncorporate sector falls, until it equals the after-tax return in the corporate sector. The effect on wages and labor shifts is indeterminate in direction.

The magnitude and, for wages, the direction of these adjustments depend on how easily capital and labor can be substituted for production in each sector, how willing consumers are to substitute corporate and noncorporate products, and the original allocations of capital and labor.

The important insight of the Harberger model is that, given reasonable assumptions about the behavioral relationships, the tax is generally borne by capital. In some cases, capital can bear more than 100 percent of the tax and in some less than 100 percent of the tax, but, overall, there is a tendency for the tax to fall on capital. (Generally, the tax is more likely to fall more heavily on capital when the noncorporate sector finds substitution of labor for capital difficult but the corporate sector can substitute easily.)

In the process of making these adjustments, resources are misallocated in the economy: too much capital relative to labor is used in the noncorporate sector and too little in the corporate sector, causing inefficient production. In addition, prices are distorted, causing too little corporate production. Most models of the corporate tax have produced welfare costs equivalent to a loss of about 0.5 percent of income, a not insignificant amount.

The original Harberger model had many simplifying assumptions: perfect competition, fixed total quantities of labor and capital, a closed economy, and a single representative consumer. It also did not reflect certain real-world circumstances: that the corporate tax was imposed not based on the product produced but rather on the form of operation, that corporations could employ untaxed debt finance, and that personal-level taxes differed between the corporate and noncorporate sectors and could be al-

tered by the firm's distribution policy.

Harberger's original finding of tax incidence has stood up surprisingly well to a variety of challenges. Some variations in the modeling of the tax, such as the addition of sectors or allowing monopoly profits, do not alter the general expectation that the tax would fall on capital rather than labor income. Much of the development of the model was directed at adding more detail to the model: more sectors, models more representative of the structure of the economy (such as the inclusion of intermediate goods), heterogeneous consumers, heterogeneous capital, and more sophisticated ways of measuring the marginal effective tax rates (see, for example Ballard et al., 1985; Fullerton and Henderson, 1989).

There are several issues, however, that deserve some discussion. I suggest that none of them alter the answer to the incidence question, although they do have implications for economic efficiency. These include (1) fundamental structural changes; (2) implications of marginal taxes and the individual tax, including the reasons for dividend payments; (3) debt finance; (4) open-economy models; and (5) growth models where the supply of capital is not fixed.

Fundamental Changes in the Structure of the Model

Harberger's model actually explores a tax imposed on capital used to produce a particular type of good. The corporate tax, however, is imposed only on incorporated firms, and even so, for small corporate firms, the law allows partnership taxation to be elected. The Harberger model does not allow taxed and nontaxed firms to produce the same product and, indeed, when faced with the actual corporate tax rules, the model implies that no corporate firms would exist (since there are no economies of scale).

Several different methods of explaining the coexistence of corporate and noncorporate sectors have now been explored, all of which tend to relate in some fashion to size of firms. Gravelle and Kotlikoff (1989) suggest that it is size that is central—large corporate firms benefit from scale advantages, while small firms benefit from entrepreneurial ability; hence, each form of production can coexist given an imperfectly elastic supply of entrepreneurial skills. Gravelle and Kotlikoff (1993) explore another alternative that allows corporate and noncorporate firms to produce differentiated products; this approach was also used by Fullerton and Rogers (1993) in their recent life-cycle model. Although the nature of the differentiation is not clear, size might also play a role in this model (*e.g.*, corporate products may be characterized by consistency and predictability; noncorporate products by flexibility and the "personal touch"). A third approach discussed by Gravelle and Mackie (1992) assumes that corporate and noncorporate investments may be imperfect substitutes in portfolios, so that equal rates of return might not be required—a differentiation that may also depend on less risk taking and more liquidity in the large market for corporate securities, and more information in the case of smaller noncorporate equity investments.

It is likely that all of these explanations play some role in allocating the corporate tax. In general, however, all of these models tend to reach the same conclusion as the original Harberger model—a tendency for the tax to fall on capital. They are likely, however, to increase the estimated cost of distortions. The Harberger model, in empirical applications, was based on averaging the corporate and noncorporate taxes within an industry, which had the effect of diluting the tax differential. This effect is important because the welfare cost rises with the square of the tax wedge. Moreover, some of these models suggest greater substitutability of resources between noncorporate and corporate firms within the same industry, than between firms in different industries. For example, even a conservative estimate using a disaggregated version of the Gravelle and Kotlikoff (1989) model suggested a welfare cost of one percent of consumption, even after the lower rates and reforms in 1986 (see Gravelle, 1989).

Perhaps in part because the Harberger approach was not challenged for many years, there has been little empirical research to establish the degree of substitutability of corporate and noncorporate capital directly (rather than indirectly *via* the structure of the model and the basic behavioral parameters of production and consumption). Gordon and MacKie-Mason (1991) report small substitution effects, but they exclude the heavily noncorporate, capital-intensive sectors of agriculture and real estate where the largest distortions might, in theory, occur.

Marginal Tax Rates, Personal-Level Taxes, and the Treatment of Dividends

The initial empirical applications of the Harberger model analyzed a tax imposed on capital used in one sector, without considering the details of taxation of noncorporate firms and taxation of corporate equity at the personal level. The personal tax at the individual level does not apply in the same way that the individual noncorporate tax applies. Taxes are immediately imposed on dividends. Retained earnings are not subject to tax until gains are realized, which may be many years into the future; moreover, assets that are passed on at death receive a stepped-up basis so that this gain is never taxed. Capital gains have also, through most of history, benefited from special rates or exclusions.

Moreover, neither the corporate and noncorporate taxes on profits, nor the tax on capital gains necessarily reflected correct measures of income, which were distorted by investment incentives (such as accelerated depreciation) and by the failure to index gains and depreciation for inflation. As a practical matter, this meant that the excess tax could not be measured merely by corporate tax receipts in empirical applications, but it needed to be calculated as the excess of corporate taxation over noncorporate taxation. This effect alone poses no theoretical challenge to the Harberger model, but it does complicate measurement. Current tax models, whatever their type, generally employ more sophisticated measures of effective tax burdens that account for these factors (including timing factors).

The most straightforward way of incorporating the dividend taxes and capital gains taxes into measures of the excess corporate tax burden is simply to base the tax on the average behavior observed in the economy (*i.e.*, weighting the personal tax by the share paid out as dividends, and using average holding periods and fractions of gain realized to measure effective capital gains tax).

This recognition of personal taxes, and of imprecisely measured income, does have several implications for the structure of corporate tax models. First, it means that the excess corporate tax (the excess of the combination of corporate taxes and personal taxes on corporate source income over taxes on noncorporate income) varies from one individual to another in a progressive tax system, making equating of returns across taxpayers impossible. Thus, some sort of

portfolio effect should probably be included in any model of the corporate tax.

Second, the particular nature of tax treatment of corporate source income at the personal level gave rise to an extensive debate about the effects of taxes on dividends. As long as retained earnings are taxed more lightly than dividends, one has to confront the question of why firms pay dividends—since dividends are more heavily taxed. Even if firms wished to distribute profits (which would be necessary in any steady-state growth model where the rate of return exceeded the growth rate), they could effectively do so by repurchasing shares (causing share prices to go up).

Several theories have been advanced to explain why firms pay dividends and what the consequences of this reasoning might be for the incidence and efficiency effects of the excess corporate tax. These theories can be divided into the traditional view of dividends (where dividend taxes do matter) and the new view of dividends. [Zodrow (1991) provides a more extensive discussion of these views.]

The "new view" (King, 1977; Auerbach, 1979a, b; Bradford, 1981) begins with the presumption that dividends and capital gains are perfect substitutes and that firms cannot repurchase shares. Under the new view, dividend taxes in excess of capital gains taxes do not affect investment when that investment is financed out of retained earnings, as most such investments are. By choosing reinvestment, the stockholder is saved this excess tax—a saving that offsets, in present value, future excess dividend taxes. Like an individual retirement account, this tax does not affect the rate of return. If the conclusions of the new view are correct, and if marginal investment is mostly financed by retained earnings, the tax differential between corporate and noncorporate tax, for purposes of investment, is smaller.

The new view also suggests that dividend taxes in excess of capital gains taxes are capitalized in the value of stock—hence the "new view" is sometimes referred to as the "trapped equity" view, or the "tax capitalization view."

The traditional view of dividends was based on the notion that there was some intrinsic value to dividends. Dividends may serve a signaling function (Bhattacharya, 1979; Miller and Rock, 1985). That is, stockholders may not have full information about the profitability of a firm, and the payment of dividends might be used as a method to make it clear (through actual distribution of profits) that the firm was doing well.

Of course, this theory does not explain why firms could not use share repurchases for that same purpose, given the extra tax burdens associated with dividends. It might be that the cash dividend is the clearest signaling mechanism. Bernheim (1991) has recently proposed an explanation for cash dividends (rather than relying solely on the volume of repurchases) through a sort of "potlatch" theory of dividends—firms with a lot of profits can afford to visibly throw away resources in taxes to demonstrate their superiority.

A second theory is agency cost, advanced by Jensen (1986) and Jensen and Meckling (1976). Because of the separation of ownership and control in modern corporations and limited information, stockholders cannot make sure that managers act in their best interests. Stockholders may wish, therefore, to limit managerial discretion by requiring payment of regular dividends. Repurchasing shares may allow managers too much discretion.

Finally, shareholders may not view dividends and capital gains as perfect substitutes. Shefrin and Statman (1984) discuss several reasons that stockholders would see capital gains and dividends as different, reflecting subjective attitudes toward risk, regret, and maintaining discipline in spending and savings decisions. Transactions costs may also differentiate receipt of income from capital gains and dividends.

Although a number of empirical studies have found some evidence that dividend taxes cause dividends to fall, these studies do not necessarily provide good evidence of the traditional view, since dividend taxes can also decrease dividends in the new view as firms expand their investments to drive down the value of the firm (see Auerbach, 1979a). Some studies have found evidence of firm market values more consistent with the traditional view, however. (See Gravelle, 1994b, ch. 4 for a summary of the empirical research.)

There are, however, some more straightforward empirical problems with the new view. A fundamental presumption of this model is that share repurchases are not possible. Yet, there is no reason to believe that open-market share repurchases cannot freely occur and, in fact, many such repurchases do occur. Moreover, firms sometimes issue new shares while paying dividends, a behavior that is inconsistent with the new view.

At the same time, it is not entirely clear how the different traditional theories of tax should be incorporated into the investment decision and whether dividend taxes should simply be weighted in the investment equation based on observed shares.

Where does all of this leave us? Essentially, one might argue that the jury is still out on this issue and its implications for the incidence and efficiency of the tax. While the new view seems to be contradictory to a straightforward observation of behavior in the economy, the implications of the "new view" of the dividend tax are still that the tax falls on owners of capital—it simply tends to fall on existing owners of corporate stock. The implications in a distributional analysis are similar with both views, although a certain new facet is introduced any time a tax is capitalized.

The dividend tax debate becomes more important when economic efficiency is considered. Under the new view or any treatment that reduces the effective corporate tax burden, the excess corporate tax is much smaller, and the efficiency gains reduced. If dividends and capital gains are imperfect substitutes, however, there is an additional element of distortion imposed by the current tax treatment along with the lock-in effect for corporate capital. Gravelle (1994a, p. 89) suggests this distortion could be as much as 0.2 of a percent of consumption, and the capital gains lock-in effect might be around 0.06 percent of consumption.

The Use of Debt Finance

Another challenge to the Harberger model is the availability of debt finance. Even if corporate firms, with their large sizes, had a reason to exist, they could avoid the tax by using debt finance. Yet, U.S. corporations not only use equity capital, but they use it in substantial amounts. What explains the tendency of corporations to choose taxed equity capital?

There are several possible explanations for the use of equity capital finance: clientele effects, bankruptcy risk, agency cost, and portfolio effects. Clientele effects (Miller, 1977) were a more persuasive argument when the individual tax rate was far above the corporate rate. In that case, some individuals with high tax rates would prefer corporate equities, which would be taxed at the lower tax rate. As long as most income was retained in the firm and the individual did not need to realize capital gains, taxes on equity capital could actually be lower than taxes on debt. The clientele theory suggests that there is no real burden to the corporate tax and indeed no real corporate tax; instead, the corporate tax offers a shelter to high-income individuals. This clientele theory was not really supported by evidence (i.e., no portfolio specializations and significant dividend payments) and became largely irrelevant as the spread between the top corporate and individual rates has virtually disappeared.

The increased risk of bankruptcy can explain why firms do not choose all debt finance (Gordon and Malkiel, 1981). This theory suggests, however, that in the absence of taxes firms would use no debt at all, a condition that did not exist prior to the income tax, and that many might find implausible.

Another explanation for debt proposed by Jensen (1986) is the agency cost issue discussed with reference to dividends. Another way to limit managerial discretion is through requiring a periodic payment of interest on debt obligations. Retaining some equity finance, however, cushions against changes in cash flow (Jensen, 1986; Gertler and Hubbard, 1990); hence, this theory could explain the use of a mix of debt and equity depending on the level of the tax.

A final explanation is a portfolio explanation, in which debt is seen as an imperfect substitute for equity (because of differences, for example, in risk, transactions costs, etc.). Portfolio approaches are used by Galper, Lucke, and Toder (1988) and Gravelle and Mackie (1992).

There are a number of potential explanations for the presence of debt finance that are consistent with empirical evidence. If the clientele theory can be rejected, this aspect of corporate finance does not constitute a challenge to the incidence effects in the Harberger, or other models, of the corporate tax. It does have implications for efficiency issues, however. Debt finance reduces the differential between taxes in the corporate and noncorporate sectors, but causes a distortion between debt and equity finance. There has been relatively little empirical research on the magnitude of the substitutability of debt and equity, although such evidence that does exist suggests that it is small (see Gravelle, 1994a, ch. 4, for a discussion). Gravelle (1994a, p. 84) suggests that this distortion might be responsible for a welfare cost of about 0.2 of a percent of consumption.

Open-Economy Models

Perhaps one of the strongest challenges to the Harberger model comes from the extension of the analysis of the tax to open-economy models. It can be shown that in a small open economy, where capital is perfectly mobile and goods in international trade are perfect substitutes, the burden of capital income taxes falls on the immovable factors—in the case of the Harberger model, labor. This incidence can be explained simply by assuming each country produces one good. If goods in trade are perfect substitutes, domestic and foreign prices must be equated, and if the country is small, the price is set on the world market. If the rate of return has to be the same after tax, then the rate of return before tax must rise. The only way to allow the product price to remain fixed but the payment to capital to rise, is for the payment to labor to fall. This outcome is the result of the migration of capital out of the country, which causes

the wage rate to fall relative to the price of capital.

As shown by Gravelle (1994a), relaxing any of these three assumptions will shift part of the tax burden away from labor, and back to capital. Maintaining the assumptions of perfectly substitutable capital and goods, the tax will fall on capital in proportion to its share cf the worldwide capital stock. If capital is imperfectly substitutable [and there is evidence that capital is, and particularly equity capital is, as discussed in Gravelle (1994b, p. 232)], then the burden is much more likely to fall on capital. In that case, the after-tax rate of return can fall— indeed, if capital is perfectly immobile then all of the burden of the tax would fall on capital. Similarly, if goods in trade are imperfect substitutes (and there is evidence that this is the case), so that prices can rise for the domestic good relative to the foreign good, then the pretax price of capital can rise without necessarily causing the price of labor to fall. Essentially, imperfect substitutability of either capital or goods acts to effectively close the economy for purposes of tax incidence. For the empirical relationships commonly estimated, the findings of the original Harberger model—that the tax falls largely on capital—hold up.

Varying the Supply of Capital and Labor: Growth Models

The Harberger model and all of the variations up to this point do not allow the stock of capital to change through a savings response. Growth models of any tax, however, introduce further complications in the form of a time dimension. One must now distinguish between the burden on individuals living in the near-term and in the long-run equilibrium and the incidence would then refer to lifetime incidence, rather than being a cross section in a single year.

The use of growth models where capital and labor can be varied introduces many new complications into the analysis of the incidence of any tax, which are beyond the scope of this survey. [Several growth models have been developed that can be used to study the corporate tax; *e.g.*, Fullerton and Rogers (1993), Gravelle and Kotlikoff (1995); see Gravelle (1994, ch. 2) for a survey of growth models.] Certain observations, however, can be made.

First, if the savings response to a tax increase is negative, the burden of the corporate tax partially falls on labor in the long run, as the contraction in the total capital stock drives down the wage. At the same time, it is not clear that the corporate tax has caused the capital stock to fall, even on a theoretical basis (that answer depends in part on the disposition of the proceeds of the tax); empirical evidence on the response of savings to changes in the rate of return is mixed [see Gravelle (1994b, ch. 2) for a summary of this evidence].

Second, the relationships between sources of income and level of income (*i.e.*, high-income individuals have more capital income) tend to be muted in a life-cycle model that accounts for individuals' changing incomes and changing amounts of capital income over time. That is, part of the reason for an association between high income and capital income, is that individuals tend to have both higher incomes and more capital incomes later in their lives. So, even if the corporate tax falls on capital (because savings does not respond to changes in the rate of return), this incidence may not contribute as much to progressivity.

IMPLICATIONS FOR REFORM

Although some troubling issues remain, especially about the magnitude of the distortions caused by the corporate tax, the corporate tax appears to produce large distortions relative to its yield. Thus, there is some payoff to a fundamental reform. Nevertheless, the evidence also generally supports some role for the corporate tax in maintaining the progressivity of the tax system. Moreover, the revenue yield of the tax is of considerable concern during these austere years. In addition, concerns about the feasibility of an administrable revision may preclude certain options (such as full partnership taxation).

There are several ways in which the excess corporate tax can be reduced. The most common methods used in other countries provide dividend relief—and this relief could be provided by (1) exclusion at the personal level, (2) a deduction at the firm level, or (3) a credit-imputation method under which the firm withholds dividend taxes and the individual shareholder takes a credit for these taxes. The latter two methods preserve tax progressivity, and the last method can maintain some tax on otherwise tax-exempt entities (including foreign shareholders). Full partnership taxation could also be achieved, at least in theory, by providing (4) a credit-imputation method for both dividends and retained earnings. Overall relief from double taxation could also be provided through (5) elimination of individual-level taxes on dividends and capital gains.

In 1992, the Treasury Department undertook an extensive study of various methods, in which they addressed the first four of these methods. Ultimately, of these four methods, they favored exclusion at the personal level. They suggested that the firm-level deduction, which was actually proposed in 1984, did not allow the flexibility of imposing some tax on tax-exempt shareholders. The other methods were viewed as undesirable due to their complexity. (The

Treasury argued for the traditional view of dividends; if the new view is correct, such general dividend relief would be largely a windfall and should, perhaps, be confined to new issues, as suggested in a proposal of the American Law Institute.)

The Treasury also explored a new and much more far-reaching approach—the Comprehensive Business Income Tax (CBIT). This proposal would tax all business income—both from debt and equity—at the firm level. Firms would not be able to deduct interest, but this interest would not be taxed to the recipient.

CBIT has a number of very attractive features, given the criteria already discussed earlier. It would eliminate virtually all of the existing distortions, it would not lose revenue (thus meeting both revenue and distributional objectives), and it would be relatively simple to administer.

CBIT, as a relatively far-reaching proposal, does face some problems (see Sunley, 1992, for a discussion). Disallowing the deductibility of interest for unincorporated firms might meet some resistance, particularly on existing debt contracts, so a phase-in and perhaps some options for small firms may be necessary. (For new debt, the lack of taxability in the hands of the recipients should lower the interest rate.) A similar concern would apply to mortgage interest. It would be possible to carve out some of these debt instruments permanently, but measures would need to be taken to ensure that they are taxed in the hands of recipients, even tax-exempt entities.

A potentially more intractable problem arises for debt supplied by foreigners. In many cases, this income is taxed in the home country, and without some relief from that tax, the flow of debt capital could be discouraged significantly.

Perhaps the best policy would be a gradual movement in the direction of CBIT. The dividend exclusion, even a partial one, would not be inconsistent with the eventual adoption of CBIT. An intermediate position is the elimination of personal-level taxes on both dividends and capital gains, which taxes equity at the firm level, as does CBIT. Relief at the personal level might be financed by some restrictions on interest deductibility or perhaps inflation indexing of interest deductions and payments. Any such revisions could also allow partial rather than full exclusions.

An important lesson that should be retained is that a partial movement toward eliminating the excess tax may nevertheless be well worthwhile, since the excess burden of a tax rises with the square of the tax. The welfare gain per dollar of revenue may, therefore, be quite large, even with only a partial movement toward a neutral system.

REFERENCES

Auerbach, Alan J. "Share Valuation and Corporate Equity Policy." *Journal of Public Economics 11* (June, 1979a): 291–305.

Auerbach, Alan J. "Wealth Maximization and the Cost of Capital." *Quarterly Journal of Economics 93* (August, 1979b): 433–46.

Ballard, Charles L., Don Fullerton, John D. Shoven, and John Whalley. *A General Equilibrium Model for Tax Policy Evaluation.* Chicago: University of Chicago Press, 1985.

Bernheim, B. Douglas. "Tax Policy and the Dividend Puzzle." *Rand Journal of Economics 22* (Winter, 1991): 455–76.

Bhattacharya, Sudipto. "Imperfect Information, Dividend Policy, and the Bird in the Hand Fallacy." *Bell Journal of Economics 10* (Spring, 1979): 259–70.

Bradford, David. "The Incidence and Allocation Effects of a Tax on Corporate Distributions." *Journal of Public Economics 30* (February, 1981): 1–22.

Fullerton, Donald and Yolanda K. Henderson. "A Disaggregate Equilibrium Model of The Tax Distortions Among Assets, Sectors, and Industries." *International Economic Review 30* (May, 1989): 391–413.

Fullerton, Donald and Diane Lim Rogers. *Who Bears the Lifetime Tax Burden?* Washington, D.C.: The Brookings Institution, 1993.

Galper, Harvey, Robert Lucke, and Eric Toder. "A General Equilibrium Analysis of Tax Reform." In *Uneasy Compromise: Problems of a Hybrid Income Consumption Tax,* edited by Henry J. Aaron, Harvey Galper, and Joseph Pechman, 59–108. Washington, D.C.: The Brookings Institution, 1988.

Gertler, Mark and R. Glenn Hubbard. "Taxation, Corporate Capital Structure, and Financial Distress." In *Tax Policy and The Economy,* edited by Lawrence Summers, 43–71. Cambridge: MIT Press, 1990.

Gordon, Roger and Jeffrey K. MacKie-Mason. "Taxes and the Choice of Organizational Form." NBER Working Paper No. 3781. Cambridge, MA: National Bureau of Economic Research, 1991.

Gordon, Roger and Burton Malkiel. "Corporation Finance." In *How Taxes Affect Economic Behavior,* edited by Henry J. Aaron and Joseph A. Pechman, 131–98. Washington, D.C.: The Brookings Institution, 1981.

Gravelle, Jane G. "Corporate Tax Incidence in an Open Economy." In *Proceedings of the Eighty-Sixth Annual Conference on Taxation.* 173–8. Columbus: National Tax Association-Tax Institute of America, 1994a.

Gravelle, Jane G. "Differential Taxation of Capital Income: Another Look at the 1986 Tax Reform Act." *National Tax Journal 42* No. 4 (December, 1989): 441–65.

Gravelle, Jane G. *The Economic Effects of Taxing Capital Income.* Cambridge: MIT Press, 1994b.

Gravelle, Jane G. and Laurence J. Kotlikoff. "Corporate Taxation and the Efficiency Gains of the 1986 Tax Reform Act." *Economic Theory 6,* forthcoming, 1995.

Gravelle, Jane G. and Laurence J. Kotlikoff. "Corporate Tax Incidence and Inefficiency When Corporate and Noncorporate Goods are Close Substitutes." *Economic Inquiry 31* (October, 1993): 501–16.

Gravelle, Jane G. and Laurence J. Kotlikoff. "The Incidence and Efficiency Costs of Corporate Taxation When Corporate and Noncorporate Firms Produce the Same Goods." *Journal of Political Economy 97* (August, 1989): 749–90.

Gravelle, Jane G. and James B. Mackie III. "The Real and Financial Efficiency Costs from Corporate Tax Integration: Results from Three Simulation Models." In *Proceedings of the Eighty-Fourth Annual Conference on Taxation.* 140–7. Columbus: National Tax Association-Tax Institute of America, 1992a.

Harberger, Arnold H. "The Incidence of the Corporation Income Tax." *Journal of Political Economy 70* (June, 1962): 215–40.

Jensen, Michael. "Agency Costs of Free Cash Flow, Corporate Finance, and Takeovers." *AER Papers and Proceedings 76* (May, 1986): 323–9.

Jensen, Michael and William Meckling. "Theory of the Firm: Managerial Behavior, Agency Costs, and Ownership Structures." *Journal of Financial Economics 3* (October, 1976): 305–60.

King, Mervyn A. *Public Policy and the Corporation.* London: Chapman and Hall, 1977.

Miller, Merton H. "Debt and Taxes." *Journal of Finance 32* (May, 1977): 261–75.

Miller, Merton H. and Kevin Rock. "Dividend Policy Under Asymmetric Information." *Journal of Finance 40* (September, 1985): 1031–51.

Shefrin, Hersh M. and Meir Statman. "Explaining Investor Preference for Cash Dividends." *Journal of Financial Economics* (June, 1984): 253–82.

Sunley, Emil. "Corporate Integration: An Economic Perspective." *Tax Law Review 47* (Spring, 1992): 621–43.

U.S. Department of Treasury. *Report on Integration of the Individual and Corporate Tax Systems.* Washington, D.C.: U.S. Government Printing Office, January 1992.

Zodrow, George R. "On the 'Traditional' and 'New' Views of Dividend Taxation," *National Tax Journal 45* No. 4 (December, 1991): 497–510.

CHANGING VIEWS OF THE CORPORATE INCOME TAX

PETER BIRCH SØRENSEN*

INTRODUCTION

Under a "classical" corporate tax system such as that prevailing in the United States, income from equity-financed corporate investment is taxed twice: at the corporate level a tax is levied on corporate profits after deduction for interest payments, and at the shareholder level dividends and realized capital gains on shares are subject to full personal income tax.

Over the years, many economists have argued that this system of "double taxation" significantly reduces the overall investment level and drives capital from the corporate sector into lower yielding projects in the noncorporate sector. Influenced by this line of argument, many governments in the OECD area have introduced measures to alleviate the double taxation of corporate-source income, *e.g.*, by granting a credit for the underlying corporate tax against the personal tax on dividends, and/or by offering favorable personal tax treatment of capital gains on shares.[1]

On the other hand, some economists have claimed that the traditional view

*Economic Policy Research Unit, Copenhagen Business School, 1366 Copenhagen K, Denmark.

greatly overstates the distortionary effects of a classical corporate tax system, implying that double tax relief may cause a considerable loss of government revenue without generating much stimulus to investment.

It is clearly important for public policy which view of the corporation tax is the more correct one. This article attempts to explain in a nontechnical manner the different viewpoints on the nature and impact of the corporate income tax. I will focus on the effects of double taxation of corporate-source income on the cost of corporate capital, defined as the minimum pretax rate of return a corporate investment project must earn to be profitable. To limit the scope of the paper, the emphasis will be on theoretical ideas, with no systematic review of empirical evidence. In the first two parts of the paper, I will abstract from the complications caused by international capital mobility, but the third part will address the special problems for corporate tax policy arising in the open economy.

TAXATION AND THE COST OF CORPORATE CAPITAL

In Table 1 I have tried to summarize the most well-known competing theories of

TABLE 1
ALTERNATIVE VIEWS OF THE "CLASSICAL" CORPORATE TAX SYSTEM

Theory	Influence of Nontax Factors on Corporate Financing Decisions	Marginal Source of Finance	Marginal Use of Profits	Cost of Corporate Capital[a]	Effect of Dividend Tax Relief
"Old" view[b]	important	new equity important	dividend payments	high above market interest rate	significant stimulus to corporate investment
Neutrality view[c]	unimportant	debt	financial investment in capital market	equal to market interest rate	no stimulus to investment
"New" view[d]	unimportant	retained earnings	dividend payments	slightly above market interest rate	windfall gains to existing shareholders; no investment stimulus
"Nucleus" theory of the firm[e] — growth phase	unimportant	at time of establishment: new equity after time of establishment: retained earnings	reinvestment in real capital	starting very high above market interest rate, but falling over time	significant stimulus to the establishment and growth of new corporations
"Nucleus" theory of the firm[e] — maturity phase	unimportant	retained earnings	dividend payments	slightly above market interest rate	windfall gains to existing shareholders; no investment stimulus

[a] The statements in this column assume true economic depreciation.
[b] Elaborated by numerous writers over the years, but heavily influenced by Harberger (1962, 1966).
[c] Reaching its most developed form in Stiglitz (1973).
[d] Developed and elaborated by King (1974a, b, 1977), Auerbach (1979), Bradford (1980, 1981) and Sinn (1985).
[e] Developed by Sinn (1991b).

corporate income taxation.[2] The statements regarding the cost of capital assume that taxable profits are equal to the true economic profits, i.e., that depreciation for tax purposes corresponds to the true economic depreciation of the firm's assets.[3] The following sections provide some explanatory remarks to the table.

The "Old" View of the Corporation Tax

According to the traditional view—also referred to as the "old" view—a classical corporate tax system will distort the financing as well as the real investment decisions of corporations. Since interest payments are deductible from the corporate income tax base, hence escaping double taxation, there is a tendency for debt finance to be substituted for equity finance. Moreover, since the shareholder's personal tax on capital gains is deferred until the time of realization, whereas his dividend income is taxed immediately, corporations are induced to generate capital gains to shareholders by retaining part of their profits rather than paying them out as dividends. To some extent, the substitution of debt finance for equity finance and the replacement of new equity by retained profits will reduce the impact of taxation on the cost of corporate capital. However, according to the old view, corporations will still wish to rely on some amount of equity finance at the margin, including some amount of new equity. The double taxation of corporate equity income will therefore reduce the overall level of saving and investment and drive the required pretax rate of return on corporate investment above the pretax rate of return required in the noncorporate sector. As a result, too little capital is allocated to the corporate sector, and too much is allocated to the noncorporate sector, as seen from society's viewpoint.

To explain why corporations would want to use some amount of equity finance at the margin despite the tax-preferred status of debt finance, the holders of the old view typically argue that high debt-equity ratios generate certain invisible costs stemming from the risks of financial distress and bankruptcy. At some leverage ratio well below a hundred percent the rise in these costs will outweigh the tax benefits of increased reliance on debt finance.

The old view also assumes that shareholders have a nontax preference for dividends over capital gains on shares. Other things equal, shareholders will thus require a lower after-tax return on shares in corporations with higher dividend pay-out ratios. Up to a point, the corporation is therefore able to reduce its cost of equity finance by raising its pay-out ratio. Since new share issues increase the ability of the corporation to pay dividends to existing shareholders, it becomes optimal for the value-maximizing corporation to rely to some extent on new equity rather than using only retained profits as the source of equity finance. In principle, the corporation will raise its dividend pay-out ratio to the point where the marginal nontax

benefits from increased dividend payments are just offset by the tax penalty on dividends, with the tax penalty being equal to the difference between the personal tax rate on dividends and the effective personal tax rate on (accrued) capital gains on shares.

Proponents of the old view do not always make very clear why shareholders would require lower net returns on shares with higher dividend pay-out ratios. The most popular hypothesis is that dividends serve as a signal to the stock market that the corporation is financially healthy and faces bright earnings prospects. Critics have found this theory rather unconvincing, arguing that a corporation faced with profitable investment opportunities should retain and reinvest its profits rather than paying them out.

The Neutrality Hypothesis

The critics of the old view tend to downgrade the importance of nontax factors for corporate financing decisions. The point of departure for these sceptics is the so-called Modigliani–Miller theorem, according to which shareholders would be indifferent to the corporation's financial policy in a world without taxes, since investors would always be able to neutralize the effects of the firm's borrowing and dividend policy on the risk-return profiles of their personal portfolios by selling from or borrowing against their portfolios. If the various modes of finance are in fact equally attractive from a nontax point of view, it follows that the corporation should rely exclusively on the source of finance that is most favored by the tax system.

In most countries, this mode of finance would be debt, because equity-financed investment tends to be subject to double taxation. If debt is used as the marginal source of finance, and taxable profits coincide with actual profits, it will be profitable for the corporation to carry its real investment to the point where the risk-adjusted marginal pretax rate of return is just equal to the (deductible) market rate of interest before tax. In other words, the optimal investment policy of the corporation would be identical to the optimal policy in a hypothetical world of zero taxes, and the corporation tax would be neutral, falling only on the inframarginal profits exceeding the market interest rate.

Stiglitz (1973) argued that the corporate income tax will also be neutral if the total corporate and personal tax burden on retained earnings is lower than the personal tax on interest income so that finance by retentions is tax-preferred to debt finance. In this situation—which Stiglitz believed to prevail in the U.S. before the 1981 tax reform—the corporation should undertake retentions-financed real investment until the marginal rate of return becomes equal to the market interest rate, and the remaining profits (if any) should be used for financial investment in the capital market. In the absence of nontax benefits from dividend payments, it is not rational to pay out any dividends if distributions are penalized by the tax system, and if financial investment undertaken through the corporation is taxed more lightly than financial investment undertaken directly by the shareholders themselves.[4] Furthermore, it would obviously not be rational for the corporation to carry out real investment with a return below the market interest rate when it could alternatively invest in financial assets. It should be clear that such a tax regime is really equivalent to a regime of debt finance: to increase its real investment by one dollar, the corporation will have to reduce its financial investment by one dollar, so the opportunity cost of real investment is the interest rate that

might have been earned in the capital market. In short, the cost of corporate capital equals the going interest rate, and again the corporation tax falls only on the inframarginal investments with returns above the market rate of interest.

The "New" View

The neutrality hypothesis does not square with the observations that most corporations do tend to pay dividends on a regular basis and that they rarely rely exclusively on debt finance at the margin. The so-called "new" view of the corporation tax assumes that corporations pay dividends and accepts the fact that firms will typically wish to use some amount of equity finance at the margin. However, according to the new view there is no convincing reason why shareholders should prefer a dollar of net dividend to a dollar of net capital gain on shares. Instead, it is argued that a mature corporation earning sufficient profits should meet all of its need for equity finance through retentions and should pay out only the remaining profit as dividends. A mature corporation operating under a classical corporate tax system should never substitute new share issues for retained earnings, since this would transform lightly taxed capital gains on shares into more heavily taxed dividends.

Since the new view assumes that retained profits are the marginal source of corporate finance, it implies that the corporation's marginal investment will generate an additional capital gains liability for shareholders, because increased retentions will tend to raise the market value of outstanding shares. If the combined corporate and personal tax burden on retentions (i.e., the sum of the corporate income tax on retentions and the personal tax on capital gains on shares) exceeds the shareholder's personal tax on interest income, the required rate of return on corporate investment will exceed the market interest rate.

On the other hand, the new view has the striking implication that taxes on *distributed* profits are *neutral*. While it is true that dividend taxes reduce the shareholder's income from additional investment, they also reduce his opportunity cost of allowing the firm to retain profits for further investment. Thus, if the total corporate and personal tax burden on a dollar of distributed profits is 50 cents, the shareholder only has to give up a net income of 50 cents for each dollar retained for investment by the corporation. This 50 percent reduction of the opportunity cost of investment fully compensates for the 50 percent dividend tax levied when the profits on the extra investment are ultimately paid out, leaving the shareholder's net return unaffected by the tax burden on distributions. Hence, taxes on dividends have no influence on the cost of corporate capital, but are merely capitalized in share prices in order to ensure that investment in shares is just as attractive as investment in interest-bearing assets, despite the double taxation of dividends. One may also say that equity is "trapped" within the corporation in the sense that the funds accumulated within the firm will inevitably have to bear the dividend tax, whether distributions are made now or later. For a constant dividend tax rate, an investment policy that maximizes the present value of distributions before dividend tax will therefore also maximize the present value of dividends after tax. Hence, the neutrality of the dividend tax.

The new view thus implies that measures to alleviate the double taxation of dividends will not stimulate corporate investment, leading only to a windfall gain to existing shareholders and a corresponding loss of government revenue.

According to the new view, policymakers should focus instead on the double taxation of *retained earnings* resulting from the coexistence of the corporate income tax and the personal tax on capital gains on shares. However, since the effective tax rate on accrued capital gains is typically rather low because the tax is deferred until the time of realization of the gain, the new view also suggests that the problem of double taxation is not very serious and that the cost of corporate capital is probably not very far above the market interest rate, even in countries like the United States where realized long-term capital gains on shares are included in the personal income tax base.[5]

Reconciling the Old and the New View: The "Nucleus" Theory of the Firm

If revenue-generating dividend taxes are neutral, one might be tempted to conclude that policymakers should *increase* the tax burden on dividends rather than worry about measures to alleviate the existing double taxation. This conclusion would be too hasty, however, since the new view explained above applies only to mature firms earning sufficient profits to be able to meet their need for equity finance through retained earnings. Holders of the new view do not deny that newly established firms or rapidly growing firms that have to rely on new share issues will face a higher cost of capital when dividends are subject to double taxation. Since shareholders are not entitled to a tax deduction for their purchase of shares, their opportunity cost of investment will not be reduced by the dividend tax rate, as is the case when the firm finances investment by withholding dividends. The net return to investment will therefore be reduced by the full amount of the dividend tax, and the cost of capital will be correspondingly higher, when new equity is the marginal source of finance and marginal profits are paid out as dividends.

It would thus seem that the old view may be relevant for immature or rapidly growing firms even if the new view provides a correct description of mature firms. Yet, it has been argued by Sinn (1991b) that the cost of capital for an immature firm will be even *higher* than predicted by the old view. The old view suggests that a corporation that is about to be set up should immediately issue the amount of shares necessary to carry investment to the point where the marginal return just compensates for the extra tax on dividends relative to interest income. However, Sinn (1991b) points out that if retentions are taxed more lightly than distributions, it may be optimal for a corporation in the start-up phase to issue a smaller amount of shares than this investment rule would suggest. The reason is that the tax system provides an incentive to postpone investment until the firm begins to make profits so that it can finance investment out of tax-preferred retentions. If it only has a limited number of investment projects with above-normal rates of return, the new firm foregoes the possibility of financing these investments by "cheaper" capital (retentions) at a later date if it raises new equity today in order to implement all projects at once. The loss of the opportunity to use a cheaper mode of finance at a later stage represents an additional opportunity cost of current investment for the immature firm that must be added to the cost of capital.

According to Sinn (1991b), a new corporation should therefore issue only a limited amount of new shares at the time of foundation—*i.e.*, it should start only with a small "nucleus" of equity—in order to carry out only the most profitable of its planned investment projects.

The remaining projects with relatively high returns should be financed exclusively out of retained earnings in the subsequent growth phase of the firm, and no dividends should be paid during this phase, since this would transform lightly taxed capital gains into heavily taxed dividends. The greater the tax discrimination against distributions relative to retentions, the lower should be the initial injection of equity, and the greater should be the volume of investment financed by retentions in the subsequent growth phase. The growth phase comes to an end when the capital stock has expanded to the point where additional investment no longer yields above-normal rates of return. The corporation then enters the stage of maturity, where net investment becomes zero and where profits are paid out as dividends. In this phase, the "trapped-equity" argument applies, *i.e.*, the dividend tax becomes neutral, and the cost of capital becomes equal to the value implied by the new view. The point is, however, that under very mild conditions the initial cost of capital is even *higher* than suggested by the *old* view at the time the firm is set up. Moreover, the cost of capital remains above the value predicted by the new view during the drive to maturity. The reason is that the gradual fall in the marginal productivity of capital during the growth phase will generate a gradual capital loss to shareholders for which they must be compensated by an above-normal rate of return on the corporation's real investment.

Notice the paradoxical implication of this dynamic theory of the corporate firm: the double taxation of dividends will drive up the cost of capital during the growth phase where the firm does *not* pay dividends and no dividend tax is collected, whereas the dividend tax will be neutral in the maturity phase where dividends are actually paid and the tax begins to yield revenue!

NEW DIRECTIONS IN THE THEORY OF
CORPORATE INCOME TAXATION

Accounting Conventions, Accelerated Depreciation and the Cost of Corporate Capital

While we have so far assumed true economic depreciation, depreciation for tax purposes is in fact often allowed to exceed the true rate of depreciation. By being able to move the deduction for depreciation forward in time, the firm essentially obtains an interest-free loan from the government. This interest-free "tax debt" reduces the firm's need to rely on other sources of finance and may have important implications for the cost of capital, as we shall see below.

Traditionally the economic literature on corporate income taxation has also tended to neglect the existence of legal constraints on the amount of dividends that the corporation may distribute.[6] In practice, however, all OECD countries apply some such constraint with the purpose of protecting the equity base of the corporate sector. In the absence of "free" reserves accumulated in the past, the legal dividend constraints essentially imply that current dividends cannot exceed some measure of current after-tax corporate earnings. This is important because it constrains the firm's ability to take advantage of the tax-preferred status of debt finance by increasing its borrowing in order to increase its dividend payments. As a consequence of this limitation on borrowing, the cost of capital will be higher than it would be if firms could fully exploit the advantages of debt finance.

As Kanniainen and Södersten (1994a) have shown, the exact implications for the cost of capital will depend on the exact form of the dividend constraint, which in turn is related to the accounting conventions used in the country. The

Anglo-Saxon countries plus a few other OECD countries adhere to the convention of *separate reporting*, which means that the profits shown in the public accounts drawn up for the shareholders need not coincide with the profits registered in the tax accounts. Roughly speaking, these "two-book" countries allow corporations to distribute the after-tax profits recorded in the public accounts minus the amount of taxes deferred through accelerated depreciation. It can be shown that this convention enables the firm to finance all of its marginal investment by a combination of regular debt and "tax debt" stemming from tax deferrals, if it borrows to the maximum extent allowed by the dividend constraint. Because the tax debt is interest free, the cost of capital will then fall below the market interest rate in the presence of accelerated depreciation, and a rise in the corporate income tax rate will *reduce* the required return by increasing the value of tax debt; a phenomenon sometimes referred to as the "taxation paradox." Still, one can demonstrate that the cost of capital will be higher than it would be if the legal dividend constraint did not force the firm to reduce its borrowing and to increase its retentions by an amount equal to its tax deferrals.

While separate reporting prevails in the Anglo-Saxon world, the majority of OECD countries practice *uniform reporting*, requiring that the profit shown in the public accounts must coincide with the profit recorded in the tax accounts. In these "one-book" countries, the dividend cannot exceed the amount of *taxable* profit after tax. This means that the corporation is forced to retain not only the amount of taxes deferred (*i.e.*, the tax rate times the amount of accelerated depreciation); in fact it must retain the entire amount by which depreciation for tax purposes exceeds the true depreciation of its assets. In this way, the firm is forced to rely more on retained earnings and less on tax-preferred debt finance, so uniform reporting implies a higher cost of capital than separate reporting.

From the corporation's cash flow constraint, it is possible to show that if dividends are not allowed to exceed after-tax taxable profits, the amount of borrowing can be no greater than the firm's gross investment minus the depreciation recorded in the tax accounts. Hence, when the dividend (borrowing) constraint is binding, depreciation for tax purposes will always correspond to gross investment minus borrowing, *i.e.*, the depreciation taken in the tax accounts will equal the equity-financed part of new investment. This means that the firm's equity-financed investment is immediately written off in the tax accounts. The corporate income tax therefore becomes *neutral*, for while the tax does confiscate part of the cash inflow from new equity-financed investment, it also finances a corresponding part of the investment outlay through the immediate write-off. In short, the corporation tax will tend to work like a neutral cash flow tax under uniform reporting, at least if there are no nontax factors discouraging corporations from borrowing to the maximum extent allowed by the dividend constraint.

However, this analysis does not imply that the cost of corporate capital is entirely unaffected by the parameters of the corporate tax system under uniform reporting. It can be shown that the possibility of accelerated depreciation will still reduce the cost of capital if the effective personal tax rate on capital gains is lower than the personal tax rate on interest income. When the dividend constraint is binding, an increase in deductions for depreciation requires the firm to reduce its borrowing and increase its retentions by a corresponding amount.

As we have just explained, this switch from debt finance toward equity finance does not generate an additional corporate income tax burden, due to the extra deduction for depreciation. At the individual investor level, the substitution of retained earnings for debt implies that personal taxes on interest income are replaced by personal taxes on capital gains on shares. If capital gains are more lightly taxed, the total tax burden on investment therefore goes down, and hence the cost of capital is reduced when the corporation takes advantage of accelerated depreciation.

Monitoring Costs, Dividend Constraints, and the Cost of Capital: The "Nordic" View

According to the above analysis, a corporation wishing to minimize its cost of capital will have a tax incentive to exploit deductions for accelerated depreciation to the maximum possible extent. Nevertheless, as Kanniainen and Södersten (1994b) pointed out, public corporations in Sweden and Finland have consistently failed to exploit all available deductions for depreciation and various reserve funds, even in cases where they might have eliminated their corporate tax liability altogether by doing so. Kanniainen and Södersten suggest that this puzzling behavior may be explained by the existence of nontax benefits from borrowing combined with the borrowing constraint implied by uniform reporting. As already noted, a binding dividend constraint under uniform reporting means that there is competition between the use of debt finance and deductions for depreciation. If there are important nontax benefits from debt finance, it may be profitable for the corporation not to exploit all available allowances in order to increase its borrowing. In that case, an increase in the maximum rate of depreciation allowed by the tax code will obviously fail to stimulate corporate investment. Since the corporate income tax rate is likewise neutral under uniform reporting, we arrive at the striking hypothesis that neither the rate nor the definition of the base of the corporation tax has any impact on the cost of corporate capital in the majority of OECD countries adhering to uniform reporting!

What are the nontax benefits from debt finance responsible for this result? The explanation offered by Kanniainen and Södersten (1994b) starts from the observation that shareholders and corporate managers do not necessarily have identical interests.[7] In the presence of imperfect and asymmetric information, corporate managers may therefore need to be monitored to ensure that they stick to an efficient, value-maximizing behavior. Still, the individual shareholder will often have little incentive to incur the costs of monitoring, because the benefits of improved management efficiency will be shared with all other stockholders in the firm. Shareholders will therefore wish the corporation to turn regularly to the external capital market, since the suppliers of debt capital (*e.g.*, banks) have an obvious interest in monitoring the firm to make sure it is run efficiently so that the risk of bankruptcy is minimized. The use of debt finance will thus help to reduce the shareholders' costs of monitoring corporate managers, and if the saving of monitoring costs is sufficiently large, the controlling shareholder may want the corporation to forego some available tax allowances in order to make room for increased corporate borrowing.[8]

A Modified Nordic View

However, as pointed out by Sørensen (1995), if debt finance reduces shareholder monitoring costs by exposing managers to the scrutiny of professional agents in the capital market, there are reasons to believe that the use of new equity finance will likewise tend to reduce monitoring costs for the firm's owners. For instance, when the corporation issues new shares, its affairs will often be reviewed by an investment banker or by underwriters of stock, and such reviews may help to expose management inefficiencies.

If the saving of monitoring costs associated with new share issues is non-negligible and the tax penalty on dividends relative to capital gains is not too large, it may be profitable for the firm to issue new shares while at the same time paying dividends to existing shareholders, as is sometimes observed in practice. Within such a regime, one can show that if certain restrictions on the parameters of the monitoring cost function are satisfied, a fall in the tax burden on distributed profits will stimulate the use of new share issues. This in turn will reduce the marginal monitoring costs associated with a rise in the corporation's capital stock, thereby encouraging its real investment, in accordance with the old view of dividend taxation (see Sørensen, 1994, 1995, for details).

On the other hand, if the monitoring cost saving stemming from new share issues is small and/or the tax penalty on dividends is large, the theory suggests that mature corporations will not wish to resort to new share issues but will instead rely only on a combination of debt and retained earnings. In that case, we are back to the regime of corporate tax neutrality analyzed by Kanniainen and Södersten (1994b).

The recent theories stressing the importance of accounting conventions for the cost of corporate capital are summarized in Table 2. As stated in the table, the presence of monitoring cost savings from debt finance does not eliminate the firm's incentive to take full advan-

TABLE 2
EFFECTS OF THE CORPORATE TAX SYSTEM UNDER ALTERNATIVE ACCOUNTING REGIMES[a]

| Accounting Regime | Role of Monitoring Costs | | |
	unimportant	significant monitoring cost savings from debt finance	significant monitoring cost savings from external finance
Uniform reporting ("One-book" system)	corporate income tax rate neutral dividend taxation neutral investment stimulated by accelerated depreciation	corporate income tax rate neutral dividend taxation neutral accelerated depreciation ineffective	corporate income tax rate non-neutral dividend taxation non-neutral accelerated depreciation ineffective
Separate reporting ("Two-book" system)	corporate income tax rate non-neutral ("taxation paradox") dividend taxation neutral investment stimulated by accelerated depreciation		corporate income tax rate non-neutral dividend taxation non-neutral investment stimulated by accelerated depreciation

[a]The table summarizes the findings of Kanniainen and Södersten (1994a, b) and Sørensen (1994, 1995). All results reported in the table are based on the assumption that marginal profits are paid out as dividends.

tage of allowances for accelerated depreciation under separate reporting (see Sørensen, 1994, Appendix). The reason is that this accounting regime does not constrain the use of debt finance to the same extent as the regime of uniform reporting.

It should be added that the monitoring-cost theory sketched here is not the only possible explanation why corporations in "one-book" (uniform-reporting) countries may not wish to exploit all available depreciation allowances. As Cummins, Harris, and Hassett (1994) have pointed out, firms in one-book countries may also be reluctant to claim all potential tax benefits if reductions in taxable income may be misinterpreted by financial markets as signals of lower profitability. Indeed, these authors find empirical evidence that investment in one-book countries is less sensitive to tax-law changes than investment in "two-book" countries allowing separate reporting. This underscores the importance of analyzing a country's accounting regime

when evaluating the incentive effects of the corporation tax.

TAXATION OF CORPORATE-SOURCE INCOME IN THE OPEN ECONOMY

We have so far ignored the complications arising from the openness of the economy. In the remainder of the article we shall briefly consider how the corporate tax system affects the incentive to undertake domestic corporate investment when the economy is open to international capital mobility.[9]

Taxes on Saving Versus Taxes on Investment

With capital mobility it becomes crucial to distinguish taxes on *saving* from taxes on *investment*. In a closed economy, this distinction is unimportant because any tax that tends to reduce the level of saving will also discourage investment, and *vice versa*, due to the equilibrium condition that saving must equal investment. By contrast, in the open economy, domestic asset returns need not adjust to

equilibrate aggregate saving and investment, because any difference between
the two magnitudes may be accommo-
dated through capital exports or capital
imports. Hence, taxes on the return to
saving undertaken by domestic residents
may primarily tend to discourage domestic saving and to stimulate capital imports without significantly affecting domestic investment, whereas taxes on the
return to capital invested in the domestic
economy may primarily induce a fall in
domestic investment and a concomitant
capital outflow without much change in
the domestic savings level.

As emphasized by Boadway and Bruce
(1992), the personal tax on dividends
and shareholder capital gains is a tax on
saving, whereas the corporate income
tax is more appropriately categorized as
a tax on investment. In the OECD area,
the personal income tax is based on the
residence principle, implying that individual shareholders are liable to tax on
their worldwide income, whether it originates from domestic or from foreign
sources. Formally, most OECD countries
also tax corporations registered in the
country on a worldwide basis, offering a
credit for taxes already paid to foreign-
source countries. Yet, in practice, the
corporate income tax comes closer to a
tax based on the *source* principle, under
which income is taxed only in the country where it is earned.

There are several factors tending to turn
the formally residence-based corporation
tax into a *de facto* source-based tax. For
one thing, half of the OECD countries
exempt dividend income from foreign-
controlled corporations from domestic
corporate income tax, unless the dividend originates from a tax-haven country.

Second, even when income from foreign
subsidiaries is liable to domestic corpo-

rate income tax, as in countries like the
United States, the United Kingdom, and
Japan, the domestic tax is usually deferred until the time the income is repatriated in the form of dividends. As Hartman (1985) pointed out, this practice of
deferral means that the "trapped equity" argument of the "new" view applies to income from foreign direct investment: if a foreign subsidiary finances
investment by retaining profits abroad,
the parent company avoids the dividend
tax on repatriations, and this reduction
of the opportunity cost of foreign investment compensates for the domestic dividend tax imposed when the profits are
ultimately repatriated. Hence, for investment by mature foreign subsidiaries using retentions as the marginal source of
finance, only the foreign corporate income tax affects the cost of capital, as
would be the case under a pure source-
based tax system.

Third, since the home countries of parent companies offer a foreign tax credit
only up to the limit given by the amount
of domestic tax on the foreign income,
foreign direct investment will be subject
only to foreign corporation tax whenever
the effective foreign tax rate exceeds the
effective domestic corporate tax rate.

Fourth, when it comes to foreign portfolio investment, the domestic residence
country typically does not grant any tax
credits for the foreign corporation tax on
the corporate profits underlying the
shareholder's portfolio income.

Thus, to a first approximation, it does
not seem misleading to assume that the
corporate income tax works essentially
like a source-based capital income tax.
To the extent that a rise in the corporate income tax rate would tend to reduce corporate investment in a closed
economy, it will therefore have an even
stronger negative impact on domestic in-

vestment in the open economy where the higher domestic tax burden may be avoided by channeling corporate investment abroad.

Will the Corporation Tax Vanish in the Open Economy?

This observation has led some writers to suggest that source-based capital income taxes like the corporation tax may tend to vanish in the long run as international capital mobility becomes near-perfect.[10] The idea is that if the government of a small open economy cannot tax foreign-source corporate income, it cannot impose any tax burden on the domestic owners of corporate capital when capital mobility is perfect. If the government levies a tax on corporate income from domestic investment, corporate capital will tend to flee the country since the after-tax return offered on foreign investment is unchanged. In principle, this process will continue until the pretax rate of return on domestic corporate investment has risen by the full amount of the domestic tax. The tax burden is thus fully shifted onto the owners of internationally immobile factors such as labor and land, because the capital flight reduces the demand for these factors. However, since it is more efficient to impose explicit taxes on the immobile factors rather than taxing them indirectly *via* a corporate income tax that distorts investment decisions, a rational government seeking to minimize the deadweight loss from taxation should rely solely on direct taxes on immobile factors and should impose no corporate income tax (or any other source-based capital income tax) at all!

If governments actually followed this prescription, the traditional worries about the double taxation of corporate-source income might soon become obsolete. However, there are several reasons why the corporate income tax will hardly vanish in the long run, despite the growing international mobility of capital. First of all, it may be politically infeasible to impose high explicit taxes on immobile factors, and the government may therefore have to tax these factors indirectly through the source-based corporate income tax, even though this involves a higher efficiency cost. Second, because of local factors, multinational corporations will sometimes be able to earn above-normal returns by investing in a particular country. The corporation tax enables the domestic government to capture some of these "location-specific rents" without deterring investment. Third, the international mobility of direct business investment is unlikely to become quite perfect. A reallocation of production activities and physical capital across countries usually involves considerable adjustment costs. Consequently, it will often be unprofitable for multinationals to relocate their activities in response to (modest) tax differentials. Fourth, as long as some important capital-exporting countries like the United States continue to offer credits for taxes on foreign-source income, it would be inefficient for capital-importing countries not to impose a source-based corporation tax in order to shift revenue from the foreign to the domestic Exchequer without deterring foreign investors.[11]

The Effects of Domestic Double Tax Relief in the Open Economy

Since the corporate income tax is likely to survive, it is still relevant to ask how measures to alleviate the double taxation of corporate-source income will affect domestic corporate investment in the open economy?

Consider first the simplified case of a small open economy with a national stock market that is perfectly integrated in the international stock market. All shares in domestic corporations are thus traded in the world stock market, and given the smallness of the domestic economy, stock prices are determined by the arbitrage behavior of foreign investors. The international price of shares in domestic corporations determines the domestic cost of equity finance, *i.e.*, the rate of return after corporation tax (but before personal tax) that a domestic corporation must be able to offer on its equity-financed investment, whether investment takes place at home or abroad.

Suppose now that the domestic government decides to integrate its corporate and personal income taxes, say, by offering a dividend tax credit to domestic residents holding shares in domestic corporations. Clearly, this makes domestic shares more attractive for domestic investors who therefore increase their demand for shares in domestic firms. However, if foreign investors do not receive the dividend tax credit, the increased demand from domestic investors will just induce foreigners to sell part of their domestic shares to domestic residents, without any noticeable effect on stock prices. Since the relative tax treatment of domestic and foreign shares is unchanged from the viewpoint of foreign investors, the price of domestic shares will also have to stay the same for the large foreign investor group to remain in portfolio equilibrium. As a consequence, the dividend tax credit will fail to reduce the cost of equity finance for domestic corporations, and will only serve to shift part of the shares in domestic firms from foreign to domestic owners without stimulating real domestic investment.

To obtain a fall in the domestic cost of corporate capital it would be necessary to extend the dividend tax credit to foreign shareholders, since this would make domestic shares relatively more attractive for international investors. Alternatively,

the domestic government could decide to relieve double taxation at the *corporate* level, say, by allowing all dividends or an imputed return to equity to be deducted from the domestic corporate income tax base. The above analysis is of some relevance since most OECD countries with integrated corporate tax systems have preferred to alleviate double taxation at the shareholder level and have typically only granted dividend tax relief to domestic holders of domestic shares.[12] Notice, however, that while tax relief to domestic shareholders may fail to stimulate domestic corporate investment, it does tend to eliminate the distortion in favor of investment in the noncorporate sector of the economy. Since a dividend tax credit reserved for domestic shareholders will increase a domestic investor's after-tax return on shares, it will also raise his required return on domestic noncorporate investment. Of course, the price to be paid for this intersectoral equalization of the cost of capital is a fall in investment in the noncorporate sector.

Double Tax Relief and the Role of Small Private Companies

When the assumptions made in the previous section are relaxed, there may be cases where double tax relief aimed at domestic shareholders will succeed in stimulating domestic corporate investment. For instance, the tax discrimination in favor of domestic shareholders may become so strong that all shares in domestic companies end up being held domestically. In that case, the "marginal" shareholder is no longer a foreign investor, and domestic share prices will then be bid up by policy measures that make shareholding more attractive for domestic investors.

Even if the prices of shares in large public corporations continue to be dominated by the arbitrage behavior of foreign investors, a realistic analysis should allow for the existence of smaller private companies in which the shares are not traded internationally. Such companies are often controlled by owner-managers who may not consider their shares to be perfect substitutes for shares in large public corporations. It is therefore conceivable that the required return on shares in private unquoted companies may be reduced through domestic double tax relief even if the prices of internationally traded shares remain unaffected. However, this outcome is not certain, as demonstrated by Sørensen (1994, pp. 40–43) within a portfolio model in which investors hold internationally traded bonds, internationally traded shares in public corporations, and nontraded shares in private corporations. Even though domestic shareholder tax relief will shift demand from bonds toward shares in general, it may also induce a shift of asset demand from nontraded to traded shares. This will be the case if the initial pretax return on nontraded shares is very low relative to the initial pretax return on traded shares. In that case, the reduction of tax on shareholder income will cause a much greater increase in the after-tax return to traded shares compared to the increase in the net return on nontraded shares, causing a portfolio shift away from the latter asset type. A sufficient (but far from necessary) condition for dividend tax relief to stimulate the demand for nontraded shares is that the pretax return on these shares is no lower than the pretax return on traded shares (see Sørensen, 1994). In that case, one can be sure that domestic shareholder tax relief will reduce the cost of equity finance for domestic private corporations.

Concluding Remarks

Though we have left out many important topics and contributions, our quick journey through the theory of corporate income taxation may have left a rather flimsy picture. The different views of the corporation tax do indeed lead to rather different predictions regarding the influence of tax policy on the cost of corporate capital. However, a review of the many competing hypotheses does at least serve to focus attention on the crucial factors that will determine the incentive effects of the corporate tax system: What is the marginal source of finance preferred by corporations? What (if any) are the important nontax factors determining corporate financial policy and how is this policy modified by tax considerations? What is the identity and tax status of the marginal shareholder? In particular, is the marginal shareholder a foreign or a domestic resident, and is he liable to personal tax or not? What is the nature of the accounting regime and how do accounting conventions constrain the corporation's ability to pay dividends?

Furthermore, the extent of disagreement over the incidence of the corporation tax should not be exaggerated. Few economists would claim that the corporate tax system is literally neutral, and the inventors of the various tax neutrality propositions reviewed in this article probably see these propositions only as useful antidotes to exaggerated claims that the corporation tax causes huge distortions. There is broad agreement that the double taxation of dividends hampers the growth of young and expanding firms, even if there is less agreement on the importance of dividend taxes for mature corporations. Finally, the need to distinguish between taxes on saving and taxes on investment when analyzing the impact of the different components of the corporate tax system in the open economy is by now well established.

Future theoretical and empirical research will hopefully help to resolve those issues that are still unsettled.

ENDNOTES

Without implicating them in any way, I wish to thank Robin Boadway, Vesa Kanniainen, and Jan Södersten for stimulating discussions of the topics covered in this paper. I also wish to acknowledge an intellectual debt to Hans-Werner Sinn, whose writings on capital income taxation have been a continuing source of inspiration. The activities of the Economic Policy Research Unit are supported by a grant from the Danish National Research Foundation.

[1] In an interesting recent report, the U.S. Treasury (1992) has analyzed various methods of eliminating the double taxation of corporate source income. See also OECD (1991) for an overview of OECD practices.

[2] For more detailed surveys, see Auerbach (1983), Poterba and Summers (1985), Sinn (1991a), or Sørensen (1995).

[3] In the next part of the paper, we shall consider the complications arising from deviations between taxable profits and true economic profits.

[4] For the corporation to have a positive market value, it must ultimately return cash to its shareholders. Stiglitz (1973) assumed that this would be done by liquidating the firm at some point.

[5] Critics have argued that the surge in share repurchases observed in the United States during the last decade undermines the assumption underlying the new view that cash distributions to shareholders take the form of dividends. However, as Sinn (1991a, sec. 7.1) has demonstrated, a corporation financing its marginal investment by new share issues (or, equivalently, by a reduction in share repurchases) and using its marginal profits to repurchase shares would in fact have exactly the same cost of capital as implied by the new view.

[6] Exceptions to this rule are King (1974a), Boadway and Bruce (1979), Boadway (1980), and Sinn (1985). However, Kanniainen and Södersten (1994a) were apparently the first writers to undertake a truly systematic investigation of the impact of existing legal constraints on the cost of corporate capital.

[7] This idea is central to the various "agency-cost" theories of corporate finance, e.g., Easterbrook (1984), and Jensen (1986).

[8] Notice the stark contrast to the old view, which assumes that there are costs (rather than benefits) associated with debt finance.

[9] This part of the paper draws on Sørensen (1994, part III). For a more comprehensive survey of capital income taxation in the open economy, see Slemrod (1988).

[10] See, e.g., Gordon (1992) and Razin and Sadka (1991).

[11] Of course, this begs the following question: Why are the governments of capital-exporting countries apparently willing to give away revenue for nothing through the mechanism of foreign tax credits? One potential explanation, offered by Gordon (1992), is that capital-exporting countries face difficulties in enforcing taxes on foreign-source income. To prevent a capital flight, which would also erode the domestic capital income tax base, governments of capital-exporting countries therefore offer a foreign tax credit, thus providing an incentive for capital-importing countries to impose a source-based capital income tax rather than playing the role of tax havens.

[12] This discrimination against border-crossing investment in shares may be part of the explanation why national stock markets still seem somewhat segmented.

REFERENCES

Auerbach, Alan J. "Wealth Maximization and the Cost of Capital." *Quarterly Journal of Economics 94* (1979): 433–46.

Auerbach, Alan J. "Taxation, Corporate Financial Policy and the Cost of Capital." *Journal of Economic Literature 21* (1983): 905–40.

Boadway, Robin W. "Corporate Taxation and Investment: A Synthesis of the Neo-classical Theory." *Canadian Journal of Economics 13* (1980): 250–67.

Boadway, Robin W. and Neil Bruce. "Depreciation and Interest Deductions and the Effect of the Corporate Income Tax on Investment." *Journal of Public Economics 11* (1979): 93–105.

Boadway, Robin W. and Neil Bruce. "Problems with Integrating Corporate and Personal Income Taxes in an Open Economy." *Journal of Public Economics 48* (1992): 39–66.

Bradford, David F. "The Economics of Tax Policy Toward Savings." In *The Government and Capital Formation*, edited by G. M. von Furstenberg. Cambridge, MA: Ballinger Publishing Company, 1980.

Bradford, David F. "The Incidence and Allocation Effects of a Tax on Corporate Distributions." *Journal of Public Economics 15* (1981): 1–22.

Cummins, Jason G., T. S. Harris and Kevin A. Hassett. "Accounting Standards, Information Flow, and Firm Investment Behavior." NBER Working Paper No. 4685. Cambridge, MA: National Bureau of Economic Research, 1994.

Easterbrook, Frank H. "Two Agency-cost Explanations of Dividends." *American Economic Review 74* (1984): 650–9.

Gordon, Roger H. "Can Capital Income Taxes Survive?" *Journal of Finance 47* (1992): 1159–80.

Harberger, Arnold C. "The Incidence of the Corporation Income Tax." *Journal of Political Economy 70* (1962): 215–40.

Harberger, Arnold C. "Efficiency Effects of Taxes on Income from Capital." In *Effects of Corporation Income Tax*, edited by M. Krzyzaniak. Detroit: Wayne State University Press, 1966.

Hartman, David G. "Tax Policy and Foreign Direct Investment." *Journal of Public Economics 26* (1985): 107–21.

Jensen, M. D. "Agency Costs of Free Cash Flow, Corporate Finance, and Takeover." *American Economic Review 76* (1986): 323–9.

Kanniainen, Vesa and Jan Södersten. "The Importance of Reporting Conventions for the Theory of Corporate Taxation." Uppsala University Department of Economics Working Paper No. 1994:5. Uppsala, Sweden: Uppsala University, 1994.

Kanniainen, Vesa and Jan Södersten. "Costs of Monitoring and Corporate Taxation." *Journal of Public Economics 55* (1994b): 307–22.

King, Mervyn A. "Taxation and the Cost of Capital." *Review of Economic Studies 41* (1974a): 21–35.

King, Mervyn A. "Dividend Behaviour and the Theory of the Firm." *Economica 41* (1974b): 25–34.

King, Mervyn A. *Public Policy and the Corporation.* London: Chapman and Hall; New York: Wiley and Sons, 1977.

Organisation for Economic Co-operation and Development. *Taxing Profits in A Global Economy—Domestic and International Issues.* Paris: OECD, 1991.

Poterba, James and Lawrence H. Summers. "The Economic Effects of Dividend Taxation." In *Recent Advance in Corporate Finance*, edited by E. Altman and M. Subrahmanyam. Homewood, IL: Irwin, 1985.

Razin, Assaf and Efraim Sadka. "International Tax Competition and the Gains from Tax Harmonization." *Economics Letters 37* (1991): 69–76.

Sinn, Hans-Werner. *Capital Income Taxation and Resource Allocation.* Amsterdam: North-Holland, 1987. Translation of *Kapitaleinkommenbesteuerung.* Tübingen: Mohr, 1985.

Sinn, Hans-Werner. "Taxation and the Cost of Capital: The 'Old' View, the 'New' View and Another View." In *Tax Policy and the Economy 5*, edited by David F. Bradford. 25–54. 1991a.

Sinn, Hans-Werner. "The Vanishing Harberger Triangle." *Journal of Public Economics 45* (1991b): 271–300.

Slemrod, Joel B. "Effect of Taxation with International Capital Mobility." In *Uneasy Compromise: Problems of a Hybrid Income Consumption Tax.* Washington D.C.: Brookings Institution, 1988.

Stiglitz, Joseph E. "Taxation, Corporate Financial Policy, and the Cost of Capital." *Journal of Public Economics 2* (1973): 1–34.

Sørensen, Peter Birch. "Some Old and New Issues in the Theory of Corporate Income Taxation." *EPRU Economic Studies* No. 2. Copenhagen: Copenhagen Business School, 1994.

Sørensen, Peter Birch. "Some Old and New Issues in the Theory of Corporate Income Taxation." *Finanzarchiv 52*, 1995, forthcoming.

U.S. Treasury. *Integration of the Individual and Corporate Tax Systems.* Washington, D.C.: Government Printing Office, 1992.

THE AMERICAN RETAIL SALES TAX: CONSIDERATIONS ON THEIR STRUCTURE, OPERATIONS, AND POTENTIAL AS A FOUNDATION FOR A FEDERAL SALES TAX

JOHN L. MIKESELL[*]

Abstract - *Americans are familiar with the retail sales tax. Therefore, it is not surprising that Congress would consider such a tax as a way to tax consumption expenditure, should it choose to shift from the present federal structure that emphasizes income taxation. While the sales taxes are impressive revenue producers for state and local government, the taxes are poorly designed as consumption taxes: they tax too few household services, they exempt too many household purchases of goods, and they tax too many business inputs, especially capital asset purchases. State and local sales tax rates are relatively low, so compliance appears not to be a major problem, and economic distortions, while real, have not been a great difficulty. The much higher rates needed to replace the federal income tax would create many more problems. Most national governments choose the credit-invoice value-added tax if they seek substantial revenue from an indirect consumption tax. That is almost certainly a better option than the retail sales tax for a national indirect consumption tax in the United States as well.*

[*]School of Public and Environmental Affairs, Indiana University, Bloomington, IN 47405.

INTRODUCTION

Retail sales taxes have been an American fiscal success.[1] The tax that Mississippi initiated in 1932 by converting its fractional rate general business tax into a two percent tax on retail sales gave the state a tax that produced considerable revenue at low statutory rates and could be easily collected in relatively painless amounts on each transaction. These taxes gave states an alternative to help them weather the collapse of property tax revenue during the Great Depression. The spread of the tax was dramatic: by 1938, 26 states (plus Hawaii) had adopted the tax. After that fiscal catastrophe, retail sales taxes provided important support for the considerable increase in state government in the post–World War II era.

Retail sales taxes have now been the largest single source of tax revenue for states for 50 years, currently yielding more than $130 billion annually. In fiscal 1994, these taxes produced more revenue than any other tax for 23 of the 50 state governments. Revenues amount to a bit more than one-third of all state tax revenue; 12 states collect 40 percent or more of their tax revenue from their general sales tax. These sales taxes also yield ten percent of local government revenue, a share so low only because of the near-total domination of the property tax in the finances of local school districts. The retail sales tax is a vital contributor to the finances of state and local government as the only broad-based tax on consumption in the United States revenue system.

The sales tax seems the model of simplicity to the customer making a purchase: the tax is added easily and conveniently to the price at the time of purchase. That appearance is misleading. As Simons (1950, p. 9) wrote many years ago, the sales tax "is a simple tax only in the sense that most people have no part in its technical operation." Because the tax levied by the states excludes many business and household purchases and requires vendors to distinguish which sales are exempt and which are taxed, business compliance with and government administration of the tax is far more complex than its appearance at the cash register. Nevertheless, state sales tax compliance seems to reach levels that federal income tax collectors can only dream about, although good data on the question are sparse: a Tennessee study (Adams and Johnson, 1989) estimated

the percentage of sales tax voluntarily reported against total tax liability at 95.9 percent in that state, and a Washington state study (Washington Department of Revenue, 1990) estimated its rate to be 98.3 percent.[2] Few believe sales tax compliance rates to be a severe problem, although that belief stems more from faith rather than from research.

Because the retail sales tax has been so productive for state governments, it is not surprising that some propose a national retail sales tax as a replacement for federal income taxes in the pursuit of fundamental tax reform. It does offer one alternative for moving the federal revenue system from heavy reliance on income taxes toward taxation based on consumption. However, such a change requires a clear understanding of the structure of the state retail sales taxes and what problems a heavier use of these taxes might create. The following sections will examine the logic of the retail sales tax, the extent to which state sales taxes are structured according to that logic, and the potential for a national sales tax that follows the design of these state taxes.

THE IDEA OF A RETAIL SALES TAX

A retail sales tax as a practical application of consumption taxation does have considerable appeal for improvement of national economic prospects and for improvement of fairness in the distribution of the cost of government. More than 40 years ago, Kaldor (1955) made the case for consumption as an equitable basis for taxation, particularly in regard to complications of defining a comprehensive income base: "...each individual [measures tax capacity] for himself when, in the light of all his present circumstances and future prospects, he decides on the scale of his personal living expenses. Thus a tax based on actual spending rates each individual's spending capacity according to the yardstick which he applies to himself. Once actual spending is taken as the criterion all the problems created by the non-comparability of work-incomes and property-incomes, of temporary and permanent sources of wealth, of genuine and fictitious capital gains resolve themselves; they are all brought into equivalence in the measure in which they support the actual standards of living" (1955, p. 47). Assigning a higher tax burden to those who spend more surely represents an ability-to-pay standard consistent with consumer sovereignty and market choice. How much the consumer believes he or she can afford to purchase from the private market becomes the standard according to which a portion of the cost of government will be distributed. Furthermore, by being collected on each transaction instead of on some end-of-year accounting, the retail sales tax variant of the consumption tax is particularly convenient for taxpayers.

The consumption base also has a strong foundation on grounds of economic efficiency, particularly as an alternative to a tax on income. As Cnossen and Sandford (1988, p. 32) note, switching from income to consumption tax bases "will reduce the difference between the pre-and-post tax return to saving that encourages taxpayers to consume rather than save, so saving will be encouraged by the change and the growth path of the economy may subsequently move upwards." This effect has generally defied precise measurement in the United States, partly because of the difficulty of understanding what influences private saving and partly because the country has no experience with a tax solely on household consumption. Nevertheless, to end the

disincentive to save that results from taxing the returns to saving under an income tax, and thus possibly to improve the prospective path of real economic growth, provides a tempting argument for consumption taxation. One prominent advocate of the national retail sales tax maintains that substituting it for the income tax would produce "...a capital formation boom with strongly increased productivity, higher paying jobs, and new investment from around the world" (Lugar, 1995, p. 3).

A retail sales tax following the ideal of a tax on consumption expenditure would require two structural principles (Due and Mikesell, 1994, p. 16):

"a. It should apply to all consumption expenditures, and thus to all sales for consumption purposes, at a uniform rate. Failure to do so will distort relative outputs of various goods and services, discriminate among various families on the basis of consumer preferences, and, frequently, complicate compliance and administration because of the need to distinguish between taxable and nontaxable items and among sales at various rates.

"b. It should apply only to consumption expenditures, and thus not to savings or to purchases for use in production. Taxation of savings or uses of savings would contradict the consumption intent of the tax. Taxation of production inputs has several undesirable consequences, including that of producing a haphazard and unknown final pattern of distribution of burden among various families."

The retail sales tax is limited to consumption expenditure by suspending application of tax to business purchases. Businesses apply tax to their sales, except when the purchaser provides suspension documentation—a certificate of exemption—ordering that the retail sales tax not be applied. The certificate identifies (1) the purchaser as a registered business eligible to make exempt purchases and (2) the business use of the item that makes it nontaxable.[3] When the suspension system works, no business in the chain of production and distribution bringing product to the household consumer would have paid tax on its purchases, because each business would have presented its tax suspension certificate to the seller. The consuming household is not a registered business, can offer no suspension certificate, and must pay the tax on its purchases. Through the suspension process, the tax rests uniformly and exclusively on household consumption. If business purchases of what they use to produce what they sell are entirely excluded and all household purchases of goods and services are taxed, the retail sales tax will be a tax on final sales to consumers—a general consumption tax.

Because state sales taxes miss the standard, they do not have all the advantages claimed for a tax on general consumption expenditure. The taxes now are partial taxes on both household consumption and business input purchases. Surprisingly enough, many states continue to have sales taxes that discourage capital formation by taxing the acquisition of many business inputs, including real capital assets.

AMERICAN RETAIL SALES TAXES AND THE IDEAL

Forty-five states plus the District of Columbia (all states except Alaska, Delaware, Montana, Oregon, and New Hampshire) and more than 6,000 local governments levy retail sales taxes. Among the sales tax states, statutory rates ranged from three percent (Colorado) to seven percent in mid-1996, with a mean of 5.18 percent. Seventeen states levied rates of six

percent or higher. That is considerably increased from the range in 1970 from two percent (five states) to six percent, with a mean rate of 3.54 percent. Furthermore, only one state levied a six percent rate and only five levied a five percent rate. The pace of rate increases has declined during the 1990s, as strong state finances have reduced the need to increase rates.

Although states tend to copy law from their neighbors, no state sales tax exactly matches any other and the different structures take dramatically different shares of their state economies. Nevertheless, the sales taxes share some elements. (1) All are levies "imposed upon the sales, or elements incidental to the sales, such as receipts from them, of all or a wide range of commodities" (Due, 1957, p. 3). (2) All have a system for suspending tax on items purchased for resale so that the cost of inventory to a retailer will not include sales tax paid on its acquisition. (3) All levy rates of one percent or higher on retail transactions. (4) All encourage, if not require, separate quotation of the tax in each transaction except in special circumstances and all but Arizona prohibit retailers from advertising that they will absorb or refund the tax (Due and Mikesell, 1994). Beyond those elements, the coverage choices dramatically influence the nature of the tax base.[4]

Table 1 shows the retail sales tax yield for each state in fiscal 1994. Highest per capita yields, after adjusting for statutory rates, are in Hawaii, New Mexico, South Dakota, Nevada, and Arizona; the yield per percentage point in those states averages $159 per capita. The lowest yields are in Rhode Island, West Virginia, Pennsylvania, Oklahoma, and Vermont: the yields averaged only $70. The high yield states have particularly

TABLE 1
AN INTERSTATE COMPARISON OF SALES TAX BASES, 1994

State	Adjusted Sales Tax Revenue ($ Thousand)	Adjusted Sales Tax Revenue as Percent of Tax Revenue	Per Capita Sales Tax Revenue per 1% Tax Rate ($)	Sales Tax Revenue as Percentage of Personal Income per 1% Tax Rate
Alabama	1,340,142	28.1%	79.42	0.44%
Arizona	2,463,337	43.5%	120.90	0.63%
Arkansas	1,211,806	38.2%	109.79	0.65%
California	16,871,660	34.0%	89.47	0.40%
Colorado	1,125,265	27.1%	102.60	0.46%
Connecticut	2,184,089	32.2%	111.14	0.38%
Florida	10,042,360	56.4%	119.96	0.55%
Georgia	3,370,936	38.4%	119.45	0.59%
Hawaii	1,268,686	42.4%	269.12	1.12%
Idaho	544,145	33.7%	96.05	0.52%
Illinois	4,794,082	31.0%	79.60	0.34%
Indiana	2,601,382	35.7%	90.45	0.45%
Iowa	1,388,742	33.6%	98.17	0.49%
Kansas	1,297,170	35.3%	103.65	0.50%
Kentucky	1,855,338	32.6%	80.81	0.46%
Louisiana	1,888,695	43.1%	109.43	0.62%
Maine	617,008	35.0%	82.92	0.43%
Maryland	2,220,825	29.3%	88.72	0.36%
Massachusetts	2,303,139	20.9%	76.25	0.30%
Michigan	4,538,124	29.4%	113.78	0.51%
Minnesota	2,848,810	32.9%	103.96	0.47%
Mississippi	1,586,879	47.7%	84.94	0.54%
Missouri	2,195,890	37.2%	98.48	0.48%
Nebraska	743,240	34.7%	91.59	0.44%
Nevada	1,184,850	49.8%	125.11	0.53%
New Jersey	3,778,427	28.0%	79.68	0.29%
New Mexico	1,267,035	41.9%	153.25	0.90%
New York	6,117,517	18.6%	84.17	0.33%
North Carolina	2,574,512	24.5%	91.04	0.47%
North Dakota	296,557	33.5%	92.97	0.50%
Ohio	4,479,907	31.6%	80.70	0.39%
Oklahoma	1,096,600	25.7%	74.79	0.42%
Pennsylvania	5,134,300	30.0%	71.00	0.32%
Rhode Island	412,820	28.7%	59.17	0.27%
South Carolina	1,685,727	37.4%	92.01	0.52%
South Dakota	371,251	56.3%	128.70	0.66%
Tennessee	3,081,250	53.8%	99.23	0.51%
Texas	11,709,340	60.2%	101.94	0.52%
Utah	984,287	40.7%	103.18	0.60%
Vermont	220,777	26.5%	76.10	0.38%
Virginia	2,178,352	27.1%	95.00	0.42%
Washington	4,169,570	43.0%	120.06	0.53%
West Virginia	756,622	29.6%	69.21	0.40%
Wisconsin	2,427,900	28.8%	95.55	0.46%
Wyoming	199,428	27.0%	107.44	0.53%
District of Columbia	509,857	20.4%	144.23	0.47%

Source: U.S. Bureau of Census: *State Tax Collection: 1994.* Sales tax collections are adjusted according to the Due and Mikesell technique (1994) to allow for inconsistencies caused by census reporting peculiarities, nonstandard rates, and special excises levied in lieu of expanded sales tax coverage in some states.

broad-based coverage and, except for South Dakota, distinct tourist economies; the low yield states have generous exemptions. However, even more information about the structural differences can be garnered by comparing yield per percentage point of tax as a percentage of state personal income. The broadest by this comparison (Hawaii, New Mexico, South Dakota, Arkansas, and Arizona) average 0.79 percent of personal income, compared with an average of 0.30 percent for the narrowest (Rhode Island, New Jersey, Massachusetts, Pennsylvania, and New York). That means, holding size of economy constant, each percentage point of tax from the broadest coverage taxes will yield more than twice the revenue of the narrowest coverage tax. While these states all levy a sales tax, the legislative choices made in structuring each tax have caused dramatically different tax bases. Major differences include the taxation of household purchases of goods, taxation of services, and exclusion of business purchases.[5]

The Taxation of Household Purchases of Goods

Retail sales taxes are typically general taxes on the purchase (or sale) of tangible personal property and selective taxes on certain purchases (or sale) of service. States have chosen, however, to exempt certain household purchases of goods from the tax. State legislatures understand that households with low annual income spend a higher portion of that income than do higher income households and seek to avoid the appearance of a regressive tax under which tax liability as a fraction of income declines with household income.[6] They respond by removing certain expenditure categories from tax. Exemption favors households with relatively greater preference for the

exempt commodity, reduces revenue from the given statutory rate, makes collection more difficult for vendors and tax authorities, and may distort use of productive resources. The presumption is against exemption unless there are extraordinary reasons otherwise, and any exemption goes against the principle of general consumption taxation.

Food exemptions

States exempt food purchased for preparation at home to reduce regressivity and thereby remove roughly one-fifth of all household consumption on goods from the tax base.[7] The exemption makes the sales tax more vulnerable to business recessions, causes tax payments by families to vary according to preferences for food, and complicates compliance and administration (Mikesell, 1996b). Furthermore, Congress requires those states choosing to otherwise tax food to exempt purchases made with food stamps, as a price for participation in the program. Only 19 states, all west of the Mississippi River, now tax food fully, 25 exempt food fully, and three provide a reduced rate.[8] Twenty-five years ago, the numbers were reversed: 28 states taxed food, 16 exempted food, and 1 state provided a reduced rate.

Items subject to an excise

Motor fuel, tobacco product, and alcohol beverage taxes are the most important examples of excised items that states have exempted from their retail sales taxes. An excise implies economic or social reasons for placing an extra tax burden on the consumption of the excised item. To then exempt the taxed items from the general tax makes no sense. Only ten states apply their retail sales tax to motor fuel: Arizona, California, Georgia (taxed at one percentage point less than the basic rate, plus a one percent special sales tax), Hawaii, Illinois, Indiana, Michigan, New York, South Carolina, and West Virginia. Most states now tax liquor and tobacco products, although Mississippi exempts alcoholic beverages, Virginia exempts state liquor store sales, and Colorado and Texas exempt cigarettes.

Prescription medicine and health related products

States regularly exempt consumer purchases of medicines and other goods related to sickness or health. Only New Mexico offers no exemption for prescription medicines. A number of states also exempt over-the-counter medicines. These states include Florida, Illinois (taxed at a lower rate), Maryland, Minnesota, New Jersey, New York, Pennsylvania, and Rhode Island. When the exemption is limited to prescriptions, compliance and administration remains relatively easy. Adding other health products requires difficult interpretations about what should be exempt and complicates the collection process, as well as erodes the notion of a tax on consumption.

Clothing

A half-dozen states—Connecticut, Massachusetts, Minnesota, New Jersey, Pennsylvania, and Rhode Island— exempt some clothing purchases, presumably under the assumption that exempting these necessities improves fairness of the tax. Evidence suggests that spending patterns across income classes are such that this exemption gives greater relief to high-income as opposed to low-income families (Schaefer, 1969). It therefore reduces revenue yield and makes collection of the tax somewhat more difficult, without the desired equity effect.

Utilities

Many states exclude from tax major utilities—electric, gas, water, and intrastate telephone—purchased by residential customers. Even fewer states tax interstate telephone charges. Until 1989, states believed that such taxes would violate the commerce clause of the constitution and thus avoided taxing these charges. The U.S. Supreme Court (*Goldberg v. Sweet*, 488 US 452, 109 S. Ct. 582, 585 (1989)) held that they do not, but states have been slow to react.

This brief review shows that the retail sales taxes are not general taxes on household consumption of goods, but rather taxes that exempt broad categories of consumption. Each exemption (1) violates the logic of a general consumption expenditure tax, (2) reduces revenue yield from any particular advertised tax rate, and (3) complicates compliance and administration. Most have been adopted to improve perceived fairness of the system and to provide tax relief. However, other means —notably annual rebates or credits offered through other portions of the overall tax system—can provide assistance at lower revenue cost and with less economic distortion. While retail sales tax coverage of the purchases of goods is broad, these taxes certainly are not uniform taxes on household consumption of goods.

Taxing Services

A tax on consumption should not treat household expenditure on goods, e.g., the purchases of a television, differently than household expenditure on a service, e.g., the repair of that television. Both are consumption expenditures. In practice, the retail sales tax more often than not reflects the pattern for such taxes established in the 1930s: the base is simply defined to be tax purchases of tangible personal property. Taxation of services usually amounts to a legislative afterthought, often limited to transient lodgings, rental of tangible personal properties, property repairs and installation, and admissions, and not all taxes go even that far. For instance, many taxes do not tax the servicing of items that are taxable when sold. States have been especially reluctant to tax professional services provided by physicians, dentists, lawyers, accountants, and casualty insurers.

State sales taxes can be generally divided into three broad groups for taxation of service purchases (Due and Mikesell, 1994; Research Institute of America, 1996):

General coverage

This coverage excludes services rendered by employees to employers and a few categories such as financial intermediation. All service purchases are taxed unless the statute specifically exempts them. No retail sales tax fully integrates taxation of services with taxation of goods, but Hawaii, New Mexico, and South Dakota provide the broadest coverage, the first two from their adoption and the latter by later expansion.

Extensive taxation of services

Repair, installation, maintenance, and other services associated with tangible personal properties are taxed, along with a long list of specifically identified services (parking, landscaping, pest control, laundry and dry cleaning, and cable television are common examples). Medical, optical, and dental care, legal services, and other professional services seldom are taxed, however. Iowa, Minnesota, and Texas provide the broadest list in terms of economic significance of the taxed services

(although Minnesota misses repair and installation services). Other states with similarly extensive taxation of services include the following: Arkansas, Connecticut, Florida, Kansas, Louisiana, Mississippi, New Jersey, New York, Ohio, Pennsylvania, Tennessee, Utah, Washington, West Virginia, Wisconsin, and Wyoming.

Limited or no coverage of service purchases

The tax applies to purchases of tangible personal property and makes no concerted attempt to tax services. A few selected services may be specifically taxed, but some of the states involved tax no services at all. The 23 states not previously mentioned in the other categories fall into this one.

A consumption expenditure tax that includes household purchases of services would have significant fiscal advantages. First, taxing services will increase the yield from any given statutory tax rate. The impact depends on what services are added and what purchases are already in the tax base. Adding household purchases of repair, installation, and maintenance of tangible personal property and services rendered by commercial establishments—including those for personal care—can increase revenue by 10 to 15 percent, much of that from services related to automobiles. Taxation of privately provided services—babysitting, housecleaning, etc.—is not administratively feasible and taxation of medical and dental services may create unacceptable social problems. Furthermore, evidence suggests that the broader base will grow somewhat more rapidly, because a growing percentage of household spending is on services rather than commodities (Duncombe, 1992).[9] National income data show that, from 1985 through 1994, the service component of personal consumption spending increased at an annual rate of 7.4 percent, compared with a rate of 5.1 percent for the goods component. Not all that service spending would reasonably be taxed, but the difference between the rates for services and for goods illustrates the pattern.

Second, taxing services can reduce discrimination according to household preferences. Without taxing services, persons with high preferences for services pay less tax than equivalently situated consumers with lower prefer-ences for services. The impact on regressiveness is not so clear. Evidence shows existing taxes with broad-based extension to services leave the tax regressive to income levels of around $30,000, above which the tax is roughly proportional (Fox and Murray, 1988). Siegfried and Smith (1991) find that the short-lived extension of the Florida sales tax to selected services in 1987 reduced regressivity. However, whether adding services to any existing goods-oriented sales tax would reduce regressivity depends crucially on what the existing tax has exempted (and taxed) and what services are added.

Finally, limiting the tax to commodities causes difficult problems when goods and services are sold together. Examples include computer programs (purchase of the physical disk or the service of the program?) and glasses (the physical eyeglasses or the services of the optometrist?), although there are also problems with repair charges that involve both materials and labor.

Taxing services does, however, present puzzles. First, firms selling services are frequently small. The firms are often highly specialized and there are few economies from large size because the labor content of the value of the

product is considerable. As a result, administration would be more difficult for the authorities and compliance would involve small firms with less skill and sophistication with the tax system. The authorities can deal with the problem by taxing the purchases of such service firms, thus letting their custom-ers pay the tax indirectly. That is generally the approach many value-added taxes (VATs) use when they exempt small businesses from collecting tax on their sales, but not from paying tax on their purchases. This is implicitly the approach used by American states: businesses selling services do not have tax suspended on their purchases. Where the labor content of the final sales to the consumer is high, however, a considerable portion of consumption expenditure will go untaxed.

Second, many services have mixed use, being purchased by both households and businesses. For example, attorneys work for both businesses and house-holds. The retail sales tax requires the seller to segregate business use from private use at purchase, apply tax to the proper transactions and be prepared to justify the remainder, and separately account for the two flows. The burden can be a problem for the seller. And the tax authorities face a similar set of tasks on unraveling flows on audit. To prevent the complications, retail sales taxes characteristically exclude difficult service transactions from the base—and, for good measure, exclude the simple ones as well.

Excluding Business Purchases

The business purchase exemption maintains the logic of a tax on house-hold consumption, keeps the tax from discouraging capital investment by being imposed on purchases of machin-ery and equipment, and reduces a barrier to state economic development. The exemption is critical to prevent the tax from applying to multiple stages in the production and distribution chain and the tax pyramiding that results. The truth of the state retail sales taxes does not follow that model.

In practice, retail sales taxes exempt items purchased for resale and components or ingredients of items to be produced for sale. Many also exempt industrial and agricultural machinery purchased for production, but not all do. A few states, including California, Nevada, South Dakota, Washington, Wyoming, and Hawaii, fully tax industrial machinery purchases and a number of states exempt only machinery purchased for new and expanded production or tax such purchases at a preferential rate. The states also vary dramatically in the extent to which their taxes exempt consumables, fuels, and utilities, even when clearly used in production.[10] A number of states turn the concept of consumption tax entirely on its head by taxing business purchases of fuels and utilities, while exempting their purchase by households. State sales taxes by no means remove business purchases from the tax.

States face considerable temptation to include business purchases in their retail sales tax base. Goods purchased for business use are just as physically "finished" or final as those purchased by households. By that standard, there is no difference between a refrigerator purchased by a restaurant and a refrigerator purchased by a family, except possibly the size. Both customers are "final." Taxing both purchases increases revenue from any given statutory rate, and including both seems to avoid a business tax preference. However, the tax on the restaurant purchase becomes part of operating cost, no less than the cost of labor, supplies, or other purchases of the firm. The refrigerator, although physically finished, is not economically final because it contributes to the production of a good or service bought by a household. The critical element for tax policy is not whether the product is finished but rather whether the purchase is household consumption or business cost.

Including business purchases creates two problems. First, these extra costs get hidden from customers, being reflected in final prices by varying amounts that depend on market conditions and on the extent to which businesses purchase taxed inputs. Thus, embedded sales tax paid by households would differ according to the sort of purchases made, rather than being a uniform percent of consumption. Second, taxing inputs distorts production decisions. The tax discourages investment in production and distribution equipment by reducing the net return from their acquisition and depressing the prospects for economic development. Joulfaian and Mackie (1992, p. 102) present the problem: "Sales taxes on purchases of capital assets can be fairly large. For some assets, the combined state and local sales tax rate can be nearly as high as 6 percent of the sales price. Furthermore, sales tax rates vary dramatically across investments, averaging 4.2 percent for equipment, 1.6 percent for structures, and 0 percent for inventories and land. Thus, sales taxes can affect both the overall average incentive to save and invest, as well as the allocation of investment across assets." In other words, American retail sales taxes, as they are structured, do not have the benign (or even encouraging) effect on investment that a consumption tax should to have. Furthermore, vertically integrated firms able to avoid purchasing from outside suppliers have an extra competitive advantage, and distortions are likely to reduce domestic capital investment and economic growth.

Unfortunately, exempting business purchases appears to favor households over businesses, so removing intermediate goods from tax has proven to be a difficult legislative challenge. Legislatures have had difficulty understanding that exempting business purchases represents a refinement to apply the tax to the defensible base, not an unwarranted tax advantage for business. And, at least as important, it is an argument that the voting public and the media have difficulty understanding. Therefore, the typical state sales tax base includes a sizable chunk of business purchases that simply do not belong in a consumption tax.

There is no entirely satisfactory estimate of the extent to which business purchasers bear the impact of state sales taxes. All evidence does indicate that the portion is substantial, although it obviously differs according to the structure of each state tax and the nature of the state economy. One study (Ring, 1989) estimated the national average to be 41 percent of the tax paid by business purchasers, with a range from around 20 percent (Maryland and Virginia) to 65 percent (Wyoming and Louisiana).[11] Individual state studies also estimate the business share to be considerable. For instance, Texas estimated the share there to be 58 percent while Iowa estimated its share to be 39 percent (Due and Mikesell, 1994). A sizable component of the tax base is business purchases, and much of the tax paid by these businesses will be reflected in higher prices of goods made by these inputs, although the impact on prices will undoubtedly not be uniform.

A NATIONAL RETAIL SALES TAX?

Retail sales taxes and VATs offer two economically equivalent alternatives for collecting a broad indirect, transaction-based tax on consumption expenditure. The taxes differ only in how they are administered. The VAT applies to each transaction in the flow of output to the consumer; in its most common variant, each business pays tax on its purchases but is reimbursed from tax collected on its sales. By that means, only the household consumer bears the tax, business purchases having been removed from tax by the refunding process. The retail sales tax applies only to the final consumer purchase, business purchases having been exempt by the suspension certificate. The two apparently dissimilar taxes differ only (but importantly) in the mechanism they use to relieve business purchases from tax, allowing the tax to apply to consumption.

Most national governments have selected the VAT, rather than the retail sales tax, as their general consumption tax. More than 100 countries around the world, including all those in Europe, all of Latin America, Japan, and Canada levy the tax; only the United States and Australia of the large industrial nations do not levy it. Countries have generally adopted the VAT for administrative advantages, especially when rates are high: the VAT more easily and completely excludes producers goods from tax, more completely includes consumer services in the base, and appears to provide a better defense against evasion (OECD, 1995). Nevertheless, the retail sales tax is familiar to Americans. It is reasonable to consider that collection method if the federal tax system is to move toward greater reliance on taxes on consumption.[12] However, reflections from state experience should enlighten and caution Congress as it weighs the options.

Higher Reliance and Higher Rates

To replace the federal income taxes with a retail sales tax would mean much heavier use of the tax than the United States has experienced: the federal individual income tax alone produced over $590 billion in fiscal 1995, roughly four and one-half times the $132 billion generated by all state sales taxes, and the corporate income tax produced $157 billion more (OMB, 1996; Bureau of Census, 1996). A national retail sales tax sufficient to replace existing federal individual and corporate income taxes would require a remarkably high rate. If the base of the national tax mirrored the median state sales tax (in fiscal 1994, Minnesota, with each one percent of tax rate generating 0.467 percent of personal income), then a national rate of 25.5 percent would be needed to replace the federal taxes. Copying the broadest tax would require a rate of 11 percent; copying the narrowest, a rate of 44 percent.[13] The message is clear: a national sales tax to replace the federal income taxes would require a rate considerably higher than the rates states now levy. Furthermore, the national tax would be on top of existing state and local rates—presumably these governments would not be forced to find other revenues when the federal government stepped in—and the combined rates would almost certainly be global records for such taxes!

States can operate their sales taxes with their many imperfections as consumption levies because the statutory rates are relatively low. Purchasers and vendors generally comply, but the rates are low enough to keep the stakes from evasion relatively low. Imposing an American retail sales tax at replacement rates would almost certainly produce untenable economic distortions and increase compliance problems. One observer of retail sales taxation guesses: "At 5 percent, the incentive to evade tax is probably not worth the penalties of prosecution; at 10 percent, evasion is more attractive, and at 15–20 percent, becomes extremely tempting" (Tait, 1988, p. 18). At the rates speculated here, evasion would be remarkably profitable and administration would become a greater challenge.

To the extent business purchases remained in the tax, vertically integrated firms able to acquire production assets without purchasing them from another business would enjoy considerable competitive advantage, and the tax applied to the purchase of capital assets would discourage investment. Furthermore, the embedded tax on business purchases would create difficult problems in international trade. It is impossible to know to what extent the sales tax is included in business cost at the point of export. Therefore, trade rules do not allow rebate of the tax. Adding a high but embedded and non-refundable national sales tax to American products would create challenging competitive adjustments on international markets. Relatively low retail sales tax rates now do not present a major problem. That would change with the much higher national retail sales tax added on.

Taxing Consumption?

A national retail sales tax generally following the pattern of the state taxes would not be a general and uniform tax on consumption. State retail sales taxes are *partial* consumption taxes and *partial* business purchase taxes. They exempt many household purchases of goods, are narrowly selective in their coverage of household service purchases, and apply to a wide array of business inputs, including the purchase of capital assets. This hybrid tax would not have the performance influences on savings, investment, and economic development that a uniform and general consumption tax would have. State experience shows the political difficulty in getting the retail sales tax structured as a tax on consumption. Legislatures see many options for excluding consumption expenditure from tax in the pursuit of distributional equity or to boost regional causes.

However, the problem may be fundamental. The technique of tax suspension probably has inherent administrative limits in the completeness of business purchase exclusion it can achieve. Suspension places the burden of parsing between business purchases and household purchases on the vendor, not a tax authority, and the vendor has an inherent competitive incentive to grant the suspension. Hence, tax administrators face a continual need to police acceptance of suspension certificates. Authorities tighten to prevent evasion through misuse of suspension authority, but tightening makes tasks more difficult for vendors. Loosening makes evasion easier.

Could Congress devise a politically feasible approach to taxing household consumption so that the base closely approaches the consumption ideal, meets contemporary ideas about fairness in taxation, and keeps up with change in the economy? Could Congress manage to suspend more completely the tax on intermediate goods to protect investment, avoid economic distortion, and accommodate international competitiveness? Would Congress—the collective author of the current federal individual and corporate

income taxes—be less susceptible to the pressures that have created the American state sales taxes than have the state legislatures?

Concerns About Compliance and Administration

A federal tax piggybacked on the existing state taxes would be completely inappropriate for a national tax because of the considerable state-by-state differences in the tax. For instance, a shopper buying a suit in New Jersey would pay the national sales tax; the shopper's cousin buying an identical suit in Pennsylvania would not pay the tax. Such differences would create major disruptions in interstate trade (adding the federal tax rate to existing state differentials would make cross-border shopping remarkably attractive on high-ticket items), as well as cause substantial differences in effective federal sales tax rates among the states. Determining the tax in the five states without a sales tax would be an interesting matter for Congress. Should such piggybacking be attempted, states would find it in the best interests of their citizens to adjust their sales taxes to the narrowest base possible as a means of minimizing their national tax burden.

Congress could prevent differences in effective rates across states by adopting its own national tax base. A distinct federally designed national retail sales tax might be a uniform and non-distorting consumption tax, avoiding all the imperfections that have emerged from the state legislatures. Experience with other federal taxes should cause some considerable skepticism about Congressional ability to pursue such purity in taxation, but even if the remarkable were to happen, there would still be problems. Vendors, the gatekeepers in any retail sales tax, would have to sort purchases as to taxability between the state and federal systems, and tax authorities would have to ensure that each sort was accurate. Of course, the federal government could force states to use the new federal base, but that would mean considerable loss of fiscal sovereignty. States have considerable experience in simultaneous administration of multiple taxes, so the primary new problem would be with compliance rather than administration.

As noted earlier, the extremely high combined national sales tax rate would change the stakes for taxpayer compliance. Most national governments have concluded that the clearer audit trail offered by VATs administered by the credit-invoice approach is important as an enforcement tool for high rate consumption taxes, and they reject the retail sales tax administrative approach. Congress needs to be prepared with considerable enforcement resources and zeal if it wants to prevent tax cheats from having a competitive advantage, given the much higher rewards to evasion with the high national tax rate. The compliance experience with the much lower state rates is probably irrelevant.[14]

Conclusions

Retail sales and use taxes have been a vital component of state and local government revenue systems since their inception during the Great Depression. They took over the slack left by the collapse of the real property tax and supported the considerable growth in state governments in the last half-century. They continue as the most important single tax levied by state governments, and they yield considerable revenue for support of local government. Structural problems, however, suggest that they would not be the best sort of general consumption tax if the federal government were to replace its income taxes. At the high rates required to yield enough revenue to replace the income taxes, problems of evasion and higher reward from avoidance, distortion caused by incomplete exclusion of business purchases, and narrow coverage of consumer services diminish the attractiveness of the retail sales tax. The taxes are not general taxes on consumption expenditure, and they do not have all the economic advantages associated with such taxes.

What are the conclusions for the American tax system? State and local governments should perfect their retail sales taxes as consumption expenditure levies. Surely the case for taxation of consumption being made at the national level has considerable validity for subnational taxes as well. The typical retail sales tax would need to be extended to professional services sold to households, personal services, and repair-and-installation sorts of services associated with goods whose purchase would be taxable. Producer purchase exemptions would need to be extended broadly to business inputs. These policy changes would improve the "capital-investment" aspect of tax climate and would dramatically reduce the number of sales tax cases in the judicial system. Neither broadening to services nor narrowing to exclude business purchases would be politically easy—if so, states would surely have made the changes years ago. Sales taxes are also challenged by marketing systems that lack a physical presence within the state —sales by catalog, telephone, computer network, etc. Constitutional restrictions prevent states from requiring such vendors to register for the tax, even as this marketing technique becomes more prevalent. Although some such merchants voluntarily agree to collect tax, Congress certainly could help states by devising some mechanism for enforcing this tax.

Attempting to levy a national tax as a supplement to state sales taxes would be folly. There is simply insufficient uniformity in what states tax and exclude to allow a linked federal tax to be fair and efficient. On the other hand, a separate national retail sales tax would complicate the work of state tax collection, increase the problems that businesses face in complying with multiple tax bases, and tax on a base not equal to household consumption. Other countries probably have it right when they select VATs to raise considerable revenue at the national level, because, in practice, such taxes using the credit-invoice method more fully exclude business purchases from tax, more completely tax household purchases than do retail sales taxes, and leave a better trail for enforcement.[15]

ENDNOTES

John F. Due, Matthew Murray, and Joel Slemrod made helpful suggestions on an earlier draft.

[1] It is now generally an American tax: among the industrialized countries, only state and local governments in the United States and provincial governments in Canada levy the retail sales tax. Switzerland and some Scandinavian countries did use the tax, but all have now replaced it with VATs. Other countries with some sort of retail sales tax include Namibia, some states in India, and parts of the former Soviet Union (for instance, the Kyrgyz Republic).

[2] The Washington study estimated compliance of only 59.7 percent for the compensating use tax, however. The compensating use tax, a companion to all state and many local sales taxes, is applied to the use of taxable items bought without payment of sales tax, normally because the vendor was out-of-state. Successful administration remains a puzzle.

[3] Its close relative, the VAT, removes business purchases from the tax by refunding, through credit or rebate, tax paid on their purchases.

[4] The taxes in Hawaii (the general excise tax) and New Mexico (the gross receipts tax) are considerably different from the other taxes considered here. Both will be included in this analysis, however, because each has the basic features of a retail sales tax, including being accompanied by a compensating use tax.

[5] Other differences include the taxability of nonprofit organization purchases and sales. States differ in terms of whether organizations will be exempt specifically or by category, what organizations or categories will be exempt, and whether sales as well as purchases will be exempt (Mikesell, 1992). Local retail sales taxes generally, but not always, follow the base of their state. Therefore, in the discussion here, comments about state sales taxes should be understood to apply also to local taxes within the state.

[6] Regressivity is far less if the horizon of measurement expands from the current year to lifetime or permanent income (Poterba, 1989). State legislatures, however, seem more concerned with annual patterns.

[7] The estimate is based on "Selected NIPA Tables"(1996) and data from the Consumer Expenditure Survey.

[8] The Georgia reduced rate is part of a phase-in to full exemption on October 1, 1998.

[9] Not all service purchases are fast growing, however, and business purchases of services, those not suitable for inclusion in the tax, grow most rapidly (Dye and McGuire, 1991).

[10] For more detail on the taxation of production inputs, see Due and Mikesell (1994).

[11] On the basis of Consumer Expenditure Survey data, Ring (1989) estimates what consumer sales tax payments should be for each state. He then attributes the difference between this estimate and actual collection to tax paid by producers. The approach has many flaws—CES categories do not align well with state tax laws, CES data do not reflect state-by-state differences in household expenditure behavior, any flaws in tax administration artificially reduce the business share, etc.— but these estimates are the national standard by default, despite the fact that they often conflict with evidence from detailed individual state studies.

[12] This section will consider a federal retail sales tax patterned generally after the American sales taxes. The National Retail Sales Tax Act of 1996, H.R. 3039 (introduced March 6, 1996), by Representatives Schaefer, Tauzin, Chrysler, Bono, Hefley, Linder, and Stump is radically different; a critical analysis of that proposal appears in Mikesell (1996a).

[13] Bartlett (1995) uses a different estimating approach, but his range from 15 to 30 percent is similar.

[14] See Murray in this volume for some thoughts on this question.

[15] See Mikesell (forthcoming) for a comparison of the fundamental differences between the retail sales and value-added approaches to general consumption taxation.

REFERENCES

Adams, Virginia N., and Kirk L. Johnson. "Estimating the Sales Tax Gap." Tennessee Department of Revenue 1989 Workshop on Tax Administration. Nashville: Tennessee Department of Revenue, 1989.

Bartlett, Bruce. "Replacing Federal Taxes with a Sales Tax." *Tax Notes* 68 (August 21, 1995): 997–1003.

Bradford, David F. "The Case for a Personal Consumption Tax." In *What Should Be Taxed: Income or Expenditure?*, edited by Joseph A. Pechman. Washington, D.C.: The Brookings Institution, 1980.

Case, Bradford, and Robert Ebel. "Using State Consumer Tax Credits for Achieving Equity." *National Tax Journal* 42 No. 3 (September, 1989): 323–37.

Cnossen, Sijbren, and Cedric Sanford. *Taxing Consumption*. Paris: Organisation for Economic Co-operation and Development, 1988.

Due, John F. *Sales Taxation*. Urbana, IL: University of Illinois Press, 1957.

Due, John F., and John L. Mikesell. *Sales Taxation, State and Local Structure and Administration*. 2d ed. Washington, D.C.: Urban Institute Press, 1994.

Duncombe, William. "Economic Change and the Evolving State Tax Structure: The Case of the Sales Tax." *National Tax Journal* 45 No. 3 (September, 1992): 299–314.

Dye, Richard, and Therese McGuire. "Growth and Variability of State Individual Income and General Sales Taxes." *National Tax Journal* 44 No. 1 (March, 1992): 55–66.

Fox, William, and Matthew Murray. "Economic Aspects of Taxing Services." *National Tax Journal* 41 No. 1 (March, 1988): 19–36.

Joulfaian, David, and James Mackie. "Sales Taxes, Investment, and the Tax Reform Act of 1986." *National Tax Journal* 45 No. 1 (March, 1992): 89–105.

Kaldor, Nicholas. *An Expenditure Tax*. London: Allen and Unwin, 1955.

Lugar, Dick. "The Lugar Plan to End the Income Tax." Statement delivered to the Cato Institute, Washington, D.C., April 5, 1995.

Mikesell, John L. "Sales Taxation of Nonprofit Organizations: Purchases and Sales." In *Sales Taxation, Critical Issues in Policy and Administration*, edited by William F. Fox. Westport, CT: Praeger, 1992.

Mikesell, John L. "A National Retail Sales Tax? Some Thoughts on Taxing Consumption the American Way." *State Tax Notes* 10 (July 8, 1996a): 105–9.

Mikesell, John L. "Should Grocery Food Purchases Bear a Sales Tax Burden?" *State Tax Notes* 11 (September 9, 1996b): 751–4.

Mikesell, John L. "Is the Retail Sales Tax Really Inferior to the Value Added Tax?" In *The Sales Tax in the 21st Century*, edited by Matthew Murray and William Fox. Westport, CT: Greenwood Publishing (forthcoming).

Office of Management and Budget. *Historical Tables, Budget of the United States Government, Fiscal Year 1997*. Washington, D.C.: Government Printing Office, 1996.

Organisation for Economic Co-operation and Development. *Consumption Tax Trends*. Paris: OECD, 1995.

Poterba, James M. "Lifetime Incidence and the Distributional Burden of Excise Taxes." *American Economic Review* 59 No. 4 (May, 1989): 325–30.

Research Institute of America. *1996 Guide to Sales and Use Taxes*. New York: Research Institute of America, 1996.

Ring, Raymond. "The Proportion of Consumers' and Producers' Goods in the General Sales Tax." *National Tax Journal* 37 No. 2 (June, 1989): 167–79.

Schaefer, Jeffrey M. "Clothing Exemptions and Sales Tax Regressivity." *American Economic Review* 59 No. 4 (September, 1969): 596–9.

"Selected NIPA Tables." *Survey of Current Business* 76 (July, 1996): 5–28.

Siegfried, John, and Paul Smith. "The Distributional Effects of a Sales Tax on Services." *National Tax Journal* 44 No. 1 (March, 1991): 41–53.

Simons, Henry C. *Federal Tax Reform*. Chicago: University of Chicago Press, 1950.

Tait, Alan A. *Value Added Tax: International Practices and Problems.* Washington, D.C.: International Monetary Fund, 1988.

U.S. Bureau of the Census. *1994 State Tax Collection Data by State* [Homepage of U.S. Census Bureau], [Online]. Available: http://www.census.gov/ftp/pub/govs/www/sttax94.html [1995, Access Date: December, 1996].

U.S. Bureau of the Census. *1995 State Tax Collection Data by State* [Homepage of U.S. Census Bureau], [Online]. Available: http://www.census.gov/ftp/pub/govs/www/sttax95.html [1995, Access Date: December, 1996].

Washington Department of Revenue. *Washington State Excise Tax Noncompliance Study.* Olympia: Department of Revenue, 1990.

WOULD TAX EVASION AND TAX AVOIDANCE UNDERMINE A NATIONAL RETAIL SALES TAX?

MATTHEW N. MURRAY*

Abstract - *A national retail sales tax has surfaced as a potential replacement for the current system of federal income taxation. A primary concern is that the revenue-neutral required tax rate may easily exceed 30 percent, leading to tax base erosion through widespread avoidance and evasion. This paper examines specific avenues for avoidance and evasion for both firms and individuals under a comprehensive national sales tax and discusses implications for the underground economy. The analysis shows that opportunities for avoidance and evasion will be sustained, not eliminated, by a change in tax structure. Unfortunately, lack of experience in administering a high-rate, indirect tax system precludes definitive statements regarding the likely extent of tax base erosion under a national sales tax.*

INTRODUCTION

The current regime of personal and corporate income taxation evokes strong criticism. The income taxes give rise to substantial efficiency losses, administrative and compliance costs are viewed as excessive, and the IRS is perceived by many to be overly intrusive. The search for potential replacements to the federal system of income taxation has led many in the direction of some form of broad-based consumption tax, ranging from a value-added tax (VAT) (and its close cousins, the various flat taxes) to a national retail sales tax (NRST).

Until recently, there was little serious discussion of an NRST as a replacement for the personal and corporate income taxes. An important reason for the shift in sentiment in favor of an NRST is the growing perception of success of state/local governments in administering the current retail sales tax.[1] But in many respects this is an illusion. Yes, the current state/local retail sales tax is a productive revenue source that gives rise to modest compliance costs for most firms and inconsequential compliance

*Department of Economics, The University of Tennessee, Knoxville, TN 37996-4170.

costs for final consumers. But the retail sales tax, as currently structured across the states, is not the neutral, broad-based consumption tax that appears in the textbook. An extensive array of final sales on services and other activities escape taxation. The retail sales tax also falls heavily on business input purchases, with studies suggesting that about 40 percent of all revenues are derived from taxes on intermediate sales (Ring, 1989). And while compliance with the retail sales tax is quite good (aside from the mail order sales problem and the growing electronic commerce problem), a primary reason is that current tax rates are modest, giving rise to only modest incentives for evasion and avoidance. Finally, administrative and compliance costs are low when compared to other taxes, but the retail sales tax has largely avoided dealing with difficult-to-tax sectors, including the array of services.[2] The comparative advantage of the states in administering a retail sales tax, and the business community's familiarity with complying with the same tax, simply does not extend to the broad-based NRST envisioned by some.

Several proposals have surfaced for an NRST. Former Indiana Senator Richard Lugar has discussed a federal sales tax with a 17 percent rate, but has produced few specifics. Advocacy groups, including Citizens for an Alternative Tax System and Americans for Fair Taxation (AFT), also have pushed for a federal sales tax. The AFT has examined some of the specific aspects of a broad-based NRST, although details have not been released as of this writing. The most detailed approach to date is the National Retail Sales Tax Act of 1996 (H.R. 3039), introduced in the House of Representatives on March 6, 1996, by Representatives Schaefer, Tauzin, Chrysler, Bono, Hefley, Linder, and Stump (hereafter, referred to as the S-T proposal).

The AFT and S-T proposals share many common features.[3] Each would supplant the current structure of federal income taxation and estate/gift taxation. The base of each would seek to tax comprehensively virtually all final consumption (including the sales of nonprofit and government enterprises). Intermediate sales would enjoy suspension of tax under both systems. The AFT proposal would further require tax payments on dual-use input purchases (i.e., purchases easily divested for personal use), with rebates available after taxpayer filing of information reports. Equity concerns would be met through rebates available to all households, administered by the Social Security Administration through employers. The states would administer the NRST to exploit their current comparative advantage in sales tax administration.[4]

A major concern of these proposals is the required tax rate. The S-T proposal specifies a 15 percent rate, whereas the AFT proposal calls for a 23 percent rate. But many observers argue that the rate of a revenue-neutral NRST might easily exceed 30 percent (for example, Bartlett, 1995). Coupled with state/local sales tax rates, the combined tax rate on final sales to consumers might approach and even surpass 40 percent. An important question arises as to whether a sales tax rate of this magnitude is enforceable. Unfortunately, there is no modern experience to draw from on administering a broad-based, high-rate indirect tax.[5]

The potential for base erosion through tax evasion and tax avoidance provides the motivation for this paper. If base erosion under an NRST proves to be substantial, the fundamental revenue, efficiency, and equity goals of the tax system will be compromised. The remainder of this paper explores specific avenues for tax avoidance and tax evasion under an NRST, focusing first on firms and then on individuals and households. A separate section explores implications for the underground economy.

AVOIDANCE AND EVASION ISSUES FOR FIRMS

A neutral sales tax that did not fall on input purchases would give rise to no avoidance incentives for firms.[6] However, should the sales tax fall on purchased inputs, distortions will arise over input choices (including self-supply though vertical integration) and location choices. There is no evidence on how the sales tax impacts input choices and little specific knowledge of how state/local sales tax rate and base differentials influence firm location. However, since taxes generally tend to have modest effects on firm location decisions[7] and most inputs presumably would be freed of tax under a broad-based NRST, and because international sites may entail higher costs, any location distortions would be quite small.

An NRST would provide an incentive for firms to register in order to be freed of the tax burden on purchased inputs. An important potential side benefit is improved compliance by having more firms (and their information reports) under the tax net. The breadth of the base of the NRST ultimately would dictate the number of taxpayers that would have to be registered and the difficulties that would be encountered by tax administration. Since there has been no detailed and comprehensive assessment of a national sales tax, inferences on this question must be drawn from recent analyses of a federal VAT.[8] The GAO's (1993) study of a federal VAT assumed a relatively broad base and provides a reasonable point of departure.[9] The assumed tax base excludes rental housing, owner-occupied housing, and financial intermediation services, but includes education, health, and nonprofit and government service providers. The estimated number of registered taxpayers is 24.4 million. But many more taxpayers may require registration, depending on the specific way in which an NRST is structured. For example, comprehensively adding owner-occupied housing to the tax base would potentially triple GAO's estimate of the number of registered taxpayers.[10] In general, one consequence of a broad-based sales tax is inclusion of large numbers of small taxpayers with limited revenue potential. While tax enforcement is difficult under any circumstances, such large numbers of small taxpayers further dilute scarce administrative resources.

Some retail firms, especially those with high value added (such as service providers), may choose not to register at all, in turn simply paying sales tax on their inputs.[11] These firms could then lay outside the tax net and sell their services at preferential rates. The primary administrative check on such illegitimate firm behavior is verification through use of third-party sources, such as telephone directories and professional registries, and street canvasing. A good point of departure for an NRST would be existing rosters of vendors under the state/local sales tax, although these listings would miss many firms due to the narrowness of the state sales tax base.

Due to potential tax advantages, some individuals may seek to register as firms to disguise their consumption as the purchase of business inputs. The AFT proposal provides a disincentive, since tax would be required on all intermediate purchases and vendors would have to file explicit rebate claims to be relieved of tax. (Note that this approach differs from a credit-invoice VAT in that the latter provides tax credits as opposed to rebates.) But under both the AFT and S-T proposals, traditional auditing activities will likely remain key to effective enforcement. Since the extent of the over-registration problem has not been documented under the current state/local sales tax, the consequences for an NRST are unclear.

Identification and notification of registered but nonfiling taxpayers can be automated through the administrative apparatus as is common with the state/local sales tax. Due and Mikesell (1994) note a 13 percent delinquency rate for the state sales tax, with problems confined largely to smaller firms. Primary reasons for delinquency are poor record keeping and scarce operating capital. An NRST would aggravate delinquencies, especially if firms were to pay tax on intermediate purchases and receive rebates at some future point as with the AFT proposal. The rebate system, which provides an additional control device, will require a one-time increase in firm operating capital. The resulting liquidity problem should not be severe, however, if refunds are provided expeditiously.[12] Delinquencies may also be increased under an NRST, simply because of the amount of revenue at stake. That is, some firms may be tempted to retain sales tax collections temporarily for business or personal use. However, this temptation is not so different from the incentive that arises in the context of withholding and remittance of personal income and payroll taxes for an employer and her staff. Sound enforcement and an interest penalty system that ensures that vendors do not benefit from the use of collected revenues can mitigate this problem.

Many might perceive the shift to an NRST as an opportunity to eliminate (or least reduce) misreporting problems attributable to exempt and use taxable sales, problems that plague the state/local sales tax.[13] Exempt and use taxable provisions in the state/local tax code currently give rise to extensive compliance complexities and opportunities for taxpayer abuse. But the use tax problem will be sustained. For example, a small retailer who personally consumes inventory would be required to remit use tax, as with the current state/local sales tax. Inputs acquired tax free from international suppliers would pose a particularly thorny problem of observation and verification for tax administration. The AFT proposal would likely require that tax be paid on these imports, with relief granted through tax rebates. Under the S-T tax, concerns over the acquisition of dual-use inputs generally would be met by the direct remittance of tax on purchases and subsequent access to tax credits.

Similarly, a broad-based NRST is unlikely to encompass all goods and services, and some sensitive activities, such as health and educational expenditures, may be exempt or taxed at preferential rates.[14] Definitional problems would most certainly arise regarding legitimate expenditures. Moreover, any rate variations would increase tax complexity and lead to greater noncompliance.[15] The taxation of specific categories of consumption, such as financial, insurance, and housing services, would also add complexities to the tax code.[16] For financial and insurance services, problems arise due to the absence of explicitly paid market prices for many services and the investment nature of many expenditures. The problem is even more acute for housing services, which represented 26.1 percent of personal consumption spending on services and 14.2 percent of total personal consumption spending in 1993.[17] Taxation of rents would require registration of huge numbers of taxpayers who would have to distinguish between business and individual consumers, in much the same way that vendors must separate taxable from nontaxable sales under the state/local sales tax. Addressing these and other issues will add to the complexity of the tax, raising administrative and compliance costs. At the same time, voluntary compliance can be expected to decline and opportunities for abuse will expand.

Incentives to underreport gross sales and taxes withheld would increase with the rate of the NRST, and successful evaders would have a potentially enormous competitive advantage over legitimate vendors. Of course, firms and individuals may be able to evade existing income tax liabilities, providing a mechanism to offer products at better than competitive prices under the current tax regime. Yet the ultimate extent of any competitive advantage hinges on administrative features and relative incentives to evade across income and sales tax regimes. Administrative features determine the relative *ability* to evade income versus sales taxes. To the extent a sales tax is more easily evaded, which may or may not be the case, the compliance problem would grow under an NRST. Equally important are incentives, which may be appreciably different under a sales tax versus an income tax regime. Should a retailer choose to evade his income taxes, the total amount of tax that can be evaded is equal to taxable income times the tax rate. And if the rate of sales taxation is equal to the rate of income taxation, the return to a dollar of underreporting is the same for each tax. But taxable retail sales will, in general, exceed

income, in most instances by a wide margin. Accordingly, the amount of tax a nonfiling retailer can save increases substantially under a high-rate national sales tax because of the concentration of revenues at the retail level. This consideration suggests an even stronger competitive advantage and a more serious compliance problem for the sales tax cheat relative to the income tax cheat.

Misreported gross sales are not a serious problem under the existing sales tax, in part because enforcement relies on cross verification with federal and state income taxes. (Similarly, the European VATs operate side-by-side with income taxes.) The multiple tiers of information reporting, coupled with independent enforcement activities undertaken by federal, state, and local tax administrators, provide numerous opportunities to verify taxpayer reports. Enforcement of an NRST would be hampered if the tax supplanted the personal and corporate income taxes, although it is not clear how significant the problem would be.

A potentially serious problem would arise under the AFT proposal as firms fraudulently overstate refund claims for taxes paid on input purchases and goods/services purchased for resale. A primary concern is simply the volume of transactions that would be subject to taxation and rebate. In effect, the AFT approach to business tax relief yields a dual-use turnover tax that provides refunds on all intermediate purchases.[18] The magnitude of turnover will be enormous for the economy as a whole, far in excess of the value of final sales. Accordingly, vast amounts of revenue would be at stake at the preretail level. Under a system of suspension, revenues are simply foregone and the worst case scenario is no tax revenue; under a rebate (or VAT credit) system, tax administration could incur deficits in the extreme (if unlikely) case of uncontrollable abuse. One mitigating factor is that under the AFT proposal firms must make formal misstatements to the revenue authorities, as opposed to simply misstating their intentions to other firms through presentation of exemption certificates. This psychological consideration, which is often discussed as a unique strength of the credit-invoice VAT, is of unknown practical value.[19]

In general, misreporting problems probably would have less to do with large retailers (with systematic and centralized accounting systems) than with smaller retail and service firms. Likely problem areas would correspond to those sectors that give rise to problems for the state/local sales tax (and the VAT), including repair services (automobiles, appliances, and homes), trade contractors (electricians, plumbers, and carpenters), personal services, agricultural products and services (veterinarians, landscaping, and food products), and retailing generally. Three administrative controls will be necessary to ensure reasonably accurate sales tax reporting. First and foremost is a sound penalty system that provides certain and unequivocal sanctions for misreporting and fraud. Second, the reporting system for business input purchases must support auditing activities. Generally, all input transactions on the part of buyer and seller should be documented so that detailed paper (or usable electronic) trails are produced for all purchases.[20] This would yield an audit trail similar to that under the credit-invoice system of the VAT.[21] Third, there must be a good system of audit selection for sales tax vendors that seeks to identify firms with atypical reporting patterns. Unfortunately, the states have had limited

success in developing objective and systematic audit selection systems for the state and local sales tax.[22]

AVOIDANCE AND EVASION ISSUES FOR INDIVIDUALS

Under the current state/local sales tax, individuals have four legal options to reduce tax liabilities: change spending patterns toward favorably taxed items; make purchases and pay sales tax in low-tax jurisdictions; choose one's location of residency in a low-tax region; and self-provide otherwise sales-taxable goods and services. The first two options, encouraged under the existing state/local sales tax, would largely vanish under a uniform-rate NRST.[23] However, if one views tax exempt casual sales as "favorably taxed," an exception arises under S-T, since there would be a *de minimis* exemption of $2,000 per person per sale, with a $5,000 annual limit. This provision would be exploited by taxpayers, especially at high tax rates, using traditional mechanisms, such as garage and yard sales, and flea markets. But new services also may be developed to facilitate and promote consumer-to-consumer sales. For example, firms could aggressively market the use of electronic bulletin boards to link buyers and sellers, collecting fees for their services. While the fees would be sales taxable, the transactions between buyer and seller would be exempt up to *de minimis* levels. Monitoring by tax administrators would be extremely difficult. Moreover, effective enforcement would require maintenance of records for all consumers engaged in casual sales, causing registration rosters to balloon.

Similar administrative and avoidance problems would arise from international purchases. (See below for a discussion of the evasion aspects of this same issue.) The S-T tax would provide a *de minimis* exemption of $400 of goods per person per entry and an annual limit of $2,000 per person. The incentive introduced by a high-rate NRST would induce abuse. For example, depending on specific statutory legislation, offshore marketers may be able to offer a shipping service for products shipped tax free from abroad directly to each member of a household.[24] As with casual sales, administrative enforcement would require maintenance of import records for all individuals acquiring goods/services from abroad.

It is unlikely that the switch to a national sales tax would have appreciable impacts on residency location patterns.[25] One reason is that under source-based income taxation one need only change the situs of receipt of income, whereas under a destination-based sales tax one must change the situs of residence to avoid the tax, which entails high costs.[26] An equally important consideration is the counterfactual. That is, to the extent that individuals confront roughly comparable burdens under the existing income tax versus an NRST, there is little motivation to change country of residence. This consideration suggests that any incentives to emigrate may be highest for the elderly. The reason is that the assets and savings of the elderly have already been taxed under the system of income taxation and the introduction of a national sales tax would substantially increase their lifetime tax burden. But even the elderly would have little motivation to emigrate since they would likely confront some form of indirect tax (admittedly at a lower rate) in the new country of residence.

The potential for self-provision of sales taxable items has received little more than speculation. Households may, for example, choose to engage in home production activities, such as gardening and home maintenance, to avoid payment of sales taxes. As with potential migration responses, a key consideration is the counterfactual to an NRST. Clearly, the returns to home production—tax savings on home-produced goods and services that would otherwise be sales taxable—would rise under an NRST. But elimination of the income tax would at the same time raise the relative returns to market work. Moreover, an important offsetting influence to engage in home production would be the significantly higher tax rate on the household's purchased inputs. On net, it would appear that little change in aggregate home production would take place in response to movement from an income tax to an NRST.

International "border shopping" and tax evasion are serious threats to the viability of an NRST. In general, for border shopping to be classified as avoidance as opposed to evasion, taxpayers must either pay sales tax in the jurisdiction of purchase or directly remit use tax in the jurisdiction of consumption.[27] Since an NRST would be a destination tax, taxpayers will be required to pay use tax on imported goods and services beyond *de minimis* levels as noted above. But collecting such taxes is problematic. Under the S-T, reliance would be placed on the import duty administration, although enforcement would be difficult except for directly imported tangible products. Yet, even with tangible products, complete enforcement would prove impossible (and costly) unless every traveler and his possessions were carefully scrutinized. The S-T tax also would require returns to be filed by taxpayers if use tax is to be paid. Despite the existence of mechanisms to accommodate direct use tax payments by consumers (primarily through income tax reports), state experience with administration of the use tax and voluntary taxpayer filings has been dismal at best.[28] Admittedly, many final consumers are unaware of their current use tax obligations. This situation would not likely change appreciably following implementation of an NRST. As a result, the international border shopping problem will likely translate into a tax evasion problem as consumers simply choose not to remit their required use tax liability.

As Due (1986) notes, the use tax problem (for businesses and individuals) is the most important reporting problem for the state/local sales tax. At the same time, overall evasion on *in-state* sales is estimated at less than five percent of revenues (Due, 1974). Estimates for 1994 indicate an *interstate* tax gap on mail order sales alone of $3.3 billion, or 2.4 percent of state sales and use tax collections (ACIR, 1994). Since the latter estimates apply only to tangible personal property (as opposed to services and electronic commerce, for example), they understate the revenue losses to state and local governments, potentially by a wide margin. Moreover, the existing tax gaps pertain to a much lower rate of sales taxation than would be the case under an NRST.

The importation of services, especially the direct delivery of electronic and information services, will represent a specific challenge to tax administration. The problem is complicated by limited state experience (or experience in the context of other indirect taxes) in administering a sales tax on intangibles in general and telecommunications and information services in particular.[29] As a result, a broad-based NRST would enter uncharted waters with no good practical experience to draw upon. Since legal, accounting, financial, information,

education, and other services could conceivably be produced abroad, a serious use tax problem may emerge. At the same time, there are two constraints that may naturally rein in transactions involving such activities. First, certain services that require close contact between buyer and seller, like health, repair, and many personal services, simply would not lend themselves to abuse via international and electronic commerce. Second, buyers of services are broadly interested in quality, and foreign suppliers may not be in a position to assure quality and back up their sales. For example, buyers of educational services may be interested in obtaining a degree or certificate of advancement through a recognized and fully accredited institution. Similarly, buyers of insurance and financial services will want to know that they are dealing with a viable and legitimate enterprise that will back up its sale. In general, consumers will want to have recourse should they be displeased with their purchase, but this may not be possible with foreign suppliers.

The bottom line is that it would be extremely difficult to track and tax the purchase of both intangible services and tangible products obtained from international marketers. Long-term growth in direct marketing and more recent growth in electronic commerce, coupled with the tax advantages arising from successful sales tax evasion, will contribute to erosion of the base of a national sales tax. It is simply not realistic to expect consumers to file returns for many of their purchases, as would be required under the S-T tax, and collection from many foreign sellers would be precluded by the absence of nexus. The tax collection problem will be aggravated by the tax administrator's inability to observe inherently unobservable transactions involving electronic commerce; observing transactions involving tangible products will come only at high cost. Collection efforts might be redirected to third parties, including common carriers, telecommunication service providers, or credit card companies. However, such a step would be unprecedented. Imposing collection burdens on third parties raises compliance costs substantially to parties largely incidental to the transaction itself, and may expose the same firms to the risks of the audit lottery.[30]

A new compliance concern would also surface under an NRST as some low-income consumers seek to take advantage of mechanisms intended to alleviate the regressivity of the tax.[31] The S-T proposal would provide a family consumption refund and the AFT proposal would provide a wage-conditioned rebate, each to be available to all families and each to be administered through the existing apparatus of the Social Security system. The rebate programs are similar since they are based on the sales tax rate applied to reported wage income up to the poverty level of income. Employers would administer the rebate by withholding less Social Security tax for each worker, increasing take-home pay. The Department of Treasury would then reimburse the Social Security Administration, so that there would be no reduction in trust fund balances. Since the rebate is available to all households and there is no cutoff for relief (i.e, those with income greater than the poverty level of income enjoy the full value of the rebate), there is no incentive to underreport wage income.[32]

For those with income below the poverty level, there is an incentive to report income since the individual gains by the amount of the sales tax rate for every dollar of wage income reported.

Unfortunately, this same incentive may be exploited by some low-income individuals who game the relief system to their own advantage through fictitious work arrangements. For example, consider two households with income below the poverty level.[33] If the households agree to exchange day care duties for an equal wage, the families would have access to refundable tax credits. A similar scheme could apply to illegal-source as opposed to legal-source income. The only binding constraint on such activities is the poverty ceiling for low-income relief and the tax administrator's ability to observe wage income.

IMPLICATIONS FOR THE UNDERGROUND ECONOMY

While the discussion above has focused on specific avenues for evasion and avoidance, a more general question is how the switch from a system of income to sales taxation might alter taxes generated from the underground economy. Unfortunately for proponents of an NRST, the answer is not much.

Consider first the case of the evasion of legal-source income on the part of an individual entrepreneur or a small retailer. In the case of an income tax, the evader may pay little or no income tax and maintain a pricing advantage over competitors. Now assume the income tax is replaced by a retail sales tax, so that all of the evader's consumption is subject to sales tax. On first appearance, it seems as if the evader is now within the tax net since the income that previously escaped tax is now taxed on the uses side. However, the rise in post-tax prices that would accompany the new NRST would allow the evader to raise the price for his services by the amount of the tax and potentially retain the receipts for personal use. So while tax is paid on the vendor's personal consumption, the vendor may now retain sales tax receipts in the same way income taxes were not paid under the income tax counterfactual. The result is no increase in net revenues collected from the evader.[34] In fact, since final sales will exceed income, a similar tax rate potentially would mean *less* revenue for the successful evader of sales taxes.

Consider next the evasion of illegal-source income.[35] Under an income tax, the recipient of illegal-source income would likely report no income and hence pay no income tax. Similarly, after the switch to an NRST, no sales tax revenue would be generated unless the entrepreneur engaged in illegal behavior collected and remitted tax on his sales, an unlikely scenario. It might be argued that the entrepreneur's tax bill rises by the amount of the sales tax imposed on personal consumption. But there remains no increase in net collections, insofar as the production and sale of these purchases flowed through the formal (as opposed to the underground) economy. The reason is that the value added that underlies the value of the final product would have been taxed on the sources side of the household budget under the alternative income tax system. So, instead of no income tax being generated on illegal-source income, the sales tax would collect no revenue on illegal sales.

One consequence of these considerations is that the only real gain from a national retail sales tax is the perception that members of the underground economy are paying tax. This may have important value if these perceptions enhance the voluntary compliance of other taxpayers.

A second and somewhat more subtle consequence is that the switch to a sales tax regime will likely change the way in which many of the same firms and individuals seek to game the tax system to their own advantage. Based on state experience with the sales tax, small firms and service providers tend to have rather dismal compliance patterns.[36] For example, a recent study of the sales tax gap in Iowa (State of Iowa, 1995) found the largest gaps associated with firms with average annual taxable sales of less than $250 thousand. A similar pattern emerges for the income tax, as illustrated by 1992 estimates showing that 47.2 percent of the legal-source income tax gap was attributable to nonfarm sole proprietorships.[37] The experience abroad with single and multistage sales taxes provides further evidence that smaller firms have poorer compliance patterns (Tait, 1988; Bird, 1967). Hence, a switch from an income tax to a national sales tax regime will likely switch the mechanism the same parties exploit in reducing their tax liabilities. Under the personal and corporate income taxes, individuals and firms may not record sales and may overstate deductions and credits to reduce taxable income. Under an NRST, individual entrepreneurs may choose not to charge tax on sales, underreport sales, and overstate refund claims or abuse the system of suspension. Similar activities may be undertaken by corporate entities to relieve themselves of tax liability.

Conclusions

The degree of compliance with any tax hinges on the rate and base structure, which introduces incentives and opportunities for abuse; attitudes, which determine whether taxpayers exploit opportunities for abuse; and tax administration, which provides oversight, enforcement, and control. A high-rate NRST would benefit from relatively positive taxpayer attitudes toward compliance that prevail in the United States. At the same time, incentives and opportunities for both tax avoidance and tax evasion will be sustained, although the specific avenues for reducing one's tax liability may change. Moreover, administrative enforcement will be hampered by the high costs associated with observing taxable transactions (especially in the context of services), not unlike the current system of income taxation.

There are certain features of the proposals for an NRST that may retard abuse, including the S-T tax's requirement of tax (and subsequent provision of tax credits) on dual-use inputs and the AFT's use of rebatable input taxes and formal filings with the tax administration. But there will be ample avoidance opportunities, including *de minimis* provisions for international purchases and casual sales, and potentially serious evasion problems associated with the concentration of revenue at the retail stage and input credit fraud.

On balance, the lack of experience in administering a high-rate, broad-based indirect tax means that it is impossible to say whether evasion and avoidance would be more or less pronounced under an NRST than under an income tax (or VAT) regime. Will the tax base whither? Probably not. Will there be radical improvement in compliance patterns? Probably not. Unfortunately, the available evidence does not allow a more unequivocal statement.

ENDNOTES

The author thanks Peter Mieszkowski, Joel Slemrod, and George Zodrow for comments. Financial support was provided by the National Tax Research Committee.

[1] See Mikesell in this issue for a discussion of the current system of state/local sales taxation.

[2] For the state sales tax, Due and Mikesell (1994) showed administrative costs as a percent of revenue varying between 0.4–1.0 percent. Due and Mikesell (1983) provided a more comprehensive listing of states, with administrative costs averaging about 0.7 percent of collections. This is similar to estimates for the European VAT of about 0.7 percent (Sandford, Godwin, and Hardwick, 1989) and for the U.S. personal income tax of 0.6 percent (using the estimate of IRS spending on the income tax of $5 billion, taken from Slemrod, 1996). Compliance costs show considerably more variation. For the U.S. sales tax, compliance cost estimates fall between 2.0–3.8 percent of revenues (research summarized by Cnossen, 1994). Sandford, Godwin, and Hardwick estimated compliance costs of the U.K. VAT at 3.7 percent of collections. In Slemrod, it is argued that compliance costs are likely in the range of $70 billion for the personal and corporate income taxes, or about nine percent of combined income tax revenues in 1995. Hall (1996) provides strikingly higher estimates for the U.S. income taxes, totaling 20.1 percent of collections. Hall estimates that the Armey–Shelby flat tax plan would cost 1.2 percent of collections to comply with, versus 4.6 percent for the USA tax plan and 1.0 percent for the S-T NRST.

[3] Burton and Mastromaro (1996) provided a favorable review of the S-T proposal. Bartlett (1996) and Mikesell (1996) provide critiques.

[4] The S-T proposal would compensate taxpayers filing monthly reports through a credit equal to the greater of $100 or 0.5 percent of revenue collected. This extension of "vendor's compensation" to compliant firms is similar to practice under the state/local sales tax. Due and Mikesell (1983), now somewhat dated, reported that nearly half of the states provide vendor's compensation, usually a flat percentage of gross collections (from 1.0–3.6 percent). Sliding scales are also common, with more support for smaller firms, consistent with their relatively higher compliance costs. The S-T plan would go further than traditional state practice by providing a tax credit equal to 50 percent of the purchase price of any new equipment required to comply with the tax. States administering the S-T tax on behalf of the federal government would be allowed to keep 1.0 percent of collections.

[5] Combined state/local sales tax rates remain, with few exceptions, below ten percent. A simple average of the VAT's standard rate in the OECD was 17.1 percent in 1995 (OECD, 1995). Due (1986) noted that many countries switched from variants of the retail sales tax to VATs because of the belief that compliance would be less of a problem. Some of these countries had relatively high indirect tax rates, including Sweden (10 percent), Norway (13.6 percent), Iceland (20

percent), and Zimbabwe (over 20 percent). Yet there is no specific evidence of a growing compliance problem in the face of rising tax rates. Moreover, Stranger (1973), Egret (1973), and deMoor (1973) note no reduction in evasion in Norway, France, and the Netherlands, respectively, following the switch to a VAT. There are instances of specific excise tax rates well in excess of 30 percent, including the state excise taxes on cigarettes and motor vehicle fuels. ACIR (1985) estimated the cigarette tax gap at 5.4 percent of collections in 1983, with 70 percent of the loss due to sales on Indian reservations. The Council of Governor's Policy Advisors (1996) estimated that the elimination of fuel tax evasion would yield a 6.5 percent revenue gain for the average state. These gap estimates are much lower than the corresponding estimates of 20 percent for the personal income tax (Slemrod, 1992) and 22.7 percent for the corporate income tax (Rice, 1992), and compare favorably to gap estimates for the VAT (OECD, 1988; Oldman and Woods, 1983). A primary explanation for the relatively low gap estimates for the excise taxes on cigarettes and fuel is the unique apparatus of enforcement, including extensive monitoring and controls at pre-retail stages. But even these enforcement mechanisms can break down in the face of high tax rates. For example, in the 12-month period following Michigan's cigarette tax hike from 25 to 75 cents a pack, cigarette sales in Michigan plummeted 31 percent (Lee, 1996).

6   As used here, avoidance refers to any legal mechanism to reduce tax liabilities. If all input purchases and goods acquired for resale were tax exempt, firms would have no tax burden to avoid.

7   Bartik (1991) provided a comprehensive review of the business location literature.

8   Dronenburg (1995) examined a federally administered consumption tax and concluded that only 7.3 million taxpayers would need to be registered. But this estimate applies to a sales tax that parallels the existing state structure, rather than a broad-based consumption tax as envisioned by an S-T or AFT.

9   Roughly the same number of firms would be required to register under both a comprehensive VAT and a comprehensive NRST. Under a VAT, registered firms at both the preretail and retail levels would pay tax and have access to relief on input purchases. Under a retail sales tax, revenues would be collected on final sales of any type from registered taxpayers, while all entities engaged in firm-to-firm sales would need to be registered to receive relief of tax on intermediate sales.

10 There were 44.9 million owner-occupied homes in the United States in 1993 (Statistical Abstract of the United States 1993, 1993).

11 Due and Mikesell (1994) reported that over-registration is a more serious problem than under-registration with state and local sales tax.

12 The S-T tax would allow tax credits on dual-use input purchases to be applied to tax collections on final sales in the same month in which taxes on inputs were paid; if refunds are warranted, they are to be provided within 60 days. Dual-use inputs are defined as goods/services for which 25 percent or more of sales are to consumers.

13 The use tax is imposed on the consumption of goods for which sales tax has not been applied in the jurisdiction of purchase. An example is the tax-free purchase of an automobile in one state, and the subsequent registration of the vehicle and payment of use tax in the resident jurisdiction.

14 The AFT proposal would exempt expenditures on tuition and job-related coursework.

15 Agha and Haughton (1996) found that multiple VAT rates are associated with a higher degree of noncompliance.

16 Such complexities can give rise to compromises in structural design. One compromise, common with the VAT, is to zero rate final sales from tax and at the same time deny suspension on input purchases. This second-best approach allows the labor component of value added to escape tax.

17 The Monthly Labor Review (June, 1996) provides a breakdown of consumption spending for 1993 and projections for 2005.

18 Similarly, a VAT is a turnover tax that provides tax credits on intermediate sales. The volume of tax credits under a VAT would far surpass the value of final retail sales, as with the AFT rebate system.

19 Shoup (1973) states "It is psychologically more difficult for most taxpayers to file a false return than file a false statement with a vendor." It is this aspect of the VAT that the AFT rebate system seeks to mimic. But this and other self-enforcement features of the VAT credit-invoice system are likely overstated. For example, it is often argued that there is an incentive for firms to ensure that tax is shown on purchase invoices so that traders have access to credits. But the incentive for taxpayers is to ensure tax is shown, not necessarily that tax has been paid. VAT invoice fraud is not well documented, but it does exist (Egret, 1973; Tait, 1988). In a similar vein, it is argued that cheating at preretail stages will mean more revenue at subsequent stages of production due to the absence of invoiced tax payments. But this argument once again ignores the possibility of invoice fraud across stages of production. Finally, there is no VAT credit system at the final retail stage, and there is evidence of underreported final sales (Egret; Cnossen, 1981). The real strength of VAT's credit-invoice system is the rich paper trail that potentially allows for improved verification

opportunities. This strength is not, however, an inherent feature of a VAT, since comparable information reports could be required under rebate and suspension systems.

20 New modes of payment and the increased use of electronic modes of payment have created some problems for taxpayer information reporting under the state sales tax. A good example is the corporate purchase card, essentially a credit or debit card that allows firms to streamline purchasing procedures. But data support systems must ensure that adequate information reports are generated for all transactions. See Lippman and Smith (1996).

21 The existence of comprehensive paper trails does not ensure improved tax administration and tax compliance. The reason is that it is costly for tax administrators to verify and assimilate taxpayer information reports. Experience with the VAT in this context is not encouraging. Han (1990) discussed Korea's ill-fated efforts to make comprehensive use of VAT invoice data in the early 1980s.

22 See Due and Mikesell (1994) and Murray (1995).

23 If state/local rate and base differentials are sustained after implementation of an NRST, they will continue to distort consumption behavior. Moreover, the returns to successful evasion will be increased. Should preferential rates or exemptions be extended to consumers under an NRST, further distortions in consumer spending behavior can be expected. Indirect evidence on consumption distortions is provided by rapid growth in mail order sales, which outpaced growth in the gross national product during the 1970s and 1980s (ACIR, 1994). More direct evidence was offered by Mikesell (1970), who reviewed the early evidence on the impact of sales tax rate differentials and found substantial taxpayer responses. Mikesell's independent analysis produced an elasticity with respect to the sales tax rate of between 1.7 and 11.0. Walsh and Jones (1988) found that grocery store sales in West Virginia responded sharply to the phase out of the sales tax on food.

24 Statutory language also would have to be carefully crafted and customs enforcement would be needed to avoid the "drop shipment" problem encountered by the states. With drop shipments, a good is sold to an out-of-jurisdiction reseller who receives a resale exemption. But the reseller does not take direct possession, instead shipping the product directly from the manufacturer to the final consumer. (See Madsen and King, forthcoming, for the state aspects of this problem). A similar scheme might be developed by off-shore resellers who buy goods directly from manufacturers, receive an export exemption, and then have the product shipped by common carrier directly to the consumer. If the off-shore marketer does not have

nexus, tax remittance by the final consumer or the manufacturer would be required.

25 The only comprehensive treatment of subnational taxes and expenditures on household location patterns is Fox, Herzog, and Schlottmann (1989). They find no significant sales tax effects on domestic household migration patterns.

26 While the sales tax is a destination tax, in practice, destination commonly means the point of sale. The complementary use tax is intended to ensure that items (generally only tangible commodities) purchased tax free in one jurisdiction are taxed in the jurisdiction of consumption. Generally, there is no apportionment of sales and use taxes across the jurisdictions in which consumption takes place.

27 The states have had difficulties in collecting excise taxes on cigarette sales on Indian lands due to legal ambiguities and limitations on state taxing authority. See ACIR (1985) and, more generally, Zelio (1995). This raises the specter of Indian reservations becoming a tax haven under an NRST. But this would not be the case (absent explicit statutory intent) since congressional acts can supersede treaties granting sovereign rights to Indians on their lands. See the Cherokee Indian Case of 1870 presented in Prucha (1990).

28 Due and Mikesell (1994) and Caldwell (1996) discussed state-by-state practice in collecting use tax.

29 Murray (1997) discusses practical problems in applying the state sales tax to telecommunication services and electronic commerce.

30 In general, third-party shippers (including common carriers and telecommunication service providers) do not know final retail price nor the nature of goods/services being shipped. Some states have sought to impose collection and remittance burdens on third-party telecommunication service providers due to the difficulty of collecting tax from buyers and the impossibility of collecting tax from sellers due to the absence of nexus. For an industry perspective on the problem, see Information Highway State and Local Tax Study Group (1995).

31 Gold (1992) noted that the primary concern of the states that administer equity-based rebate programs is nonparticipation rather than noncompliance. The federal earned income tax credit also has less than complete coverage, but there are serious compliance problems as well. See GAO (1994) and Holtzblatt (1991).

32 An "avoidance" issue would surface for low-income individuals since wage income would be preferred to nonwage income. Multiple job holders might present a separate problem if individuals sought multiple rebates.

33 See Yin and Forman (1993) for a similar example in the context of the federal earned income tax credit.

[34] If the evader is entirely out of the tax net under an NRST, there will be no opportunity for the individual to enjoy tax relief on legitimate input purchases. Hence, it again appears that the sales tax may increase the tax burden on the evader. But the income tax counterfactual must be carefully considered. Had the individual purchased inputs from legitimate vendors under the income tax regime, such purchases would have embodied the income tax burden that underlies the value added on such goods and services. The switch to a sales tax regime means the loss of these income tax revenues in exchange for the new revenues of the evader who has no exemption certificate or no access to credits for taxes paid on inputs. The net effect is no change in aggregate collections.

[35] See Armey (1995) for a discussion of this specific issue and a general critique of a national sales tax.

[36] The problem for tax administrators is aggravated by the large numbers of small firms and their limited contribution to total sales. Census data for 1992 reveal that one-third of retail trade establishments accounted for only three percent of sales; 77.8 percent of service firms accounted for 23.5 percent of sales; and 58.6 percent of construction firms accounted for 23.2 percent of sales. Almost 58 percent of retail trade establishments were either partnerships or sole proprietorships; the comparable figure for service establishments is 84.5 percent.

[37] Department of Labor (1992). This summary estimate is based on an IRS analysis that relies on the Taxpayer Compliance Measurement Program.

REFERENCES

Advisory Commission on Intergovernmental Relations. *Cigarette Tax Evasion: A Second Look.* Washington, D.C.: ACIR, 1985.

Advisory Commission on Intergovernmental Relations. *Taxation of Interstate Mail Order Sales: 1994 Revenue Estimates.* Washington, D.C.: ACIR, 1994.

Agha, Ali, and Jonathan Haughton. "Designing VAT Systems: Some Efficiency Considerations." *Review of Economics and Statistics* 78 No. 2 (May, 1996): 303–8.

Armey, Dick. "The Case Against the National Sales Tax." *Policy Review* 73 (Summer, 1995): 31–5.

Bartik, Timothy J. *Who Benefits from State and Local Development Policies?* Kalamazoo, MI: W. E. UpJohn Institute for Employment Research, 1991.

Bartlett, Bruce. "Replacing Federal Taxes with a Sales Tax." *Tax Notes* 68 No. 8 (August 21, 1995): 997–1003.

Bird, Richard M. "An Appraisal of the Colombian Sales Tax." In *Readings on Taxation in Developing Countries*, edited by Richard M. Bird and Oliver Oldman. Baltimore, MD: Johns Hopkins Press, 1967.

Burton, David R., and Dan R. Mastromaro. "The National Sales Tax: Moving Beyond the Idea." *Tax Notes* 71 No. 9 (May 27, 1996): 1237–47.

Caldwell, Kaye. *Survey Results: State Use Tax Collection.* [Homepage of Software Industries Issues], [Online]. Available: http://www.webcom.com/software/issues/docs-html/usetaxcl.html [1996, Access Date: December, 1996].

The Council of State Governments and The Council of Governors' Policy Advisors. *State Road Fund Tax Evasion: A State Perspective.* Lexington, KY: The Council of State Governments and The Council of Governors' Policy Advisors, April, 1996.

Cnossen, Sijbren. "The Netherlands." In *The Value-Added Tax: Lessons from Europe*, edited by Henry Aaron. Washington, D.C.: The Brookings Institution, 1981.

Cnossen, Sijbren. "Administrative and Compliance Costs of the VAT: A Review of the Evidence." *Tax Notes International* 8 No. 25 (June 20, 1994): 1649–68.

DeMoor, A. E. "Value Added Tax in the Netherlands." In *The Value-Added Tax in the Enlarged Common Market*, edited by G. S. A. Wheatcroft. New York: John Wiley and Sons, 1973.

Dronenburg, Ernest J. "SAFCT: State Administered Federal Consumption Tax: The Case for State Administration of a Federal Consumption Tax." Paper presented at New York University Annual State and Local Taxation Conference, New York, November 30, 1995.

Due, John F. "Evaluation of the Effectiveness of State Sales Tax Administration." *National Tax Journal* 27 No. 2 (June, 1974): 197–219.

Due, John F. "The Implications for Australia of the Experience in the United States, Canada and Other Countries with Retail Sales Tax." In *Changing the Tax Mix*, edited by John Head. Sydney: Australian Tax Research Foundation, 1986.

Due, John F., and John L. Mikesell. *Sales Taxation.* Baltimore: The Johns Hopkins University Press, 1983.

Due, John F., and John L. Mikesell. *Sales Taxation.* 2d ed. Washington, D.C.: Urban Institute Press, 1994.

Egret, Georges. "The Value-Added Tax in France." In *The Value-Added Tax in the Enlarged Common Market*, edited by G. S. A. Wheatcroft. New York: John Wiley and Sons, 1973.

Fox, William F., Henry Herzog, and Alan Schlottmann. "Metropolitan Fiscal Structure and Migration." *The Journal of Regional Science* 29 No. 4 (November, 1989): 523–36.

Gold, Steven D. "Simplifying the Sales Tax: Credits or Exemptions?" In *Sales Taxation*, edited by William F. Fox. Westport, CT: Praeger, 1992.

Hall, Arthur P. "Compliance Costs of Alternative Tax Systems." *Tax Notes* 71 No. 8 (May 20, 1996): 1081–9.

Han, Seung Soo. "The VAT in the Republic of Korea." In *Value Added Taxation in Developing Countries*, edited by Malcolm Gillis, Carl S. Shoup, and Gerardo P. Sicat. Washington, D.C.: The World Bank, 1990.

Holtzblatt, Janet. "Administering Refundable Tax Credits: Lessons from the EITC Experience." In *Proceedings of the Eighty-Fourth Annual Conference on Taxation*, 180–6. Columbus: National Tax Association–Tax Institute of America, 1991.

Information Highway State and Local Tax Study Group. "Supporting the Information Highway: A Framework for State and Local Taxation of Telecommunications and Information Services." *State Tax Notes* 9 No. 1 (July 3, 1995): 57–71.

Lee, Dwight. *The Economic Impact of Michigan's 50 Cent/Pack Cigarette Tax Increase.* Atlanta: University of Georgia, 1996.

Lippman, Michael H., and Scott D. Smith. "Taking the Fear out of Corporate Purchase Cards." *State Tax Report* 96 No. 5 (1996): 2–6.

Madsen, H. Michael, and Kimberly L. King. "Interstate Dimensions of the Sales Tax: 3rd Party Drop Shipments." In *The Sales Tax in the 21st Century*, edited by Matthew N. Murray and William F. Fox. Westport, CT: Praeger (forthcoming).

Mikesell, John L. "Central Cities and Sales Tax Rate Differentials: The Border City Problem." *National Tax Journal* 23 No. 2 (June, 1970): 206–13.

Mikesell, John L. "A National Retail Sales Tax? Some Thoughts on Taxing Consumption the American Way." *State Tax Notes* 11 No. 2 (July 8, 1996): 105–9.

Murray, Matthew N. "Sales Tax Compliance and Audit Selection." *National Tax Journal* 48 No. 4 (December, 1995): 515–30.

Murray, Matthew N. "Telecommunication Services and Electronic Commerce: Will Technology Break the Back of the Sales Tax?" *State Tax Notes* 12 No. 4 (January 27, 1997): 273–80.

Oldman, Oliver, and LaVerne Woods. "Would a Value-Added Tax System Relieve Tax Compliance Problems?" In *Income Tax Compliance: A Report of the ABA Section of the Taxation Invitational Conference on Income Tax Compliance*. Chicago: American Bar Association, 1983.

Organisation for Economic Co-operation and Development. *Taxing Consumption.* Paris: OECD, 1988.

Organisation for Economic Co-operation and Development. *Consumption Tax Trends.* Paris: OECD, 1995.

Prucha, Francis Paul. *Documents of United States Indian Policy.* Lincoln: University of Nebraska Press, 1990.

Rice, Eric M. "The Corporation Tax Gap: Evidence on Tax Compliance by Small Corporations." In *Why People Pay Taxes*, edited by Joel Slemrod. Ann Arbor: University of Michigan Press, 1992.

Ring, Raymond R., Jr. "The Proportion of Consumers' and Producers' Goods in the General Sales Tax." *National Tax Journal* 42 No. 2 (June, 1989): 167–79.

Sandford, Cedric, Michael Godwin and Peter Hardwick. *Administrative and Compliance Costs of Taxation.* Great Britain: Fiscal Publications, 1989.

Shoup, Carl S. "Factors Bearing on the Assumed Choice Between a Federal Retail-Sales Tax and a Federal Value-Added Tax." In *Broad-Based Taxes*, edited by Richard A. Musgrave. Baltimore: The Johns Hopkins University Press, 1973.

Slemrod, Joel. "Why People Pay Taxes: Introduction." In *Why People Pay Taxes: Tax Compliance and Enforcement*, edited by Joel Slemrod. Ann Arbor: University of Michigan Press, 1992.

Slemrod, Joel. "Which is the Simplest Tax System of Them All?" In *The Economics of Fundamental Tax Reform*, edited by Henry Aaron and William Gale. Washington, D.C.: The Brookings Institution, 1996.

State of Iowa. Department of Revenue. *Iowa Sales Tax Gap: Study of Registered Retailers.* Des Moines: Department of Revenue, 1995.

Stranger, Finn. "Value Added Tax in Denmark." In *Value-Added Tax in the Enlarged Common Market*, edited by G. S. A. Wheatcroft. New York: John Wiley and Sons, 1973.

Tait, Alan A. *Value Added Tax.* Washington, D.C.: International Monetary Fund, 1988.

U.S. Department of Labor. *The Underground Economy in the United States.* Washington, D.C.: Department of Labor, 1992.

U.S. General Accounting Office. *Value-Added Tax: Administrative Costs Vary Widely with Complexity and Number of Businesses.* Washington, D.C.: GAO, 1993.

U.S. General Accounting Office. *Earned Income Credit-Data on Noncompliance and Illegal Alien Recipients.* Washington, D.C.: GAO, 1994.

Walsh, Michael J., and Jonathan D. Jones. "More Evidence on the 'Border Tax' Effect: The Case of West Virginia, 1979–84." *National Tax Journal* 41 No. 2 (June, 1988): 261–5.

Yin, George K., and Jonathan Barry Forman. "Redesigning the Earned Income Tax Credit Program to Provide More Effective Assistance for the Working Poor." *Tax Notes* 59 No. 7 (May 17, 1993): 951–60.

Zelio, Judy. "States and Indian Tribes: Seeking Agreement on Taxes." *State Tax Notes* 9 No. 11 (September 11, 1995): 765–70.

LIFE UNDER A PERSONAL CONSUMPTION TAX: SOME THOUGHTS ON WORKING, SAVING, AND CONSUMING IN NUNN-DOMENICI'S TAX WORLD

MARTIN D. GINSBURG*

To tax plans old and new, I bring the certainty of a famous *New Yorker* cartoon.[1] Three staff members are reporting to their senator. The senior staffer sums up: "Sir, we've come to the conclusion that it's absolutely impossible to assemble a tax plan that *doesn't* benefit the rich."

At the threshold, I am told, I am to assume that in fall 1995, effective January 1, 1996, the 104th Congress enacts and President Clinton signs into law the USA Tax Act of 1995, S. 722, precisely in the 290-page form this grand legislation was introduced on April 25, 1995 by Senators Sam Nunn (Democratic-Georgia), Pete Domenici (Republican-New Mexico), and Bob Kerrey (Democratic-Nebraska).[2] This exorbitant assumption embraced, my task is to imagine plausible answers to the simple question, "And then what happened?"

Forecasting the tax bar's delighted response to a truly sweeping and novel legislative proposal barely off the ground is great fun. The legislation seems unlikely of enactment, surely unlikely of enactment in the form introduced, and therefore none ever will prove how wrong I was. Thus comforted, I proceed to a selective review of S. 722[3] and then hazard some tax planner responses, but preface the entire exercise with what is intended as a provoking observation. The Nunn-Domenici tax world is one in which municipal bonds pay interest in even years only, executive compensation and the yield on at least one class of each corporation's stock is paid only in odd years, and the rich with borrowed money buy raw land or works of art they admire but may not expect to keep forever.

THE PROPOSED USA TAX SYSTEM

Overview

S. 722 would do away with both the individual and the corporate income tax, and AMT as well, substituting at the individual level a broad-based, graduated (three rates) personal consumption tax—unlimited deduction for net new savings—and at the entity level (partnerships, LLCs, and

*Georgetown University Law Center, Washington, D.C. 20001.

proprietorships, as well as corporations) a flat rate (11 percent) business tax that turns out to be a subtraction-method value-added tax (VAT).[4] In addition, while the current employment tax system would persist, the individual's share of payroll taxes is a (refundable) credit against the individual tax[5] and the employer's share is a credit against the business tax.[6]

The Business Tax

The business tax is imposed on "a business entity that sells or leases property or sells services in the United States."[7] Thus, all business entities—corporations, partnerships, LLCs, and sole proprietorships—are treated alike: each is a taxpayer and none is a passthrough entity.[8] The tax rate is 11 percent and the tax base is the taxable year's *gross profit,* defined as the amount by which (1) taxable receipts (which include receipts from the sale or use of property and performance of services in the United States, exclude interest on credit sales and other financial receipts,[9] but include amounts received in providing "games of chance") exceed (2) the business entity's deductible amounts for the taxable year.[10]

Deductible amounts include "the cost of business purchases in the taxable year," and business purchases expansively include the acquisition of property, the use of property (*i.e.*, rental payments), and the acquisition of services, in each case for use in a business activity in the United States.[11] However, every expenditure is not a business purchase. Some major exclusions:[12]

(1) Payments for use of money or capital, explicitly interest and dividends.[13]

(2) The acquisition of "savings assets"[14] or "financial instruments," the latter defined[15] as properties remarkably similar to savings assets.

(3) Premiums for life insurance.[16]

(4) Compensation expenses—wages, salaries, retirement plan contributions, premiums for life, health, disability, or other insurance benefiting the service provider or her family, various other fringe benefits, and the cost of property purchased to provide compensation—if the service provider is an employee of the business entity.

In sum, for the U.S. business leasing or selling goods or services, operating gross receipts—but not dividends, interest, and other "financial" income—are included in the tax base and the cost of business purchases—a term that includes rental expense and compensation paid for services furnished by independent contractors—is deductible,[17] but neither now nor ever may the business enterprise deduct dividends, interest expense, or employee compensation.

Now, not *every* purchase by a business entity is a "business purchase." In particular, the acquisition of unimproved land will qualify if the business entity rents out the real estate (at full value),[18] but will not qualify as a business purchase if the land will be held for speculation, subdivision or other development, leasing on a temporary basis, use not commensurate with underlying value (*e.g.*, a temporary parking lot pending construction of an office building), or simply an indefinite future use in a business activity.[19] In any of these circumstances the business entity, denied a purchase deduction, will hold the land at a basis equal to its undeducted purchase price. If in a subsequent year the land is put to full current business use (*e.g.*, when improvements on the land are placed in service), cost is deductible as a business purchase at that time.[20] Also, to take the polar case, if the business entity acquired land as rental property and thus took an immediate deduction for the entire cost, and in a sub-sequent taxable year the realty ceases to qualify as rental property (because put to a nonbusiness use by, *e.g.*, having been leased at a below-market rent),[21] the realty (and any associated debt) "shall be treated as distributed by the business entity to its owners."[22]

An individual in her human-being capacity is not a business entity conducting a business activity, but an individual engaged in business activity is, with respect to that, a business entity subject to the business tax.[23] An individual proprietorship running the corner newsstand is an example; an independent contractor is another; individually owned property leased full-time for full and fair rent is yet another. The need for an exception is patent. If an employee were deemed a business entity and her employment its business activity, wages could be taxed three times: first to the employer (no deduction for wages paid employees in computing the business tax base); a second business tax, this time on the employee's business entity; and third, the individual tax that is imposed on the employee herself.[24] S. 722 avoids the employee's second tax, announcing that the performance of services by an employee for a business entity employer is not a business activity for purposes of the business tax.[25] Additionally, and sensibly, "business activity" does not include casual or occasional sales of property used by an individual (other than in a business activity).[26]

A successful business entity in the throes of expansion, new factory, new offices, new equipment, materials, and inventory, in a given year will have aggregate business purchases far in excess of its taxable receipts. The difference is a loss,[27] and while the loss cannot be carried back to obtain an immediate refund of business tax previously paid, under the business tax it is a loss carryover good for 15 years.[28] Of course, if a number of taxable years of expansion are anticipated, the present value of that 15-year loss carryover will not be great unless it can be put to more immediate use.

The business tax's treatment of losses incurred after 1995 contrasts sharply with the treatment the business tax accords losses incurred, pre-1996, under the old regime. S. 722 announces that no deduction is allowed under the business tax for net operating loss carryovers, capital loss carryovers, or "any other loss carryovers" from the days of the income tax, and no credit carryovers are allowed either.[29] They simply go "poof."

A very different transition rule applies to embedded asset basis, the unrecovered basis as of January 1, 1996 of business assets acquired, created, or placed in service under the old regime. The business tax accords a transition basis adjustment or deduction—no poof here—by establishing four categories of business assets and allowing the aggregate basis in each category to be amortized over a set period. Unrecovered inventory costs, for example, are amortized over 3 years; depreciable property that enjoys on January 1, 1996 a remaining recovery period of less than 15 years is amortizable over 10 years.[30]

Under the pre-1996 Internal Revenue Code, whole law school courses were taught and grand careers in tax practice were made concentrating on transactions among business entities and their owners. It is too much to hope that all of the Byzantine rules and requirements of historic corporate tax law retain vitality in Nunn-Domenici's tax world. They do not. However, the new tax world presents its own challenges. To appreciate them, it is first necessary to review the proposed USA tax for individuals because contribution and distribution transactions and business combinations implicate both entity-level business tax considerations and individual tax considerations.

The USA Tax for Individuals

The individual tax component of the new system imposes a tax on personal consumption at graduated rates (up to 40 percent). For those who prefer a tie to the familiar, the new individual tax has been described as "a broader-based individual tax with an unlimited deduction for net new saving . . . imposed using a three-tier graduated rate schedule."[31] The individual tax proposal departs from recognized cash flow consumption tax design, and attracts the description of an "income tax with an unlimited deduction for net new saving," by excluding borrowed money from the tax base (and concomitantly allowing no deduction for interest payments and debt repayments) while allowing, some of the time and perhaps a lot of the time, a deduction for savings generated with borrowed money.[32]

Gross income for the taxable year is all income from almost every source derived—wages, salary, and other compensation for services; most fringe benefits including the cost of employer-financed health insurance; distributions from business entities including dividends, interest, rents, and other compensation for use of capital; life insurance proceeds; and gains on asset sales[33]—but does not include gifts and bequests,[34] amounts that are treated as taxable receipts of a business entity under the business tax,[35] and tax-exempt bond interest.[36]

The important changes are on the deduction side. Child support payments are now deductible (like alimony)[37]; the individual tax law continues to afford a personal exemption ("personal and dependency deduction" in the new world) for each exemption reflected in the tax re-

turn[38]; and an enlarged standard deduction, redesignated the Family Living Allowance, now is available to taxpayers whether or not they itemize deductions.[39] On the other hand, few itemized deductions persist; reidentified "USA deductions,"[40] they are a homeowner deduction (old law's home mortgage interest deduction but without the home equity line),[41] a philanthropic transfer deduction (old law's charitable contribution deduction, modestly modified),[42] and a new education deduction of up to $2,000 of qualified higher-education expenses of each eligible student (the taxpayer, the taxpayer's spouse, and the taxpayer's dependents), but limited to a maximum annual education deduction of $8,000.[43]

However, among post-1995 deductions the Big Pineapple is the unlimited deduction for net new saving. In S. 722 it is called, in search of the perfect acronym, the Unlimited Savings Allowance, and is announced to be "intended to reflect the amount of net new savings other than new savings attributable to borrowings or tax-exempt interest."[44] As Professor Warren has demonstrated with great care, some algebra, and a dozen simple examples,[45] S. 722 is rather more complicated and, as Professor Kaplow convincingly argues, will attract a full measure of responsive taxpayer manipulation.[46]

More than a century ago, Private Willis assured us that in Great Britain everyone born into the world alive is either a little Liberal or a little Conservative.[47] Stability there. In the United States after 1995, on the contrary, without regard to political persuasion everyone decently wealthy will be a net saver in some (perhaps odd-numbered) years and a net dissaver in other years. Transition, from old tax to new, is the first reason but by no means the only reason.

Net saving in any year equals what you put into savings in excess of what you withdraw (above any available basis you may have in the withdrawn asset or account).[48] Net withdrawal is the reverse.[49] The savings deduction is not simply for the year's "net savings," however, and a net withdrawal in any year does not inevitably attract individual tax liability. There is more to it.

"Deductible net savings," [50] which does reduce individual tax, is (1) the year's net savings minus (2) a number you get by adding up these three so-called nontaxable sources of funds—(a) your nonexempt debt as of the end of the taxable year over your nonexempt debt at the beginning of the taxable year,[51] plus (b) any interest you receive during the year on tax-exempt bonds,[52] plus (c) the basis (normally from pre-1996 investments) of savings withdrawn this year.

Thus, if in 1996 you (1) enjoy gross income of $500,000 and save $400,000 more than you withdraw from savings, but during the year you foolishly (a) borrow $135,000 to buy cars for the family, (b) receive $250,000 of municipal bond interest, and (c) discover that incident to this year's modest savings withdrawals you also "withdrew"—forget for the moment how—$40,000 of historic basis, your deductible net savings are limited to $10,000.[53]

What happens to the other $390,000 of net savings, on which you have just been taxed? Obviously you should not be taxed on this same amount later, when you withdraw funds from savings to repay debt, live riotously, or whatever. The USA Tax mechanism to allow later tax-free withdrawal of the previously taxed $390,000 is a general basis account[54] to which is added at the end of 1996 $390,000—the lesser of (1) your net savings ($400,000) or (2) your "nontaxable sources of funds" ($390,000). Well and good, but there is another way to see it: Neither borrowing nor receiving tax-ex-

empt interest nor recovering historic basis is a smart idea in a year in which you are a net saver.[55]

Is there no way quickly to free up the basis you amassed in savings during the days of the income tax? Indeed there is, provided you did not amass much: Not more than $50,000 in "qualified savings assets," which are all the savings assets you have on January 1, 1996, excluding only (1) your ownership interest in a non-public business entity to which you regularly provide services and (2) if you so elect, your retirement accounts.[56] If you are a small fish, so described, say $45,000 in aggregate basis, this $45,000 of "transition basis" electively is deductible one-third ($15,000) each year in 1996, 1997, and 1998, with a year-to-year carryover of any unused deduction,[57] and your asset basis is properly and promptly reduced to zero. However, if you (together with your spouse) are a more than $50,000 savings basis fish, it is transition basis that is zero[58] and your asset basis remains what it was, doing you no good so long as you continue to qualify as a net saver.

Suppose in 1996 your gross income was small and, choosing not to invest this year, you instead withdraw $40,000 from savings and expend it along with your $135,000 of borrowed money and $250,000 of municipal bond interest. You are a 1996 net dissaver. Neither tax-exempt income nor borrowings, whether exempt or nonexempt, go into the tax base of a net dissaver, and your "net includable withdrawal income" —the amount that is to be added to your 1996 tax base—is limited to that $40,000 withdrawal from savings, less your basis if any allocated to the savings asset you disposed of, and in all events less the balance in your general basis account (which is thereby reduced dollar-for-dollar).[59]

For potential net dissavers, as you can see, it pays to have a sizable general basis account.

In sum, in 1996 you borrow or otherwise obtain and consume all sorts of money, but you are taxed on little if any of it. In all likelihood, you will not concern yourself about the tax until the future year in which you repay your debt. A strange sort of consumption tax, is it not?

A few miscellaneous notations will wrap up this brief introduction to the USA individual tax and its centerpiece, the Unlimited Savings Allowance. While a great many purchases give rise to additions to savings—payment of a life insurance premium, even a term life insurance premium, is a somewhat unexpected example[60]—some do not. Savings assets do not include investments in land whether made directly or through investments in business entities whose "primary purpose" is investment in land.[61] Thus, the investor in undeveloped land or in a land company obtains no current deduction and holds the property at a basis reflecting her investment.

Savings assets also do not include "cash on hand,"[62] a collectible[63]—a Picasso painting, a Rodin sculpture, the Hope Diamond—or "the investment in any business entity, the purpose of which is to hold collectibles for appreciation."[64] Amounts contributed to a hobby activity—pleasurable, revenue generating, but not intended to earn a profit—are not additions to savings.[65]

The receipt of a gift or bequest is not gross income.[66] An in-kind transfer of a savings asset is not a taxable withdrawal from savings by the donor.[67] Transfer of cash or a bank account is a withdrawal by the donor and (if the cash is then invested) an addition to savings by the donee.[68]

As noted earlier, amounts that are treated as taxable receipts of a business entity under the business tax—for example, my proprietorship supplies to third parties my "independent contractor" professional services as a chef for the occasional great family dinner—are not gross income to me under the individual tax.[69] My individual tax liability will mature when I receive a payment or distribution from my proprietorship.

Finally, sprinkled about the USA Tax statute are antiabuse provisions, sad testimonials to the drafters' quite reasonable fear that the tax bar is poised to do them in. In paranoid focus, for example, are (1) an *inter vivos* gift "made primarily to effect a transfer of tax liability to a taxpayer in a lower tax bracket,"[70] which I would have accounted a fairly trivial concern at this late date in our tax history; (2) acquiring a savings asset "with funds borrowed for the purpose of increasing the taxpayer's Unlimited Savings Allowance";[71] and (3) taxpayers "borrowing against their savings to consume rather than withdrawing their savings."[72] The last two concerns are not trivial, but antiabuse rules of this sort suggest, not that the problems are thereby solved, but rather that there are basic flaws in the Unlimited Savings Allowance.

Transactions Among Business Entities and Their Owners

Contributions

A cash contribution to business entity B by individual A is a saving by her (but not a net saving if the cash is withdrawn from a different investment) under the individual tax, and is not a taxable receipt by B under the business tax.[73] If A contributes to B property that A has just bought from Z for the purpose, it is as if B bought from Z with cash furnished by A.[74] If A contributes to B personal use property—property used by A at any time other than in a business activity[75]—B has no income or deduction and enjoys a carryover basis in the property[76] and A is given no addition to savings[77] but is awarded basis in her interest in B equal to the lesser of her basis in the p.u. property or its fair market value.[78] A's contribution to B of a financial asset is, I would guess, a carryover basis transaction in which neither A nor B has any income or deduction under, respectively, the individual tax and the business tax.[79] Finally, if A contributes services to B for an ownership interest, B is awarded no deduction[80] and A, having received a savings asset, has no net income.

A's contribution to B of an asset used by A in a business activity is a transfer, not by A the human, but by a business entity to a business entity. That transaction implicates only the business tax and under it neither entity has a deduction or a taxable receipt. If the transfer were in cash, the results would be the same.[81]

Distributions

For both liquidating and nonliquidating distributions, General Utilities stays repealed. Indeed, repeal is extended to all business entities and is not limited solely to corporations. B's initial distribution to A is a sale to A at fair market value as reasonably determined by B.[82] Under the individual tax, it is a savings withdrawal by A, but if the property is a savings asset or is converted to business use, for A this much of it is a wash.[83] Additionally, under the business tax, real property will be treated as distributed if used by B for a nonbusiness purpose for more than an insubstantial period of time during the taxable year.[84]

There are two exceptions to the rule that in-kind distributions are fully taxable to B. First, if the distributee is a controlling business entity—the direct or indirect owner of more than 50 percent of the capital or profits interest in B—it is nonrecognition and tax attribute carryover for both parties.[85] Second, if p.u. property is distributed by B to A and A originally con-

tributed that property to B, then (1) in computing B's gain on its deemed sale to A fair market value equals the p.u. property's basis plus any enhancements in value attributable to business purchases with respect to the property,[86] and (2) A's basis in the p.u. property is equal to her basis in that property at the time of contribution (but not more than her predistribution basis in B) and her basis in B is concomitantly reduced.[87]

If the distribution is not just p.u. property back to the contributor, there is one point on which it matters if B's transfer to A is or is not a distribution in "complete liquidation" of B: If A has basis in her interest in B, under the USA individual tax she can offset that basis (allocating to cash, savings assets, and other property received) only if B's distribution is in complete liquidation.[88]

Finally, the dividing up of a business entity—a spin-off, split-off, or split-up—triggers no immediate business tax consequence.[89] At the individual investor level no income is realized (one savings asset has become two) and her basis, if she has any, will be allocated among her new and old entity holdings proportionate to relative values.[90]

Sale of Business Assets

We consider here the class of transactions in which one business entity (T) transfers some or all of its assets to another business entity (P) for consideration that does *not* include equity (e.g., "corporate stock") in P or in a P subsidiary.[91] Under the business tax, T has sold assets and the consideration received is allocated among those assets applying the rules of current Code § 1060, subject to the ability of T and P to reach a mutually binding and reasonable allocation agreement.[92] Alternatively, if P acquires from T substantially all of either T's assets or a line of business of T or "a separately standing business" of T, P and T may jointly elect to treat the acquisition as if it were the acquisition of stock of a business entity holding the assets transferred, a transaction that is subject to the merger and stock acquisition rules of § 213 and not to the asset acquisition rules.[93]

If the "treat as a stock sale" election is not made, or indeed cannot be made because P has not acquired substantially all of the relevant T assets, there is one rule left to consult. If T's business predated 1996, T almost certainly holds transition basis assets and is amortizing transition basis in up to four categories.[94] Because all transition basis has been reallocated to amortization accounts, the respective transition basis assets have no basis.[95]

What happens to T's transition basis property amortization accounts when T makes a big sale of assets to P but there is no election to treat the transaction as a sale of stock? The answer is, nothing—T keeps the accounts—*unless* P and T jointly elect to have P assume the amortization deductions attributable to the assets sold.[96] The election is available only for a "substantial sale"[97] and, if it is made, T's taxable receipts on the asset sale are reduced by the unamortized accounts' balance and P's cost of the business purchase is reduced by the same amount.

Mergers and Stock Acquisitions

Tax simplification is on the horizon. Under the business tax, nothing happens. At the entity level, T and P, no income, no deduction, and T's loss carryovers and other tax attributes (*e.g.*, transition basis amortization accounts) are inherited by P. In the USA business tax there are no "don't traffic in NOLs" rules similar to current Code §§ 382 through 384, or even to § 269. In the business tax no one has heard of the continuity of interest doctrine, and that seems a very good thing.[98]

At the individual investor level, A's exchange of T stock or other T ownership interest for P stock or other P ownership interest is a nontaxable exchange of savings assets, with substituted basis if A has basis in T. If in the exchange A receives cash "boot" in addition to P stock, the boot is a withdrawal from savings under the USA individual tax.

A final observation on asset transfers to and from business entities. If T owns as one of many assets an operating factory building worth $1 million and transfers the building to P for $1 million cash, T has a $1 million taxable receipt and P a $1 million deduction. The results are the same if P pays T with a P debt obligation or with stock of X, a corporation unrelated to P. The latter arrangement should be disaggregated, viewed as if P paid T $1 million in cash and T then used the cash to purchase the X stock from P (on which deemed sale of a financial asset P would not be subject to USA business tax).

But if P pays T by delivering to T $1 million of P stock, as I read the proposed statute[99]—a reading that may be faulty to be sure—T does not have a taxable receipt and P has no deduction, just a carryover of T's (presumably zero) basis. Restated in pre-1996 terms, Code § 351 is shorn of its 80 percent control requirement and now applies all over the place.

One may view in a similar way the rule for contributions of p.u. property by individual A to widely-held business entity P in exchange for P stock.[100] A has no income and gets no deduction, and instead holds the P stock at a basis equal to her basis in the p.u. property, reduced by any encumbrance on the property to which P succeeds. P has no income and gets no deduction, and inherits A's basis in the p.u. property. These would be the tax results under current Code §§ 351, 357, 358, and 361, if § 351 did not contain an 80 percent control requirement.

AND THEN WHAT HAPPENED?

The proffered review of S. 722 is selective in attempting to suggest some of the provisions and positions that seem likely to confuse the tax advisor, or attract her responsive tax plan, or some of each. In what follows, I will try to put a measure of flesh on the collection of bones.[101]

Before the January 1, 1996 Effective Date

NOLs and Other Carryovers

Because carryovers will go poof on January 1, 1996, they should if possible be promptly converted to a tax attribute that will survive the changeover. Basis will survive, under both the USA individual tax and (usefully converted to transition basis amortization) the USA business tax.

Sell the right amount and sort of appreciated property (*i.e.,* capital gain property with appreciation sufficient to match the capital loss carryover).

If you are an individual selling investment assets, put the proceeds (cash, which is basis on the hoof) in your bank account *not* in your brokerage account.

If you are a corporation with an NOL and the appreciated assets you would sell are difficult to transfer to a third-party, even with a leaseback, do not despair. Organize a 99-percent owned partnership (see to it that the other 1 percent is in friendly hands) and contribute the appreciated assets to the partnership. Just before you do this, be sure that you have filed a consent under Code § 341(f)(2) and that one of your more-than-5-percent shareholders promptly thereafter sold at least one of her shares to anyone other than her spouse.[102]

Corporate Debt Restructure

After 1995 a business entity will not be allowed an interest deduction. Retire cor-porate debt in 1995. Substitute lease financing. A nice thought: If you have assets eligible for installment sale, sell for a buyer's note that will come due in 1996 and leaseback. It would appear that the 1996 gain will be taxed under the USA business tax, which may mean, if the buyer's note is viewed as a financial asset, no business tax at all.

Individual Debt Restructure

Money borrowed before 1996 for consumption or to purchase a savings asset will, if not repaid until after 1995, attract disadvantageous tax consequences under the USA individual tax. This is because post-1995 interest on pre-1996 debt is not deductible (unless the debt is a home mortgage), while the earnings used to pay the interest are includable in the individual's gross income. The individual is well advised to pay, before the end of 1995, all 1995 interest that is deductible under Code § 163, and to repay the debt before the end of 1995 if the necessary funds can be raised without attracting significant income tax liability.[103]

Postpone Excess Investment Gains

Other than to offset losses that will otherwise go poof, see "NOLs and Other Carryovers" above, gains on investment assets are best deferred to 1996 when they will be exempt from USA business tax and deferrable under the USA individual tax through the Unlimited Savings Allowance. Those who appreciate tax deferral (or tax elimination) but wish to lock up an economic profit will consider the acquisition of a put option, a short sale against the box, or an equity swap. It is unclear, at least to me, how the USA Tax reacts to each of these strategies.

Fattening Individual Bank Accounts

Under the USA individual tax asset basis survives transition, but all asset basis is not equally available for use. Basis in an individual's adjusted general basis account is best because it is most available. Basis in investment securities held in a brokerage account is poor because it is stacked last on withdrawals. Basis in a bank account is good because it will promptly become part of the general basis account. It is good planning to fatten the bank account and slim down the brokerage account, prior to 1996, provided it is done in a way that does not trigger undesired 1995 gains.

Consider Combining Business Activities

Under the USA business tax, a business entity that has business purchases in excess of taxable receipts in any year has generated a loss that cannot be carried back and can be carried forward 15 years. If Ms. A owns two business entities, the one just described and another that every year generates substantial taxable receipts in excess of business purchases, she will be grumpy, and rightly so, if she cannot offset the losses in business 1 against the profits in business 2 each year.

Under the USA Tax Act it is wonderfully unclear if and when the results of operations of two business activities can be combined.[104]

Postponing a restructure until after 1995 is possible, but prudence argues for restructuring now so that the business activities are properly configured at all times commencing the January 1, 1996 effective date of the USA business tax. Thus, Ms. A might now transfer both businesses to a single corporation, or one business to a parent corporation and the other business to its wholly owned subsidiary. If each business is currently in a separate partnership, the two partnerships might be combined into one or might be incorporated into a single entity or into a parent-subsidiary corporate configuration.

Consider Postponing the Sale of Your Home

If you have lived in your home at least 3 years out of the last 5, are 55 years of age, and contemplate a sale gain that will not exceed $125,000, you should sell before the close of 1995.[105] Otherwise, for reasons explored hereafter, you should consider waiting until next year or the year after.

Fund Your Issue

If you can afford it—and what tax planner would wish to represent a taxpayer of only slender means?—be sure that on January 1, 1996 each of your children and grandchildren owns qualified savings assets (cash in the bank, publicly traded securities) that have an aggregate basis of $50,000 or a little bit less, but in no event even a penny more.[106]

Consider Divorce

The USA individual tax presents its unfair share of marriage penalties. If on January 1, 1996 your son and daughter-in-law own qualified savings assets with an aggregate basis of just under $100,000, no transition basis adjustment for them.[107] If they divorce the week before and divide their qualified savings assets equally, on January 1, 1996 each will be under the $50,000 Plimsoll Line and each will enjoy happy years of transition basis deductions. Should only one of them have outside income, payments to the other of alimony and child support[108] will take care of that.

Divorce may be in your interests, as well as in the interests of your kids. The new deduction for qualified higher-education expenses is up to $2,000 for each eligible student, but the maximum annual deduction is limited to $8,000.[109] If you have eight children you currently are higher educating at $2,000 per year each,[110] marriage is imposing a significant penalty. Divorce, split the children four a piece, and equalize incomes by paying and receiving alimony. You will double the annual education deduction, from $8,000 to $16,000.

Does it matter what sort of school the kids attend? A so-called "white flight" institution, I believe, would not qualify as an eligible education institution under new § 10(b)(2)(B).[111] Now, how about a parochial school?

By the way, maintaining two households rather than one joint return, your aggregate family living allowance will increase from $7,400 to $10,800.[112]

After 1995: Some Planner's Tools

Facing the USA individual and business taxes, the planner will think about the tools the statute places at hand.

(1) Investments are immediately deductible, but with exceptions. One exception is the purchase of a collectible, the Hope Diamond or a Picasso painting, or something a bit cheaper. A second exception is land if the land is not currently leased for a full and fair rental. Simply holding cash in hand (rather than in the bank) generates no deduction. Thus, by the investment she makes or does not make, the taxpayer can elect for the current year saving/deduction or no saving/no deduction.

(2) In any year, a savings deduction, otherwise available, is reduced by the amount of net nonexempt borrowing in that taxable year. Net nonexempt borrowing is the excess, if any, of nonexempt debt at year-end over nonexempt debt at the beginning of the year. Thus, if the taxpayer incurs $1 million of nonexempt debt in year 1 and, paying

interest currently, maintains the debt balance through the close of year 2, the taxpayer has no "net nonexempt borrowing" in year 2, and on down the years so long as the taxpayer maintains the debt position.[113]

(3) In applying the Unlimited Savings Allowance and the deferred-income adjustment,[114] each taxable year stands on its own. The USA individual tax contains no rule of the sort found in Code § 1231(c) under which a later year's tax reporting changes in consequence of an earlier year's reporting of a different transaction. Thus, it is entirely possible to arrange an individual's financial affairs to alternate years of net saving and years of net dissaving.

(4) Ms. A, an individual service provider to P, a business entity, may be P's employee, in which event the compensation paid by P for her services is not deductible in computing P's business tax liability. However, the relationship can be established as a "loaned employee" arrangement in which Q, a different business entity (Ms. A may or may not have an ownership interest in Q), employs A and seconds her services to P for a fee paid by P to Q.[115] In this configuration, P's fee payment is deductible by P and is income to Q; for its compensation payments to A no deduction is awarded Q. If P is currently profitable while Q enjoys a sizable post-1995 business tax loss, the arrangement will be attractive to all parties and the pricing will reflect the tax benefit Q through its intermediation has conferred on P.[116]

(5) The USA business tax bifurcates sale proceeds, when goods or services are sold on credit, into a (taxable) payment for the product or service and a payment for delay that is not income to the seller and is not de-

ductible by a business entity buyer. If, however, the customer is an individual, not a business entity, she can deduct neither component of the price and presumably is indifferent to the relative size of its segments.

Some Illustrations of Life and Work Under the USA Tax Act

A Basic Strategy for the Truly Rich

Here is the basic strategy, in a few simple steps.

Withdraw Opening Basis in 1996. The USA business tax converts a business entity's 1996 opening basis to deduction streams that are essentially unaffected by subsequent taxpayer actions. The USA individual tax does not follow that sensible course when the aggregate basis of savings assets exceeds $50,000. The individual taxpayer is obliged to plan for it, and if she is rich—ample pre-1996 savings— she should do just fine.

(1) Early in 1996 shift investment basis to the general basis account by (a) a simple election in the case of bank accounts[117] and (b) selling all marketable securities and closing all brokerage accounts.[118] (It is okay for the moment to open a new brokerage account with a new broker and reestablish investment positions.) Selling a savings asset at a loss is fine for this purpose: the loss goes directly to the general basis account.[119]

(2) Shift a reasonable part of the investment portfolio into tax-exempt bonds that pay interest only in even years (of which the first is 1996).[120] It is safe to predict that once the USA Tax becomes law, there will be lots of product like this available for acquisition.

(3) Shift a reasonable part of the investment portfolio to stocks and bonds that pay cash dividends and cash in-

terest only in odd years (1997 will be the first). Once again, after 1995 there should be lots of product available.

(4) Renegotiate the compensation package so that the bulk of cash compensation is payable only in odd years (1997 will be the first).

(5) Before the end of 1996, withdraw in cash from savings an amount equal to a fair part of the total general basis account. This is a net withdrawal year, obviously, and hence this recapture of historic savings basis will not be taxable.

(6) Take the largest part of 1996's tax-free money—historic savings basis plus tax-exempt interest—and before the close of 1996 buy either (a) the Hope Diamond (or other collectibles of ensured value)[121] or (b) land that is *not* leased for a full rental appropriate to its underlying value.

(7) Consume the rest of the tax-free money in 1996. Prepay some 1997 consumption if you can (buy the 1997 vacation package now).

Save in 1997. In 1997 the taxpayer will receive large amounts of gross income in the form of dividends, interest, and compensation. She should invest as much of the funds as possible in taxable securities that yield only in odd years, and in tax-exempt securities that yield only in even years. These investments are 1997 deductions against 1997 gross income.

The taxpayer needs money for consumption in 1997. Her sale of the Hope Diamond, or the real estate, or an appropriate part of either, will generate consumable funds but not gross income.

And on Down the Line. In 1998 the taxpayer again has low gross income and again will be a net dissaver, recapturing another part of the general basis account. These funds plus tax-exempt interest finance 1998 consumption, the purchase of collectibles and land, and even some prepayment of 1999 consumption.

In 1999 it is back to saving, coupled with any necessary consumption withdrawals, not from savings, but from land and collectibles.

Sell Your Fine Home

Mr. H owns Tara, a fine home. His basis is $5 million and the property is worth $15 million. Mr. H is happy at Tara, but willing to move to equivalent housing.

In 1996 Mr. H sells Tara for $15 million cash. He promptly purchases a new principal residence, Boutwell. He pays the $15 million purchase price $3 million in cash and $12 million by executing a long-term note secured by a mortgage on Boutwell.[122] Mr. H invests his surplus $12 million cash in collectibles, land, consumption, and anything but savings assets.

In subsequent years Mr. H saves much gross income as it is received, and never acquires savings assets with any of the $12 million. Over time the collectibles and land are turned back into cash and the cash consumed. Mr. H never borrows against his savings.

This example is to be tested against the § 58 antiabuse rules none of which, I believe, hits the mark.

Long-Term Nonexempt Borrowing

In 1996 wealthy Ms. K borrows long-term $2 million on her spotless personal credit. With the funds she purchases a tract of undeveloped land for a long-term investment. The property is operated temporarily as a parking lot and throws off only enough earnings to defray part of the carrying costs.

Property values go up and in 1999 Ms. K, revising her original investment plan, sells the land for $3 million cash. Her 1999

gross income from other sources is $1 million. Ms. K decides not to repay the $2 million personal loan—interest rates have gone up and the loan is advantageous from the viewpoint of the borrower— and, while considering her options, Ms. K invests her $3 million land sale proceeds in a money market fund at the end of 1999.

I suggest Ms. K has beaten the system, and that her 1999 USA individual tax liability is zero.

Summing Up

Many questions might be added. For example, may Mr. Rich consume in odd years and save in even years, while Mrs. Rich, filing a separate return, does the reverse? Or is it necessary to the plan that Mr. and Mrs. Rich divorce and live together in wealthy sin?

If in 1996 a corporation acquires land for business use and in 1999 that land turns into a nonbusiness asset, the USA Tax finds a deemed corporate distribution. If in 1999 a corporation acquires, with business intent, an asset that turns out to be a collectible, is there a deemed distribution?[123] Whether of land or collectibles, precisely who are the deemed distributees if the corporation is capitalized with various classes of common stock, convertible and nonconvertible preferred stock, convertible and nonconvertible debt, and warrants that are in-the-money?

Corporate stock that has a basis (from income tax days) less than current value can, after 1995, be reconfigured tax-free into (1) corporate stock with a value equal to its basis and (2) other corporate capital instruments that have value but no basis. Are the benefits to be derived from manipulating this isolated basis structure superior to the benefits to be obtained through manipulation of the general basis account?

How comfortable should the creators really be in their tax world in which NOLs are freely transferable in corporate acquisitions, and readily exportable through loaned employee and equivalent arrangements?

All of these questions and concerns, all of the suggestions for manipulation set out earlier, and the many others that time and experience would bring forth, urge that Professor Warren's "tentative conclusions" [124] concerning the superiority of a standard consumption tax model over the USA Tax's Unlimited Savings Allowance, and Professor Kaplow's determinations with regard to the recovery of preenactment basis,[125] are absolutely correct. I would only add that conjoining tax-exempt bond interest with a savings deduction for the purchase of those bonds, as the USA Tax would do, seems to me genuinely flaky. In any event, a cash flow consumption tax that (1) includes borrowed amounts in the tax base and (2) does not hold the recovery of preenactment basis hostage to taxpayers' postenactment conduct, may not solve all of the problems and eliminate all of the opportunities real life and the tax bar can produce—the rich will persevere—but it will perform measurably better the task to which the Nunn-Domenici proposals are addressed.

Conclusion

The New Yorker got it right.

ENDNOTES

1 *The New Yorker Magazine,* January 14, 1985, p. 35.
2 The April 25 introduction of S. 722 was preceded by the wide circulation (as a Special Report Supplement to the March 13, 1995 issue of *Tax Notes)* of a lengthy paper entitled "Description and Explanation of the Unlimited Savings Allowance Tax System," prepared for Alliance, USA by Ernest S. Christian and George J. Schutzer (hereafter, the "USA Explanation"). The USA Explanation is helpful in analyzing S. 722 but the

two do not inevitably match, *e.g.,* S. 722 embraces the accrual method for its business tax although the USA Explanation announced that all businesses will report on the cash method.
3 In attempting to understand just what S. 722 is attempting to do and how, I have been greatly aided by, in addition to the USA Explanation, the following more recent papers. *Description and Analysis of Proposals to Replace the Federal Income Tax* (JCS-18–95), prepared by the Staff of the Joint Committee on Taxation (June 5, 1995), hereafter "Joint Committee Pamphlet"; Alvin C. Warren, Jr., The Proposal for an "Unlimited Savings Allowance," *Tax Notes 68* (August 28, 1995): 1103, hereafter "Warren Paper"; Louis Kaplow, "Recovery of Pre-Enactment Basis Under a Consumption Tax: The USA Tax System," *Tax Notes 68* (August 28, 1995): 1109, hereafter "Kaplow Paper"; Alan L. Feld, "Nunn-Domenici and Non Profits," *Tax Notes 68* (August 28, 1995): 1119, hereafter "Feld Paper"; Bernard Wolfman, "Corporate Tax Issues Under the Nunn-Domenici Consumption Tax," *Tax Notes 68* (August 28, 1995): 1121, hereafter "Wolfman Paper." I have cribbed shamelessly from all of them.
4 Joint Committee Pamphlet 38. Thus, export sales are not taxed and imports are subject to an 11 percent import tax. S. 722 §§ 286-288.
5 S. 722 § 21.
6 S. 722 §§ 281-282. Under the business tax, excess credit is not refundable and instead carries forward a maximum of 15 years. S. 722 § 283.
7 S. 722 § 201(b).
8 While subchapters K and S of present law thus disappear, subchapter T (Code § 1381-1388 relating to cooperatives and their patrons) in large measure persists, see S. 722 § 260 (qualified patronage dividend).
9 S. 722 § 203(e) defines *financial receipts* to include interest, dividends, and other distributions by a business entity, proceeds from the sale of financial instruments including corporate stock and other ownership interests in business entities, and proceeds from annuities and life insurance policies, currency hedging and exchanges, and other financial transactions.
10 S. 722 §§ 202, 203.
11 S. 722 §§ 204, 205(a).
12 *See* S. 722 § 205(a)(3).
13 The proposed statute, S. 722 § 205(a)(3)(A),

announces an exception to nondeductibility "to the extent that a portion so paid is a fee for financial intermediation services." The proposed treatment of financial intermediation services and businesses, §§ 235-246, turns the mind to mush. Section 246, dealing with a business entity which, although not "regularly" in the business of providing financial intermediation services, engages in "significant" financial intermediation activity anyway—no doubt out of sheer perversity—strikes a ringing blow for tax simplification. I shall write no more on this perfidious subject.

14 *Savings assets* is defined in S. 722 § 53(b) to include stocks, bonds, securities, certificates of deposit, investments in partnerships and proprietorships, shares of mutual funds, life insurance policies, annuities, and "other similar savings or investment assets."

15 In S. 722 § 242(b)(3).

16 S. 722 § 238.

17 One cannot safely say immediately deductible, because the business taxpayer is ordinarily on the accrual method of accounting and the economic performance rules, Code § 461(h), apply. S. 722 § 220.

18 S. 722 § 232.

19 S. 722 § 230.

20 S. 722 § 230(d).

21 See S. 722 § 232(b)(2)(A).

22 S. 722 § 232(c). That deemed distribution, in turn, under S. 722 § 211(a) is treated as if the business entity sold the property "to its owners at fair market value." Because the business entity would have deducted the property's cost in a prior year, the property's full value is part of the entity's gross receipts for business tax purposes.

23 S. 722 § 206.

24 Alternatively, only two taxes might be imposed but, inappropriately, both would be borne directly by the employee (business tax on her business entity and personal tax on her wages) and the "true employer" would be awarded a deduction for compensation paid the employee's business entity.

25 S. 722 § 206(c)(1). The same provision announces that "business activity" does not include the performance of regular domestic household services (baby-sitting, housecleaning, lawn cutting, etc.) by an employee of "an employer that is an individual or family."

26 S. 722 § 206(b). The illustration given is the sale by an individual of her used car.

27 In fact, the loss will be greater than the described difference, by the amount of the "transition basis adjustment" for the taxable year. See S. 722 § 290 (amortization of transition basis), described below.

28 S. 722 § 207(b)(1).

29 S. 722 § 292.

30 S. 722 § 290. Depreciable property with a remaining recovery period of 15 years or more is awarded a 30-year amortization period, and nondepreciable property used in a business activity in 1996 and previously placed in service is awarded 40-year amortization provided that property, were it initially acquired by the business entity in 1996, would have been immediately deductible under the business tax.

31 Joint Committee Pamphlet 38.

32 In the standard cash flow consumption tax model, a dollar borrowed goes into the tax base and a dollar committed to saving is deducted in computing the tax base. Under that arrangement, borrowed money can increase but can never decrease the net amount that otherwise would have been subject to consumption tax, in the year of borrowing, had the borrowing not occurred.

33 S. 722 § 3.

34 S. 722 § 4(a)(3).

35 S. 722 § 4(a)(12).

36 S. 722 §§ 4(a)(4), 91. Section 4 catalogs a miscellany of other exclusions mainly derived from current law, *e.g.*, Code §§ 104(a)(2) (compensation for injury and sickness), 107 (parsonage allowance), and 119 (meals and lodging furnished for the convenience of the employer).

37 S. 722 § 5.

38 S. 722 § 6.

39 S. 722 § 7.

40 S. 722 § 8.

41 S. 722 § 9.

42 S. 722 § 11. See Feld Paper 1119–20.

43 S. 722 § 10. The maximum annual deduction is limited to $4,000 in the case of married individuals filing separate returns, and all dollar amounts are adjusted for inflation commencing 1997. See S. 722 §§ 10(d), 24.

44 S. 722 § 50(a).

45 Warren Paper 1104–8.

46 Kaplow Paper 1109–18.

47 W.S. Gilbert, *Iolanthe*, Act II (1882).

48 S. 722 §§ 52(a)(1), 53(a), (b), 54.

49 S. 722 § 52(b)(1).

[50] S. 722 § 52(a)(2).

[51] S. 722 § 55. Nonexempt debt is the principal amount of plus accrued interest on indebtedness that is not exempt debt. Exempt debt is limited to (1) principal residence debt (home mortgage), *see* § 9, but without regard to the $1 million limitation that relates to the interest deduction in § 9; (2) debt to acquire a consumer durable, up to $25,000; and (3) an additional $10,000.

[52] S. 722 § 91.

[53] Savings of $400,000 less $390,000, which is the sum of nonexempt borrowing $100,000 [equal to $135,000 less (a) $25,000 and (b) $10,000], tax-exempt interest $250,000, and $40,000 basis of savings withdrawn during the taxable year.

[54] S. 722 § 57.

[55] See Warren Paper 1105.

[56] S. 722 § 12(d).

[57] S. 722 § 12.

[58] S. 722 § 12(c)(1).

[59] See S. 722 § 52(b), defining net includable withdrawal income, and § 57 defining general basis account (GBA) to reflect for each year: (1) if the taxpayer is a net saver, a GBA increase equal to the lesser of (a) net savings or (b) nontaxable sources of funds; (2) if the taxpayer is a net dissaver, a GBA decrease equal to the net withdrawal; (3) if a savings asset having a basis is disposed of for less than that basis, an increase equal to the "loss"; and (4) an elective addition to GBA under § 57(c) when sale of a principal residence and investment of the proceeds produces a savings deduction in excess of the year's income. In addition, § 57(d) affords a one-time election in the 1996 tax return to increase the GBA by the January 1, 1996 balance of the taxpayer's bank accounts (which thereafter have no basis). It is unclear why the USA Tax does not award a similar election with respect to historic brokerage accounts; historic brokerage accounts in fact are treated far worse (a "recover basis last" approach) by § 56(a)(3).

[60] See S. 722 § 53(a)(3), USA Explanation 1559. On the other hand, proceeds of life insurance are not exempt from USA individual tax, *cf.* § 238(c) (business tax exemption), which requires the individual beneficiary to invest rather than consume the proceeds in order to postpone the tax.

[61] S. 722 §§ 53(c)(1), 1114 (land companies). However, "the activity of rental of real estate is a business activity," § 112(a), and hence the acquisition of rental real estate (fully leased for fair rent) should qualify as a deductible investment in a business entity, *i.e.*, a real estate rental proprietorship that is separately subject to the business tax, and not as a nondeductible investment in land.

[62] S. 722 § 53(c)(2).

[63] S. 722 § 53(c)(3).

[64] S. 722 § 53(c)(4).

[65] S. 722 § 113. *Cf.* Code § 183.

[66] S. 722 § 4(a)(3). Basis, if there is any, limited to fair value if lower, carries over from the donor or testator (no stepped-up basis at death). § 74.

[67] S. 722 § 56(c)(1).

[68] S. 722 § 56(c)(3).

[69] S. 722 § 4(a)(12).

[70] S. 722 § 56(c)(2).

[71] S. 722 § 58(a)(1).

[72] S. 722 § 58(c).

[73] S. 722 § 210(b)(1).

[74] S. 722 § 210(b)(2).

[75] S. 722 § 210(b)(3)(B). In the individual tax personal use property ("p.u. property") is defined with respect to personal use by A, anyone related to A, and anyone from whom A acquired the property at other than an arm's-length price. § 111(c).

[76] S. 722 § 210(b)(3)(A).

[77] S. 722 § 111(a).

[78] S. 722 § 74(b).

[79] For some reason S. 722 § 210, entitled Contribution to a Business Entity, does not appear to advert to this case.

[80] S. 722 § 210(b)(4).

[81] S. 722 § 210(a).

[82] S. 722 § 211(a).

[83] S. 722 § 75(d).

[84] S. 722 § 211(e). *Nonbusiness use* is defined in § 232(b)(2) to mean, *inter alia*, a use for which a fair rent is not paid. It is barely conceivable that the deemed distribution provision, § 211(e), is intended to apply to personal property (*e.g.*, collectibles) as well as real property, but the definitional reference in § 211(e) is solely to § 232, a provision that deals only with real property.

[85] S. 722 § 211(b)(d).

[86] S. 722 § 211(c).

[87] S. 722 § 75(d)(4).

[88] S. 722 § 75(d)(3). For an excellent discussion of the concerns focused by this differential individual tax treatment of liquidating and

nonliquidating distributions, see Wolfman Paper 1122–1123.

[89] S. 722 § 214. Allocation of tax attributes, carryovers and the like, between the entities is to be prescribed by regulations. Section 215.

[90] S. 722 § 75(c).

[91] S. 722 § 212(e). If P equity is exchanged as part or all of the acquisition consideration, the merger rules of § 213, reviewed below, govern the transaction.

[92] S. 722 § 212(a).

[93] S. 722 § 212(c). When a business entity sells stock, a financial asset, under the business tax the entity is not taxed. This election, to treat an asset sale as a stock acquisition, is current Code § 338(h)(10) in reverse. The proposed USA business tax contains nothing equivalent to current law's § 338(h)(10) election to treat a stock sale as a sale of underlying assets.

[94] See S. 722 § 290, reviewed earlier in this paper.

[95] S. 722 § 291(a).

[96] S. 722 § 291(b).

[97] More than 20 percent (in value or original cost) of T's assets are sold for total consideration that exceeds $1 million or 20 percent of T's taxable receipts of the immediately preceding taxable year.

[98] S. 722 § 213(a). The same business tax nonrecognition results obtain if P acquires, whether for cash or P stock, all or substantially all of the stock of (or other form of ownership interest in) T. Section 213(b).

[99] See S. 722 §§ 210(a)(2), 212(e)(2). See also USA Explanation 1571, which is supportive.

[100] See S. 722 § 210(b)(3), reviewed earlier in this paper.

[101] After this Nunn-Domenici paper was drafted I received from Professor Alan Feld his paper, "Living With the Flat Tax," which I promptly read with a view to stealing the flat tax concerns identified in the paper and presenting them as Nunn-Domenici concerns. But I failed. Not out of a sudden concern over propriety, but because a high percentage of the unanswered or misanswered questions identified under the flat tax are decently responded to in the proposed USA Tax Act (which presents a set of its own problems).

[102] The contribution to the partnership is a taxable exchange. See Reg. § 1.341–7(e)(2). It is irrelevant that the corporation is not in fact collapsible. Reg. § 1.341–7(a)(2)(ii).

[103] For a further discussion on preenactment individual debt, see Warren Paper 1107–8 (examples 10–12).

[104] See S. 722 §§ 301(b) (referring to proprietorships and calling for regulations), 302(a) (contemplating the filing of consolidated returns by business entities but written in a way that appears to prevent consolidation in the case of Ms. A's two businesses because she and not a business entity would be the "common parent").

[105] See Code § 121.

[106] See S. 722 § 12 (transition basis deduction).

[107] See S. 722 § 12(c)(2).

[108] Under S. 722 §§ 3(a)(7) and 5, child support and alimony are treated alike, deductible by the payor and income to the recipient.

[109] S. 722 § 10(c).

[110] This can happen. We have friends with nine children, each of whom has been educated both highly and costly.

[111] Cf. *Bob Jones University v. United States*, 461 U.S. 574 (1983).

[112] S. 722 § 7. The numbers will be adjusted for inflation beginning in 1997.

[113] S. 722 § 58 contains antiabuse rules, *e.g.*, "Borrowing to Generate Deduction," which the tax planner would consult and, employing adequate care and patience, almost certainly subdue. Decades of experience with Code § 269 lends comfort.

[114] Deferred income is defined in S. 722 § 51 as the amount of gross income that was previously deferred though the Unlimited Savings Allowance and that is treated as withdrawn from savings in a subsequent taxable year; the amount of deferred income for a taxable year is equal to the net includable withdrawal income (net withdrawal in excess of the balance in the taxpayer's general basis account) computed under § 52(b).

[115] See, *e.g.*, *Rubin v. Commissioner*, 429 F.2d 650 (2d Cir. 1970), rev'g 51 T.C. 251 (1968); *Robert E. Wilgus*, 20 T.C.M. 752 (1961); *Fontaine Fox*, 37 B.T.A. 271 (1938).

[116] A similar strategy on the asset side: Q purchases equipment on credit and leases to P; Q uses part of the rent to pay carrying costs.

[117] S. 722 § 57(d).

[118] S. 722 § 56(a)(2)(D).

[119] S. 722 § 57(b)(3).

[120] S. 722 § 122(b) makes it clear that OID accrual notions do not apply under the USA individual tax. Absent constructive receipt, it is "follow the cash."

[121] It is reasonable to anticipate that an industry will spring up to sell and to "guarantee" resale prices for collectibles so employed.

[122] Under S. 722 § 76, Mr. H would not recognize gain on his residence rollover.

[123] As pointed out in the Wolfman Paper 1121, neither the USA Tax Act as introduced nor the USA Explanation offers a clue.

[124] Warren Paper 1108.

[125] Kaplow Paper 1117–18.

LIVING WITH
THE FLAT TAX
ALAN L. FELD*

The flat tax replacement for the current federal income tax—proposed by Hall and Rabushka,[1] and endorsed by House Majority Leader Dick Armey[2] and Senator and Presidential aspirant Arlen Specter[3]— has attracted support from scholars and the general public alike.[4] Many scholars believe the flat tax will reduce the inefficiencies of the income tax, increase incentives for productive behavior, and promote savings.[5] Proponents add that the flat tax will produce adequate revenue without significantly increasing the tax burden that the personal and corporate income taxes currently impose.[6]

For the general public, the most salient attraction of the flat tax lies in its promise of simplicity. The voluminous Internal Revenue Code would follow the dinosaurs into extinction, replaced by a short and easily comprehended statute.[7] Transactions motivated by tax reduction likewise would disappear, as would the complex forms of certain business transactions. Most particularly, the prospect of filing the annual income tax return on a form the size of a postcard has captured the popular imagination.[8]

The flat tax converts the income tax into a national tax on consumption, whose

*Boston University School of Law, Boston, MA 02215.

economic effects resemble those of a value-added tax. It consists of two parts, a tax on individuals and a tax on businesses. The two taxes, taken together, create an "airtight" system for including income in the tax base once and only once, as close to the source as possible.[9] The rate is the same for both taxes. It hovers around 20% and varies with the proposal.[10] The tax on individuals generally includes only wages and other compensation paid in cash and pensions.[11] (Correspondingly, business may deduct these payments.) Dividends, interest, rent, and capital gains are not taxed to individuals. Nor may individuals claim the personal deductions currently available for mortgage interest, state and local taxes, charitable gifts, medical expenses, and the like.[12] The individual tax becomes progressive at the lower end through a personal allowance or standard deduction.[13] The earned-income credit, however, would disappear.

The business tax is intended to act as a comprehensive withholding tax on all types of income other than wages.[14] The business tax covers all businesses, including partnerships and sole proprietorships. Accounting for business transactions is intended to follow cash receipts and disbursements. The tax base consists generally of gross receipts from the sale or exchange of property, or services less the cost of business inputs, wages, and retirement contributions.[15] The tax provides current expensing of all property purchased for a business; thus, if a corporation purchases a factory, it may deduct the cost of the land, buildings, and equipment. The tax eliminates depreciation and inventory accounting, defers deductions until payment, and repeals percentage depletion. The current deduction of all business inputs has the effect of exempting from tax the future income derived from business assets, calculated at a normal rate of return.[16] Current expensing of business investment essentially converts the business income tax base into a value-added tax base. Businesses may claim no deduction for interest or dividends paid and do not include financial income when received. A special set of rules applies to banks and other financial institutions to tax income on services "bundled" with lending transactions.[17] Any excess of deductions over income carries over into the following year with interest added at the 3-month Treasury bill rate.

As this brief description suggests, the flat tax would eliminate at least four features of the current income tax system that create statutory or transactional complexity. First, the single tax rate does away with bracket arbitrage, where taxpayers with different marginal rates seek to create or use deductions at high rates and include income at low rates.[18] Second, current expensing of investment obviates the need for the existing rules to recover investment over different time periods, such as depreciation and basis. Third, elimination of the capital gain-ordinary income distinction makes it unnecessary for tax planners to seek favorable characterization for transactions. Fourth, accounting for transactions on a cash basis eliminates arbitrage between different accounting systems. For taxpayers who keep their books on an accrual basis, however, the flat tax may require an extra set of accounting books, an increase in taxpayer compliance cost. As an additional feature, by reducing the marginal tax rate, a flat tax would reduce the incentive for taxpayers to complicate their transactions for tax savings. This benefit could be duplicated under the existing income tax by reducing marginal rates without conversion to a national consumption-based tax.

Unfortunately, despite the initial simplifying effects of a flat tax, other causes of complexity in the present income tax would remain. Many of the problems and tensions that have shaped the Internal Revenue Code will mar the anticipated simplicity of the ideal flat tax. New distinctions created under a flat tax will require new solutions, inevitably embodied in the statute, and altering its initial spare form.

This paper will discuss a few areas likely to be troublesome under a flat tax. I will not address directly the merits of an income tax versus a consumption tax.[19] Nor will I discuss the important questions of economic efficiency in moving to a flat tax from the current system, nor those relating to the equitable distribution of the federal tax burden. Nor will I dwell on issues arising out of the transition to a flat tax, a subject for an entirely separate paper.[20] Also, I leave to others the questions of how much record-keeping and audit activity will be required under a flat tax.[21] Instead, the paper will assume the enactment of a flat tax in relatively pure form, and will look at the choices that taxpayers and lawmakers will have to make in adapting to the flat tax. My claim is a modest one, that the flat tax cannot achieve all its goals of a simple statute and simple taxpayer reporting at a low uniform rate and raise the revenues produced under the current income tax regime.

I begin with an examination of questions under the business tax, partly because relatively little appears to have been written about its operation and partly because flat tax proponents look to the business tax to raise a significant part of the tax revenues under the new system. I turn next to the individual tax component of the flat tax. Finally, I list a few of the groups disadvantaged by the change to a flat tax and which accordingly are most likely to press legislators for compensating benefits in the new law.

THE BUSINESS TAX

The business tax applies to all forms of business, including partnerships and sole proprietorships. The number of businesses subject to this tax would far exceed the corporations taxable under the existing corporate income tax, but virtually all of these new taxpayers already file returns either as pass-through entities or on Schedule C of the individual return. The tax base starts with gross receipts. Deductions follow for wages, retirement contributions, and the cost of business inputs. Businesses will claim no deductions for interest, fringe benefits, the employer's share of social security taxes, or state and local taxes, including property taxes.

What Counts as Business Inputs?

Current law includes all of a person's income as taxable, whether derived from business or investment. It distinguishes between an individual's investment activity and business activity for deduction purposes, favoring the latter with more liberal deduction treatment.[22] On a sale of assets, the individual can obtain the generally more favorable capital gain treatment for investment property and for most kinds of business property,[23] except inventory or property held primarily for sale to customers in the ordinary course of the trade or business.[24]

The flat tax enlarges the consequences of characterization of an activity as a business. It excludes altogether from the tax base the investment income of the individuals. It includes all business income and business expenses under the business tax.[25] Individuals under the flat tax accordingly will have an incentive to characterize receipts as derived from investment, while treating expenditures as related to business. None of the proposals state how they will patrol the frontier between an individual's business and nonbusiness activity. Failure to do so will allow aggressive taxpayer reporting that will erode the business tax base.

Example 1
Mary operates a sole proprietorship for the purchase and sale of widgets. For investment she purchases a piece of undeveloped land unrelated to the widget business. Mary receives nominal grazing fees on the land. May Mary deduct the cost of the land as an offset to the income from her widget business?

Hall and Rabushka's draft statute includes each sole proprietorship as a business, specifically including any individual with business receipts.[26] A business may file any number of business tax returns, provided all income is reported in the aggregate and that deductions are claimed only once. Mary thus may report the purchase of the land as a business input for a business of renting land for grazing purposes, and create a large first-year deduction. With the aggregate filing under the H-R proposal, the deduction will offset widget income. Mary can defer tax on income from the widget business virtually at will. The Armey and Specter bills both impose the business tax on every person engaged in a business activity, an undefined term.[27] Their tax base begins with gross active income and perhaps the word *active* is intended to exclude from the business tax activities that produce relatively passive income, like rents.[28] All versions will require rules to distinguish business income (and therefore business assets) from investment income (and assets).

If grazing land reaches the necessary minimum of activity to count as a business under the Armey and Specter proposals, will purchase of the land offset income from the widget business? Aggregate filing at the taxpayer's election is not explicit in the Armey and Specter bills; but because Mary is the taxpayer for both the widget and the grazing land businesses, the statute presumably will require her to file only one return that includes her two businesses. If so, Mary will be able to defer tax on her widget business income.

Investment in land that produces nominal income thus produces deductions to offset other business income. Will investment in art serve the taxpayer as well? Suppose Mary buys an Old Master to hang on the office wall in order to impress customers. Will that expenditure count as a business input that gives rise to a deduction? If not, will occasional rental of the painting to others qualify its purchase for immediate deduction?

In both instances, the possibility for deferral arises because current deductibility diverges far more sharply than does current law from the measure of economic change in the value of the land or the art.[29] These investments can serve a dual purpose, as business inputs and as a store of value for the owners of the business. If the investments reduce taxable business income, entrepreneurs will shelter business income with investments by their business in order to store value until the individuals need them. The erosion of the business tax base will be substantial, inefficient, and inequitable if businesses can obtain deductions by purchasing investment property from individuals who will

not be required to take the gross proceeds into income. Lawmakers might seek to correct such activity by carving passive assets out of the business input definition. The current income tax has had to determine whether to characterize property as an investment or as part of a business under the capital gain and loss provisions. The return of such questions will add a level of unanticipated complexity to the flat tax. The passive activity loss rules, occasionally cited as an example of bad complexity under current law, may return in a new guise.

Which intangibles will qualify as business inputs under the flat tax? Businesses currently deduct or amortize the costs of creating or acquiring many intangibles, including goodwill.[30] The flat tax presumably would not distinguish between tangible and intangible business inputs for purposes of allowing deductions. However, would it treat financial interests differently? For example, will the commodities futures transactions of an individual farmer constitute part of the business, producing gains and losses that enter the business tax computation, or will they fall under the investment category, with all gains and losses ignored? If farmers may deduct such hedging transactions, will individuals who take the other side of the contract be allowed to exclude the gross revenues as investment income? Complex rules for the identification of hedging transactions may be necessary to distinguish paper transactions related to a business from those that are not. If deductibility also extends to notional principal contracts and other derivative financial instruments, businesses may be able, by employing such contracts, to deduct the equivalent of interest expense, which the flat tax purports to make nondeductible.[31] Further, if hedging through financial instruments can constitute deductible investments for a business, will hedging through stock ownership similarly qualify, as when a business purchases the stock of a captive supplier or customer or other business-related investment?[32]

Finally, consider individuals who make their living as traders in stocks, securities, and other financial instruments. Under the H-R proposal, their income would constitute investment income unless the profits from their activities count as the sale or exchange of goods or services. The Armey and Specter bills would appear to treat traders as engaged in a business. Both define business taxable income as starting with gross active income. The Armey bill defines it as gross receipts from the sale or exchange of property or services in the United States, while the Specter bill defines the term as gross income other than investment income (which it leaves undefined). Both bills would have to brighten the line between the receipts from active investment by individuals, exempt from tax, and trading.

Mixed Business and Personal Assets

How much may an individual deduct when an asset serves both business and consumption functions? Suppose Martin purchases a seaside home, occupying it part of the time and renting it out during the vacation season. May he deduct the full purchase price and set it off against other business income? Current law has intricate rules to allocate expenses, including depreciation, between personal and rental use.[33] The law makes the determination on an annual basis, obviating the need to make an all-or-nothing or an intent-related decision at the time of purchase. Will the flat tax replicate the existing rules either on an initial or an annual basis?

Another common situation exemplifies other difficulties of mixed personal and business use assets.

Example 2
Olivia purchases a house and uses it as a personal residence. In year 2, Olivia rents out one room to a tenant and continues to live in the rest of the house. In year 4, Olivia stops renting the room and resumes personal use of it.

Olivia presumably enters the rental business in year 2 and rental income should be taxed as gross receipts of a business. How much may Olivia deduct as the cost of the business inputs? The H-R proposal defines the cost of business inputs as the actual cost of purchases of goods, services, and materials required for business purposes. Because Olivia incurred no actual cost in year 2, perhaps this language precludes any deduction for her house purchase. Alternatively, Olivia might be permitted to deduct some amount in year 2 for a deemed purchase of a business input, raising the further question of whether to base the deduction on her original cost or on the value of the rental unit in year 2. In either case, Olivia would have to make some allocation between the personal and business use of the property. Olivia also would allocate common expenses for the property, such as property taxes. Similar results and questions would arise under the Armey and Specter proposals.

In year 4, termination of the business use of the property gives rise to business income to Olivia under the H-R proposal,[34] in an amount equal to the value of the rental unit at that time. If this activity is Olivia's only business transaction, the business income is reduced by any carryover remaining from the earlier deduction of cost (if any). The Armey and Specter bills contain no provision for inclusion in Olivia's income. However, neither full inclusion of the value of the rental unit nor exclusion of all income in year 4 on conversion of the rental unit to personal use seems right, assuming Olivia enjoyed an earlier deduction. Exclusion would allow the deduction to offset the earlier business income without inclusion of any receipt on the sale of the property. Inclusion at current value offsets that earlier deduction but also recognizes as income any appreciation in value from the time of purchase, which may include investment income earned while the property was held for personal use. Moreover, inclusion requires payment of tax at a time when the business does not have cash.

How Will the Flat Tax Treat In-Kind Transfers?

Example 3
Suppose in example 1 that Mary, in a subsequent year, transfers the land to a newly formed corporation, Land, Inc., and later sells the stock to Norman. Norman uses the land for recreational purposes. How will Mary, Norman, and Land, Inc. be taxed?

(1) The transfer of the land to a corporation apparently does not give rise to tax to Mary under the H-R proposal. Receipt of the stock of Land, Inc. does not appear to fall literally within any of the subdivisions of the definition of business receipts. If it did, simple adjustments in business form that do not change beneficial ownership, exempt from tax currently, would become taxable under the flat tax. For other exchanges of land for stock, however, the H-R proposal may need to create a form of constructive receipt of cash. Thus, under the rule that only cash and not stock gives rise to business income, if Mary transferred the land to Boise-Cascade, a publicly traded company, for a small amount of its stock, the tax result under the current draft would be the same as in the example, no taxable inclusion to Mary. Yet Mary now would have a liquid financial investment, sale of which would not give rise to tax to Mary. A flat tax advocate might argue

that no undue benefit has accrued in this example so long as Boise-Cascade claimed no deduction for its acquisition of land for stock.

The Armey bill includes as gross active income (the minuend for determining business taxable income) the gross receipts from exchanges of property, defined in the case of an exchange as the fair market value of the property received.[35] The language thus would treat Mary's transfer to Land, Inc. as a taxable exchange, valued at fair market value. For the Armey bill (or for the H-R proposal if a constructive receipt of cash idea is introduced), some of the exceptions under current law for transfers to controlled corporations, reorganizations, or like kind exchanges may be needed to prevent interference with simple changes in form undertaken for good business reasons.

(2) Land, Inc. presumably would recognize no income under the H-R proposal on receipt of the land in exchange for its own stock, as the transaction does not fall within the definition of business receipts. Under the Armey bill, it is not clear whether the sale or exchange by a corporation of its own stock produces gross active income as gross receipts from the sale or exchange of property in connection with a business activity.

As noted, Land, Inc. probably may not claim deductions with respect to the land acquired for stock, even when it uses the land in its own business. The H-R proposal defines the cost of business inputs as the actual cost of purchases, including the actual amount paid for goods, services, and materials.[36] Stock in the acquiring corporation issued as payment probably will not be treated as an "amount paid" by the corporation, unless a constructive issuance for cash followed by a constructive purchase for cash is implied. The Armey bill also uses the phrase "amount paid," but treats the fair market value of property in an exchange as an amount paid.[37] This broad language may include a corporation's issuance of its own stock in payment. If the cost of business inputs includes payment in stock, Land, Inc. perhaps could claim deductions for the land, and both Mary and Land, Inc. would do so without any inclusion in income. In the absence of a concept of basis or basis carryover under the flat tax, Mary's prior claim of a deduction may not prevent the corporation from claiming one as well.[38]

(3) Mary's sale of stock to Norman presumably would not be taxed to Mary. Thus, from her perspective, incorporation of an expensed asset followed by a sale of the stock provides a simple way to avoid income recognition on disposition of the asset.

(4) If, after the sale of stock, Land, Inc. distributed the land to Norman, the H-R proposal would require the corporation to include the value of the land in income. The H-R proposal requires businesses to include the market value of goods and services provided to owners or employees. It is unclear, however, whether Land, Inc. must make an inclusion for Norman's use of the land; if it must, is the amount of the inclusion the entire value of the land, as a constructive distribution of the land to Norman, or its annual rental value, as the provision of services to Norman?

Neither the Armey nor the Specter proposal contains a comparable provision and no inclusion to Land, Inc. apparently would be required under either. Presumably, even if Mary had simply converted the property in example 1 from business to personal use, neither the Armey nor the Specter proposal would require the business to include anything in income. The absence of a recapture mechanism when property moves from business use to personal use by the owner creates opportunities for claiming deductions on property applied to personal consumption. If the flat tax does not tax property in kind when it leaves a business, corporations could substitute tangible property for cash in their dividend policy. Imagine how General Electric would behave if it had to pay tax on the sale of toasters but not on their distribution to shareholders, to whom all dividends came free of tax in any case. Some kind of recapture or constructive receipt by the business on a distribution of property will have to supplement the simple cash accounting the flat tax contemplates.

Who Is the Taxpayer Business?

Who must file the business tax return and pay the tax? All three versions of the flat tax seek to impose the tax on business activity, without regard to the legal form in which it operates. Apart from the personal consumption-business boundaries, explored elsewhere, the question of defining the taxpayer becomes material for a variety of purposes, including apportionment of the liability for the tax and the obligation to file a tax return. Most importantly, it can alter the amount of the tax liability, notwithstanding that all businesses are subject to the same tax rate.

Taxpayers under a flat tax generally will find it advantageous to aggregate their businesses. They can use losses currently to offset income, while they will suffer no penalty for adding two incomes together, given the absence of graduation in the tax rate. Consider the following example:

Example 4
Joan owns all the stock of corporation A, which operates at a profit of $4,000 for the year. Joan also owns 50% of the stock of corporation B, which invested in expensive equipment and has a loss of $5,000 for the year. Paul owns the other 50% of the stock of

corporation B. If the tax law treats the two corporations as separate businesses, corporation A will incur a tax of $800 on its income and corporation B will have a carryover of $5,000. If the law aggregates the two, corporation A will pay no tax currently and Corporation B will have a carryover of $1,000. If the law splits the deduction between Joan and Paul, corporation A will pay tax on $1,500 of income.

Joan generally will prefer aggregation and an immediate tax saving of $200. While the carryover will earn interest at the 3-month federal rate, and would offset a larger amount of income in the future, that rate almost certainly will understate Joan's internal rate of interest for the enterprises as well as the interest a bank would charge for lending corporation A $800.

Current law imposes strict limits on sharing of tax attributes among different taxpayers. The consolidated return regulations,[39] the S corporation restrictions,[40] and the partnership allocation rules[41] all provide complex systems for dividing income and loss among joint owners. Because all taxpayers would be subject to a single rate, flat tax advocates may advocate elimination of restrictions on the allocation of deductions, leaving the parties free to negotiate their own arrangements.

At a minimum, the law will have to specify default rules for use of deductions. Assume that some part of corporation B's deduction is absorbed by corporation A in Example 4. What tax result follows if the stock ownership of corporation B changes? Suppose, for example, that Joan uses $4,000 of deduction and then sells her B stock interest to Stephanie. Who becomes entitled to the remaining $1,000 carryover (plus interest)? Suppose B claims the full $5,000 carryover in the next year. What default rule will determine who was properly entitled to the deduction, Joan or B? How will carryovers of deductions be accounted for? Must businesses keep records of their use of deductions so that after several ownership changes the entitlement to an original purchase can be traced?

The logical conclusion of unregulated allocation of deductions would allow free transferability of losses. Historically, however, the outcry against the opportunity by wealthy businesses to purchase exemption from income tax has produced the existing restrictions on the transfer of loss corporations[42] and repeal in 1982 of the finance lease provisions of the 1981 tax act.[43]

Cash Accounting

If all business taxpayers report on the cash basis, accounting arbitrage disappears, but only if both parties report all transactions consistently. Several common transactions raise the consistency question. At a minimum, each requires specification in the statute or regulations of default rules to govern in the absence of agreement by the parties. Failure to specify such rules allows taxpayers to report inconsistently and erode the business tax base.

(1) A purchaser mails a check at the end of year 1 that the vendor does not receive until the beginning of year 2. When may the purchaser deduct the payment and when must the vendor include it in income?

Under current practice, a deductible payment occurs when the purchaser puts the check in the mail if it clears the sender's account in the ordinary course: the purchaser claims a deduction in year 1 in the example. On the other hand, the vendor includes it in income when received in year 2. Current law, however, limits the opportunity to reduce tax in this simple way. The widespread use of accrual accounting (generally mandated for taxpayers who have inventories,[44]), inventory accounting, and capitalization requirements for durable goods and long-lived intangibles all restrict deductions for year-end payments.

However, under the flat tax, the moment of payment determines the timing of deductions for business inputs. A rule like the existing one could allow a business to wipe out annual income with a large year-end payment to a supplier, who would not take the matching amount into income until year 2. While only one year's income could be deferred in this way, repetition of the year-end payment would defer the income indefinitely. The purchaser could enlarge the payment in subsequent years to take account of new increments in income.

It is not clear how the result would change under the flat tax if the vendor is a related party. Existing law tries to regulate certain related party transactions, including certain accounting-related deferrals.[45] Will the flat tax include special related-party rules?

(2) How should purchasers and sellers treat deposits made before taking possession of a business input? Are they like loans, neither deducted nor included until something more happens? If the deposit is not taken into account when made, and the purchaser loses the deposit, does the vendor have an inclusion in gross receipts for not selling the business input, does the depositor have a deduction for not purchasing a business input, or does the transaction have no tax effect? If the flat tax instead treats deposits as deductible and includible when made, some sort of recapture rule is needed if the deposit is returned in a later year.

(3) Are prepayments distinguishable from deposits or loans? Before delivery of the goods, should cash prepayments constitute gross receipts from the sale or exchange of property, includible by the vendor, and a cost of business inputs, deductible by the purchaser?

(4) How should contingent payments like options be treated?

(5) Suppose a purchaser buys a machine for 50 in year 1 and 55 in year 2. When will the purchaser deduct the cost of the machine? If the deduction matches cash payments, the purchaser will deduct the equivalent of interest, otherwise impermissible under the flat tax. Will some allocation be required in the manner of section 483? In this situation, so long as the vendor must include in income the same amount the purchaser deducts in each year, the consistency requirement of the business tax would be met.

International Transactions

The H-R proposal curtails the present worldwide jurisdiction for U.S. taxation (with complex foreign tax credit provisions and a web of treaty adjustments). It substitutes simple source-based rules under which the market value of goods and services delivered from the United States to points outside the United States is included in business receipts, the market value of business inputs brought into the United States is deducted, and income on activities abroad are excluded from the tax base.

Current law prescribes complex source rules for determining whether or not income and deductions should be attributed to the United States.[46] While many of the issues taken up in these rules concern interest and dividends, other jurisdiction-allocating rules doubtless will be needed. Moreover, rules similar to those under current section 482 for determining the arm's-length price of goods and services will become even more important under the H-R proposal. A full elaboration of the possible transactions to test these simple parameters is beyond the scope of this paper.

Summary

When put in place, the business tax will have to deal with several unresolved questions. The responses to them will create statutory complication and, in some cases, will challenge the premises of the business flat tax. The need to ensure consistency of treatment, simultaneous inclusion in income and deduction of the same amounts, between parties to transactions will produce further rules and add complexity. Some of these will seem unfair when judged by traditional standards.

THE INDIVIDUAL TAX

Income

The individual tax counts only wages and retirement payments, and permits no deductions other than a substantial standard deduction. The restrictive character of the tax base causes it to diverge from cash flows that enrich individuals. Apart from business income, taxed separately under the business tax, individuals will enjoy enrichment and suffer expenses not taken into account under this plan. The omissions may produce surprising results.

(1) Just after Arthur cashes his weekly paycheck, Betty robs him of the money at gunpoint. Under the flat tax, presumably Arthur includes the wages in income and has no offsetting deduction. Betty, on the other hand, probably has no income to tax unless she makes a practice of larceny, in which event she is in a business and should be taxed on the proceeds under the business tax. Present law, by contrast, would tax Betty and allow Arthur a deduction for theft loss, subject to certain limitations. Taxing Arthur and not Betty will be viewed as anomalous at best.

(2) Donald makes alimony payments to Charlene. Under current law, Donald deducts the payments and Charlene includes them in income. Under the flat tax, Donald has no deduction and Charlene has no inclusion in income. While the flat tax reaches a proper result in the aggregate, the parties would regard it as anomalous. Even without consideration of the transitional problems created by existing arrangements, negotiations after the flat tax is operative may fail to adjust fully for the tax differential.

(3) Fern borrows money from Euphoria Investing Co. Fern later runs into financial difficulties and, after negotiations, Euphoria reduces the amount of the loan. Under current law, Fern will have discharge of indebtedness income, unless one of several exceptions applies.[47] Euphoria would claim a bad-debt deduction.[48] Under the flat tax, Fern has no income and Euphoria has no deduction.

(4) Geraldine wins a prize on a quiz show. The business that operates the show deducts the amount paid as an expense of the business. Geraldine, however, would not include the amount in income because it is not wages or retirement benefits. The income accordingly would escape taxation. Under current law, Geraldine would include the prize in income.

The first three examples simply shift the obligation to pay tax away from the party who receives cash and who is liable for the tax under current law. They raise questions of liquidity and perceived fairness: the taxpayer who pays out cash nevertheless incurs the tax liability and must find additional cash to pay the tax. Negotiations between parties in some but not all the cases can ameliorate these concerns. Case 4 provides an example of "leakage" from the business tax in providing deductible but nonincludible payments to individuals. The structure of the law will encourage businesses to find and exploit similar opportunities.[49]

Consumption

The current income tax has wrestled with the tax treatment of a range of business expenditures that confer consumption benefits on owners or employees of a business. The H-R proposal attempts to deal with the question on the business side by excluding any deduction for purchases of goods or services provided to employees or owners unless included in business receipts. Business receipts include the market value of goods, services, and other property provided to owners or employees. The H-R proposal, however, also allows as a deductible cost of business inputs the actual cost, if reasonable, of travel and entertainment expenses for the business. The Specter bill allows deductibility of reasonable travel and entertainment expenses, using the same language as the H-R proposal, but contains no limitation on deductions for goods or services provided to owners or employees. The Armey bill contains neither provision but makes nondeductible items for personal use not in connection with any trade or business.

Example 5
Harmless Insurance Agency, Inc. employs Ivan as an insurance broker. It provides Ivan with an automobile, which he uses to commute to and from work, to meet clients and potential clients, and for personal matters. Harmless provides lunch without charge to employees on the business premises each day. Ivan occasionally takes potential clients to dinner and Harmless reimburses Ivan for the cost of some of these dinners. Clients sometimes take Ivan to dinner.

The automobile use and the meals all present different combinations of personal and business use. As an employee of Harmless, Ivan will include only the cash wages he receives and none of the consumption items Harmless otherwise makes available to him. Ivan will not deduct the cost of meals for potential clients because Ivan is not in a business. Harmless, on the other hand, will deduct all of the expenses as the cost of business inputs unless some specific restriction applies. It is not clear from the H-R proposal which of its two principles should prevail: deductibility of reasonable expenses or nondeductibiliy of benefits to employees. Under the Armey and Specter bills, Harmless apparently could deduct all the expenses.

Current law contains a web of restrictions on the deductibility of expenditures for meals, entertainment, luxury automobiles, club dues, and similar items.[50] Many of these restrictions are ineffective or redundant. Others, however, such as the limitation of deductions to half the amount spent on meals and entertainment, seem appropriate.[51] If the flat tax provides a deduction for the business and an exemption from tax to the employee for any kind of consumption, it will push businesses to compensate employees in that tax-favored form. The result will be both inefficient and inequitable.

The Taxable Unit

The flat tax provides progressivity through substantial personal allowances, referred to as a standard deduction in the Armey and Specter proposals. All three proposals significantly reduce the so-called marriage tax penalty by reason of the single tax rate bracket. The Armey proposal also enlarges the standard deduction for a joint return to double the amount for an individual, eliminating this source of marriage tax penalty as well, but creating the potential for increased marriage benefit.

Likewise, children will be entitled to a personal allowance or standard deduction. The potential exists for "kiddie tax shelters" to return, by paying children salaries out of family businesses. The salary payments would create deductions for the business, while the income would generate no tax because it is covered by the personal allowance. The Armey proposal addresses this potential difficulty in two ways. First, it requires that taxable income of each dependent child younger than 14 years of age be taxed to the parent. Second, it conditions any additional standard deduction for dependents on their not being required to file a return, a requirement that presumably would attach whenever salary income of a child exceeds the exempt amount.

PRESSURES FOR CHANGE

The effect of a revenue-neutral tax change that increases a person's tax bill resembles that of taking candy from a child. Some children suffer in silence, while others express their wrath and often get compensated for the lost sweet. We should expect pressures for change in the flat tax to come from taxpayers who lose current benefits and are unaccustomed to legislative defeat. A partial list follows:

(1) *Businesses that benefit from current special deductions.* The timber and mineral-extraction industries present two examples of businesses that receive substantial benefits under current law and would lose their relative advantage under a flat tax.[52]

(2) *Labor and labor-intensive businesses.* The flat tax influences the business decision at the margin of whether to produce goods or services using labor inputs or machinery inputs. It favors the latter, as compared with current law, in at least three ways. It provides for current deductibility of capital investment. It eliminates the deductibility under current law of the employer's share of social security tax. Certain fringe benefits, currently deductible, become nondeductible under the flat tax. All three changes make the use of la-

bor more expensive as compared with machinery and equipment.

(3) *Home owners and home builders.* Elimination of deductions for mortgage interest and real property taxes will adversely affect home owners. Estimates of the impact vary, with one industry source concluding that home owners will suffer a one-time loss in property values of $500 billion. For home builders, some predict a decline in single-family home building, which might be offset at least in part by an increase in multiple-dwelling construction. The Specter bill provides restricted deductibility of mortgage interest.

(4) *Charities and other nonprofits.* The H-R proposal eliminates current deductibility of charitable gifts and tax exemption for certain nonprofits that are not charities or community service organizations. The Armey bill retains the current tax exemptions but repeals the charitable contribution deduction. The Specter bill retains the deduction, with a ceiling of $2,500 and a limitation to cash or equivalent gifts. Charities will fear the loss of major gifts, especially of appreciated property, under all three proposals.[53]

(5) *State and local governments.* The flat tax effectively eliminates the comparative advantage that state and local governments currently enjoy in obtaining financing. Municipal bonds will enjoy no special market niche when all interest is exempt from tax. Further, nondeductibility of state and local taxes will increase their real impact and make revenue-raising more difficult. If charitable gifts become deductible, it will seem anomalous to disallow deductions for taxes to pay for services similar to those provided by charities.

If these groups and others are "compensated" under the flat tax with new tax favors, the rate will have to rise to make up the lost revenue. An increase of only a few points, however, could materially alter the attractiveness of the tax.

Conclusion

This brief survey of the business and individual tax portions of the flat tax points to several unresolved questions. Something will give way in their resolution: the revenue yield, the simplicity of the tax, or the simplicity of the business transactions that will take place. The imagination of practitioners and the need by government to preserve its chief revenue source will pull the statute in different directions and inevitably create complexity.

ENDNOTES

I would like to thank Michael Graetz, Joel Slemrod, and Alvin C. Warren, Jr. for helpful comments on an earlier draft, and my research assistant, Zachary D. Beim, for his assistance.

[1] Hall and Rabushka (1985, 1995). References to the draft statute the authors propose will be identified as "H-R proposal."

[2] Representative Armey introduced his latest flat tax proposal as Title I, Subtitle A of the "Freedom and Fairness Restoration Act of 1995" on July 19, 1995 (the "Armey bill"). A companion measure, S. 1050, was introduced in the Senate by Senator Richard Shelby.

[3] Senator Specter introduced his flat tax proposal as S. 488 on March 2, 1995 (the "Specter bill").

[4] As used in this paper, the term "flat tax" refers to this consumption-type tax and excludes a single-rate income tax.

[5] See Doernberg (1985); U.S. Dept. of Treasury, Blueprints for Basic Tax Reform 113–15 (1977). See also *Discussion of Issues Relating to "Flat" Tax Rate Proposals.*

[6] Hall and Rabushka note that high-salaried executives would pay far less tax under the individual flat tax than under the current personal income tax, but argue that, as an offset, wealthy people would incur a higher tax on business income. Any shift from wage taxation to business taxation would be progressive (Hall and Rabushka, 1985, pp. 76–9.

[7] Hall and Rabushka's draft statute runs to 5 pages, including a table of contents (Hall and Rabushka, 1985, pp. 123–7. The first

individual income tax statute after the Sixteenth Amendment covered 15 pages, including all the administrative material not included in the Hall and Rabushka draft, 63 Stat. 166–81.

[8] Many individuals already file returns on Forms 1040A or 1040-EZE with as few lines as the Hall and Rabushka postcard.

[9] Hall and Rabushka, 1985, pp. 38–41.

[10] Hall and Rabushka proposed a 19% rate. Armey has advocated a 17% rate, intended to reflect some reduction in total government expenditures; the Armey bill now proposes a 20% rate for the first 2 years. The Specter bill proposes a rate of 20%.

[11] The Armey bill also includes unemployment compensation. The H-R proposal does not include it and unemployment compensation appears to fall outside its general definition of included compensation. The H-R proposal does include workman's compensation and other payments for injury, which the Armey bill does not. The Specter bill excludes all of these payments. All three exclude payments for services performed outside the United States.

[12] The Specter bill would allow a deduction for charitable contributions and for mortgage interest, but with more severe limits than under current law.

[13] Hall and Rabushka proposed a personal allowance in 1985 of $9,000 for a married couple filing jointly and an additional $1,800 for each dependent, defined more narrowly than under current law. The Armey bill proposes a standard deduction of $21,400 for joint filers and an additional standard deduction of $5,000 for each dependent not required to file a return for the year. [The dependent must also be described in section 151(c)(1), a reference to the current requirement that the dependent have gross income of less than the exemption amount *or* be a child of the taxpayer either younger than age 19 or a full-time student younger than age 24. It is not clear under what circumstances someone who will not be required to file a return for the year nevertheless could have income over the exemption amount.] The Specter bill allows a basic standard deduction of $16,500 for joint filers and an additional standard deduction of $4,500 for each dependent, as defined in the Armey bill. Unlike the other two proposals, the Specter bill does not peg the basic standard deduction for a single individual at half the joint return amount, but at $9,500.

[14] Hall and Rabushka, 1985, p. 47.

15 The H-R proposal imposes the tax on business taxable income, defined as business receipts less the cost of business inputs, compensation, and the cost of capital equipment. The Armey bill defines business taxable income as the gross active income less similar deductions. Gross active income means gross receipts from the sale or exchange of property or services in the United States in connection with a business activity and certain export receipts. Hall and Rabushka and the Specter bill allow a deduction for the actual cost, if reasonable, of travel and entertainment expenses for business purposes, but specifically exclude from "business inputs" purchases of goods and services provided to employees or owners (unless included in business receipts). The Armey bill excludes items for personal use not in connection with any business activity. The Armey bill expressly allows a deduction for excise and sales taxes on property used in a business activity.

16 Businesses whose income exceeds the normal rate of return would pay tax on the excess. See Bankman and Griffith (1992).

17 The H-R proposal, section 102(8), includes as business receipts the market value of goods and services provided to depositors. The Armey bill, section 102(e), includes as business income the value of financial intermediation services. The Specter bill contains no such provision.

18 Tax rate arbitrage with a zero-bracket taxpayer continues to be possible.

19 See e.g., Pechman (1980).

20 Compare the discussion of transition problems in Kaplow (1995).

21 Hoven (1995).

22 Compare section 162 (trade or business deductions) with the more restricted deductions under section 212 (expenses for the production or collection of income). The latter cannot be claimed by nonitemizers and are subject to a 2 percent floor, section 67.

23 Code section 1231.

24 Code section 1221(1). See, e.g., *Biedenharn Realty Co. v. United States,* 526 F.2d 409 (5th Cir. 1976)(real estate); *Hollis v. United States,* 121 Fed. Supp. 191 (N.D. Ohio 1954) (art objects).

25 It also requires characterization of the property at an earlier time, in the year of purchase rather than the year of sale.

26 H-R proposal, section 203(a).

27 Section 102(a) of the Armey proposal and section 11(B) of the Specter bill.

28 The Specter bill simply defines gross active income as income other than investment income, without specifying how to tell them apart.

29 But cf. *Liddle v. Commissioner,* 65 S.3d 329 (3d Cir. 1995) and *Commissioner v. Simon,* f.3d (2d Cir. 1995).

30 Code section 197 allows amortization of purchased intangibles over a 15-year period.

31 For a discussion of the impact of innovative capital market contracts on income tax policy, see Warren (1993).

32 See *Arkansas Best Corp. v. Commissioner,* 485 U.S. 212 (1988).

33 Code sections 280A and 183 and regulations.

34 The H-R proposal includes as a business receipt the market value of property provided to the owners or employees of a business.

35 The Specter bill defines gross active income as income other than investment income.

36 The cost of business inputs is defined as the actual cost of purchases of goods, services, and materials required for business purposes. It includes the actual amount paid for them.

37 The Specter proposal does not contain similar language.

38 In its provision on filing units, the H-R proposal allows any number of business tax returns provided that each expenditure for business inputs is reported on no more than one return. The issue then is whether Mary's purchase of the land and the corporation's later issuance of stock for it represent one or two separate expenditures.

39 Treas. Reg. sec. 1.1502-1, *et. seq.*

40 Code sections 1361–79.

41 Treas. Reg. sec. 1.704.

42 See Code sections 269 and 382.

43 P.L. 97-248, section 209, 96 Stat. 324, 442–7.

44 Reg. sec. 1.446-1(c)(2).

45 Code section 267(a)(2).

46 See Code sections 861–5 and regulations.

47 See generally Code section 108.

48 Code section 166.

49 Structured settlements in tort provide an example under current law of the exploitation of forms of payment that allow deductions to one party and noninclusion in the income of the other.

50 Code sections 274 and 280F.

51 Code section 274(n).

[52] For a comparison of tax liability under the flat tax and under current law by sector, see Merrill, Wertz, and Shah, (1995).

[53] Compare, as to the USA tax, Feld (1995).

REFERENCES

Bankman, Joseph and Thomas Griffith. "Is the Debate Between an Income Tax and a Consumption Tax a Debate about Risk? Does it Matter?" *Tax Law Review 47* (1992): 377–406.

Doernberg, Richard L. "A Workable Flat Rate Consumption Tax." *Iowa Law Review 70* (1985).

Feld, Alan L. "Nunn-Domenici and Nonprofits." *Tax Notes 68* (1995).

Hall, Robert E. and Alvin Rabushka. *Low Tax, Simple, Tax, Flat Tax.* New York: McGraw-Hill, 1983.

Hall, Robert E. and Alvin Rabushka. *The Flat Tax.* Stanford: Hoover Institution Press, [1985], 1995.

Hoven, Vernon. "Flat Tax as Seen by a Tax Preparer." *Tax Notes 68* (1995).

Kaplow, Louis. "Recovery of Pre-Enactment Basis Under a Consumption Tax: The USA Tax System." *Tax Notes 68* (1995).

Merrill, Peter, Ken Wertz, and Shvetank Shah. "Corporate Tax Liability Under the USA and Flat Taxes." *Tax Notes 68* (1995): 741.

Pechman, Joseph A., ed. *What Should Be Taxed, Income or Expenditure?* Washington, D.C.: The Brookings Institution, 1980.

U.S. Department of Treasury. *Blueprints for Basic Tax Reform.* Washington, D.C.: U.S. Government Printing Office, 1977.

U.S. Joint Committee on Taxation Staff. *Discussion of Issues Relating to "Flat" Tax Rate Proposals.* Washington, D.C.: U.S. Government Printing Office, 1995.

Warren, Alvin C., Jr. "Financial Contract Innovation and Income Tax Policy." *Harvard Law Review 107* (1993).

THE INTERNATIONAL IMPLICATIONS OF CONSUMPTION TAX PROPOSALS

**HARRY GRUBERT* &
T. SCOTT NEWLON***

Several of the current tax reform proposals would replace the U.S. income tax system with a consumption tax. This paper examines how recognizing the international mobility of goods and capital may change the results of a closed economy analysis of these proposals. We consider the effects of the proposed tax systems on cross-border investment and trade, and on international tax administration and compliance problems. We also examine the distribution of the transition incidence of these plans between foreign and U.S. residents, and the possible reactions of other countries to a change in U.S. tax policy of this nature.

The analysis in this paper will focus largely on two of the consumption tax proposals, a "flat" tax, as Representative Armey proposed; and the Unlimited Savings Allowance (USA) tax Senators Nunn and Domenici proposed. The Armey flat tax proposal is modeled on the tax scheme Hall and Rabushka (1983, 1985, 1995) proposed, which we rely on for details of the plan.[1] Under the flat tax scheme, individuals are taxed only on their wage income (including pensions) and businesses are taxed on their cash flow measured as sales less purchases, including capital purchases and wages. Under the USA tax plan, individuals face a consumed income tax, i.e., a tax on income less savings (plus dissavings). At the business level, the USA tax imposes a substraction method value-added tax (VAT), *i.e.*, tax is paid on sales less purchases, where purchases include capital purchases but not wages.

Our focus will be largely on the business tax components of these proposals, although we note the effects of the consumed income tax, or other consumption tax variants, where they differ significantly. The proposals are compared principally to our current tax system. To examine the extent to which the results of this comparison derive from the consumption base or other features of the plans, we also consider the effects of an income VAT, which differs from a consumption VAT in that capital purchases are depreciated rather than being expensed.

Our principal conclusions are as follows:

*U.S. Treasury Department, Washington, D.C. 20220.

- Taking the effects of international capital mobility into account, a switch to a consumption base has an uncertain impact on the total U.S. capital stock. Investment in U.S. equity should increase, but debt financed investment in the United States may decrease to the extent that U.S. interest rates would fall in the absence of capital mobility.
- The integration of world debt markets is likely to substantially dampen any decline in interest rates that might otherwise occur.
- In contrast to its effects under an income tax, the exemption of foreign income under a consumption tax, including exemption of receipts of foreign royalties under the destination principle, is not likely to cause a substantial "runaway plant" effect in which multinational corporations (MNCs) shift production abroad. On the contrary, MNCs would likely shift tangible investment, intangible assets, and R&D to the United States.
- As argued by most economists, the alternative destination and origin principles for the taxation of exports and imports under a consumption tax are equivalent for international investment and trade at the margin.
- Origin- and destination-principle taxes do differ in their taxation of the inframarginal, supernormal returns of U.S. investors from foreign investments and foreign investors from U.S. investments. A consequence is that under the origin principle, but not under the destination principle, some incentive may remain for MNCs to locate production in low-tax countries to avoid U.S. tax on supernormal returns. However, this incentive is likely to be weaker than it is under the current tax system.
- Transition effects of eliminating the income tax aside, when a destination-principle consumption tax is imposed, foreigners bear no transition tax on their U.S. assets, while U.S. residents bear transition tax on both their U.S. and foreign assets. When an origin-principle consumption tax is imposed, both U.S. residents and foreigners bear the effective transition tax on their U.S. assets, but U.S. residents bear no transition tax on foreign assets held prior to imposition of the tax.
- A consumption base would provide some significant simplifications in international tax rules. For example, expense allocation rules would be largely unnecessary, as would rules affecting passive foreign income.
- In addition, a destination-principle consumption tax would eliminate incentives for income shifting by MNCs out of the United States through manipulation of their transfer prices. However, there would continue to be such an incentive under an origin-principle consumption tax.
- There would be some new complexities and tax avoidance issues. For example, under the destination principle it may be difficult to identify nondeductible foreign services and to allocate implicit service fees of financial intermediaries between foreign and domestic sources.
- A destination-principle consumption tax creates an incentive for cross-border shopping and consumption abroad, *e.g.,* through emigration.
- The reactions of foreign governments must be considered in evaluating the effects of these proposals. They may react to the extent that they find their countries less competitive in terms of the taxation of capital and they experience tax base erosion through shifting of interest expenses and, under the destination principle, transfer pricing practices.
- Perhaps surprisingly, foreign governments may not find it in their interest

to terminate their income tax treaties with the United States.

The next section of the paper summarizes features of the proposals that are relevant to the analysis. The following sections of the paper analyze the implications of the plans for the activities of MNCs, international capital flows and trade, tax-avoidance opportunities and the complexity of international tax provisions, transition incidence, and the reactions of other countries. The last section presents some concluding remarks.

RELEVANT FEATURES OF THE PLANS

The Tax Base

Both the flat tax and the USA tax have consumption bases. The flat tax and USA business tax are essentially both subtraction method VATs in that purchases of goods and services are immediately deductible, including capital expenditures. The flat tax differs from the typical consumption VAT only in that wages are deductible at the business level and taxable at the personal level. The USA individual tax is a consumed income tax in that the consumption base is arrived at by deducting from (including in) income a measure of net new saving (dissaving).

The principal significance of the consumption base is that an investment in the United States earns the pretax rate of return to capital. For a tax rate of t, a dollar's worth of capital can be bought with $1 - t$ dollars because it is immediately deductible (*i.e.*, it is expensed) and each year the investment will pay $1 - t$ of its cash flow after tax. The expensing of the capital invested and taxation of the cash flow occur at the business level under a flat tax or subtraction method VAT and at the individual level under a consumed income tax. Because the present value of the cash flow from a dollar invested at the margin should be equal to a dollar,

the value of the expensing is just equal to the present value of the tax on the future cash flow from a dollar invested at the margin, and there is no tax on the return to new capital at the margin. There is tax on inframarginal, supernormal returns because the present value of the tax on the future cash flow will exceed the value of the initial deduction. However, an investment project that is worthwhile in the absence of the tax will remain worthwhile with the tax, and the choice among investments would not be affected by the tax.

An income VAT operates on the same basis as a consumption VAT except that capital purchases are depreciated for tax purposes rather than being expensed. Under an ideal income VAT, in which depreciation allowances match economic depreciation, marginal as well as inframarginal returns to capital would be taxed. Under such a tax, returns to capital would be taxed only once at the business level, because interest and dividends would not be deductible to the business and would not be taxed at the personal level.

The current U.S. tax system departs substantially from this ideal income VAT. There is a classical corporate income tax in which equity income is taxed once at the corporate level and then again when distributed at the personal level. Interest income is taxed, if at all, only at the personal level, because it is deductible at the business level. Depreciation allowances are not necessarily related to economic depreciation, and nominal, rather than real, interest is taxed. There are also substantial tax-favored sectors, including owner-occupied housing, tax-exempt entities such as pension funds, and the state and local government sector, which benefits from being able to issue tax-exempt bonds. Noncorporate business is also taxed more favorably than corporate business.

Given these complications, it cannot be presumed that much tax is paid on capital income. In fact, in an analysis of 1983 data, Gordon and Slemrod (1988) estimated that the United States collected little revenue from the taxation of capital income. Even so, they did find that some revenue was collected, and the 1986 Tax Reform Act significantly narrowed the scope for the tax arbitrage that allowed capital income to escape tax or, in fact, be tax favored.[2] Consequently, we shall assume that the current U.S. tax system does impose some tax on capital income; however, the complications we have outlined above will prove important in analyzing the effects of the proposals on capital flows.

Dichotomy between Real and Financial Transactions

The flat tax, the USA business tax, and an income VAT all use what is called an R base (for real, as distinct from financial, transactions), a terminology adopted from the Meade Committee Report.[3] Under an R-based tax, sales of goods and services are taxed, and purchases of goods and services are deductible, but financial transactions, including the payment and receipt of interest and dividends, are ignored. This creates an issue, familiar to those who have studied the VAT, concerning the taxation of banks and other financial intermediaries.[4] In the context of this paper, one implication is that while interest is not deductible from the U.S. tax base, it still will be deductible in countries that retain an income tax.

The USA individual tax is an example of an $(R + F)$-based tax, in which real and financial transactions enter the tax base. Under an $(R + F)$ base, net increases (decreases) in financial assets are taxable (deductible). In the context of debt, this means that cash receipts from borrowing (a borrower's proceeds from the issuance of new debt or a lender's receipts of in-

terest or principal repayments) are taxable and cash payments from borrowing (a borrower's interest payments and repayments of principal or a lender's new loans) are deductible. McLure and Zodrow (1995) have proposed a consumption tax system that is the reverse of the USA tax in that the business-level tax is on an $(R + F)$ base, while the personal level tax is on an R base. Note that the treatment of interest under the R and $(R + F)$ bases is essentially equivalent. Because the present value of interest and principal repayments on a loan is equal to the amount of the loan, the deductions and inclusions for debt under the $(R + F)$ base are equivalent to ignoring debt transactions under the R base.

Nondeductibility of Interest

Under the flat tax, the USA business tax, and all VATs, including an income VAT, interest expense is not deductible at the business level and interest income is not taxed. In a purely domestic context, this change is innocuous to the extent that the elimination of interest deductibility is compensated for by the elimination of tax on interest income. However, the increase in tax from the loss in interest deductions may actually far exceed the tax saving from exemption of interest income because so much interest income is not taxed under current law. Consequently, such a change would substantially increase the tax burden on debt-financed business investment. In an open economy, the shift to interest nondeductibility becomes even more significant because foreigners already are exempt from U.S. tax on portfolio interest. Because they derive no benefit from any personal level exemption, foreigners would reduce their holdings of U.S. debt if the adoption of these proposals produced any tendency for U.S. interest rates to decline.

Origin versus Destination Principle

Consumption taxes can differ in the way that exports and imports are treated. Under the destination principle, imports are taxed (either by making them nondeductible to the importing business or by imposing an import tax) and exports are exempt.[5] This means that the aggregate base of the tax, netting out transactions between businesses and taking into account the deduction of capital expenditures, is domestic consumption of goods and services. Under the origin principle, exports are taxed and imports are not. This means that the aggregate base of the tax is domestic consumption plus net exports. The USA tax follows the destination principle, while the flat tax follows the origin principle.[6] It has been claimed that the destination principle promotes exports and domestic investment. We discuss in later sections what effects the different bases might have on trade, investment, tax-avoidance opportunities, and transition incidence.

The choice between destination and origin principles is also available for an income VAT. Under the origin principle, the tax base would be U.S.-source income, while under the destination principle, it would be U.S.-source income less net exports.[7]

Treatment of Foreign Income

Under the current U.S. tax system, U.S.-resident individuals and businesses are subject to tax on their foreign income. In the case of income earned by controlled foreign subsidiaries of U.S. MNCs, U.S. tax is generally not imposed until the income is distributed to the U.S. parent company as a dividend; this policy is known as *deferral*. At the time of income repatriation, a tax credit against U.S. tax liability is allowed for any foreign taxes paid directly on foreign income. For dividend distributions from controlled foreign subsidiaries, U.S. MNCs also receive a foreign tax credit for underlying foreign corporation taxes on the income out of which the distribution is made. The for-

eign tax credit is limited to the amount of the U.S. tax liability on foreign income, so that any foreign tax in excess of that amount cannot be used to reduce other U.S. tax liabilities. Within limits imposed by separate "baskets" for different types of foreign income, excess foreign tax credits from one source of foreign income can be used to offset U.S. tax liability on other foreign income; this is sometimes called *cross-crediting*.

Under R-based consumption taxes such as the flat tax and the USA business tax, foreign interest and dividends, as well as the foreign earnings of U.S. MNCs, are exempt. Under $(R + F)$-based consumption taxes such as the USA individual tax, all interest and dividend receipts are taxed, but investment in both foreign and domestic assets is deductible, so that capital income is untaxed at the margin whether it is a foreign or domestic source.

A business-level income tax could also exempt income from direct foreign investment, as is done in several other countries. However, income from passive, or portfolio, foreign investment could not realistically be exempted without leading to substantial erosion of the taxation of capital income.[8]

Royalty receipts from foreign licensees are in a category distinct from interest and dividend income from foreign sources because they can be thought of as payments for the export of an intangible asset, just as lease payments from a foreign lessee to a lessor of U.S. machines are payments for the export of those machines. Under current tax law, receipts of royalties from abroad are included in foreign-source income, but, in principle, they could be included in domestic income under an income tax, as generally is income from the export of goods under current law.[9]

Based on this reasoning, the taxation of royalties should be consistent with the choice of destination or origin principle.[10] Royalty receipts from abroad should be exempt under the destination principle and royalty payments to foreigners not deductible. Conversely, under the origin principle, all royalty receipts should be taxable and all royalty payments deductible.

IMPLICATIONS FOR INVESTMENT AND TRADE

Our analysis will start by considering what effects the plans might have on the behavior of MNCs. We then go on to examine the potential effects of the plans on overall capital flows, and, consequently, on the U.S. capital stock, taking into account the differential effects on debt and equity, and spillover effects from other sectors of the economy such as noncorporate business, residential housing, and state and local government.

Effects on MNC Behavior

In this section we consider the effects of moving to a consumption tax system on MNC decisions regarding the location of production, the location of intangible assets, where R&D is performed, and the financial structure of the multinational group. In examining the MNC investment location decision we implicitly treat investments as being equity financed.[11]

Location of Production by U.S. MNCs

Under R-based consumption tax proposals such as the flat tax and the USA business tax, the foreign income of U.S. MNCs would be exempt from U.S. tax. The question arises whether this exemption would make investment in low-tax foreign jurisdictions relatively more attractive than it currently is. This is the so-called runaway plant problem, wherein production is shifted to foreign jurisdic-

tions to take advantage of low tax rates. We argue that although exemption of foreign income under an income tax does lead to incentives to locate tangible capital in low-tax jurisdictions, this is not necessarily the case under a consumption tax. In fact, switching to a consumption tax likely would result in a greater preference by MNCs for investment in the United States, even as compared with investment in low-tax countries in many cases.

Table 1 presents some numerical examples that illustrate the effects of the different tax systems on the production location choices of MNCs. The examples are constructed so that the foreign income tax rate is substantially lower than the domestic tax rate. For purposes of simplicity, the foreign tax rate is 10 percent, and the domestic (U.S.) tax rate is 25 percent, whether on an income or a consumption base. The pretax rate of return to investment in a machine is assumed to be equal to 10 percent in each location. For simplicity, it is assumed that there is no depreciation of the machine. The cost of the machine and the value of its output are assumed to be the same in each location, thereby implicitly establishing the consumption tax as following the origin principle.[12]

The first two columns of Table 1 illustrate the situation when the domestic tax is on an income base. Columns 1 and 2 show the global neutrality of the tax system if foreign income is taxed with a credit provided for foreign taxes paid; taxes do not affect the location choice. Column 2 illustrates the case when there is no deferral of tax on the foreign income (i.e., all earnings are treated as being immediately repatriated as dividends) and no cross-crediting. We turn to the effects of those complications below. The results in rows 11 and 12 show that under these assumptions the tax system is neutral to the

TABLE 1
INVESTMENT LOCATION CHOICE UNDER INCOME AND CONSUMPTION TAXES

	Domestic Income Tax			Domestic Consumption Tax	
	Domestic Investment 1	Foreign Investment with Foreign Tax Credit 2	Foreign Investment with Exemption 3	Domestic Investment 4	Foreign Investment 5
(1) Cost of machine	100	100	100	100	100
(2) Tax deduction for machine	0	0	0	25	0
(3) Net cost of machine (1) − (2)	100	100	100	75	100
(4) Net return before tax	10	10	10	10	10
(5) Foreign income tax	—	1	1	—	1
(6) Net return after foreign tax (4) − (5)	10	9	9	10	9
(7) Domestic tax liability	2.5	2.5	0	2.5	0
(8) Foreign tax credit	—	1	—	—	—
(9) Total domestic taxes paid (7) − (8)	2.5	1.5	0	2.5	0
(10) Total taxes paid (5) + (9)	2.5	2.5	1	2.5	1
(11) Net return after tax (4) − (10)	7.5	7.5	9	7.5	9
(12) Rate of return (11) ÷ (3)	7.5%	7.5%	9%	10%	9%

Assumptions: domestic income or consumption tax rate = 25 percent; foreign income tax rate = 10 percent; pretax rate of return on investment in each location = 10 percent; no depreciation; and consumption tax is R base and origin principle.

location choice for investments. An investment with a pretax return of $10 (10 percent) leaves an after-tax return of $7.5 (7.5 percent) to the investor whether it is undertaken in the foreign country or at home.

Column 3 shows the after-tax return from locating the production in the low-tax foreign country when foreign income is exempt from tax. Comparing the results in columns 1 and 3, illustrates that when the domestic tax is on an income base, exemption of foreign income provides an incentive to locate the project in the low-tax foreign jurisdiction, because the after-tax rate of return rises from 7.5 to 9 percent.

Comparison of columns 4 and 5 of Table 1 show the results for domestic and foreign investment, respectively, when the domestic tax is an R-based consumption tax. The results in row 12 illustrate that, at the margin, exemption of foreign income no longer provides an incentive for investing in the low-tax foreign country. In fact, the after-tax rate of return for domestic investment is now 10 percent, the

same as the pretax rate of return and higher than the 9 percent after-tax rate of return in the low-tax jurisdiction. This result occurs because the consumption tax does not tax the return to new investment at the margin, whereas a standard income tax at any positive rate does.

This preference for domestic investment may not, however, hold where there are supernormal returns that could be earned if the investment was undertaken in either location, i.e., if the supernormal returns are portable rather than being location-specific rents. As shown below in the discussion of the origin and destination principles, under an origin-principle consumption tax there may be an incentive to locate in low-tax foreign countries to save tax on supernormal returns. In this case, the incentive to locate in low-tax jurisdictions will largely depend on the scope for income shifting through transfer pricing practices.

Even if a switch to a consumption tax did not eliminate the incentive for MNC investment in low-tax jurisdictions in all cases, it would likely make the United

States a *relatively* more attractive location as compared with the current tax regime—and it would clearly be relatively more attractive than investment in high-tax jurisdictions. This is particularly apparent when it is recognized that the current U.S. tax regime, although it provides for taxation of foreign income with a credit for foreign taxes paid, in many respects resembles the exemption system of column 3 of Table 1 as much as the ideal foreign tax credit system of column 2. One feature pushing the system in that direction is deferral, which can substantially reduce the present value of U.S. tax on the income of foreign subsidiaries of U.S. companies. In fact, Hartman (1985) has shown that deferral can be equivalent to exemption in its effects when foreign investment is financed out of a subsidiary's retained earnings. Furthermore, the ability to cross-credit, so that excess credits from high-tax foreign income can be used to offset U.S. tax on low-tax foreign income, also can push the system towards an exemption system in its effects. Where a U.S. MNC has excess foreign tax credits overall, there is effectively no U.S. tax on additional income from a low-tax foreign source. Based on calculations using 1990 data, Grubert and Mutti (forthcoming) show that the average effective U.S. tax rate on the foreign income of U.S. MNCs from active investments is remarkably low, about 2 percent when calculated using a standard definition of foreign income and *negative* if foreign income is defined to exclude royalty receipts.

Is the relative increase in the incentive for U.S. MNCs to invest in the United States a good thing from the perspective of national or global welfare? Table 1 can again provide some insight on this issue. Comparison of columns 4 and 5 shows that in deciding where to locate production, under a consumption tax a U.S. MNC would compare the pretax return in

the United States—which in this case is the same as the after-tax return—with the after-foreign-tax return abroad. From the perspective of the national welfare, the consumption tax clearly results in the correct comparison, because the United States only receives the after-foreign-tax return to foreign investment.[13]

From the perspective of global welfare, this is not the appropriate comparison. To maximize the efficiency of the international allocation of capital, taxes should not affect the decision where to locate capital. This is the case in column 2, where the credit for foreign taxes means that the project that earns a 10 percent rate of return in both jurisdictions before tax earns an equal rate of return (7.5 percent) in each jurisdiction after tax. However, as explained above, the effects of the current tax system depart substantially from the simple example in column 2 in the direction of the exemption system of column 3, so that there is a tax motivation for investing in low-tax countries. Consequently, switching to a consumption tax may cause a shift away from investment in low-tax countries, which would tend to improve global efficiency. However, this move in the direction of global efficiency must be balanced against the reduced incentives for U.S. investment in high-tax countries. In fact, a consumption tax would give all U.S. MNCs greater incentives to reduce foreign taxes and thus would cause a shift of investment from high-tax countries to the United States and other low-tax countries (e.g., from Germany to Ireland) at the expense of global efficiency.

Location of Production by Foreign MNCs

In the case of investment by a foreign MNC, the effects of moving to a consumption tax may vary depending on the tax rules of the home country. Where the home country exempts foreign income,[14] the story illustrated in Table 1 still holds true, and investment in the United States would become relatively more attractive. Where the home country taxes foreign income and provides a foreign tax credit,[15] the story is somewhat more complicated. To the extent that the reduction in United States tax on capital income results only in a reduction in the home country foreign tax credit, the U.S. is merely ceding tax revenue to the home country fisc without affecting the MNC's investment incentives. However, as discussed above, deferral and cross-crediting should enable many MNCs to keep a significant part of the benefit from eliminating taxes on income from new capital.

An additional issue is whether countries that provide a credit for the current U.S. corporate income tax would also allow a credit for any portion of a consumption tax. Some countries that have considered a business cash-flow tax (as part of a consumption tax system) in place of a corporate income tax have been deterred by the perception that other countries might not provide a foreign tax credit for such taxes. Typically, countries that provide foreign tax credits do so either by domestic law or by tax treaty for taxes that look like corporate income taxes. Because the rationale for providing the credit is to preserve neutrality in the location of capital, the credit should apply to taxes imposed on capital income, such as a standard corporate income tax. Consumption taxes generally would not qualify simply because they are imposed on consumption and not on income.

There is, however, an argument for permitting a credit for a component of a consumption tax, but the argument applies only when the tax is imposed on the origin principle and there are supernormal returns, and even in this case it depends on the origin of the supernormal returns.[16] For tangible investment with normal returns, an investment in the United States at the margin would not be affected by the provision of a home country credit because the initial reduction in credits when the investment is expensed, and U.S. tax is reduced, exactly offsets the value of the credits from the U.S. tax on the future returns from the investment. Also, as we show below, under a destination-principle consumption tax, foreign investors would effectively bear no U.S. tax on normal or supernormal returns, so that no home country credit for U.S. taxes would be called for. However, as explained below in the discussion of the origin and destination principles, under an origin-principle consumption tax, investment in the United States would bear a tax on supernormal returns. In this case, the lack of a home country foreign tax credit for the U.S. tax on supernormal returns might discourage investment in the United States as compared with countries that imposed taxes that were creditable in the home country. However, this disincentive to investment in the United States could only arise to the extent that the supernormal returns were not specific to the United States and could be earned if the MNC operated in other locations. Moreover, if the supernormal returns were attributable to intangible assets, then appropriate application of transfer pricing rules would lead the supernormal returns to be taxed in the United States only if the intangible asset was created in the United States, and, consequently, the U.S. tax, and its creditability, would have no impact on the decision where to exploit the intangible asset. Of course, the application of transfer pricing rules is unlikely to be perfect.

Given the narrowness of the creditability issue, it seems likely that moving to a consumption tax would lead to increased investment in the United States by foreign MNCs whether or not other countries provided credits for any part of the U.S. tax.

Origin versus Destination Principle

It is often claimed that a destination-principle consumption tax, because it exempts exports and taxes imports, promotes exports and discourages imports. There is great intuitive appeal to the idea that the exemption of tax on exports would encourage firms to locate production to supply foreign markets in the United States rather than abroad, and the tax on imports would encourage firms to replace imports with domestic production.[17] Economists have long held that this notion is a fallacy and that, for flat rate consumption taxes, the destination and origin principles are equivalent in their effects on trade and investment at the margin.[18] We will briefly run through this argument here.

We start with the balance of payments identity: $X + NII = M + dFK$, where X is merchandise and service exports, NII is net investment income receipts, M is imports, and dFK is the net change in the holdings of foreign assets. We distinguish here between the export of "real" services such as computer software, included in X, and investment income, which is frequently included in the service account in the balance of payments.

As explained previously, the aggregate base of a consumption tax is domestic consumption under the destination principle and domestic consumption plus net exports $(X - M)$ under the origin principle. If capital is not mobile, so that trade must balance at each moment in time, $X = M$ and the equivalence of the bases is straightforward. A tax on imports is the same as a tax on exports because exports are being exchanged for imports and the same burden is imposed on that exchange irrespective of whether the tax is nominally on imports or exports. Now suppose that investment abroad is possible and consider the effect of a net increase in the holding of foreign assets.

This has to be financed with an increase in exports relative to imports, since investment income cannot change immediately (because it is determined by the initial holding of foreign assets). In real terms, the foreign assets are being acquired in exchange for U.S. exports. The net exports will be in the current origin-principle base but not in the current destination-principle base. However, on the margin, an extra dollar of foreign investment will finance future imports (purchased with the investment income) with a present value of $1 (because trade must balance over all time). In real terms, the real return to the marginal foreign investment is paid out in a stream of future imports that is equal in present value to the value of the U.S. exports that financed the foreign investment. Thus, taxing the current marginal export is equal in present value terms to taxing the stream of imports generated by that marginal export, and the tax bases are equivalent at the margin.

A numerical example may help to make clear the equivalence between the bases at the margin. Table 2 extends the example presented in Table 1 to consider the investment location choice under destination- and origin-principle taxes.

To start we must first consider the effects of the different tax bases on relative price levels as shown in row 1. As illustrated, switching from an origin- to a destination-principle consumption tax causes the foreign price level to fall relative to the domestic price level by a proportion equal to the consumption tax rate. To see why this must be so, consider an export good that, under the origin-principle tax, sells for $1 in both locations. If the switch is made to the destination principle, and there are no price-level adjustments, equilibrium cannot be maintained, because a good that can be sold for $1 domestically garners $1 if exported plus a rebate of

TABLE 2
LOCATION CHOICE FOR TANGIBLE INVESTMENT UNDER DESTINATION- AND ORIGIN-PRINCIPLE
CONSUMPTION TAXES

	Destination-Principle Tax		Origin-Principle Tax	
	Domestic Investment 1	Foreign Investment 2	Domestic Investment 3	Foreign Investment 4
(1) Foreign price/domestic price	0.75	0.75	1	1
(2) Cost of machine	100	75	100	100
(3) Tax deduction for machine	25	0	25	0
(4) Net cost of machine (2) − (3)	75	75	75	100
(5) Net return before tax	10	7.5	10	10
(6) Foreign income tax	—	0.75	—	1
(7) Domestic tax	2.5	0	2.5	0
(8) Total taxes paid (6) + (7)	2.5	0.75	2.5	1
(9) Net return after tax (5) − (8)	7.5	6.75	7.5	9
(10) Rate of return (9) ÷ (4)	10%	9%	10%	9%

Assumptions: domestic consumption tax rate = 25 percent; foreign income tax rate = 10 percent; pretax rate of return on investment in each location = 10 percent; and no depreciation.

consumption tax equal to 25¢. To restore equilibrium, the relative foreign price level must fall so that a good selling for $1 domestically only gets 75¢ abroad.[19] It is easy to show that the same argument holds for imports as well.

Returning to the example in Table 2, this means that under the destination principle the domestic cost of the machine is $100 and the foreign cost only $75. However, although the real net output of the machine is assumed to be the same in both locations, because of the price-level difference, its value is 25 percent lower in the foreign location, as illustrated in row 5. The consequence is that there is no difference in the results under the destination and origin principle at the margin. In each case, the pretax and after-tax rates of return to domestic investment are the same, 10 percent. And in each case, the after-tax rate of return to foreign investment is 9 percent.

While the origin and destination principles are equivalent in their effects on international trade and investment at the margin, they differ in the presence of supernormal returns. Comparing rows 9 and 10 of Table 2, under the destination principle, the higher rate of return for the domestic investment goes along with a higher dollar return per machine, whereas under the origin principle, the higher rate of return for the domestic investment goes along with a *lower* dollar return. Under the destination principle, the U.S. MNC effectively gets the benefit of expensing for foreign investment, because the after-tax cost of the investment is the same abroad as it is at home, but tax is also effectively paid on the stream of cash flow returning from a foreign investment by a U.S. MNC. In real terms, the rebate of tax on the U.S. exports that finance the foreign investment is equivalent in value to the foregone expensing for a domestic investment, and the tax on the stream of imports that represents the real return to the foreign investment is equivalent to the tax on the cash flow from a domestic investment.

Under the origin principle, there is no equivalent to expensing for foreign investment, because the pretax cost of investment is the same at home or abroad, but there is no effective tax on the returning cash flow from the foreign investment. In real terms, there is no rebate of tax on the U.S. exports that finance the foreign investment, but there is also no tax on the stream of imports that represents the real return to the investment. Under the origin principle, the lack of expensing for foreign investment represents, in effect, a prepayment of tax on the return from foreign investment. However, if there are supernormal returns to the investment, then the prepayment of tax on the initial foreign investment under the origin principle is smaller than the present value of the effective taxes that would be paid under the destination principle, and the difference is equal to the present value of the tax on the supernormal returns. Therefore, the U.S. MNC's supernormal returns bear tax under the destination principle whether they are earned at home or abroad. It follows also that a foreign MNC's supernormal returns from U.S. investment escape U.S. tax under the destination principle but not under the origin principle.

Note that under the destination principle a U.S. resident can avoid U.S. tax on the return to investment—whether it is a foreign investment or a domestic investment—if he moves abroad. In that case the real return from the investment does not incur an import tax. The tax cannot be avoided under the origin principle because it is effectively prepayed. Under the origin principle, the U.S. resident does, however, avoid tax on the return from the foreign investment if it was made prior to the date when the tax was imposed. In that case there would have been no prepayment of tax on the foreign investment and no tax on the consumption financed by the investment return. These points will be important in our discussion of tax-avoidance and transition incidence issues below.

Location of Intangible Assets

In addition to affecting MNC decisions concerning the location of their physical capital and production facilities, switching to a consumption tax system could also influence MNC decisions as to where to exploit intangible assets such as patents and know-how. Under current law, U.S. companies with excess foreign tax credits have an incentive to exploit a U.S.-created intangible asset abroad because the royalty income that returns to the United States can escape both U.S. and foreign tax. This occurs because the royalty payments are generally deductible in the foreign country and, being classified under U.S. law as foreign-source income, excess foreign tax credits can be used to offset any U.S. tax liability on the royalty. In contrast, a consumption tax generally would not influence the choice between exploiting an intangible asset at home or abroad.

A numerical example is again useful to illustrate this point. Once again the distinction between origin- and destination-principle consumption taxes must be dealt with. As already discussed, we would expect that under a consumption tax royalty receipts from abroad would be treated as payments for an export, and therefore would be exempt under the destination principle and taxed under the origin principle. The exemption of foreign royalty receipts may create the appearance that a destination-principle tax favors foreign exploitation of intangible assets in order to avoid U.S. tax, but appearances can be misleading.

Table 3 presents the case of an intangible asset that produces $100 of value added if used in the home country, yielding a return after tax of $75. It produces the same real output if used abroad. Under the origin principle, the returning royalty of $100, which captures the value of the intangible,[20] is taxed, yielding the same after-tax return of $75.[21] Under the destination principle, the returning royalty is untaxed, but the 25 percent foreign-domestic price differential that exists under the destination principle means that the value added, and the required royalty, is

TABLE 3
LOCATION CHOICE FOR INTANGIBLE ASSETS UNDER DESTINATION- AND ORIGIN-PRINCIPLE
CONSUMPTION TAXES

	Domestic Use 1	Foreign Use	
		Destination- Principle Tax 2	Origin- Principle Tax 3
(1) Foreign price/domestic price	—	0.75	1
(2) Value added by intangible before tax	100	75	100
(3) Royalty required	—	75	100
(4) Domestic tax	25	0	25
(5) Return after tax, (2) or (3) − (4)	75	75	75
(6) Return after (foreign) tax if no royalty paid	—	67.5	90

Assumptions: domestic consumption tax rate = 25 percent; foreign tax rate = 10 percent; and intangible asset creates same real output in each location.

only $75. Thus, the consumption tax, whether it follows the origin or destination principle, does not distort the choice of location for exploiting the intangible asset if appropriate royalties are paid.[22]

What if the appropriate royalty is not paid? Where there is imperfect enforcement of transfer pricing rules, MNCs are able to set royalties the do not fully capture the value of an intangible asset being transferred between members of the MNC group. The issue here is closely related to the issue of supernormal returns discussed earlier, because supernormal returns apparently earned by an MNC in one country may actually be the result of an intangible asset created in another country. Row 6 of Table 3 illustrates the case in which no royalty at all is paid for the transfer of the intangible asset to the foreign location. The results are different under the destination and origin principles. Under the destination principle, the MNC gains no benefit from shifting the intangible income to the foreign location, and loses to the extent that there is any foreign tax on that income. Under the origin principle, the MNC gains as long as the foreign tax rate is lower than the domestic tax rate. Thus, the possibility of tax avoidance through transfer price manipulation may provide an incentive to locate intangible assets in low-tax foreign countries under an origin-principle tax, but not under a destination-principle tax.

To summarize, movement to a consumption base would eliminate the incentive for locating U.S.-created intangible assets abroad that is created under our foreign tax credit system when a company has excess foreign tax credits. Under an origin-principle consumption tax, there would still be an incentive to move intangible assets to low-tax jurisdictions to exploit transfer pricing opportunities, but this incentive would be little different than it is under the current income tax. The greater neutrality in the tax treatment of intangible assets that would be achieved under the consumption tax proposals is not, however, inherent to the consumption base. The same neutrality could be achieved under our income tax if royalty receipts were treated as domestic-source income. In that case, excess foreign tax credits could not be used to eliminate U.S. tax on receipts of royalties from abroad. Under an income VAT, the same neutrality would hold as long as royalty receipts were treated consistently with the origin- or destination-principle treatment of exports and imports under the tax.

Location of R&D

MNCs sometimes also face a decision about the location of their investment in the creation of intangible capital through R&D.[23] Because these investment expenditures are currently expensed in the United States and most other countries, consumption tax treatment would not represent a direct change.[24] There likely would be some modest shift in R&D activity to the United States because U.S. companies would no longer have to allocate a portion of R&D expense against foreign income as they do under current U.S. tax rules. This allocation represents a partial disallowance of deductions for R&D expense for firms that have excess foreign tax credits, because the deduction is against foreign income that bears no U.S. tax in any case. Thus, replacement of current rules with a consumption tax system would eliminate a tax rule that provides some disincentive to perform R&D in the United States.

Here again the result is not inherent to the consumption tax aspect of the proposals. If under our income tax all royalties were treated as domestic-source income, then it would make sense to allocate all R&D expenses against domestic income, thereby eliminating the tax incentive to locate R&D activities abroad.

Location of Debt

Because under the *R*-based flat tax and USA business tax plans (or, for that matter, an income VAT) interest expense would no longer be deductible in the United States, but would, presumably, remain deductible abroad, U.S. and foreign MNCs would have an incentive to shift debt to the books of their foreign affiliates.[25] The extent to which this would happen depends on the substitutability of borrowing by foreign affiliates for borrowing by a U.S. affiliate. There is some empirical evidence for such substitutability.[26] The revenue costs of such debt shifting would be at the expense of foreign fiscs and not the United States.

Overall Effects on Net Capital Flows, Interest Rates, and the Capital Stock

While replacement of the current income tax with a consumption tax is likely to increase the amount of business investment in the United States, the overall effect on net capital flows and the capital stock is more difficult to determine. To examine this issue we need to take into account differences in effects on debt- and equity-financed investment, and tax-favored sectors such as owner-occupied housing, noncorporate business, tax-exempt bonds, and entities such as pension funds and nonprofits.

Because the relative change in the tax treatment of debt- and equity-financed investment is of particular importance in the analysis, it is useful to outline first what we are assuming about the relationship between the two forms of finance in capital market equilibrium. The returns to debt and equity presumably reflect the division of risk among the owners of the different types of claim. However, debt and equity are not perfect substitutes; otherwise, given the current tax bias in favor of debt finance, there would be no equity-financed investment. We assume that a tax change directed at debt, such as the nondeductibility of interest, will lower interest returns relative to equity returns because there are risk-averse investors with a preference for debt. Similarly, an influx of risk-averse investors will lower interest rates relative to equity returns. We assume that the trade-off between risk and return can change in response to changes in tax provisions as well as changes in the distribution of investor preferences.

We start the analysis by examining the effects of consumption taxes in a closed economy. After describing the changes in this economy when consumption taxes are introduced, we see how those effects

Closed Economy Analysis

may be altered by the international mobility of goods and capital.

We start by considering the corporate sector of the economy in isolation. It should be clear that the after-tax rate of return on equity investment goes up very dramatically in the movement to a consumption base. Rather than equity investors bearing a double tax on corporate income, as under our classical income tax, on the margin they receive the full pretax return to capital.

The effect on interest rates and debt-financed investment is less obvious. Debt investors should now receive a higher after-tax return because of the elimination of tax at the personal level. However, the effect on interest rates depends both on investors' demands and the interest rates companies are willing to offer in view of the real return to capital and the tax system. Consider the extreme case, in the initial classical income tax, of an investment with 100 percent debt financing and no inflation. Assuming economic depreciation, before the tax at the personal level bondholders will just receive the pretax return to capital because the interest return is deductible at the corporate level. The switch to expensing and nondeductibility of interest in a consumption VAT leaves interest rates that companies offer unchanged. The value of the current expensing is just equal to the present value of the interest deductions lost. Companies are still willing to offer the same pretax rate of return to bondholders, because expensing just offsets the nondeductibility of interest.

In this 100 percent debt financing case, interest rates will only fall if there is an increase in saving and a resulting lower pretax return to capital. If we reintroduce equity into the economy, interest rates can rise or fall because companies will ad-just their financing choices while capital owners adjust their portfolio choices. Because interest is now nondeductible, while the treatment of dividends at the business level has not changed, companies will offer less debt and more equity for given corporate-level returns, and this will tend to lower interest rates. However, capital owners may insist on higher interest rates in order to compete with higher after-tax equity returns. The net effect of arbitrage between debt and equity by businesses and capital owners is uncertain.[27] The nondeductibility of interest can be expected to lower interest rates relative to equity returns, but because expensing will raise the overall return to capital, interest rates may still rise in absolute terms.

Overall, the case that Hall and Rabushka (1995) made for a large drop in interest rates, based solely on the elimination of taxes on corporate capital income, does not seem strong, even in a closed economy. Hall and Rabushka seem to ignore the implications of capital expensing for the interest rates that companies are willing to offer.

These results may be altered in several respects if we consider the effects of the empirically important noncorporate sector, owner-occupied housing, tax-exempt bonds issued by state and local governments, and the many tax-exempt entities such as pension funds that receive investment income free from tax at the shareholder level.

Under the consumption tax proposals, the (approximately 10 percent of total) debt in the form of tax-exempt bonds would lose its advantages over taxable business debt. If mortgage interest deductibility is eliminated, as in the flat tax but not the USA individual tax, investment in home ownership would lose its tax-favored status. These changes would lead to shifts of capital out of the state and local government and nousing sectors to the business sector, dampening the rise in business equity returns brought about by the shift to a consumption tax and tending to lower interest rates for business investment. The noncorporate sector would also lose its tax advantage over the corporate sector, so that capital would shift to the corporate sector, further dampening the rise in after-tax returns to corporate equity and lowering interest rates.

On the other hand, the large amount of investment income currently received by tax exempts means that the increase in saving induced by a consumption tax is likely to be much weaker than would otherwise be predicted.[28] This would tend to accentuate the rise in equity returns and moderate any decline in interest rates. Nevertheless, it appears likely that the shift of capital out of the state and local and housing sectors would more than offset the effect of the smaller increase in saving. Taking into account these complicating features of the U.S. capital market, on balance it seems likely that interest rates would fall. After-tax equity returns would probably still rise, but by somewhat less than would be expected if the corporate sector were considered in isolation.

Open Economy Effects

The extent to which the open economy would alter the results just presented depends largely on the degree to which capital is internationally mobile. There has been substantial controversy on this subject.[29] We cannot resolve this issue here, but examination of cross-border asset holdings indicates that, at the least, there is a significant degree of integration of global debt markets. Federal Reserve Board and Bank for International Settlements data indicate that cross-border lending in U.S. dollars is comparable in size to borrowing by U.S. business.[30] These data on the worldwide pool of dol-

lar assets suggest a substantial elasticity in the supply of debt to U.S. business.[31]

To the extent that portfolio debt capital is internationally mobile, the downward pressure on interest rates, caused largely by the reduction in borrowing by the housing and state and local sectors described above, would cause an outflow of debt capital. Because the return to debt capital is currently untaxed at the corporate level (because interest is deductible), and by law portfolio interest is exempt from any withholding tax, foreign debt investors obtain no direct benefit from the tax changes and any tendency for dollar interest rates to fall will make foreign currency debt relatively more attractive. In addition, because the tax treatment of foreign and domestic interest income would be the same for U.S. residents, a fall in dollar interest rates would make foreign currency debt more attractive to them as well.

In an open economy, there is an additional factor that may reinforce the downward pressure on U.S. interest rates. As discussed previously, the nondeductibility of interest in the United States is likely to lead MNCs to shift borrowing to the books of their foreign affiliates. If this debt continues to be in dollars, which would seem likely because borrowing in dollars is now likely to be cheaper, there would not be much effect on U.S. interest rates. However, if more borrowing is in foreign currencies, there will be a greater tendency for U.S. interest rates to fall.

The resulting outflow of debt capital due to the shift of capital from the housing and state and local sectors would tend to dampen the decline in U.S. interest rates predicted by the closed economy analysis. In the polar case of perfect capital mobility, there would be no decline at all in U.S. interest rates. The extent of this effect depends on the elasticity of demand for capital in the business sector relative to the elasticity of the worldwide supply of debt to the U.S. business sector. It is not necessary to believe in a high degree of international debt mobility to expect that any decline in interest rates that would occur in a closed economy would be substantially reduced in an open economy.[32]

To the extent that equity capital is internationally mobile, the rise in after-tax equity returns in the United States brought about by the shift to a consumption tax would lead to an inflow of equity capital. However, as described above, the shifts of U.S. capital from the noncorporate business, housing, and state and local sectors to the corporate sector should restrain the rise in corporate equity returns. Because foreign investment in U.S. equity is concentrated in the corporate sector, the inflow of equity is likely to be significantly dampened by the shift of domestic capital into the corporate sector.

The net result of the equity inflows and debt outflows is uncertain. Because debt capital is likely much more mobile than equity capital, the debt outflows could be larger than the equity inflows, leaving a net capital outflow. Investment in the U.S. business sector would increase, but the capital that flows out of the housing and state and local sectors might in part go abroad. If the domestic savings response to the increase in after-tax returns to capital is relatively small, the result could conceivably be a decline in the U.S. capital stock.

Even if replacement of the current income tax system with a consumption tax resulted in net capital outflows and a decline in the U.S. capital stock, this does not necessarily mean that the United States would lose from the transition. The gains from a more efficient allocation of capital within the U.S. economy might

outweigh any losses from resulting capital outflows.

The role of debt outflows described above is not limited to reforms that involve a consumption base. In fact, these effects would be even larger under an income base, such as an income VAT, that provides for nondeductibility of interest because there is no benefit of expensing to offset the elimination of interest deductibility. If interest rates remained stable because of the integration of world debt markets, the cost of debt-financed business capital in the United States would rise substantially. This effect could outweigh the benefit to equity in the form of the dividend exemption that would go along with such a reform. Grubert and Mutti (1994) simulated the effect of "backward integration" of corporate and personal income taxes, which is similar to an income VAT in its treatment of capital income, and found that even with moderate international mobility of debt investment the U.S. capital stock could decline by more than 5 percent in the long run.[33]

EFFECTS ON SIMPLICITY AND TAX-AVOIDANCE OPPORTUNITIES

Positive Effects on Simplicity and Compliance

Because foreign income need not be defined under a consumption tax, the tax code's source rules and the associated rules to allocate expenses between domestic and foreign income could be substantially simplified or would become unnecessary. Under an origin-principle consumption VAT or flat tax, expense allocation rules would be entirely irrelevant. All purchases by a U.S. business would be immediately deductible. Under a destination-principle consumption VAT, such as the USA business tax, the treatment of purchases would be the same, except that payments for imported goods, services, or intangible assets would effectively be nondeductible. Export sales would be exempt under a destination-principle tax, but all expenses would remain deductible in order to relieve the tax burden on all earlier stages of production. Under either of these forms of consumption tax, interest allocation rules would be unnecessary, because interest would not be deductible.

Under an income tax, it would, in principle, also be possible to eliminate perhaps the two most important expense allocation rules. First, because under an income VAT interest is also nondeductible, interest allocation rules would be irrelevant. Second, if under an income tax all royalty receipts from abroad were treated as domestic income, rather than being treated as foreign income as under current law, then it would be logical to allocate all research and development expense against domestic income.

The foreign tax credit rules provided under current law would become unnecessary under a consumption tax regime. These rules contain substantial complexity, including, for example, nine separate foreign tax credit baskets for different types of foreign income and look-through rules to retain the character of income when passed through tiers of foreign subsidiaries, and there are associated complications such as the need to determine the "earnings and profits" of foreign subsidiaries according to U.S. tax rules. The extent to which these rules realistically could be simplified within an income tax regime is uncertain. Many of the complexities result from attempts to achieve reasonable policy objectives, such as limiting the incentive to move passive or other investments to low-tax jurisdictions that is created when excess foreign tax credits can shield the related income from U.S. tax. Although exemption of foreign-source income would eliminate

these rules, it would greatly accentuate the incentive to shift investment (and profits through transfer pricing) to low-tax jurisdictions.[34]

As a general rule, a U.S. shareholder in a foreign corporation, whether an individual or a company, pays no tax on the income earned by the foreign corporation until it is distributed. This creates an incentive for MNCs to avoid U.S. tax by having a foreign subsidiary in a low-tax jurisdiction hold passive investments. It creates an incentive for any U.S. taxpayer, corporate or individual, to hold passive investments in low-tax foreign jurisdictions through the vehicle of a foreign corporation. The tax code contains some fairly complicated rules that counteract this incentive by providing for current taxation of income from such investments.[35] A related compliance concern is that tax evaders may escape U.S. tax on investment income by keeping their money in secret accounts in tax havens, presenting a difficult enforcement challenge for the tax authorities. Because investment income is untaxed under a consumption tax, there no longer would be any tax motivation to keep passive investments abroad, and these rules and compliance concerns would be irrelevant.

Interest deductibility under standard income tax systems creates the incentive for MNCs to arbitrage across countries with different tax rates by shifting their borrowing out of low-tax countries and into high-tax countries. The U.S. earnings stripping and interest allocation rules are designed to limit this kind of arbitrage. They would clearly be unnecessary under a consumption tax system in which interest is not deductible.[36] As noted already above, this result is not, however, inherent only to the consumption base, because an income VAT would also disallow interest deductions.

One of the more problematic areas of international taxation arises because of the need for MNCs to set internal transfer prices for transfers of goods, services, and intangibles across borders between different members of the multinational group. These transfer prices directly affect the amount of income reported in each jurisdiction. A compliance problem can be created because an MNC will have an incentive to set these prices so as to shift income from high-tax jurisdictions to low-tax jurisdictions. The U.S. tax rules incorporate the internationally accepted standard for setting transfer prices, which is that they should be set at the level that would have prevailed had the parties been dealing at arm's length. However, application of this standard can be problematic and can involve considerable compliance and administrative burdens. The volume and variety of these transactions is high, and they can involve the transfer of unique goods, services, or intangible assets that are difficult to value because there are no comparable transactions between unrelated parties.

Whether transfer pricing problems remain an issue under a consumption tax depends on whether the origin or destination principle is adopted. Under a destination-principle consumption tax, such as the USA business tax, transfer prices would no longer be relevant to the determination of U.S. tax liabilities because a company's tax base would be equal to its domestic sales less its domestic purchases. Because export sales (and, presumably, royalty receipts from abroad) would be exempt and imports (and royalty payments to foreign parties) effectively nondeductible, the prices established for such transactions would not affect the U.S. tax base. Therefore, opportunities to use transfer prices to reduce U.S. taxes would be eliminated. However, because transfer pricing profits into the United States would not increase U.S. taxes, there would be an incentive to shift profits out of other countries and into the United States.

Under an origin-principle consumption tax, such as the flat tax, transfer pricing would continue to be an issue for U.S. taxes, because export sales would continue to be taxable and imports deductible. As is true under our current tax system, the magnitude of the incentive to shift income out of the United States through transfer prices would depend largely on the U.S. tax rate.[37]

Returning to table 3, columns 2 and 3 of row 6 illustrate the transfer pricing incentives for royalty payments under the origin and destination principles. The results in this row are derived assuming that no royalty is paid to the United States, so that an additional foreign tax, at a 10 percent rate, is paid on the profits shifted into the foreign country. Under the destination principle, the net return is only 67.5, less than if the royalty had been paid, because an additional foreign tax is incurred without any reduction in U.S. tax. Under the origin principle, however, the net return is 90, greater than the return if the appropriate royalty had been paid.

Under an income VAT, the advantageous properties of the destination principle with respect to transfer pricing incentives are somewhat diminished. Incentives for shifting profits through transfer pricing would still exist for imports of capital equipment. The import would be taxed at the border, but the company would not have a fully offsetting current deduction for the purchase, because the cost of the capital equipment would be depreciated rather than being expensed. The difference between the price of the equipment and the present value of the depreciation deductions would create an incentive to lower the stated price. In addition, if foreign income was taxed and a foreign tax credit provided under either a destination- or origin-principle income tax, there would be incentives to shift income to low-tax countries when excess foreign tax credits could offset additional U.S. tax on foreign income.

New Complexities and Tax Avoidance Problems

Identifying taxable imports and exempt exports under the destination principle

The experience of countries that impose VATs shows that application of a destination-principle consumption tax can create compliance problems and complexities due to the need to distinguish between deductible domestic purchases and effectively nondeductible imports, and between taxable domestic sales and exempt exports. The extent of these problems depends on the controls at the border, the type of consumption tax (subtraction method versus invoice-credit method), and the type of imports or exports (merchandise or services).

The problem for imports is reduced if the credit-invoice method is used, because a company would presumably only get a credit for taxes on its purchases if it can show that those taxes have actually been paid, either at the border on imports or at an earlier stage of domestic production. Under the subtraction method, the problem for merchandise imports is also much reduced if, as in the USA business tax, there is a tax at the border, because then the importing business does not have to distinguish between deductible and non-deductible expenses. However, if under a subtraction method tax there is no tax at the border, the problem can be substantial because a company must distinguish between domestic purchases and imports—only the former are deductible—even though the goods may be identical.

Although it is relatively straightforward to impose a tax on merchandise imports, it is not so easy in the case of imported services. For example, foreign software, ad-

vertising, or consulting services could be transmitted by report, disk, or over a satellite. Tax auditors would presumably rely on billing addresses, but because domestic addresses could easily be arranged, a series of transactions might have to be examined.

An additional level of complexity would be added in cases in which a service was provided partly domestically and partly from abroad. For example, an international consulting firm might prepare a report to which both its New York and London offices had contributed. The fee for this report would need to be divided into two separate components representing compensation for the services performed by the two different offices. In principle, this division does not affect the total tax base, as long as the component that does not bear import tax is included in the receipts of the New York office for U.S. tax purposes. Additional difficulties with respect to financial services provided by financial intermediaries are discussed below.

Consumers would also have the incentive to use foreign services, such as credit-card processing. Cross-border shopping could also be an issue. International mail order for merchandise would not seem to create a new problem as long as customs duties are imposed on packages, as under the current system.

Compliance problems would also arise in identifying true exports. Goods could be shipped from one U.S. port and landed in another. Problems of this kind have been encountered in the case of ozone-depleting chemicals, whose domestic use is subject to a high tax under current law.

These problems would be particularly severe if a destination-principle VAT was imposed at a high rate, such as would be required to replace the income tax entirely. If the states followed suit and replaced their sales taxes with a VAT modeled off the federal VAT, the combined tax rate would likely be high in comparison to other VAT countries. The USA proposal, however, does not contemplate an unusually high tax rate as compared with other VAT countries, because it is combined with a consumed income tax on individuals.

Are Financial Intermediaries More of a Problem in an Open Economy?

The familiar problem of financial intermediaries in R-based consumption tax schemes, such as a VAT, arises because of the dichotomy between real and financial transactions. Interest payments and receipts are ignored. Therefore, services provided in exchange for interest rate spreads, *e.g.*, transactions services to consumers instead of higher interest rates on their checking account balances, are not subject to tax.

This problem would seem only to exist for services to consumers. If untaxed financial services are provided to a business, it gets no deduction (or credit) but has to pay tax on the final sale. The same is true for loan expenses incurred by a bank on its business loans. Tax will be paid on the full gross product of the loan at the business (borrower) level. In addition, some financial services, such as investment management, are often investment rather than consumption. These services are provided with the object of producing a higher return from the investor's capital. The value of the goods or services produced with that capital is taxed. In these cases all the proper tax can be collected when the goods and services are sold to consumers, and the imputation of interest spreads on loans, as Hall and Rabushka (1995) proposed, seems largely unnecessary. With equal tax rates for all business taxpayers, the failure to impute income to one of the stages is offset by the absence of a deduction at the next stage.[38]

International transactions would not seem to exacerbate the problem of untaxed financial services to a great extent. Under the destination principle, service exports would be exempt, and service imports by business nondeductible, anyway. The problem in this case would be largely limited to the direct import of services by consumers. Under the origin principle, the distortions created might be greater, because service exports should be taxed and imports deducted; however, the direct import of services by consumers would no longer be an issue, because such services should be untaxed anyway.

If it is deemed necessary to impute service fees to the transactions of financial intermediaries, then international transactions will add some complexity. It will be difficult to determine the appropriate allocation of imputed fees to foreign customers.

Reclassifying Sales Receipts as Interest

Because of the dichotomy between real and financial transactions, R-based consumption taxes create an incentive to reclassify part of the taxable sales price of a good sold to consumers as nontaxable interest on an installment sale. In an open economy, this incentive also exists under the origin principle for sales to foreigners in an income tax country because only the sales component would be taxable in the United States but the foreigner can deduct both sales and interest components. Similarly, the incentive exists under the origin principle to overstate the purchase price component of imports and understate the interest component. Note that this is essentially a variant of the transfer pricing problem, but these transactions need not be with related parties. The potentially large magnitude of trade receivables could make this a significant problem.

Consumption Abroad

Because the base of a destination-principle consumption tax is consumption in the United States in each period, it can create an incentive for residents to avoid the tax by consuming abroad. One way to do this is through vacationing abroad. Perhaps more importantly, a retiree might avoid the tax by emigrating to some country that imposed a lower consumption tax, or no consumption tax at all. Under a destination-principle VAT, the tax savings from emigration would show itself through the tax-induced difference between the U.S. and foreign price levels. Under a personal consumption tax such as the USA individual tax, a U.S. taxpayer could benefit from the deduction for savings while accumulating wealth, and then avoid tax when subsequently dissaving by emigrating. The USA individual tax reduces this incentive to some extent by taxing citizens and green card holders on their dissaving, even if they no longer reside in the United States, and by continuing to tax former citizens and green card holders under some circumstances.

The incentive to emigrate would not exist under an origin-principle tax such as the flat tax. There would be no tax-induced difference between the foreign and domestic price levels. In real terms, the tax on any income earned in the United States is not rebated at the border when it is used to finance foreign consumption, as it is under a destination-principle consumption tax.

TRANSITION INCIDENCE

Some of the more problematic issues associated with adoption of a consumption tax relate to transition impacts.[39] In a closed economy, perhaps the major transition impact is that, in the absence of transition rules,[40] imposition of a consumption tax has the effect of imposing a one-time tax on the existing stock of wealth in the economy.[41] In general terms, with the transition the existing stock of wealth is taxed when it is consumed. In an open economy, an additional issue is the distribution of transition impacts between foreign and U.S. investors. In particular, the issue is to what extent foreign investors in U.S. assets and U.S. investors in foreign assets bear the transition tax. It turns out that the distinction between origin and destination principles is crucial. To simplify the analysis, we examine the international transition effects of introducing a consumption tax while largely ignoring the effects of eliminating our income tax.

We start by considering a 100 percent equity ownership of a U.S. asset existing at the time the consumption tax is introduced. Introduction of a flat rate consumption tax involves taxing at a given rate all the future cash flow from the asset, if the cash flow is used to finance consumption in the United States. Now consider the effect on a foreign holder of that equity interest if the consumption tax is imposed on the destination principle. In this case, the purchasing power in terms of U.S. consumption of the stream of cash flow from that equity interest will have fallen in proportion to the tax rate at the business level. However, recall that the foreign price level will also fall relative to the U.S. price level in proportion to the tax rate. Therefore, the real value to the foreign investor of the cash flow from the U.S. equity interest will not change, and the foreign investor escapes any transition burden from the introduction of a destination-principle consumption tax. Because the real return to a U.S. investment is effectively paid out to foreigners in U.S. exports, the tax on that return is rebated at the border. On the most basic level, a destination-principle consumption tax falls on domestic consumption in each period, so it should not be a surprise that a foreign investor escapes the burden of the tax.

Now turn to the transition effect of imposing a destination-principle tax on a U.S. owner of a foreign asset. In this case, the cash flow from the foreign asset is not directly affected by the tax; however, the relative increase in the U.S. price level means that the cash flow declines proportionately in terms of U.S. purchasing power. More fundamentally, the real return to the U.S. owner of a foreign asset is paid out in imports to the United States, and those imports are taxed under the destination principle. Therefore, the U.S. owner of the foreign asset bears the transition impact of the tax in full, as long as he continues to consume in the United States.

Consider next an origin-principle consumption tax. In this case, there is no change in relative price levels brought about by the introduction of the tax. Therefore, in contrast to the case of a destination-principle tax, the foreign equity holder bears the transition burden of the origin-principle tax in the same way as any domestic equity holder would. At the same time, a U.S. owner of foreign assets escapes the transition impact altogether. In real terms, the exports that represent the real return to the foreign investor receive no rebate of tax under the origin principle, and the imports that represent the real return of the U.S. owner of foreign assets are not taxed.

One conclusion from this analysis is that an origin-principle consumption tax could be expected to impose more of its transition burden on foreigners, to the extent that transition rules do not otherwise affect the burden. This may be viewed as an attractive feature to the extent that it represents a lump-sum transfer from foreigners to the United States. Given that the U.S. net foreign asset position is currently negative, the United States would gain more from the transition tax on the U.S. assets of foreigners than it would

lose in transition tax on foreign assets held by U.S. residents.

By focusing on the transition impact on equity holders, we have ignored the effects on debt. In general, the analysis of those effects will be little different from the closed economy analysis in which the distribution of transition losses between debt and equity holders depends largely on the price-level adjustment that occurs with the transition and the terms of outstanding debt contracts (*e.g.*, whether bonds are indexed).

REACTION OF OTHER COUNTRIES

In the discussion so far we have implicitly assumed that other countries would not change their tax policies in response to the replacement of the U.S. income tax with a consumption tax. In fact, other countries might well react to the extent that the U.S. policy change threatened to cause significant capital flows to the United States at their expense and to erode their tax bases through MNCs shifting debt from their U.S. books and, under a destination-principle tax, transfer pricing profits into the United States.

Other countries might move to protect their tax bases from the effects of MNC debt shifting by instituting rules to limit interest deductions, such as thin capitalization rules and rules to allocate interest deductions among the members of an MNC group. Such a reaction would likely have little direct effect on the United States, unless policies were targeted specifically at U.S. MNCs.

Of more consequence would be the pressure other countries might feel to reduce their taxes on capital income. This pressure would come both from the shifting of debt from the United States to those countries and from the likely flows of equity investment from those countries to the United States. The ultimate result could be lower taxes on capital income worldwide, and, consequently, the effects on capital flows to the Unites States that were posited above would be muted.

Whether the overall effect of these changes would push the global economy toward or away from efficiency is unclear. A uniformly lower level of capital income taxes would likely lead to fewer distortions in the allocation of capital across countries and a globally increased return to saving. However, in order to replace lost revenue from capital income taxes, governments are likely to have to raise other taxes, in particular, taxes on labor income, either directly or, following the U.S. lead, through increased reliance on consumption taxes.

Tax Treaties and Withholding Taxes

The analysis to this point has not yet dealt with the implications of moving to a consumption tax system for our network of tax treaties. The United States currently has bilateral tax treaties with more than 40 countries. These treaties provide substantial benefits to cross-border investment by, among other things, lowering withholding tax rates on cross-border income flows, scaling back the tax reach of host countries, and preventing discriminatory treatment of foreign investment by host countries. Most provisions of these treaties apply only to taxes on income, and the United States would be unilaterally eliminating its income tax. The question therefore arises whether other countries would perceive themselves as unilaterally providing benefits to U.S. investors and receiving little in return under their treaties. In that case, foreign countries might be tempted to terminate their treaties with the United States. It turns out, however, that U.S. tax treaty partners would have incentives to maintain their treaties with the United States, particularly if the United States retained its

statutory withholding taxes on income payments to foreigners.[42]

Under current law, the United States imposes a 30 percent withholding tax on payments of dividends, interest (other than portfolio interest, which is exempt), and royalties to foreigners. These rates are generally substantially reduced under tax treaties, sometimes to zero for direct investment interest and royalties, and 5 percent for direct investment dividends. If the United States retained its statutory withholding taxes, treaty partners with significant investment in the United States would stand to lose, at the least, the substantial benefit of the treaty withholding rate reductions, but they might lose even more. Under the nondiscrimination articles of these treaties, a treaty partner is not permitted to impose a greater tax burden on the resident individuals or companies of the other country than it imposes on its own residents. Although these withholding taxes fall only on foreigners, they are not considered to violate the nondiscrimination article because they are deemed to be imposed in lieu of the income tax on resident recipients of such payments. Because under the consumption tax plans generally no tax is imposed on resident recipients, the withholding taxes might be viewed to violate the discrimination article.[43] In this case, residents of treaty partners would face no withholding tax at all if the treaty was retained, but a 30 percent tax if it was terminated.

U.S. tax treaty partners might also be deterred from terminating their tax treaties because they might not wish their higher statutory withholding tax rates to apply to U.S. investors. They might rightly be concerned that this would make their country an even less competitive location for U.S. investment, particularly because the United States would no longer provide a foreign tax credit.

Conclusions

International considerations can significantly alter the projected effects of replacing our income tax system with a consumption tax. The net effect of moving to a consumption tax on the U.S. capital stock could be positive or negative, because while equity capital would flow into the U.S. business sector, debt capital might flow out of the United States. Even in the event that the U.S. capital stock declined, the overall effect on U.S. national welfare is uncertain. To a large extent, the outflows of capital would be the result of a more efficient allocation of capital across the different sectors of the U.S. economy. In addition, the shift of investment by U.S. companies from abroad back to the United States might increase U.S. welfare, because part of the return from foreign investment is captured by foreign taxes, while all of the return from domestic investment remains in U.S. hands. On the other hand, the United States would give up some tax revenue from foreign equity investment in the United States (foreign debt investment in the United States is already largely untaxed). Without knowledge of the magnitude of these various effects, the bottom line is uncertain. Detailed simulation modeling would be required to place bounds on the likely effects.[44] The reactions of other countries may also be significant and should be taken into account.

International considerations also raise new issues in evaluating consumption tax proposals. As we have described, a consumption tax would permit substantial simplification of our complicated international tax rules and would eliminate certain compliance problems in some cases. However, there would also be some new administrative and compliance issues. The choice between origin and destination principles for the treatment of exports and imports turns out to have important consequences in this regard, although, contrary to what is often alleged, it does not have consequences for the promotion of exports. Balancing the administrative and compliance problems eliminated against those created would clearly be important in assessing the overall impact of the consumption tax proposals.

ENDNOTES

We thank Jay Mackie, Sheena McConnell, Barbara Rollinson, Joel Slemrod, Eric Toder, and Joann Weiner for their comments. Any views expressed in this paper are those of the authors alone and should not be construed as reflecting the views or policies of the U.S. Treasury Department.

[1] We also refer to the text of H.R. 2060, the bill introduced by Representative Armey in the House of Representatives on July 19, 1995.

[2] Merrill, Wertz, and Shah (1995) find that tax revenues from nonfinancial corporations would rise under the USA business tax and the Armey flat tax at plausible tax rates. However, their analysis reveals nothing about the total tax burden on capital income. Their comparison ignores the taxation of capital income at the personal level under the current tax system. They also attribute taxes on wages to the corporate tax burden under the USA business tax but not under the current tax system or the flat tax. Tax burdens clearly do not depend on who sends the checks to the Internal Revenue Service.

[3] See Institute for Fiscal Studies (1978).

[4] Because interest income and interest expense are ignored, financial intermediaries will have a negative tax base due to their purchase of goods and services from other firms. The implications are discussed later in this paper.

[5] Our use of the term *exempt* here describes a situation that is technically described as "zero rating." In the context of a credit-invoice VAT, this means that no tax is paid on the export and credit is allowed for taxes paid by suppliers, so that no tax is paid on the value of the export at any stage in its production.

[6] According to the General Agreement on Tariffs and Trade (GATT), indirect taxes, but not direct taxes, may be administered according to the destination principle. Although there is no evident economic mean-

ing to the distinction between direct and indirect taxes, this would apparently make it difficult for the flat tax proposals to be administered on the destination principle, presumably because wages are not included in the business tax base.

[7] If wages are not in the tax base, a destination-principle tax would be difficult to implement, even apart from GATT problems. The rebate would apply only to the capital component of exports and, more important, some capital component would have to be imputed to imports.

[8] If foreign income is included in the base of an income VAT, which would be necessary to ensure neutrality in investment location choices from a global perspective, the mechanics of the foreign tax credit limitation may not be straightforward because of the elimination of deductions for interest (and possibly wages.) Exempting foreign income under an income VAT would be the equivalent of providing a front-loaded IRA for foreign investment under the destination principle and a back-loaded IRA for foreign investment under the origin principle.

[9] The expected present value of rental payments for the use of property over the life of the property should be equal to the market value of the property. Because under current tax rules proceeds from the sale of property by U.S. residents are generally treated as U.S.-source income, neutrality in tax treatment would require rental receipts to be treated as U.S.-source income as well.

[10] The proposals themselves are vague on this point. The USA tax proposal appears to include royalty receipts in the base, but does not mention royalty payments in the context of deductions nor does it discuss their treatment under the destination principle. The Armey proposal appears to be completely silent on the subject of royalties.

[11] This reflects the fact that there are restrictions on the extent to which MNCs can treat contributions of capital to a foreign subsidiary as debt, and the bulk of U.S. direct investment abroad and foreign direct investment in the U.S. is in fact characterized as equity. Although direct investment may also be financed partly with local debt, our subsequent discussion of interest rate effects indicates that taking local debt finance into account would only reinforce the conclusions drawn here.

[12] As discussed below, there would be a domestic-foreign price differential under a destination-principle tax. We consider the implications of this price differential below.

[13] We ignore the potential reactions of other countries, which are discussed below. Gordon (1992) shows that the foreign tax credit may be optimal from a national standpoint when such reactions are taken into account.

[14] These countries include Canada, France, Germany, and The Netherlands.

[15] As in the case of Japan and the United Kingdom.

[16] McLure and Zodrow (1994) present this argument.

[17] See, e.g., the claims in Alliance USA (1995) regarding the USA tax.

[18] See Grossman (1980), Dixit (1985), and Feldstein and Krugman (1990) for recent demonstrations of this point.

[19] In reality the fall in the relative foreign price level would occur through some combination of changes in the exchange rate, the foreign price level, and the domestic price level.

[20] Actual amounts could differ to reflect the transfer of risk; however, accounting for a risk premium would not affect the results of the analysis.

[21] We are assuming here that the royalty is deductible against any foreign income tax and that there is no foreign withholding tax on the payment. The presence of a foreign withholding tax would make foreign use of the intangible relatively less attractive.

[22] It is possible that a consumption tax would be implemented in which the treatment of royalties was inconsistent with the general destination- or origin-principle treatment of exports and imports of goods and services. If receipts of royalties from abroad were taxed under a generally destination-principle tax, it would be the equivalent of a double tax on the income from the intangible because the imports financed by the income flow from abroad are taxed as well. If royalties from abroad were exempt under a generally origin-principle tax, the income from the intangible would be consumed effectively free of U.S. tax because the imports financed by that income flow are not taxed.

[23] Marketing activities can also create intangible assets, but there may be less flexibility in location choice because these activities are frequently market specific.

[24] There might, however, be indirect effects. For example, because all investment would be expensed, R&D and advertising would no

longer be favored relative to investment in tangible capital.

25 This is likely also to be true for an $(R + F)$-based tax such as the McLure and Zodrow (1995) proposal. As explained above, the inclusion of new borrowing and deduction for payments of interest and principal is equivalent to the nondeductibility of interest under the R base.

26 See Altshuler and Mintz (1994) and Froot and Hines (1995).

27 An additional complication of uncertain empirical significance is the effect of inflation on interest rates. Inflation should tend to raise real interest rates when interest is deductible because the inflationary premium is deductible. If interest is no longer deductible, this factor disappears and interest rates could fall as a result. There does not, however, seem to be much empirical evidence for increased interest rates because of the interaction of inflation and tax rates.

28 The Gordon and Slemrod (1988) results would suggest that the overall tax on capital does not decline substantially.

29 For evidence on this issue, see Feldstein and Horioka (1980), Frankel (1991), French and Poterba (1991), and Baxter and Crucini (1993), among many others.

30 Federal Reserve Board data show that credit market borrowing by corporate and noncorporate nonfinancial U.S. business was $3,885 billion at the end of 1994. Bank for International Settlements data give total net international financing in international markets at $5,830 billion at the end of 1994. Banks reported cross-border claims in dollars of $2,345 billion. Also, there were Eurobonds and notes in dollars at the end of 1994 equal to $915 billion. These cross-border holdings in dollars do not include foreign investments in dollar debt not included in bank claims or Eurobonds, e.g., private holdings of U.S. Treasury bonds or corporate bonds.

31 Huizinga's (forthcoming) evidence that banks pass on part of the benefits of home country credits for foreign withholding taxes on interest also suggests substantial mobility of debt capital flows.

32 For example, the prediction of Hall and Rabushka (1995) that interest rates would fall by a full 2 percentage points seems much too high.

33 This effect might be ameliorated if the nondeductibility of interest payments was converted to a withholding tax on interest and dividends, which might be creditable in the home country or could be relieved for foreigners by law or tax treaty. Alternatively, the adverse effect on debt flows would be avoided if all taxation of capital income was imposed at the personal level.

34 We know of no country that is a significant source of cross-border investment that exempts all foreign income. Most "exemption" countries exempt only foreign income from active businesses and not income from passive foreign investments. Some countries also exempt foreign income only from selected countries, e.g., countries with which they have a tax treaty or that are not considered tax havens. The associated rules create considerable complexity.

35 These are the Passive Foreign Investment Company rules and parts of the subpart F rules.

36 As noted previously, $(R + F)$-based consumption taxes do provide for interest deductibility, but because new borrowing is included in the tax base and repayments of debt deducted, the treatment of debt is equivalent in present value terms to interest nondeductibility.

37 There might be a need to adapt some of the provisions in the current tax code that serve as backstops for the transfer pricing rules, such as the foreign base company sales income provision of the subpart F rules.

38 Under the flat tax the financial services problem would be even narrower, because the wage component of the value of those services would be taxed.

39 See Sarkar and Zodrow (1993) for a review of some of the major transition problems.

40 The USA tax proposal contains transition rules to ameliorate this impact, but they add considerable complexity. In addition, estimates of large increases in savings from moving to a consumption tax are generally predicated on the lack of any transition rules. See, e.g., Auerbach and Kotlikoff (1987).

41 This transition impact could be moderated to the extent that the elimination of income taxes increased the after-tax yield to wealth holders. In this case, the initial transition losses in wealth are offset to a greater extent the longer the wealth holder can take advantage of the higher after-tax yields, i.e., the longer the period before the wealth is consumed. However, this moderating influence may be diminished by international capital flows, since any rise in domestic after-tax yields would be moderated by an inflow of foreign capital.

[42] It appears to us that the USA tax plan intends to retain these withholding taxes, but we could not determine whether that was the case under the Armey flat tax.

[43] The USA individual tax might be an exception, because receipts of dividends and interest are included in the tax base.

[44] Goulder, Shoven, and Whalley (1983) concluded that a consumption tax that increases U.S. welfare in a closed economy would decrease U.S. welfare when international capital mobility is taken into account. Their explanation is that the consumption tax leads to a large capital outflow and a loss to the United States of business-level taxes that would be collected by foreign countries. However, in contrast to the proposals analyzed here, they assume a savings deduction at the personal level combined with a corporate income tax that provides a foreign tax credit. As we have seen, a business-level consumption tax is likely to result in less equity investment abroad and less foreign tax being paid.

REFERENCES

Alliance USA. "Description and Explanation of the Unlimited Savings Allowance Income Tax System." *Tax Notes 66* No. 11 (March, 1995): 1483–575.

Altshuler, Rosanne and Jack Mintz. "U.S. Interest Allocation Rules: Effects and Policy." *International Tax and Public Finance 2* No. 1 (May, 1995): 7–35.

Auerbach, Alan and Laurence J. Kotlikoff. *Dynamic Fiscal Policy.* Cambridge: Cambridge University Press, 1987.

Baxter, Marianne and Mario Crucini. "Explaining Saving-Investment Correlations." *American Economic Review 83* No. 3 (June, 1993): 416–36.

Bradford, David F. *Untangling the Income Tax.* Cambridge, MA: Harvard University Press, 1986.

Dixit, Avinash. "Tax Policy in Open Economies." In *Handbook of Public Economics*, edited by Alan Auerbach and Martin Feldstein. Amsterdam: North-Holland, 1985.

Feldstein, Martin S. and Charles Y. Horioka. "Domestic Savings and International Capital Flows." *Economic Journal 90* (June, 1980): 314–29.

Feldstein, Martin and Paul Krugman. "International Trade Effects of Value-Added Taxation." In *Taxation in the Global Economy*, edited by Assaf Razin and Joel Slemrod, 263–78. Chicago: University of Chicago Press, 1990.

Frankel, Jeffrey A. "Quantifying International Capital Mobility in the 1980s." In *National Saving and Economic Performance*, edited by Douglas Bernheim and John Shoven. Chicago: University of Chicago Press, 1991.

French, Kenneth R. and James M. Poterba. "Investor Diversification and International Equity Markets." NBER Working Paper No. 3609. Cambridge, MA: National Bureau of Economic Research, 1991.

Froot, Kenneth A. and James R. Hines, Jr. "Interest Allocation Rules, Financing Patterns, and the Operations of U.S. Multinationals." In *The Effects of Taxation on Multinational Corporations*, edited by Martin Feldstein, James R. Hines, Jr., and R. Glenn Hubbard. Chicago: University of Chicago Press, 1995.

Gordon, Roger H. "Can Capital Income Taxes Survive in Open Economies?" *The Journal of Finance 47* No. 3 (July, 1992): 1159–80.

Gordon, Roger H. and Joel Slemrod. "Do We Collect Any Revenue from Taxing Capital Income?" In *Tax Policy and the Economy*, vol. 2, edited by Lawrence Summers. Cambridge, MA: The MIT Press, 1988.

Goulder, Lawrence H., John B. Shoven, and John Whalley. "Domestic Tax Policy and the Foreign Sector: The Importance of Alternative Foreign Sector Formulations to Results from a General Equilibrium Tax Analysis Model." In *Behavioral Simulation Methods in Tax Policy Analysis*, edited by Martin Feldstein, 333–64. Chicago: University of Chicago Press, 1983.

Grossman, Gene M. "Border Tax Adjustments: Do They Distort Trade?" *Journal of International Economics 10* (February, 1980): 117–28.

Grubert, Harry and John Mutti. "International Aspects of Corporate Tax Integration: The Contrasting Role of Debt and Equity Flows." *National Tax Journal 47* No. 1 (March, 1994): 111–33.

Grubert, Harry and John Mutti. "Taxing Multinationals in a World with Portfolio Flows and R&D: Is Capital Export Neutrality Obsolete?" *International Tax and Public Finance* (forthcoming, 1995).

Hall, Robert E. and Alvin Rabushka. *Low Tax, Simple, Tax, Flat Tax.* New York: McGraw-Hill, 1983.

Hall, Robert E. and Alvin Rabushka. *The Flat Tax.* Stanford: Hoover Institution Press, [1985], 1995.

Hartman, David. "Tax Policy and Foreign Direct Investment." *Journal of Public Economics 26* (February, 1985): 107–21.

Huizinga, Harry. "The Incidence of Interest Withholding Taxes: Evidence from the LDC

Loan Market." *Journal of Public Economics* (forthcoming).

Institute for Fiscal Studies. The Meade Committee Report. *The Structure and Reform of Direct Taxation*. London: Allen and Unwin, 1978.

McLure, Charles E. and George R. Zodrow. "Creditability of the Cash Flow Tax." Unpublished submission to the Treasury Department, October, 1994.

McLure, Charles E. and George R. Zodrow. "A Hybrid Approach to the Direct Taxation of Consumption." In *Proceedings of Frontiers of Tax Reform*. Washington, D.C.: Hoover Institution, 1995.

Merrill, Peter, Ken Wertz, and Shvetank Shah. "Corporate Tax Liability Under the USA and Flat Taxes." *Tax Notes 68* No. 6 (August 7, 1995): 741–5.

Sarkar, Shounak and George R. Zodrow. "Transitional Issues in Moving to a Direct Consumption Tax." *National Tax Journal 46* No. 3 (September, 1993): 359–76.

CHAPTER 3

THREADING THE FISCAL LABYRINTH: SOME ISSUES IN FISCAL DECENTRALIZATION

RICHARD M. BIRD*

Abstract - *Fiscal decentralization in many guises has become a central concern around the world. This paper discusses several aspects of this complex subject that have turned out to be important in policy work on the issue in a number of countries.*

First, I discuss briefly the meaning and rationale of fiscal decentralization. There is much that has to be disentangled before one can approach the issue in a particular policy setting, including distinguishing between the problems of federal finance and fiscal federalism.

Second, I review the issue of the choice of local revenue sources from the perspective of establishing efficient local governments, including the roles of user charges, property taxes, and income taxes.

Finally, I sketch some considerations with respect to the design of intergovernmental transfers from the same perspective, with particular emphasis on the desirability in many settings of transfers that are both conditional and equalizing.

INTRODUCTION

In recent years, there has been a worldwide revival of interest in fiscal decentralization. The so-called "countries in transi-

*University of Toronto, Toronto, Ontario, Canada.

tion" of eastern Europe, for example, are busily setting up new systems of local and intergovernmental finance (Bird and Wallich, 1993). Many developing countries are turning to various forms of fiscal decentralization as one way of escaping from the traps of ineffective and inefficient governance, macroeconomic instability, and inadequate economic growth in which so many of them have become mired in recent years.[1]

Similar, if less dramatic, pressures are at work in developed economies attempting to reshape their intergovernmental fiscal structure to be more in tune with the realities of the "postwelfare state" era (Bennett, 1990).[2] At one extreme, the threat of national disintegration has led Canadians to focus as never before on such traditional issues as tax assignment (Ip and Mintz, 1991) as well as on the broader political and economic aspects of federalism.[3] In Europe, new federal states are emerging (Spain, Belgium), and decentralization is being studied extensively even in such centralized countries as the United Kingdom and France (Bennett, 1990). The latest "new federalism" in the United States has resulted in increased attention to such concepts as fiscal competition (Kenyon and Kincaid, 1991) and fiscal equalization.[4]

Issues of fiscal decentralization, broadly conceived, are thus in the air everywhere—and, indeed, are already on the ground in many different guises in different parts of the world. Economic theorists are theorizing about fiscal decentralization, applied economists are attempting to pin it down in numbers, and policy economists are busily flying around the world dispensing advice about it.[5] But just what is meant by fiscal decentralization? What advice does the academic literature suggest should be given? And how does this advice relate to what is actually taking place in the real world?

Although I cannot answer such broad questions here, this paper is intended to provide some guidance to policy advisers and researchers who wish to find their way through the fiscal labyrinth of local and intergovernmental finance in any country. I focus on a few issues that have turned out to be important in my experience as a policy economist who has worked on various aspects of fiscal decentralization in a variety of different settings over the years.[6]

The paper is organized in three main sections. First, I discuss what fiscal decentralization is and why it is a matter of policy concern. Second, one critical decision invariably concerns the revenue-raising powers of local governments.[7] I consider briefly some factors affecting the choice of local revenues, with particular attention to the neglected case for user charges and the relative merits of local property and income taxes. Finally, in many ways, the design of transfer systems lies at the heart of central-local relations. I discuss several issues in transfer design in the last section, with particular emphasis on the case for conditional but equalizing transfers.

FISCAL DECENTRALIZATION: WHAT AND WHY

"Fiscal decentralization" seems often to mean whatever the person using the term wants it to mean. Broadly speaking, however, two quite different approaches may be taken to the concept. One views decentralization from the top down. The stimulus may be, for example, to make the life of the central government easier by shifting deficits (or at least some of the political pressures resulting from deficits) downward.[8] Or it may be a desire on the part of the central government to achieve its allocative goals more efficiently by delegating or decentralizing authority to local governments.[9] An additional goal may (or may not) be to increase the level of national welfare. In any case, this top-down approach suggests that the main criterion for evaluating fiscal decentralization should be how well it serves the presumed national policy objectives.

In contrast, the second approach to fiscal decentralization is from the bottom up. This approach stresses both political values—improved governance in the sense of local responsiveness and political participation, for example—and, again, allocative efficiency. Sometimes efficiency is explicitly defined in terms of improving welfare—the "decentralization theorem" of Oates (1972), for example, or the broader notion of increased scope for dynamic innovation that may be traced back to the Federalist papers. In other instances, such less individualistic concepts as "local autonomy" and "accountability" may be brought into play. Whatever the specifics of such "localist" arguments—and the variations are infinite, as Prud'homme (1991) and Dafflon (1992) emphasize in different ways—the appropriate criterion for evaluating fiscal decentralization differs sharply from that in the top-down approach.

A first problem in analyzing any aspect of fiscal decentralization in a specific setting is therefore to determine whether a "good" fiscal decentralization is one which better achieves the goals of the central government (or improves national welfare as a whole, if one prefers) or one which frees local governments most from central dictates (or, if one prefers, improves local welfare most). Decentralization may have many virtues: it may, for instance, improve accessibility, local responsibility, and the effectiveness of government. But it is not likely to produce exactly the expenditure pattern the central government would choose to implement except in the unlikely case that the goals of central and local government precisely coincide. In a heterogeneous society, as a rule, it is not possible for the central government to have its cake (decentralize decision-making to local governments) and eat it too (have the same decisions made). Conflicts between central and local governments as to what should be done are inevitable even if each government tries faithfully to serve the interests of its (different) constituents. A choice of perspective is thus essential in approaching issues of fiscal decentralization.

Federal Finance and Fiscal Federalism

Another way to approach the critical issue of whose preferences dominate is to distinguish between two varieties of fiscal decentralization, which may be loosely labeled federal finance and fiscal federalism.

In "federal finance," as I define it, jurisdictional boundaries and the assignment of functions and finances are basically taken as fixed at some earlier "constitutional" stage and not open to further discussion in normal circumstances. Moreover, the degree of fiscal and regulatory harmonization attained and, for that matter, the degree to which an internal common market exists are matters to be determined jointly by both levels of government in some appropriate political (constitutional) forum rather than simply assuming consensus on these goals exists (Bird, 1989). In addition, both levels of government may properly pursue their own distributive policies (Tresch, 1981), again with no presumption of central dominance. In this federal setting, intergovernmental transfers are often both

equalizing and unconditional, as, for example, Shah (1991) emphasizes. Finally, the appropriate analytical framework is essentially a bargaining situation between principals—what one Canadian author (Simeon, 1972) has called "federal-provincial diplomacy." In some countries (Canada, Switzerland), this may not be a bad description of federal-state relations (Dafflon, 1992; Bird, 1986). It is not, however, the world I want to discuss here.

That world is instead the traditional world of "fiscal federalism" or "multilevel finance," as set out by Oates (1972). In this framework, in principle, everything—boundaries, assignments, the level and nature of transfers, *etc.*—is up for grabs. Moreover, the central government's policy preferences are clearly dominant (in practice, if not so clearly in theory). The appropriate analytical framework in this setting is clearly a principal-agent model in which the principal (the central government) may alter jurisdictional boundaries, local government revenue and expenditure responsibilities, and intergovernmental fiscal arrangements in its attempt to overcome the familiar agency problems of information asymmetry and differing objectives between principal and agent.[10]

Of course, many qualifications might be introduced to soften or modify the dichotomy sketched earlier. For example, as political scientists emphasize, the central function of government is not simply to deliver services, as economists tend to stress, but also to manage conflict—and a central way in which governments everywhere manage conflict is through distributive policy. Indeed, a government, whether "local" or central, that is not concerned with distribution is not so much a government as a particular organizational structure for delivering certain services.

Nonetheless, partly in the interest of brevity and partly because I do not consider it critical in the fiscal federalism model (as interpreted here), the distributive aspect of local finances is not considered further in the present paper. In practice, the principal manifestation of distributional concern at the local level is often through the free provision of public services; a secondary aspect is concern for the distributional effect of local revenues. These two distributional factors combine perniciously to bias many against local user charges, as noted later. They also have long bedeviled discussion of local general taxes. Since my approach to the fiscal federalism model is, in essence, to view local governments as a firm (club), I set these aspects aside in order to concentrate on what I argue is the main, allocative task of local government: to give its constituents what they want and are willing to pay for. In addition, of course, as many have noted, the ability of small governments to effect distributional goals in an open economy is very limited.[11]

I emphasize—indeed, exaggerate—the contrast between these two quite different "models" of fiscal decentralization for two reasons. First, it is critical to distinguish these two broad approaches in principle because the implications for policy design that follow from them are very different, especially with respect to the design of intergovernmental transfers, as discussed later.[12] Second, in my judgement, except for central-state relations in a relatively few "truly federal" states, it is the second approach—fiscal federalism—that is the right way to analyze fiscal decentralization issues in most cases.[13]

Since almost all of the academic literature on decentralization already adopts this approach, this appears to be good news for the policy analyst. Unfortunately, in practice, that literature offers surprisingly little guidance to some of the key questions that arise with respect to fiscal decentralization. Economic analysis, like democratic theory, does provide a strong rationale for the establishment of local governments that are responsive to the wishes of their citizens instead of being simply the instrumentalities of central planners. People have different preferences for public services— some may be more concerned with good roads and others with good schools, for example. Moreover, many services (including roads and schools) are consumed in a spatially differentiated pattern. It seems to follow from these facts that the most efficient allocation of public sector resources can be secured only if such services are provided (and paid for) by governments responsive to those most directly affected.

Unfortunately, the apparent strength and simplicity of this conclusion dissipates quickly when other considerations, economic and political, are taken into account. The existence of benefit and cost "spillovers" from one jurisdiction to another, for example, suggests that larger governmental units are needed to internalize such externalities. Moreover, the unit cost of collecting revenues from most lucrative tax sources is much less for national than for local governments. On the other hand, as Buchanan and Tullock (1962) demonstrated, the cost of political decision-making (in terms of the nonsatisfaction of preferences) rises as the population covered expands. Little is known of most of the relevant magnitudes, but the extreme variation in the spatial dimension of virtually every governmental function and subfunction suggests that the "optimal" government structure is likely to be as complex in theory as it is in practice in most countries (Bird and Hartle, 1972).[14]

Even if theory provided a clearer guide to either the design of jurisdictional boundaries or the assignment of taxes and expenditures, the role played by local governments in practice in any country is, of course, primarily determined by the extent to which central governments choose, for reasons of administrative efficiency or political choice, to utilize such governments as taxing and, especially, spending agents. In this respect, perhaps the main practical guidance emerging from the theoretical literature may be argued to be the benefit model of local finance.[15]

The Benefit Model of Local Finance

The basic rule of efficient expenditure assignment is to assign each function to the lowest level of government consistent with its efficient performance. So long as there are local variations in tastes and costs, there are clearly efficiency gains from carrying out public sector activities in as decentralized a fashion as possible.[16] The only services that should be provided centrally are those for which there are no differences in demands in different localities, where there are substantial spillovers between jurisdictions that cannot be handled in some other way (e.g., by contracting or by grant design), or for which the additional costs of local administration are sufficiently higher to outweigh its advantages. In short, leaving aside the important distributive question, almost all public services (except national defence, foreign policy, and a surprisingly few others) should probably be delivered at the local level, with local decision makers deciding what services are provided, to whom, and in what quantity and quality and with local taxpayers paying for the services provided.[17]

In practice, although there are some functions (e.g., maintenance of streets) that are local everywhere, the allocation of functions to local governments varies considerably from country to country, with the principal differentiating factor apparently being the extent to which local governments are given an independent (as opposed to executing) role with respect to primary education.[18] Since the United States lies at one end of the spectrum in this respect, it is not surprising so much American discussion of local and intergovernmental finance is really about education finance.

In any case, the essential economic role of local government is to provide to local residents those public services for which they are willing to pay. Local governments must be accountable to their citizens for the actions they undertake at least to the extent those citizens finance those actions. Accountability is the public sector equivalent of the "bottom line" in the private sector. Accountability, in this sense, clearly requires that local governments should, whenever possible, charge for the services they provide, and, where charging is impracticable, they should finance such services from taxes borne by local residents except to the extent that the central government is, for reasons such as those mentioned previously, willing to pay for them. Where the central government does pay, local governments should be accountable to the central government to the extent the services they provide are financed by transfers. Public sector activities are unlikely to be provided efficiently unless the lines of responsibility and accountability are clearly established in these ways.

In principle, local governments should not only have access to those revenue sources that they are best equipped to exploit—such as residential property taxes and user charges for local services—but they should also be both encouraged and permitted to exploit these sources without undue central supervision. Unless local governments are given some degree of freedom with respect to local revenues, including the freedom to make mistakes (for which they are accountable to their citizens), the development of responsible and responsive local government will remain an unattainable mirage.

There are, of course, dangers in permitting local governments even limited freedom. One danger in the eyes of some is that they will not utilize fully all the revenue sources open to them, thus allowing the level and quality of public services to deteriorate below the standard considered desirable, at least by those who think this way. But this is not a real problem. If the service in question is one of national importance (*e.g.*, research) or one in which there is a strong national interest in maintaining standards (*e.g.*, poverty alleviation or some other distributional goal), it should be nationally funded at least in part and its achievement monitored. If it is not a matter of national interest, why should the national government be concerned? If the local electors do not like what their local government does, or does not do, they can (try to) throw the rascals out at the next election.[19] The freedom to make mistakes and to bear the consequences of one's mistakes is an important component of local autonomy.

Another danger, more salient from an economic perspective, is that local governments may attempt to extract revenues from sources for which they are not accountable, thus obviating the basic efficiency argument for their existence. "Tax exporting," like benefit spillovers, generally requires central intervention if local governments are to operate efficiently. Although some local taxation of business may, of course, be warranted on "benefit" grounds, as noted subsequently, it is thus often desirable to limit local government access to taxes that, in many instances, may be presumed to fall mainly on nonresidents, such as most natural resource levies, preretail stage sales taxes, and, to some extent, nonresidential real property taxes.[20]

LOCAL OWN-SOURCE REVENUES

User Charges

The first rule of local finance should be: "Wherever possible, charge." For efficiency, charges should be levied on the direct recipients of benefits, whether residents, businesses, or "things" (real property).

While user charges are likely to be viewed by hard-pressed local officials solely as a potential additional source of revenue, their main economic value is to promote economic efficiency by providing demand information to public sector suppliers and to ensure that what the local public sector supplies is valued at least at (marginal) cost by citizens. This efficiency objective is particularly important at the local government level, since the main economic rationale for local government in the first place in the perspective adopted here is to improve efficiency. Whenever possible, local public services should therefore be charged for—of course, at properly set prices (Bird, 1976)—rather than given away. Attempting to rectify fundamental distributional problems through inefficiently pricing scarce local resources is almost always a bad idea, resulting in little, if any, equity being purchased at a high price in efficiency terms.[21]

Although in most countries much less use is made of charging at the local level than seems desirable and many of the charges that are levied are poorly designed from an efficiency point of view, at least three types of local "charge" revenue exist almost everywhere: (1) service fees, (2) public prices, and (3) specific benefit charges.

By "service fees" I mean license fees (marriage, business, dog, vehicle) and various small charges levied by local governments essentially for performing specific services—registering this or providing a copy of that—for identifiable individuals. Charging people for something they are required by law to do may not always be sensible—for example, if the benefit of (say) registering births or deaths is general and the cost is specific—but, on the whole, there is seldom much harm, or much revenue, in thus recovering the cost of providing the service in question.

In contrast, by "public prices" I mean the revenues received by local governments from the sale of private goods and services (other than the cost reimbursement just described). In principle, prices of locally

provided services to identifiable private individuals—whether public utility charges or
admission charges to recreation facilities—
should be set at the competitive private
level, with no special tax or subsidy element included.[22]

A final category of charge revenue is "specific benefit taxes." Unlike service fees and
public prices, these revenues do not arise
from the provision or sale of a specific
good or service to an identifiable private
individual. Unlike "prices" which are voluntarily paid—although like "fees" which are
paid for services that may be required by
law—taxes represent compulsory contributions to local revenues. Nonetheless, specific benefit taxes are (at least in theory)
related in some way to benefits received
by the taxpayer. In contrast to such general benefit taxes as fuel taxes levied on
road users as a class or local taxes in general viewed as a price paid for local collective goods (discussed later), specific benefit
taxes relate to the specific benefits supposedly received by specific taxpayers.

Examples abound in local finance: special
assessments, land value increment taxes,
improvement taxes, front footage levies,
supplementary property taxes related to
the provision of sewers or streetlighting,
development exactions and charges, deline-
ation levies, and so on. Most such charges
are imposed either on the assessed value
of real property, changes in that value, or
some characteristic of that property (its
area, its frontage, its location).

The importance of all these forms of
charging is, in principle, much greater than
the relatively small amounts of money generally collected from this variegated group
of levies. To the extent that a local government is viewed primarily as a provider of
services, as was suggested previously, and
the benefits of those services can be attributed specifically to individual citizens, properties, or businesses (or small groups), the
appropriate policy is clearly to charge the

correct (roughly marginal cost) price. Only
thus will the correct amounts and types of
service be provided to the right people,
that is, those willing to pay for them.

As much as there is to be said for charging
for local services, however, experience to
date in most countries is not very encouraging. Even where the common philosophical objections to pricing in the public sector can be overcome, the prices charged
are seldom those needed for efficiency.
The potential for improved user charge finance as a means of financing local government thus remains more potential than
reality.[23] In practice, the most important
decisions in local government finance thus
inevitably concern the design and implementation of local taxes and intergovernmental transfers, the subjects of the balance of this paper.

What is a Local Tax?

In the first place, a "truly local" tax might
be defined as one that is (1) assessed by a
local government, (2) at rates decided by
that government, (3) collected by that government, and (4) whose proceeds accrue
to that government. In reality, however,
taxes often possess only one or two of
these characteristics.

For example, the proceeds of an income or
sales tax may accrue in whole or in part to
local governments, but tax rates are set by
the central government, which also as-
sesses and collects the tax. This situation is
common in many countries with so-called
"shared" taxes. In many ways, such a
shared tax is more like a central government grant allocated to local governments
either in proportion to the amount of central income tax collected locally or in accordance with some (centrally determined)
formula.

On the other hand, what looks like a central tax and a related transfer program may
really be a local tax. Some intergovernmental transfers, for example, in effect simply

return taxes to the regions in which they were collected in the first place. If the local government determines the tax base and rate and receives all the revenues, the only role the central government plays is as a collection agent, presumably because it has a comparative advantage in tax collection and the local government has contracted for its services in this respect. In this case, there is no intergovernmental transfer at all, except in the narrowest accounting sense.

While it is thus sometimes difficult to figure out just what are local taxes, it can be argued that the most important characteristic of a local tax is the freedom of the local government to determine the tax rate. Local governments may have large receipts from what appear to be local taxes, but if they can neither set the tax rate nor determine the tax base, it is difficult to see how they can be accountable to their consituents at the margin, as both democracy and efficiency require.

Characteristics of a Good Local Tax

The characteristics to be sought in an "ideal" local tax from the point of view of local and central governments are not necessarily compatible. A partial listing might include the following.

(1). The tax base should be immobile to allow local authorities some leeway in varying rates without the tax base vanishing.

(2). The tax yield should be adequate to meet local needs and sufficiently buoyant (*i.e.*, expand at least as fast as expenditures) over time.

(3). The tax yield should be stable and predictable over time.

(4). The tax should be perceived to be reasonably fair by taxpayers.

(5). The tax should be easy to administer efficiently and effectively.

(6). It should not be possible to export much, if any, of the tax burden to nonresidents.

(7). The tax base should be visible to ensure accountability.

Both levels of government may agree on the first five of these characteristics, but only the central government is likely to be concerned about the last two.

More generally, not everyone would agree that all these characteristics are necessarily desirable; *e.g.*, is it unequivocally good that local governments should be insulated from either the tax base consequences of their tax rate choices or from inflation (Oates, 1975)? In reality, since central governments set the rules and generally take the best-yielding taxes for their own use, as a rule, local governments are unlikely to have sufficient access to tax sources to free them from some dependence on transfers. Nonetheless, unless local governments have some degree of freedom to alter the level and composition of their revenues, neither "local autonomy" nor local accountability is a meaningful concept. In particular, as emphasized earlier, rate flexibility is essential if a tax is to be adequately responsive to local needs and decisions.

The Choice of Local Taxes

The purpose of local taxes is to finance locally provided collective public goods for local residents. If such goods are truly "public" in the sense of accruing equally to all residents of the jurisdiction *and* if redistribution to other than national standards is not an aim of local public policy *and* if administrative (and compliance) costs are left out of account, the best source of local revenue might perhaps be an equal per capita levy, such as the poll tax, which also has the virtue of being economically neutral or efficient in the sense of giving rise to no excess burden.

In practice, however, local poll taxes that differ from place to place are easy to evade by moving. Even those who do not flee may be hard to tax: the low efficiency costs of the poll tax seem likely to be purchased at the expense of high administrative and compliance costs (Smith, 1991). Moreover, since some residents—property-owners, people with school-age children, or whoever—benefit more than others from the provision of local public services, there may be reason for some local residents to pay more than others.

If the demand for local public services is income-elastic, a benefit case can be made for a local income tax or, more feasibly, given the high administrative costs of separate local income taxes, a local surcharge on the central income tax. If the enjoyment of such services is associated with consumption (rather than residence), a benefit case can similarly be made for a local tax on consumption, which would in practice almost certainly have to take the form of a retail sales tax. And, finally, if the benefits of local public services are enjoyed in proportion to the value of real property, there is obviously a case for a local property tax.

Local Property Taxes

In practice, the property tax remains the main source of revenue for local governments in a number of countries, particularly, of course, the English-speaking countries in which it has been well-established historically (Bird and Slack, 1991). Moreover, there are good reasons for taxing real property. A tax on real property may, for example, make good sense as part of the tax system as a whole: although relatively expensive to administer, in many ways, the property tax scores quite well in terms of both its efficiency and its equity aspects. Moreover, if levied at the local level, a property tax may, as noted earlier, serve as a good means of financing local public services.

Nonetheless, as experience in a number of countries has shown in recent years, there is often widespread resistance to property taxation. The recent poll tax ("community charge") fiasco in the United Kingdom, which, like the earlier "Proposition 13" movement in the United States, originated initially as a reaction to rising property taxes, illustrates the strength and political importance of the resistance to property taxes in some countries, as well as the fact that not all possible replacements are necessarily desirable, or desired! Dislike of the property tax (like the poll tax) seems to result in part from the visibility of the tax and in part from certain inherent problems in its administration.

Local taxes on real property are more visible than other taxes for several reasons. First, unlike the income tax, the property tax is not deducted at source but often has to be paid directly to the municipality by taxpayers in periodic lump-sum payments. Taxpayers who pay taxes directly to the government tend to be more aware of the size of their tax bill than those whose take-home pay is reduced by weekly or monthly tax deductions. The need to make periodic large payments may well add to the accountability and responsibility of local governments, but it also increases the sensitivity of taxpayers to even nominal increases in taxes.

Second, the inelasticity of the property tax has a similar effect. Since the base of this tax does not as a rule increase automatically over time, the periodic nominal increases in property tax bills needed to maintain real revenues when price levels rise require increased tax rates.[24] In terms of political accountability, this need to confront the people with the cost of government again represents a virtue of the property tax. Again, however, the downside is the heightened visibility of nominal tax increases and the accompanying political resistance.

Third, local property taxes, of course, finance such municipal services as roads, garbage collection, and (in some countries) education. The quantity and quality of these services (or their absence) is thus readily linked to the property tax. When potholes develop in their streets, taxpayers are understandably quick to question the taxes that supposedly finance street repair.[25] Once again, the very feature that makes the property tax a good source of local government revenue in principle makes it especially vulnerable to political resistance.

Other problems result from property tax administration. As a rule, property is supposed to be assessed on the basis of its market value, usually defined as the price struck between a willing buyer and a willing seller in an arm's length transaction. In reality, however, for both political and technical reasons, discrepancies usually arise between assessed values and market values within classes of property, between classes of property, and across municipalities. Since taxpayers can easily compare their property taxes with those of similar properties in their neighborhood, such discrepancies lead both to specific assessment appeals and to general pressure for tax relief.

In sum, experience suggests that there are at least two substantial constraints on the use of property taxes for local finance. First, although the administration of the tax can be improved, it is difficult to administer in a horizontally equitable fashion, particularly when prices are changing rapidly. It will therefore always be hard to levy very heavy taxation on this base. Indeed, international experience suggests that heavy reliance by local governments on the property tax means they will continue to be heavily dependent on intergovernmental grants to finance their activities (Bird and Slack, 1991).

Second, the temptation to indulge in politically painless but economically inefficient (from a national perspective) "tax exporting" means that some constraint should ideally be placed on local taxation of nonresidential property (Thirsk, 1982). While

there is much to be said for local taxes on residential property, there is little case for allowing local governments a free hand in taxing business, whether such taxes take the form of the nonresidential property tax, corporate income taxes, or local "business" taxes based on gross sales, type of business activity, or other indicators. Some such levies may, of course, be justified on benefit (efficiency) grounds—as well as, more arguably, on "entitlement" grounds (Musgrave, 1983)—but they should always be strictly constrained in order to preclude localities from attempting to shift the costs of services to outsiders.

Local Income Taxes

The principal alternative (or supplement) to property taxes is some form of local income tax, generally levied as a supplement to national income taxes.[26] Since property taxes can only be pushed so far, if more local "own-source" revenue is desired— either to expand the size of local activities or to make local governments more self-reliant— there is much to be said for supplementary ("piggybacked") local income taxes. Indeed, if a country wants its local governments to be *both* large spenders *and* less dependent on grants, it must, it appears, provide them with access to the personal income tax, probably in the form of locally established surcharges on the national income tax (or, if a different degree of progressivity is desired, local rates on the national tax base).

Like the property tax, such a tax would be visible and, hence, in principle satisfy the criteria of political responsibility and accountability.[27] However, the fact that income tax revenues tend to grow with less political fuss, while presumably good news for local officials, suggests that in practice increased reliance on local income taxes should be viewed with mixed feelings. On the other hand, since an income tax is usually perceived as more progressive than a property tax, it scores higher than the latter on equity grounds—although, as emphasized earlier, the relevance of this in the local context is arguable.

The principal argument against local income taxation is administrative, but a properly designed "piggyback" system can readily handle this problem. Most of the other arguments raised against such taxes have no merit. For example, contentions that local income taxes necessarily induce inefficient fiscal competition or inefficient resource allocation are at best incomplete and in general misleading. In line with the benefit model of local government, local taxes simply constitute the price of local public services and (provided they are not exported) have no adverse effects on resource allocation or on fiscal competition. On the contrary, their allocative effects are desirable, as is the competition they may induce in lower cost provision of desired public services.[28] If the functions local governments are supposed to carry out are important and the case for financing them from local taxes strong, international experience suggests strongly that local income taxes are the most promising source of local finance (Bird and Slack, 1991).

THE DESIGN OF INTERGOVERNMENTAL TRANSFERS

Almost irrespective of local revenue sources, transfers between central and local governments are an important feature of the public finances of many countries. A well-designed system of intergovernmental transfers is thus essential to any decentralization strategy. Unfortunately, the traditional literature on fiscal federalism (Oates, 1972), which emphasizes interjurisdictional externalities, both fails to explain most of the transfers found in the real world and makes impossible informational demands.[29]

No simple, uniform pattern of transfers will be suitable for all circumstances. Since one size will not fit all, the first task of the fiscal tailor is to know as much as possible

about his client. As tailors know, for example, one should not place much credence in promises to lose weight—or, in this case, reduce expenditures!

In particular, since transfers reflect closely the nature of a country's political system, their inherently political nature must be taken into account without being hamstrung by it. One way to do so is simple, if somewhat artificial: focus on the *effects* rather than on the *instruments* used to achieve them. In this perspective, transfers as such are neither good nor bad: what matters are their effects on such policy outcomes as allocative efficiency, distributional equity, and macroeconomic stability. If, for example, the sole objective of fiscal decentralization is the efficient delivery of public services, as I suggest should be the initial assumption of economic analysts (other than in federal finance settings), all that matters is how transfers affect the effectiveness and efficiency of public sector operations.

What is critical about intergovernmental transfers is thus not who gives them, or who gets them, or what the details of program design are, but solely their effects on policy objectives.[30] The idea is thus simply to "get the prices right" in the public sector in the sense of making local governments accountable to their citizens for the actions they undertake, to the extent those citizens finance those actions, and to taxpayers in general, to the extent the finance comes from transfers.[31] This focus on results suggests some significant characteristics that desirable transfer programs are likely to possess whatever the context. In terms of process, for example, good transfers should be both transparent and predictable and should also accommodate the diversity of the country in question.

Since local governments should be accountable to the central government to the extent they are financed by transfers, in this model, there is no role for completely unconditional transfers.[32] As argued earlier, this principal-agent framework (as opposed to a local autonomy model) seems to describe the reality of central-local fiscal relations in most nonfederal countries and state-local relations even in federal countries. Local governments can and should make decisions on such matters as bus routes and when and how often the garbage is collected, but they should not, if education and health are matters of national interest, be free to decide (with central funds) who gets educated or whether local health care centers should be provided even if such functions are, for efficiency or other reasons, carried out at the local level.

The implications of this approach for the design of transfers may be further illustrated by considering the basic tasks assigned to transfers in most fiscal systems: closing the fiscal gap, equalization, pricing externalities, stretching the central budget, and achieving political objectives.

Closing the Fiscal Gap

As a rule, transfers constitute the principal way in which countries achieve what is sometimes called "vertical fiscal balance," that is, ensure that the revenues and expenditures of each level of government are approximately equal. For various reasons, both economic and political, central governments usually have much greater revenue-raising capacity than do local governments. Intergovernmental transfers are one mechanism by which some of the revenues accruing to the center are transferred to finance the deficits of lower levels of government.[33]

Although all transfers from higher level to lower level governments help close the fiscal gap, it is useful to consider vertical fiscal balance in an accounting sense as achieved when expenditures and revenues (including transfers) are balanced for the *richest* local government, measured in terms of its capacity to raise resources on

its own.[34] Fiscal gaps will still remain for all poorer local governments, but such "gaps" are better considered in relation to the problem of achieving *horizontal* fiscal balance (within the local government sector).

Equalization

Horizontal fiscal balance or equalization, as it is usually called, is controversial not least because, like decentralization itself, it is a concept with many different interpretations. For example, if horizontal fiscal balance is interpreted in the same "gap-filling" sense as vertical fiscal balance, what is implied is that sufficient transfers are needed to equalize revenues (including transfers) and the *actual* expenditures of each local government.

Such "fiscal dentistry" makes no sense, however. Equalizing the actual outlays of local governments in per capita terms (*i.e.*, raising all to the level of the richest local government), like making up all gaps between actual outlays and actual own-source revenues for all local governments, ignores differences in local preferences. Moreover, from the perspective of the central government, such equalization ignores local differences in needs, in costs, and in own revenue-raising capacity. Finally, equalizing actual outlays discourages both local revenue-raising effort and local expenditure restraint, since, under this system, those with the highest expenditures and the lowest taxes get the largest transfers.

For these reasons, in all countries with formal systems of equalization transfers (for example, all developed country federations apart from the United States), the aim is either to equalize the *capacity* of local governments to provide a certain level of public services or to equalize the actual *performance* of this level of service by local governments. The performance criterion, which adjusts the transfer received in accordance with the *need* for the aided service (and which may also allow for cost differentials), is generally more attractive to central governments: the level of service funded is determined centrally, and the transfer can be made conditional on the provision of that level of service. Unfortunately, unless an adjustment is made for differential fiscal capacity, that government which tries least again gets most.

Capacity equalization aims to provide each local government with sufficient funds (own-source revenues plus transfers) to deliver a (centrally) predetermined level of services.[35] Because transfers are based on measures of *potential* revenue-raising capacity (such as taxable assessed values equalized to adjust for differences in the ratio of assessed to market values in different localities, or the so-called "representative tax system"[36]) and not on actual revenues, in principle, no disincentive to fiscal effort is created.

On the other hand, only if the standard revenue-raising capacity which the grant is intended to provide is set at the level of the richest local government will full horizontal fiscal balance (full equalization), as defined earlier in the sense of closing all gaps, be achieved. For any lower standard, such as the average revenue-raising capacity of local governments, the disabilities of below-average localities relative to those that are above average will obviously remain.[37]

In this framework, the basic case for an equalization transfer is twofold. First, as argued in Feldstein (1975) and the next section, such a transfer may be needed to enable poorer local governments to respond efficiently to central transfers intended to generate the correct level of externalities. Second, it may also be needed to enable local governments, acting as agents of the central government, to provide an adequate "minimum bundle" of public services to citizens. Such transfers should, of course, not be unconditional but should rather be conditioned on both capacity *and*

performance, in the sense of actually providing the specified package of services.[38] Both the incorporation of an appropriate measure of capacity in any general transfer formula and the implementation of an adequate central government system for monitoring local government performance are therefore essential to effective fiscal decentralization in this framework.[39]

Getting Intergovernmental Prices Right

The transfer rationale with the strongest basis in the economic literature is that the local activity in question may spill over to other jurisdictions. The correct matching rate is, in this approach, set by the size of the spillovers. Basically, a matching grant program designed to encourage the optimal provision of public services should therefore vary primarily with the nature of the activity, that is, depending on the level of associated externalities.

Since, however, no country has achieved full equalization of local fiscal capacities, a uniform matching level offering the same price to all local governments will yield nonuniform responses in rich and poor localities (Feldstein, 1975). Even if revenue bases are fully equalized, need or cost differentials may require an equalization element in matching grant formulas. For example, per capita grants for roads in sparsely populated and mountainous regions may be larger (as in Switzerland, for example), because the per capita cost of achieving any particular standard of road service will obviously be higher.

The basic problem with the spillover approach to the design of matching grants, however, lies not in such concerns but in the simple fact that no one, anywhere, seems to have a good idea of the magnitude of spillovers associated with particular services. Indeed, there are few aspects of local government finance that seem more likely to repay careful empirical research. At present, the spillover argument appears to provide at most a rationale for central government support of some local expenditures: it almost never indicates *how much* support is needed, and a priori the required matching ratios found in practice (*e.g.*, 10–20 percent) as a rule seem likely to be far too low for allocative efficiency.

Stretching the Central Budget

A quite different rationale for matching grants arises from the simple existence of a central government budget constraint.[40] To maximize expenditure on any service, the optimal way to allocate a given total transfer among localities is inversely related to the price elasticity of local demand for the service (assuming no cross-price elasticity effects). In practice, however, it is almost as difficult to estimate the relevant price elasticities as to measure spillovers. All transfers have income effects, and all grants for specific activities have price effects, but in reality we have little idea of the size of either the income or the price elasticities of demand for local public goods.[41]

Nevertheless, as implied earlier (Feldstein, 1975), it may often be useful for matching grants to be inversely correlated to the income level of the recipient government. This approach differs from the general equalization argument discussed earlier for three reasons: (1) specific services are designated, perhaps because they are thought to entail spillovers or perhaps because they are considered especially meritorious; (2) the specific level of service to be provided is also established; and (3) the payment of the grant is conditioned on that level of the specified services in fact being provided. The higher the income elasticity, the higher the matching rate needed for low-income recipients (to offset the higher local expenditures on the aided service in higher income areas). The higher the price elasticity, the lower the matching rate needed to achieve a given level of total expenditures. In practice, this analysis yields a case for varying the matching rate inversely with in-

come levels even when only the allocative effects (and not the distributional effects) of matching grants are considered.[42]

The matching rate for each program may be thought of as having two components. The basic matching rate for each service reflects the degree of central government interest in the provision of that service (whether that interest is motivated by concern over spillovers, the "merit good" nature of the activity, or simply the desire to implement some plan). This basic rate could then be increased inversely to a uniformly determined measure of fiscal capacity.[43] The matching rate faced by any particular locality for any particular program would then be higher the greater the degree of central interest and the lower the (expected) degree of local enthusiasm (price-elasticity) and ability (income-elasticity) to support that program. The exact structure of the final formula for any service could likely be determined only after a period—perhaps a prolonged period—of trial and error, of observing the results of formulas, such as those now in place, and adjusting them as necessary to approximate more closely to the (centrally) desired outcomes. Unfortunately, nowhere in the world does there appear to be evidence of such an iterative approach at work nor is there much evidence anywhere of research that is helpful in designing matching rates.[44]

Achieving Political Goals

Finally, even the purest analyst of intergovernmental fiscal relations must deal with the reality of political transfers. It may be necessary, for example, to transfer some resources to jurisdictions that do not, strictly speaking, need them in order to make it politically feasible to transfer needed amounts to other jurisdictions.[45] It may also be essential to transfer resources simply in order to keep some economically nonviable local governments alive for political reasons—to salvage regional pride, to provide jobs for local supporters, or for some other reason.[46]

From an economic perspective, what is important is minimizing any collateral damage in the course of achieving the political ends of transfers. For example, transfers that simply finance local deficits or that are entirely discretionary in nature are invariably bad from the perspective taken here.

On the other hand, it may be quite sensible for central governments in effect to make individual contracts with particular local governments—though preferably for a period of years rather than on an annual basis and preferably in an open and agreed fashion. Given the diversity of many countries and the usual political necessity to have nominally uniform laws, only such a contract approach may be able to provide the necessarily nonuniform terms needed to secure the desired outcomes at least cost. The design and limits of such "asymmetrical fiscal federalism" have, unfortunately, so far received little attention. In any case, as with the design of governments, an optimal system of transfers might appear on the surface to be as complex, diverse, and apparently arbitrary as the transfers that actually exist in many countries. But the complexity and diversity would almost certainly be quite different in character from that found in practice, and the system would be both more transparent and predictable.

Conclusions

In this paper I have covered so much ground so rapidly, and to some extent in such a cavalier fashion, that it may be useful to conclude by recapitulating briefly the main points I have tried to make. The first point is simply that it is critical to understand clearly the objectives and context of fiscal decentralization in any country before analyzing any component of the process. I assume here that, in the usual (nonfederal) case, the primary objective is to improve efficiency and that the appropriate perspective to adopt is that of the central government. In reality, of course, other objectives, and other perspectives, are often relevant and need to be taken into account. Nonetheless, I would argue that the more or less standard economic approach suggested here is still likely to provide the best starting point in most cases.

Given this starting point, I then limit the discussion to two of the principal public finance problems that invariably come up when fiscal decentralization is discussed— assigning local revenues and designing intergovernmental transfers. From the efficiency perspective, I argue that local revenues should clearly be as benefit-related as possible. To the extent local public services can be financed from user charges and specific benefit taxes, they should be. Moreover, local general taxes should also be considered primarily from a benefit perspective. Property taxes have some attractions from this perspective, but local income taxes levied in the form of proportional surcharges on central taxes look even better in many instances, subject in both cases to limits on the ability of local governments to export tax burdens (unmatched by benefits) to nonresidents.

As for intergovernmental transfers, I argue that not only are such transfers almost invariably necessary in practice if local governments are responsible for significant expenditures but that a good case can generally be made for some degree of capacity equalization. On the other hand, I suggest that (apart from the federal case which is not discussed here) such transfers should always be conditioned on local expenditure performance.

Finally, I should stress two important caveats. The first is simply to emphasize that, even with all the footnotes and asides, many issues and qualifications that may be critical in particular circumstances have not been adequately discussed here. I have attempted only to sketch one possible way into, and out of, the intergovernmental fiscal labyrinth that has proven helpful in practice in a number of very different circumstances. Mapping the entire maze in any country, let alone in more general terms, must be left for those who view these problems from a superior perspective to that available in the trenches.

Such mapmaking is the essential role of economic theory, and much of what I have said is, of course, based in large part on the work of the many fine theorists who have worked on these issues. Nonetheless, the second caveat I would like to emphasize is simply that there are few issues in fiscal practice which require more specific institutional knowledge than those related to fiscal federalism. The approach I have suggested—define a single clear objective (efficiency from a national perspective) and cling tightly to the thread of the benefit model—is, I think, often a useful one. But exactly what this approach implies in any particular setting is something that can be decided only on the basis of close study of the local terrain and careful exploration on the ground. In this, as in so many other areas of public economics, what we seem to need at the moment is less more imaginative sketches of what may (or should) exist than more careful reporting and analysis of what does exist and how it works.

ENDNOTES

I am grateful to the World Bank for a period as a Research Fellow that led me to think about this subject and to the late (and much missed) Dan Holland and the Morris Beck Award for providing the occasion to write this paper. I am also grateful for helpful comments on earlier drafts from William Dillinger, Ned Gramlich, and Joel Slemrod and to many colleagues—including Amaresh Bagchi, John Bossons, the late John Graham, Ken Messere, Richard Musgrave, Guillermo Perry, Govinda Rao, Anwar Shah, Enid Slack, Christine Wallich, Eduardo Wiesner, and Heng-fu Zou—for useful discussions on some of these points. Naturally, none of those named is in any way responsible for what I have written.

[1] See Bahl and Linn (1992) and Shah (1991) for examples.

[2] For other recent collections of papers on this topic, see Prud'homme (1991) and Owens and Panella (1991).

[3] See Boadway (1992), Fallis (1992), and Boadway et al. (1991).

[4] See, for example, Ladd and Yinger (1989) and Downes and Pogue (1992). In addition, there has been considerable interest recently at the supranational level in tax harmonization (Kopits, 1992) as well as in a wider range of traditional fiscal federalism issues (Walsh, 1992). Such concerns are most obvious in the European Community but also arise to some extent within such nascent regional groupings as NAFTA. Discussion of such issues, however, would take me well beyond what can be attempted here.

[5] See Inman (1989) and Oakland (1992) for two recent samplers of theoretical and empirical work in the United States. For a more international view, see Prud'homme (1991), which also contains some examples of the sort of policy advice being dispensed by the profession; on the latter, see also the various papers in Bennett (1991) and Owens and Panella (1991).

[6] Many of the issues that are prominent in the theoretical literature have either never come up in (my) practice or, if they have, are not sufficiently resolved in the literature to provide useful guidance. For this reason, some important topics (such as the Club and Tiebout models) that dominate other surveys of this area are not discussed here. For useful reviews of much of the relevant theoretical literature, see Wildasin (1986) and Rubinfeld (1987); see also Oates (1990, 1991).

For those interested, much of the experience on which I draw has been set out in more detail in other works: see, for example, on developed countries—Bird (1986) and Bird and Slack (1991, 1993); on developing countries—Bird (1980, 1984, 1990); and on the countries in transition—Bird and Wallich (1993).

[7] Where applicable—a point discussed briefly in the following section on federal finance and fiscal federalism—"local" is to be read throughout as encompassing "state and local". Similarly, "central-local" may sometimes refer to "central-state" (in what I call the "fiscal federalism" model) as well as to "state-local."

[8] As Gramlich (1987) argues, there may sometimes be a useful stabilization role for at least some larger subnational governments. Although this point cannot be further discussed here, experience from Argentina to Russia suggests that it would indeed be useful to pay much closer attention to the stabilization implications of multilevel finance under a wide variety of economic and institutional conditions.

[9] "Delegation" refers to a situation in which local governments act as direct agents for the center in executing certain functions on its behalf, in contrast to "decentralization" in which both implementation authority and at least some say in what is done are transferred to local governments. In both cases, but especially of course in the latter, there are obvious principal-agent problems. Both these concepts should be distinguished from "deconcentration," which refers solely to the dispersion of responsibilities within the central government structure to regional branch offices.

[10] For a recent example of the application of agency theory to fiscal decentralization, see Ferris and Winkler (1991).

[11] Note that locally determined distributive policy may as well act against as in support of centrally determined policy. As Tresch (1981) and Boadway and Flatters (1982) have emphasized in different ways, it is a moot question "who comes first (or last)" in this sequence of decision-making. The assumption here, however, is that, while this question is very real in the "federal finance" model, it does not have to be answered in (my version of) the "fiscal federalism" model, because there is only central distributive policy.

Of course, it may prove to be administratively or otherwise convenient for local governments to act as agents implementing centrally determined distribution policies, including those related to subsidized distribution of particular services. But when they do so, as argued subsequently, their provision of such services should be both monitored and (largely) financed by the central government.

[12] For a related argument with respect to tax harmonization, see Bird (1984a) and (1989); incidentally, the latter paper also attempts to distinguish more clearly between political unions (federations) and economic unions (*e.g.*, common markets).

[13] Bird (1986) sets out at length my views on how to analyze the federal finance case, including an argument that the United States is considerably less federal (as I define it) than such countries as Canada and Switzerland.

[14] Of course, the complexity found in practice is most unlikely to resemble that suggested by theory. Bird and Slack (1993), for example, discuss the very limited role theoretical and empirical research have played in the extensive restructuring of local government in Canada in recent years. See also Skaburskis (1992) for a political scientist's view of this restructuring.

[15] See Break (1992) for a recent view of the benefit and ability models and Break (1980) for an earlier treatment. As I have argued elsewhere (*e.g.*, Bird (1980)), the actual distributive effects of local policies, intended or otherwise, may of course be relevant from the point of view of the central government (as from the—different—point of view of the local government). My point here, however, is that the benefit model provides a much more useful guide to the issues of fiscal decentralization than the ability model, which both focuses solely on distributive concerns and completely neglects the critical connection in the local context between expenditures and revenues.

[16] Many local public facilities—fire protection, parks, *etc.*—provide differential "tapering" benefits to residents located at different distances from the facility. The precise location of facilities within a local jurisdiction may thus be important from the point of view of both efficiency and "spatial equity" (Truelove, 1993). This question cannot be further discussed here, however.

[17] Since the efficiency benefits of decentralized service provision may, of course, be realized by a sufficiently discriminating central government, the case for local decision-making from this perspective rests largely on the argument that it is less costly for local than for central authorities to obtain and act on the necessary information concerning local preferences.

[18] In countries with important intermediate (state) governments, the range of functions assigned to these governments is much wider. Many such countries are, of course, formally federal, although relatively few appear to be "truly federal" in the sense discussed briefly earlier. In any case, the role of intermediate governments is yet another addition to the long list of important questions that cannot be further discussed here.

[19] Of course, unhappy citizens could also migrate, a la Tiebout (1956), to someplace they like better. On the whole, however, emphasizing the "voice" (vote) option seems more appropriate in the accountability framework suggested here. Changing residence is not like changing toothpaste or car models: the costs are much greater, and it seems more sensible to consider moving as a last-ditch option that will be exercised only after (possibly repeated) electoral defeat.

[20] One way to deal with this problem to some extent may be to establish a uniform set of tax bases for local governments (perhaps different for different categories, such as big cities, small towns, and rural areas), with a limited amount of rate flexibility being permitted in order to provide room for local effort while restraining unproductive competition and unwarranted exploitation.

My colleague John Bossons has suggested another interesting approach to this problem: establish a band of say ±10 percent of the national average effective rate on (say) nonresidential property and allow free deviation within this band while inducing initial outliers to move to the accepted range by imposing penalties equal to the revenue gains (or losses) represented by their "excess" deviation. Of course, much more work is needed on this and other ways of, as it were, supporting local government cartels, assuming it is considered desirable to do so.

[21] For an extended treatment of pricing public services, see Bird (1976). Despite what is assumed in the present paper, distributive concerns are always so important in practice that more research is definitely needed on the incidence of alternative systems of charging (or otherwise financing) local services.

[22] Of course, there are many qualifications (*e.g.*, optimal departures from marginal-cost pricing) that need to be taken into account in practice: for extensive discussion of local service pricing in various areas, see Mushkin (1971), Bird (1976), and Bailey (1988).

[23] For an example, see the analysis of development charges in Canada in Slack and Bird (1991).

[24] In a few countries that have suffered high inflation, mainly in Latin America, assessed values are adjusted periodically by some price index, but this is the exception. The general rule is that the property tax base, unlike the income or sales tax base, is increased only when deliberate administrative action is taken to increase it.

Moreover, as noted subsequently, since the property tax base, unlike the income or sales tax base, is determined administratively in the first place (*i.e.*, not based on observed market transactions), it is inherently more arbitrary and hence subject to challenge—and the changes needed to cope with inflation invariably provoke such challenges.

25 The link between spatially specific local services (roads, streetlighting, *etc.*) and taxes is not nearly so strong for local sales or income tax. I pay the taxes on my house, and I expect the street in front of my house to be adequately constructed and maintained. The linkage between street maintenance and the extra 5 percent I pay at the local shopping mall, or a larger payroll deduction, is much more tenuous.

26 As mentioned earlier, any local sales tax would have to be a retail sales tax. In most countries other than the United States, there is an important national sales tax which is not levied solely at the retail level. No one has yet satisfactorily resolved the political and technical problems of either levying a retail sales tax at one level and a value-added tax at another (as Canada now does) or permitting both levels of government to tax value-added (as in Brazil). For this reason, I focus here solely on local income taxes. Incidentally, the much-discussed European Community experience is, of course, quite different: what is at issue there is the coordination of VATs among jurisdictions at the same level, not the coordination of VATs at different levels.

27 This assumes the local income tax applies to local residents only. There may, of course, be a limited case on benefit or possibly "entitlement" grounds for taxing non-resident workers as well, but any such tax should presumably be confined to a low-rate payroll levy to avoid undue tax exporting. Again, this interesting subject cannot be further discussed here.

28 Of course, there is much more to be said, both pro and con, about fiscal competition; see, for example, Kenyon and Kincaid (1991).

29 The same is true of the related, but not identical, literature on the actual financial arrangements found in federal states (Bird, 1986), which also does not explain much of reality.

30 An implication of focusing on allocative efficiency as the relevant policy objective is that jurisdictional (or place, or regional) equity is irrelevant to the design of intergovernmental transfers except as noted subsequently. Transfers are thus not judged on how or whether they contribute to such inherently vague aims as restoring regional balance or alleviating regional disparities.

Whether one accepts this perspective or not, it is often essential to put arguments on regional equity as much aside in practice as possible for at least two reasons. First, little is known about the relation between regional transfers and regional growth in any case. Second, taking a position on regional matters is invariably a recipe for political controversy in any country.

31 This argument implicitly assumes some degree of local democracy in the sense that local citizens should also determine what services they get (and have to pay for, at least at the margin)—an implication that is also consistent with allocative efficiency—but this important question is not further discussed here. Of course, accountability in this sense is not necessarily easy to achieve in practice, as demonstrated by the abortive British poll tax (Smith, 1991).

32 In what may be called "truly federal" (as distinct from formally federal) countries, where the traditional political arguments for equalization transfers to foster nationhood and federation are important (Courchene, 1984), such transfers should properly be unconditional (Shah, 1991). There appears to be no reason, however, to treat local governments as "sovereign" (autonomous) in the same way as states in such a federal system.

33 Of course, such fiscal gaps may also be closed, and vertical fiscal balance restored, by transferring revenue-raising power to local governments, by transferring responsibility for expenditures to the central government, or by reducing local expenditures or raising local revenues. In all countries, however, there invariably remains sufficient mismatch in the revenues and expenditures assigned to different levels of government—even if both are assigned solely on efficiency grounds—for an important balancing role to be assigned to intergovernmental fiscal transfers.

34 The more usual approach is to treat the subnational level as a whole when analyzing vertical balance; see, for example, Hunter (1977) and, for a considerably more sophisticated approach, Hettich and Winer (1986).

35 Differentials in the cost of providing services may or may not be taken into account. Note that it is important to distinguish fiscal capacity equalization (among jurisdictions) from considerations of horizontal equity (among individuals): the two are not necessarily connected. The discussion here concerns only the former. For discussion of an efficiency argument for equalization (in the sense of horizontal equity among individuals rather than capacity equalization among jurisdictions) that does not fit within the framework adopted here, see Boadway and Flatters (1982) and Musgrave and Musgrave (1993).

36 Originally developed under the auspices of the ACIR (1962), this approach has for 35 years been the foundation of the extensive Canadian federal-provincial equalization system (Boadway, 1980) although not without criticism (Courchene, 1984; Bird and Slack, 1990).

37 The only exception is when the positive transfers required to bring those below the average up to the average are financed by negative transfers from those above the average (as in the *finanzausgleich* of Germany and the similar system in Denmark). More generally, the effects of any grant system are obviously determined in part by how the grants are financed (Musgrave, 1961), but this important question cannot be discussed further here.

38 Such services could, of course, also be provided centrally, but it is assumed here that it has been determined to be administratively or politically advisable to provide them at the local level.

39 On the other hand, it is probably not advisable to include explicit measures of fiscal effort in such formulas for a number of reasons. First, the measurement of fiscal effort

is considerably more complex than usually seems to be realized (Bird and Slack, 1990). If, for instance, tax bases are sensitive to tax rates, then the usual measures overestimate capacity in low tax-rate areas (and hence underestimate the effort needed to increase tax rates) because the base will decline if the rate is increased. Second, putting too much weight on fiscal effort in allocating grants unduly penalizes poorer areas, where, by definition, a given percentage increase in effort (as usually measured) is more difficult to achieve (Bird, 1976a). The problem giving rise to the need for equalization in the first place is that the capacity (tax base) of poor areas is too low not that their tax rates are too low. Imposing an additional penalty on poor localities in a transfer program that almost invariably falls far short of equalizing fiscal capacity seems hard to justify. Third, including actual tax rates in the formula undesirably opens it to gaming by recipients (Courchene, 1984).

40 Gramlich (1977, p. 222) presents an argument along roughly these lines as a possible explanation for the surprising prevalence of closed-end conditional grants in the United States.

41 The elasticity estimates obtained in empirical studies are generally critically dependent on the models used. Moreover, it is still the case that most such estimates found in the literature are based on the median voter model, which leaves out of account both the fact that governments do more than one thing at a time and the entire supply (political-bureaucratic) side of the public sector. This is one area, however, in which substantial progress is being made, especially in the United States; in addition to some of the studies in Inman (1989) and Oakland (1992), see, for example, Renaud and van Winden (1990).

42 The same arguments apply if local governments are viewed as agents of the central government in carrying out particular activities, whether the level of such activities is the same or different in different localities.

43 Capacity is preferable to income in this context for two reasons. First, as discussed earlier, what is relevant is the ability of the local government to raise local revenues from local citizens, which may be only loosely related to (for example) per capita income. Second, as also discussed earlier, it is important to distinguish the equalization role of intergovernmental transfers from purely distributional goals, which should presumably be focused on people not places. Unfortunately, while the work of Ladd and Yinger (1989) and others has done much to improve measures of fiscal capacity in the U.S. context, elsewhere, similar studies are sadly lacking.

44 On the contrary, what evidence there is suggests that the equalization elements found in many transfer formulas reflect more political than economic concerns; see, for instance, the discussion of Switzerland in Bird (1986).

45 In analogy to social security which, to some extent, transfers unneeded amounts to the well-off in order to make needed transfers to the poor politically acceptable, this may perhaps be labeled the social security argument for transfers.

46 Bird (1984) labels this rationale for municipal grants in Colombia the "survival of the unfittest."

REFERENCES

Advisory Commission on Intergovernmental Relations. *Measures of State and Local Fiscal Capacity and Tax Effort.* Washington, D.C.: Government Printing Office, 1962.

Bahl, Roy W. and Johannes Linn. *Urban Public Finance in Developing Countries.* New York: Oxford University Press, 1992.

Bailey, S.J. *Practical Charging Policies for Local Government.* London: Public Finance Foundation, 1988.

Bennett, Robert J., ed. *Decentralization, Local Governments and Markets: Towards a Post-Welfare Agenda.* Oxford: Clarendon Press, 1990.

Bird, Richard M. *Charging for Public Services: A New Look at an Old Idea.* Toronto: Canadian Tax Foundation, 1976.

———. "Assessing Tax Performance in Developing Countries: a Critical Review of the Literature." *Finanzarchiv 34* (1976a): 234–55.

———. *Central-Local Fiscal Relations and the Provision of Urban Public Services.* Canberra: Australian National University Press for the Centre for Research on Federal Financial Relations, 1980.

———. *Intergovernmental Finance in Colombia.* Cambridge: Harvard Law School International Tax Program, 1984

———. "Tax Harmonization and Federal Finance: A Perspective on Recent Canadian Discussion." *Canadian Public Policy 10* (1984a): 253–66.

———. *Federal Finance in Comparative Perspective.* Toronto: Canadian Tax Foundation, 1986.

———. "Tax Harmonization in Federations and Common Markets." In *Public Finance and Performance of Enterprises,* edited by M. Neumann. Detroit: Wayne State University Press, 1989, pp. 139–51.

———. "Intergovernmental Finance and Local Taxation in Developing Countries: Some Basic Considerations for Reformers." *Public Administration and Development 10* (1990): 277–88.

Bird, Richard M. and Douglas G. Hartle. "The Design of Governments." In *Modern Fiscal Issues: Essays in Honour of Carl S. Shoup,* edited by Richard M. Bird and John G. Head. Toronto: University of Toronto Press, 1972, pp. 45–62.

Bird, Richard M. and Enid Slack. "Equalization: the Representative Tax System Revisited." *Canadian Tax Journal 38* (1990): 913–27.

———. "Financing Local Governments in OECD Countries: the Role of Local Taxes and User Charges." In Owens and Panella, 1991, pp. 83–97.

———. *Urban Public Finance in Canada,* 2nd ed. Toronto: John Wiley and Sons, 1993.

Bird, Richard M. and Christine Wallich. "Fiscal Decentralization and Intergovernmental Relations in Transition Economies: Towards a Systemic Framework of Analysis." Washington, D.C.: Country Economics Department, World Bank, February, 1993.

Boadway, Robin W. *Intergovernmental Transfers in Canada.* Toronto: Canadian Tax Foundation, 1980.

————. *The Constitutional Division of Powers: an Economic Perspective.* Ottawa: Minister of Supply and Services, 1992.

Boadway, Robin W. and Frank Flatters. "Efficiency and Equalization Payments in a Federal System of Government: a Synthesis and Extension of Recent Results." *Canadian Journal of Economics, 15* (1982).

Boadway, Robin W., Thomas J. Courchene, and Douglas Purvis, eds. *Economic Dimensions of Constitutional Change* (2 vols.). Kingston, Ontario: John Deutsch Institute for Study of Economic Policy, 1991.

Break, George F. *Financing Government in a Federal System.* Washington, D.C.: The Brookings Institution, 1980.

————. "Ability and Benefit Model Guidelines for State-Local Tax Reform." *State Tax Notes 2* (March, 1992): 338–40.

Buchanan, James M. and Gordon Tullock. *The Calculus of Consent.* Ann Arbor: University of Michigan Press, 1962.

Courchene, Thomas. *Equalization Payments.* Toronto: Ontario Economic Council, 1984.

Dafflon, Bernard. "The Assignment of Functions to Decentralized Government: from Theory to Practice." *Environment and Planning C: Government and Policy 10* (August, 1992): 283–88.

Downes, Thomas A. and Thomas F. Pogue. "Intergovernmental Aid to Reduce Disparities: Problems of Definition and Measurement." *Public Finance Quarterly 20* (1992): 468–82.

Fallis, George. *The Costs of Constitutional Change.* Toronto: James Lorimer and Company, 1992.

Feldstein, Martin S. "Wealth Neutrality and Local Choice in Public Education." *American Economic Review 65* (1975): 75–89.

Ferris, James M. and Donald R. Winkler. "Agency Theory and Intergovernmental Relations." In Prud'homme (1991), pp. 155–66.

Gramlich, Edward M. "Intergovernmental Grants: a Review of the Empirical Literature." In *The Political Economy of Fiscal Federalism,* edited by W.E. Oates. Lexington: Lexington Books, 1977.

————. "Subnational Fiscal Policy." *Perspectives on Local Public Finance and Public Policy 3* (1987): 3–27.

Hettich, Walter and Stanley Winer. "Vertical Imbalance in the Fiscal Systems of Federal States." *Canadian Journal of Economics 19* (1986): 745–65.

Hunter, J.S.H. *Federalism and Fiscal Balance.* Canberra: Australian National University Press, 1977.

Inman, Robert P., ed. "New Research in Local Public Finance." *Regional Science and Urban Economics. 19* (1989): 347–562.

Ip, Irene and Jack M. Mintz. *Dividing the Spoils: the Federal-Provincial Allocation of Taxing Power.* Toronto: C.D. Howe Institute, 1992.

Kenyon, Daphne and John Kincaid, eds. *Competition among State and Local Governments.* Washington, D.C.: Urban Institute, 1991.

Kopits, George, ed. *Tax Harmonization in the European Community: Policy Issues and Analysis.* Washington, D.C.: International Monetary Fund, 1992.

Ladd, Helen F. and John Yinger. *America's Ailing Cities: Fiscal Health and the Design of Urban Policy.* Baltimore: Johns Hopkins University Press, 1989.

Musgrave, Richard A. "Approaches to a Fiscal Theory of Political Federalism." In *Public Finances: Needs, Sources, Utilization,* National Bureau of Economic Research. Princeton: Princeton University Press, 1961.

————. "Who Should Tax, Where and What." In *Tax Assignment in Federal Countries,* edited by Charles E. McLure, Jr. ed., Canberra: Centre for Research on Federal Financial Relations, Australian National University, 1983.

Musgrave, Richard A. and Peggy B. "Tax Equity with Multiple Jurisdictions." Paper Prepared for Ontario Fair Tax Commission, January, 1993.

Mushkin, Selma J. *Public Prices for Public Services.* Washington, D.C.: The Urban Institute, 1971.

Oakland, William H., ed. "Financing State and Local Government." *Public Finance Quarterly 4* (October, 1992): 413–589.

Oates, Wallace E. *Fiscal Federalism.* New York: Harcourt Brace Jovanovich, 1972.

————. "'Automatic' Increases in Tax Revenues: the Effect on the Size of the Public Budget." In *Financing the New Federalism: Revenue Sharing, Conditional Grants, and Taxation,* Resources for the Future, Washington, 1975.

————. "Decentralization of the Public Sector: an Overview." In Bennett (1990), pp. 43–58.

————. "Fiscal Federalism: an Overview." In Prud'homme (1991), pp. 1–18.

Owens, Jeffrey and Giorgio Panella, eds. *Local Government: an International Perspective.* Amsterdam: North-Holland, 1991.

Prud'homme, Remy, ed. *Public Finance with Several Levels of Government.* The Hague/Koenigsteing: Foundation Journal Public Finance, 1991.

Renaud, P.S.A. and F.A.A.M. van Winden. "Behavior and Budgetary Autonomy of Local Governments: a Multi-level Model Applied to the Netherlands." *European Journal of Political Economy 7* (1991): 547–78.

Rubinfeld, Daniel L. "The Economics of the Local Public Sector." In *Handbook of Public Economics* (2 vols.), edited by Alan J. Auerbach and Martin Feldstein, Amsterdam: North-Holland, 2: 571–645.

Shah, Anwar. "Perspectives on the Design of Intergovernmental Fiscal Relations," WPS 726. World Bank, Washington, D.C.: Country Economics Department.

Simeon, Richard. *Federal-Provincial Diplomacy,* Toronto: University of Toronto Press, 1972.

Skaburskis, A. "Goals for Restructuring Local Government Boundaries: Canadian Lessons." *Environment and Planning C: Government and Policy 10* (1992): 159–77.

Slack, Enid and Richard M. Bird. "Financing Urban Growth through Development Charges." *Canadian Tax Journal 39* 1991: 1288–1304.

Smith, Peter. "Lessons from the British Poll Tax Disaster." *National Tax Journal 44* (December, 1991): 421–36.

Thirsk, Wayne R. "Political Sensitivity versus Economic Sensibility: a Tale of Two Property Taxes." In *Tax Policy Options in the 1980s*, edited by W.R. Thirsk and J. Whalley, Toronto: Canadian Tax Foundation, 1982.

Tiebout, Charles M. "A Pure Theory of Local Government Expenditures." *Journal of Political Economy 64* (1956): 416–24.

Tresch, Richard W. *Public Finance: A Normative Theory.* Plano, TX: Business Publications, Inc., 1981.

Truelove, M. "Measurement of Spatial Equity." *Environment and Planning C: Government and Policy 11* (1993): 19–34.

Walsh, Cliff. "Fiscal Fedralism—an Overview of Issues and A Discussion of their Relevance to the European Community." Discussion Paper No. 12. Canberra: Federalism Research Centre, Australian National University, February, 1992.

Wildasin, David. *Urban Public Finance.* New York: Harwood Academic Publishers, 1986.

A POLICYMAKER'S GUIDE TO FISCAL DECENTRALIZATION

EDWARD M. GRAMLICH*

Fiscal decentralization has been an important topic among public finance economists for nearly 40 years now, but recently it has become important in the real world as well. The United States has, in effect, implemented a decentralization strategy as it has tried to cut its federal government budget deficit, largely by reducing state and local grants. For Canada, fiscal decentralization is tied up closely with the Quebec issue, and, for Germany, with the unification issue. The European Community is beginning to worry about fiscal decentralization issues in connection with policy harmonization—what policies and/or conventions should be harmonized and what need not be? Many developing countries are also groping with decentralization issues as they try to find a way to manage the public sector side of their growth process.

Decentralization has always been understood to mean the proper location, by level of government, of various taxes, spending programs, grants, and regulations. What types of spending should be conducted by what levels of government, what types of taxes should be assessed by what levels of government, how should grants help fill in gaps, and how should regulations be harmonized? On the one hand, taste differences across jurisdictions argue for separate policies—governments in jurisdiction x should do what the voters in jurisdiction x want. On the other hand, the existence of benefit spillovers across jurisdictions and the potential migration of taxpayers and spending beneficiaries across jurisdictional lines make things complicated. These factors suggest that indvidual jurisdictions do not operate in a vacuum, can make things easy or difficult for other jurisdictions, and should not behave independently. The tension between cooperation and competition among jurisdictions has always been the key element in analyzing fiscal decentralization strategies.

Bird's paper in this volume tries to develop a handy guide to decentralization strategies for policymakers. Bird focuses particularly on taxes and grants—what principles should be kept in mind in designing sensible policies for each? I want to develop a similar guide to decentralization strategies but from a different perspective. I look at guides for policy with respect to each of Richard Musgrave's (1959) three public sector branches of government—allocation, distribution, and macroeconomics. Most of my specific policy suggestions are similar to Bird's, though there are a few differences. But whether the suggestions are the same or different, it is illuminating to develop this guide from a different perspective.

*The University of Michigan, Ann Arbor, MI. 48109

ALLOCATION BRANCH

On the spending side, the basic allocation issue involves the spatial domain of benefits from public service programs. Oates (1972) showed how jurisdiction size can be determined by the balance between competing forces—the welfare loss from taste differences, which argues for small jurisdictions, and the welfare gain from burden sharing, which argues for large jurisdictions. His decentralization theorem called for public services to be supplied by the jurisdiction covering the smallest area over which benefits are distributed. A corollary says that, if the decentralization theorem is followed, efficiency can be further promoted by having central government grant arrangements to insure that those living outside the jurisdiction pay their appropriate marginal share of the benefits of public services.

Using this logic, schools, roads, police, and fire services affecting only one area would be provided by the local government or a special district covering that area, perhaps with matching grant support. On the other hand, interstate highways, national defense, and foreign aid affecting larger groups of areas would be provided by the national government. This split of spending responsibilities, in fact, does seem to be more or less that realized in most countries with federal structures. Normally, there are even matching grants to finance the local services, though, as pointed out subsequently, the structure of these grant programs generally falls short of the efficiency ideal.

On the tax side, the key issue is factor mobility. Suppose some factor is mobile across local boundaries but not across national boundaries. Trying to extort fiscal residuals from the factor at the local level or have local governments tax the factor more than the value of local public service benefits received by the factor will simply drive the factor out of the jurisdiction. The lesson is

almost the opposite of the spending decentralization theorem: once they have paid for their benefits received, factors or activities should be taxed at the highest level possible to cut down on mobility effects.

This disjuncture leads to what Bird calls the vertical imbalance problem. If many spending programs are conducted by lower levels of government and most taxes are assessed by higher levels of government, lower levels of government may find it impossible to finance themselves without grants from the higher level. This provides one rationale for general purpose grants from higher levels of government to remedy this vertical imbalance.

But before instituting such grants, there are several caveats. As implied previously, mobile factors should respond as much to benefits received as to taxes paid; hence, local service user fees or taxes can be assessed to pay a portion of the costs of government. Second, as Bird argues, user fees on households are also an excellent form of local finance. Among other advantages, user fees automatically solve the spillover problem because outsiders automatically pay their appropriate marginal share of service benefits received. Third, even if local user fees have been used as much as possible, there are still other local taxes, many of which can be assessed on immobile bases and which can finance a broad array of local public services. Fourth, Walsh (1985) has argued against vertical imbalance grants on management grounds: with these grants, government officials at lower levels of government become primarily grant procurers or rent seekers rather than economical managers of public affairs. With all these caveats, it is unclear how important a rationale for general purpose grants is provided by the vertical imbalance argument. There may ultimately be some imbalance and rationale for general purpose grants, but it may also be that, over the relevant ranges, local user fees and taxes on immobile sources can provide plenty of revenue to finance all lower level government spending called for by the spending decentralization theorem.

Beyond user fees, what taxes on immobile sources can be used to finance local governments? Bird praises the local income tax, which is certainly worthy of more serious consideration and use around the world. The most common existing local tax is, of course, the local property tax. This should be acceptable too because it falls largely on land or relatively immobile homeowners, but some property wealth does consist of mobile industrial capital. This suggests a split treatment for local property taxes: while homeowners can be assessed full property taxes, industrial capital should only be assessed property taxes equal to the marginal costs of provision of sewers, roads, and other public services.

On the grant side, even if there were no vertical imbalance grants, there should still be grants to correct for benefit spillovers. Especially if the decentralization theorem is followed, there will be outsiders who benefit from local public spending and should pay some of the cost. Coasian bribes are possible, but central government grants are a more feasible way to handle these spillovers.

Using this rationale, central government grants should be open-ended price subsidies for particular types of spending, with the central matching rate roughly equal to the share of marginal benefits realized outside the jurisdiction. Throughout the world, most central government matching grants are not of this form. Existing central government grant programs generally feature very high central government matching rates, enough to encourage overspending at the local level, but then have this subsidy capped so that, at the margin, there is no price subsidy at all. As has been pointed out many times, this form turns a

supposed price subsidy grant into an income subsidy grant and definitely does not solve the spillover problem. The remedy is to uncap the grant and make the central government matching rate conform to the marginal share of benefits received inside and outside the jurisdiction.

There is one unconscious way in which central governments often give open-ended price subsidies. If state or local taxes are deductible against the national income tax, the marginal tax cost of a dollar of local revenue is the complement of the marginal central government income tax rate. It may be that this slight reduction in local tax cost is an appropriate correction for externalities in general, but there are many problems. First, there is no obvious reason why the national marginal income tax rate gives the proper externality correction. Moreover, if many income taxpayers do not itemize deductions, deductibility is horizontally inequitable, lowering tax costs in wealthy jurisdictions but not poor jurisdictions (Gramlich, 1985).

Bird makes the common claim that it will be difficult to estimate the marginal share of outsider benefit and thereby to determine ideal central government matching rates on grants. Obviously, these shares will not be easy to estimate, but based on the United States experience, I have always felt that even crude estimates will make such efficiency improvements that the attempts should be made. For highways and other transportation projects, it is possible to count users, license plates, truck weight, *etc.* to determine marginal benefit shares. For pollution control projects, it is possible to measure the changes made by the project and determine the location of gains. For human investment projects, users can be counted directly. There will be some grants where the estimation is difficult, but these matching rates could be set at average shares, one-half, or other politically acceptable numbers. The issue certainly is not insuperable, and the potential efficiencies are significant.

A different sort of real world puzzle under the allocation heading involves the role of intermediate governments, such as states in the United States and Australia, provinces in Canada, and Lander in Germany. These governments all have historical institutional roles in federal systems, they have often come together to form the nation, and they are often constitutionally responsible for their local governments. From the standpoint of historical evolution or administrative convenience, perhaps it makes sense to have these intermediate governments, but from an economic standpoint, the rationale could be questioned. There do not seem to be many spending programs that confer benefits over a statewide area, as opposed to a local, regional, or national area. Perhaps the evolution of federalism and/or decentralization will see states and other intermediate governments gradually decline in power; perhaps there could be a development of grants that go directly from the national government to local or regional authorities. The United States already has a few such grants.

DISTRIBUTION BRANCH

There are generally two types of distributional programs in modern societies—human capital type programs aimed at helping people earn higher incomes in the long run and income transfer type programs aimed at protecting peoples' incomes in the short run. Both types of programs could be lodged at either a higher or lower level of government and both raise a series of policy issues.

The key issue for income transfer programs is the spatial horizon of altruism. Taxpayers give income transfer benefits in the first place either as a form of social insurance or because they care about the welfare of their fellow citizens suffering poverty. If the motive is social insurance, over what geo-

graphic span is that to be—do taxpayers want programs that operate throughout their locality, state, or nation? If the motive is altruism more generally, again which fellow citizens are these—those in the same locality, state, or nation? If the relevant area is a nation, transfer benefits should be nationwide, or at least there should be a nationwide floor on benefits. If the relevant area is a state or locality, transfer benefits should extend just to that area.

There are further complications on the recipient side. Recipients do seem to migrate across jurisdictional lines in search of higher transfer benefits, at least to some degree. This raises the cost to any state or locality in raising its own transfer benefits to the level its own taxpayers might prefer—the higher benefits attract recipients from other areas and thus extend the geographic domain of benefits beyond what the voters might have preferred. It is possible to have residency rules that eliminate this distortion, but many intermediate governments do not have or cannot enforce such rules. This is an effective externality, and, in fact, Boadway and Wildasin (1984) have proposed dealing with it by open-ended matching grants from the central government to the sponsor government, just as if there were normal benefit spillovers.

Another issue has been raised in the United States, where pure unconditional income transfer programs have never been very popular with voters. In recent years, there have been attempts to combine income transfers with work—to make benefits contingent on working, to put recipients through job search training or skills training, and so forth. There are many ways in which such combinations can be effected, and there is no one preferable way for all regions of a country, for all types of labor markets. The United States has let states experiment with innovative work-transfer programs, hence giving added programmatic justification for lower level involvement. Similar arguments could be made for homeless shelter or other service programs where local conditions would matter greatly.

Because all potential transfer recipients may not reside in one local or state area and because there is some migration, transfer programs should not be left entirely up to lower state or local governments. At the same time, because feelings of taxpayer altruism may be somewhat stronger for residents of one area than across the whole nation, because local conditions matter in service programs and because states or localities might be valuable innovators, transfer programs should not be entirely national either (as Bird seems to assert). To me, the optimal design is for mixed programs with some base national level of benefits and optional state supplementation and other mechanisms for combining services with transfers.

The most prominent human capital program is elementary education, though there are others as well. The tradition in most countries is to conduct public schooling at the local level, with parental involvement in the operation of the schools.

The local role is an established tradition that is likely to persist and has a justification similar to that for programs that combine transfers with work. But there is a long-run income distribution impact of public schooling that argues for some broader interest as well. Local communities vary widely in wealth and/or income, and if, as is suggested by econometric evidence (Inman, 1978; Feldstein, 1975), public schooling is a normal good, rich communities will in general spend more on education and have better public schools than poor communities. This quality disparity will be magnified if, as seems likely, the public safety costs of schooling depend inversely on community wealth or income. Leaving the financing of public schooling entirely up to localities will then lead to systematic differences in the quality of schooling received by students from rich and poor districts and will tend to perpetuate income differences.

There are essentially three ways to break this link. One approach is simply to centralize some base level of spending on public schools. The problem with this approach is that there would be no equalization above the base level. A second approach is to give unconditional grants to bring spendable resources in poor jurisdictions up to those in wealthy jurisdictions. The problem with this approach is that if grants are unconditional, they are unlikely to be spent entirely on public schools and spending disparities will persist. The best third, and preferred, approach is to use the district power equalization approach of Feldstein (1975), which features open-ended matching grants with the matching rate set so that, on average, spending will be equalized across rich and poor jurisdictions. There could also be a hybrid approach, with uniform base level spending and district power equalization above that.

As one final point regarding education, Hanushek (1991) has been arguing that focusing entirely on education finance, as opposed to the structure of incentives, may actually set back the cause of educational reform. Since spending is only very loosely tied to educational output, reforms that focus only on spending are unlikely to be successful. Financial reforms may be a necessary condition for broader educational reform, but they are only that—attention to the underlying incentives for teaching and learning is also important. If nothing else, this reemphasizes how important it is to have lower levels of government involved in the process of educational reform.

MACROECONOMIC BRANCH

Musgrave (1959) actually called this the stabilization branch, but I use the broader macroeconomic branch because the requirements of macropolicy have changed in recent years. The traditional closed-economy Keynesian view of macroeconomics was that fiscal policy should stabilize the economy around full employment, period. The newer view, really open economy view, is that now that economies are open with flexible exchange rates and free mobility of capital, fiscal policy has very weak stabilization effects and stabilization should be primarily the role of monetary policy. What fiscal policy then does is to set a country's national saving rate, which determines the composition of its output between consumption and investment and its living standards in the long run. Fiscal policy does have stabilization impacts when exchange rates are fixed, but most of the world is now ultimately on flexible rates (or at least fixed rates that often must be changed in response to shocks).

In the traditional closed economy Keynesian view, macropolicy was viewed as the responsibility of central government monetary and fiscal policy and not at all the responsibility of lower levels of government. Even in those days there was apparently no thought that macrodemand or supply shocks might operate differentially across different regions of a country—raising output and employment in some regions and lowering it in others. Now that economies are open, it is quite clear that macrodemand or supply shocks can often have these differential effects (Courant and Deardorff, forthcoming), and, since central government fiscal policy has a limited stabilization effect anyway, the time seems right for some new thinking about decentralization strategies.

I have tried to argue (1987) that the appropriate way to discharge responsibilities in the new world is to let the world economy set interest rates, have the national government set fiscal policy to determine the nation's saving rate, and then give lower governments the ability to operate

some limited fiscal stabilization policies. This permits these governments to counter demand or supply shocks to some degree. Unlike the national government, since lower governments are on fixed exchange rates, lower government fiscal measures are likely to have stronger output effects than national measures, contrary to the previous impression. The way in which lower governments can operate stabilization policy is for governments to build up their asset stocks in good years and run down these assets in bad years, or to borrow in bad years and repay in good years. The United States has a scheme whereby states can and do borrow from the unemployment trust fund to implement such a system, and it seems important for areas, such as the European Community, to plan similar arrangements.

POLICY SUGGESTIONS

Since this paper is ultimately a guide for policymakers, I wrap things up by collecting the main policy suggestions resulting from the discussion. I also compare my position on each issue with that of Bird.

(1) I am in general agreement with Bird that public services should be provided by the lowest level of government possible, or the jurisdiction spanning the smallest area over which benefits are distributed. If those outside the jurisdiction receive some of the marginal benefits of these public services, the best cure against underspending is open-ended matching grants, with the matching rate equal to the share of the marginal benefits received by outsiders.

(2) I am also in agreement with Bird that user fees and local income, land, and property taxes are valuable forms of local finance and should be adopted to the extent possible, hopefully with enough revenue potential that vertical imbalance grants would not be necessary. But local property taxes should not be assessed on mobile industrial capital beyond the level of services

received, for such taxes will just drive that capital out of the jurisdiction.

(3) Whereas in his preferred fiscal federalism model, Bird takes the traditional view that distributional programs should be entirely a national responsibility, I feel these programs should be a mixed responsibility. The national government should set a base level of benefits and use matching grants to equalize tax prices for human capital programs. Local governments can then supplement the national floor transfer benefits and manage both these transfer programs and the human capital programs.

(4) Like Bird (again in his preferred fiscal federalism model), I see no strong rationale for unconditional grants anywhere in the system. Matching grants are preferred ways of dealing both with benefit spillovers and with disparate abilities to finance human capital distributional programs.

(5) In a proposition that Bird takes no position on, I feel that the national government should take responsibility for manipulating fiscal policy to determine national saving rates and generally not worry about discretionary fiscal stabilization policy. National business cycles can be counteracted by monetary policy and regional cycles by subnational governments running rainy day funds or borrowing from designated trust funds.

ENDNOTE

I have benefitted from the helpful comments of Richard Bird, Paul Courant and Joel Slemrod.

References

Boadway, Robin W. and David E. Wildasin. *Public Sector Economics*, 2nd ed. Toronto: Little, Brown and Company, 1984.

Courant, Paul N. and Alan V. Deardorff. "Amenities, Nontraded Goods, and the Trade of Lumpy Countries." *Journal of Urban Economics*, forthcoming.

Feldstein, Martin S. "Wealth Neutrality and Local Choice in Public Education." *American Economic Review 65* (March, 1975): 75–89.

Gramlich, Edward M. "The Deductibility of State and Local Taxes." *National Tax Journal 38* (December, 1985): 447–465.

Gramlich, Edward M. "Subnational Fiscal Policy." *Perspectives on Local Public Finance and Public Policy: A Research Annual*, 1987, *3*, 3–27.

Hanushek, Eric A. "When School Reform May Not be Good Policy." *Harvard Journal on Legislation 28* (Summer 1991): 425–456.

Inman, Robert P. "Testing Political Economy's 'As If' Proposition: Is the Median Voter Really Decisive?" *Public Choice 33* (1978): 4:45–66.

Musgrave, Richard A. *The Theory of Public Finance.* New York: McGraw-Hill, 1959.

Oates, Wallace E. *Fiscal Federalism.* New York: Harcourt, Brace, Jovanovich, 1972.

Walsh, Cliff. "Reforming Federal Financial Relations: Some Radical (Or Are They Conservative) Proposals." Mimeo, 1985.

FISCAL DECENTRALIZATION AND ECONOMIC DEVELOPMENT

WALLACE E. OATES*

The point of departure for my contribution to this symposium is the striking contrast in the extent of fiscal centralization of the industrialized and the developing countries: government in the developing nations appears to be far more centralized (as measured by existing fiscal indices) than in the industrialized countries. This marked differential in degrees of fiscal centralization is widely documented. Over two decades ago in an empirical study of fiscal federalism (Oates, 1972), I found, for a sample of 58 countries, that measures of fiscal centralization were significantly and negatively correlated with levels of per capita real income. And, more recently, using a sample of 43 countries, my sample statistics (1985) revealed an average share of central-government spending in total public expenditure of 65 percent in the subsample of 18 industrialized countries as contrasted to 89 percent in the subsample of 25 developing nations. In terms of public revenues, the average share of central governments in the developing countries was in excess of 90 percent![1]

These measures thus suggest that central government in the developing countries assumes the lion's share of fiscal responsibility. Bird (1986), among others, has expressed some legitimate reservations concerning the validity of fiscal data from the developing nations and the resulting summary measures of the sort I have just cited. There are, in particular, some serious problems regarding the extent of coverage and comparability. Moreover, there is considerable variability among countries within the samples. Nevertheless, the generalization that the developing countries are characterized by relatively high degrees of fiscal centralization appears to stand up pretty well. There are various kinds of corroborating evidence. Writing some 37 years ago, for example, Martin and Lewis (1956) observed that "The weakness of local government in relation to central government is one of the most striking phenomena of under-developed countries" (p. 231).

While this systematic difference in fiscal centralization across industrial and developing countries is a well-established property of fiscal structure, its meaning and implications are much less clear. What are we to make of this? In particular, is fiscal decentralization a "cause" or a "result" of economic development? Or, more likely, is it a more complex outcome of the interplay of a variety of forces that accompanies economic growth?

A better understanding of these relation-

*University of Maryland, College Park, MD 20742.

ships is important, for there is much current interest in the potential contribution of fiscal decentralization to economic development. Shifting greater responsibility to local authorities is seen by many as a way to break the "grip" of central planning and mismanagement that has bedeviled efforts to set poorer nations on a course of self-sustaining growth. Both political leaders within the developing countries and advisors from without have sounded the call for decentralization as a mechanism to make policy more responsive to local needs and to involve the local populace in processes of democratic governance. As de Valk (1990) points out, it is interesting in this regard that this "resurgence of interest in decentralization" appears to have less of a political focus and more of a concern with increasing "effectiveness and efficiency" in development planning and implementation (p. 5).

From a sharply contrasting point of view, the growth of the local public sector may be seen as largely the result of economic development. The contention here is that, as economies mature and incomes rise, the economic gains from fiscal decentralization emerge. At some point, it becomes worthwhile to differentiate outputs in local jurisdictions according to local demands. This appears to be the view, for example, of Bahl and Linn (1992), who argue that "Decentralization more likely comes with the achievement of a higher stage of economic development" (p. 391) and that the "threshold level of economic development" at which fiscal decentralization becomes attractive "appears to be quite high" (p. 393). From this perspective, it is economic development that comes first; fiscal decentralization then follows.

My purpose here is to explore somewhat more systematically the sources and implications of this observed inverse relationship between fiscal centralization and the level of economic development. I begin with a more historically oriented exploration of

the trends in fiscal centralization that yields a very different picture of the matter from the cross-sectional pattern just cited. From this perspective, I turn to some of the issues that Bird raises in his paper, putting them in the context of the developing countries.

THE EVOLUTION OF THE LOCAL PUBLIC SECTOR

Let me begin by returning to the Bahl-Linn thesis that a major role for the local public sector tends to emerge at the later stages of economic development. This view is based largely on the modern theory of local finance that envisions the local sector as responding to a variety of different tastes for local services. There are two strands to the argument. First, the local sector is seen as responsive to local demands. Making use of the median voter model or other models embodying some sensitivity to voter preferences, the analysis of local finance envisions the local sector as providing outputs of local services that are closely tailored to the demands of the local constituency. In the median-voter framework, the equilibrium level of local services mirrors faithfully the median of the preferred levels of outputs of local residents.

The capacity of the local sector to satisfy consumer preferences is enhanced by a second dimension to the theory of local finance based on consumer mobility. Drawing on the famous Tiebout model (1956), this strand of the literature describes a world of mobile households that "vote with their feet" by choosing as a jurisdiction of residence a community which provides the most desirable fiscal package. Thus, both through responsiveness to the local electorate and through fiscal mobility (the "voice" and "exit" options as Hirschman (1970) has called them), the local sector makes an important contribution to efficient resource allocation by ensuring that individuals, as in their choices of private goods, are able to obtain outputs of local services that equate fairly accurately marginal benefits and costs.

The Bahl-Linn contention is that this vision of the local sector has descriptive and normative power primarily in the industrialized countries. The local sector functions very differently in developing countries; it is sometimes a manipulative and exploitative instrument. It is only at well-advanced stages of economic development that a responsive local sector, like that sketched out previously, can be expected to emerge.

This view would seem to imply that, from the perspective of the evolution of the local public sector over time, we should expect to observe a continuing growth in the relative importance of local finance. This suggests that we might gain some insight from supplementing our cross-sectional data on fiscal centralization with some time-series studies of the evolution of local finance.

Some limited empirical work on this matter exists. I have pulled together elsewhere (Oates, 1975) data on a few industrialized countries, and Wallis and I (Wallis and Oates, 1988) have assembled a detailed body of twentieth century data on the U.S. public finances. These data, covering the last century or so, describe a process that does not correspond at all well to the view described earlier. In fact, if we pick up the story late in the nineteenth century, we find a very striking process of public-sector *centralization* in progress. In the United States, for example, the central-government share of total government spending was only around 30–35 percent at the turn of the century; by 1955, this share had risen from about one-third to two-thirds of public expenditure. Likewise, for the United Kingdom, the central-government share of total expenditure rose from 57 percent in 1895 to 75 percent in 1955 (Oates, 1975).

Thus, the trend in vertical fiscal structure

over most of this period was toward increased fiscal centralization. This led de Tocqueville in *Democracy in America* to the ". . . opinion that, in the democratic ages which are opening upon us . . . centralization will be the natural government" (1980, vol. II, p. 296). In a like vein, Bryce (1901), writing at the turn of the century, saw centralization as a prevailing tendency; in his view, ". . . the centripetal forces are permanent and secular forces, working from age to age" (p. 844), and he notes ". . . the normal tendency to aggregation and centralization" (p. 844) in the public sector. McWhinney (1965) has gone on to enshrine "Bryce's Law," the proposition that ". . . federalism is simply a transitory step on the way to governmental unity" (p. 105).

This surely does not sound like a process of growing reliance on local government! It is certainly true, of course, that the trend toward increased centralization was hastened in the first half of the twentieth century by cataclysmic events. Two World Wars and the Great Depression placed heavy demands on central governments. Such violent social disruption and the predominant role for central government that it produced gave rise, in the view of Peacock and Wiseman (1961), to certain "displacement effects" that were never fully rectified after the events. Central government took on, and never relinquished, its predominant role in the public sector.

The evidence does suggest, however, that centralizing tendencies played out around the middle of the twentieth century. Fiscal centralization ratios for most of the industrialized countries appear to have peaked in the 1950s and, since that time, have actually declined modestly (Oates, 1975; Pommerehne, 1977). These more recent trends appear to have belied any simplistic notions of increasing fiscal centralization. What we seem to be observing is a more complicated process with both decentralizing and centralizing forces at work, a process that is resulting, for example, in devolution in a number of OECD countries and, at the same time, in a new top layer of government in the European Community!

A historical view thus presents a much more complex and less clear view of the relationship between fiscal decentralization and economic development. What are we to make of this regarding the current state of the developing nations? My own sense is that the historical experience of the industrialized nations is, in this particular respect, of limited relevance to the developing countries. This is largely because the latter have a very different starting point for their process of economic growth. As Conyers (1990), among others, stresses, "Most less developed countries inherited relatively centralized systems of government from their colonial powers, and in the first years of independence there was often a tendency to maintain—if not strengthen—central control and centralized systems of planning, in order to encourage a sense of national unity and reinforce the new government and its policies" (p. 16). Many of these countries have thus effectively initiated their modern statehood with highly centralized government sectors. They have not undergone the kind of evolution that seems more characteristic of the industrialized countries.

This suggests that the potential of fiscal decentralization for facilitating economic development has to be evaluated largely in terms of the particular circumstances of the developing countries in their current state. The evolution of the public sector in the industrialized countries may contribute some insights, but it is unlikely to provide a "model" for the evolution of the public sector in the developing countries. I might add here that I think there is some truth in the Bahl-Linn contention that economic growth creates an environment favorable to the gains from fiscal decentralization (Oates, 1975). But it does not follow from this that local government finance has little

to offer the developing countries at this juncture in history. This issue requires consideration on its own terms. In the next section, I offer some thoughts on all this, drawing on Bird's useful treatment of decentralized finance.

FISCAL DECENTRALIZATION TO FACILITATE ECONOMIC DEVELOPMENT

The basic *economic* case for fiscal decentralization is the enhancement of economic efficiency: the provision of local outputs that are differentiated according to local tastes and circumstances results in higher levels of social welfare than centrally determined and more uniform levels of outputs across all jurisdictions. Although this proposition has been developed mainly in a static context (see my treatment of the "Decentralization Theorem,' 1972), the thrust of the argument should also have some validity in a dynamic setting of economic growth. There surely are strong reasons, in principle, to believe that policies formulated for the provision of infrastructure and even human capital that are sensitive to regional or local conditions are likely to be more effective in encouraging economic development than centrally determined policies that ignore these geographical differences. There is, incidentally, no formalized theory of such a relationship between fiscal decentralization and economic growth; it would probably be useful to work through such a theory (in which investment programs are "jurisdiction-specific") to determine the parameters on which these gains depend and some idea as to orders of magnitude.

While some basic theory would be helpful here, such theory does not come to terms with the fundamental issue of how local government actually works in developing countries. The economic case for decentralized finance is based on the presumed responsiveness of local governments to the welfare of their respective constituencies. But is there good reason to believe that such responsiveness exists? As Conyers (1990) argues, ". . . decentralization may increase the participation of people at the local level, but sometimes it is only a small privileged elite group who get to participate" (p. 18). And such elites may pursue their own narrowly focused self-interest. In short, will decentralization simply involve exchanging a central "tyrant" for a local tyrant with resulting policies that do not address the welfare of the local populace?

The whole issue of corruption is a closely related matter. Myrdal (1968) among others has made much of the debilitating effects of corruption on efforts to promote economic growth. Is there reason to expect that such practices are likely to be more or less prevalent at local, as contrasted to more centralized, levels of government? There exists little systematic evidence that I know of that sheds much light on these questions of the operation of decentralized finance, but they are clearly matters of great importance. While there is a compelling case, in principle, for decentralized finance, the case is obviously compromised if local government fails to perform.

In this regard, it does seem to me that certain conditions must be satisfied if local government is to have the capacity to perform effectively. These are conditions that Bird stresses in his paper and that effectively give local officials the scope for autonomous fiscal decisions and which provide the right kind of signals and incentives. I want here to echo Bird's emphasis on two particular conditions.

First, local authorities need their own independent sources of revenues. There is an important issue of "balance" in the vertical structure of revenues. Intergovernmental grants from central to local governments have an important role to play in the fiscal system, but they cannot be excessive. In some developing countries, such intergovernmental transfers account for the largest share of local revenues. This can under-

mine the autonomy and vitality of decentralized decision-making. If local governments are to have real and effective fiscal discretion, they must raise a significant portion of their funds from their own revenue sources. This is important for two reasons. First, in a political setting, central funds nearly always come with strings attached. If regional and local governments are heavily dependent on transfers from above, it is inevitable that central intrusion into expenditure decisions will be pervasive. Decisions concerning the menu and levels of local programs will become the result of negotiations between central and local authorities, undercutting local fiscal independence. Second, heavy reliance on grants destroys the incentives for responsible local decisions. It is essential that localities in choosing to expand or contract various programs consider carefully the cost of these decisions. If funding comes from "above," there may be little real economic cost to the locality associated with these decisions. Funding from own revenues, *especially at the margin* of local programs, is critical if decentralized choice is to play its proper role in the fiscal system.

The second condition, closely related to the first, concerns the nature of own revenues. In his paper, Bird devotes considerable attention, quite rightly, to the "characteristics of a good local tax." It is important in the vertical "assignment" of revenue instruments to ensure both that local taxes do not induce distorting movements of economic goods and activity *and* that they are tied, at least roughly, to benefits in order to provide the right sorts of cost signals to the community on local fiscal decisions. This second issue is not so easy in developing countries because of the absence of the requisite institutions for revenue administration. Korea presents an interesting case in this regard. Oh (1991), in his discussion of the ongoing devolution of the public sector in Korea, describes the shift of certain parts of the tax base to local government. Local government in Korea is coming to play a greater role in the raising of its own revenues, which, as we have discussed, is essential to the development of real local autonomy. At the same time, however, we find that the major tax being transferred to local government is the tobacco tax. While this tax is indeed the source of considerable revenues and puts local government on a sounder fiscal footing, it is not a very "good" local tax by Bird's criteria.

The property tax is, in my view, quite a good local revenue source, especially in conjunction with local user fees wherever possible. Requiring local property owners to pay for local services is both reasonably fair and provides the requisite cost signals to the community. But many developing countries do not have the administrative capacity at present to implement property taxation. There is, incidentally, much interest in all this, and there are ongoing efforts to provide assistance in the development of property tax systems in several developing countries. This is an important issue.[2]

In sum, decentralized finance appears, in principle, to have a potentially useful role to play in economic development. But the translation of this potential into a real contribution to economic growth depends on a number of crucial conditions regarding the responsiveness of local institutions to local welfare which, in turn, depends importantly on the proper structure of fiscal institutions.

ENDNOTES

I am grateful to the Institutional Reform and the Informal Sector (IRIS) Program at Maryland for its support of my research on fiscal decentralization and economic development.

[1] Other studies have produced comparable findings. Bahl and Nath (1986), for example, found an average central government share in total public spending of 85 percent in their sample of developing countries. See also Pommerehne (1977) and Wasylenko (1987).

[2] See Bird (1992) and Bahl and Linn (1992) for extended treatments of these taxation issues in developing countries.

REFERENCES

Bahl, Roy W. and Johannes F. Linn. *Urban Public Finance in Developing Countries.* Oxford: Oxford University Press, 1992.

Bahl, Roy W. and Shyam Nath. "Public Expenditure Decentralization in Developing Countries." *Government and Policy* 4 (1986): 405–18.

Bird, Richard M. "On Measuring Fiscal Centralization and Fiscal Balance in Federal States." *Government and Policy 4* (1986): 384–404.

———. *Tax Policy and Economic Development.* Baltimore: Johns Hopkins Press, 1992.

Bryce, James. *The American Commonwealth.* New York: MacMillan, 1901.

Conyers, Diana. "Centralization and Development Planning: a Comparative Perspective." In *Decentralizing for Participatory Planning?*, edited by P. de Valk and K. Wekwete. Aldershot: Avebury, 1990.

de Tocqueville, Alexis. *Democracy in America.* New York: Alfred Knopf; the Henry Reeve text as revised by Francis Bowen, 1980; original copyright, 1945.

de Valk, Peter. "State, Decentralization and Participation." In *Decentralizing for Participatory Planning?*, P. de Valk and K. Wekwete. Aldershot: Avebury, 1990.

Hirschman, Albert O. *Exit, Voice, and Loyalty.* Cambridge: Harvard University Press, 1970.

Martin, Alison and W. Arthur Lewis. "Patterns of Public Revenue and Expenditure." *The Manchester School of Economic and Social Studies 24* (September, 1956): 203–44.

McWhinney, Edward. *Comparative Federalism,* 2nd ed. Toronto: Toronto University Press, 1965.

Myrdal, Gunnar. *The Asian Drama,* Vol. II. New York: Twentieth Century Fund, 1968.

Oates, Wallace E. *Fiscal Federalism.* New York: Harcourt Brace Jovanovich, 1972.

———. "Searching for Leviathan: an Empirical Study." *American Economic Review 75* (September, 1985): 748–57.

———. "The Changing Structure of Intergovernmental Fiscal Relations." In *Secular Trends of the Public Sector,* edited by H. Recktenwald. Paris: Editions Cujas, 1975, pp. 151–62.

Oh, Yeon-Cheon. "The Allocation of Tax Bases between the Central and Local Governments in Korea." In *Public Finance with Several Levels of Government,* edited by R. Prud'homme. The Hague: Foundation Journal Public Finance, 1991, pp. 54–68.

Peacock, Alan and Jack Wiseman. *The Growth of Public Expenditure in the United Kingdom.* Oxford: Oxford University Press, 1961.

Pommerehne, Werner W. "Quantitative Aspects of Federalism: a Study of Six Countries." In *The Political Economy of Fiscal Federalism,* edited by W. Oates. Lexington, MA: D.C. Heath, 1977, pp. 275–355.

Tiebout, Charles. "A Pure Theory of Local Expenditures." *Journal of Political Economy 64* (October, 1956): 416–24.

Wallis, John J. and Wallace E. Oates. "Decentralization in the Public Sector: an Empirical Study of State and Local Government." In *Fiscal Federalism: Quantitative Studies*, edited by H. Rosen. Chicago: University of Chicago Press, 1988, pp. 5–32.

Wasylenko, Michael. "Fiscal Decentralization and Economic Development." *Public Budgeting and Finance 7* (1987): 57–71.

FEDERALISM AND REDUCTIONS IN THE FEDERAL BUDGET

JOHN M. QUIGLEY* & DANIEL L. RUBINFELD*

INTRODUCTION

Our national constitution incorporates built-in tensions of economic federalism, enumerating certain powers for the central government, while reserving others for the states. The historical resolution of these tensions has a complex political and economic history.[1] Given the substantial inertia that is built into the U.S. federalism system, it is not surprising that the current set of economic responsibilities has evolved only slowly during the past two centuries.

Almost 15 years ago, it appeared that a new period in federal relations would begin when the Reagan administration proposed to reverse the long-term trend toward the centralization of financing of government services. The Reagan proposal sought to return to states and localities all financial responsibility for income redistribution (Aid to Families with Dependent Children (AFDC) and food stamps) as well as control over more than 60 federal programs targeted to low-income households, including education, community development (e.g., water and sewer programs), transportation, and social services. This was to be accomplished, in part, by a cut in specific grant programs and, in part, by the consolidation of other programs into a single block grant program.

The Reagan federalism initiatives forced a serious rethinking of the evolutionary path of the public economy, which had moved the financial and managerial responsibility for public goods and services steadily upward to the national level. While the core reforms of the Reagan "New Federalism" proposal never became law, the Reagan budgets significantly curtailed the levels of federal support for state and local governments. This curtailment was bifurcated: Federal support for spending on local goods and services declined dramatically, but federal support for distributional programs, especially those involving health care, increased substantially over the past decade and a half.

The budget issues that have divided the Clinton Administration and the 104th Congress mirror those of the Reagan initiative in many ways. Rather than

*University of California, Berkeley, CA 94720.

marking a reversion to the New Federalism of the 1980s, the current debate may well signify the beginning of a new period of retrenchment in American federalism. The debate puts the presumptions of our entire federalist system under scrutiny and asks whether the current structure of responsibilities is appropriate to the 21st century.

There are at least two ways in which appeals to federalist principles can affect the revenue requirements at the federal level, the size of the federal deficit, and the economic relationship between central and local governments. These include "mandates," direct orders from the central government, and "grants," powerful but indirect incentives provided by the federal government. The second and third sections analyze the positive aspects of these two facets of federalism. The fourth section provides a more normative discussion and some brief conclusions.

BUDGET CUTTING THROUGH MANDATES?

Federal mandates—directives to state governments—are a built-in feature of America's federal structure. Mandates reflect the constitutional division between the enumerated responsibilities of national government and those reserved to the states by the Bill of Rights (in the tenth amendment).

At one level, the appropriate use of mandates encompasses fundamental questions of governance. Where in the system of governments should a policy be made? Who should be charged with the execution and implementation of a given policy? How much flexibility in execution should be afforded? Who should bear the costs of compliance?

These philosophical and normative issues once dominated the budgeting policy debate. However, a narrower and more recent focus on "unfunded federal mandates" presupposes answers to these questions and invites the conclusion that central government directives have been used to save federal dollars by imposing expenditure responsibilities on state and local governments.

Federal mandates include a variety of distinct forms, encompassing differing rationales, costs, and levels of direction of state activity by central authorities. One indirect form of federal control, through conditional grants, is considered in the next section. In this section, we consider other more direct forms. These include direct orders, cross cutting requirements, crossover sanctions, and statutory preemptions.[2]

An economic taxonomy of federal government mandates is somewhat elusive. Table 1 presents our categorization of mandates by their economic rationale and the type of activity regulated. Objectives for federal mandates include the reduction of spillovers across states, the imposition of national standards, and the reflection of national norms. The first two are clearly efficiency enhancing rationales: air and water quality standards encourage concerted action by adjoining states on efficiency grounds. The requirement that highway access be provided uniformly for 40-ton trucks ensures a market for these vehicles. The prohibition against automotive fuel economy regulations by the states protects scale economies in auto design. In addition, many federal mandates are imposed on the basis of the third criterion, fairness—to ensure equal treatment of citizens across states (in antidiscrimination mandates or in drinking rules), equal access to mandated services (e.g., unemployment

TABLE 1
ECONOMIC TAXONOMY OF FEDERAL MANDATES

	Rationale		
Type of Activity	To Reduce Spillovers	To Impose National Standards	To Reflect National Norms
States must:			
1. Produce some good	clean air	highways appropriate for large trucks	unemployment insurance
2. Produce in a specified way	specific tests for drinking water	—	union wages in construction
3. Regulate firms and consumers (or refrain from regulation)	handgun waiting period	refrain from regulating fuel economy	drinking age at 21

insurance), or other forms of equal treatment (as in the removal of asbestos from schools).

The growth in the number of federal mandates, their complexity, and their costs to state and local governments was pointed out forcefully at the beginning of the Reagan administration (see Koch, 1980, for a characteristically sharp statement). In response, much more systematic information about the fiscal dimensions of proposed mandates is now available. (see Gullo, 1990; Barr, 1990).

Increased attention to the existence of mandates and their costs during the 1980s did little, apparently, to reduce the growth of federal mandates. For example, one count of conservatively defined statutory mandates reported that Congress enacted only one mandate in the 1930s, one in the 1940s, none in the 1950s, nine in the 1960s, and 25 in the 1970s. According to this definition, Congress enacted 27 more statutory mandates during the decade of the 1980s (ACIR, 1995).[3]

The increase in the number and complexity of mandates during the 1980s and 1990s raises the possibility that the federal government has been

"saving" money by imposing fiscal burdens on lower levels of government. There is some documentation from the 1970s and 1980s supporting the second part of the statement—the increased financial burden on lower levels of government.[4]

There have been several recent efforts to increase further the salience of federal mandates and to make their costs more transparent. For example, the National Conference of State Legislatures now maintains and publicizes a "catalog" of federal mandates imposed on the states. In addition, recent legislation (the Unfunded Mandates Reform Act of 1995) provides a rather carefully constructed definition of those mandates which "impose an enforceable duty" on lower levels of government. This legislation requires the Congressional Budget Office to prepare timely cost estimates for mandates expected to cost as little as $50 million.

Several credible cost estimates are available for the most important mandates imposed on state and local governments. The Environmental Protection Agency has produced estimates of the magnitude of costs imposed on central and lower level governments by the most important environmental mandates of the 1980s. These are summarized in Table 2. Clean air, water, and land conservation, together with chemical requirements and multimedia mandates, impose costs of about $13 billion annually on the federal government and about $31.6 billion on state and local governments. (Other costs to households and private firms, not shown, are estimated to add an additional $76 billion to the bill).

The U.S. Advisory Committee on Intergovernmental Relations has calculated that mandates relating to the education of the handicapped, together with the Americans with Disabilities Act, impose costs of $1.3 billion annually on state and local governments. The Fair Labor Standards Act is estimated to impose annual costs of slightly less than half a billion dollars. Price Waterhouse has surveyed city governments about the costs imposed by federal mandates. The firm estimated that the ten most important mandates will increase the costs borne by city governments by about $54 billion during the next five years.

These expenditures are certainly substantial, and they may be quite burdensome to the state and local governments required to undertake them. Nevertheless, from the viewpoint of the federal budget process, the numbers are really quite small. The cost estimates, $30 billion or more annually,

TABLE 2
COST ESTIMATES FOR MAJOR UNFUNDED MANDATES
(THOUSANDS OF 1994 DOLLARS)

Type	Federal Costs	State and Local Costs	Note
A. Annual costs			
Air quality[a]	$ 1,202	$ 1,318	Clean air act, radon gas
Water quality[a]	8,437	19,974	Clean water act, safe drinking water, marine protection
Land conservation[a] environmental	1,765	8,226	Resource recovery, comprehensive response
Chemical requirements[a]	413	125	
Multimedia[a]	1,175	18	
Education of handicapped[b]	—	643	
Asbestos[b]	—	164	
Disabilities act[b]	—	664	
Fair labor standards[b]	—	484	
B. Aggregate costs to cities[c] 1994–98	—		
Underground storage tanks	—	$ 1,040	
Clean water and wetlands	—	29,303	
Clean air	—	3,652	
Resource Recovery and Conservation Act	—	5,476	
Safe drinking water	—	8,644	
Asbestos	—	746	
Lead paint	—	1,628	
Endangered species	—	189	
Disabilities act	—	2,196	
Fair labor standards	—	1,121	

[a]Environmental Protection Agency, Report of the Administrator, *Environmental Investments: The Costs of a Clean Environment*, Island Press, 1991, pp. 8-51, Table 8-12A. (Estimates are for 1988 in 1994 dollars.)
[b]U.S. Advisory Commission on Intergovernmental Relations, *Federally Induced Costs Affecting State and Local Governments*, Information Report M-193, September 1994, pp. 13 and 15. (Estimates are for 1991 in 1994 dollars.)
[c]Price Waterhouse, *Impact of Unfunded Federal Mandates on U.S. Cities*, Second Printing, December 1994, p. 4.

are on the order of two percent of federal expenditures. We must conclude that, although mandates may provide a battle cry for states' rights, they have not provided a substantial opportunity for offloading federal expenditures to the states.

INTERGOVERNMENTAL GRANTS: REFORM OR BUDGET CUTTING?

As noted above, federal edicts can require expenditures by state and local governments—expenditures which can substitute directly for federal outlays. Consequently, these edicts can be used to reduce the central government deficit. Federal grants-in-aid to lower governments also impose spending requirements and stipulations on recipients. Moreover, they involve substantial central government expenditures. As a result, federal deficit reduction can be achieved by tightening state spending requirements and simultaneously cutting grant-in-aid programs. If these programs are cut or modified in form, the conditions of receipt will change, as will the incentives of state and local governments to continue the provision of the affected public services.

We note that even general revenue sharing, in effect between 1972 and 1982, imposed some relatively modest restrictions on recipient governments (Nathan, 1975). Most restrictions on grants-in-aid apply explicitly to categories of expenditure by lower level governments, and many involve matching programs. As a result, as currently constituted, these programs stimulate the provision of state and local services.

Reforms in the intergovernmental grant system can therefore have two significant effects. First, changes in regulations governing federal programs may provide

ample opportunity for intergovernmental grants to be cut in magnitude and changed in form—the result could be a substantial budget reduction by the central government. Second, both cuts and reformulations of grant programs may lead to substantial reductions in state and local spending on programs such as health and welfare. We treat each of these issues in turn.

Reversing the Trend: Budget Cuts

Figure 1 reports the trend in federal government grant activity during the past three decades. In real terms, federal grants-in-aid quadrupled during the period, from under $50 billion to more than $210 billion (in current dollars). Importantly, more than one-fourth of this substantial increase has been registered in the last five years. Between 1989–94, federal grants in aid to state and local governments increased by more than $68 billion—from 2.4 to 3.2 percent of GDP.

Spending on grants exceeded 17 percent of federal spending in the late 1970s. The Reagan years saw a steady drop in the importance of grants, to about 11 percent of federal spending. However, since 1989, grants have increased again, up to roughly 15 percent of outlays.

Figure 2 reports trends in grants to state and local governments for the four largest expenditure categories: transportation, education and training, health, and income security.[5] As the figure indicates, there has been little change in the pattern of federal grants for transportation. The pattern of grants for education and training is more complex, but the current level of grant expenditures is substantially lower, in real terms, than it was in the late 1970s. The same cannot be said for federal grants for

FIGURE 1. Grants to State and Local Governments

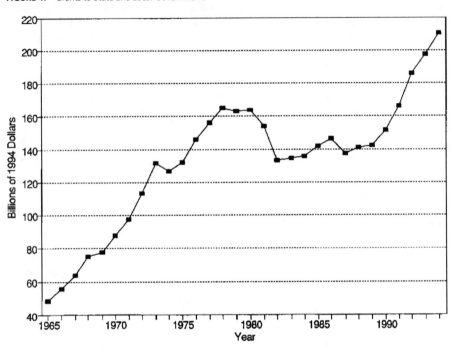

Source: *Budget of the United States Government,* Fiscal year 1996, Historical Tables, Tables 10.1, 12.1.

income security and for health. Grants to state and local governments for income security have risen steadily, from $15.7 billion in 1965 to $38 billion in 1989 (in current dollars). Since 1989, federal grants have risen sharply by $13.5 billion, or by more than one-third.

The increases in grants for health have been nothing short of explosive. Federal government grants to state and local governments increased from $2.8 billion in 1965 to more than $32.8 billion by 1985 (again, in current dollars). During the past decade, however, grants for health care have almost tripled, to $86.3 billion. The exponential growth of health care grants has continued—health care grants have doubled in the past five years alone.

Figure 3 reports the trend in federal grants to local governments for payments to individuals. Chief among these are, in order, medical care (chiefly Medicaid), public assistance (chiefly AFDC), housing assistance, and nutrition programs (not including food stamps). As the figure indicates, the trend between 1965–1980 is flat—grants for payments to individuals were something less than 35 percent of the total. The explosion since 1980 has almost doubled the fraction of grants to lower levels of government which are passed through as payments to individuals.

Similarly, there is a steady growth in dollar expenditures for grant payments to individuals until 1989—and an

FIGURE 2.   Major Categories of Federal Grants

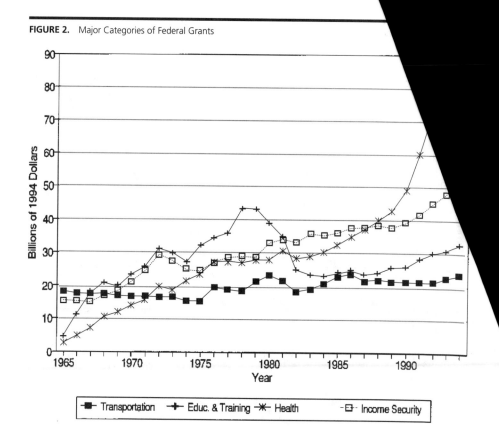

Source: *Budget of the United States Government,* Fiscal Year 1996, Historical Tables, Tables 10.1, 12.2.

explosive increase thereafter. These grants have *increased* by $53.4 billion in the past five years.

The trend in federal grants to state and local governments for payments to individuals is quite different from the trend in other types of grants-in-aid. Since the mid-1970s there has been a systematic decline in programmatic grants for education, transportation, and the production of local services and an increase in the extent of grants for payment to individuals—principally for medical care.[6] Since 1991, grants for

medical care have exceeded *all* grants for goods and services provided to state and local governments.

The debate over whether the grant levels of the 1970s or even the 1980s were reasonable and appropriate will certainly continue for many years to come, as the specific public programs supported are reviewed and evaluated. Whatever one's view on the merits of specific programs, a serious commitment to deficit reduction implies changing the trends in federal expenditures on these programs. Indeed, much

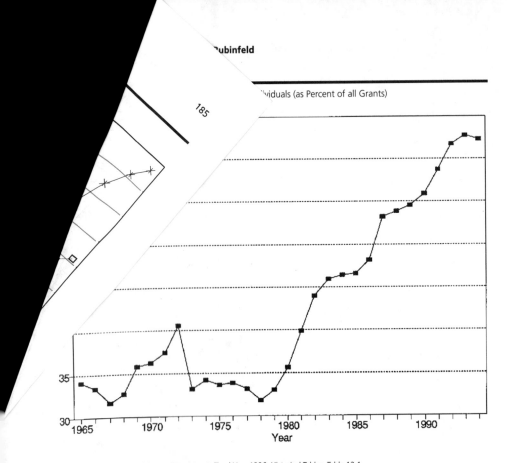

viduals (as Percent of all Grants)

Source: *Budget of the United States Government*, Fiscal Year 1996, Historical Tables, Table 12.1.

of the current rhetoric for "reform" of health care and AFDC is explicitly motivated by deficit reduction efforts. No picture of budgetary reform can be complete, however, without considering the implications for the programs themselves of proposed changes in the federal system of intergovernmental aid. We now turn briefly to the possible effects that changes in grant programs will have on the state and local public sectors.

Local Governments' Response

Most state and local governments operate under balanced budget constraints. It is not surprising, therefore, that the aggregate of state and local budgets is in modest surplus rather

than deficit. More to the point, however, the aggregate surplus has generally been declining for a decade.[7] Seen in this context, we should expect many states would choose not to provide equivalent services if they were given responsibility for health and welfare programs without the funding to support them.

The outcome of protracted budgetary debates between the Republican congress and the Democratic executive is unclear. There are clear incentives, however, to reform or replace current health and welfare programs—heavily subsidized by the federal government through a system of open-ended matching grants—by block grants of fixed size. For example, AFDC is currently an open-ended matching program in which the price subsidy provided by the federal government varies inversely with state income, ranging from 50 to 78.6 percent. Medicaid matches state spending at the same rate as AFDC.[8] Even without any change in funding levels or other regulations, a switch from matching programs with price and income effects to block grants without price effects will lead to a reduction in state and local spending.

The state and local government responses to specific policy changes will vary substantially depending on current budgetary pressures and on preferences. Depending upon the regulations governing program change, we should expect that cuts in current programs will be very substantial. A review of the evidence on price and income elasticities of demand for transfer programs suggests the reasons. Recent work by Chernick (1996) provides some estimates of the responses of state and local governments to a programmatic change in which AFDC and Medicaid were converted to block grants. He suggests that the shift would raise the average price of a dollar of AFDC benefits and Medicaid outlays from 45 cents to one dollar.[9]

The magnitude of the spending response of lower levels of government will depend heavily on the size of the relevant elasticities and the course of reductions in federal spending on block grants. Even if federal budgetary cuts were small to begin with, they would almost certainly grow over time. Current proposals cap future increases in program expenditures at the federal level. The response magnitude also depends on the extent to which states alter their benefit levels to compete with other states—a decline in one state's

benefits could lead (through a "race to the bottom") to substantial decreases in benefits offered by other states. At the high end in terms of predicted responses are Gramlich (1985) and Craig and Inman (1986), whose work suggests reductions in AFDC spending of from 70 to 85 percent. At the other extreme are Moffitt (1984, 1990) and Craig (1993), who suggest that substitution effects will reduce AFDC benefit levels by about 9 percent.

A large body of econometric evidence on state welfare spending and state AFDC benefit levels suggests that price elasticities are rather large, income elasticities are relatively small, and there is little substitution of food stamps for other forms of public welfare. Thus, studies by Gramlich (1982, 1985), Gramlich and Laren (1984), and Craig and Inman (1986) all find that the form and level of federal matching programs have substantial effects upon the amount of redistribution undertaken by the states. These studies are consistent with declines in benefit levels or state welfare spending of 70 to 85 percent. In contrast, two papers by Moffitt (1984, 1990) find smaller price elasticities and somewhat larger income elasticities— both of which would moderate the disastrous effects predicted by the others in moving to block grants.

The views of Gramlich and Laren (1984) and others are based, in part, upon the evidence that states responded to court-mandated increases in beneficiaries (arising from the "right to travel" rulings) by restricting benefits. This suggests that there will be a race to the bottom in the provision of welfare benefits as each state reacts in turn to the cuts in welfare levels proposed in neighboring states by cutting their own benefit levels. To the extent, however, that states are able to create constitutionally acceptable devices for restricting benefit levels of new entrants, or more generally that states do not respond closely to the choices of benefit levels of neighboring states, the race may not be as extreme as suggested by Gramlich and Laren.

There is much less econometric evidence on the determinants of state spending on Medicaid. (An early review is by Inman, 1985.) Chernick's more recent review (1996) concludes that "the small number of studies of Medicaid price responses suggest that the absolute magnitude of the income and price elasticities is greater than for AFDC." If true, these findings imply even larger estimates of the effect of block granting on spending reductions for Medicaid and public medical care by the states.

This evidence is not conclusive. But, given that many states have become more fiscally conservative, and given the tightness of their budgets, we conclude that the effects of this reform upon program beneficiaries would be very substantial.

Apparently, only one factor could mitigate the substantial reductions in aggregate spending on transfer programs which would accompany the termination of current federally supervised matching grants—a large increase in x-efficiency accompanying a shift in control to state governments. Indeed, there are extravagant claims that the states are more creative and innovative in designing welfare programs, and they are better managers of these programs. Curiously, these claims are made more forcefully about transfer programs than about other government activity. There is little doubt that a shift to state administered block grants will involve less bureaucracy and will give more

flexibility to states.[10] Beyond this, there is little or no systematic evidence about creativity or innovation.

Anecdotal evidence is not reassuring. It is reported that efforts to computerize child support and welfare payments in Maryland have been "disastrous"; the system will be two years late and 67 percent over budget. News accounts have estimated that Florida "lost" $170 million on food stamp errors, and state officials have acknowledged $28 million in "mistakes" in the Medicaid program. California's new welfare computer system is now estimated to be $455 million over budget, about 90 percent, and will not accommodate the volume of transactions necessary.

As far as management is concerned, one state's Secretary of Human Services suggests that passage of these federalism initiatives will be like "flying blind into a fog."[11]

Interpretation and Conclusions

The consensus normative model of federalism, summarized in Wallace Oates' 1972 book *Fiscal Federalism*, gives to the central government responsibility for financial oversight of those public activities distinguished by significant externalities involving spatially dispersed populations, while leaving to local governments responsibility for those public activities for which spatial spillovers are limited or absent. The guiding principle is to internalize all economic externalities at the smallest level of government possible—a principle formalized by Oates in his "decentralization theorem."[12] Decentralization to small collectives is favored since taste differences can best be accounted for by the political process if decision makers most closely represent their constituents. As Oates put it more recently (1994, p. 130), "The tailoring of outputs to local circumstances will, in general, produce higher levels of well-being than a centralized decision to provide some uniform level of output across all jurisdictions . . . And such gains do not depend upon any mobility across jurisdictional boundaries."

The traditional consensus was that regulation of markets, national defense, public health, economic stabilization, and redistribution policies are best handled at the centralized, or national, level of government, while education and the maintenance and protection of private and public property are best left to decentralized state or local levels of government. The current political debate questions this view.

The normative model that comes closest to making the case for a decentralized system of local governments is the Tiebout model. In the simplified Tiebout model, there are no spillovers across jurisdictional boundaries. When a Tiebout government decides to engage in an activity such as primary education, the benefits are obtained only by the residents of the jurisdiction. When benefits and costs do extend beyond the local boundaries, the "optimal" fiscal unit is a higher level of government.

These spillovers can create competitive incentives that lead to further and more significant inefficiencies. For example, states can be encouraged to relax their environmental controls to encourage business migration. The net result is a race to the bottom, leading to regulatory standards that vary from state to state and which would be significantly more lax than states would prefer if common national standards were set (Revesz, 1992).

A further case for a national standard can be made on nonefficiency grounds. When there is support for a particular national norm, a centralized policy that reflects that viewpoint may be appropriate, regardless of whether there are significant spillovers. Thus, "fairness" may require that all individuals receive equal access to public services and, more generally, equal treatment under the law. Alternatively, fairness can involve a judgment about the appropriate allocation of economic entitlements, including judgments about progressive taxation.

By themselves, the presence of spillovers is not sufficient to undo the efficiency of a Tiebout economy. For example, if a public good benefits two or more Tiebout communities, a Coasian bargain *might* arise in which joint production internalizes the externality. With costly bargaining, a higher level of government can facilitate and enforce the bargain.

Perhaps the two most important examples of the failure of Coasian bargaining in a decentralized public economy are the agreement to redistribute income to needy households and the agreement to manage jointly the overall macroeconomic performance of the economy. Perhaps redistribution policy should allow for regional differences (Pauly, 1973); yet regional agreements—particularly interconnected regional agreements—may not emerge because of strategic bargaining. If so, a national redistribution policy that explicitly grants some degree of local choice is the second-best compromise. Similarly, strategic bargaining between localities would most certainly prevent the design of a coordinated macroeconomic policy—as it did during the days of the Articles of Confederation. The only recourse, when a voluntary agreement cannot be reached, is a coercive, nationally directed fiscal policy.

We continue to adhere to the national consensus that poor and elderly U.S. residents should have access to minimum levels of health care. On the basis of this national norm alone, centralized regulation of health care is desirable. Further, however, destructive competition among states will lead to the underprovision of both health and welfare benefits. (Again, see Gramlich and Laren, 1984.) As a result, there is a powerful case for minimum national standards for both programs, financed centrally.[13]

It is clearly too early to know the direction in which U.S. federalism will move with much certainty. However, the current budgetary debate suggests strongly that we are entering a new period in fiscal federalism—a period marked by "restrained federalism." In this more limited federalist economy, the central government will encourage state responsibilities for a number of public regulatory and spending programs.

This review of the linkages between federal and lower levels of government does suggest three conclusions.

First, an increasing burden of federal mandates for expenditures has been placed on the states and local governments by the central government. Despite increasing attention to this issue during the past decade, the level and extent of unfunded mandates continue to grow. However, the evidence also indicates that these mandates provide only limited opportunities for budget reduction at the federal level. Cumulative state and local expenditures engendered by preemptions, direct

orders, and crossover mandates are significant and large from the local perspective but are rather small in comparison with expenditures from the federal budget.

Second, the rapid rise in federal grants to local governments does provide a significant opportunity to reduce the budget of the central government by appealing to federalist principles. The federalist principles are dubious. They involve the assertion that benefit levels in transfer programs are better decided locally and that program operations and standards are better managed locally. We have seen no systematic evidence suggesting a better management capacity by local government. Further, while there may be gains from state experimentation with new programs, and with new ways to administer old programs, we recognize the fact that, under our current system, states already have substantial flexibility to experiment.

The budget opportunity arises from the shift from open-ended matching grants for substantial programs to block grants of fixed size whose increase can be controlled centrally. We are persuaded by the evidence that there are moderate price elasticities and small income elasticities at the local level. Given the real possibility of a race to the bottom as well, this suggests that budget savings at the federal level will be achieved by drastically reducing the aggregate size of these programs. This reduction could, of course, be put off temporarily by the addition of a "hold harmless" clause to any new block grant programs. With a hold harmless clause, a condition of receipt of a block grant would be that the state maintain nominal benefits at current levels.

Third, since budgetary savings arise from capping the future growth of these programs, the savings arise in some part from the elimination of federally imposed rules for eligibility and program participation. It is elimination of the entitlement aspects of the programs that permits them to be devolved to the states. Removal of this mandate imposed on states and localities can generate substantial budgetary savings to the central government (at the expense of low-income people), but it will substantially change the nature of federalism in the United States.

ENDNOTES

This is a considerably revised and shortened version of Quigley and Rubinfeld (1996). We acknowledge the comments and suggestions of Roy Bahl, Roger Gordon, and Robert Inman, and we are grateful to Scott Susin for research assistance. Financial support for this research has been provided by the Fisher Center for Real Estate and Urban Economics, University of California, Berkeley.

1 See, for example, Scheiber (1966) for a discussion.
2 These and other distinctions in the extent and definition of mandates are discussed in Conlan (1991) and Musso and Quigley (forthcoming).
3 Another study (Conlan, 1991) reported that more than half of all federal preemption statutes enacted since the founding of the republic had been passed since 1970.
4 See, for example, Lovell et al (1979), Muller and Fix (1980), and Singh et al. (1988).
5 These are gross categories. For example, the category "income security" includes substantial expenditures by the Departments of Agriculture and Housing and Urban Development as well as expenditures by the Department of Health and Human Services.
6 See Quigley and Rubinfeld (1996) for a more detailed and qualified discussion.
7 See Gramlich (1991, Figure 1). The National Income Accounts surplus began to decline in 1983, while the operating surplus has generally fallen since 1972.
8 Specifically, the federal matching rate is $1 - 0.45(S^2/N^2)$, where S is state per capita income and N is national per capita income. See ACIR (1992) for an extensive discussion.
9 The price would be higher than one dollar if the Food Stamp program were to continue to tax AFDC benefits.

10 Gold (1995) develops these points.
11 These anecdotes are reported in *Business Week* (Kelly et al.,1995) and by Babington (1995) among other popular sources.
12 This theorem is closely related to the concept of "subsidiarity" which appears frequently in the current debates over the governmental structure of the European Union. See, also Breton (1965).
13 This conclusion is more detailed (and qualified) in Quigley and Rubinfeld (1996).

REFERENCES

Advisory Commission on Intergovernmental Relations. *Medicaid: Intergovernmental Trends and Options*, A-119. Washington, D.C.: ACIR, 1992.

Advisory Commission on Intergovernmental Relations. *Federally Induced Costs Affecting State and Local Governments*, M-193. Washington, D.C.: ACIR, 1994.

Advisory Commission on Intergovernmental Relations. *Federal Mandate Relief for State, Local and Tribal Governments*, A-129. Washington, D.C.: ACIR, 1995.

Babington, Charles. "Overloading the States." *Washington Post*, October 23–29, 1995, National Weekly Edition.

Barr, Calvaresi. "Cost Estimation as an Anti-Mandate Strategy." In *Coping with Mandates: What Are the Alternatives?*, edited by Michael Fix and Daphne Kenyon, 49–56. Washington, D.C.: The Urban Institute, 1990.

Breton, Albert. "A Theory of Government Grants." *Canadian Journal of Economics and Political Science* 31 (1965): 175–87.

Chernick, Howard. "Fiscal Effects of Block Grants for the Needy: A Review of the Evidence." Department of Economics, Hunter College and Graduate Center, CUNY. Revised, mimeo. January, 1996.

Conlan, Timothy J. "And the Beat Goes On: Intergovernmental Mandates and Preemption in an Era of Deregulation." *Publius* 21 (1991): 43–57.

Craig, Steven G. "Redistribution in a Federalist System: Can the Federal Government Alter State Government Behavior?" Department of Economics, University of Houston, September, 1993.

Craig, Steven G., and Robert P. Inman. "Education, Welfare, and the 'New Federalism': State Budgeting in a Federalist Public Economy." In *Studies in State and Local Public Finance*, edited by Harvey Rosen. Chicago: Chicago University Press, 1986.

Environmental Protection Agency. *Environmental Investments: The Costs of a Clean Environment.* Washington, D.C.: Island Press, 1991.

Gold, Steven D. "Impacts of the Revolution in Federal Policies on State and Local Government." *NTA Forum*, No. 22 (Summer, 1995).

Gramlich, Edward M. "Reforming U.S. Fiscal Arrangements." In *American Domestic Priorities*, edited by John M. Quigley and Daniel L. Rubinfeld, 34–69. Berkeley: University of California Press, 1985.

Gramlich, Edward M. "Federalism and Federal Deficit Reduction." *National Tax Journal* 40 No. 3 (September, 1987): 299–313.

Gramlich, Edward M. "The 1991 State and Local Fiscal Crisis." *Brookings Papers on Economic Activity*, 2 (1991): 249–87.

Gramlich, Edward M., and Deborah Laren. "Migration and Income Distribution Responsibilities." *Journal of Human Resources* 19 No. 4 (Fall, 1984): 489–511.

Gullo, Theresa A. "Estimating the Impact of Federal Legislation on State and Local Governments." In *Coping with Mandate: What are the Alternatives?*, edited by Michael Fix and Daphne Kenyon, 41–8. Washington, D.C.: The Urban Institute, 1990.

Inman, Robert P. "Fiscal Allocations in a Federalist Economy." In *American Domestic Priorities*, edited by John M. Quigley and Daniel L. Rubinfeld, 34–69. Berkeley: University of California Press, 1985.

Kelly, Kevin, Richard A. Melcher, Susan B. Garland, Wendy Zellner and Bureau Reports. "Power to the States: Are They Ready?" *Business Week* 34 No. 36 (August, 1995): 48–56.

Koch, Edward I. "The Mandate Millstone." *The Public Interest* (Fall, 1980): 42–57.

Lovell, Catherine H. *Federal and State Mandating on Local Governments: An Exploration of Issues and Impacts.* Riverside, CA: University of California, Riverside, 1979.

Moffitt, Robert. "The Effects of Grants-in-Aid on State and Local Expenditures: The Case of AFDC." *Journal of Public Economics* 23 (1984): 279–306.

Moffitt, Robert. "Has State Redistribution Policy Grown More Conservative?" *National Tax Journal* 43 No. 2 (June, 1990): 123–42.

Muller, Thomas, and Michael Fix. "The Impact of Selected Federal Actions on Municipal Outlays. In *Government Regulation: Achieving Social and Economic Balance*, Vol. 5. Washington, D.C.: Government Printing Office, 1980.

Musso, Juliet, and John M. Quigley. "Intergovernmental Fiscal Relations in California: A Critical Evaluation." In *Infrastructure, Economic Growth, and Regional Development*, edited by David Batten. New York: Springer Verlag, forthcoming.

Nathan, Richard P. *Monitoring Revenue Sharing.* Washington, D.C.: The Brookings Institution, 1975.

National Conference of State Legislatures. *1994 Mandate Catalog*, Special Edition. Washington, D.C.: Hall of the States Mandate Monitor Database, 1994.

Oates, Wallace E. *Fiscal Federalism.* New York: Harcourt, Brace, Jovanovich, 1972.

Oates, Wallace E. "Federalism and Government Finance." In *Modern Public Finance*, edited by John M. Quigley and Eugene Smolensky. Cambridge: Harvard University Press, 1994.

Pauly, Mark. "Income Redistribution as a Local Public Good." *Journal of Public Economics* 2 No. 1 (February, 1973): 35–58.

Perloff, Harvey S., and Richard P. Nathan, eds. *Revenue Sharing and the City.* Baltimore: John Hopkins Press, 1968.

Price Waterhouse. *Impact of Unfunded Federal Mandates on US Cities.* 2d printing. Washington, D.C.: Price Waterhouse, 1994.

Quigley, John M., and Daniel L. Rubinfeld. "Federalism as a Device for Reducing the Budget of the Central Government." Robert D. Burch Center for Tax Policy and Public Finance Working Paper. Berkeley: University of California, Berkeley, 1996.

Revesz, Richard. "Rehabilitating Interstate Competition: Rethinking the 'Race to the Bottom' Rationale for Federal Environmental Regulation." 67 *New York University Law Review* 1210, 1992.

Scheiber, Harry N. "The Condition of American Federalism: An Historian's View." Subcommittee on Intergovernmental Relations to the Committee on Governmental Operations, U.S. Senate, October 15, 1966.

Singh, Jasbinder . *Municipal Sector Study: Impacts of Environmental Regulations on Municipalities.* Prepared by Policy Planning and Evaluation, Inc. for the U.S. Environmental Protection Agency, Washington, D.C., September, 1988.

ISSUES RAISED BY THE NEW FEDERALISM

STEVEN D. GOLD*

INTRODUCTION

The November 1994 elections reignited interest in many fundamental issues. The assignment of functional roles to local, state, and federal governments, the appropriate balance between the public and private sectors, and the types of grants provided by the federal government all could be significantly altered. As this is written in early 1996, it is not clear whether major policy changes will be enacted before the November elections, but the probability appears to be high that federal policies will be significantly altered no later than 1997.

This paper addresses the implications of these developments for the country and for public finance research. In terms of research needs, it is concerned with two primary questions: How can research be improved so that it is better able to explain the policy choices that state and local governments are making? What can be done to make research more useful to state policy makers?

*Urban Institute, Washington, D.C. 20037.

THE CONTENT OF THE DEVOLUTION REVOLUTION[1]

Devolution refers to passing responsibility down to another level of government. It is difficult to discuss for several reasons. First, it is inherently complicated, with numerous important effects on states and citizens and major differences in how various states will be affected. Second, as the cliche says, the devil is in the details. Some approaches to reducing federal aid and increasing state flexibility have very different effects than others. Third, the welfare and Medicaid systems would be fundamentally altered, confronting state governments with new choices. There is enormous uncertainty about how they would respond. Fourth, the time horizon matters: the short-run effects of devolution are likely to differ considerably from the long-run effects.

The New Federalism embodied in the Republican revolution has three major aspects affecting state and local governments. (1) They would receive less federal aid. (2) Some of the most important aid programs would be changed from matching to nonmatching grants. (3) States would have more flexibility in operating programs. A major uncertainty is the size of the aid reductions in relation to the benefits from increased flexibility.

Aid Reductions

The driving force in reducing aid is the effort to balance the federal budget by the year 2002. Aid to states will bear a disproportionate share of the spending reductions needed to balance the budget because the three largest spending categories—Social Security, defense, and interest payments—are likely to be cut relatively little if at all. In the reconciliation bill vetoed by the president in late 1995, aid would have been reduced approximately 26 percent in 2002.[2] If there is a budget agreement, the eventual aid reduction will probably be less than 26 percent because the federal tax reduction will be smaller and more optimistic economic assumptions have reduced the prospective deficit in 2002. But the aid reduction would still be substantial, probably on the order of 15–20 percent.

This projected reduction is from what aid would have been under current federal law. In nominal dollars, the total amount of aid would increase. It is important, however, to disaggregate aid. The entire nominal increase between 1995–2002 is attributable to Medicaid, which accounted for about 40 percent of total aid in 1995. Excluding Medicaid, aid would fall in nominal dollars. It should also be recognized that the baseline from which the aid reductions are calculated does not reflect the impact of inflation on discretionary programs in some years.

Federal aid represents between a quarter and a third of state government resources.[3] A 15–20 percent reduction from what aid would have been in 2002 implies that, other things being equal,

state revenues will be about five percent lower than they would have been in that year. Spreading this reduction over seven years, we can say that total revenues will grow about 0.7 percent less per year than they otherwise would have.

Whether states can absorb this reduction without having to reduce services or increase revenues depends on how fast current services spending and revenue are growing. If the growth rate of revenue were at least 0.7 percent higher than the growth rate of spending, states could adjust to the loss of federal aid without having to cut back spending or raise taxes and fees. However, it appears that most states are not so fortunate. Indeed, many seem to have structural deficits. (A common strategy for states has been to shift their fiscal problems, such as by relying increasingly on tuition to fund higher education, cutting back on aid to schools and other local governments, and pushing costs into the future. Each of these shifts represents a failure to maintain current services).

This does not imply that states face an immediate fiscal catastrophe. In fact, aid reductions will be gradually phased in, so they will not be particularly dramatic at first but rather will grow steadily over time. Besides, many states have accumulated substantial reserve balances that can provide a cushion to help them absorb aid cutbacks at first. But those balances represent nonrecurring revenue, and they would disappear fast if a recession occurred.

Some observers may discount long-term projections in the belief that policies would probably be changed before 2002, resulting in smaller cutbacks. Whether that assumption is accurate depends, in part, on whether a constitutional amendment to require a balanced federal budget is adopted. If it were, it would be much more difficult to avoid large aid reductions in the out-years.

Another imponderable is how well the economy performs. The federal government's projections assume that eliminating the deficit would raise the growth rate of the economy. If that occurred, it would help states in two ways—federal aid reductions would not have to be as large because the federal deficit would be smaller, and state tax revenue would grow more. Assumptions about stronger economic growth rate (and the positive effect of deficit reduction on the level of interest rates) are, however, extremely uncertain.

Shift from Matching to Nonmatching Grants

At least as important as the amount of grants is their form. By proposing a shift from open-ended matching grants to block grants for Medicaid, Aid to Families with Dependent Children (AFDC), and some smaller programs, the reforms incorporated in the budget reconciliation act would have significantly decreased the incentive for states to spend their own money on the affected programs. Since 1965, the federal government has paid from 50–83 percent of the cost of Medicaid and AFDC, so it cost states only 17–50 cents to increase their spending for those programs by a dollar. Under block grants, it would cost a dollar for states to spend a dollar.[4] Thus, the devolution revolution would reduce not only federal spending but also state spending. It is really a prescription for lower government spending.

The virtual abandonment of open-ended matching grants[5] is inconsistent with the view that such grants are needed to stimulate the production of services that produce external benefits. It appears that the externality argument for welfare and Medicaid spending is being rejected. People seem not to accept the idea any longer that there are production externalities—for example, that poverty breeds crime and that welfare tends to reduce it. At the same time, belief in consumption externalities appears to be waning—the idea that one person's welfare is affected adversely if others are in poverty.[6]

Another important implication of adopting block grants is that the amount of financial aid provided by the federal government to states will not automatically respond during a recession. States usually experience serious fiscal problems when the economy contracts, because tax revenue is depressed and the caseloads of programs such as Medicaid and welfare grow substantially. During the most recent recession these developments were partially offset by a large increase in federal aid. Between 1990–1992, state spending rose 20.4 percent while state tax revenue was growing only 9.1 percent. A 34.3 percent federal aid increase made it much easier for states to avoid deficits or painful spending reductions and tax increases (Gold, 1995a). Although some Congressional proposals include contingency funds to augment certain block grants if unemployment rises sharply, states would not enjoy a large increase in federal aid during the next recession as they have in the past.

The automatic growth of federal aid caused by the recession of the early 1990s suggests that the full implications of switching to block grants will really not be felt until the next recession occurs. Eliminating open-ended matching grants means that the state budget crunch will be much more severe during a recession than it has been during the downturns of the past several decades.

On the other hand, the federal deficit will not increase as much in recessions as it has done in the past. There is, however, not perfect symmetry. States cannot run up big deficits as the federal government can. Their efforts to stave off deficits will tend to destabilize the national economy.[7]

Enhanced Flexibility

The New Federalism would give states the freedom to redesign programs in more efficient and effective ways, but the quantitative magnitude of the benefits from increased flexibility is uncertain. The advantages gained by reducing paperwork are probably not worth a great deal in comparison with the loss of funding that is associated with the block grants,[8] but the relaxation of regulations could be more significant. Freedom from the voluminous rules governing how programs must be operated could yield substantial efficiency gains, particularly if the federal government has been prescribing standards that are higher than local citizens desire. Advocates of devolution point to the results of welfare and Medicaid waivers as indications of the kind of changes that will occur. For example, Oregon and Tennessee used waivers to substantially expand Medicaid coverage, and Wisconsin was able to significantly reduce welfare caseloads in two counties.

The gains from enhanced flexibility depend on how creative the states are and how sweeping the block grant legislation turns out to be. Some of the freedom that state officials seek involves allowing them to reduce their own

spending, to cut off beneficiaries of programs, to reduce service standards, or to shift costs to others (e.g., by repealing the Boren Amendment that has forced states to pay higher rates to hospitals and nursing homes than they otherwise would have). Such provisions help states fiscally but do not necessarily make programs more efficient.

Historical Perspective

The New Federalism rolls back the clock in some ways to before the Great Society and in other respects to before the New Deal. By fundamentally changing Medicaid, it affects one of the major legacies of the Great Society. By abolishing AFDC, it undoes a guarantee that was established as part of the New Deal.

But while the New Federalism would fundamentally change the *form* of those programs, it does not come anywhere near returning us to where we used to be in terms of the *amount* of aid provided. Federal aid is currently 3.2 percent of GDP. That is less than the peak level of 3.6 percent in the late 1970s, but it is higher than in any year before 1973. The comparable figure in 1965 was 1.9 percent, and in 1940, 0.9 percent.

If federal aid were cut 20 percent from its 1995 level, it would be no lower than it was in 1992. After falling in the early 1980s and growing relatively slowly through most of the remainder of that decade, the amount of aid began to rise rapidly in 1989. Just four years later it had grown from $124 billion to $194 billion. Most of this increase occurred automatically, without explicit initiatives from the federal government. As explained above, much of it reflected the recession that led to surging demand for social services (defined broadly to include health, income security, and direct services). Another part was caused by spending increases related to new federal mandates. But part also was the result of state actions that shifted costs to the federal government, particularly for Medicaid.[9]

De Facto Devolution

As this is written in early 1996, the stalemate between the president and Congress has brought a halt to what once seemed an irresistible march toward block grants and adoption of a balanced budget plan. Nevertheless, it appears very likely that much of the devolution agenda will continue to advance.

Two points can be made. First, many states already have waivers permitting them to escape from a large number of the federal regulations that have governed welfare and Medicaid programs, and the administration appears ready to approve more waivers liberally. The end of "welfare as we know it" is already occurring, with 37 states having welfare waivers of some kind (varying from far reaching to minor). The same thing is happening to Medicaid.

Second, momentum toward reducing the federal budget deficit appears likely to continue. If it does, aid to states will be curtailed, probably resulting in a reduction of the proportion of state revenue coming from the federal government. This amounts to de facto devolution, although it will occur more gradually than if it were compressed into seven years.

Whether a big budget agreement is reached in 1996 or 1997, the federal system appears likely to change fundamentally. The issues are how fast it changes and how it changes.

WHAT IS NEEDED TO IMPROVE RESEARCH

If the New Federalism is actually enacted, it will eventually stimulate considerable research by specialists in public finance and public policy. A thorough discussion of the pitfalls and priorities for such research would consider such issues as how welfare and Medicaid reform affected work effort, family structure, the nonmarital birth rate, and access to health care. This review will focus on a narrower set of issues, those dealing with state tax and spending policies.

Unfortunately, unless major changes are made in how public finance research is conducted, it is likely that a large portion of that research will fail to recognize critical features of the state fiscal landscape. This will significantly impair its usefulness.

It would exceed the scope of this article to discuss all of the improvements that are needed to improve the relevance of research for the real world of state governments. Rather, two important issues will be addressed here: using appropriate data and focusing on some of the key subjects that have received inadequate scrutiny.

Data

One of the main limitations of much existing research is the use of inappropriate data. In some cases, this is due to a mistake on the part of the researcher. But, in many situations, the relevant data are somewhat difficult to obtain.

Most studies of state spending and tax policies use data published by the U.S. Census Bureau. Those data are adequate and appropriate for testing many theories, and sometimes they are the only option available. Census data, however, are often inappropriate and too dated to be useful for understanding recent developments.

Timeliness is one serious problem. As of March 1996, the most recent information on state finances from the Census Bureau was for fiscal year 1993, which ended in June 1993 for most states. [10] For local finances, the most recent data were for fiscal year 1992. Such old information is of limited value in analyzing state and local policies in 1996 because major changes have occurred in the interim. For example, since 1993, the rate of growth of Medicaid spending and federal aid have slowed sharply, states have switched from raising taxes to cutting them, and corrections spending increases have escalated.

Census data have a number of other important shortcomings. Two of the most important are the following:

(1) they aggregate all spending and revenue, failing to distinguish between what is in or out of the general fund; and
(2) they do not report Medicaid as a distinct category of expenditures even though Medicaid has been at the heart of state budget policy for a number of years.

The Importance of the General Fund

When governors and legislators battle about the state budget, they usually focus primarily on the general fund, which normally receives the great majority of non-highway-related state tax revenue. In some but not most states, there are also some other important tax-supported funds, particularly for school aid. The Census Bureau aggregates all funds, combining the general fund and school aid fund with others related to independent or quasi-independent authorities that were established by the state government. The difference is substantial. In 1992, for example, general fund spending was $296 billion, while the Census reported that general state spending was $612 billion. (Note that the Census refers to its most important measure of spending as *general* spending, which should not be confused with *general fund* spending; the two have nothing in common.)

The two ways of viewing spending yield very different pictures of the nature of state activity. For example, for 1992, elementary and secondary education represented 34.0 percent of general fund spending but only 19.8 percent of Census general spending. Corrections was 5.6 percent of general fund spending but only 3.3 percent of Census general spending. Interest payments on general debt were 4.0 percent of the Census measure but much less of General Fund spending.[11]

Both measures of spending are valuable, depending on the issue one is concerned with analyzing. If the focus is on the total scope of state government activity, the Census measure is preferable. But if one wants to understand what is going on in state budget deliberations, the general fund is better.

For example, in the 1970s and 1980s, there was a major expansion of activity financed by bonding, such as authorities that underwrite subsidized mortgages or help to finance environmental projects or medical facilities. This expansion received little if any state tax support, so it was largely independent of annual budget deliberations. It was captured by the Census measure but was ignored by the general fund.[12]

This emphasis on the general fund needs to be modified in two respects. First, spending earmarked for schools in a special fund is a very close substitute for the general fund. It should be aggregated with general fund spending to provide the best measure of how state spending patterns are changing. Second, there is not uniformity about how the general fund is defined across states or for a particular state over time. General fund data are more useful for comparing developments in particular states in various years than for making interstate comparisons. If a state has made a material change in what it includes in the general fund, analysts should adjust for this in their research. Fortunately, states do not often make major changes in the definition of their general funds.

Medicaid

Medicaid is the second largest program in most state budgets, exceeded only by aid to elementary and secondary education. It is also an extremely complicated program. Although approximately half of the participants are children, they account for only about one-sixth of spending. Rather, about two-thirds of the spending is for the elderly and disabled.

The Medicaid program has been changing rapidly in several dimensions. For one thing, its costs have risen sharply. In 1991 and 1992, for example, total Medicaid spending rose approximately 28 percent per year. Its financing has also been in a state of flux as states first used creative financing to shift costs to the federal government, and then the federal government gradually tightened regulations to prevent or restrict many of the stratagems employed by states. The way states paid for Medicaid in 1991 and 1992 was considerably

different from 1988, but by 1995, it had significantly changed once again.[13] To understand the real story of state finances, there is no substitute for incorporating such institutional information.

Using More Appropriate Data

If the data collected by the Census Bureau are inadequate, what should be done?[14] There are two alternatives— information from individual states themselves and reports published by national organizations of state governments. As mentioned above, little reliable analysis is available on whether state budgets are structurally balanced, which is a very important issue for understanding how state fiscal policies are changing. To resolve this issue obviously requires data that are available only at the state level. It will be discussed in the next section.

The National Conference of State Legislatures (NCSL) and the National Association of State Budget Officers (NASBO) publish numerous reports that fill in some of the gaps left by the Census Bureau.[15] Studies by Poterba (1994, 1995) and Blackley and DeBoer (1993) are examples of recent analyses that creatively used NCSL and NASBO reports to analyze state fiscal developments in the early 1990s.

Despite their great value, the NCSL and NASBO reports have some shortcomings that researchers should consider. For example, as already mentioned, states do not employ the same accounting and budgeting systems. A low year-end balance is a sign of unusual fiscal stress in most states, but some states make budget adjustments so that they always report a low balance. In addition, the projections in the reports are often misleading, tending to underestimate spending and revenue increases and year-end balances.[16] The information in the reports about periods that have already ended is more useful than the projections. The reporting methodology used by particular states has not always been consistent from year to year, making comparisons across years sometimes unreliable. Finally, the information submitted by states is occasionally influenced by political considerations. In 1993, for example, it was widely believed in Sacramento that California ended the fiscal year with a large deficit, and that is what NCSL reported. Governor Pete Wilson's administration, however, reported to NASBO that there was a budget surplus, and that is what it said. Despite such problems, the NCSL and NASBO reports are extremely useful documents on the whole.

Vital Research Subjects

Five subjects are essential for understanding state fiscal policies: whether state budgets are structurally balanced, the factors affecting discretionary tax changes, the determinants of state spending, the interactions between state and local governments, and the effects of federal aid. The first four subjects have received relatively little attention. While the fifth has been studied extensively, it requires more disaggregated research, particularly in relation to Medicaid and block grants in general. These issues are largely the same ones that would need to be studied even if no major devolution occurs. Before one can trace the effects of new federal policies, it is necessary to understand what is already occurring in state policy.

Structural Balance

The analysis of whether state budgets have structural surpluses or deficits can be divided into two parts: How rapidly will revenue from the existing tax system grow? How much will the spending necessary to maintain the current level of services increase?

In many (but not all) states, the income elasticity their state tax systems is lower than it was in the late 1970s, and tax revenue now tends to grow more slowly than total economic activity. Among the reasons for the lower responsiveness of tax revenue to economic growth are the trend toward flatter income tax rates, the adoption of indexing in 17 of the 41 states with income taxes, the movement of more households into the highest bracket of state income taxes, and the increasing economic importance of services, which are lightly taxed by state sales taxes. Unfortunately, there is little good research to document the extent of the reduction of elasticity.[17] Well-grounded estimates of elasticity using time-series data need to make adjustments for the effects of legislated changes; such information can be obtained only at the state level.

There are numerous important conceptual issues in analyzing the spending side of the state budget, such as the following.

(1) Is the concern with maintaining current services or complying with current laws? Many recent studies do not really assume current services. Rather, they often extrapolate past trends or assume that policies follow existing legislation, which may permit erosion of service levels or improvements in services.

(2) What is assumed about productivity? Traditionally, productivity improvements in the public sector have lagged, but with the emphasis on "reinventing government" in many state capitals, it may be

possible to maintain services even if spending is squeezed.

(3) What does "current services" mean in relation to local aid—maintaining real spending per person or continuing the traditional relationship between state aid and local spending?

Discretionary Tax Changes

The articles by Poterba (1994) and Blackley and DeBoer (1994) mentioned above both made important contributions to understanding why states raised their taxes during the early 1990s, but they merely represent a beginning toward filling an important information gap. Additional research is needed on state tax changes during periods when fiscal conditions are healthy as well as when they are stressed.

This issue is closely related to the question of whether states with more elastic tax systems tend to have faster growing revenue and spending. From a political point of view, it would seem considerably easier to increase revenue automatically from the nominal growth of income than to increase it by explicitly raising tax rates or expanding the tax base. In fact, however, most studies have found that the proportion of tax revenue from the personal income tax (the proxy usually used to indicate differences in elasticity) has a weak effect on revenue/spending increases or no effect at all. (Oates, 1975; Feenberg and Rosen, 1987) If that is true, it would imply that discretionary tax changes offset differences in the natural growth of revenue in response to economic changes. That would be consistent with the well-established fact that states with relatively high personal income tax rates were much more likely to reduce them in the 1980s than states with low

income tax rates (Gold, 1991). But firm conclusions about the effect of the tax system's elasticity on revenue and spending cannot be obtained until good estimates of elasticity are available.

Determinants of Spending

An important area for research would focus on the simultaneous determination of spending for the major parts of the state budget. It is widely believed but not well documented in public finance literature that Medicaid and corrections spending have, to some extent, crowded out spending for education and welfare programs. Moffitt (1990) concluded that Medicaid has crowded out welfare spending, and Wyckoff and Fossett (1996) found an impact of Medicaid on school aid, but much further research is needed along these lines. Neither of those studies took a general approach that considered all of the major budget categories, recognizing that, if more is spent on one program, less can be devoted to others.

Most research has focused on determinants of state and local spending. While that is important from some perspectives, it is also important to analyze state and local spending separately because decisions are often made independently at the two levels.

Interactions between State and Local Governments

Aside from elementary and secondary education, relatively little attention has recently been devoted to the shifting balance of spending and revenue between state and local governments. But important changes are occurring. The U.S. Census Bureau began reporting on state aid in 1957. From that year until 1988, aid fluctuated between 34–37 percent of general state spending. It fell below that level in 1989, and by 1992, the last year for which figures are available, aid was only 32.3 percent of general spending. Ladd (1991) provides one of the few recent analyses of local aid.

An important priority for future research should be the effects of devolving state programs to local governments. In view of the substantial variation that already exists among states, it should be possible to provide useful guidance to state policy makers about how to devolve programs without creating more problems than are solved.

Effects of Federal Aid

A vast amount of research has been done on the effects of federal aid on state and local spending. Little of it extends into the period from 1989–93 when federal aid soared. Little of it deals with Medicaid, which, as mentioned above, now accounts for approximately 40 percent of the total amount of aid provided. Much of the research is relatively highly aggregated, making it impossible to measure with precision the effect of differing matching ratios.

Welfare is one program that has been analyzed extensively. According to Chernick and Reschovsky's review of the literature (1995), it has been difficult if not impossible to separate the price effects of aid from the income effects because a state's matching rate depends on its per capita income. Considerable difference exists between two bodies of research, with one group of studies finding much larger price effects than the other. This issue would be extremely important if the federal government converted welfare to a block grant, which would sharply increase the price of spending on welfare from the state budget point of view. While the

literature agrees that block grants would tend to depress welfare spending to some degree, the so-called "race to the bottom" would be much faster according to some researchers than others.

The Importance of Disaggregation

One of the underlying themes of this section is the importance of disaggregation. For example, various states must be considered separately because states are not monolithic in their policies, what the Census Bureau calls welfare spending must be divided between Medicaid and cash assistance, individual spending programs must be considered to understand the effects of federal matching provisions, revenue from charges must be considered separately from miscellaneous revenue, and states must be analyzed distinctly from local governments.

The reference to local governments requires elaboration. Many of the points made here about the need for research on states apply to local governments as well. There is far less research on the fiscal behavior of counties—the fastest growing general governments in the country—than on states. From some perspectives, it is important to consider state and local policies rather than those of states or localities alone. We need both kinds of analyses—those that examine state and local governments separately and those that study them together.

Issues Raised Specifically by Devolution

Much of the research on devolution can be divided into four important areas.

(1) *Responsiveness to price changes*. How much will spending decrease if block grants substitute for matching grants?

(2) *Diversity of demands*. How much will the variation in spending among states increase? If the federal government has caused spending to rise to a much higher level than citizens of some states desire, differences in the level of spending could grow considerably. Among the factors influencing these changes will be the effect of relaxing mandates on service levels, differences in matching rates, and possible differences in the elasticity of demand for services.

(3) *Diversity of production technology*. If the federal government allows greater freedom to design programs, there should also be increased variation in how states structure and operate the delivery of services.

(4) *Distributional effects*. If the federal government eliminates the national safety net, there could be a significant increase in inequality in terms of income and services received.

In analyzing these effects, analysts should be careful to avoid the pitfall of placing too much emphasis on policies adopted in the one or two years after devolution goes into effect. The initial state response may be muted because of inertia or by reserves that can be tapped during a transition period. The long-run effects of devolution are likely to be much greater than its short-run results.

THE CONTEXT OF THE DEVOLUTION REVOLUTION

Research about the impact of the New Federalism has to consider the context in which it is occurring. State policies are already changing. One of the problems with studying states is that there are long-term trends and intermediate-term trends, and one's sense of the direction of change depends on the time period one considers. For example (Gold et al., 1996), consider the following.

(1) State taxes rose much faster than local taxes in the quarter century from 1970–95, but that is entirely because of what happened in the 1970s. Since 1985, local taxes have risen faster.

(2) Likewise, states now pay a considerably higher share of the cost of elementary and secondary education than they did in 1970, but since 1987, the state share has been trending downward.

(3) States are much more dependent on personal income taxes than they were in 1970, but in the past decade, the average effective income tax rate has not risen.

(4) Reliance on the property tax fell sharply in the 1970s, but since 1982, the property tax has rebounded, growing faster than personal income (although it still claims a much lower proportion of income than it did 25 years ago).

If one is predicting what will happen in the next five or ten years, the trends since the mid-1980s seem more significant than the longer-term trends going back to 1970. What, then has been happening to spending and tax policy? Let us consider spending first.

Expenditures

Table 1 shows that some important changes occurred in the composition of state spending between 1990–94:

(1) Medicaid rose most, growing from 9.1 percent to 12.8 percent of the budget. Among the causes of this increase were health cost inflation,

TABLE 1
COMPOSITION OF STATE SPENDING, 1990 AND 1994

	1990	1994
Elementary and secondary education	36.3%	36.2%
Higher education	14.0%	12.5%
AFDC	2.5%	2.8%
Medicaid	9.1%	12.8%
Corrections	5.2%	5.9%
Miscellaneous	32.8%	29.8%

Note: Spending consists of general fund expenditures plus other expenditures from state revenue for elementary and secondary education.
Source: See Gold and Ritchie, 1996.

the impact of the recession in raising caseloads, and the shifting of other health programs into Medicaid.[18]

(2) Corrections also rose sharply, from 5.2 percent to 5.9 percent of total spending, reflecting popular support for "get tough on criminals" policies such as "three strikes and you're in."

(3) School aid, the largest share of the budget, was stable at about 36 percent of the total. This was not a strong performance considering that schools had to contend with large enrollment increases during this period.[19] Competition from Medicaid and corrections is probably an important reason why school aid did not increase more. After the recession ended, real spending per pupil, including federal and local funds, rose much less than in other nonrecession periods during the past 50 years.

(4) Higher education was the big loser in the battle for state support, falling from 14.0 percent to 12.5 percent of spending. While part of this slippage was due to slow enrollment growth, the main reason was that states relied heavily on tuition increases to substitute for state tax support.

(5) Aid to Families with Dependent Children rose slightly, from 2.5 percent to 2.8 percent of the budget. This is not much of an increase in view of the 27.5 percent caseload increase that occurred. Real benefits were reduced in most states.

(6) The remaining programs received a smaller share of the pie, as states focused on trimming bureaucracies, shifted some health programs into Medicaid, and downsized or provided meager increases for other programs.

What would one expect under the New Federalism? If federal aid cutbacks cause state fiscal stress, the programs that fared badly in the early 1990s would probably again be losers, but block grants would cause Medicaid and welfare spending to grow less than before. Higher education and miscellaneous programs would continue to fall as a proportion of the budget, and welfare spending would also go down. Corrections spending would surely continue to grow rapidly. School aid would have to battle hard for funds, and Medicaid would rise much more slowly than it did in the early 1990s.

On another level, spending may be undergoing changes in response to the "reinventing government" movement, which can be viewed as attempting to change the production function for government services, or at least moving up to the production function from an inefficient position away from it. To the extent that this movement succeeds, lower spending may not imply reduced services.

An important issue to monitor and analyze will be how widely state responses differ. Will many states sharply reduce their spending on poverty-related programs if given the chance, as might be predicted by those who remember how backward some states were before federal programs and mandates began to expand in the 1960s? Or have states changed so much that they will maintain most services even though they are not required to?

Taxes

State tax policy has been dominated during the past several years by small net tax reductions. This followed a large number of tax increases at the start of the decade. It is precisely what normally has happened for the past 20 years, with increases during recessions and decreases in their aftermath (Gold, 1996).

It may be, however, that state tax policy is in the process of becoming more conservative. At least, that is the impression one gains from shifts in the political ideologies of many recently elected governors and legislators.

This issue is unsettled because not many proponents of tax cuts also explicitly call for large reductions in services. They usually claim that services can be maintained by increasing efficiency, or they gloss over the issue. But attitudinal surveys usually find that, while citizens like tax cuts, they do not want to lose services.

Recent experience suggests that tax cuts will tend to occur in states with relatively high tax rates and relatively elastic tax systems. The cut in high-tax states reflects the intense competition for economic development that is an important part of the environment for making state fiscal policy.

Conclusions

If the New Federalism is adopted in something like the form proposed by Congressional Republicans, the country will be in for a grand experiment. In some important ways, state governments have changed fundamentally. Starting in the 1960s, they became more representative, more competent, and much larger. If the federal government pulls back sharply, there is no precedent for telling how the states will respond.

The problem of predicting their response is complicated by some other factors. Twenty-one states now have term limits for legislators. While the effects of these newly enacted limitations are still uncertain, they are likely to reduce expertise, increase the short-term orientation of policy making, and enhance prospects for adoption of new, untested policies. In addition, nearly half of the states have constitutional or statutory spending or revenue limits that did not exist 20 years ago. Since most of those limitations make no allowance for changes in federal aid, they could present formidable barriers to state efforts to offset reduced reliance on federal aid.

The New Federalism promises to present great opportunities for public finance researchers. But if they are to take advantage of it, they will have to be more creative about obtaining data and pay more attention to institutional details than they have in the past.

ENDNOTES

The views expressed in this article are solely those of the author and should not be attributed to the Urban Institute or the New Federalism Project and its sponsors. The author appreciates helpful comments on an earlier draft by Howard Chernick, George Peterson, Len Nichols, and the editor.

[1] The term "devolution revolution" was coined by Richard P. Nathan.

[2] This estimate was prepared by the Center on Budget and Policy Priorities. For a discussion of this issue developed before the reconciliation bill was vetoed, see Lav and St. George (1996). The 26 percent figure is the decrease in the year when the budget is supposed to be balanced. Many other analyses discuss the cumulative decrease over seven years, which is a smaller percentage reduction because the aid decreases grow over time.

[3] According to the U.S. Census Bureau, federal aid was approximately 26 percent of state general revenue in 1992. One component of general revenue is miscellaneous revenue, a large portion of which is dedicated to programs that are outside the scope of annual budget deliberations, such as interest received in return for loans to companies (for economic development subsidies) or to home owners (for mortgage subsidies). Excluding miscellaneous revenue raises the proportion of state resources accounted for by federal aid.

[4] This is not necessarily true in all cases. Under one Medicaid block grant proposal, there would still be a price effect for low-spending states. That is, they would receive the maximum possible amount of federal aid only if they spent more than they were already spending.

[5] As of March 1996, it appeared likely that Congress intended to retain an open-ended matching grant for foster care.

[6] These points were suggested by George Peterson.

[7] Numerous states do have deficits during recessions. In many states, the balanced budget requirement requires that a balanced budget be enacted, but if the budget falls into deficit during the course of the year, that is acceptable. All states do, however, attempt to eliminate deficits quickly.

[8] That was the conclusion about the block grants created in 1981 according to Peterson et al. (1986).

[9] At first, states used donations from hospitals to provide their matching funds and then returned the funds to the hospitals as Medicaid reimbursements. A variation was to impose a tax on health care providers, which sometimes needed to be paid only if the provider agreed. Some of these taxes guaranteed that the provider would receive at least as much back from the state as it paid in tax. When donations were outlawed and the federal government required that hospital taxes not have "hold harmless" provisions, some states turned to intergovernmental transfers, which were like donations, except that they came from local government hospitals or university medical facilities. All of these devices allowed states to painlessly obtain more federal aid without spending any regular tax money. Another strategy was to convert a health program that was formerly funded completely by state revenue into part of the Medicaid program, thereby obtaining federal support for at least half of the cost.

[10] The fiscal year ends March 31 in New York, August 31 in Texas, and October 31 in Alabama and Michigan.

[11] There are no national figures for interest spending in general funds, but Maryland's situation is illustrative. Its general fund interest outlays are less than 1 percent of the total, while interest accounts for more than 4 percent of general spending reported by the Census Bureau.

[12] During the 1980s, such activities led to rapid increases in both interest outlays and interest earnings, making it appear as if the reach of government was growing more rapidly than was true for core activities. Much of the growth of interest revenue, for example, was not available for funding regular programs because it was balanced by higher interest expenses.

[13] Between 1990–92, for example, the proportion of state (i.e., nonfederal) Medicaid dollars obtained outside of the general fund rose from 5–19.9 percent.

[14] The National Income and Product Accounts do not provide a satisfactory alternative. Although they are much more timely than Census data, they are even more highly aggregated, both in terms of spending functions and in that they combine state and local governments.

[15] Both NCSL and NASBO publish reports on forecasts of general fund spending and revenue and year-end balances as well as estimates of those indicators for the most recently completed year. Their coverage otherwise differs, providing complementary features. NCSL publishes projections of spending increases for five major spending categories, and its compilation of legislated tax changes is more detailed and accurate. NASBO reports spending in the two most recently completed years, enabling it to incorporate later revisions than NCSL. In addition, NASBO publishes a report on state spending that shows outlays for the three past years for the major categories of spending, dividing it between general fund, other state funds, federal aid, and bonding.

[16] These biases tend to exist when the economy is expanding. When a recession occurs, revenue and balances generally are lower than projected. Spending is higher for some programs but lower for others.

[17] The first two reasons why elasticity has fallen relate to one-time changes, while the second two refer to continuing developments. For a review of what state revenue officials believe about the elasticity of their tax systems and a review of the literature, see Gold (1995b).

[18] No reliable data are available to measure how much health spending was shifted into Medicaid. The spending considered here is the sum of

general fund spending plus earmarked state spending for elementary and secondary schools. This is a rough approximation of how tax dollars are spent, except that it excludes most highway-related spending. It excludes spending paid for with federal aid, user charges, or the special devices used to help finance Medicaid.

[19] Enrollment rose 6.9 percent during this period, the largest increase since school enrollment peaked in 1973. This was, of course, much less than the increases in welfare caseloads, Medicaid rolls, and prison populations.

REFERENCES

Blackley, Paul R., and Larry DeBoer. "Explaining State Discretionary Revenue Increases in Fiscal Years 1991 and 1992." *National Tax Journal* 46 No. (March, 1993): 1–12.

Chernick, Howard, and Andrew Reschovsky. "Entitlements and Block Grants." Presented at a conference on devolution sponsored by the Economic Policy Institute (December, 1995).

Feenberg, Daniel R., and Harvey S. Rosen. "Tax Structure and Public Sector Growth." *Journal of Public Economics* 32 (1987): 185–201.

Gold, Steven D. "Interstate Competition and State Personal Income Tax Policy in the 1980s." In *Competition Among States and Local Governments*, edited by Daphne A. Kenyon and John Kincaid. Washington, D.C.: The Urban Institute, 1991.

Gold, Steven D., ed. *The Fiscal Crisis of the States: Lessons for the Future.* Washington, D.C.: Georgetown University Press, 1995a.

Gold, Steven D. "The Income Elasticity of State Tax Systems: New Evidence." *State Tax Notes* 8 No. 18 (May, 1995b): 1849–56.

Gold, Steven D. "State Tax Cuts in 1995: Is Something New Afoot?" *Public Budgeting and Finance* (forthcoming, 1996).

Gold, Steven D., and Sarah Ritchie. "State Spending Patterns Have Been Changing." *State Tax Notes* (January 15, 1996): 187–91.

Gold, Steven D., Elizabeth I. Davis, Deborah A. Ellwood, David S. Liebschutz, and Sarah Ritchie. *How Funding of Programs for Children Varies among the 50 States.* Albany: Center for the Study of the States, 1996.

Ladd, Helen F. "The State Aid Decision: Changes in State Aid to Local Governments, 1982 to 1987." *National Tax Journal* 44 No. 4 (December, 1991): 477–96.

Lav, Iris J., and James R. St. George. "Can States Assume Federal Roles?" In *Proceedings of the Eighty-Seventh Annual Conference on Taxation.* Columbus: National Tax Association–Tax Institute of America, 1996.

Moffittt, Robert. "Has State Redistribution Policy Grown More Conservative?" *National Tax Journal* 43 No. 2 (June, 1990): 123–42.

Oates, Wallace E. "Automatic Increases in Tax Revenues—The Effect on the Size of the Public Budget." In *Financing the New Federalism*, edited by Wallace E. Oates. Baltimore: Johns Hopkins, 1975.

Peterson, George E., Randall R. Bovbjerg, Barbara A. Davis, Walter G. Davis, Eugene C. Durman, and Theresa A. Gullo. *Reagan and the States.* Washington, D.C.: The Urban Institute, 1986.

Poterba, James M. "State Responses to Fiscal Crises: The Effects of Budgetary Institutions and Politics." *Journal of Political Economy* 102 (August, 1994): 799–821.

Poterba, James M. "Balanced Budget Rules and Fiscal Policy: Evidence from the States." *National Tax Journal* 48 No. 3 (September, 1995): 329–36.

Wyckoff, James, and James Fossett. "Has Medicaid Growth Crowded Out State Spending on Education?" *Journal of Health Politics, Policy and Law* (forthcoming, 1996).

FISCAL EQUALIZATION
AND SCHOOL FINANCE

ANDREW RESCHOVSKY*

There is a long tradition in the United States of local provision of elementary and secondary public education. In the early years of the nation, "public" education was financed primarily through voluntary contributions from local residents and from direct payments by parents. Only in the late nineteenth century did the responsibility for the provision and financing of public education come to rest entirely on local governmental bodies, and to rely primarily on revenues from local property taxes.

By the turn of the century, both scholars and public officials had begun to express concern about inequities across communities in the provision of public education. Along with the rapid industrialization of the country came a growing spatial variation in property wealth (Coons, Clune, and Sugarman, 1970). Although residents of property-poor communities could compensate for their lack of fiscal resources by taxing themselves at a higher rate, the spatial differences in property tax base were so large that spending per pupil on public schools was in most states highly correlated with per-pupil property wealth. This pattern of spending differences led to a call for state intervention in the fi-

*University of Wisconsin–Madison, Madison, WI 53706.

nancing of public education. In the early years of the century, a number of states responded by providing equal per-pupil (flat) grants. This began the long history of attempts by state governments at fiscal equalization in the financing of public education. In this paper, I spell out the objectives of these fiscal equalization efforts and assess the effectiveness of the mechanisms put in place to achieve fiscal equalization. I then summarize what we have learned about fiscal equalization over the past two decades, and draw a number of lessons from that experience designed to serve as a guide for future policies.

Over time, two quite distinct principles of equalization have evolved, an egalitarian principle and one that focuses on equal educational opportunity. A fiscal mechanism that achieves equal educational opportunity does so by eliminating or substantially reducing the link between the local fiscal resources available to a school district and its ability to provide public education. Equal educational opportunity is achieved if school districts have equal access to the resources necessary to provide any given amount of education. This definition focuses on the inputs into the educational process and the importance of equalizing the fiscal capacity of districts to provide equal quality education. By contrast, the egalitarian principle focuses more on the output of the educational process by calling for a system that achieves equal education for all students within a state.[1]

There exists ample econometric evidence that education is a normal good (Bergstrom, Rubinfeld, and Shapiro, 1982; Inman, 1977; Ladd, 1975; Rubinfeld and Shapiro, 1989). As long as the local property tax continues to provide a substantial portion of school district revenues, districts with large amounts of property wealth will spend more on public education and will provide higher quality public education than poorer districts.[2] In addition, the resource costs of providing any given amount of education will be higher if a district's student body includes a substantial number of pupils whose native tongue is not English, who have various learning disabilities, or who come from economically disadvantaged families. To the extent that school districts with large concentrations of these "high cost" students are also districts with relatively low property wealth, students in high-wealth/ low-cost districts will get a higher quality education than students in low wealth/ high cost districts.

These between-community differences in the provision of public education would be of limited concern if education did not play such a fundamental role in enabling individuals to function in our society. Despite the efficiency benefits of local control, there are both efficiency and equity arguments for the direct involvement of state governments and perhaps the federal government in the provision of public education. First, it is widely recognized that there are substantial benefit spillovers from the local provision of education (Break, 1967, Weisbrod, 1964). The operation of our democratic form of government at the federal, state, and local levels requires an educated electorate that is knowledgeable

about our economic, social, and political system, and capable of making informed decisions concerning increasingly complex policy issues. As Break points out, the benefits of education "rub off" on people who come in contact with the person who is educated. This contact can occur at the workplace or in the community, and can take the form of the transferral of skills, general knowledge, or culture. Furthermore, current investments in education may reduce future government spending, and hence additional taxation to finance social services or incarceration for the poorly educated. It should be emphasized that these impacts of education become external to a local community because of the high rate of residential mobility in the United States.

In addition to these spillover arguments, the state and federal financing of public education is usually justified on distributional grounds. Because the future well-being of children is so dependent on the quality and quantity of education they receive, there is a widespread belief that decisions about its provision should not be left entirely to the preferences of parents and their neighbors.[3] The increasingly strong link between the level of education received and the level of earnings suggests that differences in educational quality related to community wealth will tend not only to perpetuate existing income inequalities, but to increase income differences between students educated in fiscally weak and fiscally strong communities.

THE GOALS OF FISCAL EQUALIZATION

The discussion in the previous paragraphs suggests that there are ample reasons for state governments to be concerned with both the level and the distribution of spending on public education that arise from the heavy reliance on local government financing. This concern, however, does not translate into a single concept of fiscal equalization. In fact, the experience of the past few decades suggests that there are a number of often inconsistent definitions of fiscal equalization, some of which may be unrelated to the efficiency and equity arguments presented above. Thus, any discussion of the effectiveness of policies to achieve equalization must start with a clear statement of the objectives. A review of policies used in the 50 states to achieve fiscal equalization makes it clear that states are pursuing a number of different objectives, all in the name of school finance equalization. In the following paragraph, I spell out what appear to be the major objectives of fiscal equalization as applied to public education. The discussion of fiscal equalization both in the literature and in public policy debates tends to focus on per-pupil expenditures on education. Expenditures would provide a good measure of actual educational services if the costs of providing any given amount of education were relatively equal across districts. As emphasized by Ladd and Yinger (1994) in their article in this issue, the relevant costs are those that reflect differences in the characteristics of local school districts or in the composition of student bodies, and are beyond the control of local school officials. Evidence exists that these costs vary dramatically across school districts (Chambers, 1978, 1980; Ratcliff, Riddle, and Yinger, 1990; Wendling, 1981). Although discussions of fiscal equalization should account for these cost differences, much of the literature and most school finance court decisions discuss the objectives of fiscal equalization in terms of per-pupil expenditures.

One possible objective of fiscal equalization is to guarantee that educational expenditures per pupil are not a function of the taxable wealth of local school districts. This objective, referred to as

wealth neutrality, was strongly championed as a goal for fiscal equalization in an influential book by Coons, Clune, and Sugarman (1970). They suggest an approach to the distribution of state aid called *district power equalization* (DPE). District power equalization can be achieved through the use of a variable matching rate formula, where the state matches local educational spending by providing a larger share of local spending to districts with lower levels of per-pupil property wealth. A DPE formula thus provides low-wealth districts with higher matching rates (and correspondingly lower tax-prices) than high-wealth districts. In essence, the formula works by guaranteeing an equal tax base to every school district. State aid is equal to the difference between the actual revenue raised from its own tax base and the taxes that would be raised if the district had a tax base equal in size to the guaranteed base. In a pure DPE scheme, school districts with property tax bases larger than the guaranteed base would be required to return to the state all property tax revenue raised in excess of what would be raised from the guaranteed base given their chosen tax rate.[4] For expository purposes, I use the term DPE formula to refer to any matching rate formula in which the matching rate is inversely related to per-pupil property wealth and in which aid is proportional to spending. In the school finance literature, DPE formulas are often called percentage equalizing or guaranteed tax base formulas.

In a well-known article, Feldstein (1975) demonstrated that under normal circumstances a DPE formula will not achieve wealth neutrality. Wealth neutrality requires that the elasticity of per-pupil spending with respect to district property wealth be equal to zero. Feldstein argues that there is no reason to believe that the tax rate choice by school districts will not be influenced by district wealth. He shows that for wealth neutrality to be achieved, the elasticity of tax-price with respect to wealth must be equal to minus one times the ratio of the wealth elasticity of spending to the price elasticity of spending. By definition, the DPE formula requires that the elasticity of tax-price to wealth equals one. Thus, a DPE formula will achieve wealth neutrality only in the case where the absolute values of the tax-price and the wealth elasticities are identical. Econometric evidence, however, suggests that wealth elasticities are generally greater than price elasticities (Bergstrom, Rubinfeld, and Shapiro, 1982; DiPasquale, 1979). We thus expect a positive elasticity of per-pupil education expenditures with respect to wealth to remain, despite the distribution of state aid through a DPE formula. This means that despite the fact that low-wealth communities benefit from high matching rates while high-wealth communities face low or zero matching rates, spending per pupil in high-wealth communities is generally higher than spending in low-wealth places.

Although a DPE formula cannot be expected to achieve wealth neutrality, it will achieve, in its pure form, what has come to be called taxpayer equity. The use of a DPE formula guarantees that if two districts choose the same property tax rate, the allocation of state aid allows them to provide equal levels of spending per pupil. However, the use of a DPE formula does not require that any school district pick a particular tax rate, and hence it does not guarantee the equalization of per-pupil spending among districts. Thus, the goal of a DPE formula is the equal treatment of taxpayers, not the equal treatment of students.

A third possible goal of fiscal equalization is to guarantee that each school district has the resources available to provide an *adequate* level of public education at a *reasonable* local tax rate. Although the expressions adequate and reasonable are obviously normative, the representative tax and expenditure systems of the U.S. Advisory Commission on Intergovernmental Relations and the need-capacity gap measures developed by Bradbury et al. (1984) use national and statewide average figures as their normative foundations. A state government trying to achieve this goal would provide more aid to school districts that had relatively low fiscal resources or, through no fault of their own, faced relatively high costs of providing their student population with any given level of education. This goal, which provides the foundation for the work of Ladd and Yinger (1989), differs in two fundamental ways from the goal of taxpayer equity discussed above.[5] First, this approach explicitly considers jurisdictional differences in the costs of providing public services; second, this approach compensates school districts for cost and resource deficiencies that exist in reaching a specific spending or service-level goal. Although the achievement of this goal calls for more aid for school districts in the weakest fiscal condition, it does not require that recipient districts levy a minimum level of taxes or spend at an adequate level.

The fourth equalization goal is to guarantee that each school district provides an adequate level of public education at a reasonable local tax rate. This goal is achieved by requiring each school district to levy a property tax at a state-mandated rate as a precondition for receiving state equalization aid. This is a more limited measure of equity than wealth neutrality or taxpayer equity because it focuses on guaranteeing that each district provides an acceptable minimum level of education. The logic of this approach, which can be implemented through the use of a *foundation* formula, arises from the premise that education is of sufficient importance for functioning in society that it should be guaranteed to all students.

The final equalization goal is one of providing all children with equal education. If the costs of education were equal everywhere, this goal could be met by mandating equal per-pupil spending everywhere within a state. To the extent that costs vary across districts, equality of education can be achieved by allowing additional spending in high-cost districts. Supporters of this egalitarian view argue that since education, like justice, provides access to a wide range of economic and social opportunities throughout our society, it should be equally available to everyone.

The easiest way to achieve equal spending is through the statewide funding of education. Although equality of spending will clearly result in wealth neutrality, it comes at the cost of destroying local control and sacrificing the efficiency gains from allowing local preferences for education to determine the level of provision. It should also be obvious that equal spending for all students is in effect an unattainable goal because those with sufficient resources always have the option to exit from the public education system. In fact, a careful econometric study by Downes and Schoeman (1993) provides evidence that a large increase in private school enrollment in California is attributable to substantial reductions in the local school district share of educational funding and limitations on spending increases by high-wealth districts, both of which were instituted in order to comply with state Supreme Court decisions in the *Serrano* case.[6]

Regardless of which equalization goal is pursued, the presumption is that equal-ization will be financed through state taxation. The impact of each goal on the distribution of income clearly depends, in large part, on the particular mix of state revenues used to finance equalization.

THE ROLE OF THE COURTS

Although there is not space in this paper to review fully the actions that states have taken over the past several decades to achieve various fiscal equalization goals, it is important to describe briefly the major role the courts have played in defining the terms of the school financing debates.

The equalization of school finance came to the center of the public agenda with the landmark ruling by the California Supreme Court in *Serrano v. Priest* (1971). The Court ruled that California's heavy reliance on the local property tax violated the state and federal constitutions because it had made children's education a function of the property wealth of the community in which they lived. In the original *Serrano* case, the court adopted wealth neutrality as a standard by which to judge the constitutionality of California's system of school financing. In a 1974 ruling by a trial court, which was upheld by the Supreme Court in a 1976 ruling, the court indicated that the implementation of a DPE formula would provide an acceptable remedy. One interpretation of this decision is that the court assumed (incorrectly) that a district power equalizing scheme would be successful in achieving wealth neutrality (Friedman and Wiseman, 1978).

In a similar case, *San Antonio Independent School District v. Rodriguez* (1971), a federal district court in Texas ruled that substantial variations in per-pupil spending as a result of differences in local property wealth were not permissible under the equal protection clause of the Fourteenth Amendment. However, on appeal, the U.S. Supreme Court in 1973 reversed the state court decision, effectively removing the federal courts from further school finance litigation. Since that time all school finance litigation has been based on claims that state systems of school financing conflict with education and equal protection clauses in state constitutions. Whether successful or not, these cases have been feasible, because in all but two states, state constitutions explicitly list education as a mandated function of state government.[7] In fact, in 33 of the 48 states that mandate state responsibility for education, education is the only public service mentioned in the state constitution.

Since 1971, as a result of court decisions or the threat of court cases, most states have made substantial changes in their school finance systems (Odden and Picus, 1992). In general, states have substantially increased their funding for education, with the states' share of total state and local government revenue for primary and secondary public education growing from 44 percent in 1970 to 53 percent in 1987, before declining to 50 percent in 1991. About one-third of the states have adopted DPE-type formulas, while several states have developed hybrid formulas that combine foundation formulas with a DPE formula for spending above the foundation level (U.S. Advisory Commission on Intergovernmental Relations, 1990).

The last few years have seen a new rash of school finance court cases. Judging from the recent decisions, state courts are broadening their definitions of fiscal equalization by moving beyond wealth neutrality and taxpayer equity. In recent cases in Texas, Kentucky, and New Jersey, the courts seem to be arguing that state constitutions require the equalization of per-pupil spending within a state.

Apparently, the equalization of fiscal resources available to school districts for the support of public education does not meet state constitutional tests. Although the specific wording differs in each state, the education clauses of state constitutions generally assert that the state government is responsible for seeing that all children receive an adequate level of education. In New Jersey, the constitution requires provision of a "thorough and efficient" education, while in Massachusetts, the constitution requires that the state "cherish" education. The problem for the courts has been to determine what level of per-pupil spending is sufficiently high to satisfy these constitutional requirements. How, in other words, does one define "thorough and efficient" education? In the earlier school finance cases, courts tended to finesse this issue by attempting to guarantee all school districts equal access to fiscal resources. In the eyes of some legal scholars, the greatest strength of wealth neutrality is that it enabled courts to avoid the extremely difficult problem of actually defining a minimum level of education or of per-pupil spending that would meet constitutional standards (Clune, 1992).

While the focus of the early court decisions was primarily on expenditures per pupil, in several recent cases, courts address issues of student performance more directly. There is also a growing recognition that equality of education, however defined, cannot be achieved unless explicit account is taken of the higher costs that are generally associated with educating children who come from poor or otherwise disadvantaged backgrounds. In Kentucky, in *Rose v. Council for Better Education, Inc.*, the court went beyond pure school financing issues and declared the entire system of public education unconstitutional. In a recent Massachusetts decision (*McDuffy*

v. *Secretary of Education*), that state's Supreme Court specified seven specific "capabilities" that an educated child must possess. In effect, the court ruled that the state must develop a system of school finance that guarantees that all children be provided with an adequate education, where adequacy is being defined in terms of a specified set of skills.

HOW EFFECTIVE HAVE EQUALIZATION SCHEMES BEEN?

Since 1970, spurred on in part by court decisions, nearly every state has enacted school finance reform measures. A number of states enacted DPE-type formulas, while others increased the foundation level of spending associated with their existing foundation formulas.[8] Finally, a few states enacted formulas that combined elements of both foundation and DPE formulas. Despite all this reform activity, there have been few across-state evaluations of the effectiveness of the various reforms in achieving their equalization goals.[9] One recent exception is a study by James Wyckoff (1992) that uses data from 49 states to compare within-state variations in per-pupil expenditures in the 1979–80 and 1986–7 academic years. He concludes that intrastate public school spending inequality decreased modestly in the majority of states during this seven-year period.[10] However, no systematic evaluation of the effectiveness of school finance reform efforts in meeting other equalization goals—wealth neutrality, taxpayer equity, and the provision of adequate education at reasonable tax rates—has been conducted.

Nevertheless, I believe that it is possible to reach some tentative conclusions about the effectiveness of the various intergovernmental aid mechanisms by studying the experiences of individual states and by observing the actions of the courts in states where the remedies

to earlier court rulings in school finance cases have been challenged.

For reasons that I will spell out below, I believe that the limited available evidence suggests that, largely for political reasons, achieving school finance equalization, particularly wealth neutrality and taxpayer equity, is by and large an elusive goal. Effective legislative solutions require either massive infusions of new state tax revenue or the reallocation of state aid from some school districts to other districts. The experience in state after state has shown that the enactment of explicitly redistributive aid policies is extremely difficult.[11] Another reason that states are ineffective in achieving equalization goals is because the instruments they choose are frequently not consistent with their desired goals. For example, states that enact a DPE-type formula often expect the formula to result in substantial increases in per-pupil spending by low spending districts and consequently a significant equalization of spending across districts. As I will indicate below, this result has generally not been forthcoming.

Because DPE formulas were originally touted as innovative mechanisms for achieving wealth neutrality and taxpayer equity and are currently used in about one-third of the states, it is reasonable to focus on their effectiveness in meeting various equalization goals. The first thing to emphasize about DPE formulas is that in none of the states that use them are they designed to achieve complete taxpayer equity. As explained above, DPE formulas operate by providing all school districts with a guaranteed tax base. Full taxpayer equity can be achieved only if the state recovers property tax revenue from districts with tax bases larger than the guaranteed base. There are, however, no states with DPE formulas that require recovery; in fact, in most states high-wealth districts receive "minimum aid." Recovery or "negative aid" has been declared unconstitutional by state courts in Wisconsin and Texas.

An alternative strategy for achieving taxpayer equity is to set the guaranteed tax base equal to the per-pupil tax base in the richest district. In that way, every district except the richest would receive state equalizing aid. This approach, however, is prohibitively expensive. For example, in Wisconsin, which sets its guaranteed tax base high enough so that last year 90 percent of all public school pupils lived in districts with per-pupil tax bases below the guaranteed base, the cost of equalization aid would have more than doubled if the guaranteed tax base had been set equal to the base in the wealthiest district (Reschovsky and Wiseman, 1993).

A second reason why states using DPE formulas fail to achieve full taxpayer equity is that they all distribute some aid in a nonequalizing fashion. As the design of newly targeted aid programs almost inevitably results in reductions in aid to some school districts, it is not surprising, given political realities, that most school finance systems include "hold harmless" grants and "minimum aid" grants even for the wealthiest of school districts. Furthermore, equalization is only one goal of state aid to school districts. Most states also distribute categorical aid designed to achieve various other purposes. Some nonequalizing grants are distributed to districts in proportion to their population of students requiring special services. These categorical aid programs are often justified as a means of compensating local school districts for the costs of satisfying state or federal mandates, especially when the mandates relate to state rather than local district objectives.

Although DPE formulas do not achieve full taxpayer equity, it is still reasonable to ask how effective they have been in weakening the link between district property wealth and the ability to provide public education. Because the purpose of a DPE formula is to guarantee that all school districts choosing any given property tax rate will be able to spend the same amount per pupil, a simple measure of the formula's effectiveness is to calculate the ratio of each district's per-pupil spending to its property tax rate and to compare the distribution of these *spending-effort ratios* across districts, with and without the receipt of equalizing aid. By definition, full taxpayer equity is achieved when all districts have identical spending-effort ratios equal to the per-pupil guaranteed tax base.[12] In a study of school finance in Wisconsin, Reschovsky and Wiseman (1994) demonstrate that the state's DPE formula achieves a substantial amount of taxpayer equity by reducing the coefficient of variation of spending-effort ratios by 59 percent.[13] Although comparable analyses have not been published for other states, the fact that Wisconsin's formula employs a high guaranteed tax base suggests that few, if any, other states could achieve greater equalization (as measured by the distribution of spending-effort ratios) than Wisconsin.

Although DPE formulas are not explicitly designed to equalize spending across districts, it appears that much of their appeal is based on the expectation by many legislators that the formulas will substantially reduce disparities in per-pupil spending by stimulating increased spending by low-wealth districts. Because DPE formulas provide larger reductions in tax-prices to low-wealth districts, per-pupil spending by low-wealth districts would be expected to increase relative to spending in high-wealth districts as long as price elasticities of demand for education are not highly inelastic.

It appears, however, that the use of DPE formulas has not eliminated low spending by low-wealth districts. As mentioned previously, courts in both New Jersey and in Texas have declared the remedies from previous court challenges inadequate, because per-pupil spending remains very low relative to spending levels in high-wealth districts. There are several possible reasons why DPE formulas have proved to be less than fully effective mechanisms for raising per-pupil spending levels in low-wealth districts. First, if price elasticities of education spending are sufficiently low, DPE formulas will reduce the variance across districts in property tax rates but do little to reduce the variation in per-pupil spending or increase the spending levels of low-wealth districts. Although the appropriate empirical analysis has not been conducted, it is possible that both price and income elasticities rise with district wealth. If low-wealth districts have particularly low price and income elasticities, DPE formulas (and foundation formulas that do not mandate a minimum local tax rate) will be ineffective in increasing spending levels by low-wealth districts. It should be emphasized, however, that one of the appeals of DPE formulas is that they allow local (parental) control over per-pupil spending levels while providing a substantial incentive for low-wealth districts to increase educational spending.

Second, although most existing estimates of price and income elasticities are based on cross-sectional data, the success of grant programs tends to be assessed by looking at changes in the distribution of per-pupil spending over time. Although hard evidence is not easy to find, it appears that grant formulas in a number of states are operating in an economic environment where a number of elements are working at cross purposes to the achievement of greater eq-

uity. For example, if central city property values are declining or growing relatively slowly, and if the state equalizing aid budget does not grow fast enough to compensate for the disequalizing pattern of property value growth, the revenue available for school may actually decline in central cities relative to their faster growing suburbs.[14] The fiscal situation of the cities can be further weakened if cities simultaneously experience cost increases attributable to a growth in enrollment of students from disadvantaged backgrounds.[15]

Finally, it should be emphasized that even if a district's spending per pupil has remained low in spite of receiving substantial amounts of aid, this does not necessarily imply that the aid has been used primarily to reduce property taxes. Between 1980 and 1988 the average starting salary of new, inexperienced public school teachers grew by 17 percent in constant dollars.[16] As long as low-wealth districts are forced to raise teacher salaries in order to attract new teachers, many low-wealth districts may well have used additional aid to finance higher teacher salaries without being able to increase their spending per pupil relative to spending in higher-wealth districts. The resulting inability of many school districts to reduce property tax rates may help explain recent statewide efforts, most notably in Michigan, to limit school property taxes.

LESSONS LEARNED AND IMPLICATIONS FOR FUTURE POLICY

Probably because there are 50 different systems of school finance in the United States, the literature includes little comprehensive analysis of the impact of the past two decades of school finance reform. Nevertheless, despite the risk of overgeneralizing, I would like to suggest four lessons that can be learned from recent attempts to achieve fiscal equalization in the financing of public education.

First, in some states, district power equalizing or guaranteed tax base formulas are reasonably effective mechanisms for achieving taxpayer equity, which is attained when the allocations of aid allow all school districts choosing the same property tax rate to provide equal levels of spending per pupil regardless of the size of their tax bases. However, for the reasons suggested in the previous section, these mechanisms are not very effective in guaranteeing that all school districts within a state spend enough money per pupil to provide all pupils with an adequate education.

Second, attempts to equalize per-pupil spending across school districts are ill-advised and are likely to prove unsuccessful. Because raising spending levels to equal those in the highest spending districts would take vast amounts of new state tax revenue, the only politically viable way to achieve equality of per-pupil spending across districts is to place a cap on spending or on spending increases by high-spending districts. Although such a strategy may be acceptable to the courts, it will ultimately fail. As indicated previously, evidence from California shows that if the public schools do not provide the education parents want for their children, those who can afford it will enroll their children in private schools (Downes and Schoeman, 1993). Furthermore, state-imposed restrictions on public school spending will undoubtedly increase the appeal of publicly funded education vouchers. Although a discussion of school choice is beyond the scope of this paper, it is certainly possible that the imposition of a universal voucher system will result in substantially less equity than currently exists in most states. Finally, the insistence by the courts that

per-pupil spending be equalized across all school districts may in some states lead to attempts to amend the education clauses of state constitutions, thereby removing the judicial underpinning for fiscal equality. In fact, shortly after the New Jersey legislature passed legislation that reduced aid to wealthy districts and placed restrictions on their spending, a group of suburban legislators introduced a constitutional amendment to replace the "thorough and efficient" education clause with one that would limit the state's educational funding obligations (Center for Educational Policy Analysis, 1993).[17]

The third lesson is that while full state funding of education can achieve equality of per-pupil spending and thereby perfect wealth neutrality, it comes at the cost of losing all local discretion over the level of per-pupil spending. Evidence from California suggests that as decisions about education spending levels move from local school boards to the state legislature, political support for public education is reduced (Fischel, 1989, Picus, 1991). California's per-pupil spending on public education went from being one of the highest in the nation in the late 1960s to being among the bottom third in the early 1990s.

Helen Ladd and John Yinger (1994) emphasize in their paper in this issue that no matter how fiscal equalization is defined, grant formulas should account for differences across jurisdictions both in resources and in the costs of providing public services. The final lesson from the experiences of the past two decades is that the failure in most states to adjust state aid formulas adequately to account for the higher costs of educating children from disadvantaged backgrounds has perpetuated disparities in educational quality and created serious deficiencies in the education provided to some children, particularly those residing in many of the nation's largest cities.[18]

I conclude that by far the most compelling equalization goal is one that requires state governments to guarantee that all children are provided with an adequate education without placing an unreasonably high property tax burden on residents. This goal can be achieved by using a cost-adjusted foundation formula, where the foundation spending level is adjusted by a cost index reflecting the costs of providing education services that are beyond the control of local school officials, and where each school district is required to levy a minimum tax rate. In order to guarantee that districts continue over time to spend sufficient resources to ensure a quality education for all children, the foundation spending level must be indexed for inflation.

By and large, the attention paid by school finance reformers to taxpayer equity is misguided. With limited fiscal resources in the public sector, we should concentrate our efforts on achieving student-based rather than taxpayer-based equity. The efficiency and equity justifications for state and federal involvement in the financing of public education are consistent with a scheme that guarantees that resources will be made available to provide all children with an education adequate to function effectively in our economy. The justification for other equity goals is on weaker grounds.

ENDNOTES

I would like to thank William Clune, Helen Ladd, Julia Murray, Allan Odden, Richard Rossmiller, Joel Slemrod, and Michael Wiseman for helpful comments.

[1] In practice, however, states pursuing egalitarian policies tend to focus on the equality of education inputs by ignoring cost factors and calling for equal per-pupil spending across all districts.

[2] In 1991, nearly 47 percent of total school district revenues in the United States came from local sources, with property taxes accounting for the lion's share of local revenue.

[3] This view is related to Musgrave's concept of a "merit good." Individuals, in this case acting collectively as residents of school districts, may undervalue education from the state or nation's standpoint. Thus, it may be appropriate either to encourage or to compel districts providing low levels of education to increase the amount and/or quality of education they provide.

[4] In practice, no states require rich districts to contribute "negative aid" to state coffers.

[5] Ladd and Yinger (1994) describe a formula to achieve this goal.

[6] The passage of Proposition 13, California's property tax limitation initiative, also contributed to the increased role state funding plays in the financing of education.

[7] The two states that do not constitutionally mandate the provision of education are Mississippi and South Carolina. In both states, education had been constitutionally mandated, but the state constitutions were amended after the U.S. Supreme Court ruling in *Brown v. Board of Education*.

[8] Foundation formulas provide each school district with a per-pupil grant equal to the difference between the state-specified "foundation" level of spending and what the local school district can raise by applying a state-specified "foundation" tax rate to its property tax base. Districts that can raise amounts in excess of the foundation receive no aid through the foundation formula. Most states require that local school districts must levy the foundation tax rate as a condition for receiving aid.

[9] A study by Stephen Carroll and Rolla Park (1983) assessed the effectiveness of school finance reform efforts in five states.

[10] Wyckoff found that inequality was reduced in 31 states during the 1980–7 period, with the median state reducing inequality by 11 percent as measured by a Theil coefficient.

[11] Recent events in New Jersey provide a good example of the political difficulties involved in school finance reform. In 1991 the Democratic controlled legislature passed a school finance plan introduced by Governor Florio that substantially increased state funding of public education by raising both sales and income taxes, while reducing state assistance to wealthy districts and increasing aid to the state's poorest districts. Largely as a result of this new legislation, the Republican party was able to gain a veto-proof majority in both

houses of the legislature and eventually unseat Governor Florio.

[12] This point is illustrated by equation 7 in Ladd and Yinger's article in this issue.

[13] Based on fiscal year 1991 data, the coefficient of variation of average tax prices in Wisconsin equals 0.14.

[14] Although they do not have data on tax base growth, Bahl, Martinez-Vazquez, and Sjoquist (1992), using data from 35 Metropolitan Statistical Areas, find that between 1977 and 1987, central city per capita incomes and employment to population ratios have both declined relative to values in their suburbs.

[15] It should be noted that because aid is inversely proportional to per-pupil property wealth, DPE (and foundation) formulas reduce the fiscal incentives of local governments to attract new tax base.

[16] This number was calculated using data from Murnane et al. (1991).

[17] The constitutional amendment was subsequently withdrawn and the provisions of the proposed amendment were incorporated into a school finance bill introduced in the legislature.

[18] Although states do not generally adjust state aid formulas for differences in costs, most states do compensate local school districts for a portion of the extra costs of providing education to various "special needs" students. This approach to "costs" tends to create substantial inefficiencies, because local districts have an incentive to classify as many students as possible as "special needs" students. Furthermore, to the extent that the allocation of state categorical aid is related to spending on programs for special needs students, districts have no incentive to operate these programs efficiently.

REFERENCES

Bahl, Roy, Jorge Martinez-Vazquez, and David L. Sjoquist. "Central City-Suburban Fiscal Disparities." *Public Finance Quarterly 20*, No. 4 (October, 1992): 420–32.

Bradbury, Katherine L., Helen Ladd, Mark Perrault, Andrew Reschovsky, and John Yinger. "State Aid to Offset Fiscal Disparities Across Communities." *National Tax Journal 37*, No. 2 (June, 1984): 151–70.

Break, George F. *Intergovernmental Fiscal Relations in the United States*. Washington, D.C.: The Brookings Institution, 1967.

Bergstrom, Theodore C., Daniel L. Rubinfeld, and Perry Shapiro. "Micro-Based Estimates of Demand Functions for Local School Expenditures." *Econometrica 50*, No. 5 (September, 1982): 1183–1203.

Carroll, Stephen J. and Rolla Edward Park. *The Search for Equity in School Finance*, A Rand Educational Policy Study. Cambridge, MA: Ballanger Publishing Company, 1983.

Center for Educational Policy Analysis. *Newsletter*, New Brunswick: Center for Educational Policy Analysis in New Jersey, Rutgers University, January, 1993.

Chambers, Jay G. "Educational Cost Differentials and the Allocation of State Aid for Elementary/Secondary Education." *Journal of Human Resources 13*, No. 4 (Fall, 1978): 459–81.

Chambers, Jay G. "The Development of a Cost of Education Index: Some Empirical Estimates and Policy Issues." *Journal of Education Finance 5*, No. 3 (Winter, 1980): 262–81.

Clune, William H. III. "New Answers to Hard Questions Posed by *Rodriguez*: Ending the Separation of School Finance and Educational Policy by Bridging the Gap between Wrong and Remedy." *Connecticut Law Review 24*, No. 3 (Spring, 1992): 721–55.

Coons, John E., William H. Clune III, and Stephen D. Sugarman. *Private Wealth and Public Education*. Cambridge, MA: Harvard University Press, 1970.

DiPasquale, Denise. *State Aid to Local School Districts: A Comparative Analysis*. Unpublished Ph.D. Dissertation. Cambridge: Massachusetts Institute of Technology, 1979.

Downes, Thomas A. and David Schoeman. "School Financing Reform and Private School Enrollment: Evidence from California." Working Paper No. 93-8, Center for Urban Affairs and Policy Research, Northwestern University, 1993.

Feldstein, Martin S. "Wealth Neutrality and Local Choice in Public Education." *American Economic Review 65*, No. 1 (March, 1975): 75–89.

Fischel, William A. "Did *Serrano* Cause Proposition 13?" *National Tax Journal 42*, No. 4 (December, 1989): 465–73.

Friedman, Lee S. and Michael Wiseman. "Understanding the Equity Consequences of School-Finance Reform." *Harvard Educational Review 48*, No. 2 (May, 1978): 193–226.

Inman, Robert P. "Optimal Fiscal Reform of Metropolitan Schools: Some Simulated Results with a General Equilibrium Model." *American Economic Review 68*, No. 1 (March, 1977): 107–22.

Ladd, Helen F. "Local Education Expenditures, Fiscal Capacity, and the Composition of the Property Tax Base." *National Tax Journal 28*, No. 2 (June, 1975): 145–58.

Ladd, Helen F. and John Yinger. *America's*

Ailing Cities; Fiscal Health and the Design of Urban Policy. Baltimore: The Johns Hopkins University Press, 1989.

Ladd, Helen F. and John Yinger. "The Case for Equalizing Aid." *National Tax Journal XLVII,* No. 1 (March, 1994): 211–224.

Murnane, Richard J., Judith D. Singer, John B. Willett, James J. Kemple, and Randall J. Olsen. *Who Will Teach? Policies That Matter.* Cambridge, MA: Harvard University Press, 1991.

Odden, Allan R. and Lawrence O. Picus. *School Finance: A Policy Perspective.* New York: McGraw-Hill, Inc., 1992.

Picus, Lawrence O. "Cadillacs or Chevrolets?: The Evolution of State Control over School Finance in California." *Journal of Education Finance 17,* No. 1 (Summer, 1991): 33–59.

Ratcliff, Kerri, Bruce Riddle, and John Yinger. "The Fiscal Condition of School Districts in Nebraska: Is Small Beautiful?" *Economics of Education Review 9,* No. 1 (1990): 81–99.

Reschovsky, Andrew and Michael Wiseman. "School Finance Reform: Where Do We Go From Here?" Statement to the Wisconsin Senate Study Committee on State Elementary and Secondary School General Equalization Aid Formula. Madison, WI, November 16, 1993.

Reschovsky, Andrew and Michael Wiseman.

"How Can States Most Effectively Meet Their School Financing Responsibilities." In *The Challenges of Fiscal Equalization for State and Local Government Finance,* edited by John Anderson. New York: Praeger, 1994.

Rubinfeld, Daniel L. and Perry Shapiro. "Micro-Estimation of the Demand for Schooling: Evidence From Michigan and Massachusetts." *Regional Science and Urban Economics 19,* No. 3 (August, 1989): 381–98.

U.S. Advisory Commission on Intergovernmental Relations. "The Structure of State Aid to Elementary and Secondary Education." Report M-175. Washington, D.C.: U.S. Advisory Commission on Intergovernmental Relations, 1990.

Wendling, Wayne. "The Cost of Education Index: Measurement of Price Differences of Education Personnel Among New York State School Districts." *Journal of Education Finance 6,* No. 4 (Spring, 1981): 485–504.

Weisbrod, Burton A. *External Benefits of Public Education.* Princeton, NJ: Industrial Relations Section, Department of Economics, Princeton University, 1964.

Wyckoff, James H. "The Intrastate Equality of Public Primary and Secondary Education Resources in the U.S., 1980–1987." *Economics of Education Review 11,* No. 1 (1992): 19–30.

THE CASE FOR
EQUALIZING AID

HELEN F. LADD* & JOHN YINGER**

Equalizing aid can be used by the federal government to equalize fiscal outcomes or resources among subnational governments, or by states to equalize outcomes or resources among local governments. Although equalizing aid can sometimes be justified in part on efficiency grounds, we focus on its primary function, namely, to achieve equity objectives.[1] The equity objective of a donor government can take many forms. The central theme of this paper is that the appropriate design for an equalizing aid program depends on the form of this objective.

Intergovernmental aid is not, of course, the only tool higher-level governments can use to assist poor or troubled lower-level governments. State governments, for example, can achieve equity objectives by altering the fiscal arrangements within which local governments operate. A state could take over from local governments the financing of certain services, such as social services, that place large burdens on a few jurisdictions,[2] or, to counter fiscal disparities in education financing, a state could encourage the merger of school districts. Hence, intergovernmental aid should be viewed as

only one tool, and not always the best tool, to achieve fiscal equity.

We place equity objectives into two classes: categorical equity, which relates to public sector spending, either on specific functions or on all functions, and distributional equity, which is aimed at equalizing the real incomes of local residents. In the following discussion, we focus on state aid to local governments.[3] For simplicity of presentation, we assume that local governments have access to only one local revenue source, a local property tax, and recognize that the local tax base *per capita* varies across jurisdictions.

Many of the specifics of what follows are well known to public finance experts. Our contributions are as follows: to incorporate cost considerations into the various aid formulas, to highlight the similarities and differences among formulas in a common framework, to highlight the role of capitalization in the discussion of equalizing real incomes, and to argue that equalizing aid is a valuable policy tool under some circumstances.

As we use the term, a local government's public service costs indicate how much a jurisdiction must spend to provide a given package of public services at a given quality level. These costs reflect both the cost of inputs and the harshness of the environment for provid-

*Duke University, Durham, NC 27708.
**Syracuse University, Syracuse, NY 13244.

ing public services.[4] Local governments that must pay more to attract employees from the private sector obviously have higher public service costs than other governments, all else equal.[5] Moreover, as first pointed out by Bradford, Malt, and Oates (1969), a jurisdiction with a harsh environment must pay more, all else equal, to obtain the same service quality. Extensive old housing, for example, raises the cost of fire protection, and a concentration of poor or disadvantaged residents raises the cost of most local public services.

In practice, costs can be derived from the coefficients of input and environmental cost factors in a multivariate regression analysis of local public spending that controls for income, price, and taste variation across jurisdictions.[6] To facilitate their inclusion in an equalizing aid formula, these estimated costs are best expressed in index form, with the index equal to one in a jurisdiction with average costs. To avoid giving inappropriate incentives to recipient jurisdictions, the cost factors included in this index should be largely, if not totally, outside the control of local public officials.

CATEGORICAL EQUITY ARGUMENTS FOR EQUALIZING AID

The most fundamental equity argument for equalizing aid is categorical equity, which exists when all citizens have fair access to public services that are thought to be particularly important to their opportunities in life.[7] Although policy makers at any higher level of government may have categorical equity objectives, the attainment of categorical equity is particularly important to states, each of which bears the primary responsibility for its system of local governments and the resulting distribution of local public services. This section presents several possible categorical equity objectives for a donor government (that

is, several possible definitions of fair access), and describes the grants needed to achieve them.[8]

Ensuring a Minimum Outcome

One widely applied categorical equity standard requires that all citizens (or students) have access to a minimum quality of public services. This standard can be applied to an individual public service, such as education or public safety, or to local public services in general.

The most direct way to achieve this standard is with a foundation grant, which ensures that each jurisdiction can reach some minimum level of spending per capita, labeled E^*, if it is willing to levy a property tax rate, labeled t^*, that is considered to be a fair minimum.[9] Both the minimum level of spending and the minimum fair tax rate are policy parameters that must be set by public officials.

With this approach, the state grant per capita to jurisdiction j, A_j, equals the minimum spending minus the local revenue that can be raised at the fair tax rate. If V_j is the property tax base per capita in jurisdiction j, then the foundation formula is

$$A_j = E^* - t^* V_j.$$

An alternative version of this formula highlights the fact that a foundation grant is a block grant, which means that it does not vary with a jurisdiction's chosen spending level, and that it is larger for jurisdictions with relatively small tax bases.[10] If V^* is defined as the tax base at which A_j equals zero, it follows immediately that $E^* = t^* V^*$ or $t^* = E^*/V^*$. Substituting this result into equation 1 yields

2

$$A_j = E^* \left(1 - \frac{V_j}{V^*} \right).$$

Note that negative grants are not allowed; jurisdictions with tax bases above V^* receive no aid.

This approach easily can be extended to include public service costs. In this case, the first policy parameter is the minimum acceptable service quality, S^*; C_j is a cost index for jurisdiction j; and state aid is the difference between the spending needed to achieve S^*, namely $S^* C_j$, and local revenue at the fair tax rate. In practice, S^* can be set equal to the minimum acceptable spending in a community with average costs, that is, with $C_j = 1$. In symbols,

3

$$A_j = S^* C_j - t^* V_j.$$

Now redefine V^* to be the tax base at which state aid would equal zero assuming a cost index equal to unity, so that $t^* = S^*/V^*$ and

4

$$A_j = S^* \left(C_j - \frac{V_j}{V^*} \right).$$

This formula describes a block grant that depends both on a jurisdiction's costs and tax base. Remember that the cost index, C_j, is defined as a jurisdictions's costs relative to the average jurisdiction; hence the terms in brackets are both expressed in relative terms.

A foundation grant makes it possible for a jurisdiction to provide the minimum acceptable service level at the fair minimum tax rate. It does not guarantee, however, that a community actually will provide this level unless it is accompanied by the requirement that the juris-

diction levy at least the minimum tax rate, t^*, to support the relevant service or services.[11]

Easing the Burden of Providing Standard-Quality Public Services

Sometimes a donor government is unwilling to require local governments to provide a specific service level on the grounds that local governments should be free to make their own decisions. Nevertheless, because some jurisdictions are fiscally disadvantaged relative to others and some service or services are viewed as particularly important, the donor government may want, without imposing a spending requirement, to help equalize the ease with which jurisdictions can achieve a specified service level. Fiscal disadvantages arise from two sources: below-average capacity to raise revenue, as measured by V_j, and above-average costs of providing the standard service quality, as measured by C_j. Hence, to successfully ease the burden of providing standard-quality public services, the donor government should give more aid to jurisdictions that have larger fiscal disadvantages, measured by what we call the *need-capacity gap*.[12] This approach makes it possible for all jurisdictions to move toward standard-quality services at a standard tax rate.

To be specific, we define a jurisdiction's need-capacity gap as the difference between its *expenditure need* and its *revenue-raising capacity*, all defined in *per capita* terms. Expenditure need is the amount of money required for the jurisdiction to provide the standard-quality services and is calculated as the standardized service quality, S', multiplied by the jurisdiction's cost index, C_j.[13] Revenue-raising capacity is the amount of money a jurisdiction could raise at a standard tax rate given its own tax base, which equals the standard tax rate, t', multiplied by V_j.[14] The need-capacity gap indicates the extent to which the revenue the jurisdiction can raise at a standard tax rate falls short of the amount it must spend to provide standard-quality public services. The meaning of "standard" must be set by policy makers; that is, S' and t' are policy parameters.

Once the need-capacity gap has been defined, the natural grant system is to close a certain portion of the gap in each jurisdiction. In symbols,

$$A_j = a + b\,G_j = a + b\,(S'C_j - t'\,V_j),$$

where a and b are policy parameters that define the aid program. Defining G' as the gap at which aid equals zero, we find that $a = -bG'$. Substituting this result into equation 5 yields:

$$A_j = b(G_j - G') = b(S'C_j - t'\,V_j - G').$$

As before, negative aid is not allowed, so jurisdictions with a gap less than G' receive no aid.

Foundation grants are a special case of this formula, in which b is set equal to one (that is, the entire gap is closed); S' is set at the minimum acceptable level of services, S^*; t' is set at what is believed to be the minimum fair tax rate, t^*; and G' is set to zero (that is, jurisdictions that can afford the minimum service quality at the fair tax rate receive no aid).

The more general form in equation 6 allows a grant program to close only part of the gap between expenditure need and revenue-raising capacity and to give some aid to jurisdictions that have negative need-capacity gaps. With b less than one and without a requirement that each jurisdiction impose at least the standard tax rate, t', the grant program

helps jurisdictions move toward the selected service level at a fair tax rate, but neither fully funds the move to this outcome nor requires it. Moreover, the amount appropriated for the grant program determines the extent of equalization. In general, there is an inverse relationship between b and the program's budget, holding G' constant; raising G', that is, excluding more jurisdictions from aid, increases the value of b that can be achieved for a given budget.[15]

Ensuring Equal Service for a Given Sacrifice

Another widely discussed categorical equity objective is to ensure that every jurisdiction willing to make a certain level of sacrifice will receive the same level of public services, regardless of its own tax base. In this context, "sacrifice" is defined as the effective property tax rate.[16] Grants to achieve this objective are called "power-equalizing" grants. In 1991–2, eight states used some form of power-equalizing grant, usually with severe restrictions, to help finance local education (Gold et al., 1992).

In equation form, this objective is to set

$$E_j = t_j \hat{V}$$

where $\hat{V}$ is a policy parameter. Since local revenue equals $t_j V_j$ and state aid equals the difference between spending and local revenue, this formula leads directly to

$$A_j = E_j - L_j = t_j (\hat{V} - V_j).$$

Now solving equation 7 for t_j and substituting the result into equation 8 yields

$$A_j = E_j\left(1 - \frac{V_j}{\hat{V}}\right).$$

This equation defines a matching grant in which the state's share of total spending, which is the term in brackets, is higher for jurisdictions with lower tax bases. Note that when the two policy parameters, V^* and $\hat{V}$, are equal, the term in brackets is the same as for a foundation formula, but this term is multiplied by actual spending in equation 9, not by the state-determined minimum spending as in equation 2. With a power-equalizing formula, in other words, a jurisdiction's aid depends both on the spending level it selects and on the divergence between its tax base and the tax base designated by policy makers.

Note also that the policy parameters in equations 9 and 2 need not be the same. The derivation of equation 9 does not assume that power-equalizing grants go only to a subset of jurisdictions. Thus, if $\hat{V}$ is set at any level below the tax base of the richest jurisdiction, the formula implies that some jurisdictions will have negative matching rates, an outcome that usually is politically unacceptable.[17] Negative matching rates can be eliminated by raising $\hat{V}$, but this action would increase the cost of the program. Instead, power-equalizing grants, as implemented, virtually always override the formula to assure a minimum amount of aid for each jurisdiction and thereby limit the extent of equalization relative to equation 9.

This type of grant also can be modified to account for a jurisdiction's costs.[18] In particular, the defining equation can be restated to say that service quality, or real spending, will depend only on sacrifice. In symbols,

10

$$\frac{E_j}{C_j} \equiv S_j = t_j \hat{V}.$$

Following the same steps as before, this equation leads to the grant formula

 11

$$A_j = S_j \left(C_j - \frac{V_j}{\hat{V}} \right).$$

Now the matching rate, that is, the state's share of total spending, depends on a jurisdiction's cost index as well as its tax base. Equation 11 differs from the cost-adjusted foundation formula, equation 4, because it is based on a jurisdiction's actual real spending (or service quality), not on a fixed minimum real spending.

Wealth Neutrality

In some of the early school finance cases, courts ruled that the wealth of the local school district should be viewed as a "suspect category," which constitutionally cannot serve as the basis for differences in the quality of education services, often measured by per pupil spending, available to pupils across the state.[19] These rulings express another possible equity objective, called wealth neutrality, which requires that variation across districts in per pupil spending, or preferably in school service levels, be uncorrelated with variation in the per pupil property tax base, a measure of wealth. Wealth neutrality could be an objective for other public services as well.

One way to achieve this outcome is to redefine school districts so that they all have the same tax base per pupil. By eliminating variation in district tax bases, this nonaid approach would assure that any remaining variation in spending or service levels was uncorrelated with district wealth.[20] Given the obvious political difficulties of redrawing district boundaries, the challenge is to design an intergovernmental aid formula that achieves the same goal.

By assuring that every jurisdiction, regardless of the size of its tax base, can generate the same revenue *per capita* (or per pupil) as the district with base V^*, power-equalizing grants appear at first to generate wealth neutrality. As pointed out by Feldstein (1975), however, this statement is not generally true. Although higher matching rates for lower-wealth jurisdictions are likely to push a system toward wealth neutrality, they also may induce lower-wealth jurisdictions to select lower (or higher) tax rates than high-wealth jurisdictions, so that a correlation between service outcomes and wealth remains despite the rule imposed by equation 7.

Feldstein (1975) also shows that, assuming a particular algebraic form for the demand for education, a wealth-neutralizing matching grant is defined by

12

$$A_j = E_j(1 - kV_j^{\beta_w/\beta_p}),$$

where k is a scale parameter, which roughly corresponds to $1/\hat{V}$ in equation 9 and which determines the overall level of spending; β_w is the elasticity of spending with respect to wealth; and β_p is the (negative) elasticity of spending with respect to price.[21] As in equation 9, the term in brackets defines a matching rate. Comparing equations 9 and 12 reveals that a power-equalizing grant is wealth-neutral only when the two elasticities in equation 12 are equal in absolute value. If they are not equal, a jurisdiction's response to the matching grant, which is determined by the price elasticity, does not exactly offset the existing impact of its wealth on service demand.

Feldstein (1975) estimates that the required exponent for V_j in this formula equals about 0.33 for cities and towns in Massachusetts in 1970. According to

this estimate, the implicit unitary exponent on wealth in the power-equalizing formula, equation 9, is too large, in the sense that it leads to a negative correlation between wealth and spending. Feldstein's estimated price elasticity is, however, much greater in absolute value than the price elasticity estimated by most other studies of local spending.[22] With a more widely accepted value for this parameter, one might conclude that the implicit exponent in a power-equalizing formula is about right or even too small to generate wealth neutrality.

The Feldstein (1975) formula is general enough to encompass public service costs. Cost factors that are uncorrelated with wealth do not influence the formula at all; if costs are uncorrelated with wealth across school districts, achieving wealth neutrality with respect to spending implies achieving wealth neutrality with respect to service quality. Moreover, so long as all cost variables that are correlated with wealth are included in the empirical analysis, and therefore influence the estimate of β_w, equation 12 leads to wealth neutrality with respect to service quality.[23]

Another way to achieve wealth neutrality would be to equalize voters' budget constraints in all jurisdictions. A constraint-equalizing grant program would consist of lump-sum grants to offset income differences across districts and matching grants to offset tax-price differences.[24] This approach has the advantage over the Feldstein (1975) approach that it does not require the incorporation of estimated elasticities into the grant formula. It costs the state more than the Feldstein approach, however, because it uses block grants instead of relying exclusively on matching grants. Given the low price elasticities found by most studies, however, the cost difference might not be too large.[25]

In conclusion, no state has attempted to implement a program that would literally be wealth-neutral. Foundation and power-equalization programs move toward this objective, at least if implemented in pure form, but they cannot achieve it. Programs that could achieve wealth neutrality are either too complicated, in the sense that they must be based on estimated elasticities, or too expensive, in the sense that they involve extensive redistribution, to be politically feasible—at least so far.

Ensuring Equal Outcomes

An even stronger equity objective than wealth neutrality is complete equality in service levels. This objective is based on the view that certain public services (education, police, or fire, for example) are so important to a person's life chances that all citizens should have equal access to them, regardless of their circumstances or the circumstances of their community.[26]

None of the plans described so far meets this objective. If they are implemented without limits and loopholes, they all move toward it, but none of them achieves full equality of outcomes. A foundation grant places no limit on the spending by rich districts; power-equalizing grants do not even achieve wealth neutrality, which is a necessary condition for equal outcomes; and wealth-neutral grants do not eliminate spending variation that is uncorrelated with wealth.

The only way we know of to meet this objective through grants is to use a foundation plan that requires each jurisdiction to set its tax rate exactly at t^*.[27] However, attempts to restrict the school tax rates of wealthy jurisdictions have proved to be unpopular and could, as emphasized by Reschovsky (1994), encourage wealthy taxpayers to send their children to private schools.[28] In principle, these political problems could be avoided if the "minimum acceptable level" were set above the spending that any jurisdiction would select, but this approach would run into another political problem: its prohibitive expense.

The Case for Equalizing Grants

In our judgement, a strong case can be made for equalizing grants to achieve categorical equity, although the appropriate form of the grants depends on the circumstances. According to their constitutions, many state governments are explicitly responsible for the character of the system that provides elementary and secondary education (see Reschovsky, 1994). We believe that a state's most fundamental responsibility in education is to ensure that every student receives a minimum acceptable level of educational services. Thus, we agree with Reschovsky (1994) that the best grant program for education is a "complete" foundation plan with a required minimum tax rate, with costs in the formula, and, we would add, with a relatively high minimum service quality.

Compared to ensuring a minimum acceptable education, the objectives of equal service per unit sacrifice, of wealth neutrality, or of equal outcomes are stronger in the sense that they require adjustments by all districts, including those that would provide high-quality education without additional assistance. However, controversy surrounding these stronger objectives inevitably leads to compromises that severely limit the extent of equalization. Some people support programs to promote equal service per unit sacrifice or wealth neutrality because those programs allow some variation in service quality even at low levels of wealth and thereby enhance choice for parents.[29] We believe that this extra choice comes at a high equity cost imposed on the students who consequently receive inadequate services. Thus, we prefer a complete foundation plan to the most widely discussed alternative, a power-equalizing grant, as well as to wealth-neutral or equal-outcome grants, and we strongly prefer a complete foundation plan to power-equalizing grants as they are typically implemented with no consideration of costs, with hold harmless clauses, and with a minimum amount of aid to each district.

Although state constitutions do not specifically mention local services other than education, this case for a complete foundation plan also can be extended to other key local public services, such as public safety. Outside of education, however, the minimum acceptable service quality may prove to be difficult for state officials to define, and a practical alternative to a foundation plan is a plan based on the need-capacity gap. This approach makes it possible to give more help to the jurisdictions that face the most severe constraints in providing these services, but it does not literally require a minimum service level. Moreover, unlike a foundation plan, this approach has the practical advantage that, holding constant the state's budget, the number of jurisdictions receiving aid (and hence the political support for the program) can be increased by lowering the extent to which state aid actually closes measured need-capacity gaps. Because the state may want to treat other local services, such as social services, the same way it treats public safety, a grant program based on the need-capacity gap also might be appropriate for all local spending.

EQUALIZING REAL INCOMES THROUGH EQUALIZING AID

Another possible objective for an equalizing grant program is to make more equal the distribution of households' real incomes. Although more direct methods for achieving this objective, such as transfer programs, social insurance, and progressive income taxation, are available, a possible role remains for equalizing grants. This role arises because low-income people cannot directly select the level of public services or taxes in their jurisdiction, and indeed may not have enough votes or political power to influence their jurisdiction's choices. If a jurisdiction in which a low-income household lives provides a service level that is far below what the household prefers, federal or state resources might have a larger impact on the household's utility if they were devoted to increasing the quality of public services than if they were devoted to transfers that directly increase the household's income. This possibility is magnified if local services are characterized by nonrivalry in consumption. Moreover, if the local tax system is regressive, so that tax reductions yield the greatest benefits to people at the bottom of the income distribution, intergovernmental grants that lead to reduced local taxes also might be worth more to low-income people than higher transfers. These are theoretical arguments; we know of no empirical work that determines whether these conditions are met.

Even if these conditions are satisfied, however, the potential of intergovernmental aid programs to boost the real incomes of low-income households may be limited by capitalization, which arises when local service quality and local tax rates affect property values.[30] In the presence of capitalization, which has been documented by many empirical studies,[31] increases in real income associated with higher service quality or lower taxes may be partially or totally offset by higher rents or housing prices.[32]

To be more specific, full capitalization implies that the benefits to tenants from grant-induced increases in service quality are canceled by rent increases and that the benefits to homeowners are confined to people who currently own property in the community. Homeowners who arrive in the future must pay a higher price to enter the community and therefore are no better off as a result of the improved services. With capitalization, therefore, an equalizing grant program appears likely to help many current low-income homeowners and current landlords (some of whom may have low incomes), but appears unlikely to help low-income renters or future low-income homeowners.

Moreover, the existence of capitalization undercuts to some degree an implicit premise in the basic objective of equalizing real incomes, namely that a person's real income depends in part on the service quality and tax rate in the jurisdiction where she lives.[33] If all households are mobile, every household with a given set of skills and preferences can achieve the same real income. Hence, because of compensation in the form of lower housing prices, low-income households who live in jurisdictions with poor public services or high taxes already are no worse off than low-income households who live in jurisdictions with excellent services or low taxes.

For two reasons, however, this capitalization argument neither completely invalidates the premise that real incomes depend on public service quality nor completely eliminates the possibility of using intergovernmental grants to equalize real incomes. The first reason is that age, disability, poverty, and discrimination reduce the mobility of many low-income people.[34] With barriers to mobility, differences in service quality or tax rates need not be fully reflected in housing prices.

The second reason is that even if low-income people are mobile, the impact of grants on housing prices depends on the solution to a complex general equilibrium problem, which does not always yield offsetting housing price changes. A general treatment of this problem is not available, but this point can be illustrated by examining several special cases.

Suppose, for example, that all low-income people live in central cities with poor public services, that these central cities contain only low-income people, and that all of these central cities receive equalizing grants. Because capitalization reflects competition among households of a given type for housing in communities with different public service levels, there is nothing to capitalize in this case. Hence, the real incomes of all low-income households are depressed by the fact that they receive low-quality public services, and raising the quality of public services in all these central cities boosts the real incomes of all low-income households without having any impact on prices. In other words, if a grant program raises service quality in every jurisdiction where low-income people live, a capitalization effect does not arise, and capitalization has no impact either on the validity of the objective or on the ability of grants to achieve it.

Wyckoff (1992) analyzes an alternative case in which there are two communities and three income classes. One community (call it the central city) contains all low-income households, the other (call it the suburb) contains all high-income households, and both contain some of the middle-income households. In this case, capitalization reflects the service demands of the middle-income households who are the households at the moving margin. Raising service quality in the central city therefore boosts the price of housing enough to keep middle-income households in equilibrium, that is, enough to offset middle-income households' valuation of the increment in service quality. This change in housing price could be higher than, lower than, or equal to the value of the public service increment to low-income households. It follows that the real income of low-income households could go down, go up, or be unchanged by equalizing grants. Wyckoff also shows that if the central city contains "a large fraction of the population of the metropolitan area, most of the relative price changes between housing prices in the two communities necessary to restore middle class indifference are accomplished by price changes in the" suburb (p. 22). In this case, intergovernmental aid has the desired effect; that is, it raises the real income of low-income households.

We conclude that capitalization weakens, but does not eliminate, the case for using intergovernmental grants to equalize real incomes. Further research is needed to determine the extent to which capitalization offsets the redistributional benefits of these grants.

Conclusions

Both state governments and the federal government have a long history of attempting to meet equity objectives through intergovernmental grants. The key step in designing an equalizing grant program is deciding on the form of this equity objective. Many different categorical equity objectives, including the guarantee of a minimum service quality and wealth neutrality, can be attained with an appropriately designed equalizing aid program, and under some circumstances equalizing grants can make a contribution to a fairer distribution of real incomes. Moreover, because all relevant equity objectives are concerned with service quality, not spending as such, grant

formulas to achieve them must account for public service costs. Although few grant programs account for costs in a systematic way, methods for doing so are readily available.

Different equity objectives and grant programs are appropriate under different circumstances. In our judgement, a complete foundation plan, that is, a foundation plan that requires a minimum tax rate, accounts for costs, and sets a relatively high minimum service level, is appropriate for elementary and secondary education. For police, fire, and other local services, grants based on the need-capacity gap provide a flexible way to focus aid on the jurisdictions that, through no fault of their own, need help the most.

ENDNOTES

[1] For a discussion of some of the efficiency arguments in favor of equalizing aid, see Ladd and Yinger (1991) and Oates and Schwab (1988). For some efficiency arguments against equalizing aid, see Oakland (1994).

[2] Around 1970, for example, many states moved the responsibility for welfare services from the city to the county or state level. See Ladd and Yinger (1991).

[3] For an analysis of the extent of equalization in existing state aid to local governments, see Yinger and Ladd (1989).

[4] The fact that household characteristics may influence the environment for providing public services leads to an important efficiency argument for equalizing grants, namely, to offset the externality imposed on jurisdictions when low-cost individuals leave. See Oates and Schwab (1988).

[5] Note that actual public wages are a poor measure of costs because they are influenced by local officials. Cost measures—and hence aid formulas—should be based on factors outside the control of local officials. For more on this issue, see Ladd and Yinger (1991).

[6] For examples of this procedure, see Bradbury et al. (1984), Ratcliffe, Riddle, and Yinger (1990), Ladd and Yinger (1991), and Ladd, Reschovsky, and Yinger (1991). Oakland (1994) states that because "spending is not a valid measure of output . . . the coefficients

produced by spending studies measure handicap only if actual budget policy compensates exactly for the handicap." This argument is not correct. The regression-based method is rigorous and requires no such assumption. See Yinger and Ladd (1991, chapter 10).

[7] Oakland (1994) discounts categorical equity objectives (except, apparently, in the case of education) because he sees no reason to think that public services are worth more to people than are private goods and services. We find categorical equity worthwhile not only because certain public services, such as education and public safety, are important to a person's opportunities, but also because a person cannot directly select the level of public services he or she receives.

[8] If many citizens believe in any of these equity objectives (or the one in the next section), then there is an efficiency gain to equalizing grants that parallels each equity objective. This is an application of the well-known theory of efficiency-improving redistribution (Hochman and Rogers, 1969). See also Ladd and Doolittle (1982).

[9] The issue of property tax capitalization, which is discussed at length in a later section, is not relevant here. The minimum service objective (along with most of the other categorical equity objectives) includes a statement about the share of a jurisdiction's tax base that represents a fair contribution to the provision of the relevant public services. The fact that a jurisdiction's property tax base may reflect the tax rate that it actually selects has nothing to do with selection of this share. One might object, however, to the use of the property tax base as a measure of a jurisdiction's capacity to raise revenue, because it reflects the jurisdiction's actual tax decisions. This problem can be solved by using a more general measure of revenue-raising capacity, which is discussed in endnote 14.

[10] Grants inversely related to a jurisdiction's tax base also may have efficiency consequences. Oakland (1994) argues that they may either offset distortions that arise when location decisions are based on tax or service levels or lower efficiency by lowering interjurisdictional variation in service-tax packages. Others have argued that these grants undercut a jurisdiction's incentive to attract more property. Because broad economic and social forces have a much larger influence on a city's tax base than anything the city can do, we do not find this argument compelling. See Ladd and Yinger (1991).

[11] An equivalent requirement is that the jurisdiction spend at least S^*C_j on the service. Note that if t^* is defined as the minimum tax rate required for a jurisdiction to be eligible for the program, instead of the minimum tax rate permitted, then some low-spending jurisdictions might choose not to participate in the grant program at all.

[12] Grants of this type were implemented by the state of Massachusetts in 1980. See Bradbury et al. (1984). Grants of this type also are described in Ratcliffe, Riddle and Yinger (1990) and Ladd, Reschovsky, and Yinger (1991).

[13] In some cases, a measure of expenditure need also must account for differences across jurisdictions in service responsibilities. See Ladd and Yinger (1991).

[14] An alternative approach to revenue-raising capacity is given by Ladd and Yinger (1991). In this approach, a jurisdiction's capacity is the amount it could raise at a standard tax burden on its residents. Ladd and Yinger show how this measure of capacity depends on a jurisdiction's income and its ability to export tax burdens to nonresidents. This approach is more complicated to implement, however, largely because export ratios are difficult to estimate, and it appears to be highly correlated with the tax-base approach used in the text. In Minnesota, for example, the correlation between the two approaches across municipalities is 0.92. See Ladd, Reschovsky, and Yinger (1991).

[15] These claims can easily be proven by substituting the formula for aid per capita, equation 6, into the program's budget constraint and rearranging the terms. This budget constraint can be written as follows:

$$B = \sum_{j=1}^{J} N_j A_j$$

where B is the total budget for the program, J is the number of jurisdictions that receive aid, and N_j is the population of jurisdiction j.

[16] This notion of sacrifice is not without problems. Jurisdictions may have other sources of revenue, for example. Philosophical objections to this notion also can be raised. See Feldstein (1975).

[17] An experiment with negative matching rates was attempted by the state of Maine but was quickly overturned by a referendum.

[18] This point was made, although not implemented, by Feldstein (1975, p. 77): "expenditure per pupil could be modified to reflect local differences in input prices or student abilities."

[19] In the 1973 Texas case of Rodriguez v. San Antonio, the U.S. Supreme Court, in a 5–4

decision, held that education was not a fundamental right and that school district wealth was not a suspect category under the United States Constitution. See Odden and Picus (1992, p. 27). Rulings by state courts have not been so definitive. For more on these issues, see Reschovsky (1994).

[20] A extreme version of this approach is to provide schools at the state level, as is done in Hawaii.

[21] Feldstein's demand function expresses the log of spending as a function of the log of wealth, the log of price (as determined by the matching rate), and the log of other variables, which may be correlated with wealth. The elasticity of spending with respect to wealth includes the direct elasticity for the wealth variable and the indirect elasticity for all other variables that affect demand and are correlated with wealth. In principle, a weaker form of wealth neutrality could be achieved with the Feldstein approach if the components of the wealth elasticity are confined to variables that are thought to be systematically, not incidentally, related to wealth.

[22] Feldstein's estimate price elasticity is −1.0. Most estimates for education fall between −0.1 and −0.5. See Inman (1979) and Bergstrom, Rubinfeld, and Shapiro (1982).

[23] As it turns out, Feldstein's equations contain no cost variables, so substituting his estimated elasticities into his formula will not yield wealth neutrality with respect to service quality, given that many other studies have found that cost factors influence education. See Hanushek (1986) or Ratcliffe, Riddle, and Yinger (1990).

[24] The precise forms of the block grant and matching grant can be found from the median voter's budget constraint. In a standard model, the block grant equals the difference between the target income (a policy parameter) and the median voter's actual income divided by the median voter's tax share (which is her house value divided by house value *per capita* in the jurisdiction). Assuming constant costs in the production of service quality, the matching rate equals the jurisdiction's cost index divided by the median voter's tax share and by the target tax price (another policy parameter). For a derivation of this type of grant in a more complex model, see Yinger (1986). Strictly speaking, this approach raises two new issues. First, it removes all systematic correlation between wealth and service outcomes, but not literally all correlation, as does the Feldstein approach. Preference differences that are correlated with wealth, for example, still might influence outcomes. Second, it assumes that it is appropriate to base grants on a majority rule (or median-voter) framework even if actual decisions diverge from what the median voter would choose. Moreover, it assumes that the median voter can be identified as the person with median income and median preferences. The conditions under which this is true are stated by Bergstrom and Goodman (1973).

[25] In addition, this approach achieves only the weaker form of wealth neutrality described in the previous endnote, which may or may not satisfy courts in school equity cases.

[26] Reschovsky (1994) points out that several state courts appear to be requiring this objective for education.

[27] One way to achieve this objective without a grant is for a state to take over provision of the service, and then to provide the same service level in each community. In Hawaii, for example, education is provided at the state level and, in principle, the same level of education could be (but undoubtedly is not) provided in each school. Another way is for the state to "take over" the local property tax. See Giertz and McGuire (1992). In Kansas, for example, every district must levy the same state-determined property tax rate and return any revenue above a certain amount to the state. Districts also can supplement their revenue with an additional local levy, although this option is scheduled to phase out. See Myers (1992).

[28] A description of a debate over restrictions on the tax levy for high-wealth districts can be found in a case entitled "Funding Schools in Washington State" in Gomez-Ibanez and Kalt (1990).

[29] Oakland (1994) criticizes equalizing aid programs for diminishing efficiency-enhancing variation in public service outcomes. However, efficiency does not require variation in outcomes associated with income or wealth; instead, it requires that communities with different preferences at any given level of income or wealth be allowed to make different choices.

[30] For more detailed discussions of this issue, see Yinger (1986) or Wyckoff (1992).

[31] For a review of existing studies with a focus on tax capitalization, see Yinger et al. (1988).

[32] Although the impact of public service quality on rents is not literally an example of "capitalization," because it does not involve an asset price, it generally is included in the concept of capitalization. In addition, note that when many urban areas are considered, service quality or tax differences also could be

partially or fully offset by wage differences. Moreover, one cannot get around capitalization by giving higher transfers to individuals in low-service or high-tax jurisdictions. Any program in which benefits depend on residence runs into the problem of capitalization.

[33] A similar point is made by Oakland (1994). In discussing differences resulting from higher wage costs, he says: "To equalize for these premia would be to doubly compensate individuals for disamenities."

[34] Racial and ethnic discrimination continues to be a severe barrier to mobility. For a review of evidence from the 1989 Housing Discrimination Study, see Yinger (1993).

REFERENCES

Bergstrom, Theodore C. and Robert Goodman. "Private Demand for Public Goods." *American Economic Review 53* (June, 1973): 280–96.

Bergstrom, Theodore C., Daniel L. Rubinfeld, and Perry Shapiro. "Micro-Based Estimates of Demand Functions for Local School Expenditures." *Econometrica 50* (September, 1982): 1183–1205.

Bradbury, Katharine L., Helen F. Ladd, Mark Perrault, Andrew Reschovsky, and John Yinger. "State Aid to Offset Fiscal Disparities Across Communities." *National Tax Journal* (June, 1984): 151–70.

Bradford, David F., R. A. Malt, and Wallace E. Oates. "The Rising Cost of Local Public Services: Some Evidence and Reflections." *National Tax Journal 22* (June, 1969): 185–202.

Feldstein, Martin S. "Wealth Neutrality and Local Choice in Public Education." *American Economic Review 65* (March, 1975): 75–89.

Giertz, J. Fred and Therese J. McGuire. "Regional and State-Wide Property Tax Base Sharing For Education." In *Proceedings of the 85th Annual Conference of the National Tax Association—Tax Institute of America* (1992): 190–94.

Gold, Steven, David Smith, Stephen Lawton, and Andrea C. Hyary. *Public School Finance Programs of the United States and Canada.* Albany, NY: The Nelson A. Rockefeller Institute of Government, 1992.

Gomez-Ibanez, Jose A. and Joseph P. Kalt. *Cases in Microeconomics.* Englewood Cliffs, NJ: Prentice-Hall, 1990.

Hanushek. Eric. "The Economics of Schooling." *Journal of Economic Literature 24* (September, 1986): 1141–75.

Hochman, H. M. and J. D. Rogers. "Pareto Optimal Redistribution." *American Economic Review 59* (September, 1969): 542–57.

Inman, Robert P. "The Fiscal Performance of Local Governments: An Interpretative Review." In *Current Issues in Urban Economics,* edited by P. Mieszkowski and M. Straszheim, 270–321. Baltimore: Johns Hopkins University Press, 1979.

Ladd, Helen F. and Frederick C. Doolittle. "Which Level of Government Should Assist Poor People?" *National Tax Journal 35* (September, 1982): 323–36.

Ladd, Helen F., Andrew Reschovsky, and John Yinger. "City Fiscal Condition and State Equalizing Aid: The Case of Minnesota." In *Proceedings of the 84th Annual Conference of the National Tax Association—Tax Institute of America, 1991.* 42–49.

Ladd, Helen F. and John Yinger. *America's Ailing Cities: Fiscal Health and the Design of Urban Policy.* Updated ed. Baltimore: Johns Hopkins Press, 1991.

Myers, Will S. "Local Government Implications of Recent Trends in State Education Finance." In *Proceedings of the 85th Annual Conference of the National Tax Association—Tax Institute of America* (1992): 184–89.

Oakland, William. "Fiscal Equalization: An Empty Box?" *National Tax Journal 47,* No. 1 (March, 1994).

Oates, Wallace E. and Robert Schwab. "Economic Competition Among Jurisdictions: Efficiency Enhancing or Distortion Inducing?" *Journal of Public Economics 35* (1988): 333–54.

Odden, Allan R. and Lawrence O. Picus. *School Finance: A Policy Perspective.* New York. McGraw-Hill, 1992.

Ratcliffe, Kerri, Bruce Riddle, and John Yinger. "The Fiscal Condition of School Districts in Nebraska: Is Small Beautiful?" *Economics of Education Review* (January, 1990): 81–99.

Reschovsky, Andrew. "Fiscal Equalization and School Finance." *National Tax Journal 47,* No. 1 (March, 1994).

Wyckoff, Paul Gary. "Capitalization, Equalization, and Intergovernmental Aid." Unpublished Manuscript, 1992.

Yinger, John. "Access Denied, Access Constrained: Results and Implications of the 1989 Housing Discrimination Study." In *Clear and Convincing Evidence: Measurement of Discrimination in America,* edited by M. Fix and R. Struyk, 69–112. Washington, D.C.: The Urban Institute Press, 1993.

Yinger, John. "On Fiscal Disparities Across Cities." *Journal of Urban Economics 19* (May, 1986): 316–37.

Yinger, John, Axel Boersch-Supan, Howard S. Bloom, and Helen F. Ladd. *Property Taxes and House Values: The Theory and Estimation of Intrajurisdictional Property Tax Capitalization.* New York: Academic Press, 1988.

Yinger, John and Helen F. Ladd. "The Determinants of State Assistance to Central Cities." *National Tax Journal 62* (December, 1989): 413–28.

FISCAL EQUALIZATION: AN EMPTY BOX?

WILLIAM H. OAKLAND*

Fiscal equalization is the process through which a central government makes funds available to lower level governments with the objective of reducing the degree of inequality in the revenues that such governments can raise using their own revenue instruments.[1] While the proximate objective is concerned with revenues, the ultimate objective may be to reduce inequalities in public expenditure.[2] Equalization policies have been advocated on both efficiency and equity grounds. In this essay, we shall critically examine these arguments and demonstrate that the case for equalization is weaker than generally thought. Nevertheless, a case can be made for a policy which is directed to assist those governments with constituencies which are disproportionately poor. While such a policy could be labeled as equalization, it may more properly be viewed as an extension of the logic of centralizing the costs of income redistribution in a federal system.

FISCAL DISPARITIES

The flip side of equalization is the concept of fiscal disparities—*i.e.*, those differences that equalization is supposed to remove.[3] We begin the discussion,

therefore, by identifying alternative measures of fiscal disparities that have been discussed in the literature.

In the broadest sense, fiscal disparities can be defined as differences in fiscal effort required to achieve a particular fiscal outcome. Some authors have been content to define outcomes in terms of revenues, while others have been more ambitious, measuring fiscal outcomes in terms of levels of public services.[4] Some even propose to measure outcomes in terms of achievement of certain standards, such as test scores or levels of public safety. Such distinctions are clearly important, affecting both the scope and character of an equalization program; hence, they will be given separate treatment below.

Similarly, the concept of fiscal effort is central to our concerns. Two principal candidates have been suggested. One measures fiscal effort in terms of tax rates, while the other measures effort in terms of the fraction of income of resident taxpayers surrendered in the process. The first approach has most commonly been identified with the Advisory Commission on Intergovernmental Relations (ACIR), which has developed the concept of the Representative Revenue Structure (RRS).[5] Simply put, the RRS is a vector of the average effective tax rates on all tax bases in use. The ACIR uses

*Tulane University, New Orleans, LA 70118.

the RRS to construct an index of fiscal capacity, defined as the ratio of the revenues that a jurisdiction would collect if it were to impose RRS tax rates to what the average jurisdiction would collect using the same tax rates. The inverse of the fiscal capacity index represents the surcharge on average tax rates necessary to collect the average revenue.

The income burden approach to fiscal effort has been advocated by Yinger (1986) and Ladd and Yinger (1989), among others. This concept is more transparent than the RRS measure. However, its implementation may be much more controversial because of uncertainties about the ultimate incidence of many taxes, especially with respect to tax exporting and importing. Consequently, the data requirements for it are an order of magnitude greater than for the RRS.

Clearly, the two approaches to fiscal effort are closely related. Indeed, if income were the only tax base, they would be identical. But, in the United States, property taxes dominate many local revenue structures and sales taxes are the major tax source of state governments. Moreover, when more than one tax base is employed, the measures may diverge. Among other things, different taxes can afford different possibilities for shifting to nonresidents. Alternatively, there could be differences in proportions of nonexported taxes.[6]

While the income burden approach is more relevant to issues of tax incidence, the tax rate approach is more germane for issues relating to tax base mobility. Equalization policy may thus be directed to either or both measures of disparity.

EQUITY

As with most public policy initiatives, equalization of fiscal disparities has been defended on both efficiency and equity

grounds. Similarly, the same considerations have also been used by critics of equalization policy.

Horizontal Equity

An equity case for equalization has been advanced by Yinger (1986), who proposed the principle of "Fair Compensation." This principle states that the average tax burden, relative to income, required for the standard bundle of public services should not depend upon one's community of residence. This can be interpreted as an application of horizontal equity.[7] It is also similar to a position advanced by James Buchanan (1950) nearly a half century ago in his classic paper, "Federalism and Fiscal Equity." There, he advocated the equalization of taxpayer surplus among communities, where surplus measures the differences between benefits from public services and taxes paid for such services.[8]

At first blush, Fair Compensation has intuitive appeal. It seems to be a straightforward application of an important canon of income taxation—*i.e.*, individuals with like income should pay like taxes. However, when extended to the finance of local government services, it acquires an added dimension, because it tacitly implies that the price of public services should be income dependent. In effect, all income classes would surrender the same fraction of their income for the standard bundle of services. Consequently, Fair Compensation can also be seen to have an important dimension of vertical equity.

However, the relation of Fair Compensation to vertical equity is markedly incomplete. Why should equalization be limited to public consumption? Are not differences in private consumption a more important source of vertical inequity? Furthermore, the extension of Fair Compensation logic to private consumption would result in total egalitarianism, certainly well beyond the goals of equalization, or of vertical equity for that matter. This arises because the cost of goods and services are expressed as budget shares. All individuals thus face the same budget set—100 percent. Moreover, outlays for particular goods and services would be the same regardless of level of consumption.

Alternatively, one might defend the limitation on the grounds that publicly provided services are so unique and basic to life that they should be provided on an egalitarian basis. However, with the possible exception of elementary and secondary education and some minimum level of law and order, locally provided public services are not fundamentally more important than the goods provided in the private sector. Arguably, food is more basic than garbage collection, clothing is more essential than recreation, and outlays for health are more important than public transportation.[9] Moreover, real decisions are at the margin, and what is true for a category as a whole may not be true for increments in that category. There is no evidence that marginal outlays for public services, even on education, are more important than marginal outlays on other private goods. In short, the burden of proof remains with those who argue for the primacy of public services.

Vertical Equity

If the major source of disparities is caused by differences of income distribution among communities, one might defend equalization on income redistribution grounds. Holding expenditure levels constant, taxes as a fraction of income will tend be lower in those communities with above average income and *vice versa*. Hence, a policy which equalizes the costs of public services would redistribute income from "rich" communities to "poor" communities.

Clearly, such an approach is a clumsy means for achieving vertical equity. For one thing, other factors, such as the ability to export taxes to nonresidents, will influence the burden a community actually faces. For another, communities are seldom homogeneous with respect to income. There is no guarantee that equalization funds would be spent for the benefit of the poor residents of a community. Indeed, to the extent that such funds reduce tax rates, benefits will redound to the relatively affluent within the community. Even if the funds are spent directly on behalf of the poor, the benefits may be captured by others. For example, housing subsidies for poor households may end up simply raising rents, with no increase in the consumer surplus from housing services. While the latter is admittedly an extreme example, it points to the difficulty in targeting public programs. For the case at hand, the benefits of equalization grants will almost certainly accrue to the rich as well as to poor residents of recipient communities. Thus, if the primary objective of equalization is to reduce interpersonal income disparities, it would be dominated by a policy which provides direct grants to poor individuals.

Equality of Opportunity

While it may be difficult to construct a general case for equalization on equity grounds, it may be possible to do so for particular goods and services such as public elementary and secondary education. In recent years, courts have increasingly rejected financing arrangements which afford affluent communities unlimited ability to exercise their superior economic resources with respect to public schooling. Even before court activism, however, equalization schemes at the state level were widespread. Apparently, the underlying motives are equality of opportunity and increasing social and economic mobility. However, it has become increasingly clear that even complete equalization is not sufficient to guarantee equality of educational outcome, or even to guarantee equality of public resources.[10] This seems to have prompted some courts to require total state financing of public education.[11] However, even such a sweeping reform may not succeed if affluent families opt out of the public education system.[12]

Property Rights

Lastly, an equity case might be advanced for the sharing of the bounty provided by natural resources. Not all regions are equally blessed with natural resources such as mineral deposits, proximity to cheap transportation and/or power, and climatic advantages. Through tax and regulatory policies, communities are frequently able to tap these resources, providing a windfall to community residents through superior public services and/or lower local taxes.[13] A case may well be made for the sharing of such windfalls among a wider polity than the jurisdiction in which the resource is physically located.[14] Equalization grants may be one means for achieving such an objective. It should be emphasized, however, that the fundamental equity issue here is one of property rights. Whether resource wealth should be considered as a local, state, or national resource involves complex issues and its resolution may well rest upon the principle of "right is might" rather than moral principles. Nevertheless, as we shall argue below, considerations of economic efficiency may also provide support for such policies.

ECONOMIC EFFICIENCY

In a world of mobile tax bases, interjurisdictional tax differentials can influence the location of such tax bases. Communities which can afford lower tax rates can attract a greater share of business activity and other tax bases. To the extent that higher tax rates do not reflect higher costs of doing business, relocations based on tax differentials are often socially wasteful. Similarly, the fear of losing tax base may discourage communities from undertaking productive public expenditure. Since the loss (gain) of tax base involves a gain (loss) to some other tax jurisdiction, there is no aggregate welfare loss associated with relocations caused by increased expenditures. Hence, the gain or loss of tax base should not be considered in deciding how much to spend in the public sector. Narrowing of tax rate and/or tax burden differentials *via* equalization would ameliorate both of these apparent distortions.

However, the process of equalization may actually introduce distortions of its own. In particular, disparities of tax burden may be necessary to achieve an efficient articulation of taxpayers' demands for public services. Moreover, equalization may discourage efficient reallocation of population and economic activity among jurisdictions. In effect, it would prop up inefficient entities. The latter consideration induced Buchanan to recant his advocacy for the equalization of taxpayer surpluses.[15] He pointed to the need to maximize the sum of public and private output, which would generally call for taxpayer surplus to differ among jurisdictions.

Like most controversies, there is merit to both sides of the argument. The efficiency consequences of equalization depends upon the underlying source of the disparities. A discussion of this issue follows.

SOURCES OF FISCAL DISPARITY

Income Distribution

A major source of fiscal disparity arises from asymmetries in income distribution.

Simply put, the higher the average income, *caeteris paribus*, the lower the tax effort required per unit of public services. Hence, the effort required for the "standard package" of services would be negatively correlated with income. However, such variations are not necessarily symptoms of resource misallocation. Indeed, they may signal just the opposite. The sorting of people into communities with different income characteristics may be a manifestation of the Tiebout mechanism, where people "vote with their feet." Because the demand for most public services is income elastic, income heterogeneous communities are likely to provide a fiscal outcome not favored by any class.

If local taxes were levied on a benefit basis, such as through head taxes or user fees, people would tend naturally to sort themselves into homogeneous communities.[16] There is no reason to presume that the actual tax effort expended would be constant across communities. Nevertheless, with benefit taxation, there would be no fiscal incentive for households to change communities.[17] A policy of equalization in such an environment might distort the true cost of public services in all communities. In "poor" communities, public services might appear artificially cheap, since part of their costs would be covered by grants, with the opposite effect in affluent communities.[18]

Thus, rather than being supportive of equalization, efficiency considerations weigh against the use of intergovernmental grants that narrow fiscal disparities arising from interjurisdictional income differentials. Such efficiency losses should be offset against any alleged equity gains.

Cost Differentials

In recent years it has become increasingly fashionable to measure fiscal disparity inclusive of interjurisdictional cost differentials.[19] Such variation can arise from two main sources: (1) differences in factor input costs and (2) differences in the effectiveness of public inputs in producing public output.

From the standpoint of efficiency, the equalization of factor price differences is of dubious merit. Presumably, such prices measure the opportunity costs of that factor; to subsidize the costs of inputs used in the provision of public services would make such services appear artificially cheap relative to private goods and services. Moreover, it would also lead to excessive relative use of the factors being subsidized. A further inefficiency arises as people are encouraged to locate in high cost areas.

Even if one ignored these efficiency consequences, focusing only on equity arguments, equalization of factor cost differentials may be totally unwarranted. Wage premia often arise to compensate for locational disadvantages such as disamenities or higher cost of living. To equalize for these premia would be to doubly compensate individuals for disamenities.

Similar remarks would apply to differences in the productivity of public inputs. The fact that public transit is more expensive in a hilly environment is a feature of the economic map. To erase this feature through equalization is to encourage excessive populations in such areas. It would be analogous to equalizing the cost of home heating between Alaska and southern California. To erase such distinctions is simply bad regional policy.

More troublesome, however, are differences in productivity arising from the characteristics of the populations being served.[20] It is more expensive to provide public safety in inner city ghettos than in middle class suburbs. If such costs were equalized, it is not clear that people would flock to the ghettos in response.[21] Like physical handicaps, it may be deemed equitable to provide compensating assistance. However, unlike physical handicaps, the need arises from behavior which, at least to some measure, may be subject to the control of those being assisted. Most important, however, may be limitations arising from the inability to accurately measure such handicaps. Present methods utilizing multiple regression analysis of actual spending behavior have serious methodological shortcomings. By hypothesis, spending is not a valid measure of output. Hence, the coefficients produced by spending studies measure handicap only if actual budget policy compensates exactly for the handicap—a highly tenuous condition.

Natural Resource Differentials

Not only do disparities in regional natural resource endowments raise issues of equity, but they are likely to be a source of spatial misallocation of mobile resources, particularly labor resources. The problem is a result of the freedom people have to move among jurisdictions, and the fact that, for the most part, new residents must be given the same treatment by the local fisc as existing residents. The immobility of natural resources make them vulnerable to exploitation by local government taxation, providing revenue windfalls to area residents. Together these considerations give rise to a "problem of the commons." That is, new residents will be drawn to resource rich communities to share in the fiscal benefits provided by such resources.[22] From a spatial efficiency perspective, there will be too many people in resource rich communities and too few in resource poor regions.[23]

In principle, a policy of equalization would eliminate the fiscal benefits of superior natural resource endowments. In effect, the central government nationalizes the fiscal benefits of natural resources. However, the real issue here is one of implementability. How can we distinguish the nature and extent of local fiscal benefits made available by superior natural resources?

If the natural resource is owned directly by the local jurisdiction, one can directly observe its fiscal benefits. This would be the case of mineral royalties on state owned land. However, such instances are the exception rather than the rule. For the most part, ownership of the resource is either vested with private owners or, as in the case of environmental amenities, owned by no one. In such circumstances, it may be very difficult, if not impossible, to measure accurately the fiscal benefits of the resource. Consider taxes upon privately held mineral resources. Almost certainly, some part of such taxes will be shifted away from resource owners to others, such as workers. Here, the tax proceeds would overstate the community benefit.[24]

Even more troublesome are those resources in the common domain. Here, to enjoy the benefit of the resource requires access. This suggests that much of the net benefit of the resource will be embedded in land prices. Communities can thus collectivize portions of the resource through property taxation. Only a portion of the property tax proceeds, however, will be reflective of resource rents; the remaining will be attributable to capital investment. To separate these two elements will be difficult at best. Property taxes, however, are not the only tool the community can use to capture resource rents. Similar results can be obtained through the taxation of products which utilize the resource as an input, as in the tourist industry. Here also, tax proceeds would be an imperfect indicator of community fiscal benefit.

Further measurement issues arise if the community were to enjoy monopoly power for some goods which it exports to nonresidents. This may itself be the result of a unique natural resource or of exogenous government policy, such as identifying an area as a government center. In such circumstances, by judicious taxation of the monopolized commodity, the community may extract a still larger fiscal windfall than the resource itself would permit.[25] Just how a central government should measure such monopoly power in practice is problematic at best.

While the preceding focus has been upon measurement of the income burden of resource taxation, similar issues arise for the RRS approach taken by the ACIR. While it may be the case that tax bases of all types will be enhanced by the existence of superior resources, the connection is very loose. Enlarged tax bases will also accrue to those communities which trade off environmental amenities for the tax and employment benefits of industry. It is unlikely that even the most sophisticated determinants of location study could disentangle resource and environmental induced industry.

IMPLICATIONS FOR PUBLIC POLICY

Wither Equalization Aid?

Our analysis suggests that there can be both equity and efficiency justifications for a policy of equalization. The strongest equity case involves the reduction of disparities of educational opportunity so as to foster social and economic mobility. Fairness also dictates the equalization of the costs of compensatory services arising from inherent citizen attributes. A third, but less compelling, motive is to share natural resource wealth among

the polity as a whole. On the negative side of the ledger, equalization is not properly suited to resolve problems of vertical equity. Also not persuasive is the position that differential income burdens imposed by a standard bundle of public services should be eliminated. Finally, we have the issues of feasibility. Equalization aid is an unwieldy instrument to equalize fiscal outcomes. Our experience with public school aid suggests that even the most aggressive equalization will allow considerable disparity to remain. As for compensatory services, measurement errors bedevil policy formulation.

On the efficiency side, the case is much weaker. Indeed, the equalization of disparities arising from income distribution or costs may have negative consequences for economic efficiency. Only when disparities arise from differences in natural resource endowment can equalization improve resource allocation. However, there are serious weaknesses in our ability to identify such resource endowments.

These considerations suggest that equalization efforts should be carefully tailored to the objective being sought. If the objective is equality of educational opportunity, the focus should be upon outcomes rather than the burden that would be hypothetically imposed if a standard bundle of educational services were purchased. On the other hand, if the objective is to narrow disparities arising from natural resources, the focus should not be upon broad measures of burden which are influenced by income distribution and/or input cost differentials.

Moreover, the difficulty in quantifying local natural resource wealth may dictate that the central government tax goods complementary with that resource, using the proceeds to finance its own services.[26] Finally, if the objective is to level the playing field for "disadvantaged" citizens, policies should be targeted with regard to the number of such disadvantaged and research should be focused on identifying the consequences of the disadvantage.

In none of the aforementioned cases is there a use for broad measures of fiscal disadvantage as advanced by Ladd and Yinger (1989) or by the ACIR. By design, both measures incorporate the effect of disparities arising from income distribution and both are subject to serious measurement errors. The Ladd–Yinger measure requires the estimation of tax exporting and importing, for which we currently have little empirical basis. The ACIR approach, by contrast, is based upon the assumption that the existence of a tax base implies taxable capacity, whether or not the tax is exported or borne by local residents. Moreover, if a community trades environmental quality for an industrial tax base, this will increase its taxable capacity and decrease its equalization aid.

Centralizing the Public Service Costs of the Poor[27]

A major impetus for equalization aid has been the fiscal plight of major United States central cities. Almost without exception, the cities are facing a chronic fiscal crisis. Much of the responsibility for this crisis is attributable to the concentration of poor households within the boundaries of the central city. Obviously, poor households contribute little to the tax base, and major concentrations of the poor are known to increase the need for public services. Historically, the central city has had a superior resource base with which to offset this disadvantage. However, the last generation has seen a marked decrease in this comparative advantage. Hence, the belief is that equalization aid, particularly that which takes into account the extra public ser-

vice needs of the central city, would help ease the fiscal plight of the city.

As with other objectives, however, equalization may not be the optimal tool with which to address the problem of the central city. It would make far more sense to confront the problem directly by targeting aid to the poor. That the federal government is the appropriate agency to conduct income redistribution is generally conceded. In practice, an overwhelming share of the "safety-net" system is funded at the federal level. Curiously, however, this effort has stopped at providing for the private consumption of the poor. In fact, however, the poor are major consumers of local public goods and services. Given that most taxes are driven by income, however, the poor do not fully pay for the public services they consume. The balance is made up through taxes on other taxpayers. As mentioned, historically, the central city was the seat of much of the resource rents within the urban area. This enabled it to maintain services without putting an undue burden on mobile tax bases, such as affluent households and business capital. The rapid increase in the share of the city's population which is poor and the erosion of resource rents has translated into higher taxes for mobile taxpayers and/or substandard services. Both of these have lead to further outmigration of mobile tax bases. This cumulative deterioration of the central city could be ameliorated or even reversed if the federal government would follow its own logic with regard to the safety-net system and extend its support to the public good consumption of the urban poor. The costs of such a program would be relatively modest, amounting to but a small fraction of the current welfare system. Moreover, it would be relatively easy to implement. All that would be required is an estimate of the cost of the safety-net level of public services to be supported and an identification of the size of the group to be served. In the aggregate, the effect of such a program would appear to be equalizing by conventional measures. However, at the individual city level, the extent of effective equalization would likely show great variability. The latter would be a reflection of how an equalization approach would fail to meet an identified social need.

Summary and Conclusion

In conclusion, the case for fiscal equalization is far less persuasive than commonly thought. As a means of addressing inequities it is poorly targeted and often seems based on a dubious primacy of public goods and services. It is also clumsy as a means of equalizing regional disparities in resource endowments, which may give rise to both inequities and inefficiencies. These advantages are manifested in numerous and often subtle ways, not subject to accurate measurement. They are also difficult to disentangle from revenue disparities arising from income differentials, which are not suitable objects of equalization. Lastly, there is potential for considerable mischief in the extension of equalization to cover cost disparities in the provision of public services, as is espoused by the other authors in this symposium. With few exceptions, to equalize cost disparities is tantamount to repealing the reality of the economic map and would encourage wasteful location decisions.

While the objectives sought by those advocating equalization policies are often noble ones, they can usually be accomplished more effectively by policies which more carefully target the problem at hand.

ENDNOTES

1 Pearce, *MIT Dictionary of Modern Economics* (1992, p. 129).

2 This clearly seems to be the focus of the other two papers in this symposium. However, revenue disparities remain the root of the issue.

3 This section draws heavily from Oakland (1994).

4 The Advisory Commission on Intergovernmental Relations (1971) is most readily identified with the revenue approach. More recently, this approach was adopted by Bahl *et al.* (1992). Cost adjusted disparities have been proposed by Bradbury *et al.* (1984).

5 See the ACIR's *Measuring the Fiscal Capacity and Effort of State Local Areas* (1971 and subsequent periodic updates).

6 The differences between the two measures is dealt with in detail in Oakland (1994).

7 Since it applies only to the average burden, however, it may fail to equalize the burden for all citizen-taxpayers. This would be the case, for example, if the tax burden of local taxes is not proportional to income. For example, if tax burdens are regressive, equalizing average tax burdens would result in higher tax burdens on those well-to-do taxpayers residing in "rich" communities than in "poor" communities.

8 However, Buchanan has since recanted this position. See Buchanan and Wagner (1970).

9 While it is the case that we sometimes observe public intervention into individual choices of private goods, *e.g.*, food stamps and public housing, these programs effectively provide fungible resources which do not restrict individual choices.

10 Among the first to make this argument was Feldstein (1975).

11 Complete state financing is not necessary to have the same effect. A similar result could be obtained by requiring local governments to contribute money to the equalization fund and placing a cap on the money any local government can spend. This is the policy adopted by California.

12 Downes and Schoeman (1992) have shown that private school enrollments in California have increased markedly since the *Serrano* decision. Furthermore, Fischel (1989) has argued that political support for public education has eroded substantially in that state. Both of these effects will widen disparities in educational outcomes.

13 Population mobility could dissipate, if not eliminate, the regional advantages of superior resources. This would convert the problem

into an efficiency issue, as discussed below. However, if population is imperfectly mobile, an equity issue would remain. Moreover, the benefits of resources would often be imbedded in site values. There would remain the issue of equity, as put forth by Henry George.

[14] The term landowner could be substituted for jurisdiction. See the preceding note.

[15] See Buchanan and Wagner (1970).

[16] Since tastes also influence demand for public services, the argument for sorting should be in terms of "effective demand" classes, where the latter reflect both taste and income differentials. This would not affect the conclusions of this section.

[17] In the more likely event of taxes based on income, there may be some tendency for lower income groups to prefer heterogeneous communities, because they are able to purchase public services at a subsidized cost. To prevent such mixing, zoning restrictions may be necessary.

[18] The marginal cost of public services would not be affected by equalization grants. Hence, there could only be a nondistorting "income" effect from equalization grants. However, if community residents misperceive the average cost of public services to be their marginal cost, distorted public service levels would result. In either event, the incentive for income stratification would remain, since the different income classes would still differ in terms of desired levels of expenditure. See Oates (1979).

[19] This approach is widely used in recent studies of education. Recently, it was applied by Ladd and Yinger (1989) to the measurement of urban fiscal disparties. It is also adopted by the other papers in this symposium.

[20] Bradford et al. (1969) were among the first to relate population characteristics to productivity of public inputs.

[21] Some conservatives might argue that to make life in urban ghettos more pleasant is to decrease the incentive to work to gain the resources necessary to leave such places.

[22] In the absence of local government activity, the problem of the commons would not arise, because land rents would adjust to offset any benefit from natural resources. It is precisely by taxing such land rents, directly or indirectly, that local governments can bring some of the benefits of natural resources into the public sphere. Once captured by the public sector, natural resources are subject to common issues.

[23] Although the text focuses on human re-

sources, similar remarks apply to mobile capital resources.

[24] In addition, tax proceeds could reflect differences in the extent to which jurisdictions choose to exploit mineral resources.

[25] The argument here parallels that of the optimal tariff.

[26] In effect, the central government would preempt local taxation of the resource. Such was the case for the United States windfall profits tax, which captured the much of the surplus created by OPEC-induced price increases.

[27] The policy outlined here was first advocated in Oakland (1979).

REFERENCES

Advisory Commision on Intergovernmental Relations, Measuring the Fiscal Capacity and Effort of State and Local Areas. M-58. Washington, D.C.: U.S. Government Printing Office, 1971.

Bahl, Roy, Jorge Martinez-Vazquez, and David Sjoquist. "Central City-Suburban Fiscal Disparities." Public Finance Quarterly 20 (October, 1992): 420–32.

Bradbury, Katherine, Helen Ladd, Mark Pernault, Andrew Reschovsky, and John Yinger. "State Aid to Offset Fiscal Disparities Across Communities." National Tax Journal 37 (June, 1984): 151–70.

Bradford, David, R.A. Malt, and Wallace Oates. "The Rising Cost of Local Public Services: Some Evidence and Reflections." National Tax Journal 22 (June, 1969): 185–202.

Buchanan, James. "Federalism and Fiscal Equity." American Economic Review 40 (September, 1950): 583–99.

Buchanan, James and Richard Wagner. "Federal Fiscal Equalization." In The Analysis of Public Output, edited by J. Margolis. New York: National Bureau of Economic Research, 1970.

Downes, Thomas and David Schoeman. 1992. School Financing Reform and Private School Enrollment: Evidence from California. Northwestern University. Mimeo.

Feldstein, Martin. "Wealth Neutrality and Local Choice in Public Education." American Economic Review 65 (March, 1975): 75–89.

Fischel, William. "Did Serrano Cause Proposition XIII?" National Tax Journal 45 (December, 1989): 405–19.

Ladd, Helen and John Yinger. America's Ailing Cities, Baltimore: Johns Hopkins Press, 1989.

Oakland, William. "Central Cities: Fiscal Plight and Prospects for Reform." In Current Issues in

Urban Economics, edited by Peter Mieszkowski and Mahlon Straszheim. Baltimore: Johns Hopkins Press, 1979, 322–58.

Oakland, William. "Recognizing and Correcting for Fiscal Disparities." In *Fiscal Equalization for State and Local Government Finance*, edited by John Anderson. Westport, CT: Greenwood Publishing, 1994.

Oates, Wallace, "Lump-Sum Intergovernmental Grants Have Price Effects." In *Fiscal Federalism*

and Grants-in-Aid, edited by Peter Mieskowski and William Oakland. COUPE Papers on Public Economics 1. Washington, D.C.: The Urban Institute, 1979.

Pearce, David. *The MIT Dictionary of Modern Economics.* 4th ed. Cambridge, MA: MIT Press, 1992.

Yinger, John. "On Fiscal Disparities Across Cities." *Journal of Urban Economics 19* (May, 1986): 316–37.

HOW WOULD YOU KNOW A GOOD ECONOMIC DEVELOPMENT POLICY IF YOU TRIPPED OVER ONE? HINT: DON'T JUST COUNT JOBS

PAUL N. COURANT*

INTRODUCTION

There is an enormous amount of literature on the effectiveness of state and local economic development policies. Most of the empirical literature by economists [very nicely summarized by Bartik, a major contributor (1991)] has been devoted to measuring how effective various kinds of policies are, with the effects measured in terms of employment, business starts, and new branch plants, among other things. Put baldly, what I want to argue here is that, with a few notable exceptions, the existing literature reflects a great deal of effort that could have been better spent asking different questions. What we should seek to measure in our assessments of local economic development policies is changes in the level and distribution of economic welfare.

The connection between welfare on the one hand and jobs, branch plants, investment, *etc.* on the other is by no means obvious or straightforward. What *is* straightforward are some standard propositions about the welfare economics of government intervention in the economy. These may be summarized in an entirely familiar way—unless there is either market failure or dissatisfaction with the income distribution generated by market outcomes, there is no persuasive rationale for government intervention. There is, of course, plenty of market failure that government may be able to ameliorate,[1] and there are many reasons to want to change the distribution of income. My claim here is that economists concerned with economic development should direct more effort to evaluating the potential for improving economic welfare (local, state, national, or international, depending on the circumstances) as distinct from measuring (in however intricate, difficult, and sophisticated ways) the consequences of development programs. To the extent that politicians refuse to listen to us, preferring words of one syllable ("jobs,

*Department of Economics and Institute of Public Policy Studies, University of Michigan, Ann Arbor, MI 48109-1220.

jobs, jobs"), it is our duty as economists to attempt, at least at the edges, to help them to understand that jobs are not coterminous with benefits, and that both jobs and benefits generally entail costs.

POLICY GOALS AND THE POLICY LITERATURE

Wassmer (1993) reports, using somewhat dated sources, that 28 states have explicit tax abatement policies that are designed to stimulate local economic development, and that 28 states (not necessarily the same ones) have other economic development policies. Bartik (1994) provides further evidence that state and local development policy is ubiquitous and nontrivial in magnitude. As a practical matter, state and local (and, indeed, national) policy regarding economic development seems to be primarily concerned with "creating" jobs.[2] When pushed, it turns out that policymakers strongly prefer "good jobs," the meaning of which is subject to considerable debate, especially during elections. Approximately, good jobs seem to be jobs that are fairly secure, pay well enough, and carry sufficient benefits so that a family whose adults are employed at between one and two such jobs can own a home, be reasonably insured against medical and other disasters, take occasional vacations, and send children to college.[3] Policymakers are often especially interested in manufacturing jobs because they tend meet the criteria for "good jobs." Indeed, economic development policy is often explicitly directed at increasing manufacturing employment. Against a backdrop of over a decade of declining manufacturing employment nationwide, this emphasis makes for a number of apparent policy failures.[4]

It is interesting to note, given politicians' almost universal interest in increasing employment, that the lion's share of resources devoted to economic development at the state and local level is used to subsidize capital, rather than labor. While it is quite likely that capital subsidies at the local level increase local employment, it is very unlikely that a capital subsidy of a given dollar amount would increase labor demand by more than a labor subsidy of the same magnitude.

Jobs may be the outcome of most interest to policymakers and politicians, but the empirical literature examines many outcome measures of development programs. These include, among other things and with many variations by industry and many different detailed definitions: new plant openings; average growth rate of state product; employment growth; changes in output; new branch plants; foreign direct investment in manufacturing; small business starts; changes in personal income (usually *per capita*); labor intensity of manufacturing; high-tech employment; new capital expenditure; value-added in manufacturing; size of new branch plants; value of business building permits; number of relocating manufacturing firms; amount of industrial land.[5] Studies that use these measures have been employed at the state, substate region, and local levels. Consistent with the special emphasis that policymakers place on manufacturing, a disproportionate number of these studies emphasize either manufacturing as a whole or some subset of manufacturing industries. Also, it is fair to say that most of the literature, and most of the policy effort, has involved fiscal incentives, mostly on the tax side. In principle, however, most of what I have to say in this paper should be applicable to any kind of development incentive.

PROBLEMS WITH THE EMPIRICAL LITERATURE IN ITS OWN TERMS

There would seem to be three general reasons why one might want to measure the effect of various policies on any or all of the list of outcome measures given above. (1) It might be that labor demand is the outcome of interest, and that other outcome measures (other than employment itself) are thought to be good proxies for labor demand, or to be part of processes that lead to increased labor demand. (*E.g.*, increased investment, adding to the capital stock, increases the value of the marginal product of labor, and hence labor demanded.) (2) It might be that the outcome measures are of interest, or of value, in their own right. For example, one could have a scientific interest in the processes that generate Gross State Product. Or one could have a political interest in processes that generate rents for valued constituencies. (3) It might be that the outcome measures are good proxies for, or are part of a process that generates, economic welfare.

Whatever the reasons for undertaking these measurements (other than purely scientific interest), the user of the research needs to know the relationship(s), if any, between the variable being studied (*e.g.*, increases in new branch plants in a specific manufacturing industry as a share of all business starts in a state) and variables that are of policy interest. Suppose that someone establishes, with great precision, the relationship between, say, general inventory taxes and the establishment of branch plants for muffler-parts suppliers in a specific state in the Midwest. Suppose that the relationship is fairly powerful, and that it has the right sign—cutting the tax increases the number of branch plants. *Without further explicit modeling of the industry and of the state's economy, the preceding information does not tell us whether a reduction in inventory taxes will increase employment in the state, employment in manufacturing in the state, or even employment in the muffler-*

-parts industry in the state. (That it also does not tell us whether state income or welfare would rise or fall goes without saying.)

Unless the inventory tax was on the downward-sloping part of the Laffer curve, the reduction in inventory taxes will generally reduce state government revenues. Given that most states operate under balanced budget requirements, the government will respond, in some combination, by raising other taxes and cutting expenditure. These responses will make the state a less attractive place to live and do business for everyone whose benefits from the inventory tax reduction are less than lost benefits from the other tax increases and spending cuts. There will be changes in the composition of labor supply and local product demand that will, generally, be opposite in sign to what happens in the muffler-parts and related industries. The net effect of the cut in inventory taxes on total employment, manufacturing employment, and income could plainly go either way.[6] Without a specific model of the relationship between a given outcome measure (muffler-parts branch plants, in this example) and something that is of policy interest (*e.g.*, employment and income in the state, or net economic welfare of different groups), knowing a lot about what drives the outcome measure is of little or no value for helping to formulate good policy. Such models, or even discussions of why we might want to measure given outcomes of development policies, are conspicuous by their absence in this literature.[7]

Why Do Estimated Effects Vary So Much?

There is enormous variation in the estimated effects of taxes on the various outcome measures associated with business location and business activity. In his paper in this symposium, for example,

Bartik reports that the long-run elasticity of business location (measured across all of the outcome measures of the studies he has looked at) with respect to taxes is probably between −0.1 and −0.6. One obvious reason for the large range, implicit in the muffler-parts example and well recognized in much of the literature, is that the uses to which tax revenues are put will generally affect the attractiveness of different locations. Many studies of the effect of development policies attempt to deal with this problem by including measures of government spending, especially in areas thought to be of value to capital, as control variables. As it turns out, these help—studies that include measures of public services are more likely to find significant effects of taxes, with the right sign (Bartik, 1991, p. 39). Even so, there remains large variation, and there is also a great deal of variation in estimates of the effect (on various measures of business location and activity) and levels of public spending on specific services. (Bartik, 1991, Appendix Table 2.3)

I think that this kind of imprecision in measured effects is unsurprising, and derives from geographic heterogeneity that is extremely difficult to correct for statistically. A dollar of spending on a given public service (*e.g.*, education) will generate different consequences depending on the quality and policies of the school district, or of the complementarities between education and what local industry is doing. No plausible level of disaggregation is going to pick these differences up. The effects will, in fact, vary by place, the controls for such variation will be imperfect, and, willy nilly, studies that look at different places and times will obtain different estimates of the effects of independent variables as measured. When controlling for the effects of public spending, be it on education, roads, or anything else, looking for an average

effect means averaging the very different effects in places where government is well and badly run, or run with varying goals and under varying conditions.

The same sort of argument applies to studies of the effect of taxes, especially when such studies do not control for the content of spending. It matters how good (as well as how large) the spending side is. Similar arguments apply to large variances in the estimates of the effects of industrial parks, other summary measures of "business support" and "business climate." In all of these cases, what the policy or program actually does will vary geographically in ways that are extremely difficult to control for. Thus, studies done in different places will (if well done) measure different effects, and studies done across many places will produce averages that may not be applicable to any place in particular.[8]

Implications

Knowing the *average* effects of, say, property-tax rates and spending on highways is not very valuable in any particular policy setting. In the empirical literature on economic development, the estimated range of effects typically includes both signs and substantial (for policy) differences in magnitudes on both sides of zero. The policymaker who infers that her town (or state) would act like the average from some set of studies would be much better advised to pursue the question of how much her town (or state) looks like places that have large, small, positive, or negative effects. The average just is not much help when the variances are large and the cause of the large variance is unmeasured, real, policy-relevant heterogeneity.

So far, what I have said seems unusually dismal, even for economics. The line of argument that I have taken here suggests that in order to make practical use of existing and similar empirical work on the effects of economic development policies, we need to do considerably more work, of a very difficult type; we need to characterize what it is about specific localities that can be associated with particular estimates of the parameter values of interest. Fortunately, there is another way: a great deal of practical information on where to look for good government policy can be derived from straightforward applications of well-known propositions in welfare economics.

WELFARE ECONOMICS AND FACTOR MOBILITY

With exceptions too rare to be considered here, local and state economies are small and open: their enterprises and their residents are price takers with respect to traded goods, including traded factors of production. Capital will locate in a given place only if the after-tax return is at least as high there as anywhere else. Labor will be supplied in a given place and to a given activity only if a worker with given tastes and endowment can do at least as well there as elsewhere, given the wage, other working conditions, taxes, and the prices of both traded and nontraded goods. All of this greatly constrains what local economic policy can accomplish. A consequence of those constraints is summarized in the following proposition:

Proposition 1

If (1) the local economy exhibits the usual diminishing marginal returns to factors (technically, production sets are convex); if (2) existing taxes on mobile factors of production are levied on the benefit principle, if (3) there is no non-frictional unemployment, and if (4) the costs of local economic development policy are locally borne; any policy that subsidizes local business location must reduce economic welfare in the local economy.

Of course, each of the numbered assumptions of Proposition 1 may not hold. It is also possible [and pursued extensively by Bartik (1991)] that economic development policies have desirable distributional effects. In light of the fact that direct redistribution at the state and local level is very difficult, there may be a second-best case for using development policy for distributional ends.[9] My claim, to be pursued for most of the rest of this paper, is that only when distributional considerations are adduced, or one or more of the assumptions made above do not hold, can there be a cost-effective role for local development policy. This claim has strong implications for research on economic development policy. It tells us where to look for productive policy opportunities.

For now, let us assume that the four assumptions do hold, and, in the interest of proving the proposition, examine the behavior of economic development policies in a local economy to which they apply. Consider a local economy that produces output X by means of a production function that uses land (L), labor (N), and capital (K). For our purposes it does not much matter what the particular output of the local economy might be. All that matters is that X is something of value that can be traded, either directly or indirectly, with the rest of the world at a known price. In essence, the local economy is being modeled as a single, profit-maximizing firm (but without any market power) that produces valuable "stuff." Assume that the amount of land available to the local economy is fixed. In the long run, the supply of capital to the local economy is assumed to be perfectly elastic at a national (or world) real interest rate r.[10]

FIGURE 1. The Size of a Local Economy

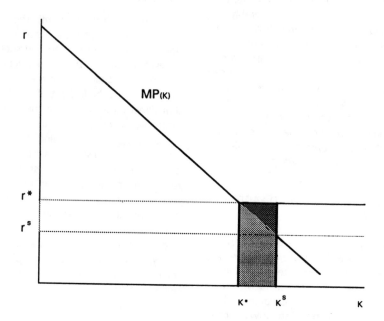

Figure 1 depicts one way to determine the equilibrium size of a local economy in this model. The figure shows an augmented demand and supply of capital to the locality. On the vertical axis is the net real annual return to a dollar's worth of capital—the amount of income, after depreciation, that a dollar's worth of capital will yield when invested in the local economy. The horizontal axis measures the amount of capital invested in the economy. The downward-sloping curve is the marginal product of capital schedule.[11]

In equilibrium, the returns to capital in the rest of the world and the local economy must be equal, at r^*. Thus the amount of capital in the local economy will be K^*. This, given a labor supply function to the locality, will also imply an equilibrium amount of employed labor, N^*. All of these equilibrium values

are determined by market forces. These equilibrium quantities will depend, of course, on tastes, technologies, world prices, and other economic circumstances.

Development Subsidies in the Model

Given a set of economic circumstances, market forces will determine the size of a local economy, as depicted in Figure 1. Basically, there are two broad ways in which government policy might be used to change the equilibrium. One is to try to change the demand schedule—to make capital (and, although not shown, labor) more productive, shifting the demand curve out and increasing equilibrium output. The second way is to subsidize the employment of capital (or labor) in the local economy. In this latter case, which is the subject of this discussion, the marginal product curve stays put, and policy induces a movement along the curve.

There are many ways for governments to subsidize capital. Here, for simplicity, we treat them all as direct reductions in the cost of employing capital in the local economy. Effectively, at least for new capital (quantities above K^*) the supply curve given by r^* is shifted downward to r^s, and the quantity of capital employed is increased, from K^* to K^s. Recognizing that eventually all capital will have once been new, a case can be made that in the long run a subsidy program shifts the supply curve down along all of its length. This is shown in the dotted line.

What are the costs and benefits of a subsidy of this type? The dollar value of the increased annual local output is given by the lightly shaded area under the marginal product of capital curve from K^* to K^s. (Each point on the marginal product curve gives the output attributable to a small increment of capital. Adding up these amounts, increment by increment, yields the area under the curve as the total increase in output.) The annual cost of generating this output is simply the cost of renting the use of the extra capital ($K^s - K^*$) on the national market—a rectangle of length $K^s - K^*$ and height r^*. Plainly, costs exceed benefits, by the area of the darkly shaded triangle.

The preceding establishes Proposition 1 when there are no preexisting taxes. In the well-behaved case of this model, it *never* pays localities to provide capital subsidies. The subsidies may indeed generate increased employment and output, but the benefits of this cannot be worth the cost. Basically, the subsidies are analogous to what might go on if a locality decided to engineer a gold rush on land that had no gold. The local government could go out and buy the gold on the open market, and incur the cost of transporting it and burying it. The gold would then surely be worth digging up, but in the end all that would be available would be the value of the gold. The costs of transport, burying, and digging would be lost forever.

This last analogy suggests some of the motivation for supporting capital subsidies. If the equilibrium demand for capital in a community were somehow larger, property values, employment, and wages would indeed be higher. Thus there is pressure on the local government to somehow create the extra demand. Policies that shift the demand curve out have the potential, as we shall see, to cover their costs, but there may be no such policies available. Proposition 1 tells us that policies that move the community along the demand curve cannot cover their costs, but they mimic the consequences of productive policies by increasing output and employment, and they are easy to implement. Moreover, the output and employment are easy to point to, where the costs of the subsidy may be widely dispersed throughout the local economy. While the public debate over such policies is invariably couched in terms of their effectiveness in increasing output and employment, the point of this discussion is that that is the wrong debate. The policies may well affect economic variables, but their certain costs exceed their maximum potential benefits.

Preexisting Taxes

For simplicity, the preceding analysis assumed no preexisting taxes on capital. More generally, as stated in assumption (2), what is required is that taxes on capital be benefit taxes. This is easily seen with reference to the figure. First, if the government taxes capital simply to raise revenue, it is obvious that the surplus lost by local users of capital exceeds the revenue gain. This is a standard excess burden argument, and is exactly symmetric with the argument against a subsidy.

Suppose instead (ruling out attempts to exploit the mobile factor as a source of revenue) that the government provides some services to capital (sewerage, for example) and that it charges, either *via* fees or *via* the tax system, the cost of providing those services. The services shift the local cost of capital downward, and the charges shift it back up. If the net effect is to reduce the cost of capital to the local economy, capital supplied and local welfare will both increase. But any further subsidy (*e.g.*, reducing the user charge below cost) will be counterproductive in exactly the same way as analyzed earlier. The locality will be using more resources to attract extra capital than the value of the output that the extra capital produces. This implies, and it is hardly news (see, *e.g.*, Oates and Schwab, 1988; Gordon, 1986), that the optimal tax on mobile capital is zero, except for user charges.[12] Thus, for the welfare-maximizing local government, subsidy of capital for purposes of business location is undertaken only at net cost, and is bad public policy.[13] There is no reallocation, given that the subsidy is locally borne, that can make this otherwise. The costs of subsidy simply exceed the benefits.

Of course, if preexisting taxes are greater than benefit taxes, the preceding becomes an argument for tax abatements on new investment. This would allow a jurisdiction to continue to raise revenue on fixed capital that is already in place (at this point, the tax is a tax on pure rent) while charging new capital prices that are commensurate with benefits. Indeed, it may be that increases in mobility over time have served to lower the optimal rate of local taxation on capital, and that this is part of an expla-

nation of the increasing use of tax abatements over time. In the long run, perhaps, the abated taxes are set approximately equal to user charges.

Note that the research question implied by this line of speculation involves measurement of the costs (to municipalities) and benefits (to capital) of providing municipal services. These costs and benefits are surely affected by second-best considerations arising from various government programs and regulations, including welfare programs and minimum wages. Careful measurement of how much winners would win and losers would lose would be useful in setting both the levels of services provided and the prices, *via* taxes or other means, to charge.[14] All of this, however, would be quite independent of, for example, the elasticity of manufacturing branch plant starts with respect to property-tax rates.

WHAT'S WRONG WITH THIS PICTURE?

With respect to both the empirical literature and the political discourse on local economic development policy, the preceding excursion into theoretical welfare economics seems to be almost irrelevant. Why is this so, and what should we make of it?

Explanations for the disjuncture between theory and practice here fall into three types. First, there is the possibility (indeed, the certainty) that some or all of the four assumptions used to support Proposition 1 do not hold. A second set of explanations has to do with distributional considerations, including both traditional concerns with equity and equally traditional political motivations for using government to redistribute in favor of particular interests. A third possibility is that there is something special about jobs that is not captured by either the standard leisure-income trade-off or by concerns with the income distribution, leading to a justification for placing extra value, over and above standard welfare measures, on policies that increase local employment.[15]

Below, I argue that each of these classes of explanation implies a different agenda for policy-relevant research. Each of the agendas implied involves activities quite different from looking for empirical regularities between development policies and the various outcome measures that abound in the literature.

Preexisting Taxes and Cost Exporting

I have already made an argument for tax abatements, as a temporary policy, when preexisting taxes on mobile factors exceed benefit taxes. (The appropriate permanent policy, of course, is to implement benefit taxes in the first place.) It is also easy to make an argument that, from the perspective of the local community, development incentives that fail a general benefit-cost test can pass a local test to the extent that someone outside the locality is bearing the cost. Thus, returning to Figure 1, a capital subsidy that is paid for by the state government, or by some federal program to enhance international competitiveness, has very low local cost; it shifts the cost of capital down, and increases employment and locally generated output without necessitating increased taxes or reduced services, except for the locality's share in the larger unit of government. Just how much of local and state development policy can be attributed to violation of the assumption that the unit of government that calls the tune pays the piper, I do not know.[16] In any case, the fact that the local government does not bear all of the costs of a given development initiative does not mean that it can ignore measurement of the benefits.

Unemployed Labor

When there is unemployed labor (in excess of frictional unemployment) the opportunity cost of labor is less than the wage. Thus, policies that increase employment are less costly (more beneficial) by the difference between the wage and the opportunity cost for the workers who are hired. Given that people are generally unwilling to work for nothing, this difference is generally less than the wage itself.[17]

Whether unemployment, and the resulting difference between the wage and the reservation wage, would warrant the use of local resources to generate increased labor demand will depend, among other things, on the cause of the unemployment. If the unemployment is due to a temporary recession, and could reasonably be expected to disappear with the next upturn in the business cycle, the preferred policy instrument is some sort of countercyclical demand stimulus, not a long-term increase in the area's business activity. Such a policy might be a national policy with intended local or regional impact, or it could be a state-level countercyclical policy.[18] In any case, few proponents of fiscal or other policies to enhance local development would count reductions in cyclical unemployment as important benefits of such policies.

Much more important, from the perspective of state and local development policies, is structural unemployment, which prevents residents of an area from finding work at their reservation wage (presumably some fraction of the wage that they used to be paid) for an indefinite period of time, and which is not due to cyclical problems. Here, using the relentlessly neoclassical approach that I have taken so far in this paper, what is at stake from an efficiency perspective are the transaction and transportation costs associated with workers leaving the area for better opportunities elsewhere.[19] If workers who become structurally unemployed choose to stay in their old location, it must be that the advantages to them of staying outweigh any net income advantages that could be derived from moving. Subsidies paid to employ such workers locally would enhance their well-being, but, at best, would be pure transfers between the payers and the recipients.[20] Because moving uses real resources, however, it is possible that there exists some subsidy to employment at the initial location, smaller in present value than the moving costs, that would enhance overall economic efficiency. If the level of subsidy at which the worker would be just indifferent between leaving and staying exceeds the costs of moving, it would be cheaper for the payers of the subsidy to simply subsidize moving costs. Any payment above moving costs is at best a pure transfer, with both excess burden and appropriation of benefits by immigrants to the area assuring that a good deal of the subsidy would be lost to initial residents of the community.

There may also be important distributional issues associated with structural unemployment. If relatively low-income workers (laid-off industrial workers are the case that comes to mind) are structurally unemployed, increasing the local demand for their services, even at some efficiency cost, may be desirable public policy, depending on the costs of doing so and the other alternatives available. Moreover, to the extent, nontrivial in many urban areas, that inner-city residents are structurally unemployed because of racial discrimination in housing and labor markets, the distributional argument is all the more powerful.[21] But notice that these justifications for development policy depend crucially on who gets the jobs, and that it is highly plausible that direct subsidies to labor demand in the inner city will be more effective than, *e.g.*, branch plant openings at some unspecified location in the state.

The discussion in this section raises the empirical question of whether, and over what time period, increased employment that arises from stimulating local employment demand is derived from the local (potential) labor force, as distinct from immigration to the local area.[22] Blanchard and Katz (1992), in an influential paper, find that regional (state) demand shocks have *no* long-term effect on the employment rate in the region, which implies that all of the benefits of increased employment from such shocks accrue, in the long run, to immigrants to the region. Most of the literature on the effects of local demand shocks, as summarized and added to by Bartik (1992), suggests that there probably are long-term effects, with between 10 and 40 percent of increased employment accounted for by local residents, primarily through increased labor force participation. The debate turns on a number of issues of specification that I will not review here, but it is at least plausible that, for a one-shot, permanent increase in labor demand, there are some lasting effects on local employment for a decade or more, although these are a fairly small fraction of the total change in employment.[23] This is an area where more empirical work would be of considerable value. The question here is not the effect of any particular development strategy, but of the consequences for employment, especially local employment, of a demand shock from any source.

Nonconvexities (Market Failures)

The remaining assumption of Proposition 1 was that marginal factor returns in the local economy are diminishing in the usual way. This would imply, in Figure 1, that the $MP(K)$ curve slopes down. When there is market failure of the usual kinds (public goods, externalities, natural monopolies, information asymmetries), there is the possibility that government policies to correct the market failure could enhance economic efficiency. In terms of Figure 1, such policy would shift the $MP(K)$ curve up. If such a shift increased the value of local output by more than the cost of implementing the policy, the policy would pass a benefit-cost test, and would enhance economic efficiency. (Public infrastructure that is complementary with private production is the standard example here.) Precisely because government is the leading candidate to correct market failures, and because, in such cases, one can see clearly a connection between what the government does and increases in the net value of local output, many commentors on local economic development policy [including myself, and Bartik (1994), in his "memo" to local officials] have argued that what government should do is govern well. It should do an efficient and effective job of providing local public goods, services, and regulations.[24]

Black and Hoyt (1989) consider a related instance of public sector nonconvexities, in which the local government produces public goods with a technology that exhibits increasing returns to scale. In this case, a larger city can produce its public outputs at reduced average cost, leaving some surplus to be divided between existing residents (more public service per tax dollar) and new ones (a subsidy to locate in the jurisdiction). That this is theoretically possible at some city sizes is clear enough; it is unclear how important this may be in light of the fact that there are also ubiquitous congestion externalities in large cities.

There are a number of reasons why the $MP(K)$ curve for a local economy might slope up, over some range. Should this be the case, increases in inputs could increase the value of the economy's (but not an individual firm's) output by more than the cost of the increase in input.

This would create an argument for subsidies.

Suppose, for example, that excess capacity, in the sense of marginal cost being less than average cost, is ubiquitous in local commercial industries, such as grocery stores, laundries, etc. An increase in demand arising from any source, including increased population due to economic growth in the area, would increase profits for these local enterprises. This implies that there is some room to subsidize mobile factors that might be induced to locate in the area. Of course, the profits would induce entry into the relevant commercial operations, and would generally erode in the long run. Both the initial and terminal equilibria in this story would be monopolistically competitive, with zero profit, but during the transition, while the economy was growing, preexisting operations would make profits. And some activities might make profits even in the long run, provided that technology and the size of the market were such that a new entrant would not be profitable. (*E.g.*, in a small town, one drug store has some monopoly profit, while two would lose money.)[25]

Related to the preceding example is the possibility of general agglomeration economies—reductions in the average cost of all economic activity in an area that take place as a result of an increase in activity. These could take the form, fashionable in trade theory lately, of increased and valuable variety in consumer goods and intermediate goods. They could also arise as a result of what urban economists call "localization economies," in which synergies across suppliers and producers in a given industry reduce costs in that industry as the size of operations in the local industry increases.[26] It is based on this idea that so much of practical development policy is aimed at occasioning new innovations in a specific locality. Silicon Valley, and earlier in the century, Detroit, are both examples of areas where there proved to be enormous localization economies in growing industries, economies that generated rents and quasi rents for decades.

Although a given local economy may have unexploited agglomeration economies, and therefore be a candidate for welfare-enhancing development subsidies, it seems very unlikely that most of the local economies (including some very large ones) that engage in development subsidies are in this position. Rarely, if ever, does one see explicit efforts to measure agglomeration economies in prospect, and rarely, if ever, does the local city council adduce such claims in support of its development plans. Moreover, it is perhaps instructive that the urban economics literature on welfare and city size tends to focus on the opposite case, where there are unpriced congestion externalities, generally leading urban areas too big, relative to their optimum, rather than too small.[27]

To the extent that agglomeration economies are localization economies that arise in particular industries, or that scale economies relative to the size of the market allow for long-term profits in specific industries, arguments for subsidy in local economies perfectly mirror the arguments for strategic trade policy at the national level. These arguments also have the same (in my view, generally fatal) weakness. We simply do not know enough about *which specific industries* to subsidize to have any realistic hope of doing more good than harm by engaging in subsidies.[28]

At the national level, a good argument can be made for subsidizing industrial research and development, because many studies show that the return to these activities is very high—perhaps 25 percent.[29] This argument is weaker at the local level, because local economies are so open—not only does the R&D need to be profitable, but it needs to lead to increased *local* economic activity in order to warrant local subsidy. Building a local development strategy around subsidizing the innovation that will spawn the next Silicon Valley is likely to be about as successful as building a strategy around the possibility that there is a lot of gold buried in your backyard. It is possible, but not likely, and not worth it on average. Moreover, if there is a payoff to subsidizing just the "right" activity, the relevant research involves finding the specific seeds of agglomeration that would pay off. This is quite different from finding the average effect of tax rates on branch plant expansions.

Distribution and Rent Seeking

One reason that local governments may engage in development policies is that there is a winning political coalition that benefits, even if the aggregate benefits are negative. Oates and Schwab (1988) work out a case in which workers in a town are willing to tax themselves and other residents (taken to be rentiers and commuters to other localities) in order to attract capital and bid up the wage. Landowners in the town like the strategy even better, because the immigration that will tend to reduce the real wage to approximately its original level will tend to bid up rents. Similarly, it is not too far-fetched to imagine a pro-subsidy coalition of landlords and owners of fixed capital that produces for local markets. By taxing everyone to subsidize increased capital input (and, hence, employment and population), the coalition could increase its rent and profit at the expense of other residents. And, recall that if the costs of subsidy are not locally borne, the expense may be exported altogether.

Something Special about Jobs

Economists view labor as a cost. We infer from the standard model of utility maximization that workers supply labor to the point where the marginal rate of substitution of income for leisure is equal to the wage. An extra hour of leisure, then, is worth the wage, and an extra hour of work requires the wage as compensation. Mayors, undergraduates, presidents, union officials, and (other?) folks in bars *say* that they view labor (or, at least, jobs) as benefits. They count as benefits of public programs (and location-specific capital subsidies) the added employment, sometimes as jobs, sometimes as increased payroll. Rather than simply asserting that we are right and they are wrong, I take a little space here to explore what noneconomists might have in mind, and to suggest that it behooves economists to think hard about these issues.

First, it is worth noting that the transactions and transition costs associated with leaving one's current place of residence in response to structural unemployment may be quite large. Selling one house and buying another uses up perhaps 15 percent of the house value; moving itself may cost thousands of dollars. There are nontrivial capital losses involved in losing a good deal of location-specific knowledge that is of both social and economic value. Children who are attached to their social setting add to these costs. I can easily believe that for many households, willingness to pay for finding reasonable employment near home, rather than having to leave the area, could be worth a year's pay or more. Annualized, that would support a noticeable tax, which would support a noticeable subsidy for attracting industry that would add to employment demand. And, for households that are unusually attached to a given location, the willingness to pay would be higher still.[30,31,32]

(Of course, all of these arguments apply only to areas in which the existing population faces structural unemployment or the risk of same.)

There is also a fair amount of evidence in the psychology literature that having a job is of considerable value to people. People who lose their jobs have increased incidence of mortality and morbidity, and reduced well-being on various psychological measures. They are also at increased risk of violent behavior, both domestically and elsewhere. Some of the studies that support these generalizations were undertaken in countries where the unemployed draw very nearly the same pay as they did when employed, allowing, at least in the short term, isolation of the effects of being paid from employment *per se*. Notice that the increased incidence of crime and of health problems provides a social interest in maintaining employment in a locality. Some of the costs of unemployment will show up as negative local externalities, both technical and pecuniary.

Where the psychology literature seems weakest, however, is in longitudinal studies of individuals, and those studies that do exist tend to show that the long-term effects are fairly small. The strongest finding in the literature is that, just as economists would predict, unemployment is less onerous the greater the income from other sources.[33] I have not been able to find any psychological studies on the effect of continued unemployment in an environment in which there is persistent high unemployment, except in a very old literature on the great depression. O'Brien's (1986) summary of that literature again shows that economic deprivation is the most consistent factor associated with psychological difficulties arising from unemployment.

Having a (good) job is an important element of social status (including the status derived from having a good income). Having a place in the local community, and knowing how to function there, is a valuable asset. Perhaps households view economic development programs as a sort of insurance against loss of the ability to earn a reasonable income in a place where they have valued social attachments. They may also have difficulty separating their ability to earn income in their current location from their ability to earn it at all. Thus, if employment is a valued part of an individual's functioning, the individual may tend to place a higher value than is warranted on having employment here and now, versus having it at an uncertain time and place.[34] It is very hard to diversify one's own time and human capital. We (economists) may know that transactions costs are "all" that is really at stake, but those costs may be high enough (and may be perceived to be very high) so that households will pay a good deal to try to insure against incurring them.

Unfortunately, there may be few effective means for providing such insurance. The problem that local economies are subject to immigration makes things especially difficult. Policies that diversify and expand employment opportunities will generally benefit newcomers as well as those who pay for the policies initially. Related, and equally depressing, is the fact that policies designed to shore up such places as old whaling villages and mill towns must fail if they are based on subsidizing increasingly unproductive activities. There may be a high willingness to pay to insure a way of life in a place of one's choice. Providing effective insurance of this kind, at any price, is something that we simply do not know how to do.

Local employment is easy to measure, is of some value in itself, is highly correlated with local (pretax) income, and very highly correlated with returns to fixed local factors, including housing and immobile capital. (Notice that owners of these fixed factors will generally not care whether new employment is held by local residents or immigrants.) Perhaps that is enough to explain why job creation is such a special object of political and policy attention. It is not enough to allow us to infer how much a local economy should be willing to pay to generate a job of given characteristics.

A RESEARCH AGENDA—MEASURE WELFARE

Governments interested in increasing local economic welfare should, broadly, be doing two things: efficiently providing local public services, broadly construed, and taxing mobile factors according to the benefit principle. Many local public goods may be of value in economic development. Information about local land and labor markets, and about state regulations, has the characteristics of a public good. Specialized training programs may be efficiently run by local units of government, and could provide valuable services to capital and to local labor that is looking for local work.[35] None of the preceding, however, justifies fiscal incentives to industrial location, except insofar as preexisting taxes exceed benefit taxes.

There are many things that economists and policymakers interested in economic development need to know more about. Most of these things, however, are going to be case-specific—average information about behavioral responses to some policy, drawn from a heterogeneous population of local and state economies, simply cannot convey much that is relevant to deciding whether Warthog Falls will be made better off by making an infrastructure investment aimed at attracting light manufacturing. On the other hand, the kind of specific information that Bartik (1994) suggests that the federal government should collect, in his "memo to the president," would be very valuable.

Reading through this paper, I come up with the following list of potentially productive research areas, all helpful to supporting a good benefit-cost analysis (with measure of distributional effects) of state and local economic policy.

- Undertake careful measurements of the benefits to mobile factors, and costs to local government, of providing government services. (Localities should then produce such services to the point where there is no marginal surplus, and charge, by some mechanism, marginal cost.)
- Calculate, case by case, the locally borne cost of development incentives. (This is of local value. Higher levels of government may want to take steps to see that the costs they bear are in line with the benefits that they receive.)
- Where distribution is important, study who gets the jobs and incomes from various interventions. Do not merely count "jobs."
- Look for potential agglomeration economies and ways to exploit them. Be skeptical even when it looks like you have found them. If there seems to be a payoff to subsidizing just the "right" activity, research should delineate just why and where Proposition 1 fails.
- Begin a program of research, jointly between economists and psychologists, to measure just how much (on average) members of a population are willing to pay for the existence of a local job with various sets of characteristics, where the characteristics include the amount of time the job lasts and the probability that it is available to a local resident.
- Work on figuring out how to tell the general public, and politicians, that the mechanisms that "create jobs" are, in

the long run, dependent on the characteristics of labor supply. In the short and medium runs, there is very little that localities can do to efficiently stimulate the demand side except in unusual cases. In other words, try to figure out how to sell the basic welfare economics of this issue.

Much that is in the existing literature, including many studies that attempt to measure the cost of generating a job (often a bit vague as to duration and quality), will also be helpful in undertaking benefit-cost analyses of local policy. But the literature as it stands tells us very little about what the policy ought to be for. If we go back to basics, and require that policy enhance welfare, and point to the mechanism(s) by which private markets are failing to maximize welfare, we may improve the quality of policy, and the focus of policy-relevant research.

ENDNOTES

I am grateful to Tim Bartik, Ned Gramlich, Dick Porter, and Joel Slemrod for valuable discussions and comments on earlier drafts. I am especially grateful to Slemrod for talking me into writing this paper, which I have been meaning to get around to for years.

[1] I do not mean to suggest that market failure necessarily means that goverment intervention is warranted. However, absent market failure or second-best arguments (e.g., making up for other government-created distortions), we can be fairly confident that government intervention will reduce economic efficiency.

[2] Politicians love to claim that they create jobs. Academics try to resist the claim. For example, Bob Woodward (1994, pp. 262–3) reports: "She [Laura Tyson] agreed to supply a representative from the Council of Economics Advisers to the [budget] War Room. Her one hesitation was that she didn't want the Council to be part of a spin organization. . . . For instance, she insisted that the team agree to attribute the job growth of 8 million to the economy, not to Clinton's plan."

[3] Until fairly recently, a good job would have been defined as one job that could produce sufficient income to support the living stan-

dard outlined in the text. By now, it is expected that both adults in a traditional family will provide significant labor supply.

[4] The absolute level of manufacturing employment peaked in 1979. The share of manufacturing in total nonagricultural employment has been declining more or less steadily since the end of World War II.

[5] The preceding long sentence is an extreme abridgment of Appendix 2.2 in Bartik (1991). Appendix 2.2 lists 82 studies, all of which use taxes as explanatory variables. There are dozens of other studies that consider the effects of nontax development policies on a long list of possible outcomes.

[6] I admit that it is pretty unlikely that state employment in the muffler parts industry would fall, but even that is not impossible. Plants in this state could be induced by the tax structure to specialize in operations that have high ratios of inventory to other inputs, causing a national reallocation of labor away from the state even as total activity in the state increased.

[7] They are not entirely absent, of course. For example, Papke (1994) is very clear about what she is measuring, and what she is not, in her study of enterprise zones in Indiana.

[8] In general, these averages will be biased toward zero unless an appropriate correction is made for location-specific fixed effects on the outcome variable. As Bartik points out, studies with fixed effect correction tend to find larger (and better-signed) impacts of fiscal variables, but even these studies, at best, permit accurate estimates of the *average* marginal impact of a given independent variable.

[9] See Gramlich (1985) and Oates (1972) for standard arguments for why redistribution is best undertaken at the national level. Gramlich himself (1987) is not entirely persuaded by these arguments. Feldstein and Vaillant (1994) provide evidence that wages adjust very rapidly to state-level attempts at redistribution, rendering those attempts unsuccessful even in the short run. Redistributive development policies, of course, may be subject to the same difficulties as local tax-transfer schemes, leading the winners to migrate in and the losers to migrate out. There may be political reasons, however, why higher-level governments, especially states, find it easier to redistribute in the guise of development than to do so directly.

[10] I assume labor to be imperfectly mobile, in that there is a distribution of tastes for location-specific attributes, so that an increase in the local wage will induce finite immigration,

and a reduction will induce finite emigration. The same qualitative behavior could be obtained in a standard urban model in which there was perfectly elastic labor supply but a congestion externality in population size. In any case, the condition stated a few paragraphs back must hold—labor must be paid enough so that the utility of workers with similar tastes and endowments is as high in the location under consideration as is available anywhere else in the world.

[11] Technically, the marginal product of capital schedule shown in the figure does not hold all other inputs constant, as in the normal construction of this type. Rather, it is drawn on the assumption that there is fixed stock of land and that labor and capital are combined optimally. If the production function is homogeneous of degree one in all three inputs and generally well behaved, the downward slope is assured. One class of production functions that meet these conditions are those given by $X = g(L)xf(K,N)$, where $F(K,N)$ is concave in each argument. The results sketched in this discussion can be easily proved if $f(K,L)$ is assumed to be homothetic and $g(L)xF(K,N)$ is homogeneous of degree one.

[12] I am intentionally sweeping a good deal under the rug by asserting the equivalence of a user fee and some form of benefit tax. As a practical matter, it is unusual that any direct or indirect tax will exactly coincide with a fee for government services rendered. However, George Break (1994) makes the argument, with which I agree, that for municipal services, which are mostly roads and public safety, given that water and sewer are already covered by user charges, a property tax is not a bad approximation of a user charge. The argument does not apply, of course, to public education, which is also often financed by property taxes.

[13] The same argument can be made for labor, to the extent that labor is mobile. However, capital is the mobile factor of interest in an analysis of most local economic development policies.

[14] A number of papers are focused on measurement of tax competitiveness, by which is meant the extent to which a given jurisdiction's taxes fall on capital or, sometimes, "business." Gentry and Ladd (1994) measure competitiveness as effective tax rates relative to other states, without taking into consideration either economic efficiency *per se* or the benefit side of the state budget. Tannenwald (1994) attempts to measure the net return to capital in Massachusetts relative to other

states, but also does not control for the benefit side.

[15] Indeed, casual conversation between economists and human beings on the subject of jobs generally reveals that often we are not talking about the same thing. It is very difficult, when teaching benefit-cost analysis, to persuade students that labor employed on a project should be treated as a cost, rather than the "job created" treated as a benefit, even when all of the local unemployment is frictional.

[16] The literature on intergovernmental grants abounds with studies in which demand for local activities of various kinds depends on the tax price of those activities. Grants (and, also, Industrial Revenue Bonds, as well as other development incentives), depending on their type, can alter the tax price. I know of no general study of the local tax prices of development incentives. In the case of tax abatements, however, the tax price is generally quite high, because the abated tax would have been deductible by the recipient.

[17] If I understand real business cycle theory, proponents of the theory would argue that the difference is zero, leaving no benefit, at least on this score, from reducing unemployment, although I do not know how real business cycle theorists treat regional cycles in unemployement. Bartik (1991, Ch. 7) estimates the value of foregone leisure at a maximum of 74 percent of increased earnings. His estimate is based on long-run effects, however, not on currently unemployed labor. It is not uncommon (see, *e.g.*, Haveman, 1983) to treat the full increase in income attributable to hiring the unemployed as a benefit of increasing employment. This implicitly assumes that there is no value of leisure for the unemployed—that the reservation wage is zero.

[18] See Gramlich (1987) for an argument in favor of subnational countercyclical policy.

[19] It is in this formulation, of course, that the relentless neoclassical perspective is at greatest variance with the way in which both politicians and people seem to think about employment demand. Later, I consider explicitly the possibility that the transactions costs of moving are quite large, and that there is something about the value of jobs that standard economic analysis simply misses.

[20] The actual case falls well short of a pure transfer. As we shall see shortly, a large fraction of employment subsidies eventually go to new immigrants to a local area, implying that, from the perspective of initial residents, a good deal of the subsidy is wasted, depending on the compass of their altruism.

[21] See Holzer (1989) on spatial mismatch. Bartik (1991) has done the best work on measuring these kinds of distributional effects.

[22] Immigration is plainly of no direct value in reducing unemployment or adding to the stock of jobs available to local residents. Of course, fixed factors have an interest in immigration, which will generally lead to an increase in demand for their services.

[23] The Blanchard–Katz specification requires that in any stable model, total employment eventually returns to the growth path that it was on before the shock. The rapidity of the return, however, still matters for the efficacy of local demand-generating policy.

[24] See Courant (1989), Ross *et al.* (1984), Bartik (1990), and Herzog and Schlottman (1991). Herzog and Schlottman's summary and conclusion to a conference on local development policies was, basically, that the best development policy is good government.

[25] See Eaton and Lipsey (1976).

[26] Krugman (1991) makes much of this. See O'Sullivan (1993) for a standard urban economics treatment.

[27] See, for example, Henderson (1988, Ch. 9). Henderson and other urban economists generally believe that agglomeration economies are important reasons for the existence of cities, but that market forces tend to determine city sizes in a range where diseconomies of congestion are larger, at the margin, than any remaining agglomeration economies.

[28] See Krugman (1993, 1994, Ch. 10). See also Jones (1994).

[29] Schultze (1992, p.303).

[30] Of course, this should show up as a willingness to work at a relatively low wage. However, there may be constraints, of exactly the mysterious kind that prevent labor markets from clearing in recessions, that prevent workers with low reservation wages from actually finding work at those wages. For at least a significant period of time, they can be unemployed at a higher wage as long as some workers who look like them are employed at that higher wage.

[31] Bartik, Butler, and Liu (1992) find that for low-income renters the WTP to stay in the current house, rather than move elsewhere in a city, can be as high as 20 percent of annual income for households with long tenure. Homeowners contemplating leaving a geographic region could be expected to suffer some multiple of that amount. Bolton (1992) provides an extended discussion on how the value of "place" can be looked at in terms of benefit-cost analysis.

[32] An alternative take on the problem is to note that it is often good for people to experience some variety in life, and that many people report that involuntary moves proved to be positive events in their lives. Still, this is hardly the dominant view in discussions of local employment growth.

[33] See O'Brien (1986) for reviews of the literature.

[34] Jobs may constitute capabilities essential to the attainment of important functionings, in the sense discussed by Sen (1992). Sen, however, does not discuss employment *per se*, and I would feel better about this line of argument if he had.

[35] Holzer (1993).

REFERENCES

Bartik, Timothy J. "The Market Failure Approach to Regional Economic Development Policy." *Economic Development Quarterly 4*, (November, 1990): 361–70.

Bartik, Timothy J. *Who Benefits from State and Local Economic Development Policies.* W.E. Upjohn Institute. Kalamazoo, MI, 1991.

Bartik, Timothy J. "Who Benefits from Local Job Growth, Migrants or the Original Residents." *Regional Studies*, 1992.

Bartik, Timothy J. "Jobs, Productivity, and Local Economic Development: What Implications Does Economic Research Have for the Role of Government?" *National Tax Journal 47*, No. 4 (December, 1994): 847–61.

Bartik, Timothy J., J. S. Butler, and Jin-Tan Liu. "Residential Mobility and the Value of a Sense of Place: An Application of Maximum Score Estimation." *Journal of Urban Economics*, (1992).

Black, Dan A. and William H. Hoyt. "Bidding for Firms." *American Economic Review 79*, No. 5 (December, 1989): 1249–56.

Blanchard, Olivier and Lawrence Katz. "Regional Evolutions." *Brookings Papers on Economic Activity 1* (1992): 1–75.

Bolton, Roger. " 'Place Prosperity vs. People Prosperity' Revisited: An Old Issue with a New Angle." *Urban Studies 29* No. 2 (April, 1992): 185–203.

Break, George F. "The Big Four of State-Local Tax Finance: Under Siege in a Changing World." *NTA Forum* (Spring/Summer, 1994): 1–5.

Courant, Paul N. "On the Process of (State and Local) Economic Development and the Substance of Economic Development Policy." Unpublished manuscript. Ann Arbor, MI, 1989.

Eaton, B. C. and R. G. Lipsey. "The Non-Uniqueness of Equilibrium in the Loschian Location Model." *American Economic Review 66* No. 1 (March, 1976): 77–93.

Feldstein, Martin and Marian Vaillant. "Can State Taxes Redistribute Income." *National Bureau of Economic Research* Working Paper No. 4785 (June, 1994).

Gentry, William M. and Helen F. Ladd. "State Tax Structure and Multiple Policy Objectives." *National Tax Journal 47* No. 4 (December, 1994): 747–72.

Gordon, Roger H. "Taxation of Investment and Savings in a World Economy." *American Economic Review 76* (December, 1986): 1086–1102.

Gramlich, Edward M. "Reforming U.S. Federal Fiscal Arrangements," In *American Domestic Priorities: An Economic Appraisal*, edited by John M. Quigley and Daniel L. Rubinfeld. Berkeley, CA: Univ. of California Press, 1985.

Gramlich, Edward M. "Subnational Fiscal Policy." In *Perspectives on Local Public Finance and Public Policy, A Research Annual*, 1987.

Haveman, Robert. "Evaluating Public Expenditure Under Conditions of Unemployment." In *Public Expenditure and Policy Analysis*, 3rd ed., edited by Haveman and Margolis, Ch. 8. Boston: Houghton Mifflin, 1983.

Henderson, J. Vernon. *Urban Development.* Oxford, United Kingdom: Oxford University Press, 1988.

Herzog, Henry W. and Alan M. Schlottmann. *Industry Location and Public Policy.* Knoxville, TN: Univ. of Tennessee Press, 1991.

Holzer, Harry J. "The Spatial Mismatch Hypothesis: What Has the Evidence Shown?" East Lansing, MI: Michigan State University, 1989, unpublished research.

Holzer, Harry J., Richard N. Block, and Marcus Cheatham. "Are Training Subsidies for Firms Effective? The Michigan Experience." *Industrial and Labor Relations Review 46*, No. 1 (July, 1993): 625–36.

Jones, Ronald W. "America's High-Tech Industries: Tyson's Policy Proposals." *Journal of the Economics of Business 1*, No. 1 (1994): 151–7.

Krugman, Paul. *Geography and Trade.* Cambridge, MA: MIT Press, 1991.

Krugman, Paul. "What Do Undergraduates Need to Know About Trade?" *American Economic Review 83*, No. 2 (May, 1993): 23–26.

Krugman, Paul. *Peddling Prosperity.* New York: W.W. Norton, 1994.

Ladd, Helen F. and William Gentry. "State Tax Structure and Multiple Policy Objectives." *National Tax Journal 47* No. 4 (December, 1994): 747–72.

Oates, Wallace A. and Robert Schwab. "Economic Competition Among Jurisdiction: Efficiency Enhancing or Distortion Inducing?" *Journal of Public Economics 35* (1988): 333–54.

Oates, Wallace A. *Fiscal Federalism.* Kent, United Kingdom: Harcourt Brace Jovanovich, 1972.

O'Brien, Gordon E. *Psychology of Work and Unemployment*, Chs. 1, 8, and 9. New York: John Wiley and Sons.

O'Sullivan, Arthur M. *Urban Economics.* Homewood, IL: Irwin, 1993.

Papke, Leslie E. "Tax Policy and Urban Development: Evidence from the Indiana Enterprise Zone Program." *Journal of Public Economics 54* (May, 1994): 37–49.

Ross, Doug, Paul Courant, Peter Eckstein, Sandra Gleason, John Jackson, James Ken- worthy, David Verway, and John Yinger. *The Path to Prosperity: Findings and Recommendations of the Task Force for A Long-Term Economic Strategy for Michigan.* Lansing, MI, 1984.

Schultze, Charles L. *Memos to the President.* Washington, D.C.: Brookings, 1992.

Sen, Amartya. *Inequality Reexamined.* Cambridge, MA: Harvard University Press, 1992.

Tannenwald, Robert. "Massachsetts' Tax Competitiveness." *New England Economic Review* (Jan/Feb 1994): 31–49.

Wassmer, Robert. "The Use and Abuse of Economic Development Incentives in a Metropolitan Area." *Proceedings of the Eighty-Sixth National Conference, National Tax Association.* St. Paul, MN, 1993.

Woodward, Bob. *The Agenda.* New York: Simon & Schuster, 1994.

JOBS, PRODUCTIVITY, AND LOCAL ECONOMIC DEVELOPMENT: WHAT IMPLICATIONS DOES ECONOMIC RESEARCH HAVE FOR THE ROLE OF GOVERNMENT?

TIMOTHY J. BARTIK*

INTRODUCTION

State and local "economic development programs"—programs that assist individual businesses with tax or financial subsidies, or special public services, in order to increase local jobs or improve local businesses' competitiveness—have become prominent and controversial. I receive several phone calls a month from reporters about the latest round in the state subsidy wars—such as Alabama's 1993 subsidies of $250 million for a new Mercedes plant, or South Carolina's 1992 subsidy package of $100 million for a new BMW plant. (Schweke, Rist, and Dabson, 1994, p. 23). The reporters seem most interested in criticisms that this is a waste of government resources. Is economic development, as argued by the Illinois Tax Foundation, "the newest form of pork"? (Ylisela and Conn, 1990).

*W.E. Upjohn Institute for Employment Research, Kalamazoo, MI 49007-4686.

Can economics research say anything useful about whether economic development policies can be effective? My answer is yes. Economics research suggests that traditional economic development policies of "buying growth," using various financial and tax subsidies, have a high cost per job created. Benefits large enough to justify such costs are more likely in economically distressed areas, in which the unemployed are more desperate for jobs and much of the existing public infrastructure is underutilized. Newer economic development policies, which provide services to enhance business productivity, may improve economic efficiency, but need careful evaluation. Such productivity-oriented services may make sense for low unemployment as well as high unemployment areas.

I will consider the implications for economic development policies of three types of economics research. First, there are the implications of economists' philosophy about what justifies government intervention in private business decisions. Second, there has been extensive empirical research on how local economic growth responds to taxes, and how local growth affects local labor markets. Third, there are several recent studies on the effectiveness of specific economic development programs.

WHAT ARE ECONOMIC DEVELOPMENT PROGRAMS TODAY?

Most of the public resources for economic development go to tax subsidies and other financial subsidies to encourage firms to locate or expand in a particular governmental jurisdiction. Examples of such subsidies include: property-tax abatements; low-interest loans; tax exempt bonds to finance business expansion; wage subsidies; free land and infrastructure. Reliable statistics on these subsidies are rare. Data on the magnitude of economic development tax expenditures are only available for three states: Michigan, New York, and Louisiana. In Michigan, annual revenue foregone through property-tax abatements exceeds $150 million, over $16 *per capita* (Citizens Research Council, 1986). In New York State, state and local tax breaks promoting economic development exceed $500 million annually, over $27 *per capita* (Regan, 1988). In Louisiana, industrial business property-tax exemptions cost over $270 million annually, over $60 *per capita*. (Schweke, Rist, and Dabson, 1994).

These tax expenditures vastly exceed government spending for economic development. Surveys indicate that annual city government spending for economic development averages around $3 per capita (National Council for Urban Economic Development, 1991; Poole, Kennedy, and Butler, 1993). Total state economic development agency spending in the United States is around $1.3 billion annually, around $5 *per capita* (National Association of State Development Agencies, 1992). Some government spending

for economic development also is devoted to financial subsidies for business location or expansion.

This emphasis on tax breaks for large new facilities and expansions has a strong political rationale. A ribbon cutting at a new plant or plant expansion attracts attention. Providing a tax break allows a governor or mayor to take credit for good news. Much of the cost of this tax break may be deferred to the future.

State and local efforts to buy growth have intensified over time. For example, Kentucky in 1988 began a 6 percent wage subsidy program for new firms locating in high unemployment counties. Kentucky has since expanded the geographic scope of this program. Kentucky's aggressive wage subsidy has been imitated by Ohio, Oklahoma, Mississippi, and Alabama (Schweke, Rist, and Dabson, 1994, pp. 14, 38).

Although the spotlight is on "smokestack chasing," many state and local governments, since the early 1980s, have devoted resources to a new approach to economic development, which emphasizes providing customized services to help businesses improve their competitiveness. Such "new wave services" include: providing businesses with advice and technical assistance on modernization options; helping businesses figure out how to export; helping businesses with worker training; helping potential entrepreneurs and small businesses develop better business plans and locate financing. Such services are usually focused on small and medium sized businesses, which have the greatest needs for such services. Examples of "new wave" services include the following:

(1) the Edison Technology Center program in Ohio, in which local techni-

cal centers associated with universities provide manufacturers with advice on technology innovation and upgrading;

(2) Pennsylvania's Industrial Resources Center program, in which the state has contracted with quasi-private centers to help manufacturers with a variety of modernization, training, and management issues;

(3) the many community colleges in the United States that are aggressively creating customized training programs to serve business needs, usually with some state subsidy—the community colleges in the Carolinas are the most well-known examples;

(4) the export assistance offices in virtually every state economic development agency and many local economic development agencies—the Port Authority of New York and New Jersey runs a well-known program;

(5) efforts to encourage "industrial networks" in which businesses cooperate to solve their problems—for example, the Northern Economic Initiatives Corporation in northern Michigan helped a group of furniture manufacturers to cooperatively hire a productivity consultant and share shipping costs;

(6) the over 500 Small Business Development Centers around the United States, initially funded by the U.S. Small Business Administration, which provide small businesses with management advice and help in locating financing;

(7) the many entrepreneurial training programs around the country, often targeted at women (the Women's Self-Employment Project in Chicago), welfare recipients (the Self Employment Investment Demonstration sponsored by the Corporation for Enterprise Development), or the unemployed (demonstrations run by the states of Washington and Massachusetts).

These "new wave" economic development services are modestly funded. Although exact figures are scarce, only a small part of the $8 *per capita* in state and local economic development spending goes to such programs. Even if such economic development services were enormously expanded, they would still be minuscule compared to the United States economy. These programs face the problem of scale: how can these programs, with such limited resources, significantly affect the overall United States economy?

MARKET FAILURE AND ECONOMIC DEVELOPMENT PROGRAMS

As Courant discusses in his article in this symposium, economists have a well-developed philosophy about when government should intervene to affect local job growth. Economists presume that government should *not* intervene unless job growth is "mispriced" because of "market failure," the failure of private markets to work efficiently. In a perfectly efficient world, when an additional job is created, the worker in that job is paid wages equal to the value he or she places on their time in their alternative activities if that job had not been created—*e.g.*, child care, looking for another job, attending school or training programs, leisure. In addition, in this imaginary perfectly efficient world, the new job will generate tax revenues exactly equal to the additional roads, public schools, and other public services associated with this job growth. In the real world, job growth may often be "mispriced" in that its benefits and costs are unbalanced—workers may be substantially better off from becoming employed, and state and local governments may receive fiscal benefits or costs from additional job growth.

Additional job growth is more likely to have social benefits in persistently high unemployment, economically declining areas. In high unemployment areas, many unemployed individuals will be desperate for a job, but unable to obtain one. These individuals will receive substantial benefits from obtaining the jobs provided by growth. In low unemployment areas, most individuals who desperately want a job can obtain one without additional job growth. The remaining unemployed will on average be less intense in their desire for a job. The benefit from employing such individuals in the jobs provided by growth will be less.[1]

Areas that have declined in employment and population will also have greater fiscal benefits from job growth. Such areas will have underutilized public infrastructure and services. Adding jobs or preventing further decline may require little additional public spending. In rapidly growing areas, additional job growth will require investments in roads, schools, and other infrastructure. Case studies have indicated that such infrastructure costs often exceed the tax revenues from new job growth. For example, a 1989 study of Montgomery County, Maryland indicated that each new office job produced county revenues per year of $410, whereas the new highways required for that job would cost $347. Altshuler and Gomez-Ibanez comment that "with such a slim margin, little tax revenue was left over to fund other county services that the office building might require (such as sewer, water, solid waste, police protection, or fire protection), let alone those required by the households of employees" (Altshuler and Gomez-Ibanez, 1993, p. 85).

There may also be a "market failure" rationale for government intervention to provide "new wave" economic development services, which target the productivity of small and medium-sized businesses. Private markets in information and training are imperfect. Such imperfections may impede productivity growth. Small businesses and potential entrepreneurs may have inadequate training in starting up and managing a business. Small and medium-sized business may not know enough about their options in technology, worker training, and exporting. Small businesses may also underinvest in worker training because of worker turnover.

There are private markets in information and training—consultants for example. But information is a peculiar commodity because it is difficult to evaluate the quality of information before one has consumed it. Uncertainty about quality may inefficiently restrict demand. In addition, training for managers and workers may sometimes be difficult to finance.

Claiming a "failure" in markets in information and training for small and medium-sized businesses does not justify every government-sponsored service that claims to correct these problems. Maybe some firms that lack information deserve to fail. Propping these firms up with free services would be a mistake. In addition, such programs face the challenge of providing services that firms value. Providing such services to firms is only efficient if the value of the information and training exceeds the costs of these services. Evaluating whether this is the case is important.

The nature of the potential market failure in information and training markets suggests that firms should be required to pay for some of the costs of such services, rather than being given free services. If the service is valuable, the firm should be willing to pay part of the costs. Fees also help stretch limited public dollars further. A given public budget for economic development can then support services to more firms.

GEOGRAPHIC SPILLOVERS OF ECONOMIC DEVELOPMENT PROGRAMS

Another standard "welfare economics" issue for any state or local government policy, including economic development, is what are the spillover effects or "externalities" on other states or local areas. For state and local policies that buy job growth, the success of one area causes negative externalities for other areas. Extra job growth in one local area will *in part* (not necessarily totally) come at the expense of reduced job growth in other local areas.[2] This tradeoff is obvious when two states are competing for a Mercedes plant. But even when a state or local area attracts small business growth, that additional growth will usually reduce the sales of businesses located elsewhere, hurting their job growth.

These negative externalities reduce the national economic benefits of local competition for jobs. But even if national employment is unaffected, there may still be some net national benefits—or costs—of local competition for jobs. Net national benefits are more likely if the local areas that most aggressively "buy growth" are high unemployment areas. Even though greater job growth in high unemployment areas comes at the expense of low unemployment areas, this redistribution of jobs will yield net employment and fiscal benefits. The extra jobs in high unemployment areas will go to individuals who desperately need jobs, whereas the reduced jobs in low unemployment areas will be taken away from individuals who could easily obtain a job anyway. Reallocating growth from booming areas to declining areas allows greater use of existing infrastructure, and less spending on new infrastructure.

In contrast, if low unemployment, booming areas are the most aggressive in "buying growth," job competition will have net national costs. Redistributing jobs from declining to booming areas will take jobs away from individuals who desperately need jobs, and provide jobs for individuals who could have obtained jobs anyway. This redistribution will also require more infrastructure spending.

Because the benefits of extra growth are lower for already booming areas, one could argue that high growth areas will not aggressively pursue growth. But political and economic elites may have strong private reasons for preferring pro-growth policies. Greater job growth will increase land prices and the prices charged by firms serving local markets (Bartik, 1991a).[3] Local banks, newspapers, and real estate developers will benefit from growth and have political clout (Logan and Molotch, 1987).

Economic development policies that enhance business productivity may also increase the efficiency of the national economy. Consumers throughout the nation benefit if businesses in one area can provide better-quality products at a lower price.

One might mistakenly think that improving local business productivity lacks national benefits because a more productive local economy will attract business activity from other local areas. But reallocating resources toward more productive uses increases national economic efficiency. Business competition also can appear to lack national benefits, because some businesses lose. For example, if Gateway Computers develops a cheaper way to make higher quality computers, it will take sales away from Compaq, but there would be net benefits even if total computer sales are unchanged. Reallocating resources toward better, cheaper computers enhances economic efficiency. Similarly, if Pittsburgh economic development agencies do a better job than Milwaukee agencies in improving the productivity of local small businesses, and as a result economic activity shifts from Milwaukee to Pittsburgh, this increases national economic efficiency.

JOBS TO PEOPLE VERSUS PEOPLE TO JOBS

I have argued that one rationale for local economic development policies in high unemployment areas is that such policies bring jobs to the persons who most need them. An alternative to bringing jobs to people is bringing people to jobs. Is promoting economic development in high unemployment areas preferable to encouraging unemployed workers to move to low unemployment areas?

It makes sense to give unemployed workers better information on job opportunities in other cities and states. But if workers have or are given good information, it is unclear that subsidizing them to move makes sense. Workers suffer large psychological costs from moving out of their home labor market, with its familiar people and places (Bartik, 1991a, pp. 64–66). If workers know the alternatives but reject moving, a policy of subsidizing workers to move seems unduly paternalistic.

Subsidizing firms to provide jobs in high unemployment areas also distorts a particular type of location decision, those of businesses rather than workers. But in this case we are subsidizing firms in order to have them recognize the effects of their job creation on another group, unemployed workers. This is different from subsidizing someone to change their behavior for their own good.[4]

RESEARCH ON STATE AND LOCAL FISCAL POLICY AND ECONOMIC GROWTH

Although there is little research on the effects of state and local tax incentives and other *special* financial incentives for economic development, there has been extensive research on how *general* state and local taxes and public services affect local economies. This research suggests that economic development incentives may be costly per net new job created.

Most of this research has focused on how differences in taxes and public services across states or metropolitan areas affect the growth of states or metropolitan areas. My 1991 book, *Who Benefits from State and Local Economic Development Policies?*, summarizes 48 studies of taxes and growth in different metropolitan areas and states (Bartik, 1991a). Based on these 48 studies, if a state or metropolitan area reduces state and local business taxes by 10 percent, without changing its public services, and without other states or metropolitan areas changing their fiscal policies, then business activity in that state or metropolitan area on average seems to increase in the long run by around 3 percent. (In other words, the long-run elasticity of state or metropolitan area economic activity, with respect to state and local business taxes, is on average estimated to be around −0.3.) Because studies differ, there is some uncertainty about this estimated effect of taxes. I argue in my book that the "true" average effect of a 10 percent reduction in state and local taxes is likely to be somewhere in between a 1 percent increase in business activity and a 6 percent increase in business activity (*i.e.*, the long-run elasticity is between −0.1 and −0.6).[5]

State and local spending on public services has a positive effect on local economies. This positive effect is large enough that some studies have found that a balanced budget increase in taxes, and spending on education or roads, will boost a state's economy (Bartik, 1989; Helms, 1985; Munnell, 1990). For business tax cuts to boost a state economy, they must be financed by increases in personal taxes or reductions in spending that does not provide services valued by business.

There has also been some research on how differences in property-tax rates within a metropolitan area affect the growth of suburban communities. Based on this research, a 10 percent reduction in an individual community's local business property taxes—for example, a reduction from 2.0 percent of property value to 1.8 percent—will, assuming other communities leave their property-tax rates unchanged, increase business activity in the community by around 20 percent. (In other words, the elasticity of a local community's business activity with respect to property taxes is around -2.0.) (Bartik, 1991a, b) How can the large effects of taxes on one community be reconciled with the modest effects of taxes on a metropolitan area? The most plausible reconciliation is that most of the increase in one community's business activity due to lower property taxes comes at the expense of other communities in the metropolitan area.

What implications does this research on the effects of *general* state and local taxes have for programs that target *special* incentives on a few firms and companies? The implications depend on whether development agencies can target incentives on firms that are the most responsive to local costs. My own view is that such targeting is usually a failure. Economic development agencies cannot read the minds of firms to tell whether a subsidy is really needed. The political pressure to extend incentives to all firms that qualify is great. [This has been

termed the "reverse potato chip rule: when it comes to tax breaks, it is hard to give away just one." (Glastris, 1989, cited in Schweke, Rist, and Dabson, 1994)]. Finally, there is no evidence from research that new branch plants, the most common targets of state and local incentives, are any more responsive in the long run to state and local taxes than are existing, smaller firms.

Hence, it seems plausible that the cost per job created from incentive programs is quite similar to the cost per job created from reducing overall state and local business taxes. Based on the average estimated effect reported above—an elasticity of around -0.3 for studies of metropolitan areas or states—general tax reductions or special tax incentives will have an *annual* cost to state and local governments per job created of $4,000. This calculation takes into account the extra tax revenue gained from firms for whom the tax reduction or subsidy did affect the location decision, as well as the cost of giving tax reductions or subsidies to firms that would have located or expanded in the area anyway.[6] The $4,000 annual cost is conservative in that it ignores the extra public service costs caused by new jobs.

It is important to understand the meaning of this estimated $4,000 annual cost per job created. First, this is an ongoing cost. Each year the job is in existence, the state or local government will have to pay a subsidy or give up tax revenue of $4,000. The present discounted value of the cost per job created would be much greater than $4,000. Second, although the average job created pays more than $4,000 annually, this need not imply that the benefits of job creation exceed the costs. Unemployed workers place value on their time, so being hired for a job will have benefits less than the wages paid. In addition, a portion of the jobs created by economic development subsidies will go to in-migrants, reducing the benefits to the original residents who pay for development subsidies. The benefits of local job creation are discussed later in this article.

There is uncertainty in this cost estimate. Some studies show greater tax effects on location decisions, whereas other studies show no effects whatsoever. As Courant points out in his article in this symposium, the costs per job created may vary from one local economy to another. We could provide better policy advice if we had more precise estimates of the effects of specific tax incentives in different local economies.

But despite the uncertainty, most evidence is consistent with the belief that economic development subsidies, in most state or metropolitan areas, are likely to have significant costs per job created in a metropolitan area. Contrary to some claims, tax and financial incentives are *not* a free lunch for a state or metropolitan area. These programs do not create enough jobs and new tax revenue that the programs have little or no net cost. Some states or metropolitan areas may perceive sufficient benefits from new jobs that a $4,000 annual cost of creating a new job could seem reasonable. But this cost is high enough that a state or metropolitan area should think carefully about whether aggressively using tax subsidies to attract new business activity will have net benefits.

Another implication of this research is that small communities within metropolitan areas may be tempted to engage in incentive wars, with little net benefit to the metropolitan area. If a 10 percent reduction in a community's business property tax rates increases local business activity by 20 percent, then a community can raise revenue by lowering business property taxes—if no other community in the metropolitan area re-sponds by lowering its property taxes. In the real world, other communities in the metropolitan area will respond. Communities will lose more tax revenue and gain fewer jobs then they initially expected.

RESEARCH ON EFFECTS OF JOB GROWTH ON LOCAL LABOR MARKETS

There is much evidence that stronger local job growth has significant long-run labor market benefits for local residents. A 10 percent increase in jobs in a metropolitan area in the long run increases local employment rates by 2 percent. To put it another way, in the long run, around one in five of the new jobs created go to the original local residents, and the other four go to in-migrants. A 10 percent increase in metropolitan employment also increases long-run real wages in the metropolitan area by around 2 percent. This increase in real wages occurs because individuals in a growing local economy are able to get and keep jobs in higher-paying occupations. (See Bartik, 1991a for a review and estimates, and Bartik, 1993c for more recent evidence.)

Local residents are able to sustain these real income gains in the long run even though local job growth leads to significant in-migration. In the short run, with limited in-migration, local residents are able because of growth to obtain jobs they otherwise would not have obtained. These jobs provide job skills. Because of these job skills, local residents are permanently better off because of a one-time surge in local job growth.

The percentage increase in income from local job growth is greater for disadvantaged groups. High school dropouts gain more than college graduates, African-Americans gain more than whites, and the lowest-income quintile families gain more than the average family (Bartik, 1991a, 1993a, 1994).

A worker's labor market fortunes are more affected by the job growth of his or her metropolitan area than the job growth of the particular city or county in which the worker resides (Bartik, 1993b). Metropolitan areas are the best definition of a "labor market," within which job-related opportunities tend to equalize for similar individuals.

The benefits of metropolitan job growth are significantly greater for jobs with a high wage premium, that is jobs that pay well relative to the skills required (Bartik, 1993b, 1994).[7] A shift in a metropolitan area's industry mix toward higher-wage-premium industries not only increases wages, but also increases labor force participation.

RESEARCH ON ECONOMIC DEVELOPMENT PROGRAMS TO IMPROVE PRODUCTIVITY

There have been few evaluations of economic development programs that seek to improve business productivity. Those evaluations that have been done, however, suggest that such programs can be effective.

Several studies suggest that *industrial extension services* and *small business development centers*, which provide businesses with information and training about modernization, exporting, worker training, or management, can be helpful. A survey of business clients of Ohio's Edison Technology Center Program found that one-third of the businesses believed that assistance from the Edison program had helped them to increase sales, profits, market share, or employment (Mt. Auburn Associates, 1992). A survey of business clients of Pennsylvania's Industrial Resource Center program found that 20 percent of the businesses reported increased revenue because of the program, and almost half reported cost reductions due to the pro-

gram (KPMG Peat Marwick, 1993). A survey of clients of Oregon's Small Business Development Center program found that one-fourth believed that the program had greatly increased their profits (Public Policy Associates, 1992).

A word on evaluation methodology. Economists are suspicious that survey respondents may lie about their evaluations. But several features of these surveys and programs suggest that these evaluations are reliable. There is no requirement that businesses must claim services were essential in order to get the service. Furthermore, if the service was useless, what is the incentive for businesses to claim it was useful? These surveys allowed respondents to be anonymous. Finally, both the Ohio and Oregon evaluations supplemented surveys with business focus groups, which confirmed the survey results.

Surveys of clients of business assistance programs can be helpful with program design if different programs are evaluated using the same survey. Survey results from different programs can be compared to see which approach is most effective.

Comparisons of surveys suggest that business information programs are more effective when programs are *locally run*, with extensive *business involvement*. For example, the most effective Edison Centers are those with extensive business influence over program design, whereas those Centers dominated by university administrators get lower ratings from their business clients. In Oregon, the 19 locally run Small Business Development Centers were more highly rated by business clients than Oregon's other small business service programs, which delivered services through a single state office.

A recent study suggests that *entrepreneurial training* programs can significantly increase the rate at which potential entrepreneurs start up new businesses. The U.S. Labor Department has sponsored experiments in the states of Washington and Massachusetts in entrepreneurial training for unemployment insurance recipients. In these experiments, UI recipients interested in entrepreneurship were randomly assigned to treatment and control groups. The treatment groups received training and assistance in developing a business plan, and a lump-sum payment of their remaining UI benefits if they achieved business planning goals. In Massachusetts, 47 percent of the treatment group entered self-employment, compared to 29 percent of the controls, whereas in Washington State, 52 percent of the treatment group entered self-employment, compared to 27 percent of the controls (Benus, Wood, and Grover, 1994).

Another study indicates that *customized job training* assistance can improve business productivity (Holzer *et al.*, 1993). Holzer *et al.* evaluated Michigan's industrial training grant program for manufacturing firms undergoing modernization. The evaluation compared firms that received training grants with firms that applied for grants too late in the fiscal year. The state program awarded grants on a "first come–first serve" basis to all firms that met eligibility criteria. Holzer *et al.* found that firms that received grants did more job training afterwards than nongrantees, and their product scrappage rates declined more. Product scrappage rates declined enough that the training seemed cost-effective. A key issue is why firms did not pursue such training on their own.

Holzer's study could be criticized on the grounds that firms that applied too late for grants may also be less capable in other ways. This criticism is not supported by the data, which suggest that assisted and unassisted firms were quite similar.

CONCLUSION: ADVICE TO POLICYMAKERS

To summarize the implications of research for economic development policy, I will conclude with two memos: one to a governor or mayor, the other to the President.

To: Governor or Mayor of Jurisdiction X. Re: three things you can do to improve your jurisdiction's economic development policies.

(1) *Target tax/financial subsidies for economic development more carefully.* Because tax and financial subsidies for economic development are expensive per job created, they should be used more thoughtfully then they are at present. Such expensive subsidies make more sense for high unemployment areas. Because the unemployed are more desperate for jobs in high unemployment areas, even expensive subsidies may have benefits exceeding costs. In low unemployment areas, many persons obtaining jobs because of an economic development program could have obtained jobs anyway. Adding jobs in a boom area will also require expensive new infrastructure. The high costs of subsidizing new jobs may not be worth it in low unemployment, fast growing areas. Tax and financial subsidies for new jobs make more sense if the jobs pay a high *wage premium*, that is, they pay well relative to the skills required. High-wage-premium jobs will provide more desirable jobs for local residents. In addition, higher-wage jobs will have greater multiplier effects on the local economy, as the higher wages lead to a greater boost to local consumer demand.[8]

Tax and financial subsidies should have rules to guide when subsidies are to be given and their amount. For example, the rules might increase the subsidy for a higher-wage plant that employs more local residents. Without rules, political pressures may lead to excessive subsidies for large projects.

(2) *Economic development policies should place more emphasis on improving business productivity.* Because research suggests that economic development services to improve business productivity can be effective, state and local governments should place more emphasis on this area. More effort should be devoted to programs to train entrepreneurs, provide advice to small and medium-sized businesses, and help small and medium-sized businesses with worker training. Such programs may be more cost-effective than tax subsidies to large companies, even if they do not allow for high-publicity ribbon cuttings.

These productivity-related services to business should be regularly evaluated, by surveys of business clients and comparisons of assisted and unassisted firms, to monitor their effectiveness and suggest program improvements. Program managers should focus these programs on filling gaps where private markets have problems providing information for improving productivity. Where possible, fees should be charged business clients to partially cover the cost of these services: this stretches limited public dollars and shows whether these services are valued.

(3) *Metropolitan cooperation in economic development programs is essential.* Competition for jobs among jurisdictions within the same metro-

politan area uses public resources without changing overall labor market opportunities in the metropolitan area. A metropolitan area is one labor market. If the goal of economic development policy is to improve labor market opportunities, economic development should be coordinated within a labor market area.

To: President Clinton.
Re: two things you can do to improve the effectiveness of government economic development efforts.

(1) *Use limited federal resources to expand and standardize evaluations of economic development programs.* Because of the budget deficit, the federal government is unlikely to devote sufficient resources to economic development services to make a significant different in the overall United States economy. Furthermore, there is some evidence that locally controlled economic development services are more effective. With limited federal dollars, it would be more effective to encourage improvements in the quality of local economic development programs, particularly economic development programs that improve productivity. Local governments lack sufficient incentive to support evaluations. The benefits of high-quality evaluation accrue to governments around the nation, not just the government conducting the evaluation. Federal funding should support evaluations of state and local economic development programs, and support disseminating the results of such evaluations.

Evaluations would be more useful if they were done similarly for different states and cities, so that the effectiveness of different programs could be compared. Standardization of out national leadership and funding. One first step would be to develop a standard survey form for business clients of economic development programs.

(2) *The national interest would be served by discouraging state and local governments in areas with low unemployment rates and booming economies from providing large financial and tax subsidies for economic development.* Political pressures lead to large tax subsidies and financial subsidies for large companies making location decisions. In low unemployment areas, the local employment benefits from these subsidies are more than offset by the losses to high unemployment areas that do not succeed in attracting the large company.

It is undesirable to eliminate all economic development programs, because some of these programs help promote business productivity. It also is undesirable to prevent high unemployment areas like Detroit from competing for new business. What we should try to do is discourage low unemployment, prosperous areas from offering excessive financial subsidies to new business.

It is infeasible to eliminate all financial subsidies for economic development, given the many thousands of jurisdictions and companies involved in such subsidy programs and the enormous political pressures encouraging such subsidies. What may be desirable and feasible is to *limit*—not eliminate—the *types* of subsidies provided to a few large companies. For new plant location decisions or expansion decisions that exceed some number of workers or dollar amount of investment, federal community development block grant assistance or industrial development bond authority could be reduced if an area provides "unproductive" subsidies to affect that location or expansion decision. The penalty for providing such subsidies would be greater for low unemployment areas. "Unproductive" subsidies would be defined as discretionary subsidies provided to one firm that would not have any permanent effect on the local economy if the firm leaves. Under this definition, a tax abatement or free land for a company would be an "unproductive" subsidy. On the other hand, building a new access road or training a firm's workers would not be considered an unproductive subsidy, because some benefit from this spending would still continue if the firm left the area. A proposal similar to this was reportedly included in an early draft of Vice President Gore's Reinventing Government Task Force on the Commerce Department.

Such a proposal might be welcomed by many governors and mayors. This limited federal intervention would enable more states and cities to resist the political pressures of trying to claim credit, by using large subsidies, for large companies' location or expansion decisions. The limitation of such subsidies would free up some state and local resources for more productive approaches to economic development, whether through productivity-oriented economic development programs, general improvements in public services, or general tax reductions. Finally, this approach would still give considerable latitude to high unemployment areas to help create new jobs for local residents.

AFTERWORD: COMMENTS ON COURANT'S PERSPECTIVE

Although this might not be apparent to some readers, Paul Courant and I are in general agreement in our perspective on local economic development policy. Both of us emphasize that policymakers and researchers should spend more time thinking about and measuring the *ultimate benefits* of local economic development policy. Policymakers and researchers need to focus on the benefits of such programs for the unemployed, different groups of workers, the local fiscal situation, and the productivity of the local economy. Job creation in and of itself should not be seen as the ultimate goal of economic development programs.

Where Courant and I differ is my greater emphasis on the value of research on the costs and effectiveness of economic development programs in creating jobs and enhancing productivity. Although there is uncertainty in current research, I would argue that we do know some useful things: tax incentives for economic development are not self-financing, but have significant costs per job created; some programs that promote productivity appear to be effective. We need to continue this line of research. Even as we learn more about the labor market and fiscal effects of job growth, we will need to have more precise information about how different economic development programs in different cities affect job growth. Furthermore, we need much more research on the "new wave" economic development programs, which seek to promote business productivity. Can such programs play a significant role in increasing the competitiveness of American industries? How can such programs be best designed? The answers to such questions may be important to the long-term performance of the United States economy.

ENDNOTES

I appreciate the helpful comments of Joel Slemrod, Randy Eberts, Paul Courant, and George Erickcek on earlier versions of this paper. Claire Vogelsong and Ellen Maloney provided their usual superb secretarial assistance.

1 Using economic jargon, in high unemployment areas the gap between wages actually paid and the "reservation wage" of the unemployed will be greater. The "reservation wage" of an individual is the lowest wage for which that individual would be willing to work.

2 Whether national job growth on net goes up or down is a complicated issue. If local governments compete by subsidizing labor demand, and national labor supply is not completely inelastic, a partial equilibrium analysis would lead us to expect some increase in equilibrium national employment. Whether a general equilibrium analysis would also make such a prediction depends on the macroeconomic model used. Furthermore, as Courant points out, most local development subsidies are nominally subsidies to capital. But because the subsidies are conditioned on the number and quality of jobs provided, they also have some of the character of a labor demand subsidy.

3 From an economic efficiency perspective, these increases in local land prices and other local prices are a transfer of resources between different groups, and do not represent a net gain for society.

4 Formally, suppose unemployed workers in city X have benefit W from getting a job and moving costs M from moving to get one. We reduce a typical firm's profit by D by inducing them to create one more job in city X. If workers have full information, M must exceed W, and no subsidy can be efficient. But it is possible that W can exceed D, and a subsidy for firm job creation may be efficient. Some economists will argue that workers and firms on their own should be able to make such a deal to create jobs. In an imperfect world, however, government may sometimes be the best available mechanism to reach such deals.

5 These elasticity estimates combine studies that look at business taxes with studies that look at overall taxes. Elasticity estimates do not seem to depend on the tax measure. It is reasonable to assume that the effects estimated for overall taxes are attributable to the business taxes included in that overall tax measure.

These elasticity estimates also combine results from studies that use different measures of business activity, for example total local employment, gross state product, and plant starts. These differences in dependent variable do not lead to systematic differences in estimated tax effects, so I refer in the text simply to effects on local business activity.

6 The calculation is as follows. The tax elasticity

of private employment with respect to state and local business taxes (E) is defined as $(dJ/J)/(dT/T)$, where J is the number of jobs, dJ is the change in the number of jobs, T is the tax rate, and dT is the change in the business tax rate. The percentage change in revenue from a tax cut, dR/R, will approximately equal $dT/T + dJ/J$. Substituting and rearranging, one obtains $dR/dJ = (R/J)[1 + (1/E)]$. R/J is state and local business tax revenue per job, which is about $1,620 per job in the United States With a value of -0.3 for E, one obtains $dR/dJ = -\$3,780$.

The figure of $1,620 for state and local business taxes per private employee comes from three sources. Total state and local tax revenue in fiscal year 1989 was $469 billion (U.S. Bureau of the Census, 1988–89). The most recent estimate of the business share of state and local taxes is 31 percent. (U.S. ACIR, 1981). Private nonagricultural employment in the United States averaged 89 million during fiscal year 1989 (U.S. Bureau of Economic Analysis, 1991).

[7] These "wage premia" are often referred to by economists as "efficiency wage premia." Wage premia are estimated by relating wages to a worker's education, experience, and other characteristics, and dummy variables for industry. These industry wage differentials are large and persistent over time (Krueger and Summers, 1988; Katz and Summers, 1989).

[8] *National* targeting of high-wage industries, or any particular industry type, is controversial among economists [see, for example, the debate over the paper by Katz and Summers (1989)]. Local development policy that targets industry is somewhat different, for three reasons. (1) We already are targeting at the local level, and the question is whether to do so randomly or by some rational formula. (2) There are clearly greater benefits for local residents from higher-wage-premia jobs, in wages, employment rates, and multiplier effects. The national benefits of such targeting are more unclear. (3) The diversity of different local jurisdictions limits the damage from mistaken targeting.

REFERENCES

Altshuler, Alan A. and Jose A. Gomez-Iba-nez. *Regulation for Revenue: The Political Economy of Land Use Exactions.* Washington, D.C.: The Brookings Institution, 1993.

Bartik, Timothy J. "The Effects of Metropolitan Job Growth on the Size Distribution of Family Income." *Journal of Regional Science* (November 1994), forthcoming.

Bartik, Timothy J. "The Effects of Local Labor Demand on Individual Labor Market Outcomes for Different Demographic Groups and the Poor." *W. E. Upjohn Institute for Employment Research Working Paper 93–23.* Kalamazoo, Michigan: W.E. Upjohn Institute for Employment Research, 1993a.

Bartik, Timothy J. "Economic Development and Black Economic Success." *Upjohn Institute Technical Report No. 93–001.* Kalamazoo, Michigan: W. E. Upjohn Institute for Employment Research, 1993b.

Bartik, Timothy J. "Who Benefits From Local Job Growth, Migrants or the Original Residents?" *Regional Studies 27,* No. 4 (September, 1993c): 297–311.

Bartik, Timothy J. "The Effects of State and Local Taxes on Economic Development: A Review of Recent Research." *Economic Development Quarterly 6,* No. 1 (February, 1992): 102–10.

Bartik, Timothy J. *Who Benefits from State and Local Economic Development Policies?* Kalamazoo, Michigan: W. E. Upjohn Institute for Employment Research, 1991a.

Bartik, Timothy J. "The Effects of Property Taxes and Other Local Public Policies on the Intrametropolitan Pattern of Business Location." In *Industry Location and Public Policy,* edited by Henry W. Herzog, Jr. and Alan M. Schlottmann, 57–80. Knoxville, TN: The University of Tennessee Press, 1991b.

Bartik, Timothy J. "Small Business Start-Ups in the United States: Estimates of the Effects of Characteristics of States." *Southern Economic Journal* (April, 1989): 1004–18.

Benus, Jacob M., Michelle Wood, and Neelima Grover. *A Comparative Analysis of the Washington and Massachusetts UI Self-Employment Demonstrations.* Report prepared for U.S. Department of Labor, ETA/UIS by Abt Associates, Inc. Bethesda, MD, January, 1994.

Citizens Research Council of Michigan. "Municipal Government Economic Development Incentive Programs in Michigan." *Citizens Research Council of Michigan Report No. 280.* Detroit, MI, February, 1986.

Glastris, Paul. "Holdup in the Windy City." *U.S. News and World Report* (July 17, 1989): 41.

Helms, Jay L. "The Effect of State and Local Taxes on Economic Growth: A Time Series Cross Section Approach." *The Review of Economics and Statistics* (February, 1985): 574–82.

Holzer, Harry J., Richard N. Block, Marcus Cheatham, and Jack H. Knott. "Are Training Subsidies for Firms Effective? The Michigan Experience." *Industrial and Labor Relations Review 46* No. 4 (July, 1993): 625–36.

Katz, Lawrence and Lawrence Summers. "Industry Rents: Evidence and Implications." *Brookings Papers on Economic Activity* (Microeconomics issue, 1989): 209–90.

KPMG Peat Marwick. *Customer Satisfaction Survey of the Pennsylvania Industrial Resource Centers.* Harrisburg, PA: Pennsylvania Department of Commerce, 1993.

Krueger, Alan and Lawrence Summers. "Efficiency Wages and the Inter-Industry Wage Structure." *Econometrica 56*, (March, 1988): 259–64.

Logan, John and Harvey Molotch. *Urban Fortunes: The Political Economy of Place.* Berkeley, CA: University of California Press, 1987.

Mt. Auburn Associates. "An Evaluation of Ohio's Thomas Edison Technology Centers." Final report submitted to the Ohio Department of Development. Somerville, MA, December, 1992.

Munnell, Alicia H. "How Does Public Infrastructure Affect Regional Economic Performance?" *New England Economic Review* (September/October, 1990): 11–33.

National Association of State Development Agencies. *NASDA 1992 State Economic Development Expenditure Survey.* Washington, D.C.: National Association of State Development Agencies, 1992.

National Council for Urban Economic Development. *Trends in Economic Development Organizations: A Survey of Selected Metropolitan Areas.* Washington, D.C.: National Council for Urban Economic Development, 1991.

Poole, Kenneth E., Tanya Kennedy, and Elizabeth Butler. *Survey of Public Economic Development Agencies: Summary of Results.* Washington, D.C.: National Council for Urban Economic Development, 1993.

Public Policy Associates and Brandon Roberts & Associates. 1992. *Oregon Small Business Services Evaluation.* Lansing, MI. Final Report.

Regan, Edward V. *Government, Inc.: Creating Accountability for Economic Development Programs.* Chicago: Government Finance Officers Association, 1988.

Schweke, William, Carl Rist, and Brian Dabson. *Bidding for Business: Are Cities and States Selling Themselves Short?* Washington, D.C.: Corporation for Enterprise Development, 1994.

U.S. Advisory Commission on Intergovernmental Relations. *Regional Growth: Interstate Tax Competition.* Report A-76 (March), revised version of Table A-1, Figures for 1977. Washington, D.C. 1981.

U.S. Bureau of the Census. *Government Finances: 1988–89.* Washington, D.C.: U.S. Government Printing Office, 21.

U.S. Department of Commerce, Bureau of Economic Analysis. *Survey of Current Business,* (January, 1991): S-10.

Ylisela, James, Jr. and Sandra Conn. *Helping Small Business: DCCA's Promise and Failure.* Springfield, IL: Illinois Tax Foundation, 1990.

CHAPTER 4

PUBLIC FINANCE IN THEORY AND PRACTICE
ALAN J. AUERBACH*

INTRODUCTION

Economists are accustomed to being asked
questions they cannot answer. Policy analysts are accustomed to answering them.
Academic research, with its often inconclusive findings, is not always well-suited to
the needs of the policy process, which requires answers. As a result, the information
and advice that policymakers receive often
ignores valuable lessons that academic research, and indeed very basic economic
reasoning, can provide.

The challenge to academic economists is to
provide information that can be used by
policymakers, without altering the message
itself. Part of this process involves educating the "consumers" about the nature of
economic research, to help them accept
the fact that in some instances their question may have no clear answer or may in
fact be the wrong question. Despite the
limits to what economic theory and empirical evidence can tell us, there are often
valuable lessons to be learned from the application of simple economic principles.

In this paper, I will try to illustrate the challenges facing economists involved in the
tax policy process and some of the lessons
we can offer using two issues of central
concern, the measurement of the revenue

*University of Pennsylvania, Philadelphia, PA 19104–6297.

and distributional effects of proposed tax
changes. Each of these subjects is dealt
with in considerably more detail in two recent publications of the Joint Committee
on Taxation (1992, 1993).

REVENUE ANALYSIS

Revenue estimation *per se* is rarely covered
as a separate subject in the academic public finance curriculum, and it has been the
focus of relatively little academic research.
Yet, a growing share of the staff time of
economists at the Joint Committee on Taxation (JCT) and the Treasury's Office of Tax
Analysis (OTA) is spent in the production
of revenue estimates for specific legislative
proposals. A typical revenue estimate presents an agency's prediction of "the"
change in tax revenue (or expenditures)
that will result over a period of time, typically five fiscal years, if a particular proposal is adopted.

The importance of revenue analysis in the
policy process has grown over the years
with the institution of specific budget control measures that impose restrictions on
taxes and expenditures based on official
revenue estimates. For example, under the
Budget Enforcement Act of 1990, a proposal that results in the loss of tax revenue
must be offset by one that raises at least
as much. However, despite the attention
that the revenue estimates themselves receive, there has been relatively little

thought given to what information the estimates actually convey and the role they *should* play in the policy process, along with other relevant information about proposals. There are several issues that deserve particular mention.

Uncertainty

No matter how high the quality of data and the skill of the econometrician, any statistical estimate carries with it a measure of error. Indeed, the conditions under which government revenue estimators labor are far more unfavorable than those faced by the academic researcher. Often, revenue analysis must be performed quickly and in the absence of any reasonable empirical research or the appropriate data. Yet existing rules and institutions leave no room for confidence intervals (which indicate the range of variation in the estimates that cannot reasonably be ruled out), the normal method of indicating the degree of statistical uncertainty.[1]

If each revenue estimate were provided with such a range of error (which itself would often be hard to gauge), legislators might realize just how limited the information was and would be warned to depend less on revenue estimates (and more on other relevant considerations) in making policy decisions and budget rules. Unfortunately, economists have not succeeded in communicating to legislators the inevitability of this uncertainty—and that those outside government who offer "rival" estimates with more precision than is technically feasible are not better economists, but simply not economists.

The Nature of the Experiment

Even if revenue estimates could be made without statistical error, arriving at meaningful estimates still requires many assumptions about the nature of the "experiment" under consideration. These questions include the government's revenue and spending policy responses in current and future years that will offset any change in revenue and the specification of the "baseline"—what would happen if the proposal were not adopted.

For example, suppose an increase in the federal excise tax on tobacco were proposed. Armed with the aggregate elasticities of demand and supply for tobacco, we still do not know how the revenue to be raised will be used. Will other taxes be reduced? Will expenditures increase? When will the offsetting changes in revenues or expenditures occur? The answers to these questions should affect the revenue estimate itself, for they influence the behavioral response, even if no offsetting fiscal changes are anticipated in the current year. Finally, once we have predicted the new level of revenue to be raised under the excise tax, relative to what initial level of revenue should we measure this new revenue level in order to determine the change in revenue?

The revenue estimating process has developed conventions to deal with many of these ambiguities, including "offsets" to take account of changes in other taxes and expenditures, but there is no "correct" set of assumptions to make and the conventions can produce counterintuitive results. For example, if the existing excise tax were about to expire, then the revenue estimate would measure revenue relative to a zero rate of tax, even if everyone already expected that the tax would be renewed at least at its current level. If the excise tax were replaced with an equivalent tax levied at the same rate directly on households in proportion to their tobacco consumption, the estimated revenue would change because of the convention that holds nominal GDP fixed. Because indirect taxes are included in GDP and direct taxes are not (this a convention imposed by national income accountants), the overall level of household expenditures inclusive of the tobacco tax would be presumed higher under the direct tax than the indirect one.

With such inherent ambiguities, the added pressure of budget enforcement rules has wrought havoc, leading legislators to seek ways of "raising revenue" without really doing so. Given that a five-year budget "window" is used to measure each proposal's revenue effects, a proposal can be altered in arbitrary ways to change the amount of estimated revenue for budget periods beyond the first five years. For example, choosing to make what is intended to be a permanent tax increase expire after five years has no effect on the initial five-year revenue estimate but allows legislators to "count" the revenue again and again as they extend the date of expiration in subsequent years, relative to the baseline that does not include the tax.[2]

The Meaning of the Numbers

Revenue estimates have a number of uses. Whatever their limitations, they typically help legislators determine the general scope and magnitude of a provision under consideration. However, they are used for much more than this. Given the current nature of the budget process, the revenue estimate for a proposal is used to tell us how much the proposal increases or reduces the corresponding year's budget deficit. But even if we can resolve the ambiguities just discussed, what does the change in the budget deficit actually tell us? Unfortunately, it may provide little information about the proposal's macroeconomic effects or how the fiscal burden is being shifted among taxpayers.

While policymakers are accustomed to thinking of a deficit-reducing measure as being contractionary, alleviating pressure on interest rates and imposing more of the fiscal burden on current generations, recent history provides us with many counter examples to these presumptions.

In 1992 alone, Congress considered several "revenue-increasing" proposals that in all likelihood would have reduced the present value of revenues collected from current taxpayers. Though the proposals differed in their specifics, each offered taxpayers a net (in present value terms) tax reduction to induce them to accelerate payments. Whether the taxpayer was prepaying the tax on an IRA withdrawal to put the funds into a more attractive "back-end" IRA or accepting the government's compromise offer regarding the disputed amortization of intangible assets, he or she was paying more tax during the budget period but less overall; this was how voluntary participation was guaranteed. Yet these proposals were treated as if they improved the government's fiscal position and were used to relax the constraints imposed by the budget process.

Some have reacted to this sort of gamesmanship by suggesting stricter rules to attempt to distinguish "good" from "bad" revenue increases. However, such arbitrary procedures have no objective principles to guide them and are bound to discourage perfectly reasonable proposals simply because they happen to have the timing characteristics of "budget gimmicks." The problem is really too fundamental to be dealt with in this way, for it reflects serious defects in the concept of deficit accounting itself.

Simply put, the annual budget deficit does not provide answers to our questions about fiscal performance. The problem is not the lack of inflation adjustment or a capital budget. As long as we look at a one-year, or even a five-year, deficit forecast, "timing games" are inevitable, and policy will be distorted by a bias toward adopting policies that, by chance or by design, deliver less of their revenue loss, or more of their revenue gain, during the relevant budget period.

What solution does economic research suggest? If we wish to determine the fiscal impact of a policy, we must know not only its long-run budget impact—the present value of the revenues it generates or loses—but also who bears the burden of these changes. While indicating the long-run revenue consequences of a policy represents an improvement over current practice, a policy—an increase in the level of pay-as-you-go social security benefits, for example—could change revenue in no year but still have "deficit like" effects by shifting resources from the young to elderly.

This combination of looking at long-run budget effects *and* their distribution among cohorts leads to the calculation of *generational accounts* as an alternative to deficit accounting.[3] A generational account equals the present value of taxes, net of transfers, that each generation can expect to pay in the future, based on current policy. By considering how proposals affect the accounts of different generations and the residual of government obligations being left to future generations, we can gain a better indication of the shifting of fiscal burdens that underlies any prospective policy change.

Generational accounting is a methodology that is still under development but already being used by the government.[4] A frequent criticism of generational accounting, and even of more modest attempts at calculating a proposal's long-run revenue consequences, is that information about the distant future is very imprecise and should not be used as a basis for current decisions. However, there is little rationale for discarding partial information in favor of ignorance. The perceived advantages of restricting attention to the short run are even less convincing once one recognizes the uncertainty already inherent in the revenue estimating process.

Should budget enforcement rules be based on generational accounting? Generational accounts have the capacity to provide information that deficit accounting cannot. But, in cynical hands, even generational accounting can be distorted, through the use of inappropriate economic assumptions

about the future. While budget enforcement rules based on generational accounting would represent an improvement over the current practice, I am unconvinced that policymakers who lack the will to make hard decisions can rely on such rules to make them do so.

The Problems of Ambiguity: Behavioral Effects

An important issue in the revenue estimation process in recent years has been the extent to which behavioral effects are taken into account. The general rule followed at the JCT and other agencies is to incorporate behavioral effects at the "micro" level but not at the "macro" level. Thus, while demand and supply responses in individual markets and changes in the composition of consumption or investment may be incorporated, estimates by the JCT (or OTA) take the aggregate output, employment, and prices forecast by CBO (or OMB) as given. For example, the revenue loss generated by an investment tax credit will account for shifts in the mix of investment, but not the increased investment, output, employment or prices that such investment shifts may cause.

Whether to include such macroeconomic "feedback" effects is perhaps the most controversial question in revenue estimation. But the controversy is not really about whether taxes have macroeconomic effects: essentially *all* taxes have macroeconomic effects. The question is whether revenue estimates should incorporate these effects. Because the underlying goal of revenue estimation is unclear, so is the answer to this question.

As a start toward an answer, it helps to consider the question in terms of the three issues already discussed. First, short-term macroeconomic forecasts, say, about the level of output, involve an additional type of uncertainty not present when forecasting the composition of output, namely, uncertainty about the ability of fiscal policy to influence macroeconomic activity. Without making such uncertainty explicit, incorporating feedback effects places the estimator in the very uncomfortable position of having to claim confidence in an estimate in which no sensible person could have much confidence.

Second, the feedback effects cannot be estimated without knowledge of the implicit macroeconomic policy response to the particular proposal—how fiscal and monetary policy will react to incipient changes in output and the price level. Finally, it is not immediately clear that we wish to know the net revenue impact of a proposal. One of the purposes of estimating revenue, admittedly served rather poorly by the current process, is to determine how the intergenerational fiscal burden is affected by a proposal. As I will discuss further in the next section, there is an important distinction between tax revenues and the tax burden, and a better measure of the tax burden may actually be provided by estimates that ignore all or some behavioral effects. This does not necessarily indicate that we should ignore feedback effects, but certainly makes the decision a more complex one.

DISTRIBUTIONAL ANALYSIS

Analyzing the distributional effects of fiscal changes is an exercise in tax incidence, one of the basic tools of analysis in public finance. However, like revenue analysis, distributional analysis often confronts a serious lack of information, because many of the proposals that must be evaluated require a level of detail that outstrips available information. As with revenue analysis, there are many questions to answer and conventions to adopt before the distributional effects of a proposal can be specified, statistical difficulties notwithstanding. Here again, perhaps the most important contribution that economics has to offer is guidance in framing the discussion, identi-

fying which questions to ask and what information is useful.

What Should the Horizon Be?

In economics, the simplest incidence analysis takes place in a static context. We ask who bears a particular tax, without paying much attention to the element of time. As the previous discussion of revenue estimation suggests, time can be an important element in determining the revenue effects, and hence the burden, of a particular tax. In the case of the consumption tax, for example, the horizon used to evaluate incidence affects the degree of measured progressivity or regressivity, because annual variations in income among individuals tend to overstate longer run differences in their ability to pay. The life-cycle model of consumption predicts that individuals will smooth consumption over their lifetimes, supporting consumption during their relatively low-income retirement years by saving during their relatively high-income working years. The same prediction comes from the permanent income hypothesis, which suggests that household consumption will smooth out transitory shocks to income.

As in the case of revenue analysis, an attractive solution is to shift to a lifetime perspective, to measure the burden a tax imposes over each generation's lifetime. This approach could then be extended by looking within each generation at the burden on different income classes.[5] However, the use of short horizons in the revenue estimation process makes it difficult to adopt the lifetime approach in performing distributional analysis. The challenge, then, is to develop an approach that, like a lifetime incidence calculation, is not sensitive to the timing of an individual's tax payments, but is still based on a shorter time horizon.

One method, recently adopted by the JCT, is to associate all taxes with the earning of income, regardless of when the taxes are actually paid. In the case of consumption taxes, this methodology takes advantage of the fact that, under normal market conditions, a broad-based consumption tax is economically equivalent to a broad-based income tax that provides an exclusion for income from new saving.[6] Hence, the consumption taxes attributed to any individual over a five-year period are those taxes that would be paid under the equivalent tax on income from labor and preexisting assets. The approach has the effect of treating, for purposes of timing, the deduction for saving provided under a consumption tax as if it were the equivalent exemption from tax of the capital income earned on that saving.

This same methodology can also be used for consumption taxes with narrower bases, and to analyze saving and investment incentives that take what might be called the "consumption tax" form—*i.e.*, that provide a deduction for saving and a tax on dissaving—in terms of the equivalent income tax exemptions for the income from that saving or investment. The result is a consistent distributional analysis of provisions that differ with respect to timing but not substance, such as "front-end" versus back-end IRAs or investment tax credits versus accelerated depreciation.

What is the Incidence of the Corporate Tax?

As economists have struggled through the years with the question of corporate tax incidence, policy-oriented distributional analysis has dealt with the issue in a variety of unsatisfactory ways, ranging from ignoring it to arbitrarily assigning it to one group or another. Beyond making the obvious point that *someone* must bear this tax, we can improve on past approaches by recognizing that the corporate tax, like the individual income tax, has different components that may be more easily analyzed separately than as a whole.

Basic incidence theory instructs us that

shifting the responsibility for the actual payment of a tax from an individual to a corporation does not necessarily alter the incidence of the tax. A common illustration of this point is the payroll tax, the incidence of which should generally be independent of whether the employer or employee is assessed. Let us consider the implications of this point for the distribution of a corporate level tax that may be part of a system of consumption taxation.

A broad-based consumption tax can be collected in a variety of ways: at the retail level, as a retail sales tax; through the stages of production, as a credit-and-invoice value-added tax; at the individual level, as a personal consumption tax or (as noted above) as a combination of a tax on wages plus the income from capital with a deduction for new saving. With the same base and the same tax rate, the incidence should be the same (ignoring administrative differences with respect to compliance, *etc.*), and any distributional analysis should indicate this.

However, for the last variant with the tax on existing capital collected at the business level as a cash-flow tax, most of which would be collected from corporations, the simple rules often used for distributing the burden of the corporate income tax need not lead to this result. A corporate cash-flow tax would be treated as a corporate income tax with reduced collections, rather than the combination of a corporate income tax plus a deduction for new investment. Treating these components separately, and applying the timing methodology described above, provides the consistency that is desirable among the different consumption tax approaches and between each and other, equivalent, forms of taxation. The important lesson is that we cannot distribute the burden of the corporate tax without considering its form.

Distinguishing Taxes Paid from Tax Burden

The two major concepts of welfare economics used in public finance are equity and efficiency; in analyzing the effects of taxation, we ask who bears the tax burden and how taxes distort behavior. When taxes worsen economic efficiency, there is a difference between the taxes individuals pay and the burdens they bear, equal to the "deadweight loss," or "excess burden," of taxation.

In computing the incidence of a tax, one computes the burden of the tax borne by different individuals, equal for each to that individual's reduction in economic well-being. The sum of these burdens equals total taxes paid plus the deadweight loss of the taxes. The difference between the total burden and the sum of tax payments is important, because it indicates how large the deadweight loss of taxation is. But this is a measure of efficiency, not equity or incidence.

The failure to distinguish between the burden of taxation and the level of taxes paid has precipitated confusion and controversy in the interpretation of distributional analyses. For example, a reduction in the rate of capital gains taxation might have a relatively modest impact on net revenues if, by relaxing the distortion of individual realization decisions, it prompted more frequent realizations. Measured properly—and there are many additional issues involved in ensuring that this is accomplished—the total revenue loss would be smaller than the total benefit resulting from the tax reduction by the associated reduction in deadweight loss. But the size of the revenue loss is irrelevant to the question of burden. Indeed, to a first approximation, the change in the taxpayer's burden is the "income effect" of the tax change—the change in taxes that would result in the absence of any taxpayer response. Still, many individuals outside the economics profession cling to the notion that the change in taxes paid is the correct measure of total burden, with the ridiculous implication that, should a tax be so distortionary that reducing it actually increases revenue, the burden of taxation increases.

The problem is that there is no independent measure of economic efficiency in the policymaker's set of tables and hence no way of making informed decisions involving the trade-off between equity and efficiency. In principle, a measure of deadweight loss might be obtained from a comparison of revenue tables and distribution tables, since the former attempt to measure taxes paid. However, there are many problems in doing so, as not all revenue effects are necessarily incorporated in the revenue calculation and the timing conventions are different. For example, even if there were no behavioral change or associated deadweight loss, the revenue impact of a consumption tax would differ from the total burden associated with such a tax over a one-year or five-year interval unless the consumption tax burden were distributed on the same cash-flow basis as the revenue estimate, a procedure that the JCT has rejected as inappropriate. But this is simply another way of pointing out once again the rather weak connection that the revenue estimates themselves have to any underlying concept of economic burden.

Conclusions

Revenue and distributional analysis are important tax policy tools supplied by economists and supposedly grounded in economic theory and practice. Yet, as the demands of the process and the stress put on these tools increase, it is important to return to the foundations of these processes, to ask what purposes they are supposed to serve and what information they are intended to convey. Without solving all the disputes raging within the economics profession, we may progress beyond the present conditions simply by highlighting and forcing policymakers to confront the weaknesses and inconsistencies of the current methods.

Among the steps that will help us achieve this objective are the following:

(1) the provision of more complete information about the long-run and distributional effects of tax proposals;

(2) the rejection of meaningless measures of fiscal responsibility;

(3) the insistence that information on the revenue and distributional impact of proposals meets the most basic tests of economic consistency; and

(4) the refusal to provide information when such information does not exist and an indication of the quality of information that is being provided.

At worst, we may be ignored, as economists often are when their message is inconvenient—as when pointing out, for example, that the current account deficit must, by identity, equal the domestic imbalance between saving and investment[7]—but we will not be guilty of the complicity of silence.

ENDNOTES

I am grateful to the Edward Netter Research Fund for financial support and to Joel Slemrod and my former colleagues at the U.S Joint Committee on Taxation, particularly Tom Barthold and Pam Moomau, for comments on an earlier draft.

[1] This implied lack of uncertainty places the producers of revenue estimates in a very awkward position on those occasions when revenue estimates simply must be revised to account for compelling new information about taxpayer behavior.

[2] A revenue "increase" of this type included in the 1993 tax bill was the extension of the high-income phase outs of itemized deductions and personal exemptions originally introduced in 1990. In this case, though, legislators opted for permanent extension, foregoing future opportunities to "use" this revenue source.

[3] For a nontechnical description and illustration of the generational accounting approach, see Auerbach, Gokhale, and Kotlikoff (1994).

[4] See U.S. President (1992, 1993).

[5] For a recent application of the lifetime incidence approach, see Fullerton and Rogers (1993).

[6] See, for example, the discussion in Auerbach and Kotlikoff (1987).

[7] See, for example, U.S. Joint Committee on Taxation (1991).

REFERENCES

Auerbach, Alan J., Jagadeesh Gokhale, and Laurence J. Kotlikoff. "Generational Accounting: A Meaningful Way to Evaluate Fiscal Policy." *Journal of Economic Perspectives,* 1994, forthcoming.

Auerbach, Alan J. and Laurence J. Kotlikoff. *Dynamic Fiscal Policy.* Cambridge: Cambridge University Press, 1987.

Fullerton, Don and Diane Lim Rogers. *Who Bears the Lifetime Tax Burden?* Washington, D.C.: Brookings Institution, 1993.

U.S. Joint Committee on Taxation. *Factors Affecting the International Competitiveness of the United States* (JCS-6–91), May 30, 1991.

U.S. Joint Committee on Taxation. *Discussion of Revenue Estimation Methodology and Process* (JCS-14–92), August 13, 1992.

U.S. Joint Committee on Taxation. *Methodology and Issues in Measuring Changes in the Distribution of Tax Burdens* (JCS-7- 93), June 14, 1993.

U.S. President. *The Budget of the United States Government, Fiscal Year 1993,* January 29, 1992.

U.S. President. *Budget Baselines, Historical Data, and Alternatives for the Future,* January, 1993.

ON THE USE OF "DISTRIBUTION TABLES" IN THE TAX POLICY PROCESS

R. GLENN HUBBARD*

INTRODUCTION

The distribution of tax burdens (and government expenditures) is a fundamental question in both public economics and public policy. Positive and normative analyses in public economics have focused on the incidence and effects of tax and expenditure policies on the distribution of economic well-being. Tax policy debates among policymakers are grounded in no small part in policymakers' perceptions of the effects of policy changes on the distribution of economic well-being. The study of incidence is an active area of research among economists, though the contributions of recent research are not always integrated in the distributional assessments presented to policymakers.

Since 1990, the preparation of "distribution tables" has been an area of increasing activity for staff economists in the administration and Congress and for economists in private organizations advising taxpayers (and for academic economists serving in the government, as I can painfully attest). While there are many reasons for this recent growth, two seem particularly promi-

*Columbia University, New York, NY 10027; National Bureau of Economic Research, Cambridge, MA 02138.

nent: (1) the heightened concern over income inequality in the 1980s (with the attendant concerns that the federal tax system may have been partially responsible and, in any event, should be used to redress changes); and (2) the increasing ability of staff economists to prepare detailed tables quickly using modern computer technology and microsimulation models. Whatever the reason, the higher profile of distribution tables has aroused worries by economists in and out of government that the tables do not necessarily convey the appropriate information (or, in some cases, lack of information) to decisionmakers. In this paper, I argue that economic analysis has much to offer decisionmakers in forming their judgments about tax fairness.

On one level, economic analysis has made significant contributions to the study of distributional effects of government policies: it is well understood, for example, that the burden (or benefit) of a tax change is not necessarily borne by (does not necessarily accrue to) the groups that bear the legal liability to remit the tax. That is, changing the structure of taxes alters the economy's equilibrium by altering prices of goods, labor, and capital.[1] The concept of shifting the burden of the tax *is* incorporated in the distributional analysis presented by policymakers in the executive branch and Congress. There is much controversy, however, on *how* the economy's equilibrium changes in response to many taxes (for example, the corporate income tax or a broad-based consumption tax). Such controversy notwithstanding, I argue below that economic analysis contributes a framework for deciding the appropriate questions and for gathering information.

The paper is organized as follows. In the next section, I present some questions posed by economic analysis for the presentation of distribution tables and then review "answers" in practice. The following section illustrates some methodological issues in measuring the distribution of the tax burden in the context of proposals for a broad-based consumption tax at the federal level. The final section concludes by suggesting a strategy for bringing theory and practice closer together.

APPLYING ECONOMIC ANALYSIS

A basic methodological issue in distributional analysis is how to measure incidence. Economists' reflexive answer is to calculate the *compensating variation*, a monetary measure (in absolute terms or relative to lifetime resources) of the effect of a particular policy change on economic well-being. This answer is by no means a simple one in practice, since it requires the calculation of the extra resources needed to restore the individual to his or her initial level of well-being given a change in prices.[2] Most applied analyses do not attempt to calculate this measure, generally emphasizing effects of taxes on after-tax current incomes of individuals or households with different levels of pretax incomes.[3]

Economists' analytical approaches to studying incidence have generally used static computable general equilibrium (CGE) models[4] or life-cycle overlapping generations models.[5] These models permit the calculation of compensating variations for

different groups in the population at a point in time (in the case of the CGE model) and, in some cases, across different lifetime-income groups or generations (in the case of the life-cycle simulation models). As analytical devices, such models have been used to assess actual and potential tax reforms. They have not, however, been the principal guiding force in shaping distributional analysis presented to policymakers.[6]

Applied analyses of the distribution of the tax burden have been more heavily influenced by empirical studies that have proceeded in two steps: first hypothesizing the incidence of each principal tax and then using cross-sectional or panel data on households to estimate the distribution of the composite tax burden by income class (see, for example, Pechman and Okner, 1974; Browning and Johnson, 1979; and Pechman, 1985). Among academic economists, the results of such empirical studies have generated controversy both because of their reliance on *ad hoc* assumptions about the incidence of particular taxes[7] and, relatedly, because tax collections may bear a poor relation to tax burdens.[8]

Rather than examining in more detail the controversy among alternative approaches to distributional analysis, I focus below on some questions suggested by economic analysis and on answers implemented in practice. The number of alternative answers (in principle) to central questions suggests, in my view, the desirability of substantially more sensitivity analysis (or at least discussion) in distribution tables than is the case under current practice.

The Construction of Distribution Tables in Principle

It is instructive to begin by describing the essential elements of the typical tax burden distribution tables used by policymakers: (1) Which taxes are included? (2) What is the definition of income? (3) What are the underlying assumptions about incidence?

(4) What measure of the tax burden is used? (5) How are temporary tax provisions treated? "Correct" answers to these questions depend, of course, on both the professional judgment of staff economists and economic policymakers and on the purpose for which the table is used. While senior policymakers often use distribution tables to guide them in implementing "equity" goals, comparatively little review of these five questions takes place by officials, though the technical staffs of the Treasury's Office of Tax Analysis (OTA), the Joint Committee on Taxation (JCT), and the Congressional Budget Office (CBO) are keenly aware of their importance.

Which Taxes Are Included? A tax burden table may include all taxes (federal, state, and local), all federal taxes, or only a specific set of federal taxes. Criteria for inclusion depend on the purpose of the table, but in practice, judgments over how certain taxes are (or how well they can be) distributed are important.

What Is the Definition of Income? The way in which "incomes" are classified is in principle chosen to distinguish taxpaying units by their levels of economic well-being. At one level, there is interest by members of Congress and administration policymakers in very narrowly defined concepts, such as money income; at another level, economists have generally stressed broader definitions matching more closely conceptual notions of income. The common economist's measure of a household's economic income, the Haig–Simons measure of annual income, equals the annual change in the household's wealth plus the market value of consumption over the year.[9]

A second issue in defining income relates to the specification of an economic unit: income may be defined on a family basis (as a proxy for an economic unit) or on a tax return basis (which corresponds to current income tax reporting).[10] Differences in

distributional estimates from different sources sometimes reflect this distinction.

A third issue relates to the time period under consideration. Generally, distribution tables produced for policymakers are based on *current annual income*, while many analysts have argued for greater emphasis on *permanent income*.[11,12] The length of the period over which one analyzes the distributional consequences of a policy change is important for two reasons. First, the progressivity or regressivity of a tax change can be overstated in the short run to the extent that annual variations in income overestimate long-run or lifetime differences (see, for example, the discussion in Poterba, 1989; and U.S. Department of the Treasury, Office of Tax Analysis, 1992a,b).[13] Abstracting from lifetime income differences, the consumption-smoothing feature of the familiar life-cycle model predicts that differences in annual income over the life cycle are larger than differences in annual consumption (which corresponds more closely to permanent income). Second, significant reforms entail periods of transition.[14] For example, a switch from a wage tax to a consumption tax burdens the current elderly in the short run (who paid wage taxes and now in retirement must pay consumption taxes); the introduction of investment incentives reduces the value of old capital in the short run; and the introduction of an actuarially fair pay-as-you-go social security scheme benefits the first generation to participate relative to future generations.

What Are the Underlying Assumptions about Incidence? Staff economists rely on theoretical arguments and empirical evidence about the incidence of particular taxes. For many taxes (such as the individual income tax), there is broad professional agreement on incidence; for other taxes (notably the corporation income tax), there is considerably less professional agreement. Though not often scrutinized by consumers of the tables, alternative incidence assumptions can have a significant effect on tax burden distribution tables.

What Measure of Tax Burden Is Used? Tax burdens are measured in practice as the amount of taxes paid (or reduction in taxes paid); they do not incorporate notions of excess burden. The distribution tables attempt to convert "taxes paid" into indicators of the economic burden of taxes, including the effective tax rate (taxes divided by income), the percentage change in taxes, the percentage change in after-tax income, or the share of taxes paid. The choice of indicator is not innocuous: the indicators do not necessarily present the same answer regarding the progressivity of regressivity of current taxes or a change in taxes nor do they relate in the same way to theoretical measures of economic well-being.

How Are Temporary Tax Provisions Treated? Both current federal tax law and proposed policy changes often incorporate measures that are temporary. (Such provisions may be included in a distribution table or given special treatment in an ancillary table.) An additional complication arises on account of provisions with a timing element. For example, Individual Retirement Account or Keogh contributions from pretax income reduce current tax payments while increasing tax payments in future years when withdrawals are subject to tax.[15] Analysts must make decisions about how to treat such timing changes.

In addition to the questions raised above, a serious question arises as to which proposals merit the detailed distributional analysis found in distribution tables. At the risk of sounding simplistic, such analysis should be submitted only when it informs the debate. I would argue that such situations arise relatively rarely—for example, the submission of the President's *Budget* or a proposal to change significantly the structure of the tax system. I return to this issue in the conclusion.

The Construction of Distribution Tables in Practice

In part because of the flurry of interest created by the fashioning of the Omnibus Budget Reconciliation Act of 1990, the Treasury Department's Office of Tax Analysis has in the early 1990s prepared numerous distribution tables to explain current-law tax burdens and effects of tax policy changes on those burdens. As a rule, distribution tables are prepared for the use of administration officials and are not released publicly. The JCT and CBO do release distributional tables to congressional decision-makers.

The OTA, JCT, and CBO have offered answers to the five questions raised earlier.

Which Taxes Are Included? Following the work of the late Pechman (Pechman and Okner, 1974; Pechman, 1985), the CBO, OTA, and JCT staffs decided to include only federal taxes, including individual income and corporate income taxes, payroll (Social Security and unemployment insurance) taxes, and excise taxes.[16] Customs duties are not incorporated. The JCT staff has not previously distributed the corporate income tax, though their (1993) pamphlet on distributional analysis suggests that they will try to do so in the future (at least for changes in elements of the tax); the CBO and OTA do distribute the burden of the corporate income tax.

What Is the Definition of Income? The OTA, JCT, and CBO use current annual income to define income. Each staff tries to approximate economic income. The JCT uses a very narrow definition, relying almost exclusively on items reported on tax returns. Specifically, the JCT adds back to adjusted gross income tax-exempt interest, workers' compensation, nontaxable Social Security benefits, deductible contributions to Individual Retirement Accounts (IRAs), employer contributions for health and life insurance, tax preferences under the alternative tax, and net losses in excess of minimum tax preferences from passive business activities. In addition to the categories in the JCT definition, the CBO includes all government cash transfers, all cash pension benefits, the employer share of payroll taxes, and a portion of the corporate income tax.

The OTA uses the broadest annual income concept, called *family economic income* (FEI), which adds the following to adjusted gross income: a proxy for unreported and underreported income; deductible contributions to IRA and Keogh plans; nontaxable transfer payments (such as excludable income from Social Security and AFDC benefits); employer-provided fringe benefits; inside-buildup on private pensions, IRAs, Keogh, and life insurance; tax-exempt interest; and imputed rent on owner-occupied housing (Nelson, 1987).[17] In contrast to the JCT and CBO, the OTA computes capital gains on an accrual basis, adjusted for inflation, to the extent permitted by reliable data. In addition, inflationary losses of lenders are subtracted and gains of borrowers are added. Finally, the FEI includes the value of food stamps received but excludes other transfers in-kind, such as the value of public housing and Medicaid payments.[18]

To represent income units, the JCT uses tax returns. The CBO uses families but, for some distributions, also adjusts for family size by dividing each family's income by the poverty level for a family of that size. The OTA's FEI is calculated on a family, rather than on a tax return, basis. The economic incomes of all members of a family unit are added to arrive at the family's income used as a classifier in the distributions.

I noted earlier that an additional question in deciding the appropriate income concept relates to the time horizon for analysis. One option is to shift from annual measures of economic income to lifetime measures. Indeed, Fullerton and Rogers

(1993) have produced an ambitious examination of lifetime tax burdens borne by groups in the population, and staff economists at the OTA and JCT are analyzing various measures of permanent income. Lifetime incidence calculations, while informative, are not likely to become the principal summary measures for policymakers for two reasons. First, on a conceptual level, lifetime income and incidence calculations assume perfect insurance and lending markets; recent research shows that for most groups in the population, consumption moves more closely with income than perfect-market models suggest (see, for example, Carroll, 1992; and Hubbard, Skinner, and Zeldes, 1993). Thus current income provides information about economic well-being not captured by permanent income. Second, since revenue estimates are presented for relatively short horizons (generally a five-year budget period), policymakers are likely to request distributional analysis for a comparable period.[19] A related point is raised by the concern over "transition issues": To the extent that policymakers are concerned with the impacts of policies over short horizons, the incidence of the tax change may be different than that suggested by "long-run" calculations.

What Are the Underlying Assumptions about Incidence? The basic incidence assumptions used by the OTA are as follows: The individual income tax is assumed to be borne by payers, corporate income tax by capital income generally,[20] payroll taxes (employer and employee shares) by labor (that is, wages and self-employment income), excise taxes on purchases by individuals by the purchaser, and excise taxes on purchases by business in proportion to total consumption expenditures. The same incidence assumptions are used in distributing current-law burdens and proposed changes. With the exception of the corporate income tax, the OTA, JCT, and CBO follow very similar incidence assumptions.

The CBO has generally assumed that half of the corporate tax burden is borne by all capital income and half is borne by labor income. As of this writing, the JCT distributes neither the corporate income tax nor proposed changes in the corporate income tax. The JCT (1993) suggests, however, that the JCT will in the future distribute *changes* in the corporate tax burdens.

What Measure of the Tax Burden Is Used? Distribution tables prepared by the Treasury's OTA have traditionally measured tax burdens by the amount of taxes paid (or the reduction in taxes paid, for a tax reduction)—in absolute terms or in terms of an effective tax rate. While such measures provide a consistent means of distributing current-law taxes and proposed changes, they do not incorporate excess burden. The JCT and CBO economists have also traditionally measured direct tax burdens by tax payments or decreases in tax payments.[21] According to their (1993) pamphlet, the JCT staff has now adopted as measures of the tax burden effective tax rates and the percentage change in taxes paid. The CBO and (if developments during my experience are continuing) OTA staff are emphasizing the percentage change in after-tax income as a (straightforwardly computable) measure of the tax burden and proxy for the change in economic well-being.

How Are Temporary Tax Provisions Treated? The OTA staff economists define as "permanent" the law at the end of the five-year budget period. The burdens of permanent tax changes are then distributed assuming *long-run* (end-of-budget-period) behavioral responses and *current* levels of income. Temporary tax changes are indicated in *short-run* distribution tables, which incorporate the effect of the first full year of the temporary provisions. Proposed policy changes involving "timing" effects (IRAs, for example) are evaluated by the OTA at long-run levels.[22] Provisions with irregular effects on tax liabilities (such as changes in the timing of depreciation allowances) are assessed using the present value of taxes (over the budget period). When I was at the OTA, I was not always certain of the CBO and JCT procedures for distributing burdens or benefits of temporary or timing tax provisions. Prospective JCT procedures are outlined in the (1993) pamphlet.

AN EXAMPLE: DISTRIBUTING THE BURDEN OF A CONSUMPTION TAX

A number of proposals over the past two decades have suggested fundamental restructuring of the federal (individual and corporate) income tax to be financed by the introduction of a broad-based consumption tax. For example, former Treasury Secretary Brady's (1992) proposal, developed within the Office of Tax Policy during my tenure, recommended the introduction of a broad-based business transfer tax (a tax on business gross receipts with expensing of purchases from other firms, including new investment)[23] to finance reductions in individual and corporate taxes. Claims that such a restructuring would improve economic efficiency are often countered with arguments that it would be regressive. The design of the Brady proposal was influenced by distributional considerations to ensure that the package did not reduce the progressivity of federal tax burdens; similar considerations have figured into the ongoing deliberation of a proposal for a broad-based consumption tax by United States Senators Boren and Danforth.[24]

Economists generally argue that over the lifetime of a given individual, a flat-rate, broad-based consumption tax is equivalent to a flat-rate tax on wages plus a flat-rate tax on existing capital at the time the tax is introduced.[25] This equivalence arises because a consumption tax is likely to lead to price increases in the long run, reducing the purchasing power of wage income and income from existing capital. The returns to new investment are untaxed under a broad-based consumption tax.

This lifetime equivalence for a given individual does not imply that commonly produced distribution tables would generate identical answers under the two approaches. Since annual consumption exceeds measured annual income for very low-income individuals (because of transfers and unmeasured income), distributing the burden of a consumption tax proportional to consumption will make the tax appear regressive at low income levels.[26] On the other hand, distributing the burden of the tax to wage income and old capital income increases the progressivity of tax at low- and high-income levels relative to the previous case.[27]

To the extent that tables showing the distribution of the tax burden by economic income class are to represent the short-run (or medium-run) incidence of tax changes, the JCT staff's decision to distribute the burden of a broad-based consumption tax to factor incomes (wages and returns to existing capital) is appropriate. During the period of transition from an income tax to a consumption tax, the burden borne by owners of existing capital enhances the current-annual-income progressivity of a flat-rate broad-based consumption tax.[28]

The decision regarding the distribution of a broad-based consumption tax is not the only incidence assumption required in analyzing the distributional consequences of a policy change involving such a tax. For example, if a business transfer tax were used to reduce federal corporate income taxes and individual income taxes, incidence assumptions for those taxes would also be needed. If, on the one hand, the corporate income tax were borne by owners of capital, replacing corporate tax revenue with consumption tax revenue would be regressive on an annual income basis. If, on the other hand, part of the burden of the corporate tax were borne by workers and/or

consumers of corporate goods, the distributional consequences would be less regressive.[29]

An additional complication is raised by distributional assumptions accompanying incremental reforms in the direction of a consumption tax. Suppose that a series of business income tax reforms were introduced gradually: expensing of investment, phasing out of interest deductions, and phasing out of deductions for compensation. At each step, the distributional analysis should be consistent with the distributional analysis of a broad-based consumption tax (the final result of the three steps). It would be inconsistent, for example, to distribute incremental reforms on the basis of factor incomes (wage and capital income) and to distribute the final result (a consumption tax) on the basis of consumption. The approach suggested by the JCT staff in their (1993) pamphlet—to distribute the burden of a broad-based consumption tax on wages and returns to existing capital—ensures greater consistency between distributional analysis of incremental and large-scale tax reforms.

To summarize, examining the distributional analysis of a broad-based consumption tax illustrates many of the issues surrounding the design of distributional information for policymakers, including assumptions about incidence and appropriate concepts of income and time horizon.

Conclusions

As with many areas in public economics, the gap between the theory and practice of distributional analysis is noticeable to economists and policymakers. Moreover, economic researchers and staff economists often want to present guarded and qualified answers to questions about the distribution of the federal tax burden to policymakers desiring much more specific answers. The temptation to satisfy policymakers' growing appetite for distribution tables should be resisted in my view in favor of the following three-part strategy:

(1) *Staff economists should continue their efforts to instruct decisionmakers on what one can and cannot learn from distribution tables.* The (1993) Joint Committee pamphlet and the (1987) Office of Tax Analysis *Compendium* are excellent examples of this educational process. Seminars for new legislators (particularly those on tax-writing committees) or administration officials could also devote time to the examination of assumptions and judgments lying behind the distributional analysis of specific proposals.

(2) *Staff economists should stress that distributional analysis is most useful for examining the distribution of fiscal policies generally*[30] and much less useful in considering small changes in policy. Reporting of tax burden tables for the existing federal tax system, presidential budget packages, or significant reforms—accompanied by the caveats to which I referred earlier—informs the policy process. Producing such tables for a large number of individual proposals gives decisionmakers the (incorrect) appearance of exactitude and can cause confusion by drawing attention away from interactions of the effects of individual policies.[31] Specific statements qualifying such distribution tables should become a part of staff economists' response to specific requests for distributional tables for individual policy changes.

(3) *Economists engaged in research on incidence can help improve the quality of applied distributional analyses by working with staff economists in the administration and Congress.* Recent research on lifetime incidence, generational differences in tax burden, and burdens and benefits of public policies under imperfect insurance and capital markets can make potentially significant contri-

butions to applied distributional analysis.[32]

In short, economic analysis can best contribute to distributional analysis in much the same way as it can to other areas of public policy decisionmaking—by posing central questions for study, designing a framework for gathering information, and imposing basic tests for consistency of analyses communicated to policymakers. These contributions, sometimes ignored by decisionmakers, will serve those decisionmakers better than merely producing information of the type they demand.

ENDNOTES

I am grateful to Anne Alstott, Alan Auerbach, David Bradford, Bill Gale, Michael Graetz, Jim Nunns, Jim Poterba, and Joel Slemrod for helpful comments and suggestions. This paper draws on some of the (many) lessons I learned while serving as Deputy Assistant Secretary for Tax Analysis in the Treasury Department. While in no way implicating my OTA colleagues for this paper, I acknowledge that debt.

[1] For a survey of the academic literature, see Kotlikoff and Summers (1985); an excellent review of practical problems is presented in U.S. Congress. Joint Committee on Taxation, (1993).

[2] Another measure is the *equivalent variation*, which uses the after-tax-change level of economic well-being as the point of reference.

[3] Another issue relates to the disposition of tax revenue. The distributional effect of a tax policy change depends in general on whether the revenue is used to finance changes in other (current or future) taxes or government spending. Some analyses of alternative tax reforms therefore focus on differential incidence, a comparison of the distributional consequences of alternative equal-revenue tax instruments.

[4] See, for example, Ballard *et al.* (1985) and the survey in Shoven and Whalley (1984).

[5] See, for example, Auerbach and Kotlikoff (1987); Hubbard and Judd (1987); and Hubbard, Skinner, and Zeldes (1992, 1993).

[6] In another line of inquiry, research by Jorgenson and his collaborators has focused on money-metric individual welfare (incorporating compensating and equivalent variations in total expenditure by defining the concept as money measures of individual welfare corresponding to each policy, expressed in terms of a common price system; see Jorgenson, Lau, and Stoker, 1980; and Jorgenson, 1990) and money-metric social welfare (providing a complete ordering of economic policies by defining the concept as the difference between money measures of social welfare

corresponding to each policy, expressed in terms of a common price system; see Jorgenson and Slesnick, 1984). While day-to-day application to distributional analysis will probably not occur in the near future, these approaches offer valuable developments for decomposing impacts of proposed policy into "efficiency" and "equity" effects.

[7] The incidence of the corporate income tax is particularly controversial.

[8] For example, a high rate of tax on realized capital gains may raise little revenue, but generate a significant tax burden for holders of assets.

[9] As discussed later, this concept of economic income is difficult to measure. Staff economists for policymakers have used different sets of approximations of economic income.

[10] For a discussion of the distinctions among these concepts, see Nelson (1987) and U.S. Department of the Treasury, Office of Tax Analysis (1992a, b).

[11] Advocates of a permanent income measure argue that it removes transitory fluctuations in annual income and better reflects long-run well-being; advocates of a current annual income measure argue that it is better (or, at least, less controversially measured) and corresponds to man-in-the-street notions of income.

[12] A still broader question is whether to consider *intergenerational* redistribution of the tax system (see, for example, Auerbach, Gokhale, and Kotlikoff, 1993; and Auerbach, in this issue).

[13] Fullerton and Rogers (1993) conclude in their study, however, that, in practice, lifetime and annual-income incidence of the United States tax system are not markedly different.

[14] Transition effects are discussed in Bernheim (1981), Chamley (1981), Auerbach and Kotlikoff (1987), and Hubbard and Judd (1987).

[15] The net tax benefit of such tax-favored savings schemes is, of course, the sheltering of accumulated earnings from taxation (plus a gain upon disbursement of funds if the tax rate is lower at that time).

[16] For a description of taxes included by the three groups, see U.S. Congressional Budget Office (1987), Nelson (1987), and U.S. Congress, Joint Committee on Taxation (1993).

[17] In earlier work, Pechman and Okner (1974) and Pechman (1985) also incorporated in "income" imputed rent on owner-occupied housing, measures of accrued rather than realized capital gains, and noncash transfer payments. Gale (1992) reviews issues in deciding upon the appropriate income concepts.

[18] The difference between the OTA and JCT approaches to defining economic income essentially represents differences in judgments about whether existing data permit the development of information about some components of Haig–Simons income relative to the OTA's family economic income. Some of the data sets used by JCT staff for other purposes described in the pamphlet could have been applied to the construction of a more comprehensive measure of economic income. Whether imperfections in such data make more comprehensive measures less meaningful is, of course, an open question with reasonable positions on either side.

[19] A compromise approach taken by the JCT staff is outlined in U.S. Congress, Joint Committee on Taxation (1993).

[20] For a review of the issues surrounding the incidence of the corporate income tax, see U.S. Department of the Treasury (1992).

[21] A notable exception is the JCT staff's measurement of the burden of the capital gains tax as the "static" revenue loss (the change in revenue by income class, assuming no behavioral response to changes in the tax).

[22] For the case of tax-favored savings vehicles such as IRAs, the long-run effect could be characterized by the tax savings from the earnings from one year's deposits in a steady-state year. I believe that the OTA follows this procedure.

[23] The business transfer tax is a variant of a subtraction-method value-added tax. There is no reason to believe that the incidence of a subtraction-method value-added tax and the more familiar (in practice) credit-invoice value-added tax are different. For discussions of this point, see Bradford (1986); U.S. Congressional Budget Office (1992); U.S. Congress, Joint Committee on Taxation (1993); and McLure (1993).

[24] In estimating the distributional impact of the plan, the OTA used the most conservative assumptions (to satisfy the Secretary's request that the proposal not reduce overall progressivity of the federal tax system): the consumption tax was assumed to raise prices, so that its burden was distributed across households according to their consumption. Taxes on corporate capital income (which were reduced in the plan through corporate tax integration) were assumed to be borne by owners of capital. Distributional analysis for the Boren–Danforth plan is (as of this writing) being provided by JCT staff economists. As discussed later, the JCT assumes that the burden of the tax is borne by wages and old capital as the income is earned.

[25] This equivalence is true in a benchmark case in which credit and insurance markets are perfect.

[26] This assumes that prices rise because of the tax and that not all transfer payments are indexed. [Evidence in Sabelhaus (1992) suggests that consumption taxes are likely to be less regressive than previously believed when distributed this way. This is because the traditionally used Consumer Expenditure Surveys overstate dissaving by very low-income households and saving by very high-income households. Sabelhaus and the JCT staff have used the Federal Reserve's Survey of Consumer Finances data on saving rates to impute consumption. These data suggest that income is higher relative to consumption for very low-income households and lower relative to consumption for very high-income households.] The Brady proposal provided a refundable tax credit for low-income households rather than specifically indexing individual transfer programs.

[27] See, for example, U.S. Congress, Joint Committee on Taxation (1993, p. 55).

[28] This distributional approach does suggest different burdens for holders of nominal and real claims on existing capital. Nominal bondholders will not be affected by the reduction in returns to existing capital. Owners of real physical capital bear this burden.

[29] See, for example, the discussions in U.S. Congress, Joint Committee on Taxation (1993) and Fullerton and Rogers (1993). While I understand the spirit of the exercise, the JCT staff's decision that the incidence of the existing corporate tax is not well understood, but that the distribution of straightforward changes is easily accomplished, puzzled me on a technical level.

[30] I use the term "fiscal policies" to underscore the need for more effort to report to policymakers the distributional consequences of federal expenditures.

[31] My former Treasury colleague Michael Graetz told me on more than one occasion that the flurry of distribution tables produced for "1990 Budget Summit" conferees at Andrews Air Force Base crossed the border between sublime and ridiculous early in the game.

[32] One example is the discussion of intergenerational differences in federal tax burdens in President Bush's Fiscal Year 1993 Budget. That informative description built on research in Auerbach, Gokhale, and Kotlikoff (1993), with assistance from those authors.

REFERENCES

Auerbach, Alan J. "Public Finance in Theory and Practice." National Tax Journal XLVI No. 4 (December, 1993):519–526.

Auerbach, Alan J., Jagadeesh Gokhale, and Laurence J. Kotlikoff. "Generational Accounting: A Meaningful Way to Evaluate Fiscal Policy." Journal of Economic Perspectives, 1994, forthcoming.

Ballard, Charles, L., Don Fullerton, John B. Shoven, and John Whalley. A General Equilibrium Model for Tax Policy Evaluation. Chicago: University of Chicago Press, 1985.

Bernheim, B. Douglas. "A Note on Dynamic Tax Incidence." Quarterly Journal of Economics (1981): 705–23.

Bradford, David F. Untangling the Income Tax. Cambridge: Harvard University Press, 1986.

Brady, Nicholas F. "Remarks Before the Graduate School of Business, Columbia University." New York, December 10, 1992.

Browning, Edgar K. and William R. Johnson. The Distribution of the Tax Burden. Washington, D.C.: American Enterprise Institute, 1979.

Carroll, Christopher D. "The Buffer Stock Theory of Saving: Some Macroeconomic Evidence." Brookings Papers on Economic Activity (Vol. 2, 1992): 61–135.

Chamley, Christophe. "The Welfare Cost of Capital Income Taxation in a Growing Economy." Journal of Political Economy (June, 1981): 468–91.

Council of Economic Advisers and Office of Management and Budget. February, 1990. Progressivity: An Analysis of the Ways and Means Committee and Congressional Budget Office Studies. Mimeo.

Fullerton, Don and Diane Lim Rogers. Who Bears the Lifetime Tax Burden? Washington, D.C.: Brookings Institution, 1993.

Gale, William G. October, 1992. Comment on 'Trends in Federal Tax Progressivity, 1980–93.' The Brookings Institution. Mimeo.

Hubbard, R. Glenn and Kenneth L. Judd. "Social Security and Individual Welfare: Precautionary Saving, Borrowing Constraints, and the Payroll Tax." American Economic Review 77 (September, 1987): 630–46.

Hubbard, R. Glenn, Jonathan Skinner, and Stephen P. Zeldes. "The Importance of Precautionary Motives in Explaining Individual and Aggregate Saving." Carnegie-Rochester Conference Series on Public Policy (1993): forthcoming.

Hubbard, R. Glenn, Jonathan Skinner, and Stephen P. Zeldes. 1992. Precautionary Saving and Social Insurance. National Bureau of Economic Research. Mimeo.

Jorgenson, Dale W. "Aggregate Consumer Behavior and the Measurement of Social Welfare." Econometrica 58 (September, 1990): 1007–40.

Jorgenson, Dale W., Laurence J. Lau, and Thomas M. Stoker. "Welfare Comparison under Exact Aggregation." American Economic Review 70 (May, 1980): 268–72.

Jorgenson, Dale W. and Daniel T. Slesnick. "Aggregate Consumer Behavior and the Measurement of Inequality." Review of Economic Studies 51 (July, 1984): 369–92.

Kotlikoff, Laurence J. and Lawrence H. Summers. "Tax Incidence." In Handbook of Public Economics, edited by Alan J. Auerbach and Martin Feldstein. Amsterdam: North-Holland, 1985, vol. 2.

McLure, Charles E., Jr. "The Mechanics of Three Consumption Taxes." In The Value Added Tax: Coming to America?. Arlington, VA: Tax Analysts, July, 1993.

Nelson, Susan C. "Family Economic Income and Other Income Concepts Used in Analyzing Tax Reform." In Compendium of Tax Research, 1987, Washington, D.C.: U.S. Department of the Treasury, Office of Tax Analysis, 1987.

Pechman, Joseph A. Who Paid the Taxes, 1966–1985. Washington, D.C.: Brookings Institution, 1985.

Pechman, Joseph A. and Benjamin A. Okner. Who Bears the Tax Burden? Washington, D.C.: Brookings Institution, 1974.

Poterba, James M. "Lifetime Incidence and the Distributional Burden of Excise Taxes." American Economic Review 79 (May, 1989): 325–30.

Sabelhaus, John. December, 1992. "What Is the Distributional Burden of Taxing Consumption?" Congressional Budget Office. Mimeo.

Shoven, John B. and John Whalley. "Applied General Equilibrium Models of Taxation and International Trade: An Introduction and Survey." Journal of Economic Literature 22 (September, 1984): 1007–51.

U.S. **Congressional Budget Office.** *The Changing Distribution of Federal Taxes: 1975–1990.* Washington, D.C., 1987.

U.S. **Congressional Budget Office.** *Effects of Adopting a Value-Added Tax.* Washington, D.C., 1992.

U.S. **Department of the Treasury.** *Integration of the Individual and Corporate Tax Systems.* Washington, D.C.: U.S. Government Printing Office, January, 1992.

U.S. **Department of the Treasury, Office of Tax Analysis.** "Household Income Changes over Time: Some Basic Questions and Facts." *Tax Notes* (August 24, 1992a).

U.S. **Department of the Treasury, Office of Tax Analysis.** "Household Income Mobility during the 1980s: A Statistical Assessment Based on Tax Return Data." *Tax Notes* (June 1, 1992b).

U.S. **Congress, Joint Committee on Taxation.** *Methodology and Issues in Measuring Changes in the Distribution of Tax Burdens* (JCS-7–93). Washington, D.C., June 14, 1993.

TAXATION AND ECONOMIC GROWTH

**ERIC ENGEN* &
JONATHAN SKINNER***

Abstract - *Tax reforms are sometimes touted as having strong macroeconomic growth effects. Using three approaches, we consider the impact of a major tax reform—a 5 percentage point cut in marginal tax rates—on long-term growth rates. The first approach is to examine the historical record of the U.S. economy to evaluate whether tax cuts have been associated with economic growth. The second is to consider the evidence on taxation and growth for a large sample of countries. And finally, we use evidence from microlevel studies of labor supply, investment demand, and productivity growth. Our results suggest modest effects, on the order of 0.2 to 0.3 percentage point differences in growth rates in response to a major tax reform. Nevertheless, even such small effects can have a large cumulative impact on living standards.*

INTRODUCTION

By now, a presidential campaign is incomplete without at least one proposal for tax reform. Recent proposals suggested that by reducing marginal tax rates, or by replacing the current federal income tax with a consumption-type tax, the United States can experience increased work effort, saving, and investment, resulting in faster economic growth. For example, Steve Forbes vaulted briefly into the political limelight based almost solely on his advocacy of a flat tax which cut nearly every person's tax bill, but which was supposed to balance the budget by stimulating economic growth. The Kemp Commission suggested that its general principles for tax reform would almost double U.S. economic growth rates over the next five to ten years.[1] Most recently, presidential candidate Robert Dole proposed a 15 percent across-the-board income tax cut coupled with a halving of the tax on capital gains, with a predicted increase in gross domestic product (GDP) growth rates from about 2.5 to 3.5 percentage points.

Others have questioned whether tax reform would have such beneficial effects on economic growth.[2] If tax cuts fail to produce the projected boost in economic growth, tax revenues could decline, putting upward pressure on the deficit, worsening levels of national saving, and leading to laggard economic growth in the future. At this stage, however, there is little agreement about

*Federal Reserve Board, Washington, D.C. 20551.
**Department of Economics, Dartmouth College, Hanover, NH 03755, and NBER, Cambridge, MA 02138.

whether a major tax reform would provide an economic boon to the United States or impede economic growth.

In this paper, we reexamine the relationship between economic growth and taxation in light of the accumulated economic evidence, both from the United States and other countries. While many economists would agree with the proposition that "high taxes are bad for economic growth," we show that this proposition is not necessarily obvious, either in theory or in the data. However, we find that the evidence is consistent with lower taxes having modest positive effects on economic growth. While such growth effects are highly unlikely to allow tax cuts to pay for themselves, they can contribute to substantial differences in the level of economic activity and living standards, particularly over the long term.

SHOULD WE EXPECT TAXES TO AFFECT GROWTH? A THEORETICAL PERSPECTIVE

Before jumping into the morass of empirical evidence, it is useful to first ask the question: How does tax policy affect economic growth? By discouraging new investment and entrepreneurial incentives? By distorting investment decisions because the tax code makes some forms of investment more profitable than others? Or by discouraging work effort and workers' acquisition of skills? These questions are often addressed in an accounting framework first developed by Solow (1956). In this approach, the output, y, of an economy, typically measured by GDP, is determined by its economic resources—the size and skill of its workforce, m, and the size and technological productivity of its capital stock, k. Thus, a country like the United States might be expected to have a greater per capita output than

Mozambique because its (per capita) capital stock is so much larger and more technologically advanced and its workers have more skills, or human capital. The growth rate of economic output therefore will depend on the growth rate of these resources— physical capital and human capital—as well as changes in the underlying productivity of these general inputs in the economy. More formally, we can decompose the growth rate of the economy's output into its different components:

$$\dot{y}_i = \alpha_i \dot{k}_i + \beta_i \dot{m}_i + \mu_i$$

where the real GDP growth rate in country i is denoted $\dot{y}_i$ and the net investment rate (expressed as a fraction of GDP), equivalently the change over time in the capital stock, is given by $\dot{k}_i$. The percentage growth rate in the effective labor force over time is written $\dot{m}_i$, while the variable μ_i measures the economy's overall productivity growth.

There are two other relevant variables in equation 1, which are the coefficients measuring the marginal productivity of capital, α_i, and the output elasticity of labor, β_i.[3] For example, if there were a one percentage point increase in the growth rate of the (skill-adjusted) labor force and β were equal to 0.75, the implied increase in the economic growth rate would be 0.75 percentage point. Alternatively, if the investment rate were to rise by one percentage point and α were 0.10, the growth rate of output would rise by 0.10 percentage point.

This theoretical framework allows us to catalog the five ways that taxes might affect output growth, corresponding to each of the variables on the right-hand side of equation 1. First, higher taxes can discourage the investment rate, or the net growth in the capital stock ($\dot{k}_i$ in equation 1 above), through high statutory tax rates on corporate and individual income, high effective capital gains tax rates, and low depreciation allowances. Second, taxes may attenuate labor supply growth $\dot{m}_i$ by discouraging labor force participation or hours of work, or by distorting occupational choice or the acquisition of education, skills, and training. Third, tax policy has the potential to discourage productivity growth μ by attenuating research and development (R&D) and the development of venture capital for "high-tech" industries, activities whose spillover effects can potentially enhance the productivity of existing labor and capital.

Fourth, tax policy can also influence the marginal productivity of capital by distorting investment from heavily taxed sectors into more lightly taxed sectors with lower overall productivity

(Harberger, 1962, 1966). And fifth, heavy taxation on labor supply can distort the efficient use of human capital by discouraging workers from employment in sectors with high social productivity but a heavy tax burden. In other words, highly taxed countries may experience lower values of α and β, which will tend to retard economic growth, holding constant investment rates in both human and physical capital (Engen and Skinner, 1992). We show this graphically in Figure 1, which focuses on a fixed level of the capital stock K, shown by the width of the horizontal axis. (A similar analysis holds for labor market distortions.) Suppose that the income tax on the corporate sector, as well as subsidies to non-corporate owner-occupied housing, distort the allocation of the capital stock between the corporate (c) and non-corporate (nc) sectors. (In other countries, the distortion may arise between sectors which escape taxation such as

FIGURE 1. The Effect of Intersectoral Distortions on the Average Rate of Return

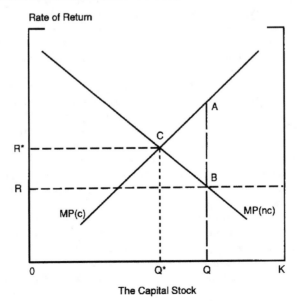

the underground economy or small-scale agriculture, versus the manufacturing sector which is easily taxed or heavily regulated.) The line denoted $MP(c)$ is the value of the marginal product of capital in the corporate sector, while $MP(nc)$ denotes the value of the marginal pro-duct in the noncorporate sector. Without any tax distortion, the profit-maximizing and most efficient point is C; the mar-ginal productivity of capital is equalized in both sectors and the economy-wide return on capital is R^*, as shown by the dotted line. (The allocation of the total capital stock, K, is Q^* units of capital in the noncorporate sector and $K-Q^*$ units in the corporate sector.) With a tax of AB on corporate capital only, there is a distortion in the allocation of capital; capital flows from the corporate to the noncorporate sector, so the new allocation is Q units of capital in the noncorporate sector and $K-Q$ units of capital in the corporate sector. The net loss in output is given by ABC, the traditional Harberger welfare loss triangle. Under some plausible restric-tions, the average rate of return for the entire capital stock, R, will correspond to the rate of return on new investment, given in equation 1 by α.[4] Hence, a distortionary tax on capital (or on labor) will be reflected in lower overall rates of return on new investment (from R^* to R), leading to laggard growth rates.

We have outlined five possible mecha-nisms by which taxes can affect eco-nomic growth. Therefore, it might appear that taxes should play a central role in determining long-term growth. However, the conventional Solow growth model implies that taxes should have *no* *impact* on *long-term* growth rates. In part, this result occurs by assumption, since productivity growth μ is assumed to be fixed and unaffected by tax policy. But this paradoxical result holds also

because of a distinction between changes in the level of GDP and changes in growth rates of GDP. For example, suppose that, in the year 2000, a "tax and spend" president is elected in the United States and tax rates are increased by ten percentage points across the board. (Ignore the effects of the extra government spending on the economy.) The extra tax distortion reduces labor supply and investment, causing a sudden decline in *short-term* growth rates. But once the U.S. economy had adjusted to the harsh new tax regime, it would revert back to its original growth path, albeit at a lower absolute level than it would have been in the absence of the tax hikes. (In the Solow model, both investment and labor supply growth revert back to their original rates determined by long-term population growth.) In other words, the simple Solow model implies that tax policy, however distortionary, has no impact on long-term economic *growth rates*, even if it does reduce the *level* of economic output in the long-term.

So then how can taxation affect output growth rates? We focus on two possible mechanisms. The first is that when the structure of taxes changes, *short-term* output growth rates would be expected to change as well along a possibly lengthy transition path to the new steady state. If one believes that the Dole or the Forbes tax reform would expand output by five percentage points and it takes ten years to make the transition to the new steady state, growth rates will be higher, on average, by about 0.5 percentage points during this period before settling back down to their long-run values.[5] Ten years is a long-term horizon for presidential candidates but is still the short-term in the Solow model. And these short-term effects are clearly important, since they result in a permanent increase in GDP.

The second possibility arises within the context of the new class of "endogenous growth" models (e.g., Romer, 1986; Lucas, 1990). In these models, the stable growth rate of the Solow model, stapled down by technology and workforce productivity growth, is replaced by steady-state growth rates which can differ, persistently, because of tax and expenditure policies pursued by the government (e.g., King and Rebelo, 1990). The endogenous growth framework emphasizes factors such as "spillover" effects and "learning by doing," by which firm-specific decisions to invest in capital or in R&D, or individual investments in human capital, can yield positive external effects (e.g., on μ) that benefit the rest of the economy. In these models, taxes *can* then have long-term, persistent effects on output growth. However, the question still remains: what is the magnitude of these tax effects on economic growth?

A number of recent theoretical studies have used endogenous growth models to simulate the effects of a fundamental tax reform on economic growth.[6] All of these studies conclude that reducing the distorting effects of the current tax structure would permanently increase economic growth. Unfortunately, the magnitude of the increase in economic growth is highly sensitive to certain assumptions embodied in the economic models used in these studies, with little empirical guidance or consensus about key parameter values. Consequently, these studies reached substantially different conclusions concerning the magnitude of the boost in growth rates. At one extreme, Lucas (1990) calculated that a revenue-neutral change that eliminated all capital income taxes while raising labor income taxes would increase growth rates negligibly. At the other extreme, Jones, Manuelli, and

Rossi (1993) calculated that eliminating all distorting taxes would raise average annual growth rates by a whopping four to eight percentage points.[7] (An "across-the-board" reduction in distortionary tax rates in these models, rather than complete elimination of distortionary taxes, would be expected to have a smaller positive effect on economic growth.) Most recently, the simulation model in Mendoza, Razin, and Tesar (1994) suggests relatively modest differences in economic growth of roughly 0.25 percentage points annually as the consequence of a 10 percentage point change in tax rates.

These simulation models of endogenous growth fail to provide a comfortable range of plausible effects of taxes on growth and thus tend to raise more questions than they answer. Moreover, they are likely to miss many relevant characteristics of the U.S. tax system. No macroeconomic model allows for the possibility of a firm undertaking financial restructuring to reduce taxable income, or of timing issues in deferred taxes, or the possibility of tax evasion.[8] Often the simulation analysis is performed in terms of a single flat-rate tax in the context of a (single) representative agent model. Ultimately, one needs to consider the empirical record to make informed judgments about whether tax policy exerts a strong influence on economic growth.

Below, we take three separate approaches to judge the empirical record. First, we take a quick look at the U.S. historical record to see if there is an easily discernible link between changes in U.S. tax policy and changes in economic growth across time. Second, we consider whether differences in growth rates across countries can be attributed, at least partially, to variation in tax policy. Third and finally, we survey the microlevel studies of how taxes affect specific subsectors of the economy and build up from these microlevel studies to make inferences about aggregate tax effects.

AN INFORMAL LOOK AT TAXES AND U.S. ECONOMIC GROWTH

Anecdotal stories about the U.S. tax code can sometimes have a larger impact on the policy debate than a stack of statistical studies. The Kemp Commission (NCR, 1996), for example, highlighted the complaint of one frustrated businessman:

> As an entrepreneur, I experience first hand the horrors of our tax system. It has grown into a monstrous predator that kills incentives, swallows time, and chokes the hopes and dreams of many. We have abandoned several job-creating business concepts due to the tax complexities that would arise.

While this testimony is suggestive that the tax system adversely affects incentives, it is not entirely clear whether the entrepreneur is concerned about the tax rate per se or the complexity of the tax system more generally. And we are not sure what fraction of entrepreneurs are of like mind, or how much investment is affected adversely by the tax code. For example, surveys from a few decades ago indicate that typical businesspeople did not view taxes as an impediment to business decisions; in one study conducted in Britain in the early 1960s, not a single executive out of the sample of 181 replied that they abandoned the introduction of a new plant or equipment during the past seven years because of tax changes (Corner and Williams, 1965).[9] More recent survey studies suggest a larger impact of taxation on the discount rates used to evaluate private investment projects (Poterba and Summers, 1995); even

among these tax-savvy Fortune 1000 executives, 36 percent reported that a corporate tax cut from 34 to 25 percent would not make them more likely to engage in investment projects.[10]

A slightly more rigorous approach is to look at the historical evidence from time-series changes in taxation and output growth. The Kemp Commission's report (NCR, 1996) relied on time-series comparisons to argue that the patterns are self-evident:

> America has experienced three periods of very strong economic growth in this century: the 1920s, the 1960s, and the 1980s. Each of these growth spurts coincided with a period of reductions in marginal tax rates. In the eight years following the Harding–Coolidge tax cuts, the American economy grew by more than five percent per year. Following the Kennedy tax cuts in the early 1960s, the economy grew by nearly five percent per year. . . In the seven years following the 1981 Reagan tax cuts, the economy grew by nearly four percent per year while real federal revenues rose by 26 percent.

This approach does not try to perform the "growth accounting" exercise detailed in the theoretical section, but asks simply whether there are discernible differences in GDP growth following tax cuts. We consider the latter two tax reforms in Figure 2, which shows real GDP growth rates (both total and per capita) in the United States between 1959 and 1994 in the bottom panel, with the relevant tax series graphed in the upper two panels.[11] To smooth out year-to-year volatility in GDP growth rates, we present three-year moving averages of GDP growth rates in the bottom panel of Figure 2, both for aggregate growth rates and for per capita growth rates. The two economic expansions noted above during the 1960s and the 1980s are apparent, as

FIGURE 2. Average Tax Rates, Marginal Tax Rates, and GDP Growth in the United States, 1959–95

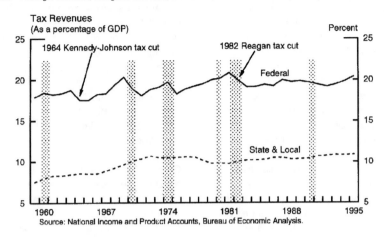

Tax Revenues
(As a percentage of GDP)

Source: National Income and Product Accounts, Bureau of Economic Analysis.

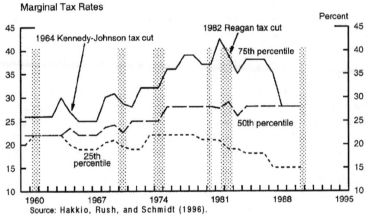

Marginal Tax Rates

Source: Hakkio, Rush, and Schmidt (1996).

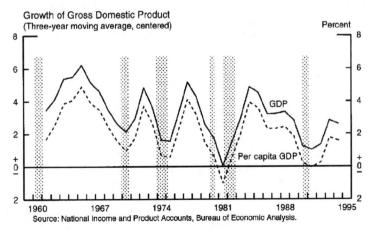

Growth of Gross Domestic Product
(Three-year moving average, centered)

Source: National Income and Product Accounts, Bureau of Economic Analysis.

are the other expansions following recessions (shown by the shaded regions). The general slowdown in economic growth over the last three decades can be seen also.

Moving to the top panel of Figure 2, we next consider the ratio of tax revenue to GDP—a commonly used measure of the average tax burden. The top line shows U.S. federal government revenue (measured on a National Income and Product Accounts (NIPA) basis) as a percentage of GDP. The lower line is state and local government tax revenue measured on a NIPA basis as a percentage of GDP. Since 1959, the average federal tax rate has risen by about two percentage points, but has generally hovered around 20 percent of GDP; the average individual income tax rate has remained relatively constant, while growth in social insurance taxes have been mostly offset by the decline in corporate and excise taxes. State and local government average tax burdens have risen by about three percentage points over the last three decades.

The Kennedy–Johnson tax cuts in 1964 resulted in a small decline in the average tax rate. Real GDP growth averaged a robust 4.8 percent over the subsequent 1964 to 1969 period. However, the extent to which this growth was caused by the tax cuts is unclear, as GDP growth had averaged over five percent in the two years *prior* to 1964.

The Reagan tax cuts also lowered the average tax rate, and real GDP growth averaged a healthy 3.9 percent from 1983 to 1989, significantly above the preceding period from 1980 to 1982 that was dominated by recession.[12] But it is a difficult task to sort out whether the strong growth during the 1980s was the consequence of supply-side effects

of lowering marginal tax rates, traditional Keynesian aggregate demand effects fueled by tax cuts and expanding defense expenditures, or a recovery that would have occurred without the tax change.[13] Indeed, Feldstein and Elmendorf (1989) suggest a somewhat different cause for the 1980s expansion: expansionary monetary policy combined with a strong dollar and active business investment.

Over the longer term, since 1959, both the average federal tax rate and the average state-local tax rate have risen— by about two and three percentage points, respectively. At the same time, average growth rates in real GDP have declined, from 4.4 percent during the 1960s to only 2.4 percent in 1986–95. These coincident trends over the last three and a half decades are consistent with the hypothesis that higher taxes have stunted economic growth. Before arriving at conclusions about taxation and growth from this single observation (which does not account for other factors that were also changing over this time period), we note that the average tax rate series is unlikely to reflect the *marginal* tax distortion, which economic theory suggests is more important in affecting economic growth through households' and firms' choices of saving, investment, and employment.

The middle panel of Figure 2 shows the marginal individual income tax rates relevant for households at the 75th, 50th, and 25th percentiles of the income distribution in each year (Hakkio, Rush, and Schmidt, 1996).[14] From 1960 to the early 1980s, marginal tax rates at the 75th percentile grew while marginal tax rates at the 25th percentile declined slightly. There was some reduction in output growth coincident with the increase in the upper-middle class marginal tax rates. However, GDP growth rates continued to fall over the past decade even as the marginal tax rates for both upper- and lower-income households declined.[15] In other words, the time-series correlation between marginal tax rates and growth rates yields a decidedly mixed picture; some decades were correlated positively, and others negatively.

Finally, we correct the first sentence of the quotation from the Kemp Commission above. The most rapid growth rates in this century were, in fact, during the period 1940–45, when output grew at 12.5 percentage points annually. During this same period, the federal tax system expanded dramatically, with median marginal tax rates rising from 3.6 percent in 1940 to 25 percent in 1945. Yet it would be ludicrous to claim on that basis that higher taxes have a positive effect on output growth, given the obvious confounding events during this period. Nevertheless, highlighting the period 1940–45 is useful for two purposes. The first is that it illustrates the risks of trying to discern incentive effects of taxation using short-term time-series data. This is a point reinforced by the experience of Sweden's tax reform, when the economy fell into a recession just after a tax reform trimming marginal tax rates substantially (Agell, Englund, and Sodersten, 1996). And second, it suggests that one should look most carefully at GDP growth rates before and after the early 1940s when the federal income tax experienced its major expansion. Stokey and Rebelo (1995) looked for this break in long-term output growth rates and were unable to find any significant difference. On the other hand, given the major disruptions in economic activity occurring during the 20th century, it may be asking too much of the data to detect

what might be very small differences in growth rates, on the order of 0.5 percentage points, caused by the distortionary effects of taxation.

More formal econometric methods may hold greater promise for uncovering the pure effects of taxation on economic growth, because that type of analysis attempts to control for other factors that affect output independently of tax policy. The problem is that time-series analysis is best suited for detecting short-term effects of changes in tax policy on output growth, which, as noted above, may reflect Keynesian expansionary effects of deficit spending or other unmeasured factors associated with tax cuts. In addition, figuring out *which* characteristics of a particular tax reform—changes in top marginal tax rates, depreciation allowances, tax progressivity, tax rates on capital gains— caused changes in growth rates is particularly problematic in aggregate time-series analysis. For these reasons, we turn our attention next to cross-country studies.

TAX POLICY AND GROWTH: THE CROSS-COUNTRY EVIDENCE

An alternative empirical approach is to draw on the experience of different countries to investigate how tax policy affects economic growth. Countries have very different philosophies about taxation and very different methods of collecting their revenue. During the past several decades, some countries have increased taxation quite dramatically, while, in other countries, tax rates have remained roughly the same. Some countries incorporated value-added taxation in the 1960s (e.g., France and Britain), while others shifted away from corporate taxation (the United States). The advantage of using such cross-country comparisons is that we can use many countries with different tax structures and GDP growth rates to test for correlation (and, one hopes, causation) between tax policy and growth.

In general, studies of taxation using cross-country data suggest that higher taxes have a negative impact on output growth, although these results are not always robust to the tax measure used. Using reduced-form cross-section regressions, Koester and Kormendi (1989) estimated that the marginal tax rate—conditional on fixed average tax rates—has an independent, negative effect on output growth rates. Skinner (1988) used data from African countries to conclude that income, corporate, and import taxation led to greater reductions in output growth than average export and sales taxation. Dowrick (1992) also found a strong negative effect of personal income taxation, but no impact of corporate taxes, on output growth in a sample of Organisation for Economic Co-operation and Development (OECD) countries between 1960 and 1985. Easterly and Rebelo (1993) found some measures of the tax distortion (such as an imputed measure of marginal tax rates) to be correlated negatively with output growth, although other measures of the tax distortion were insignificant in the growth equations.

Most empirical studies of taxation and growth are "reduced form" estimates in that they specify a linear model of output growth rates, with tax rates, labor resource growth, and investment rates on the right-hand side of the equation. However, taxes do not necessarily enter the growth accounting framework in equation 1 in a linear fashion. We explored this possibility in Engen and Skinner (1992), where the primary growth effect of tax distortions on production is hypothesized to

depress the economy-wide return on capital, α, and on labor, β (as in equation 1 and Figure 1). Using cross-country data for 1970–85, Engen and Skinner found that an increase of 2.5 percentage points in the average tax burden (total taxes divided by GDP) is predicted to reduce long-term output growth rates by 0.18 percentage points, holding constant the supply of investment and labor.

A recent McKinsey (1996) study points to the potential importance of the intersectoral allocation of capital. The study observed that Japan and Germany both had much higher rates of investment. But because U.S. investment appeared to be allocated to more profitable (i.e., higher productivity) sectors, the net increment to the effective capital stock, and hence to national income, was considerably greater in the United States, despite the lower investment rate. Similarly, King and Fullerton (1984), in their study of tax systems in the United Kingdom, Sweden, West Germany, and the United States, found a strong negative correlation between economic growth and the intersectoral variability in investment tax rates.[16]

Of course, nearly any tax will tend to distort economic behavior along some margin, so the objective of a well-designed tax system is to avoid highly distortionary taxes and raise revenue from the less distortionary ones. There is some evidence that how a country collects taxes matters for economic growth. Figure 3, reproduced from Mendoza, Milesi-Ferretti, and Asea (1996), shows the correlation among the OECD countries between income taxes and economic growth (panels A and B) and consumption taxes and economic growth (panel C), over the period from 1965 to 1991. These scatter

FIGURE 3A.   Growth and the Capital Income Tax, OECD Countries

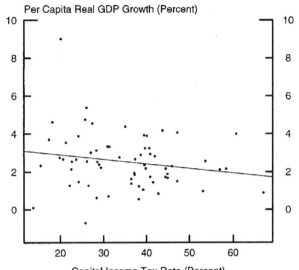

Capital Income Tax Rate (Percent)
Source: Mendoza, Milesi-Ferretti, Asea, 1996.

plots, largely confirmed in regression analysis, suggest that income taxation is more harmful to growth than broad-based consumption taxes.

It is useful to consider the growth effects of a major tax reform using these cross-country regression estimates. Suppose that marginal tax rates are cut by a uniform five percentage points and average tax rates are cut by 2.5 percent of GDP, leading to a (static) revenue loss of $185 billion annually. This hypothetical tax reform was chosen because it is on the outer fringe of politically feasible tax reform, losing more than twice as much revenue as the tax proposal supported by presidential candidate Robert Dole. Were such a plan enacted, the tax-to-GDP ratio would revert to levels last seen in 1958. As noted above, the estimated coefficient from Engen and Skinner (1992) that ignores possible changes in the supply of capital and labor implies an increase in long-term

growth rates of 0.18 percentage points. Including estimates of the responsiveness of investment to the marginal tax rate from Mendoza, Milesi-Ferretti, and Asea (1996) suggests that this hypothetical tax reduction would increase investment by 1.35 percent, boosting the predicted growth rate effect of the tax cut to 0.32 percentage points annually.[17]

SANDTRAPS IN CROSS-COUNTRY ECONOMETRIC ANALYSIS

To this point, we have been taking the results of the cross-country econometric studies at face value. Any empirical study must be treated with some caution; but, in many of the studies cited above, particularly the cross-country studies, one must be particularly careful in the interpretation of the coefficients (Levine and Renelt, 1992; Slemrod, 1995). We consider just four of these potential problems below.

FIGURE 3B.   Growth and the Labor Income Tax, OECD Countries

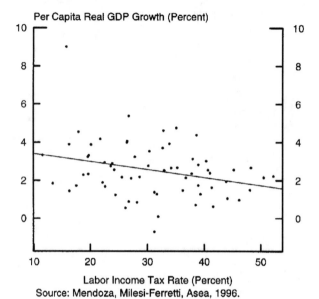

Source: Mendoza, Milesi-Ferretti, Asea, 1996.

FIGURE 3C.   Growth and the Consumption Tax, OECD Countries

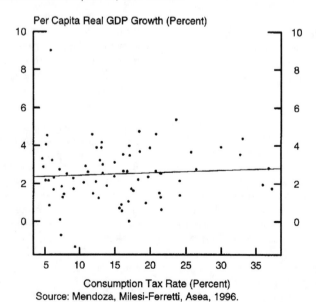

Source: Mendoza, Milesi-Ferretti, Asea, 1996.

First, studies of taxation and growth may find negative growth effects resulting from taxation, but it is more difficult to measure the potential benefits of the spending financed by the revenue collected. The combined impact of distortionary taxes and beneficial government expenditures may yield a net improvement in the workings of the private sector economy (e.g., Barro, 1990, 1991a,b). An example of the deleterious effects caused by the absence of government spending comes from the *World Development Report* (World Bank, 1988, p.144):

> According to the Nigerian Industrial De-velopment Bank (NIDB), frequent power outages and fluctuations in voltage af-fect almost every industrial enterprise in the country. To avoid production losses as well as damage to machinery and equipment, firms invest in genera-tors.... One large textile manufacturing enterprise estimates the depreciated capi-tal value of its electricity supply invest-ment as $400 per worker.... Typically, as much as 20 percent of the initial capital investment for new plants financed by the NIDB is spent on electric generators and boreholes.

That is, when the government of Nigeria did *not* provide the necessary electricity supply, private firms were forced to generate electricity on their own, and presumably at much higher cost. Clearly, a tax in Nigeria earmarked for (new) government expenditures on improving the electrical system would be likely to enhance economic growth even if the taxes distorted economic activity. The problem is that taxes are not necessarily earmarked to those expenditures most conducive to economic growth, either because of political "inefficiencies" or because of redistributional policies that may yield benefits for society but will not be reflected in robust GDP growth rates (Atkinson, 1995).[18] Thus, one

must be careful in interpreting the coefficients on tax and output growth studies to remember that these esti-mates reflect just one part—the costs—of a combined tax and expenditure system.

Second, one should be very wary of the data, particularly from developing countries with large agricultural or informal sectors where the measure-ment of income is difficult indeed.[19] Even in developed countries, it is well known that GDP measures suffer from biases and mismeasurement of produc-tivity in service sectors, for example.[20] Measuring "the" effective tax rate is even more difficult, given the wide variety of tax distortions, methods for measuring them, and variation across countries in administrative practices.

Third, there are real difficulties with reverse causation; one does not know whether regression coefficients reflect the impact of investment on GDP growth rates, for example, or the reverse influence of GDP growth rates on investment, or both effects com-bined (Blomstrom, Lipsey, and Zejan, 1996). Sometimes these biases creep in because of the way the regression variables are constructed. Suppose one wanted to estimate an explicitly short-term relationship between the change in the tax burden, typically measured as the ratio of tax revenue to GDP, and the percentage growth rate in GDP. Any positive measurement error (or short-term shock) in GDP will shift GDP growth rates up but also tend to shift the tax-to-GDP ratio down, thereby introducing a spurious negative bias in the estimated coefficient.[21] One can try to avoid such bias by introducing as explanatory variables the percentage growth rate in the level of taxation, or of government expenditures, rather than the change in the *ratio*, as above. In this case, the bias would go in the opposite direction, because countries that grow rapidly also tend to experience rapid growth in tax collection and in spending.[22] One approach for both of these problems is to use instrumental variables for changes in government spending and taxation (Engen and Skinner, 1992), although the problem still remains to find appropriate exogenous instruments.

Another "reverse causality" problem comes in deciding what factors to include on the right-hand side of a growth regression. Should one control for other factors such as inflation, political unrest, and the share of agriculture in total output? On the one hand, these are factors that could be spuriously correlated with tax policy, and one would clearly want to control for them. But, on the other hand, a shrinking share of agriculture in output, or political unrest, or inflation could be symptomatic of the underlying growth rate of the economy. During severe recessions, countries often resort to high inflation rates as a means of financing expenditures after their tax collection efforts have collapsed. This reverse causation makes it harder to argue that inflation "causes" poor economic growth, as well as making it difficult to interpret the coefficients on all other variables. In sum, reverse causality is really the Achilles' heel of the typical cross-country regression. Nearly every variable on the right-hand side of the regression is suspect.

Fourth, as noted by Slemrod (1995), countries may differ both in their tastes for government-sector spending (the demand side) and in their ability to raise tax revenue (the supply side). Suppose that more developed countries experience a lower cost of raising tax revenue,

perhaps because industrial production is much easier to tax than agricultural production. Then countries that grow quickly may also experience a more pronounced drop in their cost of raising tax revenue, which could in turn lead to more rapid growth in tax revenue. The researcher might well find a spurious positive correlation between tax rates and output growth. By the same token, countries that grow fast may exercise a greater taste for government spending (sometimes known as Wagner's law), leading to a shift to the right in the demand for government spending. As Slemrod points out, such a model would imply that, in a cross section of countries, there could be little correlation between output growth, government spending, and taxation.[23] Slemrod's point is therefore a cautionary one, that the regression coefficients one actually estimates may have little to do with the Solow-style production function written in equation 1 (see also Islam, 1995). But this point also suggests that, even if taxes affect growth rates adversely, cross-country regression models would be biased against detecting such effects.

SECTORAL STUDIES OF TAXATION AND GROWTH

Our third approach is to consider separately the effect of taxes on the disaggregated "micro" components in equation 1, such as labor supply, human capital, investment, and technological growth. We then combine these effects to arrive at an aggregate "bottom-up" measure of how our hypothetical tax reform—cutting marginal tax rates by five percentage points, and average rates by 2.5 percent—will affect output growth.[24] The advantage of this approach is a more accurate measure of how economic agents respond to tax incentives, often with data generated by natural experiments such as tax reform or other (exogenous) legislative change. There are two disadvantages to this strategy, however. First, we are unable to account for the spillover effects of both human and physical capital accumulation, as in the hypothesized correlation between the level of investment and technological innovation (Boskin, 1988). And, second, even with this disaggregated approach, there is virtually no empirical evidence on some key parameter values.

Change in the Labor Force

Consider first the effects of taxation on labor supply. The top panel of Figure 4 contains a graph that shows marginal labor income tax rates for the United States from 1965 to 1988 from Mendoza, Razin, and Tesar (1994) plotted against the average weekly hours for workers in private nonagricultural industries and also the civilian labor force participation rate. As labor income tax rates have increased, average weekly hours have declined. On the other hand, labor force participation has increased. (Although not shown, participation has generally increased for women while falling for men.) Thus, the effect of increased marginal labor taxes appears to be ambiguous based on this simple time-series examination.

A voluminous empirical literature has examined how taxes affect the labor supply of individuals within various demographic groups (e.g., Killingsworth, 1983; Hausman, 1985; MaCurdy, Green, and Paarsch, 1990; Triest, 1990, 1996; Bosworth and Burtless, 1992; Mariger, 1995; Eissa, 1996a,b). Generally, the results suggest quite modest labor supply effects of tax policy in the United States.[25] Most estimates suggest that both work hours and labor force participation for men are only mildly responsive to historically

experienced tax changes, and Heckman (1993) concludes that most of the evidence points to a relatively larger participation effect than hours effect. Estimated uncompensated tax elasticities are usually small, often in the range of zero to 0.1.[26] Recently, Eissa (1995) found that married women in high-income households are more responsive to tax changes—with tax elasticities in the range of 0.6 to 1—with approximately equal importance on hours and participation changes. However, working married women make up a relatively small part of the labor force and often have relatively tenuous ties to the labor force (Eissa, 1996a). Like men, unmarried women generally have similarly small labor supply responses to taxes (Eissa, 1996a).

For the purposes of our equation 1, we would like to know how tax policy affects the rate of change in quality-adjusted labor supply $\dot{m}$. Consider first short-term effects. If the labor supply elasticity is assumed to be 0.15 and marginal tax rates decline by five percentage points, then one might expect an increase of 0.75 percent in total hours worked. Assuming labor income comprises 75 percent of total output and the labor market transition is spread over a ten-year transition period, the net change in GDP growth rates over the short-term (ten-year) period would be 0.06 percent annually. In the long-term, however, only tax-induced changes in the accumulation of education or human capital more generally would affect the growth rate $\dot{m}$.

A number of empirical studies (e.g. Romer, 1990; Mankiw, Romer, and Weil, 1992; Judson, 1996) suggest that measures of human capital have statistically and economically important effects on economic growth, although

FIGURE 4.   Labor, Investment, and Factor Tax Rates, 1965–88

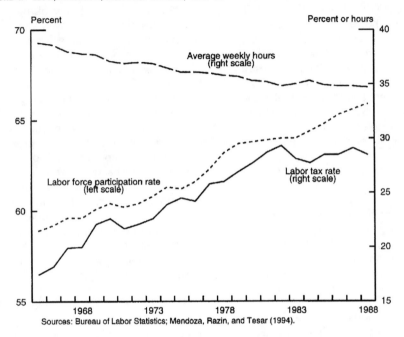

Sources: Bureau of Labor Statistics; Mendoza, Razin, and Tesar (1994).

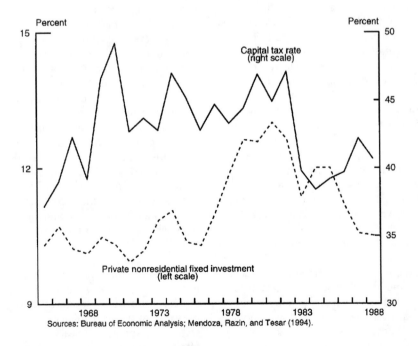

Sources: Bureau of Economic Analysis; Mendoza, Razin, and Tesar (1994).

some (e.g., Barro and Lee, 1992) estimate that the effect is quite small. However, the effect of taxes on human capital formation is quite uncertain. Theoretically, the effect is ambiguous and, not surprisingly, simulation analysis can lead to a variety of conclusions. Trostel (1993) simulates substantial long-term elasticities of human capital with respect to taxation; he suggests a long-term increase in human capital of 0.97 percent per one percentage point decrease in the marginal tax rate. Hence, our hypothetical five percentage point reduction in the marginal tax rate would be predicted to increase the stock of human capital by 4.8 percent. In equilibrium, maintaining that higher level of human capital requires an extra 4.8 percent additional net investment in human capital. Suppose that $\dot{m}_i$ were about three percent annually. The new level of equilibrium growth in human capital would rise to 3×1.048, or 3.14 percent annually.[27] Assuming the factor share coefficient is 0.75, the net effect on growth would be 0.10 percentage points.

Change in the Net Investment Rate

The bottom panel of Figure 4 shows marginal capital income tax rates for the United States from 1965 to 1988 from Mendoza, Razin, and Tesar (1994), plotted against private nonresidential fixed investment as a percentage of GDP. As has been noted before (e.g., Chirinko, 1993; Hassett and Hubbard, 1996), a simple examination of the time-series evidence suggests little relationship (and possibly a *positive* correlation) between investment and capital income tax rates. However, as before, this type of analysis is surely too simplistic.

Alternatively, Figure 5 shows a graph from data on the OECD countries comparing capital income taxes with investment rates, taken from Mendoza,

Milesi-Ferretti, and Asea (1996). There is a moderate negative correlation between tax rates and investment rates; more detailed regression analysis suggests that a 10 percentage point change in tax rates on profits could affect investment rates by at most two percentage points. It should be noted, however, that one shortcoming of these capital tax measures is that they use weighted statutory rather than effective rates, and thus they cannot account for the dramatic increase in effective marginal tax rates on capital during periods of inflation (e.g., King and Fullerton, 1984; Fullerton and Karayannis, 1993).

A number of recent studies (e.g., Auerbach and Hassett, 1991; Cummins, Hassett, and Hubbard, 1994, 1996; Chirinko, Fazzari, and Meyer, 1996) have found significant effects of tax policy on investment, suggesting a plausible range for the investment elasticity for changes in the user cost of capital in the range of 0.25 to 1. This finding is potentially important because, although Levine and Renelt (1992) find that almost all results are fragile in cross-country growth regressions, they do find a positive, robust correlation between growth and investment.

How might a change in the nature of investment decisions affect output growth? Suppose we adopt an investment elasticity of 0.5; then, a five percentage point drop in marginal tax rates should boost investment rates by 2.5 percent, or by about 0.4 percent of GDP. Assuming the net marginal product of capital is ten percent, output growth rates might be expected to grow by another 0.04 percentage points. We assume this boost in growth rate will be permanent, although in the Solow-style model, the growth effects will diminish over time.

FIGURE 5. Capital Income Taxation and Investment Rates, OECD Countries

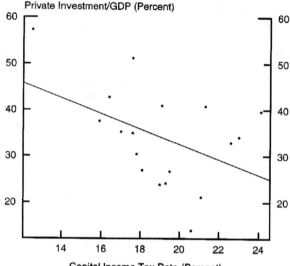

Private Investment/GDP (Percent)

Capital Income Tax Rate (Percent)
Source: Mendoza, Milesi-Ferretti, Asea, 1996.

One factor that could stifle tax-induced investment expansions is a lack of new saving to finance the increased investment. In an economy without foreign capital flows, the increased demand for investment would be financed by the additional supply of saving attracted by higher net interest rates. But simulation models (Engen, 1996) and empirical studies (Skinner and Feenberg, 1990) find little support for a strong responsiveness of personal saving to the interest rate (although, see Elmendorf, 1995, and references cited therein). The relevant source of financing for the extra investment may therefore be retained earnings of firms and foreign investors.[28] In any case, the investment elasticities gained from microlevel studies of firm investment behavior *already* reflect the additional cost or difficulty incurred by firms in providing additional financing for their investments, suggesting that the pure demand elasticities are even larger.

The Impact of Taxation on the Productivity Residual

Taxes can affect the output growth in another way, by discouraging innovations and economic organizations that result in increased levels of output, holding constant the supply of capital and labor. In other words, distortionary tax policy may permanently reduce the level of technological growth μ. Of course, by its nature, trying to determine whether the residual effect μ is caused by tax policy or by some other factor (of which there are always many candidates) is always problematic. Here, we consider two examples: the effects of tax policy on research and development and its impact on entrepreneurship.

Hall (1993) studied the impact of the tax credit on R&D spending using two sources of variation: changes in the tax code over the 1980s and differences in the taxable status of individual firms that affected their ability to take advantage of the credits. She found quite large effects: for every $1 billion lost in tax revenue, there was a $2 billion increase in R&D spending. Since R&D is about 2.5 percent of GDP (Nonneman and Vanhoudt, 1996), Hall's estimates imply that a five percentage point tax advantage to R&D would increase R&D spending by 0.25 percent of GDP. Using a rate of return to R&D spending of 30 percent (e.g., Griliches, 1988), the net effect would be a 0.075 increase in GDP growth rates.

A second possibility is that the hypothetical tax cut, for example, on capital gains, would stimulate entrepreneurship and innovation, which in turn would augment productivity growth. Poterba (1989) investigated the tax incentives faced by venture capitalists, and concluded that venture capital was only a small fraction of total capital income, so that tax cuts were a blunt sword to encourage high-tech industries. Furthermore, tax-exempt institutions provided a large fraction of start-up funds, and these institutions are not subject to income taxation.

A somewhat different picture emerges from a recent study quantifying labor hiring decisions by self-employed workers. Carroll et al. (1996) found that a six percentage point decline in the marginal tax rate of a (Schedule C) entrepreneur in the top tax bracket increased by 11 percent the likelihood of hiring at least one employee. However, the magnitude of these effects and their impact on aggregate employment are just not well enough understood to hazard a numerical estimate of their growth effects.

Summing Up

To complete our bottom-up analysis, we simply add the growth effects based on

changes in human capital, investment, and technological growth. The long-run effects of our hypothetical major tax reform are estimated to be 0.22 percentage points, while the short-term effects, which include the transitional effects of increased labor supply, increase to 0.28 percentage points.

Aside from the uncertainty inherent in nearly every empirical parameter used in these calculations, there are some further caveats. First, the calculation ignores the reduction in the sectoral distortion of capital and labor, which, in the section on cross-country regressions, was found to be important. And second, these estimates reflect a uniform reduction of five percentage points in marginal tax rates for all income-generating activities. It may be the case that tax cuts in capital gains, or tax credits for R&D, coupled with increases in consumption taxes, or a shift to a flat tax, could yield much stronger growth effects with less pronounced revenue effects. Nevertheless, these results suggest growth effects from major tax reform on the order of one-quarter of one percent per year.

LESSONS FOR POLICY

While the last word on taxation and economic growth certainly has not been heard, there are some lessons that we think can be taken from the evidence thus far.

First, we think that tax policy does affect economic growth. There is enough evidence linking taxation and output growth to make the reasonable inference that beneficial changes in tax policy can have modest effects on output growth. The implied effects from the "bottom-up" microlevel studies and the "top-down" cross-country regressions are quite close in magnitude: a major tax reform reducing all marginal rates by five percentage points and average tax rates by 2.5 percentage points is predicted to increase long-term growth rates by between 0.2 and 0.3 percentage points. Whether these effects on output growth are permanent (lasting forever) or transitory (lasting perhaps 10 to 15 years) is difficult to determine, both because our data sources do not extend for a lengthy period and because tax regimes themselves generally have such short half-lives.

Second, even these modest growth effects can have an important long-term impact on living standards. For example, suppose that an inefficient structure of taxation has, since 1960, retarded growth by 0.2 percent per annum. Accumulated over the past 36 years, the lower growth rate translates to a 7.5 percent lower level of GDP in 1996, or a net reduction in output of more than $500 billion *annually*. So the potential effects of tax policy, although difficult to detect in the time-series data, can be potentially very large in the long term.

Third, it appears highly unlikely that past tax reforms have been self-financing in the aggregate. There is evidence that tax changes focused on high-income taxpayers may be self-financing, perhaps because of changes in financial arrangements as well as shifts in economic activity (e.g., Feldstein, 1995; Feldstein and Feenberg, 1996). Of course, the historical record does not relate specifically to a flat tax or a consumption-based tax, which could have quite different effects, but we think it unlikely that any tax system could engender the long-term increases in growth rates necessary to completely pay for the tax cuts.

We want to be careful here about the context of our conclusions about taxation and growth in the policy debate over dynamic scoring. Typically, dynamic scoring of tax revenue in response to changes in the tax code involves two adjustments: one is the microeconomic change in the tax base, holding constant macroeconomic variables, and the other is the change in macroeconomic climate caused by the tax reform (Auerbach, 1996b). Here, we say nothing about the first, micro-economic effects, which could well be quite large (as in the short-term response of capital gains realization to changes in the capital gains tax cut). We simply claim that the second, macroeconomic, effect is likely to be quite modest.

Fourth, a major shortcoming with nearly all cross-country and time-series studies is the difficulty of measuring the marginal tax burden appropriately. The average tax rate does not reflect the marginal tax burdens hypothesized to affect economic decisions. Even stat-utory marginal tax rates may not ad-equately reflect the quite complex intertemporal incentive effects of a complex tax system. In many countries, tax policy is administered at the local level, where the tax collector may not even have a current copy of the relevant statutes.

Fifth, the composition of the tax system is probably as important for economic growth as is the absolute level of taxation. Countries that are able to mobilize tax resources through broad-based tax structures with efficient administration and enforcement will be likely to enjoy faster growth rates than countries with lower overall tax collec-tions assessed inefficiently. In short, the design of the tax system is likely to exert a modest, but cumulatively important, influence on long-term growth rates.

ENDNOTES

We are grateful for the very helpful comments from Darrel Cohen, Don Fullerton, William Gale, Kevin Hassett, Harvey Rosen, and Joel Slemrod. The opinions expressed in this paper are those of the authors and are not necessarily shared by the Board of Governors of the Federal Reserve System or other members of its staff.

1   The Kemp Commission was formally known as the National Commission on Economic Growth and Tax Reform (1996).

2   For examples, see Gravelle (1995) and Gale (1996).

3   The two coefficients are not measured in the same units because $\dot{k}_i$ is expressed as a ratio of GDP and $\dot{m}_i$ as a percentage change.

4   See Auerbach, Hassett, and Oliner (1994) for a discussion of how α corresponds to the (net or gross) return on capital.

5   David (1977) suggests that much of the 19th century in the United States was characterized by a transition from a low to a high capital-intensity economy. On the other hand, King and Rebelo (1993) find that traditional Solow growth models generate implausible transition paths in shifting from one equilibrium to another.

6   There is an extensive simulation literature showing transitional gains in economic efficiency using the framework of dynamic computable general equilibrium models; see Ballard et al. (1985), Auerbach and Kotlikoff (1987), Fullerton and Rogers (1993), Auerbach (1996a), and Engen and Gale (1996). Like the endogenous growth literature, the results from such studies often depend on the structure of the simulation model. In a life cycle model with perfect certainty and perfect foresight, Auerbach and Kotlikoff (1987) and Auerbach (1996a) find quite dramatic shifts in some aggregate variables (such as saving rate) during the transition to a new steady state. In a model with uncertainty about future earnings, Engen and Gale (1996) find more moderate shifts in output and saving during the transition to a new tax regime.

7   Stokey and Rebelo (1995) provide an excellent survey of this literature and explain why the theoretical simulation models differ so dramatically in their implications for growth.

8   For a discussion of these issues, see Alm (1996), Slemrod (1990, 1994, 1995), and Auerbach and Slemrod (1997).

9   Moreover, only eight percent said they had even postponed investment. Also see Holland (1969) for survey evidence on the labor supply of highly paid executives.

10 Specifically, the survey question asked whether the tax cut would reduce or increase the "hurdle rate" or the minimum rate of return required before approving internal corporate investments.

11 Including earlier periods is complicated by the fact that revised GDP figures are currently only available on a consistent basis from 1959. Also, Lindsey (1990) notes that the Coolidge–Mellon cuts in the 1920s affected only the top quarter of households as most U.S. citizens paid no income tax during that time.

12 During 1971–79, the economy expanded at an annual average rate of 3.5 percent including the recession years of 1974–75. Growth averaged 3.2 percent over the 1982–89 period.

13 Sorting out the difference between supply-side and demand-side expansions is important, since demand-side expansions tend to deflate later into recessions, while supply-side shifts correspond to permanent improvements in the productive capacity of the economy.

14 We are grateful to the authors for making this data on tax rates at different income percentiles available to us. Note that these tax rates only reflect the federal individual income tax and do not incorporate federal corporate income, earned income tax credit, payroll, or state income taxes.

15 An alternative measure of the tax distortion is the top statutory federal income tax rate. The top rate reached its zenith during the 1950s and early 1960s, when it was 91 percent. Since then it has bounced steadily downward to 28 percent, briefly, in 1988, with a jump back to 39.6 percent by 1993. (See Pechman, 1987, for a historical summary of most of this time period.) The economic expansion of the 1980s coincided with a marked decline in top marginal tax rates, leading some to conjecture a causal relationship between the cuts in top marginal rates and the economic expansion. However, taking the long view (circa 1960–88), a general decline in the top marginal rate occurred as average GDP growth rates tended to *fall*.

16 In the King and Fullerton study, based on 1980 data, West Germany exhibited the least degree of intersectoral distortion, trailed closely by the United States. In the McKinsey study, the factors identified as important—the motivation of managers to show profits, for example—are extremely difficult to quantify across countries on a consistent basis. Furthermore, as Kevin Hassett pointed out to us, the productivity of the capital stock may not necessarily be an indicator of better organization. In the absence of perfect world capital markets, a country may exhibit a higher productivity of capital because capital is scarce (that is, the capital-labor ratio is low). In this case, an increase in the capital stock might *lower* capital productivity but make the economy better off.

17 The investment effect is calculated using the first equation from Table 4 in Mendoza, Milesi-Ferretti, and Asea (1996), assuming that marginal labor and capital taxes are both cut by five percentage

points, while the output effect assumes a marginal product of capital equal to 0.10 (Auerbach, Hassett, and Oliner, 1994.) Unfortunately, we have no estimates from cross-country equations on labor supply effects.

[18] Empirical evidence from a cross section of states suggests either that government spending yields no positive growth effects (Holtz-Eakin, 1994) or that only educational spending yields positive effects (Evans and Karras, 1994). Aschauer (1989) argues that the productivity effects are quite large.

[19] The commonly used Summers and Heston (1991) data include a grade, ranging from A to D, that summarizes the authors' estimate of the reliability of the data. Engen and Skinner (1992) weighted their estimates with a numerical scale of this reliability; results were similar, although standard errors were smaller.

[20] For a nontechnical discussion, see "The Real Truth About the Economy: Are Government Statistics Just So Much Pulp Fiction?" (*Business Week*, November 7, 1994).

[21] For example, Grier and Tullock (1989) find a negative correlation between output growth and the growth of government expenditures, although they do not interpret the correlation as reflecting reverse causation.

[22] Ram's (1986) estimated positive correlation between the growth in government spending and output growth appears to be an example of this problem.

[23] The analogy is to market prices for competitive goods; regressing price on quantity (or conversely) tells the researcher nothing about the nature of the supply curve or of the demand curve without further identifying variables.

[24] This is the approach followed by Agell, Englund, and Södersten (1996) in considering the Swedish tax reform of the early 1990s. The bottom-up and top-down terminology is attributed to Slemrod (1995).

[25] Lindsey (1987), Navratil (1994), Auten and Carroll (1995), Feldstein (1995), and Slemrod (1996) find evidence of behavioral responses to tax reforms by documenting increases in reported taxable incomes following reductions in tax rates during the 1980s. However, it is difficult in these analyses of taxpayers' income to separate the effects of "real" responses—such as changes in labor supply—from the effects of compensation, timing, and reporting responses.

[26] We focus here on uncompensated elasticities, because we are considering a tax cut. However, if government expenditures are highly substitutable with market consumption goods or if Ricardian equivalence holds, one might prefer to use compensated elasticities, which are generally higher.

[27] Strictly speaking, in the growth accounting framework in equation 1, the percentage growth rate $\dot{m}_i$ will be unaffected by the higher level of human capital because human capital growth is defined in percentage terms. We instead consider an alternative renormalization in which the denominator is the pre-tax-cut level of human capital.

[28] Government tax policy could also be used to encourage saving through targeted saving programs such as IRAs or 401(k)s. While there is some debate about their effectiveness in increasing saving (see the Fall 1996 issue of the *Journal of Economic Perspectives*), the macroeconomic effects of these programs are probably not large given their modest size relative to GDP.

REFERENCES

Agell, Jonas, Peter Englund, and Jan Södersten. "Tax Reform of the Century—the Swedish Experiment." *National Tax Journal* 49 No. 4 (December, 1996): 641–62.

Alm, James. "What is an 'Optimal' Tax System?" *National Tax Journal* 49 No. 1 (March, 1996): 117–33.

Aschauer, David Alan. "Is Public Expenditure Productive?" *Journal of Monetary Economics* 23 No. 2 (March, 1989): 177–200.

Atkinson, Anthony B. "The Welfare State and Economic Performance." *National Tax Journal* 48 No. 2 (June, 1995): 171–98.

Auerbach, Alan. "Tax Reform, Capital Allocation, Efficiency, and Growth." In *Economic Effects of Fundamental Tax Reform*, edited by Henry Aaron and William Gale. Washington, D.C.: The Brookings Institution, 1996a.

Auerbach, Alan. "Dynamic Revenue Estimation." *Journal of Economic Perspectives* 10 No. 1 (Winter, 1996b): 141–58.

Auerbach, Alan, and Kevin Hassett. "Recent U.S. Investment Behavior and the Tax Reform Act of 1986: A Disaggregate View." *Carnegie-Rochester Conference Series on Public Policy* 35 (Autumn, 1991): 185–215.

Auerbach, Alan, Kevin Hassett, and Stephen Oliner. "Reassessing the Social Returns to Equipment Investment." *Quarterly Journal of Economics* 109 No. 3 (August, 1994): 789–802.

Auerbach, Alan, and Laurence Kotlikoff. *Dynamic Fiscal Policy.* Cambridge: Cambridge University Press, 1987.

Auerbach, Alan, and Joel Slemrod. "The Economic Effects of the Tax Reform Act of 1986." *Journal of Economic Literature* 35 No. 1 (forthcoming, March, 1997).

Auten, Gerald, and Robert Carroll. "Taxpayer Behavior and the 1986 Tax Reform Act." U.S. Treasury Department, Office of Tax Analysis. Mimeo, 1995.

Ballard, Charles L., Don Fullerton, John Shoven, and John Whalley. *A General Equilibrium Model for Tax Policy*. Chicago: The University of Chicago Press, 1985.

Barro, Robert J. "Government Spending in a Simple Model of Endogenous Growth." *Journal of Political Economy* 98 No. 5 (October, 1990, part 2): S103–25.

Barro, Robert J. "Economic Growth in a Cross-Section of Countries." *Quarterly Journal of Economics* 104 (May, 1991a): 407–44.

Barro, Robert J. "A Cross-Country Study of Growth, Saving and Government." In *National Saving and Economic Performance*, edited by B. Douglas Bernheim and John Shoven. Chicago: University of Chicago Press and National Bureau of Economic Research, 1991b.

Barro, Robert J., and Jong-Wha Lee. "International Comparisons of Educational Attainment, 1960–1985." Harvard University. Mimeo, 1992.

Blomstrom, Magnus, Robert E. Lipsey, and Mario Zejan. "Is Fixed Investment the Key to Economic Growth?" *Quarterly Journal of Economics* 111 No. 1 (February, 1996): 269–76.

Boskin, Michael. "Tax Policy and Economic Growth: Lessons from the 1980s." *Journal of Economic Perspectives* 2 No. 4 (Fall, 1988): 71–97.

Bosworth, Barry, and Gary Burtless. "Effects of Tax Reform on Labor Supply, Investment, and Saving." *Journal of Economic Perspectives* 6 No. 1 (Winter, 1992): 3–26.

Carroll, Robert, Douglas Holtz-Eakin, Mark Rider, and Harvey S. Rosen. "Income Taxes and Entrepreneur's Use of Labor." Working Paper No. 32, Center for Economic Policy Studies, Princeton: Princeton University, July, 1996.

Chirinko, Robert S. "Business Fixed Investment Spending: Modeling Strategies, Empirical Results, and Policy Implications." *Journal of Economic Literature* 31 No. 4 (December, 1993): 1875–1911.

Chirinko, Robert S., Steven M. Fazzari, and Andrew P. Meyer. "Business Investment and the User Cost of Capital: New Evidence from U.S. Panel Data." Emory University, Atlanta, GA. Mimeo, 1996.

Corner, D. C., and Alan Williams. "The Sensitivity of Business to Initial and Investment Allowances." *Economica* 32 No. 125 (February, 1965): 32–47.

Cummins, Jason, Kevin Hassett, and R. Glenn Hubbard. "A Reconsideration of Investment Behavior Using Tax Reforms as Natural Experiments." *Brookings Papers on Economic Activity* 2 (1994): 1–74.

Cummins, Jason, Kevin Hassett, and R. Glenn Hubbard. "Have Tax Reforms Affected Investment?" In *Tax Policy and the Economy*, Vol. 9, edited by James Poterba. Cambridge, MA: MIT Press, 1995.

Cummins, Jason, Kevin Hassett, and R. Glenn Hubbard. "Tax Reforms and Investment: A Cross-Country Comparison." *Journal of Public Economics* (forthcoming, 1996).

David, Paul. "Invention and Accumulation in America's Economic Growth: A Nineteenth Century Parable." In *Industrial Organization, National Priorities, and Economic Development*, edited by Karl Brunner and Allan Meltzer. Amsterdam: North–Holland, 1977.

Dowrick, Steve. "Estimating the Impact of Government Consumption on Growth: Growth Accounting and Optimizing Models." Australian National University. Mimeo, October, 1992.

Easterly, William, and Sergio Rebelo. "Fiscal Policy and Economic Growth: An Empirical Investigation." *Journal of Monetary Economics* 32 No. 3 (December, 1993): 417–58.

Eissa, Nada. "Taxation and Labor Supply of Married Women: The Tax Reform Act of 1986 as a Natural Experiment." NBER Working Paper No. 5023. Cambridge, MA: National Bureau of Economic Research, 1995.

Eissa, Nada. "Tax Reforms and Labor Supply." In *Tax Policy and the Economy*, Vol. 10, edited by James Poterba. Cambridge, MA: MIT Press, 1996a.

Eissa, Nada. "Labor Supply and the Economic Recovery Act of 1981." In *Empirical Foundations of Household Taxation*, edited by Martin Feldstein and James Poterba. Chicago: University of Chicago Press, 1996b.

Elmendorf, Douglas. "The Response of Household Saving to Changes in Interest Rates." Federal Reserve Board, Washington, D.C. Mimeo, 1995.

Engen, Eric. "Precautionary Saving and the Structure of Taxation." Federal Reserve Board, Washington, D.C. Mimeo, 1996.

Engen, Eric, and William G. Gale. "The Effects of Fundamental Tax Reform on Saving." In *Economic Effects of Fundamental Tax Reform*, edited by Henry Aaron and William Gale. Washington, D.C.: The Brookings Institution, 1996.

Engen, Eric, and Jonathan Skinner. "Fiscal Policy and Economic Growth." NBER Working Paper No. 4223. Cambridge, MA: National Bureau of Economic Research, 1992.

Evans, Paul, and Georgios Karras. "Are Government Activities Productive? Evidence from a Panel of U.S. States." *The Review of Economics and Statistics* 76 No. 1 (February, 1994): 1–11.

Feldstein, Martin. "The Effect of Marginal Tax Rates on Taxable Income: A Panel Study of the 1986 Tax Reform Act." *Journal of Political Economy* 103 No. 3 (June, 1995): 551–72.

Feldstein, Martin, and Douglas W. Elmendorf. "Budget Deficits, Tax Incentives, and Inflation: A Surprising Lesson from the 1983–84 Recovery." In *Tax Policy and the Economy* 3, edited by Lawrence Summers. Cambridge, MA: MIT Press, 1989.

Feldstein, Martin, and Daniel Feenberg. "The Effect of Increased Tax Rates on Taxable Income and Economic Efficiency: A Preliminary Analysis of the 1993 Tax Rate Increases." In *Tax Policy and the Economy* 10, edited by James Poterba. Cambridge, MA: MIT Press, 1996.

Fullerton, Don, and Marios Karayannis. "United States." In *Tax Reform and the Cost of Capital: An International Comparison*, edited by Dale Jorgenson and Ralph Landau. Washington, D.C.: The Brookings Institution, 1993.

Fullerton, Don, and Diane Lim Rogers. *Who Bears the Lifetime Tax Burden?* Washington, D.C.: The Brookings Institution, 1993.

Gale, William. "The Kemp Commission and the Future of Tax Reform." *Tax Notes* 70 No. 6 (February 5, 1996): 717–29.

Gravelle, Jane. "The Flat Tax and Other Proposals: Who Will Bear the Tax Burden?" *Tax Notes* 69 No. 12 (December 18, 1995): 1517–27.

Grier, Kevin B., and Gordon Tullock. "An Empirical Analysis of Cross-National Economic Growth." *Journal of Monetary Economics* 24 No. 2 (September, 1989): 259–76.

Griliches, Zvi. "Productivity Puzzles and R&D: Another Nonexplanation." *Journal of Economic Perspectives* 2 No. 4 (Fall, 1988): 9–22.

Hakkio, Craig, Mark Rush, and Timothy Schmidt. "The Marginal Income Tax Rate Schedule from 1930 to 1990." *Journal of Monetary Economics* (forthcoming, 1996).

Hall, Bronwyn. "R&D Tax Policy During the 1980s: Success or Failure?" In *Tax Policy and the Economy* 7," edited by James Poterba. Cambridge, MA: MIT Press, 1993.

Hall, Robert, and Alvin Rabushka. *The Flat Tax.* 2d ed. Stanford: The Hoover Institution Press, 1995.

Harberger, Arnold C. "The Incidence of the Corporation Income Tax." *Journal of Political Economy* 70 No. 3 (June, 1962): 215–40.

Harberger, Arnold C. "Efficiency Effects of Taxes on Income From Capital." In *Effects of Corporation Income Tax*, edited by Marian Krzyzaniak. Detroit: Wayne State University Press, 1966.

Hassett, Kevin A., and R. Glenn Hubbard. "Tax Policy and Investment." NBER Working Paper No. 5683. Cambridge, MA: National Bureau of Economic Research, 1996.

Hausman, Jerry. "Taxes and Labor Supply." In *Handbook of Public Economics*, edited by Alan Auerbach and Martin Feldstein. Amsterdam: Elsevier, 1985.

Heckman, James. "What Has Been Learned About Labor Supply in the Past Twenty Years?" *American Economic Review* 83 (May, 1993): 116–21.

Helms, L. Jay. "The Effect of State and Local Taxes on Economic Growth: A Time Series-Cross Section Approach." *Review of Economics and Statistics* 67 No. 4 (November, 1985): 574–82.

Holland, Daniel. "The Effect of Taxation on Effort: Some Results for Business Executives." In *Proceedings of the Sixty-Second Annual Conference on Taxation*, 428–517. Columbus: National Tax Association–Tax Institute of America, 1969.

Holtz-Eakin, Douglas. "Public Sector Capital and the Productivity Puzzle." *Review of Economics and Statistics* 76 No. 1 (February, 1994): 12–21.

Islam, Nazrul. "Growth Empirics: A Panel Data Approach." *Quarterly Journal of Economics* 110 No. 4 (November, 1995): 1127–70.

Jones, Larry E., Rodolfo E. Manuelli, and Peter E. Rossi. "Optimal Taxation in Models of Endogenous Growth." *Journal of Political Economy* 101 No. 3 (June, 1993): 485–517.

Judson, Ruth. "Do Human Capital Coefficients Make Sense? A Puzzle and Some Answers." Federal Reserve Board, FEDS Working Paper No. 96-13. Washington, D.C.: Finance and Economic Discussion Series, 1996.

Killingsworth, Mark. *Labor Supply.* Cambridge: Cambridge University Press, 1983.

King, Mervyn, and Don Fullerton, eds. *The Taxation of Income from Capital: A Comparative Study of the United States, United Kingdom, Sweden, and West Germany.* Chicago: University of Chicago Press, 1984.

King, Robert G., and Sergio Rebelo. "Public Policy and Economic Growth: Developing Neoclassical Implications." *Journal of Political Economy* 98 No. 5 (October, 1990, part 2): S126–50.

King, Robert G., and Sergio Rebelo. "Transitional Dynamics and Economic Growth in the Neoclassical Model." *American Economic Review* 83 No. 4 (September, 1993): 908–31.

Koester, Reinhard B., and Roger C. Kormendi. "Taxation, Aggregate Activity and Economic Growth: Cross Country Evidence on Some Supply-Side Hypotheses." *Economic Inquiry* 27 No. 3 (July, 1989): 367–86.

Levine, Ross, and David Renelt. "A Sensitivity Analysis of Cross-Country Growth Regressions." *American Economic Review* 82 No. 4 (September, 1992): 942–63.

Lindsey, Lawrence. "Individual Taxpayer Response to Tax Cuts, 1982–1984: With Implications for the Revenue Maximizing Tax Rate." *Journal of Public Economics* 33 No. 2 (July, 1987): 173–206.

Lindsey, Lawrence. *The Growth Experiment.* New York: Basic Books, 1990.

Lucas, Robert E. "Supply-Side Economics: An Analytical Review." *Oxford Economic Papers* 42 No. 2 (April, 1990): 293–316.

MaCurdy, Thomas, David Green, and Harry Paarsch. "Assessing Empirical Approaches for Analyzing Taxes and Labor Supply." *Journal of Human Resources* 25 No. 3 (Summer, 1990): 415–90.

Mankiw, N. Gregory, David Romer, and David N. Weil. "A Contribution to the Empirics of Economic Growth." *Quarterly Journal of Economics* 107 (May, 1992): 407–38.

Mariger, Randall. "Labor Supply and the Tax Reform Act of 1986: Evidence from Panel Data." Federal Reserve Board, Finance and Economics Discussion Series Paper 95-34. Washington, D.C.: Federal Reserve Board, 1995.

McKinsey Global Institute; with assistance from Axel Borsch-Supan and our Advisory Committee, Robert Solow, Benjamin Friedman, Zvi Griliches, and Ted Hall. *Capital Productivity.* Washington, D.C.: McKinsey and Company, 1996.

Mendoza, Enrique G., Assaf Razin, and Linda L. Tesar. "Effective Tax Rates in Macroeconomics: Cross-Country Estimates of Tax Rates on Factor Incomes and Consumption." *Journal of Monetary Economics* 34 No. 3 (December, 1994): 297–324.

Mendoza, Enrique G., Gian Maria Milesi-Ferretti, and Patrick Asea. "On the Ineffectiveness of Tax Policy to Alter Long-Run Growth: Harberger's Superneutrality Conjecture." Federal Reserve Board of Governors. Mimeo, 1996.

National Commission on Economic Growth and Tax Reform (NCR). *Unleashing America's Potential.* Washington, D.C.: NCR, 1996.

Navratil, John. "Evidence of Individual Taxpayer Behavior from Panel Tax Return Data." Harvard University. Mimeo, 1994.

Nonneman, Walter, and Patrick Vanhoudt. "A Further Augmentation of the Solow Model and the Empirics of Economic Growth for OECD Countries." *Quarterly Journal of Economics* 111 No. 3 (August, 1996): 943–53.

Pechman, Joseph A. *Federal Tax Policy.* 5th ed. Washington, D.C.: The Brookings Institution, 1987.

Poterba, James. "Venture Capital and Capital Gains Taxation." In *Tax Policy and the Economy*, Vol. 3, edited by Lawrence Summers, 47–68. Cambridge, MA: The MIT Press, 1989.

Poterba, James M., and Lawrence H. Summers. "A CEO Survey of U.S. Companies' Time Horizons and Hurdle Rates." *Sloan Management Review* 37 No. 1 (Fall, 1995): 43–53.

Ram, Rati. "Government Size and Economic Growth: A New Framework and Some Evidence from Cross-Section and Time-Series Data." *American Economic Review* 76 No. 1 (March, 1986): 191–203.

Romer, Paul M. "Human Capital and Growth: Theory and Evidence." *Carnegie-Rochester Conference Series on Public Policy* 32 (Spring, 1990): 251–86.

Romer, Paul M. "Increasing Returns and Long-Run Growth." *Journal of Political Economy* 94 No. 5 (October, 1986): 1002–37.

Skinner, Jonathan. "Taxation and Output Growth in Africa." Policy, Planning and Research Working Paper 73. Washington, D.C.: The World Bank, August, 1988.

Skinner, Jonathan, and Daniel Feenberg. "The Effect of the 1986 Tax Reform Act on Personal Saving." In *Do Taxes Matter?: The Impact of the Tax Reform Act of 1986*, edited by Joel Slemrod, 50–79. Cambridge, MA: MIT Press, 1990.

Slemrod, Joel. "The Economic Impact of the Tax Reform Act of 1986." In *Do Taxes Matter?: The Impact of the Tax Reform Act of 1986*, edited by Joel Slemrod, 1–12. Cambridge, MA: MIT Press, 1990.

Slemrod, Joel. "On the High-Income Laffer Curve." In *Tax Progressivity and Income Inequality*, edited by Joel Slemrod, 177–210. Cambridge: Cambridge University Press, 1994.

Slemrod, Joel. "What Do Cross-Country Studies Teach About Government Involvement, Prosperity and Economic Growth?" *Brookings Papers on Economic Activity* 2 (1995): 373–431.

Slemrod, Joel. "High-Income Families and the Tax Changes of the 1908s: The Anatomy of

Behavioral Response." In *Empirical Foundations of Household Taxation*, edited by Martin Feldstein and James Poterba, 169–188. Chicago: University of Chicago Press and NBER, 1996.

Solow, Robert M. "A Contribution to the Theory of Economic Growth." *Quarterly Journal of Economics* 70 No. 1 (February, 1956): 65–94.

Stokey, Nancy L, and Sergio Rebelo. "Growth Effects of Flat-Rate Taxes." *Journal of Political Economy* 103 No. 3 (June, 1995): 519–50.

Summers, Robert, and Heston, Alan. "The Penn World Table (Mark 5): An Expanded Set of International Comparisons, 1950–1988." *Quarterly Journal of Economics* 106 No. 2 (May, 1991): 327–68.

The World Bank. *World Development Report 1988*. Oxford: Oxford University Press, 1988.

Triest, Robert. "The Effect of Income Taxation on Labor Supply in the United States." *Journal of Human Resources* 25 No. 3 (Summer, 1990): 491–516.

Triest, Robert. "Fundamental Tax Reform and Labor Supply." In *Economic Effects of Fundamental Tax Reform*, edited by Henry Aaron and William Gale. Washington, D.C.: The Brookings Institution, 1996.

Trostel, Philip A. "The Effect of Taxation on Human Capital." *Journal of Political Economy* 101 No. 2 (April, 1993): 327–50.

TAX REFORM OF THE CENTURY—THE SWEDISH EXPERIMENT

JONAS AGELL, [*] **PETER ENGLUND,** [*]
& JAN SÖDERSTEN [*]

Abstract - *What can changes in tax structure accomplish? The Swedish tax reform of 1991 is the most far-reaching reform in any industrialized country in the postwar period. It represents a thorough application of a strategy of rate cuts cum base broadening, and it has affected a myriad of economic incentives in a more or less substantial way. This paper reviews the lessons from a major evaluation effort, sponsored by the Swedish government and involving a large number of researchers.*

INTRODUCTION

Sweden might be best known as the home of film director Ingemar Bergman and—for better or for worse—as the prototype welfare state. What might be less well known is that Sweden recently implemented the most far-reaching tax reform in any western industrialized country. Although Sweden was a latecomer to the bandwagon of world-wide tax reforms of the 1980s, with the U.S. Tax Reform Act of 1986 (TRA 86) as a celebrated example, the architects of

[*]Department of Economics, Uppsala University, S-751 20 Uppsala, Sweden.

the Swedish tax reform of 1991 (TR 91) applied the strategy of rate cuts cum base broadening in an unusually thorough manner. Under the catchy slogan "tax reform of the century," marginal income taxes were dramatically lowered and various tax shelters eliminated. According to prereform estimates, the rate cuts entailed a revenue loss on the order of six percent of gross domestic product (GDP). Measured in this way, TRA 86 stands out as a relatively modest endeavor, with a projected revenue loss of one to two percent of GDP due to rate cuts.

It goes without saying that sharply reduced income tax rates represent a sensitive political issue, particularly so in a country where tax policy used to center on the idea that a steeply progressive income tax is an efficient way of transferring resources from the rich to the poor. To understand why TR 91 gathered wide political support, both external and internal considerations are important. The integration of world capital markets during the 1980s implied that it became more difficult to tax capital income at rates that differed very much from those applicable elsewhere. Also, the major changes in the tax structures of a number of other countries provided an impulse. However, it would be wrong to view TR 91 as a mechanical response to these developments. After all, Ronald Reagan's tax policy is not a very natural source of inspiration for Sweden's Social Democrats. While many of the arguments of the proponents of TR 91 bear a striking resemblance to those put forth in the context of TRA 86,[1] their origin should be traced primarily to the domestic debate.

As early as 1978, Nobel Laureate Gunnar Myrdal complained that high marginal tax rates had turned Sweden into a "nation of wanglers." According to Myrdal (1978), the progressive income tax had created such strong incentives for high-income individuals to exploit various tax avoidance schemes (including outright tax fraud) that the Swedish tax system no longer redistributed income. Myrdal's view carried particular weight since he belonged to the political left. Parties more to the right, and quite a few economists, had for long warned that the income tax created large disincentive effects. But Myrdal seemed to suggest that also those in favor of egalitarian outcomes, and concerned less about efficiency, had reason to reconsider the role of the progressive income tax. Although Myrdal offered no hard facts to substantiate his claim, the perception that the rich could avoid their fair share of the tax burden was probably instrumental in softening the Social Democrat's traditional resistance to proposals involving lower marginal tax rates.

But there were also other influential arguments. Since the late 1970s, when inflation reached double-digit levels, there was widespread concern that the tax system promoted the wrong kind of investments. Investments in noncorporate assets, and housing in particular, were given preferential tax treatment. Many Swedish economists argued, as did many of their colleagues in the United States, that the uneven playing field created substantial efficiency losses. The nonuniform treatment of the returns on different assets also created considerable scope for a number of straightforward tax arbitrage operations, more often than not involving purchases of low-taxed assets with borrowed money. This spelled bad news for the tax collector—for several years, households claimed tax deductions to such an extent that the net revenue from taxes on personal capital income was negative.

The corporate income tax attracted similar criticism. A variety of tax allowances, and a high statutory tax rate, were once part of a deliberate strategy of stimulating firms to plow back profits into their businesses. The idea was that large and expanding firms were good for growth. During the 1980s, there was a shift in emphasis. According to the new view, the corporate tax breaks were an obstacle to efficient capital allocation. The high rates of profit retention required to take advantage of the various tax allowances created a capital lock-in effect, which prevented necessary structural readjustments. Finally, toward the mid-1980s, an overheated economy and concerns about an acute labor shortage seemed to give added weight to the argument that there was an urgent need to strengthen labor supply incentives.

TR 91 was presented as a way of remedying all of these problems in one giant stroke. According to its proponents, the reform would avoid the classical goal conflict between efficiency and income distribution. In spite of drastic marginal tax cuts, high-income earners were not supposed to gain relative to other groups. As a result of a generally more efficient economy, all strata in society should gain. Moreover, total tax revenue was not supposed to decrease—the Swedish tax take should remain the highest in the world. The revenue gains from broader tax bases were to make up for the losses from lower tax rates.

What can changes in tax structure accomplish? Did the proverbial free lunch materialize? This paper reviews the lessons from a major evaluation effort, commissioned by the Swedish government and involving a large number of foreign and Swedish researchers.[2] The next section gives a brief outline of TR 91. We proceed by discussing the considerable difficulty in evaluating a tax reform in the midst of a very sharp recession. We review the evidence on behavioral responses, and we seek to identify areas where TR 91 mattered the most. We also present an assessment of the overall effects on efficiency and equity. Our concluding remarks draw some lessons for tax reform more generally.

WHAT TR 91 IMPLIED

Prereform estimates presented by the Ministry of Finance indicated that the rate cuts for the personal income tax alone, together with additional outlays for housing and child allowances to cushion the distributional effects of the reform, would reduce revenues by an amount equivalent to between six and seven percent of GDP. Nearly 40 percent of this loss was to be recouped through a new system of taxing capital income. A broadening of the value added tax (VAT) (of 23 percent) to include goods and services previously exempted, or granted lower rates, would yield additional revenue on the order of 30 percent of the budget loss, while almost

15 percent was to be financed by elimination of loopholes and preferential rules for taxing earned income. Enlarged tax bases due to a generally more efficient economy would offset roughly five percent of the revenue loss. The reform hence brought a major reallocation of the total tax burden away from earned income to consumption and to individual capital income (including the return to housing).

A noteworthy feature of TR 91 was the move away from the principle of global income taxation toward a *dual income tax*, by introducing separate tax schedules for earned income and capital income.[3] The new taxation of earned income meant that almost 85 percent of the income earners would pay only local income tax. In 1991, the countrywide average of the local income tax was 31 percent. A national income tax of 20 percent was imposed for incomes exceeding 185,000 kronor (equivalent to U.S. $33,500, at the 1991 exchange rate), which meant that the top marginal tax rate on earned income was set at 51 percent. TR 91 implied that the marginal rate would be reduced by between 24 and 27 percentage points for large groups of full-time employees (Figure 1).

The new proportional capital income tax was set at 30 percent, and levied on dividends, interest income, and both long- and short-term realized nominal capital gains. As before, interest on all kinds of debt would be fully deductible. A stated purpose of the separate capital income tax was to reduce the value of interest deductions and to limit the scope for tax avoidance in various forms.

Although the initial ambition of TR 91 was to levy a uniform VAT (of an unchanged 23 percent) on all commercial turnover of goods and services,

FIGURE 1.   Marginal Tax Rate 1989–91 at Different Levels of Tax Assessed Income; 1 SEK = 0.181 U.S. Dollars (1991)

percent

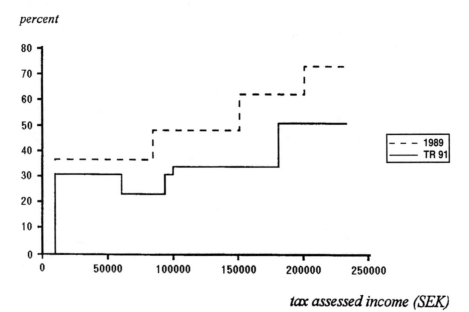

tax assessed income (SEK)

several areas have remained tax exempt. These include various cultural and social services and housing rents. Housing costs have risen as a result of the tax reform, however, partly because the VAT was broadened to include real estate maintenance, heating, and electricity. Owner-occupiers were further affected by the inclusion of expenditures on housing investment in the new VAT. Before TR 91, the tax was 13 percent.

The changes in the corporate income tax were no less dramatic. The statutory tax rate was reduced from 57 to 30 percent. In order to maintain an unchanged level of revenue from the corporate tax, the rate reduction was combined with substantial broadening of the base. The possibility to under-value inventories for tax purposes was eliminated, and the investment funds system, introduced in the mid 1950s as the main tool of a countercyclical fiscal policy, was discontinued.

Even a casual comparison reveals obvious similarities between TRA 86 and TR 91. Both reforms were far reaching with the same intent of reducing various behavioral distortions from the tax systems. The approach to tax reform was similar, combining substantial tax cuts with a broadening of the base. TR 91 was much larger in scope, both in terms of revenue effects from the rate cuts and by covering a wider range of tax instruments. Obviously, these differences partly reflect the vast difference between Sweden and the United States in the financing require-ments for the public sector. As a proportion of GDP, the total tax yield was almost 56 percent in Sweden in 1989, compared to 30 percent for the United States. However, the relative importance of different taxes, summa-rized in Table 1, is broadly similar. In both countries, there is a heavy reliance on receipts from the personal income tax and from Social Security contribu-

TABLE 1
SOURCES OF TAX REVENUE IN SWEDEN AND THE UNITED STATES

Revenue Source	Share of Total Receipts (Percent)		
	Sweden		U.S.
	1989	1991	1991
Taxes on personal incomes (including capital gains)	39.3	34.2	34.9
Taxes on corporate incomes	3.8	3.1	7.3
Social Security contributions	26.7	28.6	29.8
Payroll taxes	2.5	3.0	—
Property taxes	3.3	4.1	11.2
Taxes on goods and services	24.2	26.9	16.8
Miscellaneous taxes	0.1	0.1	0.0
Total receipts (percent)	100.0	100.0	100.0
Share of taxes in GDP (percent)	55.6	52.7	29.5
GDP (Billion U.S. 1991 dollars)	—	237	5,611

Source: *Revenue Statistics of OECD Member Countries 1965–94* (OECD, Paris, 1995).

tions. Taxes on goods and services are more important in Sweden, whereas corporate and property taxes contribute a larger share of tax revenue in the United States. The reallocation of the total tax burden brought by TR 91, away from personal income to consumption, is clearly visible.

A NATURAL EXPERIMENT?

A major reshuffling of the tax structure may seem like that rare opportunity to sharpen the estimates of the behavioral elasticities that would interest a public finance economist. However, the implementation of TR 91 was accompanied by the most severe economic downturn since the 1930s. Between 1991 and 1993 GDP fell by more than five percent, open (i.e., excluding those enrolled in various labor market programs) unemployment rose from less than two percent to more than eight percent, asset prices tumbled, and residential construction activity came to a virtual standstill. At the same time, income inequality increased and the government deficit reached record heights. In this environment, it is clearly hard to sort out cause and effect with much precision.[4] Macroeconomic time series for the years surrounding TR 91

contain very little of the kind of independent information needed to discriminate between alternative hypotheses about behavioral responses. Microeconomic panel data, allowing the analyst to control for individual variation over time, may seem like a safer bet, but there is still an obvious risk that the macroeconomic noise pollutes the microeconometric analysis.

The Swedish tax evaluation effort includes several contributions which try to make do with data sets including pre- and postreform observations. But the macroeconomic turmoil has led a number of researchers to confine attention to the information that can be gathered from an *ex ante* evaluation of TR 91. These evaluations have two ingredients in common. The first is an assessment—based on previous findings reported in the literature or on new findings based on prereform data sets—of the reasonable value of some relevant behavioral parameter. The second ingredient is a careful assessment of the change in the incentive structure implied by TR 91. This is a far from trivial exercise, since TR 91 contained several provisions with counteracting influences on the relevant incentive margin. Combining these ingredients, the *ex ante* evaluation produces a set of predicted responses, which serve the useful purpose of scrutinizing the political arguments. Do recent research and refined analysis of the incentive structure produce the kind of behavioral responses promised by the architects of TR 91?

An additional complication stems from the fact that the sharp drop in the activity level cannot be treated as independent of TR 91. Toward the end of the 1980s, the Swedish economy showed many signs of overheating.[5] Due to a high demand pressure, wage costs increased substantially, which led to eroded competitiveness in world markets. At the same time, and in the wake of financial deregulation, the indebtedness of households and firms reached very high levels. This left the Swedish economy in a vulnerable position when the international economy slowed down in the early 1990s. While the international recession may explain part of the rise in unemployment, a more important reason for the severity of the recession is probably that macroeconomic policy was firmly devoted to nonaccommodation. As had been the case previously in many other Western European countries, fighting inflation and defending an overvalued exchange rate now became the top priority for Swedish economic policymaking. As a result, manufacturing output fell sharply.

These developments, certainly unrelated to TR 91, explain a major part of the severe economic recession. But TR 91 may help to explain why the slump in the exporting sectors spread to the sheltered parts of the economy. By lowering the value of household interest deductions, TR 91 increased real after-tax borrowing costs and stimulated indebted households to sell off assets.

Also, higher borrowing costs, in conjunction with certain tax hikes aimed specifically at the housing sector, contributed to the collapse of the construction sector. These contractionary impulses amplified the downturn and contributed to a general weakening of aggregate demand.[6] James Tobin once cautioned that it takes a heap of Harberger triangles to fill an Okun gap. Whatever its long-term merits, it is easy to conclude that the timing of TR 91 was unfortunate. While part of this can be blamed on bad luck, TR 91 was designed to be implemented in a situation with fair macroeconomic wind. The official inquiry which preceded TR 91 contains a wealth of material, but there was hardly any discussion of the macroeconomic aspects.

BEHAVIORAL RESPONSES

As suggested by Slemrod (1992), the evidence about the responses to the major U.S. tax reforms of the 1980s can be interpreted as an indication of a behavioral hierarchy. The most responsive decisions, at the top of the hierarchy, are those involving the timing of transactions, followed by a variety of financial, accounting, and evasion responses. The least responsive decisions, at the bottom, concern the "real" ones, including labor supply, savings, and investment. Let us review the Swedish evidence.

Tax Avoidance

A characteristic feature of the pre-TR 91 tax system was the highly nonuniform treatment of income from capital. The returns to different assets were taxed at vastly differing rates, and the tax paid on a given income could vary systematically depending on the identity of the taxpayer, the kind of income concerned, and when it was reported for taxation.

The steeply progressive tax schedule, in combination with the treatment of children as separate taxpayers, meant that the tax burden could be reduced considerably by shifting capital income from parents in high tax brackets to children with little or no earned income. Likewise, differences among corporate firms in availability and possibilities to take advantage of various nondebt tax shields were extensively exploited. On several occasions, schemes to avoid tax were set up as joint ventures between taxpaying private corporations and tax exempt institutions in the public sector, including several Swedish cities (the operations included sale and leaseback of icebreakers, municipal sewage systems, hospital equipment, etc.).

In Sweden as elsewhere, the strategy of the tax planners was to claim deductible expenses against fully taxable income and report income in forms granted preferential tax treatment. The concessions to specific forms of household savings in the late 1970s and early 1980s provide a simple illustration of this. Savings in special bank accounts were offered a tax-free return plus an initial tax credit, which effectively implied a negative tax. However, nothing prevented households from paying for the contributions to the scheme by borrowed money and deducting the interest against earned income. The special bank account could hence easily be transformed into a *money machine*. Private pension plans, which received the equivalent of consumption tax treatment, provided similar opportunities for reaping the double benefits of tax exemption and full interest deductibility.

As in other countries, much effort was devoted to transforming corporate source income into low-taxed capital gains. Complicated schemes were set up, often involving the use of new financial instruments, where the tax legislation was either unclear or preliminary in nature. The capital gains tax provided additional opportunities for tax avoidance. Before TR 91, short-term gains on shares held for less than two years were fully taxed, while on long-term gains, the tax rate was 40 percent of the income tax rate. The holding-period distinction thus implied that a short-term loss of one krona could be used to offset the tax on a long-term gain, two and a half times as large.

The decades preceding TR 91 witnessed a continuing battle between the tax planners and the tax authorities. New and increasingly complicated rules were set up to combat tax avoidance, and at least to some extent the added complexity created new and unforeseen opportunities to avoid tax. Rather than continuing along the same path, TR 91 cut the Gordian knot by focusing on the circumstances that had opened up the tax planning, that is, the asymmetric tax rules and the high tax rates. Family transactions set up to exploit differences in the marginal tax rates between parents and children were rendered meaningless, since individual capital income was taxed at a proportional rate with no exemption. The uniform tax on capital income also meant that the tax could be levied at the source.[7] Transactions among firms driven by differences in taxpaying status were less rewarding because of the lowered statutory tax rate, while the broadening of the tax base reduced the differences in availability of tax shields between companies. The elimination of the holding-period distinction for capital gains meant a further blow to tax planning.

The balance between taxation of labor income and corporate source capital income was much discussed in the tax reform process and during the following years. TR 91 retained a difference of some 15 percentage points between the total (including payroll taxes) marginal rate on earned income and the total corporate and personal tax on profits. Hence, for owners of corporate firms active as managers, there remained a clear incentive to reclassify labor income as corporate profits. While a thorough-going attack against tax avoidance would seem to require that this incentive be eliminated, the tax legislators do in fact face a difficult dilemma posed by the increased openness of the Swedish economy. Following the deregulation of financial markets and the elimination of currency controls at the end of the 1980s, Swedish households have both legal and easy access to international portfolio investments. Though taxation of individual income from capital follows the residence principle, Swedish tax authorities in practice have little opportunity to enforce taxes on income earned abroad. The prospect of intro-ducing a functioning reporting system from foreign banks and/or a system of withholding taxes on dividends and interest payments seems bleak indeed. If, on the other hand, the tax legislators would attempt to keep domestic investors at home by more lenient taxation, the difficulties of defending the line of demarcation against labor income would magnify.

Consumption

Private consumption is normally considered to be one of the least volatile of all macroeconomic variables. In Sweden, however, consumption fell by about five percent between 1991 and 1993.[8] Can changes in tax structure explain the consumption bust? TR 91 may have had a negative impact on consumption via three channels: (1) intertemporal substitution in response to an increase in the real after-tax interest rate,[9] (2) a downward revision of expected future labor income, and (3) wealth effects due to reevaluations in asset markets, in particular, in the markets for residential real estate. Of these channels, only (3) seems to hold some promise in explaining the con-sumption bust.

With a large intertemporal elasticity of substitution, periods of high expected interest rates should coincide with rapid consumption growth, and periods of low interest rates with stagnant consumption (e.g., Hall, (1988)). However, although there are reasons to be cautious about the information that can be drawn from representative agent models and aggregate data, empirical studies in Sweden and elsewhere suggest that the intertemporal elasticity of substitution is close to zero.[10] Moreover, some basic aspects of the data are hard to reconcile with a story of intertemporal substitu-tion. Between 1986 and 1989, when consumption growth was brisk, the average real after-tax interest rate was negative. Between 1991 and 1993, when consumption growth was nega-tive, the average real after-tax interest rate was exceptionally high. If intertemporal substitution is to charac-terize the data, consumption growth should follow the opposite pattern.

When households make a downward revision of their forecasts of future labor income, consumption should fall. However, while there are good reasons to believe that permanent labor income fell during the Swedish consumption bust,[11] TR 91 is not likely an important factor. Indeed, most assessments of the efficiency effects of TR 91—discussed below—suggest that it lowered excess burdens due to tax wedges in the labor market. If anything, this effect should increase permanent income.

Capitalization effects in asset markets, whether due to TR 91 or something else, may certainly affect consumption. The consumption boom of the late 1980s was associated with an increase in real estate prices, and the bust period with decreasing prices. Of course, correlation is not the same as causation. But recent macroeconometric work indicates that variables such as real housing prices and windfalls in the housing market seem to have power in explaining aggregate Swedish consumption behavior.[12] Moreover, TR 91 led—as discussed below—to a dramatic increase in the rental cost of housing and contributed to the sharp fall in house prices after 1991. Although these housing market adjustments are unlikely to explain a very large part of the consumption bust, they seem like the most important mechanism for an adverse consumption response to TR 91.

Consumption Pattern and Asset Composition

While TR 91 may have had a small effect on the aggregate consumption *level*, it mattered more for the *composition* of consumption and savings. The move toward a broader base for the VAT implied substantial tax hikes for some previously favored consumption categories. Available data and a few econometric studies suggest that there was a strong negative demand response for some of these categories, including hotel and restaurant services and domestic tourism.[13] These responses serve as a healthy reminder of the fact that one of the guiding principles of TR 91—the purported superiority of a system with uniform tax rates on goods and services—has no obvious connection with the tax structure implied by the "inverse elasticity rule" of models of optimal commodity taxation.

Our prior was that household asset choice—at the top of the response hierarchy—was an area where TR 91 should matter. Microeconometric evidence suggested that the old tax system created strong tax clientele effects, in the sense that households tended to specialize in assets according to their marginal tax rate.[14] Macroeconometric evidence suggested that the large shifts from financial to nonfinancial savings outlets (e.g., consumer durables and housing investment) during the decades preceding TR 91 were highly correlated with after-tax returns.[15]

TR 91 removed many of the asymmetries on the asset side of households' balance sheets. The 30 percent tax rate on personal capital income mitigated the tax disadvantage of bank savings and reduced the tax premium for investments in durables and real estate. There were also important consequences for the treatment of liabilities. In the early 1980s, nominal interest expenses were fully deductible against often quite high marginal income tax rates. This created a strong incentive to inflate balance sheets by purchasing assets with borrowed money. In 1980, an individual with the marginal tax rate of an average blue-collar worker paid a real after-tax interest rate of *minus* seven percent. In 1991, when nominal interest expenses became deductible at the new flat tax rate of 30 percent and inflation was lower, the same individual paid a real after-tax interest rate of *plus* seven percent.

On balance, TR 91 gave households strong incentives to shift from real to financial savings outlets and to shrink balance sheets by selling off assets and amortizing debt. Households seem to have adjusted accordingly. In the early 1990s, net investments in tangibles and durables turned negative, and household financial savings increased dramatically. Between 1988 and 1992, net lending as a share of disposable income increased by an astonishing 13 percentage points, while the nonfinancial savings ratio decreased by more than 8 percentage points.[16] Although the rapid fall in inflation and the macroeconomic crisis played a role, calculations reported in Agell, Berg, and Edin (1995) indicate that about one-third of the increase in the net lending rate can be attributed to TR 91.

Housing

Valuing and taxing the services rendered by owner-occupied housing constitute a classical difficulty in implementing a comprehensive income tax. In Sweden, this has been handled by imputing a measure of the implicit income from an owner-occupied home at one to two percent of market value and adding this imputed income on top of other taxable income. With nominal interest income being fully taxable and interest payments deductible, this introduced substantial asymmetries in the tax treatment of housing and other sectors of the economy, and within the housing sector itself, especially with the high inflation and nominal interest rates of the 1970s and 1980s. Owner-occupied housing was tax advantaged relative to other forms of household investment, user costs of owner-occupied housing varied across households according to marginal tax rates, and owner-occupied housing had a general tax advantage[17] over rental housing. Apart from the provisions of the income tax code, housing was also favored through government-guaranteed interest-subsidized loans, a lower VAT rate for building and construction, and income-dependent housing allowances.

As a reflection of the progressivity of the tax schedule, with widely differing marginal tax rates, after-tax interest payments varied a lot across households. Before TR 91, this resulted in rental costs of owner-occupied housing ranging from two percent in the upper marginal tax bracket up to six percent at low marginal tax rates, according to calculations discussed in Englund, Hendershott, and Turner (1995). With the new flat 30 percent tax schedule for all forms of capital income, after-tax interest costs became the same for all households. Owner-occupied housing was no longer cheaper for high-income groups. But TR 91 also affected housing costs through increased VAT and reduced interest subsidies. The combined impact of TR 91 was to fundamentally transform the price structure in the housing market. Rental costs increased substantially and became essentially uniform across households.

Based on microsimulations, we predict that these cost changes should lead to an aggregate demand decrease on the order of 15 percent. Since the stock of housing capital adjusts so sluggishly, the immediate response to the reform should be on prices and new construction. Simulations with a perfect foresight model in the vein of Poterba (1984) suggest a drop in prices of around 10 to 15 percent upon announcement of TR 91 and a sharp fall in new construction.[18] These predictions of falling prices and a virtual standstill of new construction have been borne out by developments after the implementation of TR 91. The reform year of 1991 marks the peak of house prices and of the rate of new construction. Construction virtually ceased after 1992, and nominal house prices fell by a total of 19 percent from the peak in the third quarter of 1991 to the trough in the first quarter of 1993.[19] The total price fall from peak to trough is well in line with expectations, although here as elsewhere it is hard to isolate the effects of TR 91 from those of the severe recession. The timing, however, is somewhat puzzling in view of the fact that the reform could reasonably have been expected by 1989 and was certainly known when the reform bill was passed by Parliament in June 1990. The fact that it took two years until this was reflected in house prices casts some doubt on the rationality of pricing in the Swedish housing market.

When house prices started to fall, however, they did so quite rapidly. In fact, this is the first episode in modern times with falling *nominal* prices. This raises two issues. First, the capital losses of homeowners gave rise to a potentially sizable redistribution of income both vertically, since the average homeowner is higher up the income distribution than the average renter, and horizontally from homeowner to renter at the same income level. Second, falling house prices dug deep holes in the net wealth of many homeowners, even to the point of creating negative net equity. This most likely created a temporary lock-in effect, as homeowners short of equity could not put up the down payment necessary for a new house. Indeed, the transactions volume in the secondary market decreased substantially.

Labor Supply

In the public debate surrounding the reform, the potential impact on labor supply played a major role, although many economists cautioned against overly optimistic supply projections. The development of the wedge between labor costs to the employer (including wage taxes) and the after-tax remuneration of blue- and white-collar employees

(accounting for income taxes, as well as VAT and other indirect taxes) is depicted in Figure 2. We see that TR 91 marks a sharp break of a long-term trend, where by the end of the 1970s the marginal take-home pay of the average blue-collar worker had fallen to less than 30 percent of pretax labor costs. In relative terms, the increase from 1989 to 1991 was 23 percent for the blue-collar worker and as much as 76 percent for the upper-tier white-collar worker.

Although these numbers clearly demonstrate the magnitude of the reform, one should not be misled into generalizing to all groups in society. In fact, looking across a representative sample of all individuals, it appears that around a quarter saw an *increase* in the tax wedge.[20] The explanation is that a large fraction of Swedish wage earners work less than full-time at relatively modest marginal-tax rates that were not much affected by the reform, and that many households in this category are entitled to income-dependent housing allowances that were increased as part of the reform. A similar pattern with a mixture of increased and decreased marginal tax rates holds for TRA 86 (Hausman and Poterba, 1987). In fact, as is emphasized by Auerbach and Slemrod (1997, forthcoming), it lies in the nature of a reform aimed at maintaining the degree of redistribution that it is very difficult to lower marginal taxes for everybody.

Various labor supply studies, conducted before TR 91 and as part of the evaluation effort, tend to confirm the "elasticity pessimism" underlying Slemrod's response hierarchy, with labor supply at the bottom. A representative estimate of the compensated wage elasticity of hours worked among Swedish prime-age males is on the order of magnitude of 0.1,[21] but the estimates are so

FIGURE 2.   The Marginal Take-Home Pay per Dollar of Employer Costs, of Blue- and White-Collar Workers, 1952–93

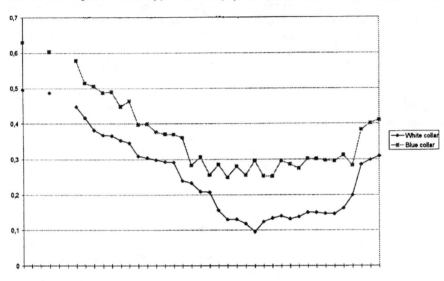

Note: Marginal take-home pay is calculated as (1-marginal tax rate)/[(1 + wage taxes)(1 + indirect taxes)]
Source: DuRietz (1994)

imprecise that the predicted hours response to the reform of the representative white-collar worker of Figure 2 has a typical confidence interval ranging from 1.5 to 15 percent. Unfortunately, there is a paucity of *ex post* studies of the impact of the reform, but the panel study of Klevmarken (1996) finds that changes in marginal wages between 1985 and 1992 were associated with statistically significant increases of the supply of hours worked, both for men and for women.[22]

Although a very large amount of research has focused on hours worked, it is possible that other margins of labor supply response may prove more important in the longer run. It is noteworthy that TR 91 implied a large change in the incentive to undertake investment in education. TR 91 lowered tax rates at higher (postinvestment) income levels, but left tax rates more or less unchanged at lower (preinvestment) income levels. Edin and Holmlund (1995) calculate internal rates of return to investing in a four-year university program. In the early 1980s, the return was four to five percent before tax and one to three percent after tax, implying effective tax rates between 40 and 90 percent depending on the year chosen as a basis for the calculations. After the reform, the effective tax rate fell to 25 percent. The impact of this reduction is not confined to formal education but applies more broadly to the choice between careers with different earnings profiles.

The Corporate Response

The new corporate tax rules meant a noteworthy departure from the previous long-standing policy of stimulating business investment in fixed capital through a combination of a high statutory tax rate and generous allowances to investing firms. The tax rate was cut almost in half, and, to keep the tax payments of the corporate sector roughly constant, the base of the tax was considerably broadened. Many of the innovative incentive provisions that had set the Swedish tax system apart were eliminated, notably the investment funds system.[23]

Though there was a widespread view among policymakers that cutting the statutory tax rate in half would itself greatly improve investment incentives, estimates using conventional methodology indicate that the corporate tax reform had little effect on the cost of capital. The base broadening largely offset the effects of the tax cut. However, TR 91 somewhat reduced the previous strong incentives to use debt rather than equity as a source of funds.[24]

An important complication in evaluating the effects of the corporate tax reform is that Swedish companies to a large extent both paid corporate income tax and abstained from fully using the generous tax allowances. A detailed study (Forsling, 1996) indicates that, over the period 1979–88, the average rate of utilization of tax allowances (deductions for depreciation, contributions to investment funds, and undervaluation of inventories) among taxpaying firms was a mere 72 percent. Only one out of five firms used the maximum allowed by the tax code. An increase in the rate of utilization from 72 to 76 percent would have been sufficient to completely eliminate all tax payments. Conventional estimates of the cost of capital or effective tax rates, assuming full utilization of existing tax allowances, may therefore give a misleading picture of the incentive effects of the corporate tax.

Recent research (Kanniainen and Södersten, 1994) has attributed this rather odd tax behavior to the uniform reporting convention used in Sweden (and several other OECD countries). Firms can distribute cash dividends only to the extent of their after-tax profits, taking account of fiscal depreciation, contributions to investment funds, etc. Hence, corporate civil law imposes a dividend constraint on using tax allowances, and, in practice, this constraint seems to have been more tight than the upper limits set by the tax code. When tax allowances on existing assets have not been fully used, an additional investment project will not affect total tax payments, that is, at the margin, the corporate tax rate is zero. Put differently, the corporate income tax is effectively turned into a tax on distributions or a cash flow tax with no impact on the cost of capital.[25] The mechanism involved here is similar to that analyzed in the literature about dividend taxation.[26] To the extent that paying dividends is the only way to get cash to the shareholders (share repurchases are disallowed in Sweden), the firm is in a "trapped equity" regime where the corporate tax is capitalized in share prices.

The possibility that large groups of Swedish firms effectively faced a zero marginal corporate tax rate makes it unclear to what extent the old tax system actually did offer an advantage to debt finance. Even the direction of change in the incentives for borrowing brought by TR 91 is unclear, as the base broadening would be expected to raise the rate of utilization of the still remaining tax shields.[27] Firms experiencing a switch from being taxed on their cash flows to being subject to a regular income tax would find the value of interest deductions increase at the margin, despite the sharp cut in the statutory tax rate. Moreover, given that the financial markets in Sweden are highly integrated with the international markets for debt and equity, it seems unlikely that the switch to the dual personal income tax with a flat rate 30 percent tax on personal capital incomes would be of much importance for corporate financial decisions. The after-tax costs of funds of the large Swedish firms are more likely determined by the operations of international portfolio investors, say, United States pension funds, than by the savings and portfolio decisions of Swedish households.

Auerbach, Hassett, and Södersten (1995) focus on the effects on business fixed investment. A model of equipment investment is estimated in order to determine which of several potential regimes best described investment behavior before the reform. Even though the regression results do not settle the issue, evidence on the use of tax allowances and investment funds generally supports the view that the pre-reform corporate tax system had essentially no effect on investment. The change in the user cost of capital due to the reform is found to be very small and swamped in recent years by the impact of the rise in real interest rates and decline in profitability. The authors conclude, "with some confidence," that the effects of TR 91 itself (as opposed to contemporaneous macroeconomic factors) on investment are likely to have been minor.

INCOME DISTRIBUTION

In the political process of selling TR 91 to various interest groups and the electorate in general, a key element was the claim that the reform would be distributionally neutral. This was interpreted in a bookkeeping sense to mean an unchanged relation between

an exogenously given distribution of pretax factor income and the distribution of income after taxes and allowances. Against this background, it was natural that a mechanical evaluation of the distributional impact along these lines was one element of the evaluation effort, although it comes natural for an economist to point to the limitations of such an exercise.

During the 1980s, a growing number of critics came to doubt whether the Swedish tax system achieved much in terms of redistribution. There were three ingredients to the critique. First, various loopholes and tax arbitrage activities created a wedge between "true" income and taxable income. Second, substitution between market labor and leisure and household production created a discrepancy between taxable income (which only derives from market activities) and potential income (which also includes the value of leisure and home production). Third, taxation based on yearly income redistributes income across different phases in an individual's life cycle, i.e., from more toward less productive ages, but it is less clear how much redistribution actually is achieved across households with different lifetime incomes.[28]

The recent study by Björklund, Palme, and Svensson (1995), however, gives little support to the critics of the old system. According to this analysis, the old Swedish tax system certainly achieved a substantial amount of redistribution of yearly incomes.[29] The amount of redistribution is not much affected by going from actual income to a measure of full income. Also, when the authors follow a panel of individuals over the period 1974–91 and take the sum of discounted income over this period as a measure of lifetime income, the conclusion is that the tax system redistributes almost as much in terms of lifetime income as in terms of yearly income. Of course, this only says something about the tax system as it evolved over this 18-year period and gives no conclusive evidence on the long-run redistributive properties of the system of the late 1980s. Nevertheless, it leads us to be somewhat skeptical about some of the more popular views of the old tax system as being void of any redistributive effect.

Björklund, Palmer, and Svensson (1995) also examine differences in pre- and post-tax Gini coefficients under the old and new tax rules. Looking at the aggregate amount of redistribution across all groups of households, the differences appear minuscule; i.e., at least in the short term (up to 1992), TR 91 seems to have lived up to the promise of "neutrality" with respect to the income distribution. This conclusion, however, conceals important differences in the structure of the tax and subsidy system. Broadly speaking, there are three counteracting differences between the old and new tax systems. First, the taxation of earned income is clearly less redistributive under TR 91. Second, with the new flat tax on capital income, tax payments become more proportional to actual capital income than under the old system, where it was possible to avoid capital taxes altogether through tax arbitrage. Since capital income is concentrated at the top of the income distribution, this tends to make the new system more redistributive than the old one. Third, child and housing allowances play a larger role after TR 91 than before. Since they largely redistribute income from households without children to families with children, TR 91 represents a shift of emphasis toward more redistribution across various phases of the life cycle rather than between households with different lifetime incomes.

By simply comparing Gini coefficients before and after taxes, one takes an unduly narrow view on income distribution. In particular, one takes the pretax distribution of factor income for granted, thereby glossing over the strong assumptions about tax incidence implicit in such an excercise. Whereas it may be reasonable for a small open economy like the Swedish one to assume that the pretax return to capital is determined in international markets and unaffected by Swedish tax policy, the assumptions about the incidence on wages merit more attention than they are commonly given by income distribution analysts. In fact, there has been a recent trend in Sweden, as elsewhere, toward more inequality of factor incomes, and one may ask if this development has been induced by tax reform to any extent. This should depend on the relative supply responses of high- and low-skilled workers and on the degree of complementarity in production between different types of labor. However, given the generally small labor supply responses, it appears unlikely that the changing wage structure has primarily been induced by changes in tax structure. In the longer run, the strengthened incentives to invest in human capital should be more important for the wage distribution. It is hard, though, to have a very definite opinion on the implications for the distributional analysis of TR 91.[30]

EFFICIENCY — A DOUBLE DIVIDEND?

A main argument of the proponents of TR 91 was that economic efficiency should improve. For many politicians, efficiency was here interpreted as a synonym for various easy-to-observe responses, such as increased labor supply and higher savings. In some quarters, there was also a hope that TR 91 should deliver an easily detectable growth bonus. For an economist, however, efficiency is defined in terms of not directly observable areas between compensated demand and supply curves, and there is no simple relation between the implied tax distortions and the magnitude of behavioral responses. Much the same goes for economic growth. According to the standard neoclassical growth model, a badly designed tax system may create important negative level effects, without the long-term rate of growth being affected. As we will see shortly, TR 91 even contained provisions which tended to *reduce* registered GDP growth but to increase consumption opportunities.

From an excess burden perspective, the most important aspect of TR 91 is that it implied a shift in the tax burden from highly taxed labor income to lightly taxed housing capital. As a consequence, the relative prices of leisure and housing consumption increased. Although there is room for disagreement on the exact magnitudes of some key behavioral elasticities, there is little reason to question the soundness of this strategy. Table 2 shows the results from an attempt at quantifying the marginal efficiency cost due to labor supply distortions of the Swedish tax system.[31] The compensated elasticities of labor

supply are chosen to reflect the range of findings in recent empirical studies.[32] The marginal tax wedges (differences between productivity and real take-home pay) for some categories of employees, before and after TR 91, account for income, payroll, and indirect taxes.

A key point is that a small behavioral elasticity matters if the marginal tax wedge is sufficiently high. The logic behind the marginal welfare cost per dollar of tax revenue implies that there is a region of tax wedges at which the efficiency cost starts to increase rapidly. At some marginal tax wedge, an additional tax hike creates additional excess burdens but no extra tax revenue. Although the table brings out the sensitivity of results to alternative behavioral assumptions, one can hardly rule out the possibility that prereform tax wedges were close to that level. The point estimates of labor supply elasticities, not to mention the confidence intervals, reported in recent studies are consistent with the view that the pre-TR 91 tax system had marked negative incentive effects.

Of course, microeconomic estimates suggesting high marginal welfare costs of taxation do not necessarily imply that

TABLE 2
MARGINAL EXCESS BURDEN PER KRONA OF TAX REVENUE (IN PERCENT)

	Compensated Labor Supply Elasticity		
	0.05	0.11	0.25
Marginal tax wedge (in percent):			
62 (average blue-collar worker, 1991)	8.2	19.0	54.7
63 (average earned income, 1991)	8.6	20.1	59.0
70.5 (average blue-collar worker, 1988)	12.7	31.6	121.8
71.5 (average white-collar worker, 1991)	13.4	33.9	139.1
73 (average earned income, 1988)	14.6	37.8	175.0
79 (average white-collar worker, 1988)	22.0	65.3	2,280.0
85.5 (average senior white-collar worker, 1988)	41.0	192.5	—
Tax rate which maximizes tax revenue	94.5	89.5	79.5

Source: Agell, Englund, and Södersten (1995).

tax cuts are in order. When there is a binding revenue constraint, lower tax wedges on labor income make sense only if other taxes can be raised in a less distortionary way. The remarkable aspect of the Swedish situation was that there was scope for a "double divi-dend." Higher taxes on housing generated a substantial part of the revenue required to finance the tax cut on labor income, but they also reduced intersectoral investment distortions. Due to the generous tax and subsidy rules, discussed above, housing investment was given a considerable advantage over investments in other sectors. Available estimates indicate (for realistic values of the debt-equity mix, inflation, etc.) that new investments in owner-occupied housing could reap a *net* marginal subsidy—the (financial) cost of capital for the prospective homeowner was well below the real rate of interest. TR 91 did much to promote a less inefficient allocation of investment resources.

The case of housing illustrates that the short-term response of an aggregate production measure, such as GDP, may provide a poor indicator of the welfare effects of tax reform. Before TR 91, household savings was channeled into an activity where the marginal produc-tivity of capital was considerably below the opportunity cost, which in an open economy can be approximated by the world real rate of interest. At the same time, the housing sector gave a substan-tial contribution to Swedish GDP. In any year, housing investment, valued from the production side, added to aggregate investments. TR 91 gave households strong incentives to redirect their savings to other uses, including net purchases of foreign assets.[33] During the adjustment phase (when the housing sector shrinks and the net foreign asset position improves), GDP

growth tends to slacken. In spite of this negative production effect, aggregate consumption possibilities tend to increase—every krona's worth of savings transferred from the housing sector to international asset markets implies that Swedish national income increases with the difference between the world real rate of interest and the marginal productivity of housing capital.

Undoubtedly, TR 91 has affected economic efficiency along a number of margins in addition to those just discussed. The reduced progressivity of the income tax has enhanced educa-tional incentives. The new corporate income tax brought about a more uniform treatment of investment projects *within* the corporate sector. The broader base for the VAT implied higher tax wedges on the "white" consumer service sector, which competes with do-it-yourself activities and services produced in the underground economy. However, in these cases, there is scant evidence on the behavioral response.

Finally, an important objective of TR 91 was to simplify the tax code, and there is reason to believe that TR 91 did much to reduce the transaction complexity of the tax system. TR 91 made it much less profitable to invest resources in a variety of tax avoidance activities. Survey evidence indicates that households' time spent on tax compliance declined substantially in the years after TR 91.[34] There is also evidence suggesting that the tax authorities got an easier work-load.

Concluding remarks

What is the verdict on TR 91 five years after its implementation? Have we seen the behavioral responses that the reform architects expected? Did the reform contribute to a more efficient economy?

Although we should keep our fingers crossed in view of the severe crisis in the Swedish economy in the early 1990s, we concur with Auerbach and Slemrod (1997, forthcoming), who argued in their survey of TRA 86 that there has been a hierarchy of responses. A number of financial activities related to tax planning were rendered meaningless and have been virtually wiped out. We have also seen large and expected effects on portfolio composition in general, with a shrinking of both sides of private sector balance sheets. Households have been induced to shift out of owner-occupied housing, resulting in falling house prices and a standstill of new construction. In the longer run, this will result in a more efficient allocation of the capital stock.

At the other end of the spectrum, major real activities such as labor supply and savings appear quite insensitive, at least as far as can be inferred from short-run behavior. Since real activities can be expected to be more important from a welfare perspective, it might be conjectured that the reform only has made a small contribution to increase the efficiency of the Swedish economy, like Auerbach and Slemrod (1997, forthcoming) conclude for TRA86. While such a conclusion may be warranted at U.S. tax rates, it is hardly correct when starting out from marginal tax rates of 70 percent and more. At such levels—close to the top of the Laffer curve—the marginal excess burden is highly nonlinear in tax rates, implying that accounting for heterogeneity and uncertainty about the correct elasticity values is very important; the expected aggregate excess burden is much larger than the marginal excess burden for the average taxpayer evaluated at point estimates of elasticities.

Although a standard efficiency calculation—comparing hypothetical equilibria

before and after the reform—unambiguously shows that TR 91 was efficiency improving, these benefits were not without costs. In fact, the reform may be viewed as an investment with quite visible short-run costs that have to be weighed against less visible, and perhaps also less certain, long-run benefits. The short-run costs of TR 91 were primarily of two types. First, by shifting savings out of real assets such as housing and consumer durables into financial assets, the reform implied a reduction of effective demand. Since the reform was implemented in a recession when output was arguably demand determined, we conclude that it led to a further deepening of the recession with accompanying short-term production losses. Second, the rapid implementation of the reform led to sizable capital losses in the housing sector, with an ensuing arbitrary horizontal redistribution across households. These observations serve as a reminder of the point emphasized, e.g., by Feldstein (1976), that one has to distinguish between tax reform and *de novo* tax design. While a comparison of the pre- and post-1991 tax systems comes out in favor of the post-1991 system, an evaluation of the reform has to weigh the long-run benefits against the short-term costs.

The costs of the reform were not unavoidable. The government took a rather careless attitude toward the transition problem. A more gradual phasein of the reform certainly would have dampened the short-run costs considerably without giving up any of the long-run benefits. While this would be a rather obvious recommendation to a benevolent dictator, things are more complex in a parliamentary democracy where one cannot tie the hands of future governments. Indeed, bringing about political consensus about a reform as far reaching as TR 91 involved a rather delicate balance of the gains and losses of different interest groups in society. If parts of the reform would have been implemented gradually or with a lag, they would also have been more susceptible to future political pressures.

Even a "tax reform of the century" implemented with such force as TR 91 did not stay unaffected for very long. Already after three years, in 1994, one could make a list of some 75 tax changes involving minor and major deviations from the original reform. Such a count of changes obviously is a cheap argument; after all, the world changes continuously, and one would hope that the tax law adapts. Nevertheless, some of the changes represent reversals of the guiding principles of TR 91. One example is the numerous changes in different VAT rates. Another is the increase of the top marginal tax rate on earned income from 50 to 55 percent. The latter change was presented as a temporary measure and part of a package to cut the growing budget deficits after 1992. While these deficits are largely attributable to the recession, they partly reflect an underfinancing of the reform by two to three percent of GDP. It is not surprising that it was easier to sell an underfunded reform package, where all groups could be portrayed as winners, than a fully financed reform, where some groups would appear as losers, at least in a short-run accounting sense.

In what direction should we expect the Swedish tax system to evolve in the future? The 1980s was a decade of tax reforms aimed at a more uniform tax structure, conspicuously ignoring much of the development in public finance since the 1970s, emphasizing the role of differentiated taxation in funding government expenditure. In the 1990s,

the pendulum of tax reform discussion has swung in the opposite direction, with a renewed emphasis on differentiation, e.g., for environmental reasons or as a means of fighting unemployment. When these factors now are being considered in Sweden, future reforms can build on a tax structure that has fewer counterproductive asymmetries than the pre-TR 91 system.

The Swedish public sector ranks among the largest in the world. As long as this remains, Swedish tax rates will inevitably be high. Our discussion suggests that, especially with a high aggregate tax rate, the structure of taxation matters. TR 91 has reduced the aggregate excess burden. However, the ever growing integration with international capital and labor markets will undoubtedly put increasing pressure on the Swedish tax system in the future.

ENDNOTES

We are grateful to Joel Slemrod for his comments on a first draft of this article.

[1] See Auerbach and Slemrod (1997) for an extensive discussion.

[2] The evaluation project is summarized (in Swedish) in Agell, Englund, and Södersten (1995) (an English version will be published by Macmillan Press.) The 1995 Autumn issue of the *Swedish Economic Policy Review* includes a selection of the background papers. A complete list of background papers is available from the National Institute of Economic Research, Box 3116, 103 62 Stockholm, Sweden.

[3] See Sørensen (1994) for further discussion.

[4] From the point of view of evaluation research, the timing of TRA 86 was more fortunate. As discussed by Auerbach and Slemrod (1997, forthcoming), the U.S. macroeconomy was well behaved in the years surrounding TRA 86.

[5] For an overview of the Swedish macroeconomic experience, see Calmfors (1993).

[6] However, compared with the international recession and the nonaccommodative exchange rate policy, TR 91 was most likely a less decisive factor. A back-of-the-envelope calculation of Agell, Englund, and Södersten (1995) suggests that TR 91 may explain about one-fifth of the sharp decline in Swedish GDP between 1991 and 1993.

[7] The Swedish Central Securities Depository handles both domestic source taxation and the withholding tax on dividends paid to foreign shareholders.

[8] For a discussion of consumption behavior in Sweden, see Berg (1994).

[9] A complication in assessing the effects of TR 91 on intertemporal incentives stems from the fact that TR 91 contained provisions with counteracting effects on the real after-tax interest rate. The lower statutory tax rate on capital income strengthened incentives, but some of the base-broadening ingredients, such as the abolishment of the favorable treatment of long-term capital gains, worked in the opposite direction. On balance, however, it seems reasonable to conclude that TR 91 implied lower effective marginal tax rates for a majority of households. This can be contrasted to the case of TRA 86, where the conclusion seems to be that the impact on savings incentives was of an ambiguous sign (Auerbach and Slemrod, 1997).

[10] For Swedish evidence on the intertemporal elasticity of substitution, see Campbell and Mankiw (1991) and Agell, Berg, and Edin (1995).

[11] A more likely factor in a drop in permanent labor income is the sharp increase in unemployment after 1991. While higher unemployment may induce consumers to revise their expectations of future labor income, it may also boost precautionary savings. When consumers are prudent, more uncertain earnings prospects can have strong negative effects on current consumption (e.g., Caballero, 1991). Although we believe that part of the increase in unemployment can be explained by the short-term contractionary impact of TR 91, the major impulses should, as already discussed, be sought elsewhere.

[12] See Agell, Berg, and Edin (1995).

[13] See, e.g., Hultkrantz (1995).

[14] See, e.g., Agell and Edin (1990).

[15] For an analysis of household asset choice, before and after TR 91, see Agell, Berg, and Edin (1995).

[16] According to the National Accounts of Statistics Sweden, household net lending is defined as the sum of borrowing and lending in the credit market, net purchases of corporate shares, individual insurance savings, and savings in other interest bearing assets.

[17] The latter advantage, however, was offset by special interest subsidies at high rates to recent-vintage rental housing.

[18] See Åsberg and Åsbrink (1994) for a presentation of the model including a discussion of the sensitivity of the results to demand and supply elasticities.

[19] These effects are qualitatively similar to, but much larger in magnitude than, those of TRA 86 according to the discussion in Poterba (1990).

[20] This fraction applies to a comparison between 1985 and 1992 for a sample of households from the HUS panel (Klevmarken et al.,1995). It

accounts for the broadening of the VAT coverage and other factors affecting the real wage.

[21] See studies by Blomquist and Hansson-Brusewitz (1990), Ackum Agell, and Meghir (1995), and Aronsson and Palme (1995).

[22] The estimated effects are quite large. Women who experience a tax decrease of more than 20 percentage points are estimated to increase yearly labor supply by 400 hours, i.e., by roughly 30 percent of average work hours. Corresponding estimates for men are 200 hours and 10 percent.

[23] See Taylor (1982) and Södersten (1989) for a discussion of the investment funds system.

[24] See Södersten (1993).

[25] For further explanation of the Kanniainen–Södersten theory, see also Sørensen (1995) in this journal.

[26] Cf. Auerbach (1979).

[27] Though data are still scant, preliminary observations seem to confirm this assumption.

[28] The two latter lines of criticism received some support from a study by Hansson and Norrman (1986), based on a cross section of households.

[29] Measuring pretax income by the sum of taxable labor income and an imputed measure of capital income (net wealth times a three percent real interest rate) and using the square-root equivalence scale to adjust for differences in household composition, the Gini coefficent based on yearly pretax income was around 0.25 during the 1980s, a quite low number by international standards. After taxes and housing and child allowances, the coefficient was around 0.20, i.e., a sizable redistribution.

[30] It should also be pointed out that the calculations reported above are confined to personal income taxes and disregard the incidence of the corporate income tax. However, as is seen from Table 1, corporate tax revenues did not change much as a result of TR 91, and assumptions about corporate tax incidence should not be crucial.

[31] See Agell, Englund, and Södersten (1995). The numbers derive from a partial equilibrium model, where an individual maximizes a single-period constant-elasticity-of-substitution utility function in leisure and goods consumption, subject to a linear income tax system, and where there is no avoidance type of response that creates a discrepancy between true and taxable income. To make life easy, it is assumed that all incremental tax revenue is returned as a lump sum (all income effects are eliminated). The marginal welfare cost per unit of tax revenue is defined as $\Delta EB/\Delta T$, where ΔEB is the change in excess burden and ΔT the change in tax revenue.

[32] The highest elasticity, 0.25, is of relevance for women's labor supply. The intermediate elasticity, 0.11, is typical for many studies of the labor supply of married prime-age males. The smallest elasticity, 0.05, is taken from a recent study on the labor supply of blue-collar workers.

[33] The drastic increase in household financial savings in the early 1990s was accompanied by a rapid improvement of the current account.

[34] See Malmer and Persson (1994).

REFERENCES

Ackum Agell, Susanne, and Costas Meghir. "Male Labour Supply in Sweden: Are Incentives Important?" *Swedish Economic Policy Review* 2 No. 2 (Fall, 1995): 391–418.

Agell, Jonas, and Per-Anders Edin. "Marginal Taxes and the Asset Portfolios of Swedish Households." *Scandinavian Journal of Economics* 92 No. 1 (January, 1990): 47–64.

Agell, Jonas, Lennart Berg, and Per-Anders Edin . "The Swedish Boom to Bust Cycle: Tax Reform, Consumption and Asset Structure." *Swedish Economic Policy Review* 2 No. 2 (Fall, 1995): 271–314.

Agell, Jonas, Peter Englund, and Jan Södersten. *Svensk skattepolitik i teori och praktik. 1991 års skattereform* (*Swedish Tax Policy in Theory and Practice. The 1991 Tax Reform*). Stockholm: Fritzes, 1995.

Aronsson, Thomas, and Mårten Palme. "A Decade of Tax and Benefit Reforms in Sweden— Effects on Labour Supply, Welfare and Inequality." Tax Reform Evaluation Report No. 3. Stockholm: National Institute of Economic Research, 1995.

Åsberg, Per, and Stefan Åsbrink. "Capitalisation Effects in the Market for Owner-Occupied Housing: A Dynamic Approach." Tax Reform Evaluation Report No. 2. Stockholm: National Institute of Economic Research, 1994.

Auerbach, Alan. "Wealth Maximization and the Cost of Capital." *Quarterly Journal of Economics* 93 No. 3 (August, 1979): 433–46.

Auerbach, Alan, Kevin Hassett, and Jan Södersten. "Taxation and Corporate Investment: The Impact of the 1991 Swedish Tax Reform." *Swedish Economic Policy Review* 2 No. 2 (Fall, 1995): 361–83.

Auerbach, Alan, and Joel Slemrod. "The Economic Effects of the Tax Reform Act of 1986." *Journal of Economic Literature* 35 No. 1 (forthcoming, March, 1997).

Berg, Lennart. "Household Savings and Debts: The Experience of the Nordic Countries." *Oxford Review of Economic Policy* 10 No. 2 (Summer, 1994): 42–53.

Björklund, Anders, Mårten Palme, and Ingemar Svensson. "Tax Reforms and Income Distribution: An Assessment Using Different Income Concepts." *Swedish Economic Policy Review* 2 No. 2 (Fall, 1995): 229–66.

Blomquist, Sören, and Urban Hansson-Brusewitz. "The Effect of Taxes on Male and Female Labor Supply in Sweden." *Journal of Human Resources* 25 No. 3 (1990): 317–57.

Caballero, Ricardo. "Earnings Uncertainty and Aggregate Wealth Accumulation." *American Economic Review* 81 No. 4 (September, 1991): 859–71.

Calmfors, Lars. "Lessons from the Macroeconomic Experience of Sweden." *European Journal of Political Economy* 9 No. 1 (March, 1993): 25–72.

Campbell, John, and Gregory Mankiw. "The Response of Consumption to Income: A Cross-Country Investigation." *European Economic Review* 35 No. 4 (May, 1991): 723–67.

DuRietz, Gunnar. *Välfärdsstatens finansiering* (*Funding the Welfare State*). Stockholm: City University Press, 1994.

Edin, Per-Anders, and Bertil Holmlund. "The Swedish Wage Structure: The Rise and Fall of Solidarity Wage Policy in Sweden." In *Differences and Changes in Wage Structure*, edited by Richard Freeman and Lawrence Katz. Chicago: University of Chicago Press, 1995.

Englund, Peter, Patric Hendershott, and Bengt Turner. "The Tax Reform and the Housing Market." *Swedish Economic Policy Review* 2 No. 2 (Fall, 1995): 319–56.

Feldstein, Martin. "On the Theory of Tax Reform." *Journal of Public Economics* 6 No. 1-2 (July–August, 1976): 77–104.

Forsling, Gunnar. "Utilization of Tax Allowances: A Survey of Swedish Corporate Firms, 1979–93." Tax Reform Evaluation Report No. 22. Stockholm: National Institute of Economic Research, 1996.

Hall, Robert. "Intertemporal Substitution in Consumption." *Journal of Political Economy* 96 No. 2 (April, 1988): 339–57.

Hansson, Ingemar, and Erik Norrman. "Fördelningseffekter av inkomstskatt och utgiftskatt" (Distributional Effects of Income Tax and Expenditure Tax). In *Utgiftsskatt. Teknik och effekter* (*Expenditure Taxation. Techniques and Effects*). SOU 1986: 40. Stockholm: Liber Förlag, 1986.

Hausman, Jerry, and James Poterba. "Household Behavior and the Tax Reform Act of 1986." *Journal of Economic Perspectives* 1 No. 1 (Summer, 1987): 101–19.

Hultkrantz, Lars. "On Determinants of Swedish Recreational Domestic and Outbound Travel."

Tax Reform Evaluation Report No. 7. Stockholm: National Institute of Economic Research, 1995.

Kanniainen, Vesa, and Jan Södersten. "Costs of Monitoring and Corporate Taxation." *Journal of Public Economics* 55 No. 2 (1994): 307–21.

Klevmarken, Anders. "Did the Tax Cuts Increase Hours of Work? A Pre-Post Analysis of Swedish Panel Data." Unpublished manuscript, Department of Economics, Uppsala University, 1996.

Klevmarken, Anders (with Irene Andersson, Peter Brose, Erik Grönqvist, Paul Olovsson, and Marianne Stoltenberg-Hansen). "Labor Supply Responses to Swedish Tax Reforms 1985–1992." Tax Reform Evaluation Report No. 11. Stockholm: National Institute of Economic Research, 1995.

Malmer, Håkan, and Annika Persson. "Skattereformens effekter på skattesystemets driftskostnader, skatteplanering och skattefusk" (The Effects of the Tax Reform on Compliance Costs, Tax Planning, and Tax Fraud). In *Århundradets skattereform (Tax Reform of the Century)*, edited by Håkan Malmer, Annika Persson, and Åke Tengblad, 5–364. Stockholm: Fritzes, 1994.

Myrdal, Gunnar. "Dags för ett nytt skattesystem!" (Time for a New Tax System!) *Ekonomisk Debatt* 6 (November, 1978): 493–506.

Poterba, James. "Tax Subsidies to Owner-Occupied Housing." *Quarterly Journal of Economics* 99 No. 4 (November, 1984): 729–52.

Poterba, James. "Taxation and Housing Markets: Preliminary Evidence on the Effects of the Recent Tax Reform." In *Do Taxes Matter?: The Impact of the Tax Reform Act of 1986*, edited by Joel Slemrod, 141–60. Cambridge, MA: MIT Press, 1990.

Slemrod, Joel. "Do Taxes Matter?: Lessons from the 1980s." *American Economic Review* 82 No. 2 (May, 1992): 250–6.

Södersten, Jan. "The Investment Funds System Reconsidered." *Scandinavian Journal of Economics* 91 No. 4 (1989): 671–87.

Södersten, Jan. "Sweden." In *Tax Reform and the Cost of Capital. An International Comparison*, edited by Dale Jorgenson and Ralph Landau, 270–99. Washington, D.C.: The Brookings Institution, 1993.

Sørensen, Peter Birch. "From the Global Income Tax to the Dual Income Tax: Recent Reforms in the Nordic Countries." *International Tax and Public Finance* 1 No. 1 (May, 1994): 57–79.

Sørensen, Peter Birch. "Changing Views of the Corporate Income Tax." *National Tax Journal* 48 No. 2 (June, 1995): 279–94.

Taylor, John. "The Swedish Investment Funds System as a Stabilization Policy Rule." *Brookings Papers on Economic Activity* 13 No. 1 (1982): 57–99.

MEASURING THE IMPACT OF TAX REFORM

ALAN J. AUERBACH[*]

Abstract - *This paper considers why so many questions about the economic effects of tax reforms remain unanswered, and draws implications for how economics can be used to evaluate and design tax changes. Tax reforms have proven difficult to assess for a variety of reasons, all related to the nonexperimental nature of empirical economic analysis. Though this makes continued reliance on theoretical predictions necessary, evaluations should distinguish clearly between theory and evidence. The paucity of evidence also militates against the enactment of major tax reforms, for dependence on such reforms limits our ability to adapt tax policy in response to new evidence.*

INTRODUCTION

The inability of economic research to provide clear and precise information about the economic impacts of tax policies has long frustrated policymakers. Although not necessarily written with this as their primary objective, the other papers in this symposium by Agell, Englund, and

[*]Department of Economics, University of California, Berkeley, CA, 94720 and NBER, Cambridge, MA 02138.

Södersten and Engen and Skinner (hereafter AES and ES) illustrate why such information has proved so hard to uncover.[1] In this brief paper, I will attempt to assess why so many questions remain unanswered and consider the implications for how economics can be used to evaluate tax reforms and how the reforms themselves should be structured.

WHY DON'T WE KNOW THE ANSWERS?

Economic theory provides researchers with powerful tools, suggesting the types of behavioral responses that are likely or feasible in response to a particular tax change. Indeed, much of what we "know" about the effects of tax reforms is really based primarily on economic theory, rather than direct observation. For example, we "know" that, other things equal, an excise tax on a particular commodity will reduce demand for that commodity, even if no such tax has been imposed in the past. Theory tells us that demand curves slope downward, and we have ample confirming evidence of this from other markets.[2] We may even "know" how responsive to the tax demand will be, based on estimates of the price elasticity of demand. Standard theory tells us that a tax-induced price increase should have the same impact on demand as any other price increase of equal magnitude, and we have no evidence to the contrary.

Useful as it is, theory does not always offer clear predictions. Sometimes, the theory itself remains in dispute. In many instances, a wide range of outcomes is theoretically possible, and only convincing empirical evidence can narrow this range of possibilities. Here, the conclusions of AES and ES as they confront major policy questions are sobering. AES find it difficult to tease out the economic effects of Sweden's "tax reform of the century," while ES can offer only tentative conclusions about the effects of taxes on economic growth, impacts that over time potentially could exert an enormous influence on a country's standard of living. Written as they are by careful and informed scholars, the papers provide a catalog of the problems confronting empirical research, which I will attempt to summarize here.

Time Is Short

Sweden's 1991 tax reform took effect as the country was entering a severe recession. AES suggest that the recession cannot be treated as entirely unrelated to the tax reform—that certain elements of the reform acted to reduce aggregate demand and that monetary policy did not adequately compensate for this. But they do not argue that the recession was due primarily to the tax reform. This leaves them with the problem of distinguishing responses to the tax reform from changes in activity resulting from the independent macroeconomic downturn. As many of the reform's predicted changes were of a smaller magnitude than the changes likely to be associated with the recession alone, their problem

is a very serious one. Ultimately, they are forced to base judgments of the reform, in large part, not on observed behavioral changes but on effects that, on the basis of theory, one should have expected the reform to produce. That is, they gain limited information from looking at what actually has happened to date.

With more time, one hopes, the cyclical factors will even out and more evidence can be uncovered. But the passage of time also inevitably brings with it other sources of behavioral change. Because economics (at least at the macroeconomic level) is not an experimental science, we will never get the clean experiment we desire.

For some changes, though, even a few more years may not be enough. Once we have enough data to control for cyclical variation, we might be able to determine the impact of a tax reform on, say, labor supply. But other questions, such as the effects of tax reform on the long-run growth rate, simply cannot be answered in the short run. As ES point out, it is important to distinguish between the short-run and long-run effects of tax policy on growth. In the short run, tax policy can affect growth by encouraging labor supply, increasing saving and capital accumulation, and improving the efficiency of the allocation of labor and capital in production. Over the longer run, once these effects have taken place, tax policy can influence the growth rate only to the extent that it has a permanent impact on the rate of technological progress. While economic research has succeeded in developing theories to trace out how these effects might occur, there is little empirical evidence that tax policy can influence a country's long-run growth rate. Indeed, there is some evidence to the contrary, that even in countries experiencing exceptional rates of growth, this growth cannot be attributed to induced changes in technology (Young, 1992). But research of this sort requires decades to be able to distinguish between transitory and long-run effects on growth.[3]

Tax Reforms Are Complex

Even when evidence is available, it is often difficult to determine what this evidence tells us about a tax reform's impact. A large-scale tax reform such as the Swedish reform of 1991 or the U.S. Tax Reform Act of 1986 (TRA 86) might have many provisions likely to influence some particular aspect of behavior. For example, if we wish to determine whether real estate investment's response to TRA 86 was consistent with theoretical predictions, and learn something of the relevant behavioral elasticities, we must take account not only of changes in depreciation provisions, marginal tax rates on ordinary income, and treatment of capital gains, but also the effects of passive loss restrictions and the changes in interest rates induced by the reform. We must account for a multitude of effects, many which are hard to evaluate. While we may have reasonably clear predictions of how a change in marginal tax rates influences investment, the incentive effects of changes in passive loss rules or similar restrictions are more difficult to quantify.

An even better illustration of this type of difficulty comes from the Swedish reform, which simplified the tax treatment of business investment by eliminating various incentive schemes, most notably the investment funds system, and compensated for this by reducing the statutory marginal tax rate. Because of the complexity of the previous tax regime, it was difficult to know how the tax system influenced investment before the reform (Auerbach, Hassett, and Södersten, 1995). Thus, it was hard to predict how the tax reform should have influenced investment. This type of problem—that we cannot estimate the effects of a tax change without knowing the effects of current provisions—seems likely to plague any major tax reform where one of the objectives is to simplify the tax system.

Sometimes, the data themselves are simply too limited to allow us to perform a serious evaluation of tax changes. For example, the typical cross-country study cited by ES considers the effects on growth of variations in the gross domestic product (GDP) shares of different types of taxes, without being able to account for the important distinction (noted by ES) between the effects of marginal tax rates and those of average tax rates or, to put it another way, between substitution effects and income effects. Even where better data are available, it is not always easy to measure these effects separately. For example, in studying the impact of TRA 86 on labor supply, it is much easier to estimate the change in an individual's marginal tax rate than the direct and indirect impacts of all provisions on that individual's purchasing power. Yet, without being able to estimate these impacts, we cannot tell how much of the observed labor supply response is due to the change in labor supply incentives.

Tax Policy Is Endogenous

Particularly in cases where long-run effects are at issue and time series from a single country are inadequate, researchers often resort to cross-country analysis as a substitute, arguing that one can evaluate the long-run effects of policies by comparing the relative performance of countries with and without the policy. Here, though, we face what ES refer to as the "Achilles' heel" of cross-country regressions— reverse causality. If countries are otherwise equal, why do they have different policies? If they are not otherwise equal (at least to the extent that we can control for observable differences), how can we be sure that the unobservable differences are not responsible both for the differences in growth and differences in tax policy, or perhaps for differences in growth which, in turn, are responsible for differences in tax policy? The answer, of course, is that we cannot be sure, nor can we often be even confident that the apparent effects of tax policy are being properly interpreted.

Careful researchers can improve their chances of full immersion in the river Styx by limiting their study to countries with similar nontax characteristics, or by controlling for unobservable differences among countries by looking at *differences* in growth rates among countries following the adoption of particular tax policies by some (the so-called *differences-in-differences* approach). But, because they do not use all available data, these approaches sacrifice some of the available information. Moreover, they do not offer a complete solution to the problem of endogeneity. There is no guarantee that our choice of comparison countries eliminates all important unobservable differences. The differences-in-differences approach also still has problems, which are discussed below.

Other Things Are Happening

For effects of a short-run nature, such as induced changes in labor supply or

investment, a major problem confronting researchers, already discussed, is the confounding influences of contemporaneous macroeconomic fluctuations in wages and employment, interest rates and profitability, etc. To control for these macroeconomic effects, which strike all individuals and firms, many studies focus on the differential effects of tax changes in cross sections of individuals or among groups. With some luck, a reform will be expected to affect the behavior of some individuals or businesses more than others, and by comparing the changes in the behavior of these groups, we may be able to identify the effects of the tax change more generally.

For example, TRA 86 reduced the marginal tax rates on high-income individuals much more than on low- and middle-income individuals. Thus, we might consider the relatively large change in the marginal tax rates of high-income individuals as a *natural experiment*; by analogy to the terminology of true experiments, high-income individuals are the "treatment" group and other individuals are the "control" group. Eissa (1995) took this approach to estimate the labor supply response of married women, and Feldstein (1995) used it to estimate the responsiveness of taxable income. Their studies found larger increases in labor supply and taxable income for those with larger marginal tax rate reductions. Comparing the differences in behavioral effects to differences in marginal tax rate changes then provides us with an elasticity of response. Armed with this elasticity, we can estimate how the remainder of the taxpaying population responds to tax rate reductions, even though we cannot observe their responses directly.

Alas, the validity of this inference depends on how well the *natural* experiment resembles a true, well-designed experiment.[4] One problem is that, unlike in the case of a random trial, the control and treatment groups in the natural experiment are not drawn from the same population. Even if high-income people respond to marginal tax rate reductions, we are not necessarily justified in assuming that low-income people would respond in the same manner to comparable marginal tax rate reductions. These groups may differ in their preferences or in their ability to adjust hours of work or to shelter income from taxation. A second problem is that macroeconomic phenomena may hit the control and treatment groups differently. During this period of increasing wage inequality, high-income individuals faced relatively higher after-tax wages not only because of reductions in marginal tax rates, but also because of increases in their before-tax wages. While it may be possible to control for relative changes in wages, there may be other differential changes that are less easily observed. Finally, as discussed above, we need to take account not only of changes in marginal tax rates, but of other tax-related changes in income and incentives. If we fail to do so, and if these other effects differ between treatment and control groups (as is likely), we may attribute to marginal tax rate changes the effects of other provisions.

Some Effects Are Hard to Measure

Some of the potentially important effects of a tax reform are difficult to observe and measure. For example, both TRA 86 and Sweden's 1991 reform attempted to reduce the disparity of treatment among types of investment, supported by the argument that this would improve the allocation of capital and thereby reduce the deadweight loss from taxation.

Unlike changes in labor supply or investment, though, changes in deadweight loss are not immediately observable. To determine how well these reforms actually did in reducing deadweight loss, it would be necessary to measure not only the extent to which capital was reallocated, but also the extent to which before-tax returns rose as a result of these shifts to more socially productive uses. Yet, it is essentially impossible to observe before-tax returns on specific types of assets.

Summary

To determine the impact of a tax reform, it is necessary not only to develop theories of that tax reform's impact, but to test the theories. The lack of controlled experiments and of the ability to measure economic changes limits the scope for performing such evaluations. Thus, even potentially important economic effects may be difficult to uncover, particularly within a period of time when such information would be most useful.

ON THE METHODOLOGY OF TAX REFORM EVALUATIONS

All of the above limitations notwithstanding, economists have learned from tax reforms and can use what they have learned, in conjunction with some basic economic principles, to help guide policy decisions. However, in light of the situation, several useful principles should be applied to the analysis of tax reforms.

Distinguish Between Assumptions and Evidence

Given the many holes in our empirical evidence, it is natural and useful to fill in the gaps in our knowledge with theoretical predictions. For example, when AES argue that the Swedish tax reform's shift away from housing subsidies "did much to promote a less inefficient allocation of investment resources," they are assuming that housing investment generates no special positive externalities, such as a homeowner's increased commitment to community service. This is a quite reasonable assumption with which most economists would be comfortable, but it is an assumption nonetheless, rather than an empirical observation.

Another common assumption that would likely be somewhat more controversial is that investments in business equipment provide no positive externalities, for this is one of the channels through which the "new" growth theory posits that technological progress can be induced. Lacking evidence of this externality, we normally exclude it from our estimates, but we should make clear that we are doing so. In short, others cannot judge the strength of our conclusions without knowing the assumptions on which they are based.

Provide a Road Map of Reported Results

Large-scale tax reforms can affect behavior through many channels simultaneously. Indicating the relative importance of different channels helps others evaluate the conclusions. For example, during the 1995 budget showdown between President Clinton and Congress, the Congressional Budget Office (CBO) provided estimates of the deficit-reducing macroeconomic feedback effects of a seven-year balanced-budget policy (CBO, 1995). CBO was quite explicit that these effects came from one source: a reduction in the crowding out of private investment, which was predicted to lead to lower interest rates and less debt service and

greater income because of capital deepening. The estimate assumed that there would be no change in the unemployment rate because of a successful coordination of monetary policy with this contractionary fiscal policy, an assumption that one might question in light of the finding by AES that the 1991 Swedish reform entailed considerable short-run adjustment costs because "the government took a rather careless attitude to the transition problem."

Another illustration comes from attempts to relate tax cuts and subsequent economic growth. ES argue that "it is a difficult task to sort out" whether the strong U.S. economic growth in the mid-1980s and the Reagan tax cuts that began in 1981 were related via traditional Keynesian stimulus or supply-side reductions in marginal tax rates. But such distinctions are important if, for example, the next tax cut we consider takes place when the economy has much less room for demand-induced expansion than it did in 1982.

Reconcile Micro and Macro Effects

Predictions can be provided either at the micro or the macro level. For example, we might say that a tax cut will increase the labor supply of married women by two percent, or that it will increase GDP by 0.5 percent. In many cases, simply asking whether microlevel and macrolevel predictions are consistent—i.e., following through on either the "bottom-up" or the "top-down" approach discussed by ES—can help determine whether the predictions make sense. Indeed, even in cases where only micro or only macro estimates are provided, we can perform our own translation in order to evaluate how realistic the predictions are.

One can think of several instances where such attempts at reconciliation have been helpful. During the last decade, considerable empirical evidence (e.g., Venti and Wise, 1992) has been put forward suggesting that a large portion of individual contributions to Individual Retirement Accounts has come through new saving rather than saving that would have been done anyway or shifts of existing assets. But this apparent increase in saving seems to have had no positive effect on aggregate saving (Engen, Gale, and Scholz, 1994). The lack of confirming aggregate evidence does not disprove the existence of individual effects, but it does force those arguing in favor of such effects to reconcile the apparent inconsistency by explaining what other factors might have caused saving to decline.

Consider the debate over the effects of a capital gains tax cut on realizations. A central controversy has been over the extent to which observed short-run elasticities overstate the long-run increase in realizations in response to a permanent tax cut. While direct evaluation of these elasticity estimates has suggested that long-run elasticities are considerably smaller (e.g., Auerbach, 1988; Burman and Randolph, 1994), this conclusion gets further support from calculations that show just how extreme the underlying change in the frequency of trading would have to be to produce such large behavioral responses (Auerbach, 1989).

A final example comes from the recent debate over how much the shift from an income tax to a simple consumption tax (such as a value-added tax, a retail sales tax, or a flat tax) would increase GDP in the short run. We can judge at least the plausibility of claims of massive growth by asking what changes in labor supply

and saving these increases would require.

Be Appropriately Humble

A tension exists between wishing to make results clear and comprehensible, on the one hand, and offering needed qualification, on the other. The conclusions that AES and ES offer to their evaluations show that one can provide information without oversimplifying or overstating one's knowledge.

IMPLICATIONS FOR THE DESIGN OF TAX POLICY

What do the findings of AES and ES imply about the design of tax policy? One sort of lesson is about the economic merits of certain tax changes themselves. AES conclude that Sweden, which started with a very complex tax structure and high marginal tax rates, improved economic efficiency through its reform aimed at simplification and base-broadening. But they also find that the changes in real behavior, such as saving and labor supply, were modest, and the transition costs considerable. Thus, the reform was beneficial, particularly for a country with Sweden's initial tax system, but not the panacea some might have predicted. ES conclude that tax policy can affect at least short-run economic growth by enough to make an important difference in a country's standard of living.

But equally important are the lessons from these two papers about the process of tax reform itself. First, major changes in tax policy are not permanent or even long-lived. AES conclude that "even a 'tax reform of the century' implemented with such force as TR 91 did not stay unaffected for very long." They point in particular to marginal rate increases that broke the spirit of the reform's trade of tax expenditures for lower rates. One notices a disturbing similarity to the evolution of tax policy in the United States since the passage of TRA 86 (Auerbach and Slemrod, forthcoming, 1997). This finding is important, because it counters one of the arguments often put forward in favor of large-scale tax reforms over more incremental ones—that the large-scale reforms overcome entrenched interests and permanently alter the political landscape, making reversion to earlier policies more difficult.

Second, the economic effects of policies are difficult to evaluate; long-run effects are the most difficult. ES conclude, for example, that we really do not know the extent to which tax policy can affect long-run growth. This, too, offers an argument against major tax reforms that produce marked changes in economic incentives, because such changes deprive us of the opportunity to learn from our mistakes.

For example, a central argument for a shift to consumption taxation is that this shift will increase individual saving. This is what accepted economic theory tells us, but we have relatively little supporting evidence. Even evidence on the efficacy of saving incentives may not be that informative regarding a move toward a broad-based consumption tax, as such incentives may work for other reasons, such as employer promotion and education.[5] At present, housing equity aside, a considerable share of the saving that most people do is through employer-sponsored pension (including 401(k)) plans. If such plans lose their tax advantage relative to other saving and cease to be offered to the extent that they are now, can we be sure that private saving will not be adversely affected? Even if we believe not, our

uncertainty should temper our willingness to experience the major transition problems associated with the shift to a major new tax system.

In short, learning by doing is an option not just for the private sector. As compensation for the potential gains sacrificed by delaying full implementation of the "best" tax policy, we have the increased certainty that it really is the best tax policy. Should the change not turn out to be for the best, we can also take comfort from the prospect that tax changes, even "permanent" ones (and, alas, even good ones), may not last very long.

ENDNOTES

I am grateful to Joel Slemrod for comments on an earlier draft of this paper.
[1] A similar conclusion follows from the consideration of the effects of TRA 86 by Auerbach and Slemrod (forthcoming, 1997).
[2] Indeed, the evidence extends beyond humans. See, for example, Kagel et al. (1981).
[3] This problem arises in other contexts in macroeconomics as, for example, we attempt to determine whether GDP cycles around a trend or follows a random walk, or whether stock markets are efficient or exhibit mean reversion. In each case, the fundamental problem is the same: we can only distinguish between the alternatives after long periods of observation.
[4] For further discussion, see Heckman (1996).
[5] See the discussion in Bernheim (forthcoming,1997).

REFERENCES

Agell, Jonas, Peter Englund, and Jan Södersten. "Tax Reform of the Century—the Swedish Experiment." *National Tax Journal* 49 No. 4 (December, 1996): 641–62.

Auerbach, Alan J. "Capital Gains Taxation in the United States: Realizations, Revenue, and Rhetoric." *Brookings Papers on Economic Activity* 19 No. 2 (1988): 595–631.

Auerbach, Alan J. "Capital Gains Taxation and Tax Reform." *National Tax Journal* 42 No. 3 (September, 1989): 391–401.

Auerbach, Alan J., Kevin Hassett, and Jan Södersten. "Taxation and Corporate Investment: The Impact of the 1991 Swedish Tax

Reform." *Swedish Economic Policy Review* 2 No. 2 (Autumn, 1995): 361–83.

Auerbach, Alan J., and Joel Slemrod. "The Economic Effects of the Tax Reform Act of 1986." *Journal of Economic Literature* 35 No. 1 (forthcoming, March, 1997).

Bernheim, B. Douglas. "Rethinking Saving Incentives." In *Fiscal Policy: Lessons from Economic Research*, edited by Alan J. Auerbach. Cambridge, MA: MIT Press (forthcoming, 1997).

Burman, Leonard, and William Randolph. "Measuring Permanent Responses to Capital-Gains Tax Changes in Panel Data." *American Economic Review* 84 No. 4 (September, 1994): 794–809.

Eissa, Nada. "Taxation and Labor Supply of Married Women: The Tax Reform Act of 1986 as a Natural Experiment." NBER Working Paper No. 5023. Cambridge, MA: National Bureau of Economic Research, 1995.

Engen, Eric M., William G. Gale, and J. Karl Scholz. "Do Saving Incentives Work?" *Brookings Papers on Economic Activity* 25 No. 1 (1994): 85–151.

Engen, Eric M., and Jonathan Skinner. "Taxation and Economic Growth." *National Tax Journal* 49 No. 4 (December, 1996): 615–40.

Feldstein, Martin. "The Effect of Marginal Tax Rates on Taxable Income: A Panel Study of the 1986 Tax Reform Act." *Journal of Political Economy* 103 No. 3 (June, 1995): 551–72.

Heckman, James J. "Comment." In *Empirical Foundations of Household Taxation*, edited by Martin Feldstein and James Poterba, 32–8. Chicago: University of Chicago Press, 1995.

Kagel, John H., Raymond C. Battalio, Howard Rachlin, and Leonard Green. "Demand Curves for Animal Consumers." *Quarterly Journal of Economics* 96 No. 1 (February, 1981): 1–15.

U.S. Congressional Budget Office. *An Analysis of the President's Budgetary Proposals for Fiscal Year 1996.* Washington, D.C.: Government Printing Office, April, 1995.

Venti, Steven, and David Wise. "Government Policy and Personal Retirement Saving." In *Tax Policy and the Economy* 6, edited by James M. Poterba, 1–41. Cambridge, MA: MIT Press, 1992.

Young, Alwyn. "A Tale of Two Cities: Factor Accumulation and Technical Change in Hong Kong and Singapore." *NBER Macroeconomics Annual*, 13–54. Cambridge, MA: MIT Press, 1992.

WHAT IS AN "OPTIMAL" TAX SYSTEM?

JAMES ALM*

Abstract - A central issue in public economics is the appropriate design of a tax system. This paper argues that previous attempts to derive an "optimal tax system" are largely irrelevant to practical tax design, because they typically ignore a range of considerations reflecting fiscal and societal institutions that are essential elements in the normative and positive analysis of taxation. In particular, the standard optimal taxation methodology often ignores the equity and efficiency effects that arise because taxes must be collected, at some cost both to the tax agency and the taxpayer, and this collection must be enforced, again at some cost to the agency and the individual. However, the paper also argues that there are ways in which many of these relevant institutional features can be incorporated into a framework more general— but also more cumbersome, at least in its most general form —than that characteristic of the optimal taxation methodology. Such a framework will never be able to capture all of the incredible complexity that characterizes the real world and that must be considered in the actual design and reform of tax systems. However, the suggested framework can enhance our understanding of appropriate tax policy in several ways: it can illuminate and quantify with a common yardstick the various trade-offs that taxes necessarily create, it can highlight the areas that require additional research, and it can provide specific guidelines that tax policies should take in particular country circumstances, guidelines that seem often likely to be significantly different than those that emerge from the optimal taxation approach.

*Department of Economics, University of Colorado at Boulder, Boulder, CO 80309-0256.

INTRODUCTION

A central issue in public economics is the appropriate design of a tax system. Such a system is usually viewed as balancing the various desirable attributes of taxation: taxes must be raised (*revenue-yield*) in a way that treats individuals fairly (*equity*), that minimizes interference in economic decisions (*efficiency*), and that does not impose undue costs on taxpayers or tax administrators (*simplicity*).

One way in which at least some of these attributes have been analyzed is in an area of research that is commonly known as "optimal taxation." This is an explicitly normative approach to tax

363

analysis that is based on standard tools of welfare economics, as applied in a world when the first-best allocation of resources and distribution of income cannot be achieved. There have been many insights from this literature (Auerbach, 1985; Stern, 1987). However, even its adherents would, I believe, admit that the practical applicability of its basic theorems has been remarkably limited to date. Indeed, there often seems a schism, if not an animosity, between those who work on the rarefied heights of optimal tax theory and those who toil in the trenches of practical tax design.

In this paper, I argue that optimal taxation as it has been practiced is in fact largely irrelevant to practical tax design, because it typically ignores a range of considerations reflecting fiscal and societal institutions that are essential elements in the normative and positive analysis of taxation. In particular, the standard optimal taxation methodology often ignores the equity and efficiency effects that arise because taxes must be collected, at some cost both to the tax agency and the taxpayer, and this collection must be enforced, again at some cost to the agency and the individual. Because most analyses in the optimal taxation tradition ignore these features, their basic policy prescriptions are unlikely to lead to an improvement in welfare, when compared to those policy rules derived from a less formal but more realistic perspective; in fact, they are even unlikely to be implemented or to be taken as serious guides to policy. Admittedly, this argument is not new (Slemrod, 1990; Bird, 1992). It is also somewhat overstated, especially given some recent work in the optimal taxation methodology that examines some of these issues. Nevertheless, I also argue that there are

ways in which many of these relevant institutional features can be incorporated into a framework more general— but also more cumbersome, at least in its most general form—than that characteristic of the optimal taxation methodology. Such a framework will never be able to capture all of the incredible complexity that characterizes the real world and that must be considered in the actual design and reform of tax systems. However, I believe that the suggested framework can enhance our understanding of appropriate tax policy by illuminating and quantifying with a common yardstick the various trade-offs that taxes necessarily create, by highlighting the areas that require additional research, and by providing specific guidelines that tax design and tax reform should take in particular country circumstances, all in a more comprehensive manner than previously undertaken. I also believe that the tax guidelines that emerge from this framework will often be significantly different than those that emerge from the optimal taxation approach. It is toward the establishment of this research framework that this paper is largely addressed.

In the next section, I discuss the standard optimal taxation methodology and present several of its more widely known results. The following sections outline some of the important considerations that have been largely ignored by this methodology and also discuss recent research on these considerations. I then present a suggestion for research that systematically incorporates the various institutional features. In the final section, I speculate on the ways in which the standard optimal tax results seem likely to be modified by these considerations.

THE OPTIMAL TAX APPROACH

The standard approach to optimal taxation is based on several methodological assumptions: the government is required to raise a specified amount of revenues; it is limited in the types of tax instruments that it has available to it, such as only commodity taxes, only income taxes, or both types; its decisions must be consistent with individual and firm optimization; and it makes its choices in order to maximize a "social welfare function," which indicates the value that society places on the welfare of different individuals.

The major results that have been derived from this framework can be classified according to the types of tax instruments that the government can select (see Auerbach [1985] and Stern [1987] for a detailed discussion of these results), as illustrated in the following subsections.

Optimal Commodity Taxes

On *efficiency* grounds, commodity tax rates should be chosen to achieve equal proportional reductions in the (compensated) demands for all commodities, so that goods with more elastic demands should be taxed at lower rates (the "Ramsey Rule"). However, on *equity* grounds, goods consumed more heavily by those with lower income (or, more generally, by those whose welfare is weighted more heavily by society) should be taxed at lower rates.

Optimal Income Taxes

On *equity* grounds, income taxes should be higher on those with greater income; indeed, under some special conditions, income taxes should be chosen to equalize after-tax incomes, thereby implying marginal tax rates of 100 percent. However, on *efficiency* grounds, marginal tax rates should be lower the more responsive are individuals in their labor decisions, the smaller is the spread in the skills of the individuals, the less concerned with equality is society, and the lower is the amount of revenue that government must collect. In fact, the marginal tax rate on the single richest individual should be zero.

Optimal Tax Mix

On *efficiency* grounds, the optimal tax mix requires simply a lump-sum income tax, and commodity taxes are not used. On *equity* grounds, both income and commodity taxes should be used in general; however, under some restrictive conditions, the optimal form of commodity tax rates that are imposed in the presence of an optimal income tax requires that the commodity tax rates be uniform, so that taxation of commodities at different rates is not optimal and only the optimal income tax is used.

The framework discussed in the previous subsections is, of course, a highly stylized one that by necessity ignores a number of relevant considerations. Still, it is a useful framework, at least in part because it forces the analyst to make explicit the trade-off between equity (*via* the social welfare function) and efficiency (*via* an array of individual and firm behavioral effects) in the choice of taxes.

For example, consider optimal commodity taxes. Commodities with more inelastic demands should be taxed more heavily in order to reduce the excess burden of taxation; however, if these goods are consumed predominantly by those with lower incomes, then equity concerns argue for lower tax rates.

Similarly, optimal income taxes must balance the equity gains that higher marginal tax rates allow with the efficiency losses that higher tax rates generate. In general, the optimal tax rules involve balancing these equity and efficiency considerations.

However, there is little dispute that the standard optimal framework ignores, or at least does not adequately consider, a number of important considerations in the design of taxes. In particular, these optimal tax rules depend primarily upon the preferences of the individuals (as well as upon the tax instruments available to government). These rules neither consider the costs imposed upon the taxpayer and the government of collecting the taxes, nor do they consider the costs imposed on the respective agents of enforcing this collection. Now if it can be argued that these considerations are sometimes relevant but seldom central to the design of taxes, then the failure to model them systematically would be irritating but unimportant. However, as I argue in the next sections, the failure to address these different costs of taxes is far from inconsequential.

INDIVIDUAL AND FIRM COMPLIANCE COSTS

Implicit in much of the optimal taxation literature is the assumption that it is costless for individuals and firms to pay their taxes. There is little question that this assumption is simply wrong, for a number of reasons.

On a purely anecdotal basis, it has been evident for some time that there are substantial individual and firm "compliance costs" from taxation. Taxpayer complaints about keeping records throughout the year, deciphering complicated tax forms, seeking professional advice, filling out returns, and the like are legion and legendary.

Furthermore, even casual economic analysis clearly indicates that we should always expect paying taxes to imply incurring costs. No one likes the loss of income from taxes, and people will clearly take actions to avoid (or reduce) their liability. It is a standard result in economics that agents will increase their actions up to the point where the marginal benefits of their actions—in this case, the reduced taxes—equals the marginal costs—or the compliance costs—of the actions. On the margin, then, the costs of paying taxes should be approximated by the tax savings from the array of legal tax avoidance schemes that taxpayers have pursued, the accuracy of the approximation depending largely upon the way in which the marginal costs of compliance increase with the extent of their magnitude.

Finally, and most importantly, there are now a number of estimates, derived from a variety of methodologies, of the actual magnitudes of the individual and firm compliance costs in the United States. For individuals, Slemrod and Sorum (1984) and Blumenthal and Slemrod (1992) use surveys of taxpayers to estimate that the compliance cost of the individual income tax may approach about seven percent of its revenues. Using a different approach based upon econometric analysis of individual tax returns, Pitt and Slemrod (1989) calculate that the compliance cost of itemizing deductions in 1982 totaled nearly 0.5 percent of revenues. On the corporate side, Blumenthal and Slemrod (1995) conclude from a survey of "large" corporations that corporate compliance costs are over three percent of total federal and state corporate income tax collections. Evidence for the United Kingdom (Sandford, 1995), Australia (Pope, Fayle, and Duncanson, 1990), and Canada (Vaillancourt, 1989) suggests that compliance costs can range from 2 to 24 percent of revenues for selected taxes.

In total, these studies clearly indicate that the compliance costs of taxation are significant, often of comparable or even larger values than the more traditional calculations of the excess burden of taxation. In part because of these results, economists have begun to add compliance costs to their standard theoretical analyses of individual taxpayer behavior (Alm, 1988; Slemrod, 1995). There is also some theoretical work that has begun to incorporate some aspects of individual compliance costs in an optimal tax framework (Slemrod, 1994; Slemrod and Yitzhaki, 1994). However, despite the insights from this work, it is still subject to some limitations: it typically examines only a limited number of tax instruments, such as those that apply to individuals only; it is based upon very stylized assumptions about individual behavior; and it seldom deals precisely with the exact nature of the compliance costs to individuals. Clearly, there is more that needs to be done to model, as well as to measure, the compliance cost of taxes.

THE ADMINISTRATIVE COSTS OF TAXATION

Although there is considerably less systematic work on the costs to the government of collecting taxes (or the "administrative costs" of taxation), the available evidence from government budgetary information clearly indicates that the budget cost of collecting individual income, business income, and sales taxes is generally in excess of one percent of the revenues from these

taxes and can sometimes be substantially higher (Vaillancourt, 1989; Sandford, 1995). Unfortunately, there is little information on how these costs vary with various policy tools; that is, it seems likely that the administrative costs change in large and discrete amounts with the scale of collections (or they may exhibit "discontinuities") and that they may also display economies of scale in their collections (or they may exhibit "nonconvexities"), but these aspects of the collection cost technology are not known.

The administrative dimension of taxation has long been recognized by tax administrators, especially those working on tax policy in developing countries (Bagchi, Bird, and Das-Gupta, 1995). However, it has not been until recently that administrative costs have been formally incorporated in the analysis of optimal taxation. Mayshar (1991) assumes that there are costs to the taxpayer and to the government from collecting a generic form of taxes and determines the conditions that characterize the optimal use of the tax. Other work has examined the optimal choice of tax instruments in the presence of positive administrative costs. For example, Wilson (1989) examines the optimal number of commodities to be taxed, where there is some cost to government from the expansion of the optimal commodity tax base; he concludes that the optimal size of the tax base balances the extra administrative costs from taxing more commodities with the efficiency (and revenue-yield) gains from the base expansion. Different aspects of the optimal administration of the individual income tax have also been considered. Stern (1982) assumes that the characteristics of the taxpayers cannot be observed with certainty, and Slemrod and Yitzhaki (1994) analyze the trade-off between more accurate measurement of income via itemized deductions and less costly measurement via the standard deduction.

These analyses have generated numerous insights. However, to repeat some points made about the analyses of compliance costs, they are also largely based on fairly arbitrary assumptions about such things as the available tax instruments (e.g., only commodity or income taxes can be used), the behavioral responses of taxpayers (e.g., taxpayers have only some particular and restrictive forms of preferences), the administrative costs to government (e.g., the administrative costs increase smoothly and continuously from policy changes), and the like. Clearly, there is more that needs to be done to model and, again, to measure the administrative cost dimension.

TAX EVASION AND ENFORCEMENT

The standard optimal tax approach assumes that individuals and firms voluntarily pay all of their tax liabilities. This assumption is wildly inaccurate. Individuals pursue many illegal avenues to reduce their payments, such as underreporting incomes, overstating deductions and exemptions, or failing to file returns. Despite obvious measurement difficulties, there is widespread evidence that tax evasion is extensive and commonplace in nearly all countries. For the United States, the most reliable estimates project the amount of unpaid federal income taxes at $127 billion for 1992, with an annual growth rate of roughly ten percent since 1973 (U.S. Government Accounting Office, 1995). Other taxes at other levels of government are also subject to nonpayment. Evidence from other countries suggests that the American experience is not an isolated one.

Tax evasion is important for many reasons. In the context of the discussion here, it affects the efficiency of the tax system by creating misallocations in resource use as agents alter their behavior—and incur costs (or "noncompliance costs")—to cheat on their taxes. Evasion also has equity effects because it alters the distribution of income in unpredictable ways. Because it causes the government to expend resources (or "enforcement costs") to reduce its magnitude and it also reduces the taxes that individuals pay, tax evasion affects the tax rates that compliant taxpayers face and the public services that all citizens receive. More broadly, it is not possible to understand the true impact of taxation without recognizing the existence of evasion. It is clearly not possible to design an optimal tax system without appropriate consideration of tax evasion and its effects on individuals and on government.

In comparison to the other areas of research discussed above, there is an extensive literature devoted to the theoretical and empirical analysis of tax evasion (Cowell, 1990). The theoretical analysis of tax evasion most often builds on the economics-of-crime model first applied to tax evasion by Allingham and Sandmo (1972). The focus of nearly all of this work is on the behavior of a representative individual who faces an individual income tax. The individual is viewed as maximizing the expected utility of the evasion gamble, weighing the benefits of successful cheating against the risky prospect of detection and punishment, and the individual pays taxes because he or she is afraid of getting caught and penalized. This approach gives the plausible and productive insight that compliance depends upon audit and fine rates. Indeed, the central conclusion of this approach is that an individual pays taxes only because of this fear of detection and punishment, and an increase in the fine or the audit rate can be shown to increase compliance. Surprisingly, an increase in the tax rate generally has an ambiguous effect on reported income in the standard model; under plausible assumptions, compliance actually rises with higher tax rates, in contrast to the common perception that higher tax rates have contributed to evasion.

However, it is clear to a number of observers that at least some forms of compliance cannot be explained entirely by the level of enforcement (Graetz and Wilde, 1985). The levels of audit and penalty rates are set so low that most individuals would either underreport income not subject to source withholding or overclaim deductions not subject to independent verification if they were purely "rational," because it is unlikely that such cheating would be caught and penalized.

In part because of this quandary, there have been numerous extensions of the basic theoretical model, to consider other factors not included in the basic theoretical model or to consider other factors not captured appropriately by the theory. These extensions include such things as government services, overweighting of low probabilities, social norms, and labor supply choices. Of particular relevance here, the theory has also expanded to include the following.

(1) Uncertainty and complexity: Individuals may not know with certainty their tax liability or the tax agency's enforcement strategy (Cronshaw and Alm, 1995).

(2) Endogenous audit selection rules: The agency may use information from the tax returns to determine strategically whom to audit, so that the probability of audit is endogenous, dependent in part on the behavior of the taxpayer and the tax agency (Reinganum and Wilde, 1985).

(3) Use of paid preparers: Paid preparers may both reduce taxpayer confusion and encourage noncompliant behavior on ambiguous items (Erard, 1993).

(4) Tax avoidance: An individual simultaneously chooses the amounts of tax evasion and tax avoidance (Alm, 1988).

(5) Structure of taxation: Some kinds of taxes are easier to evade than others (Kesselman, 1989).

To date, however, no single theory has been able to incorporate more than a few of these factors in a meaningful way, and it seems unlikely that such a general model will be forthcoming.

Empirical analysis of individual behavioral responses has also grown dramatically in the last 20 years. The main difficulty in this work is finding information on the compliance behavior of individuals. Because of this problem, the empirical work draws creatively on a variety of data sources. The most extensively used source for the United State relies on information generated by the Internal Revenue Service. Other sources include taxpayer returns, survey data, national income accounts, and laboratory experiments. In its entirety, this work suggests the following conclusions relevant to the discussion here.

(1) An increase in tax complexity leads to greater use of a tax practitioner, and the average level of noncompliance is higher for returns prepared with paid assistance (Erard, 1993).

(2) A higher audit rate leads to more compliance, at least to a point, with an estimated reported income–audit rate elasticity ranging from 0.1 to 0.2 (Dubin and Wilde, 1988).

(3) A higher fine rate leads to marginally more compliance, with an estimated reported income–fine rate elasticity less than 0.1 (Alm, Bahl, and Murray, 1993).

(4) A higher tax rate leads to less compliance, with an estimated reported income–tax rate elasticity ranging from –0.5 to –3.0. (Clotfelter, 1983).

(5) Audit rates are endogenous, in that they depend in part on the choices of taxpayers (Feinstein, 1991).

There is now also some empirical work on corporate income tax compliance (Rice, 1992) and on firm sales tax compliance (Murray, 1995).

Given the underlying data problems, this empirical work needs to be treated cautiously. Still, these results indicate that individuals incur costs and change their behavior in response to enforcement activities and that the enforcement agency can increase compliance by taking advantage of these responses in its choice of an enforcement strategy. They also clearly indicate that there are limits to strategies based only on greater enforcement.

There has also been much work on optimal government policy in the face of tax evasion, including theoretical analysis of optimal tax *cum* enforcement policies (Sandmo, 1981; Kaplow, 1990; Cremer and Gahvari, 1993; Boadway, Marchand, and Pestieau, 1994). The standard policy prescription has long been an increase in penalty and audit rates; indeed, at least the theoretical work suggests that sufficient—and draconian—increases in penalty and audit rates could substantially eliminate evasion.

However, it is unlikely that such extreme measures will actually be implemented, at least in part because there is a widespread belief that "the punishment should fit the crime." Moreover, it should be remembered that, although higher penalty and audit rates generate benefits, they also entail costs, both to the government that must use real resources in its efforts and to the individuals who suffer a loss in utility from greater enforcement. These considerations clearly suggest that government should not expand its enforcement actions to the point where an additional dollar of enforcement costs yields an additional dollar of revenues: the former involves a real resource cost to the economy, while the latter is simply a transfer from the private to the public sector (Slemrod and Yitzhaki, 1987; Alm, 1988). Instead, most analyses of the optimal amount of government enforcement conclude that optimal enforcement must equate the marginal costs of enforcement with the marginal benefits, where these benefits should include the added revenues but should also reflect the impact of greater induced honesty and the loss in individual expected utility. Consequently, it seems clear that optimal enforcement should not eliminate all tax evasion (Polinsky and Shavell, 1984). As noted above, there is also clear theoretical evidence that the optimal enforcement policy should utilize information from the tax returns in the selection of returns for audit (Reinganum and Wilde, 1985). Such "endogenous" audit selection rules are able to generate higher levels of compliance than equal cost rules in which returns are selected randomly (Alm, Cronshaw, and McKee, 1993).

A FRAMEWORK FOR ANALYSIS

It is obviously difficult to know how all these considerations will affect the standard optimal taxation rules. Indeed, it is difficult even to know where to start to analyze in a systematic way the effects of these factors on the appropriate design of tax systems.

Still, I believe that a careful examination of these factors suggests that they all involve trade-offs among essentially three main criteria:

(1) How does the choice of taxes affect the yield of the tax collections, where the yield is defined broadly in terms of the gross collections in excess of administrative and enforcement costs (*revenue-yield*)?

(2) How does the choice affect the distribution of the burden of taxation on individuals, where the burden is defined broadly in terms of the tax burden, the compliance cost burden, and the noncompliance cost burden on taxpayers (*equity*)?

(3) How does the choice affect the decisions of individuals and firms, where the decisions are defined broadly in terms of the responses of the agents to the entire tax, compliance, and enforcement parameters (*efficiency*)?

Note in particular that I do not define a separate criterion for *simplicity*. Instead, simplicity is implicitly assumed to be considered in its effects on the other three dimensions of a desirable tax system.

The omission of simplicity as an explicit measure and its incorporation in other goals is important and needs some justification; this justification also serves to illustrate the ways in which compliance, administrative, noncompliance, and enforcement costs can be incorporated in the analysis. The reasons for this omission are best illustrated by means of some examples. Consider, say, the introduction of some specific tax provision that affects individuals via the individual income tax (*e.g.*, the deduction of business-related expenses). This change is often discussed as involving a balancing of simplicity, efficiency, equity, and revenue-yield effects. The change allows the tax to be imposed on a more accurate measure of an individual's ability to pay, and it encourages, or at least does not discourage, the individual from engaging in those business-related activities that generate income. However, there are clearly added costs imposed on individuals from this feature. There are compliance costs to the individual because records of these expenses need to be maintained, and these costs reduce the individual's income. There are also added administrative costs that lower net revenues, since these deductions complicate the administration of the tax. Further, individuals may fraudulently claim these expenses, which implies that the government must expend resources enforcing the provision, at some cost both to the government and to the taxpayer. Finally, the deduction itself will generate some revenue loss to the government.

However, these various aspects will be incorporated in the standard measures of equity, efficiency, and revenue-yield.

The direct effect of the deduction on revenues enters in an obvious way, as do the impacts of the extra administrative costs and enforcement costs on government revenues net of these costs. The effects on efficiency are reflected in any lost output that arises from behavioral responses to the tax provision itself, from the individuals' efforts to establish the legitimacy of the deductions, from the noncompliance actions of the individuals, and from the enforcement activities of government, all of which are represented by the standard measure of the excess burden of taxation. The effects of the tax provision on equity are captured by the differential impact of the provision on the income of different individuals and by the weights of those individuals in the social welfare function; that is, the provision both increases an individual's income (because it generates tax savings) and decreases income (because it produces compliance and noncompliance costs), and these equity effects are measured in the social welfare function by the combination of the change in individual income and the social weights on the welfare of those individuals who experience these changes. (Note that these comments pertain to the vertical equity of taxes. The effects on horizontal equity are more difficult to determine; indeed, as argued by Kaplow (1989), even the existence of a separate notion of horizontal equity is controversial.) A separate criterion for simplicity is therefore not needed.

Or consider a change in enforcement policy (e.g., an increase in audit coverage). There is a range of effects that determines the desirability of this policy change. The government will incur some added administrative and enforcement costs but will also generate some extra revenues. The level of output will be affected as individuals change their behavior in the face of the stricter enforcement. Because different individuals will be affected in different ways, the distribution of income will also be altered, thereby creating equity effects. All of these effects will be captured by the usual standards of revenue-yield, efficiency, and equity.

Consequently, analysis of taxation requires balancing the trade-offs between equity, efficiency, and revenue-yield, where each is broadly defined and commonly measured. Still, analysis of even these three factors is obviously a daunting task. It seems to me that the best option involves a threefold strategy.

First, empirical work must continue to be performed to estimate both the magnitude of the compliance costs of different taxes and the determinants of those compliance costs (or the individual and firm "compliance cost function"). At least for the United States, most previous work has focused on the cost to individuals of the individual income tax and, to a lesser extent, on the cost to large corporations of the corporate income tax. However, there are clearly compliance costs from many other major taxes, costs that are borne largely by firms. Firms of all sizes incur costs in the collection of sales and excise taxes, payroll taxes, severance taxes, user fees, and so on; the costs incurred by "small" and "medium" size firms are largely unknown. Further, the ways in which these compliance costs are affected by different tax design features is essential in the determination of government policies but again is not known. How do compliance costs increase with special provisions of the taxes? Are compliance costs affected by progressive tax rates? What is the magnitude of the costs in the "start-up" phase of new taxes or of new tax provisions? How significant are scale economies in tax compliance? How do individuals and firms respond in their decisions to changes in government tax policies, such as an increase in the standard deduction or a strengthening of reporting requirements? These and other questions are unanswered.

Similarly, although there is budgetary information on the administrative costs of various taxes, there has been little systematic analysis of the determinants of these administrative costs and the effects of these determinants on the quantity and the quality of tax administration (the "administrative cost function"). In particular, it seems likely that there are significant fixed costs when a new tax is imposed or when the features of an existing tax are changed. For similar reasons, it seems likely that the expansion of, say, an existing sales tax to include new commodities involves a stepwise, or discontinuous, increase in costs. Also, there may well be some economies of scale, or nonconvexities, in tax administration. However, these issues have received little attention, at least by economists. Similar questions surround noncompliance (the "noncompliance cost function" for taxpayers) and enforcement (the "enforcement cost function" for tax agencies). There is clearly much scope for empirical analysis, and such analysis is a necessary input in the design of taxes.

It is, however, important to emphasize that a focus on the measurement of compliance, administrative, noncompliance, and enforcement costs does not mean that empirical work on the more common behavioral responses to taxes should be ignored. There is an enormous—and surprising—amount that we simply do not know about how individuals and firms react to taxes. Empirical work on these aspects is the central

component of the optimal design of taxes, and the analysis of these responses must continue.

Second, the equity, efficiency, and revenue-yield effects generated by these behavioral responses must be incorporated into an analysis in which they can be measured on a common scale. As argued above, these effects are captured by standard measures, known and used by economists. Note again that the consideration of (vertical) equity effects requires that explicit judgments about the relative social worth of different individuals must be made by the analyst. Such judgments are always made, perhaps especially when they are not made explicitly.

Third, I think it unavoidable that rigorous analysis of the range of considerations relevant to tax design requires numerical analysis, perhaps in a computable general equilibrium framework, in which the different considerations are sequentially layered, one atop another, until the full model captures the relevant factors. The numerical analysis would necessarily incorporate the empirical analyses of compliance cost, administrative cost, noncompliance cost, and enforcement cost functions.

The reason for reliance upon numerical analysis is easily stated. Even simple theoretical models of optimal taxation quickly become unwieldy and incapable of interpretation or generalization. At best, these models only characterize the optimal tax rules by defining the numerous conditions that must be satisfied if taxes are to be optimal; that is, these models specify a system of equations that must hold simultaneously in order for the tax rates to be optimal. However, these models do not actually determine the precise pattern of the taxes. Unless the exact forms of the various equations are specified, it is clearly impossible to solve analytically the system of equations for the actual tax rates; even with these specifications, there is obviously no guarantee that the equations can be solved for unique tax rates. Further, these models almost always assume that the various functions change smoothly and continuously, an assumption that allows the use of differential calculus. However, as discussed above, it seems likely that the various cost functions, especially the administrative and enforcement cost functions, are characterized both by large discrete changes and by economies of scale. The search for purely analytical solutions seems a dead end.

There are now many examples of numerical analyses in the optimal tax tradition. There is also a growing literature on general equilibrium modeling (Shoven and Whalley, 1992). The combination of these literatures seems a fruitful path of research. Like the standard optimal taxation approach, such a framework requires an explicit modeling of the behavioral effects of taxation, as well as an explicit recognition of the welfare weights placed on different classes of individuals. Importantly, it also requires explicit incorporation of the different cost functions. The numerical specification necessarily pertains to the characteristics and institutions of a particular country.

For example, consider the process by which optimal commodity taxes could be determined in such a framework. The analysis would begin with the simplest case, which forms the basis of the standard optimal commodity tax problem: How should tax rates on commodities be chosen to raise a specified amount of revenues when the government is concerned only with the efficiency effects of taxes and when there are no compliance costs, administrative costs, noncompliance costs, or enforcement costs? This analysis would consider a numerical representation of a specific economy in which consumer and firm decisions are modeled with functional forms whose parameter values replicate the real world outcomes of that economy. The outcome of this simulation would be the standard optimal commodity tax result that tax rates should be higher on commodities with less elastic demands.

This analysis would then be modified to incorporate efficiency and equity concerns: If individuals differ and if government is concerned with raising revenues to meet efficiency and equity goals, how should commodity tax rates be chosen? Note that this analysis requires explicit assumptions about the social worth of different individuals.

A third layer of analysis would then add the compliance costs on firms (and, perhaps, on individuals) of commodity taxes. This analysis would be based on estimates of the compliance cost function generated from empirical studies of firm behavior, and its results would indicate the effects of compliance costs on the simple optimal tax rules. A possible complication in this stage is the potential for discontinuities and nonconvexities in the compliance cost function. These are difficult to analyze in theoretical models, but there are now methods for incorporating such factors in numerical models.

A fourth layer would incorporate administrative costs, using administrative cost function estimates that allow for discontinuities and nonconvexities. A fifth layer would consider noncompliance. Some commodity taxes are easier to collect, and some are easier to evade, than others (*e.g.,* commodities versus services). How does the presence of noncompliance with commodity taxes affect the optimal commodity tax structure? The enforcement of commodity taxes would then be added in a final layer, based on the individual noncompliance and the agency enforcement cost functions. Obviously, other sequences could be usefully considered.

Similar steps can be followed for optimal income taxes. The first stage would examine the optimal form of a (linear) income tax, when the government is concerned with equity only and when there are no compliance costs, administrative issues, noncompliance problems, or enforcement difficulties; transfer (or welfare) programs would also be separately incorporated. Then the following sequence of layering would be analyzed: equity only; equity and efficiency; equity, efficiency, and compliance costs; equity, efficiency, compliance costs, and administrative costs; equity, efficiency, compliance costs, administrative costs, and noncompliance costs; and equity, efficiency, compliance costs, administrative costs, noncompliance costs, and enforcement costs. The result of this (or some other sequence) would be a much more detailed and realistic set of policy prescriptions for the appropriate design of tax policies in a specific setting.

Conclusions: Optimal Taxation In The Real World

What would be the form of the tax rules that would emerge from such a framework? It is risky to make general statements. Indeed, I think it certain that the tax rules would vary, perhaps significantly, across the different economies subject to this analysis. Tax design must always consider the particular circumstances at hand, and at present, we do not know many of the characteristics of the relevant functions. Still, my own guess is that a full analysis of these factors will lead to modification of the standard optimal tax rules, as discussed in the following subsections.

Optimal Commodity Taxes

Commodity tax rates should be largely proportional. Proportional tax rates reduce compliance costs and administrative costs because they eliminate the necessity of separate measurement of the tax bases. For similar reasons, they lower the enforcement costs to the government. Proportional tax rates also reduce the incentives for noncompliance, and they reduce the distortions from changes in the relative prices of commodities. Divergences from proportional commodity tax rates should be minimal and should largely take the form of marginally higher tax rates on goods that are unresponsive to price changes (*e.g.,* necessities, for efficiency reasons), on goods that generate significant negative spillovers (*e.g.,* alcohol or tobacco, also for efficiency reasons), on goods consumed by higher income groups (*e.g.,* luxuries, for equity reasons), and on goods for which taxes can be easily and cheaply collected (*e.g.,* goods versus services, for administrative cost and revenue-yield reasons).

Optimal Income Taxes

Income taxes should be imposed at constant marginal tax rates on broadly defined tax bases above some level of income determined by generously defined exemptions and (standard) deductions with minimal use of special tax incentives. Constant marginal tax rates reduce compliance costs by reducing the incentive to engage in tax shifting schemes; for related reasons, they reduce administrative costs. Broadly defined tax bases allow lower marginal tax rates to generate a given level of revenue, and so reduce the distorting effects of taxes on behavior, including behavior related to noncompliance. Generously defined exemptions help achieve equity goals with reduced compliance and administrative costs and imply that lower income individuals will pay negative taxes. Standard deductions reduce the equity of the income tax but lower administrative, compliance, noncompliance, and enforcement costs; in contrast, tax incentives increase the range of taxpayer and tax agency costs with uncertain impacts on their desired ends. Income taxes should also be collected by source withholding, thereby lowering compliance and administrative costs.

Optimal Tax Mix

Both direct and indirect taxes should be levied. Use of both taxes allows each tax to be imposed at lower marginal tax rates, which reduces distortions and, most likely, noncompliance. Use of both taxes also gives the government more flexibility to achieve its equity and its revenue-yield goals, especially given the limitations that administrative considerations impose on the scope and even the use of some taxes.

The optimal tax mix guidelines are the most uncertain and the most in need of additional research. It is easily established that proportional income and commodity taxes are equivalent when each is imposed on a comprehensive base. Given such equivalence, only one of these taxes need be used; indeed, the incorporation of the range of costs discussed above clearly implies that only one should be used. However, it is also easily recognized that the equivalence of

direct and indirect taxes in theory is unlikely to hold in practice. "General" sales taxes are never general, due to difficulties in administration and enforcement. Similarly, income taxes are never imposed and collected on all incomes. When it is also recognized that compliance costs for income and commodity taxes differ in both their magnitude and their incidence, that the taxes differ in their costs of collection, that some individuals are better able to evade income taxes than others while most individuals are unable to cheat on commodity taxes, that enforcement of income taxes is generally more difficult than that for commodity taxes, then in such circumstances I think it plausible that both taxes should be used. In short, it is the fact that each tax is imperfect—and that each is imperfect in different ways—that suggests that both should be used.

Although it is comforting that these broad guidelines are similar to those suggested by others (Bird, 1992), more systematic analysis of these issues is obviously needed, and such analysis may well lead to different guidelines. There is clearly a pressing need for analyses in which specific features of a particular country are incorporated and analyzed in useful and usable simulation models. I believe that such analyses serve at least three ends: they indicate and quantify with a standard measure the trade-offs that taxes necessarily create; they indicate the areas in which our knowledge is incomplete; and they provide specific guidelines for tax design and tax reform, in particular country circumstances. I also believe that the guidelines that emerge from such analyses are in most cases likely to be significantly different than those that emerge from the optimal taxation approach.

It is, unfortunately, important to keep in mind that this exercise may ultimately prove futile. The informational requirements for the kind of analysis outlined here are daunting, and there is too much that we do not and, indeed, that we cannot know. It is also impossible to consider all possible aspects that are relevant in the optimal design of tax systems; even if all of the factors discussed at length above were to be incorporated, there would necessarily remain omissions. Perhaps most important among these omissions, the optimal taxation methodology does not consider the positive aspects of the enactment and the enforcement of tax rules. The individuals who pass the tax laws have interests that may not always coincide with the somewhat amorphous notion of social welfare that is used in optimal taxation; that is, there is a political dimension to tax policies that may well outweigh the purely normative considerations at the foundation of optimal taxation (Hettich and Winer, 1988). As one example, these interests may lead individuals in authority to enact complex tax rules because of the political gains from complexity, even though such complexity may have efficiency, equity, and revenue-yield costs. Appropriate government policy must also recognize that the individuals responsible for administering and enforcing the tax rules may well need oversight as well. There is widespread evidence of corruption by government officials, and the ways in which this corruption should be controlled must be considered (Chander and Wilde, 1992).

In short, the search for a general scheme that specifies, for all countries and all times, the details of an optimal tax system is certain to fail. There are simply too many details that must be known but that are unknowable to implement fully the prescriptions of optimal tax theory. There are simply too many tax features that are possible candidates for action but that cannot be modeled to consider fully their use. Still, this should not discourage the search for specific tax design—and, especially, tax reform—guidelines that apply to a single country at a point in time and that incorporate the range of considerations discussed here. Such guidelines will necessarily be couched in general terms. However, if the guidelines are generated from models that incorporate the factors discussed here, I believe that they will offer a better map for tax policy than those derived from the standard optimal tax framework.

ENDNOTE

I have benefited greatly from comments by Richard Bird, Louis Kaplow, and Joel Slemrod.

REFERENCES

Allingham, Michael, and Agnar Sandmo. "Income Tax Evasion: A Theoretical Analysis." *Journal of Public Economics* 1 No. 3/4 (1972): 323–38.

Alm, James. "Compliance Costs and the Tax Avoidance–Tax Evasion Decision." *Public Finance Quarterly* 16 No. 1 (January, 1988): 31–66.

Alm, James, Roy Bahl, and Matthew N. Murray. "Audit Selection and Income Tax Underreporting in the Tax Compliance Game." *Journal of Development Economics* 42 No. 1 (October, 1993): 1–33.

Alm, James, Mark B. Cronshaw, and Michael McKee. "Tax Compliance with Endogenous Audit Selection Rules." *Kyklos* 46 No. 1 (1993): 27–45.

Auerbach, Alan J. "The Theory of Excess Burden and Optimal Taxation." In *Handbook of Public Economics, Vol. 1*, edited by Alan J. Auerbach and Martin S. Feldstein, 61–128. Amsterdam: North-Holland, 1985.

Bagchi, Amaresh, Richard Bird, and Arindam Das-Gupta. "An Economic Approach to Tax Administration Reform." Discussion Paper No. 3. Toronto, Canada: International Centre for Tax Studies, University of Toronto, 1995.

Bird, Richard M. *Tax Policy and Economic Development.* Baltimore, MD: The Johns Hopkins University Press, 1992.

Blumenthal, Marsha, and Joel Slemrod. "The Compliance Cost of the U.S. Individual Income Tax System: A Second Look After Tax Reform." *National Tax Journal* 45 No. 2 (June, 1992): 185–202.

Blumenthal, Marsha, and Joel Slemrod. "The Compliance Costs of Big Business." University of Michigan Working Paper No. 93-11. Ann Arbor, MI: University of Michigan, 1995.

Boadway, Robin, Maurice Marchand, and Pierre Pestieau. "Towards a Theory of the Direct-Indirect Tax Mix." *Journal of Public Economics* 55 No. 1 (1994): 71–88.

Chander, Parkash, and Louis L. Wilde. "Corruption in Tax Administration." *Journal of Public Economics* 49 No. 3 (1992): 333–49.

Clotfelter, Charles T. "Tax Evasion and Tax Rates: An Analysis of Individual Returns." *The Review of Economics and Statistics* 65 No. 3 (August, 1983): 363–73.

Cowell, Frank A. *Cheating the Government: The Economics of Tax Evasion.* Cambridge, MA: MIT Press, 1990.

Cremer, Helmuth, and Firouz Gahvari. "Tax Evasion and Optimal Commodity Taxation." *Journal of Public Economics* 50 No. 3 (1993): 261–75.

Cronshaw, Mark B., and James Alm. "Tax Compliance with Two-Sided Uncertainty." *Public Finance Quarterly* 23 No. 2 (April, 1995): 129–66.

Dubin, Jeffrey, and Louis L. Wilde. "An Empirical Analysis of Income Tax Auditing and Compliance." *National Tax Journal* 41 No. 1 (March,1988): 61–74.

Erard, Brian. "Taxation with Representation: An Analysis of the Role of Tax Practitioners in Tax Compliance." *Journal of Public Economics* 52 No. 2 (1993): 163–97.

Feinstein, Jonathan S. "An Econometric Analysis of Income Tax Evasion and Its Detection." *The Rand Journal of Economics* 22 No. 1 (Spring, 1991): 14–35.

Graetz, Michael J., and Louis L. Wilde. "The Economics of Tax Compliance: Fact and Fantasy." *National Tax Journal* 38 No. 3 (September, 1985): 355–63.

Hettich, Walter, and Stanley L. Winer. "Economic and Political Foundations of Tax Structure." *The American Economic Review* 78 No. 4 (December, 1988): 701–12.

Kaplow, Louis. "Horizontal Equity: Measures in Search of a Principle." *National Tax Journal* 42 No. 2 (June, 1989): 139–54.

Kaplow, Louis. "Optimal Taxation with Costly Enforcement and Evasion." *Journal of Public Economics* 43 No. 2 (1990): 221–36.

Kesselman, Jonathan R. "Income Tax Evasion: An Intersectoral Analysis." *Journal of Public Economics* 38 No. 2 (1989): 137–55.

Mayshar, Joram. "Taxation with Costly Administration." *Scandinavian Journal of Economics* 93 No. 1 (1991): 75–88.

Murray, Matthew N. "Sales Tax Auditing and Compliance." *National Tax Journal* 48 No. 4 (December, 1995): 515–530.

Pitt, Mark M., and Joel Slemrod. "The Compliance Cost of Itemizing Deduction: Evidence from Individual Tax Returns." *The American Economic Review* 79 No. 5 (December, 1989): 1224–32.

Polinsky, A. Mitchell, and Steven Shavell. "The Optimal Use of Fines and Punishment." *Journal of Public Economics* 24 No. 1 (1984): 89–99.

Pope J., R. Fayle, and M. Duncanson. *The Compliance Costs of Personal Income Taxation in Australia, 1987/87.* Sydney, Australia: Australian Tax Research Foundation, 1990.

Reinganum, Jennifer F., and Louis L. Wilde. "Income Tax Compliance in a Principal-Agent Framework." *Journal of Public Economics* 26 No. 1 (1985): 1–18.

Rice, Eric. "The Corporate Tax Gap: Evidence on Tax Compliance by Small Corporations." In *Why People Pay Taxes: Tax Compliance and Enforcement*, edited by Joel Slemrod, 125–61. Ann Arbor, MI: The University of Michigan Press, 1992.

Sandford, Cedric T., ed. *Tax Compliance Costs: Measurement and Policy.* Bath, United Kingdom: Fiscal Publications, 1995.

Sandmo, Agnar. "Income Tax Evasion, Labour Supply, and the Equity-Efficiency Tradeoff." *Journal of Public Economics* 16 No. 3 (1981): 265–88.

Shoven, John B., and John Whalley. *Applying General Equilibrium.* Cambridge: Cambridge University Press, 1992.

Slemrod, Joel. "Optimal Taxation and Optimal Tax Systems." *Journal of Economic Perspectives* 4 No. 1 (Winter, 1990): 157–78.

Slemrod, Joel. "Fixing the Leak in Okun's Bucket: Optimal Tax Progressivity When Avoidance Can Be Controlled." *Journal of Public Economics* 55 No. 1 (1994): 41–51.

Slemrod, Joel. "A General Model of the Behavioral Response to Taxation." University of Michigan. Mimeo, 1995.

Slemrod, Joel, and Nikki Sorum. "The Compliance Cost of the U.S. Individual Income Tax." *National Tax Journal* 37 No. 4 (December, 1984): 461–74.

Slemrod, Joel, and Shlomo Yitzhaki. "The Optimal Size of a Tax Collection Agency." *Scandinavian Journal of Economics* 89 No. 2 (1987): 183–92.

Slemrod, Joel, and Shlomo Yitzhaki. "Analyzing the Standard Deduction as a Presumptive Tax." *International Tax and Public Finance* 1 No. 1 (May, 1994): 25–34.

Stern, Nicholas H. "Optimum Income Taxation with Errors in Administration." *Journal of Public Economics* 17 No. 2 (1982): 181–212.

Stern, Nicholas H. "The Theory of Optimal Commodity and Income Taxation: An Introduction." In *The Theory of Taxation for Developing Countries*, edited by David Newbery and Nicholas H. Stern, 22–59. New York, NY: Oxford University Press, 1987.

U.S. Government Accounting Office. *Taxpayer Compliance: Reducing the Income Tax Gap.* GAO/T-GGD-95-176, Washington, D.C.: June, 1995.

Vaillancourt, Francois. *The Administrative and Compliance Costs of the Personal Income Tax and Payroll Tax System in Canada, 1986.* Toronto, Canada: Canadian Tax Foundation, 1989.

Wilson, John Douglas. "On the Optimal Tax Base for Commodity Taxation." *The American Economic Review* 79 No. 5 (December, 1989): 1196–1206.

HOW TAX COMPLEXITY AND ENFORCEMENT AFFECT THE EQUITY AND EFFICIENCY OF THE INCOME TAX

LOUIS KAPLOW*

Abstract - *Much criticism of the income tax involves administration: the enormous complexity of the system is responsible for large compliance costs, public and private, and the tax gap is large despite substantial resources devoted to enforcement. The desire for simplification and improved compliance motivates various incremental reforms as well as proposals for fundamental restructuring of the tax system. But evaluation of such changes is difficult because the underlying problems have not been analyzed in terms of the equity and efficiency concerns that animate more familiar assessments of income tax policy. This article provides a framework for a unified analysis, in which the same factors that are used to justify the choice of the tax base and the rate structure are employed to resolve problems involving complexity, compliance costs, and enforcement difficulties.*

INTRODUCTION

Is an income tax preferable to a consumption tax? Which fringe benefits should be included in the tax base? What capitalization rules should apply to exploration costs or research and development under an income tax? These and countless other questions have long been studied from the perspective of ideal tax policy, which is concerned about the equity (distributive effects) and efficiency of the tax system.

Recently, analysts have paid increasing attention to the rather significant details of implementation. Complex tax systems impose large compliance costs, which Slemrod (1995) suggests are on the order of $75 billion for the U.S. income tax. And taxes are not self-enforcing: the GAO (1995) estimates the 1992 tax gap for the U.S. income tax to be $110–$127 billion.

The magnitude of these problems of complexity and enforcement commands attention and, it would seem to many, demands action. Moreover, the significance of compliance costs and enforcement difficulties warrants

*Harvard Law School and National Bureau of Economic Research, Cambridge, MA 02138.

rethinking basic questions of tax design: perhaps tax rules or even tax systems that are desirable in principle should be redesigned in practice, sacrificing the original equity and efficiency goals to some extent for the sake of improving tax administration.

An obstacle to analysis of complexity and enforcement is the lack of an obvious common denominator. If, for example, eliminating a set of deductions would reduce compliance costs at the expense of the equity or efficiency of the tax system, how is one to decide whether the change is warranted? More broadly, if the compliance cost of an income tax is $100 billion and that of a national sales tax or VAT would be half as high, how does one decide whether the savings justifies the cost with regard to distributive objectives? Or, with regard to enforcement, if raising the IRS budget $5 billion would close the tax gap by $25 billion, is the expenditure sensible in light of the alternative of increasing tax rates sufficiently to raise the same revenue without incurring the additional enforcement costs? Of what relevance is the fact that some taxpayers currently pay 100 percent of what they owe while others pay but a small fraction of their tax obligations?

The present paper presents a conceptual framework for addressing these questions. It begins by outlining the standard method by which economists integrate the analysis of distributive objectives and efficiency. Then, this method is applied to contexts that involve typical problems of complexity and enforcement. In each instance, both the equity and efficiency implications will be identified, and it will be suggested how this framework is capable of incorporating the relevant factors in a unified analysis.

The conclusion is that a common denominator can be found, making it possible to provide more structure and coherence to policy analysis involving complexity, enforcement, and other problems of tax administration. The analysis, nonetheless, is not easy. It is necessary to state one's distributive objectives clearly and to obtain empirical evidence concerning the behavioral effects and incidence of tax reforms that affect the complexity of the tax system or the enforcement of tax rules. It is hoped that the present investigation, by defining the questions more precisely, will guide future work so that information on the most relevant questions will become increasingly available.

INTEGRATING DISTRIBUTIVE OBJECTIVES AND EFFICIENCY

When engaging in normative analysis of complex problems, economists begin by stating an objective function, often called a *social welfare function*. Conventionally, this function indicates how social welfare depends upon individuals' well-being, referred to as individuals' *utility*. Individuals' utility will depend on how individuals are affected by the relevant policy variables.

To be more specific, an individual's utility (U) might be expressed as a (positive) function of his consumption (C) and a (negative) function of his labor effort (L). Thus, a utility function may be written as

$$U(C, L).$$

The individual is assumed to choose a level of labor effort to maximize his utility. Taxes are relevant because they affect how much labor income the individual is permitted to spend on consumption.[1] Using this formulation, the analyst can determine the effect of various tax regimes on how much an individual works and thus how much income will be available for consumption. (In order to make this determination, the analyst must specify the utility function, indicating precisely the manner and extent to which the individual values additional consumption and disfavors additional labor effort. In addition, one would designate the tax schemes to be studied.) Then, given the results concerning labor effort and consumption, the analyst can compute the individual's utility level.

Once this process has been completed for a population of individuals (who may have different utility functions and face different wages), a tax scheme can be evaluated using some social welfare function. Two common social welfare functions are the utilitarian one—the summation of individuals' utilities—and the so-called "maximin" welfare function—which directs that the well-being of the worst-off individual (the one with the *min*imum level of utility) be *max*imized, without regard to the effects on others. To illustrate, the utilitarian social welfare function (W) can be expressed as

$$W = \sum_{i=1}^{n} U_i$$

where there are n individuals and U_i is the utility function of individual i. This utilitarian welfare function (like others that are usually studied) tends to favor equality, other things equal. The reason is that individuals' utility is believed to exhibit decreasing marginal utility of consumption; that is, an additional dollar is worth less to those who already have more. As a consequence, social welfare would rise if the tax system redistributed a dollar from a rich individual to a poor one. Complete equality is not, however, the optimal outcome due to the incentive effects of taxation and redistribution. Thus, there is the familiar trade-off between redistribution and incentives. A social welfare function consists, essentially, of a precise statement of how much weight should be given to the gains and losses of various individuals that arise under a designated regime.

The primary tax policy application of this method appears in the literature on the "optimal income tax." The question addressed in this literature is how redistributive the income tax should be in light of its adverse effect on incentives. The output of the analysis indicates how much revenue should be raised to fund transfers and the shape of the optimal income tax schedule (*i.e.*, whether marginal tax rates increase, at what rate, and so on). The input to the analysis has three dimensions. First, the analyst must specify the social welfare function. Second, the analyst must supply information on individuals' utility functions, such as data on the rate at which individuals trade off leisure and consumption and on the extent to which individuals value a marginal dollar more when they are poor than when they are rich.[2] Third, the analyst must employ additional data about the economy, notably concerning the distribution of skills in the population and the wages associated with different skills. Given such specifications and information, it is possible to determine what tax schedule is optimal.

The procedure just described is daunting: controversial value judgments are required in specifying the welfare function, empirical judgments must be made despite much uncertainty, and the analysis itself is challenging. But there really is no other choice. How can one expect to make coherent statements about the appropriate degree of redistribution without making explicit value judgments and offering predictions about how behavior will be affected by the tax system?

To illustrate, suppose that careful analysis demonstrated that, under existing circumstances, a highly egalitarian social welfare function would be maximized by a tax system under which the *marginal* (but not average) tax rates on the rich would be lower than those on other individuals. (The suggestion is not hypothetical, as many analyses have suggested this possibility: reducing the marginal rate on the rich may induce enough additional work effort at a small enough direct revenue cost to allow an improvement in total welfare.) A political progressive might attack the implicit policy recommendation as reactionary. But such an attack would be nonsensical. If the analysis has been performed correctly, the seemingly conservative position is truly what the egalitarian should favor. The progressive critic is merely confused, not understanding the subtle relationship between his value judgments (ends) and how different policies (means) might bear on them.

Return now to the problems of tax administration, of complexity and enforcement. The questions posed in the introduction might seem intractable, not susceptible to being reduced to a common denominator. My claim is that the framework just described, which has been employed successfully to analyze the problem of the optimal extent and form of redistribution, can be used to illuminate the problems of complexity and enforcement.

COMPLEXITY AND COMPLIANCE COSTS
Statement of the Issue

A tax system may be complex and thus involve greater compliance costs for many reasons and in many ways. For present purposes, I shall focus on one important source of compliance costs: those arising from the need to make the tax base more accurately reflect taxpayers' relative taxpaying ability. Such compliance costs may arise on account of more complex rules, for example, rules that attempt to distinguish more precisely between deductible business expenses and nondeductible personal expenses, or rules that include a range of fringe benefits in income. As another example, if imputed income from housing and other sources were to be taxed, greater compliance costs would be incurred.

It should be emphasized that the immediate costs of complexity cannot be measured by looking solely at the rules themselves. The primary source of compliance cost involves taxpayers' behavior, often involving recordkeeping, so estimates of incremental paperwork costs are usually more probative than counts of the number of pages of rules.[3] Similarly, the difficulty of an audit will usually depend upon problems of verifying the details of taxpayer behavior rather than challenges of understanding the rules themselves. Indeed, more precise rules might reduce ambiguity, easing compliance costs, or might close avenues for complicated avoidance schemes.

The very use of an income tax (or personal consumption tax) rather than a sales tax or a head tax involves the use of a substantial and complex set of rules imposing significant compliance costs on taxpayers and administrators for the purpose of assessing each taxpayer's circumstances more accurately in terms of some notion of their equitable tax burden. Thus, even fundamental tax reforms can be analyzed as an instance of changing (greatly) the degree of complexity, raising the trade-off between compliance costs and accuracy of assessment.

Many other dimensions of complexity will not be addressed directly in this investigation. Some complexity arises from poor rule writing, which involves a pure waste. Other complexity arises from rules that consciously deviate from tax principles in order to subsidize certain activities and groups (R&D, farmers, homeowners). In this case, it is easy to say that the rules should be eliminated, if they are viewed as inequitable, inefficient, and complex, their existence being attributed to special interest politics or past mistakes. In such instances, the complexity problem is merely the tail. On the other hand, if one is to take the objective of the special provisions as desirable— serving a legitimate purpose that is usefully carried out through the tax system—one could apply the present analysis. The benchmark for equitable treatment may change and behavioral effects that otherwise might be deemed inefficient (diverting resources from industrial capacity to housing) might now be viewed as efficient.

Equity Effect

The spirit of the analysis can be captured in a simple example. Suppose that two individuals each have true income of $40,000. However, unless a special deduction is provided (for a type of pure business expense), one of the individuals will have reported income of $45,000. The simple scheme, without

the deduction, overtaxes this individual. (If the marginal tax rate is 20 percent, she pays $1,000 too much.) The more complex scheme, with the deduction, taxes both individuals equally but involves additional costs (recordkeeping for the deduction, greater audit expenses to prevent fraudulent deductions, and so on).[4]

Consider also the following variation: under the simple scheme, both individuals have reported income of $40,000; but one has true income of $45,000, due to an in-kind fringe benefit. A more complex scheme—dealing with valuation and enforcement difficulties—that taxed the fringe benefit would properly measure the true income of both. A simple scheme undertaxes one individual. This variation will be skipped in the discussion to follow; the analysis is the same, but the directions of the effects are reversed.

To focus on the equity effect, suppose for the moment that behavior is fixed; that is, suppose that individuals' earnings and the extent of the business expenses governed by the rule are unaffected by deductibility. Then, the simple scheme, which allows no deduction, has the equity cost of mistaxing one of the individuals. Assuming that levying the tax on true income produces the correct level of tax, social welfare will be lower on this account.

What, exactly, is the welfare cost of this loss in equity? The overtaxed individual, by definition, pays too great a relative share of the total tax burden. (She pays $1,000 more than otherwise identical taxpayers.) One must look to the social welfare function, which contains the distributive preferences, to compute how much welfare is lower. To explain, the social welfare function indicates how welfare is affected as a function of each individual's situation. One would expect the social welfare function to place some weight on equalizing income.[5] The extent of that weight and other factors (notably, incentive effects) is what presumably determined the tax rate structure initially. The same social preferences are relevant in assessing the equity cost of overtaxing the individual with $40,000 in true income but $45,000 in taxable income under the simple system.[6.]

To be concrete, for a given specification of the social welfare function and other parameters (such as individuals' trade-off between income and leisure), one could simply compute social welfare for the case in which this erroneous specification is made. One could then, for example, compute how much government revenue would have to be "destroyed" in the case with no error in income measurement to produce the same figure for social welfare. This revenue measure—suppose it is $200 in the present example—could be taken as a measure of the benefit of proper income measurement in the present context.

The compliance cost can now be factored in directly. Suppose, for example, that all the additional compliance costs of the more complex, accurate regime are borne by the government. If this cost is less than $200, the more complex rule would increase social welfare; if the cost is less than $200, the additional complexity would be socially excessive.

More realistically, some (much) of the additional compliance cost will be borne by the taxpayer (recordkeeping, more complex instructions, and so on) and only a portion by the government (writing rules, more complex and costly auditing, and so on). The portion borne

by the taxpayer—unlike when she paid too much tax—is both an equity cost (in that she still pays, now through compliance costs, a bit more than she ideally should) and an efficiency cost (in that the added amount she pays involves a waste of resources in addition to the increase in the government's expenditures). To evaluate this situation, the analyst would compute social welfare given the actual situation that would confront the affected taxpayers and taking into account the administrative cost borne by the government. This level of social welfare would then be compared to that in the absence of the complex rule, with the resulting mismeasurement of income.

In sum, it is possible to translate compliance costs into conventional efficiency costs. It is also necessary to take into account distributive effects, primarily because it is the distribution problem that motivates expending resources to improve the accuracy of income measurement. The same social preferences that dictate the nature and extent of redistribution have direct implications for the welfare cost of inequity arising when individuals' burdens deviate from the ideal.

Comments on the Equity Analysis

One might object that the proposed analysis of complexity and compliance costs requires one to invoke an agreed-upon social welfare function, which is unavoidably controversial given the value judgments involved. But this need for choosing a welfare function should not be viewed as a problem with the framework. Rather, it is virtue because such value judgments must be made and articulated if one is to measure equity costs in a manner that will allow one to say whether it is worth a given level of real resource costs to eliminate the inequity. As suggested previously, inequity is costly only because we care about how much tax various individuals pay; that is, we care about distributive justice. We employ redistributive taxes.[7] In doing so, a decision is made to redistribute from the rich to the poor (and from the upper-middle class to the lower-middle class, and so on). Implicit in this decision is some notion of what it means to be rich and poor (suggesting some tax base) and a judgment of the *weight* attached to any given redistribution. One could develop views on these matters in two ways—through reflection and analysis or by inferring the value judgments of our society from the nature and extent of redistribution currently undertaken. Either way, some conclusion is necessary before the analysis can proceed. (Alternatively, an analyst might present results for a range of distributive norms, allowing the reader to supply a value judgment and, accordingly, identify the applicable results.) Policy recommendations that eschew this step merely hide value judgments; they cannot avoid them.

It should be useful to offer further comments about the quantification of the equity effect, short of sending someone to the computer to reassess social welfare for every incremental reform (although this is becoming rather cheap and easy these days). One obvious point is that the higher the marginal tax rate, the more important any tax base mismeasurement will be. Another is that mismeasurement is likely to have a more significant effect on social welfare in the case of lower-income individuals. (The equity cost of taxing an individual with true income of $5,000 by $1,000 too much is substantially greater than a $1,000 mistake for an individual whose true income is $40,000.[8]) Looking at the income tax in isolation, these effects seem to run in

opposite directions because higher-income individuals are in higher tax brackets. If one integrates transfer programs, however, the result is quite different. Due to welfare and tax phaseouts (EITC, child care credits, IRAs, and so on), the poor and other lower-income individuals often have very high *de facto* marginal tax rates. In that case, the equity cost of mismeasurement is unambiguously greater per dollar of error for those with lower income. (Perhaps this explains why welfare eligibility rules are often more complex than tax rules, using shorter accounting periods, measuring assets, and including additional sources of income.)

To some readers, the equity problem analyzed here may seem like one often discussed under the rubric of "horizontal inequity," which refers to the unequal treatment of equals. Observe, however, that no special horizontal equity definition or measure was needed. The social welfare function is already taken to embody social preferences concerning the distributive share each citizen should pay. The problem is that the identified taxpayer pays relatively too much, compared to the ideal. If there were no other taxpayer with true income of $40,000—and thus no unequal treatment of "equals"—this would still be a problem, and essentially to the same extent. Similarly, if the mismeasurement applied to each of a large number of taxpayers with $40,000 of true income (but not those with higher or lower true income), the problem would be magnified, not eliminated.[9]

Because the problem involves mismeasurement of a sort that reduces the degree of distributive justice in a manner already captured by the very social welfare function used to determine the tax base and rate structure, it follows that measurement of the inequity must be derived from the social welfare function itself rather than from various ad hoc equity indexes that sometimes have been proposed. This does not imply, however, that pragmatic shortcuts are unavailable. For example, analysts could examine hypothetical reforms involving, say, a $1,000 overpayment of tax by individuals with true incomes of $10,000, $50,000, and $100,000, with the social welfare costs expressed in terms of the government administrative cost that would produce indifference. (Recall the above example, in which the "cost" of the mismeasurement for a $40,000 individual was $200.) One could then produce simple charts that could be used for rule-of-thumb guidance in deciding on hosts of details. At a minimum, the suggested approach would provide ballpark estimates that would clearly resolve many questions, given the necessary data. Presumably, many reforms would not be close questions, although given that there has really been no welfare analysis of this sort to date we have little idea which reforms they would be.

The present formulation also tells us in what form we need data in order to assess reforms that affect compliance costs and tax equity. Primarily, we need to know the extent of mismeasurements by income, so that we can apply the proper weights. (Note that if mismeasurements are large for some individuals but not others, an average mismeasurement, even by income class, would not suffice.) In addition, the incremental compliance costs attributable to a more accurate regime must be estimated and their incidence determined, for if they are borne by the affected taxpayers any equity benefit from the more costly provision will be incompletely realized.[10]

Efficiency Effect

The equity analysis assumed that behavior was independent of the tax treatment. If one is talking, say, about whether to have a special provision for the blind, this assumption would be correct. (That is, providing tax breaks for the blind would be unlikely to have a significant effect on how many individuals were blind.[11]) But usually one would expect a behavioral response. If in-kind fringe benefits are not taxed, more such benefits will be provided. If a legitimate business expense is not deductible (because allowing it would be more complex), one would expect there to be less spent on that activity. Also, to the extent that the business expense was sector-specific (say, it involved only the fishing industry), that sector would then face higher costs, charge higher prices, and thereby contract somewhat. Similarly, some fringe benefits (tax-free flights for airline employees) will benefit particular industries by lowering their after-tax costs, leading to some expansion.

In the limit, such behavioral responses might totally drive out any inequity.[12] To simplify our discussion, assume that this is the case. (The case of partial behavioral response involves simply a combination of each of the two extremes.[13]) When the behavioral response is complete, the preceding equity analysis can be ignored. Workers denied the deduction will be overtaxed, but in long-run equilibrium their before-tax income must be higher, so that their after-tax income is the same as in the case in which the deduction is permitted. The difference, now, is that there will be less production in the affected sector and a bit more in other sectors because of the effect on labor costs of denying the deduction. The resulting distortion in the allocation of resources will tend to be inefficient, reducing social welfare.

This distortion is equivalent to the familiar one arising from differential taxation. For example, special depreciation rules and other tax expenditures have been criticized because they cause interindustry distortion or, within industries, distortions in the mix of inputs. These familiar efficiency problems arise when the tax system intentionally discriminates. In the present context, the discrimination is incidental, in that it results because implementing the desired rule would be administratively costly. But the effect on efficiency is precisely the same. As a consequence, the efficiency cost can be analyzed in the usual way: one measures the resulting price differences, estimates elasticities, and determines the deadweight loss due to the distortion.

To complete the welfare analysis, this deadweight loss from the distortion would be compared with the administrative cost of implementing the tax provision that avoids the initial mismeasurement.[14] As noted, if the behavioral response is complete, the analysis would consist entirely of this simple efficiency comparison, without the need to assess the previously discussed equity effect.

Accuracy in Administration

The preceding discussion emphasizes "complexity"—*i.e.*, the detail or precision of rules and regulations with regard to differentiating behavior (or

preventing spurious differentiation, such as by including in-kind fringe benefits in income) and the resulting compliance costs imposed on taxpayers. Although the discussion thus far speaks in terms of the applicable *rules*, one can also speak of the *accuracy* with which particular rules are *administered*.

To illustrate, suppose that miscellaneous employee business expenses are deductible but that similar personal expenses are not. Now, compare a gentle audit strategy and an intensive, more accurate one. (Both the probability of audit and the care with which audits are performed are relevant here, the latter having received little attention in the academic literature.) Under the gentle strategy, many mistakes will be overlooked. Moreover, taxpayers will be inclined to be aggressive, leading to systematically excessive deductions. The opportunity for such excessive deductions will vary among taxpayers (some occupations more lend themselves to attempting additional deductions without creating the appearance of obvious fraud; taxpayers will differ in their knowledge of the opportunity and their temperament with regard to compliance). As a result, the sorts of inequities and inefficiencies identified with simple, imprecise rules will arise. By contrast, an intensive strategy will correct more mistakes and, more importantly, induce taxpayers to be less aggressive in the first place. But this strategy will be more costly.[15]

In sum, the equity and efficiency analysis of the accuracy of tax administration is quite similar in structure to that of complexity and compliance costs. One can simply view loose administration and enforcement as a *de facto* simple regime, whereas with tight administration the rule that is more complex on the books will have the previously hypothesized effect of a complex rule in practice. (Put yet another way, the analysis of complex rules simply assumed that they would be enforced to a substantial extent.) This suggests that the analysis of many issues concerning the administration and enforcement of rules is quite similar to the analysis used to assess the rules themselves. The following section, which focuses directly on tax enforcement, will reinforce this view.

ENFORCEMENT

There are many tools of tax enforcement—information-reporting requirements, audits (which may vary in probability, intensity, and selection criteria), and sting operations, among others—and a range of penalties that might be utilized. Moreover, different forms of noncompliance—failing to report cash income, excessive deductions, complex business manipulations such as may arise with transfer pricing—raise diverse problems. In each context and with respect to each tool, the questions presented in the Introduction might be asked: By what criteria is one to determine whether enforcement expenditures are cost justified, in an absolute sense or by comparison to raising revenue by raising tax rates, and what is the relevance of the fact that the degree of compliance varies among taxpayers? This section provides a framework for answering these questions—one that, it turns out, is remarkably similar to that presented in the previous section addressed to complexity and compliance costs.

The Problem

For concreteness, I will focus on one of the most important sources of noncompliance for individual taxpayers,

underreported labor income. The GAO (1995) indicates that the self-employed report only 36 percent of their income and "informal suppliers" report just 11 percent of their income (compared with 97 percent compliance by wage earners), and unreported income by sole proprietors alone constitutes more than a quarter of the estimated tax gap (with other unreported income contributing more than another quarter).[16]

More precisely, suppose that there are two types of workers, employees who work for large enterprises and inevitably receive accurate W-2s indicating their true labor income, and self-employed individuals in businesses in which cash is a significant portion of gross receipts. The former have little choice but to comply, whereas the latter have significant opportunity to evade.

Now consider a proposed enforcement plan that, at a nontrivial cost, would make a significant dent in this noncompliance problem. It may involve a higher audit rate, more intensive audits when they are undertaken, greater information reporting by purchasers (*e.g.*, in sectors where there are large businesses who are buyers), or elaborate sting operations involving undercover agents. All that matters for present purposes is that there exists a strategy that would have a real effect but at a serious enough cost that it is not obvious whether it is desirable. Should the additional enforcement be undertaken?

In the academic literature, it is well understood (although not always remembered or emphasized) that the proper cost-benefit analysis does not simply compare the enforcement cost to the revenue raised.[17] Why this extremely common approach (exemplified by the heavy emphasis at hearings and in the press on revenue raised per dollar of IRS budget) is misguided can be seen in a number of ways. One is to note that enforcement costs involve the use of real resources, whereas tax receipts involve transfers. (To be sure, the government "deserves" the money and needs it, but it remains the case that uncollected taxes are not lost resources.)

Another way to look at the problem is to consider alternatives. The government can raise revenue by a slight rate increase or an addition to the enforcement budget.[18] Select the rate increase that raises the same revenue as the proposed enforcement program. The rate increase does not consume real resources the way greater enforcement expenditures do, so on efficiency grounds it might appear that the rate increase is preferable. (Rate increases are not politically popular, but neither, it turns out, are a larger IRS budget, wider information reporting requirements, and so on.) Greater enforcement, however, may have more positive equity and efficiency effects, as will now be described.[19]

Analysis

Return to the original example, in which one type of worker pays all the tax owed and the other type is able to evade substantially. In order to meet a stated revenue requirement, a higher tax rate will be required.[20] In the end, employees pay significantly more taxes on the same income than do the self-employed.

As in the discussion of complexity and compliance costs, assume first that there is no behavioral effect. In that case, there is an *equity cost*. Some individuals pay relatively too much tax; others pay relatively too little. This equity cost is precisely the sort analyzed in the

previous section and can be measured in the same manner. In place of administrative and compliance costs, one now has enforcement costs, which are analogous. Thus, assessing whether the equity cost of evasion warrants greater enforcement (instead of simply raising tax rates) involves the same sort of cost-benefit analysis as was suggested when determining whether greater complexity to provide more accurate tax treatment justified the additional compliance costs. One can compute the effect of mismeasuring relative income on social welfare and determine the welfare cost in terms of an equivalent amount of government revenue. If this cost is greater than the enforcement cost required to eliminate the problem, greater enforcement will raise social welfare.

Now suppose, more realistically, that there is a behavioral effect. To this extent, instead of an equity cost there will be an *efficiency cost*. In particular, consider individuals of a given skill level who are deciding whether to be an employee in sector A or entrepreneur in sector B. For given work effort and resulting income, the employee in sector A pays much higher taxes. This will encourage individuals to be entrepreneurs in sector B. When the labor market is in long-run equilibrium, the following will be true. First, the net, after-tax wages of the two sets of workers must be such that their utilities are the same. If that is the case, there is no equity effect. (It may appear that there is an equity effect: those in A pay taxes on all of their income and those in B do not. But those in A receive, in equilibrium, a higher before-tax wage to compensate for this difference in taxation; those in B have depressed earnings because of the additional flow of workers into B as a result of the tax differential.) Second, the tax difference causes an economic distortion: the economy has too much labor in sector B and too little in sector A.

Like the equity cost, this efficiency cost is entirely familiar. It is the same distortion that would have resulted with perfect enforcement but different tax rates in the two sectors. That is, the effect of imperfect enforcement in this instance is *de facto* a higher tax rate in sector A than in sector B. This produces the standard intersectoral distortion.[21] Moreover, it is the same sort of distortion discussed in the case of rules that were not sufficiently complex to avoid imposing different real tax burdens on individuals with similar true incomes. Thus, to assess the efficiency cost, one would again measure the elasticities, use that information to quantify the deadweight loss, and proceed to determine whether the additional expenditure on enforcement was sufficiently low to be cost justified. To indicate the potential significance of this problem, consider Alm's (1985) estimate of an aggregate distortion in excess of $100 billion from tax evasion that involves resources flowing into the underground economy.

When enforcement is imperfect, the efficiency problem is not limited to the distortions just described; there are additional inefficiencies because taxpayers expend resources directly on noncompliance. (One may operate less efficiently in order to have more funds in cash, hire less productive but more loyal individuals—perhaps relatives—to make cheating safer, and so on.) If perfect compliance could be achieved through greater enforcement, these resources inefficiently expended by individuals in sector B would be saved. For a moderate increase in enforcement, however, the story is more complicated. When enforcement is very light,

cheating might be easy and, therefore, cheap. When enforcement is increased but still not wholly effective, individuals may devote more resources to hiding income. This increase in evasion mitigates any direct equity or efficiency benefits of the greater enforcement effort and increases the resources (inefficiently) devoted to hiding income. Once such effects were measured, one could modify the analysis accordingly, allowing one to determine whether an enforcement plan increased social welfare.

Comments on the Analysis

In the present context, one would not always expect behavioral responses fully to substitute inefficiency effects for inequity. Suppose, for example, that some individuals work in sector B because they are more productive as entrepreneurs in B than as employees in A. (One reason is that their skills are more useful in industry B; another is that they have a personality that makes them a bad employee but a good entrepreneur.) Further, suppose that some of these individuals are honest; they report all income despite the ease of evasion. In the distorted equilibrium, their earnings are depressed by those who flock into sector B to take advantage of the low *de facto* taxes, but they continue to pay the full stated rate. As a result, they are worse off than those in sector B who are dishonest. Moreover, they are worse off than employees in A who, unlike themselves, receive higher before-tax wages to compensate for the fact that they pay taxes on all of their income. Thus, there is inequity with respect to these honest individuals, so a realistic account will involve both equity and efficiency effects. (This story is not far-fetched: the tax gap in many such sectors exceeds 50 percent. One possibility is that all individuals are cheating to the same extent. Another is that opportunities and temperaments vary greatly; some may be paying 100 percent and others close to 0 percent.)

It also should be noted that tax evasion has a feedback effect on optimal tax rates. If different rates could be applied to these two sectors, a higher tax might be imposed on the sector with evasion: the higher tax would offset the under-payments by workers in the sector with evasion, which would improve equity (to the extent there is not full adjustment through behavioral responses) and efficiency (by reducing the incentive for resources to flow excessively into the *de facto* undertaxed sector). One problem with this approach is that, as the tax rate in the sector with evasion is increased, individuals will evade more. This response reduces the direct benefits from the rate increase and raises the resource cost from evasion activity.

Conclusions

This paper has examined a variety of imperfections in tax administration. All of the problems studied here involve a similar trade-off: rules that more accurately measure income, more accurate administration of such rules, and greater enforcement to improve compliance all typically raise aggregate administrative costs, whether compliance costs borne by taxpayers or enforcement costs borne by the government.

The administratively cheaper approach primarily involves costs of mismeasurement. To the extent such mismeasurement is not offset by behavioral responses, the resulting social cost involves inequity: some taxpayers pay more and others less than is

warranted. It was suggested that the only reasonable way to measure these equity costs is by reference to a social welfare function, embodying the distributive objectives from which the tax base and rate structure were derived.

Often, behavioral responses will reduce or eliminate the resulting inequity, substituting inefficiency instead. This inefficiency arises because imperfect administration involves tax rates that *de facto* differ across sectors of the economy. Thus, the distortion is of a type that is familiar to tax policy analysts, so the problem can be ana-lyzed in the customary manner.

For decades, many reformers have called for simplification, ranging from elimina-tion of particular deductions to whole-sale restructuring of our tax system. Others have noted the large tax compliance gap and advocated propos-als ranging from greater IRS enforce-ment budgets to substitution of easier-to-administer taxes. What has been lacking in much of the debate, however, is a conceptual framework for assessing which reforms would increase social welfare. This paper, hopefully, will help fill that void.[22]

The present investigation is, of course, only a beginning. The framework is rather simple, whereas the range of problems and issues concerning tax complexity and enforcement are—for lack of a better term—complex. Moreover, a conceptual framework is of little use without empirical evidence.[23] The demands in the present context are substantial. Fortunately, some work has already been done. In addition, with a more concrete analytical structure in hand, it should be clearer what information is most important to collect.

ENDNOTES

I am grateful for comments from James Alm, Reuven Avi-Yonah, Diane Ring, Steven Shavell, Joel Slemrod, and Alvin Warren, research assistance from Travis Pearson, and support from the John M. Olin Center for Law, Economics, and Business at Harvard Law School. The symposium piece by Alm (1996) is in many respects complementary to this investigation.

1   This may be expressed by stating the individual's budget constraint as

$$C = wL - T(wL).$$

The term w refers to the wage rate and $T(wL)$ indicates the amount of income tax owed on income of wL. The present formulation abstracts from savings, taxation of capital income, and numerous other complications. Incorporating additional dimensions would make the problem more difficult but would not alter its essential character.

2   Information about individuals' trade-off between income and leisure is derived from empirical studies of labor supply, which typically assess the responsiveness of hours worked or labor market participation to changes in after-tax wage rates. Information about how the marginal utility of income depends on income levels can be derived from studies of behavior under uncertainty. For example, the amount that individuals are willing to pay to insure against losses of income indicates how much they value avoiding a low-income situation.

3   This characterization of the primary sources of compliance costs is borne out by the empirical work on the subject. See Arthur D. Little (1988) and Blumenthal and Slemrod (1992).

4   An extreme but important example of sacrificing accurate measurement for the sake of reducing compliance and administrative costs involves the use of presumptive taxation—e.g., estimating restaurant sales from the square feet occupied by the restaurant or measuring property values by counting the number of windows. Within the income tax, standardized depreciation schedules and the use of standard deductions and floors may serve a similar purpose. See Kaplow (1994) and Slemrod and Yitzhaki (1994).

5   If it did not, the adverse incentive effects of redistributive taxation would not be offset by any distributive benefit, so no income—or other "ability-to-pay" taxation—would be justified in the first place.

6   To simplify the exposition, I assume that the government's revenue requirement is held constant, so that the taxpayer's reduced obligation when the deduction is allowed as well as the government's additional administrative costs must be made up through higher taxes. Alternatively, other government expenditures would have to be reduced, substituting a different welfare cost. (If government expenditures are optimized, the marginal social cost of tax revenue will just equal the marginal social benefit of expenditures, so that the social welfare cost will be the same if marginal adjustments to restore budget balance are made by tax increases or program cuts.)

7   Note that even a purely proportional or moderately "regressive" tax is massively redistributive by comparison to a head tax. One cannot speak as though we have not made a substantial decision involving redistribution just because there is not that much net "progressivity"—graduation of effective tax rates—in the current tax system.

8   Under a utilitarian social welfare function, this result is due to the decreasing marginal utility of income. For more egalitarian social welfare functions, the weight of this concern would be greater. See Mirrlees (1990).

9   In the extreme, the problem would, however, vanish: if all taxpayers' incomes were overstated by the same $5,000, one could simply adjust the tax brackets by that amount—say, by giving everyone an additional $5,000 exemption—and there would be no problem at all. Thus, the problem does involve *relative* mismeasurement but not particularly mismeasurement among individuals of equal income. It also does not involve rank reversals in the income distribution. If there were no individuals within $5,000 of the large group that was mis-taxed, the equity cost described in the text would be unaffected. For further discussion suggesting that horizontal equity and concerns about rank reversals do not constitute an independent norm in the present context, see Kaplow (1989, 1995).

10 This latter point is relevant to the appropriate tax treatment of the compliance costs themselves (*e.g.*, whether they should be deductible).

11 Such tax breaks might induce some individuals to feign blindness, the type of problem addressed in the later section on enforcement.

12 This possibility has been emphasized by Bittker (1979) and Bradford (1986), among others.

13 In long-run equilibrium, one would generally expect full adjustment in many instances. Note that it is not necessary that all individuals be able to respond to the economic incentives. Assume, for example, that there are 100 workers; in the efficient (perfect income measurement) equilibrium, there are 50 in each sector; and in the distorted equilibrium (when a deduction in one sector is not permitted because of compliance costs), there are 40 in sector A and 60 in B. To reach the distorted equilibrium, it takes only 10 of the 50 who would otherwise have gone into A to work in B instead. Thus, even if most could

(would) not move, it is entirely possible that the full adjustment just described would occur. Those who were "stuck" in A would still benefit from the higher before-tax wage that prevails in equilibrium, so there would not be any equity effect.

If adjustment between sectors is partial, workers' effective tax (and thus wage) rates will differ. This difference will tend to increase the distortion in labor effort because distortion tends to rise disproportionately with tax rates. (That is, the increase in distortion with respect to those facing a higher effective tax rate will tend to be more than the decrease in distortion with respect to those facing a lower effective tax rate.)

[14] Yitzhaki (1979) has performed such an analysis in the case of commodity taxation: omitting commodities from the tax base creates distortion; including them involves greater administrative costs.

[15] It is possible that in some instances more intensive auditing would reduce costs, because taxpayers would be deterred from incurring additional costs to avoid taxation, as is discussed in the following section on enforcement. In such instances, a more accurate system would be unambiguously desirable.

[16] I will emphasize enforcement efforts that tend to affect most directly taxpayers' economic incentives to comply. Many researchers emphasize sociological and psychological factors as well, but these factors are not unrelated. For example, if there are low incentives for compliance, a large number of taxpayers might cheat; once cheating is sufficiently widespread, more honest taxpayers may lose some of their inhibitions to evasion, magnifying these effects. For a discussion of a range of factors affecting compliance and experimental evidence on their interaction, see Alm, Sanchez, and de Juan (1995).

[17] See, e.g., Kaplow (1990), Mayshar (1991), and Slemrod and Yitzhaki (1987).

[18] Another alternative is to impose requirements on the private sector, with the result that most of the administrative costs will not be reflected in the government's budget. These are, of course, real resource costs of greater enforcement regardless of who must foot the bill.

[19] As another provocative example, suppose that all taxpayers paid half of what they owed—perhaps each is able costlessly to hide half of income, whatever its level. One could spend a massive amount to uncover the hidden income. Alternatively, one could simply double the tax rate; each individual then pays twice the proper rate on half the base, for the same total tax bill. All the enforcement resources required to find and demonstrate the hidden income would be saved.

[20] As explained in note 6, one could view the resulting problem as one of reduced government expenditures, leading to a similar analysis.

[21] In addition to the previously noted distortions between industries and in the use of inputs, there is the possibility that the organizational form may be inefficient, as when individuals who would function better as employees instead become entrepreneurs. (The inefficiency may involve the bearing of risk, loss of economies of scale, problems of lack of managerial ability, and so on.)

[22] See also prior work by Kaplow (1990) and Mayshar (1991) and a range of work by Slemrod and Yitzhaki, in particular their recent paper (1995) which integrates administrative issues in the context of assessing reforms involving marginal changes in tax rates.

[23] It was also emphasized that one must choose a social welfare function, which necessarily involves value judgments. As noted, one approach is to infer such judgments from existing institutions (as by determining what social welfare function would generate a degree of redistribution close to that actually observed). On the more purely normative side, I believe that the argument for a utilitarian norm is stronger than is generally recognized. See Kaplow (1995).

REFERENCES

Alm, James. "The Welfare Cost of the Underground Economy." *Economic Inquiry* 23 (April, 1985): 243–63.

Alm, James. "What is an 'Optimal' Tax System?" *National Tax Journal* 49 No. 1 (March, 1996): 117–133.

Alm, James, Isabel Sanchez, and Ana de Juan. "Economic and Noneconomic Factors in Tax Compliance." *Kyklos* 48 (1995): 3–18.

Arthur D. Little. *Development of Methodology for Estimating the Taxpayer Paperwork Burden, Final Report to the Department of the Treasury.* Washington, D.C.: Internal Revenue Service, 1988.

Bittker, Boris I. "Equity, Efficiency, and Income Tax Theory: Do Misallocations Drive Out Inequities?" *San Diego Law Review* 16 (1979): 735–48.

Blumenthal, Marsha, and Joel Slemrod. "The Compliance Cost of the U.S. Individual Income Tax System: A Second Look after Tax Reform." *National Tax Journal* 45 No. 2 (June, 1992): 185–202.

Bradford, David. *Untangling the Income Tax.* Cambridge: Harvard University Press, 1986.

Kaplow, Louis. "Horizontal Equity: Measures in Search of a Principle." *National Tax Journal* 42 No. 2 (June, 1989): 139–54.

Kaplow, Louis. "Optimal Taxation with Costly Enforcement and Evasion." *Journal of Public Economics* 43 (November, 1990): 221–36.

Kaplow, Louis. "The Standard Deduction and Floors in the Income Tax." *Tax Law Review* 50 (Fall, 1994).

Kaplow, Louis. "A Fundamental Objection to Tax Equity Norms: A Call for Utilitarianism." *National Tax Journal* 48 No. 4 (December, 1995): 497–514.

Mayshar, Joram. "Taxation with Costly Administration." *Scandinavian Journal of Economics* 93 No. 1 (1991): 75–88.

Mirrlees, J.A. "Taxing Uncertain Incomes." *Oxford Economic Papers* 42 (1990): 34–45.

Slemrod, Joel B. "The Simplification Potential of Alternatives to the Income Tax." *Tax Notes* 66 (February, 1995): 1331–8.

Slemrod, Joel B., and Shlomo Yitzhaki. "The Optimal Size of a Tax Collection Agency." *Scandinavian Journal of Economics* 89 (September, 1987): 183–92.

Slemrod, Joel B., and Shlomo Yitzhaki. "Analyzing the Standard Deduction as a Presumptive Tax." *International Tax and Public Finance* 1 (May, 1994): 25–34.

Slemrod, Joel B., and Shlomo Yitzhaki. "The Social Cost of Taxation and the Marginal Cost of Funds." IMF/FAD Working Paper. Washington, D.C.: International Monetary Fund/Fiscal Affairs Division, 1995.

U.S. General Accounting Office. *Taxpayer Compliance: Reducing the Income Tax Gap.* GAO/T-GGD-95-176, Washington, D.C., June, 1995.

Yitzhaki, Shlomo. "A Note on Optimal Taxation and Administrative Costs." *American Economic Review* 69 (June, 1979): 475–80.

TAX POLICY FROM A PUBLIC CHOICE PERSPECTIVE

RANDALL G. HOLCOMBE[*]

Abstract - Tax policy is a product of politics, so a complete understanding of tax policy requires an explicit recognition of the political environment within which tax policy is made. The paper emphasizes the concept of political costs associated with the tax system and discusses several aspects of tax policy using a public choice approach. The paper argues that the political costs associated with taxation can be minimized by embedding the tax system within a relatively inflexible fiscal constitution. Despite the insights the public choice perspective offers, most analysis of tax policy does not take public choice considerations into account.

Despite the fact that the tax structure is a product of the political process, rarely does an economic analysis of tax policy take account of the political environment within which the tax structure is designed.[1] The political environment is important for several reasons. Most obviously, because the tax structure is a product of politics, one must understand the political process to completely understand the tax system. Furthermore, if the tax structure is designed appropriately, the collective choice process can provide a revealed preference mechanism that can help enhance the efficiency of government both on the tax side and the expenditure side of the ledger. Also, public choice analysis might lend some insight into what constitutes an equitable tax structure. The analysis that follows begins with the recognition that the political system uses resources to design tax systems, and these costs should be taken into account along with other welfare costs of the tax system.

The advice of economists has had a substantial impact on the tax structure both in the United States and worldwide. However, tax policy is the product of political decision making, with economic analysis playing only a supporting role. A closer integration of public choice theory into the analysis of taxation can help increase our understanding of the tax system and can improve the quality of advice that economists offer with regard to tax policy. Of course, much analysis of tax systems can be undertaken without an explicit recognition of the political

*Florida State University, Tallahassee, FL 32306.

system. For example, one does not need to take politics into account in order to estimate how much of a tax is shifted from the group upon which the tax is initially levied. Furthermore, public choice analysis is relatively young and not well-integrated into public finance, so this essay will present some avenues that can be explored, but there is still a substantial amount of work that can be profitably undertaken to integrate public choice analysis more fully into the analysis of taxation. While public choice theory might offer much to help advance the theory of taxation, the main focus of this essay will be policy oriented and will begin by explicitly recognizing the political costs that are created when people try to influence tax law for their benefit.

POLITICAL COSTS AS A WELFARE COST OF TAXATION

At the simplest level of analysis, the welfare cost of taxation arises because a tax causes people to substitute away from whatever is being taxed, resulting in an excess burden. In addition, economists have long recognized that administrative costs (the costs that government incurs to collect taxes and enforce tax laws) and compliance costs (the costs taxpayers incur in the process of calculating and paying taxes) are often significant and, as Slemrod (1990) notes, should be included as part of the welfare cost of the tax system. The political costs of the tax system are also significant, but are less often recognized in economic analysis. These costs include the cost to the government of legislating tax policy and, more importantly, the rent seeking costs incurred by those who want to influence tax legislation.

Rent-seeking activity occurs because people want to influence tax policy for

their benefit. Those who are being taxed continually lobby to have their taxes reduced or eliminated, and even if a group is not currently being taxed, it needs to keep an active lobbying presence to guard against taxes that might be placed on it in the future. Thus, the easier it is to modify the tax structure, the higher will be the political costs associated with taxation. When the tax structure can be easily modified, taxpayers will find it in their interests to incur political costs to try to minimize their tax burdens. Thus, Buchanan (1967) has argued the merits of a fiscal constitution, which creates a basic tax structure that can be changed only if there is substantial consensus, reducing the potential payoff from trying to lobby for tax changes that create benefits for special interests.[2] The idea that rent-seeking activity can impose significant welfare costs on an economy is relatively recent, dating to the articles of Tullock (1967) and Krueger (1974), and while simple observation reveals that the costs are substantial, there are no really good estimates of the political costs the economy incurs because of the tax system.

Holcombe (1997) estimates the annual political costs of a selective excise tax to be in excess of ten percent of the annual revenues raised, but this is a rough estimate based on limited data. Political costs in this range would exceed administrative and compliance costs combined, so if this estimate is even close, political costs are very significant.[3] One can see that, when an excise tax is levied on a narrow base, those paying the tax have an incentive to lobby for its removal. However, the tax does not even have to be levied in order to generate political costs. If the tax is being considered, the potential taxpayers have an incentive to lobby against it, resulting in political costs even though there is no tax revenue generated. [4] A tax structure that is easily modified can bring with it substantial political costs, not only because people have an incentive to lobby for changes for their benefit, but also because they must be on their guard to protect themselves from changes that could harm them. These political costs have largely been ignored by economists who have analyzed the efficiency of the tax system.

WICKSELL, PUBLIC FINANCE, AND PUBLIC CHOICE

Wicksell (1896), whose insights laid a foundation for modern public choice theory, was trying to design a more equitable and efficient tax system, so in this sense, public choice can trace its origins back to the theory of taxation. Wicksell envisioned creating a tax system that assigned tax shares to correspond to each taxpayer's benefit from the public expenditure, anticipating Lindahl (1919) pricing. Wicksell's idea was to ensure that tax shares corresponded to Lindahl prices by requiring an approximate unanimous agreement among taxpayers before undertaking public expenditures. The benefit principle is clearly embodied in the work of Wicksell and Lindahl, but so is the public choice notion that political agreement can be used as an indicator of economic efficiency. In theory, one can find the optimal level of public expenditures by summing the demands of all consumers, but in practice, revealing people's preferences for public goods is more problematic.

The political process can help reveal preferences, but under majority rule, efficiency can be assured only when taxes are levied according to the benefit principle. Otherwise, people will be revealing their preferences for receiving

benefits paid for by taxes levied on others or against paying taxes for benefits received by others. [5] Application of the benefit principle has the advantage that majority rule decision making tends to lead toward efficient outcomes. Another advantage of Lindahl pricing is that all individuals agree on the quantity of the public good to be produced, making political decisions less costly to produce. Thus, for example, it makes sense to use a gas tax to finance roads for public choice reasons, because this tax is likely to approximate the benefit principle, facilitating political agreement that will result in an optimal level of that good being produced. If another tax that does not closely correspond to the benefit principle is used, there will be a struggle between those who expect to be net beneficiaries because of their heavy use of the roads and those who expect to be net losers because they will pay the bulk of the taxes used to finance the roads. The outcome will depend upon which group has more political power. Not only will more in political costs be incurred, it will be less likely that the political decision-making process will lead toward an optimal provision of the good.

Buchanan and Tullock (1962), extending Wicksell's analysis, make the distinction between constitutional and post-constitutional rules. Constitutional rules are relatively difficult to modify, whereas postconstitutional rules can be modified more easily. In order to minimize political costs, a tax system should be designed so that the overall structure is relatively unchangeable as a part of the fiscal constitution, with some flexibility at the postconstitutional level to modify the tax system in ways that incur only small political costs. For example, the use of gasoline taxes to finance highway expenditures could be constitutionally mandated, whereas the tax rate could be adjusted postconstitutionally to reflect changes in the demand for highways. While this approximates the practice of most U.S. states, there are significant enough deviations to generate political costs. Frequently, states augment gas tax revenues with revenues from other sources to fund roads, and it is not uncommon for some gas tax revenues to be diverted away from roads to finance other expenditures.

The tax structure can be formally embedded in constitutional rules, but even when it is not, the tax structure can still be a part of the effective fiscal constitution, in the sense of generally agreed-upon tax rules. When there is general agreement on the rules, political costs are not incurred to try to modify the tax structure. When the tax structure is flexible, economic agents are encouraged to incur political costs to try to modify the tax system for their benefit.

State income taxes can be used to illustrate the fuzzy line between formal constitutional provisions and the agreed-upon, nonformalized fiscal constitution. From 1961 to 1971, when the public sector was held in higher regard by voters than it is today, nine states established personal income taxes. A tenth, New Jersey, added a personal income tax in 1976. After that, no states added income taxes until Connecticut did so in 1991. It was a controversial move that, one could argue, violated the state's implied fiscal constitution. In 1993, Texas, which did not have a personal income tax, nor a provision in its constitution to prevent income taxation, passed an explicit constitutional amendment prohibiting one. In effect, Texas had a fiscal constitution that prohibited personal income taxation, but after the Connecti-

cut experience, Texans decided to make explicit what they had always believed was a part of their implied fiscal constitution.

OPTIMAL EXCISE TAXATION

These concepts can be applied to the design of an optimal system of excise taxes. Ignoring political costs, the Ramsey (1927) rule would suggest taxing goods in inverse proportion to their elasticities of demand. A public choice approach to the problem would suggest taxing all goods at a single uniform rate to minimize political costs. A straightforward application of the Ramsey rule ignores the fact that, in reality, differential rates of excise taxation will be a product of the political system. Because of the way tax rates are set in reality, the political pressures imposed by interest groups will have much more to do with the actual structure of excise taxes than differences in demand elasticities among taxed goods. If the fiscal constitution allows different excise tax rates on different goods because in theory this could be optimal, political costs will be encouraged, and the end result of public policy is not likely to correspond with the Ramsey rule.

The Ramsey rule tells economists how the excess burden of taxes can be minimized when excise tax rates are set according to that rule. However, because tax rates are set according to the political power of interest groups, the political process will not produce a tax structure that follows the Ramsey rule in any event, and allowing differential rates of excise taxation merely opens the door for escalating political costs associated with excise taxation, increasing the welfare cost of taxation. When political costs are factored into the analysis, optimal excise taxation may well imply uniform tax rates across goods, not different rates for different goods as the Ramsey rule implies. For example, North Carolina places an excise tax of 5 cents per pack on cigarettes, and Oklahoma, which has about the same level of per capita income and per capita government expenditures, has an excise tax of 23 cents per pack. Obviously, political power has more to do with the determination of those particular taxes than the Ramsey rule.

If some goods are exempt from taxation, or are taxed at different rates, this should be a part of the fiscal constitution, and not something subject to political manipulation, bringing with it the associated political costs. For example, about half the states that have general sales taxes exempt food from taxation, and some states exempt clothing. If these aspects of the tax system are considered a part of the fiscal constitution, then there will be minimal political costs associated with them. If, however, it appears that changes in these provisions might be politically feasible, interests on both sides of the issue will incur political costs to try to change the tax structure or, on the other side of the issue, to try to maintain the status quo.

OPTIMAL INCOME TAXATION

An extensive literature on optimal taxation, summarized by Mirrlees (1976), follows the methodology of determining the optimal tax structure by maximizing a social welfare function subject to constraints, where social welfare is a function of the utilities of all individuals in the society. Buchanan (1976) criticizes this literature using an argument related to the earlier discussion on the benefit principle, because it fails to take account of the expenditure side of the budget. Of course, any use

of a social welfare function is open to the criticism that it is not possible to make the interpersonal utility comparisons that this methodology requires. But the public choice perspective raises yet another problem. Because the tax system necessarily plays a redistributive role within this framework, the optimal tax system, derived this way, is likely to imply substantial political costs as all groups try to get as much revenue transferred to them, or as little transferred away from them, as possible.

Any system of progressive income taxation inherently has this problem, because, as Hayek (1960, p. 313) notes, "Unlike proportionality, progression provides no principle which tells us what the relative burden of different persons ought to be." On this ground, Buchanan (1993) argues for proportional taxation.[6] If proportional income taxation is accepted as a part of the fiscal constitution, the political costs of an income tax system can be lowered substantially. The same argument applies to deductions, exemptions, and tax credits as methods of altering the amount of income subject to taxation. If the tax system is flexible and subject to negotiation, it invites the creation of political costs to try to alter it.

Is it possible to create this type of fiscal constitution? At the federal level, Ballentine (1992) argues that the Tax Reform Act of 1986 made the tax system more stable, and more difficult to change, which should reduce political costs.[7] At the state level, this suggests making the taxpayer's state income tax liability a percentage of the taxpayer's federal tax liability. If such a provision is accepted as a part of the state's fiscal constitution, only the rate is subject to negotiation, greatly limiting the political costs of the tax system (and the compliance costs as well).

Interestingly enough, the conclusions of the optimal tax literature following Mirrlees (1971) have pointed toward the desirability of a relatively flat rate income tax structure, even though methodologically that literature is quite at odds with the public choice approach to taxation. Taking political costs into account makes proportional income taxation look much more like an optimum without compromise. In this case, a public choice approach helps illuminate the issue of optimal income taxation, reinforcing and clarifying some of the conclusions in the literature. In other cases, such as optimal commodity taxation discussed in the previous section, a public choice approach yields conclusions more at odds with the conventional wisdom.

SOME TAXES GENERATE HIGHER POLITICAL COSTS THAN OTHERS

Taxes are the creation of the political system, and tax structures that are easily amended are likely to generate high political costs. Thus, tax systems should be a part of a stable fiscal constitution, with generally agreed-upon rules, in order to minimize political costs. One would conjecture that uniform and broad-based retail sales taxes would entail lower political costs than income taxes, for example, but despite the substantial political costs that are involved in tax reform, the issue has remained outside the national debate on whether a national sales tax or VAT would be desirable to supplement or replace the federal income tax, or whether a flat rate income tax with a redefined tax base, such as the one suggested by Hall and Rabushka (1985), would be better than the current income tax structure. Of course, states constantly tinker with their sales tax rates—and especially their sales tax bases—creating political costs there too.

Thus, the conjecture that income taxes create greater political costs than sales taxes is just that: a conjecture. It may be that a state income tax tied directly to the taxpayer's federal income tax liability incurs smaller political costs than a general sales tax, where the base is subject to redefinition at every legislative session. Economists have done little empirical work on the political costs of taxation, even though such costs are obviously substantial and are a significant component of the total welfare cost of a tax system.

TAXATION AND REDISTRIBUTION

The tax system has long been viewed as a mechanism for redistributing income. However, as Stigler (1970) has noted, in the real world, income tends to be redistributed from those who have income and wealth to those who have political power, implying that there can be substantial overlap between taxpayers and recipients of redistribution. Thus, public choice theory suggests that the pattern of redistribution produced by the political system is unlikely to conform to the normative prescriptions of more traditional public finance models. Furthermore, it is likely that, if the fiscal constitution places no constraints on the nature of redistribution, democratic decision making by itself will not lead to a stable pattern of redistribution.

If redistribution is envisioned as a zero-sum game, as in Atkinson (1995), it is unstable, because there is always a majority coalition that can target the benefits of those who receive above-average redistributional benefits and try to divide them among the coalition members. The majority coalition may temporarily be successful, giving them a larger than average share of the pie, but this makes them a tempting target for a realigned majority coalition, creating a cyclical majority. Because redistribution is at best a zero-sum game, there is no stable pattern of redistribution that can be maintained under majority rule.

Public choice theory has offered two explanations for how a stable redistributive outcome might be produced by democratic institutions. Weingast, Shepsle, and Johnsen (1981) suggest that political institutions might generate a universal coalition in which everyone agrees to a roughly equal division. As Holcombe (1986) notes, this might result in an outcome that everyone agrees to under majority rule, but that produces an inefficient outcome, leaving everyone worse off than if the redistribution had not occurred. [8] More generally, redistributive outcomes might be stable because institutions prevent them from changing, but if so, this may make them a part of the fiscal constitution, limiting the political costs they generate. Taking a different approach, Becker (1983) and Wittman (1989) argue that those in government have an incentive to redistribute in the most efficient manner possible in order to minimize the deadweight loss of redistribution and maximize the political support of officeholders. Redistribution is not a zero-sum game, but a negative-sum game, and the process is biased toward redistributive outcomes that minimize the total cost of redistribution. In other words, the process is biased toward pushing the negative sum as close to zero as possible.

Hettich and Winer (1988) follow Becker's approach, applied specifically to taxation, to develop a model of the tax structure incorporating both democratic political institutions and the more traditional public finance notion of excess burden. Following this approach, the tax system that maximizes voter support, which would be optimal in Wittman's (1989) framework, is significantly different in principle from optimal taxation as defined by Mirrlees (1976). Economists have long considered the possibility of using the tax system as a tool for redistributing income to enhance the social welfare. Taking a public choice perspective, one must recognize that redistribution is a product of a democratic decision-making process in which the beneficiaries of redistribution are more likely to be those who have political power than those who are really needy.

The tax system can also cause rent seeking to occur even when it is not explicitly used as an income redistribution tool, if the distribution of taxes is different from the distribution of benefits from government expenditures. Meltzer and Richard (1981) show why, when the decisive voter's tax share is below average, democratic decision making will create pressure for increased taxation to finance redistribution. [9] Thus, as Buchanan (1976) notes, there is an argument for applying the benefit principle of taxation to minimize the political costs of the tax system. Application of the benefit principle may also lower the more traditional measure of excess burden, if the tax acts as a price.

Buchanan (1963) makes an argument for earmarked taxes, noting that, when taxes are not earmarked, the political process may lead to a suboptimal level and mix of government expenditures. Earmarking works well when those who pay the earmarked tax are also the recipients of the benefits financed by the tax. Otherwise, as Buchanan (1967) notes, there is the incentive for potential beneficiaries to try to finance their benefits with an earmarked tax levied on another group. Again, there is a public choice argument for the benefit principle to minimize the political costs of the tax system. If tax shares do not correspond to the benefit principle, there is always the incentive for some people to engage in rent seeking for benefits that will be financed by taxes levied on others.

The tax system does not provide a good mechanism for redistribution, for two reasons. First, the explicit use of taxation as a redistributive mechanism invites the escalation of political costs. Second, the democratic decision-making process is not well-suited to enhancing social welfare through redistribution anyway, because it favors those with political power rather than those who are in need. The largest redistribution programs in the United States—Social Security and Medicare—illustrate both of these reasons. Many recipients are well-off compared to those who are paying for their benefits, and the elderly have incurred substantial political costs to make sure they retain the right to their transfers.

THE OPTIMAL SIZE AND MIX OF GOVERNMENT EXPENDITURES

Although the study of taxation is often undertaken without considering how those revenues will be spent, public choice theory has the potential to offer insight into how a tax system can be designed to encourage the optimal level and mix of government expenditures. As Samuelson (1954) noted, one problem with public expenditures is the difficulty of determining the efficient level of production. Indeed, this was the very problem that Wicksell and Lindahl were trying to solve. Building on Wicksell's approach, Buchanan (1976, 1993) has frequently argued that an optimal tax system cannot be designed without taking into account how its

revenues will be spent. One role of a fiscal constitution is to match the costs and benefits of public sector expenditures.

Holcombe (1978) argues that determining the level of government expenditures through a democratic decision-making process without the constraint of a fiscal constitution leads to a bias in favor of larger government expenditures. The reason is that political competition for the support of the decisive voter implies that candidates and parties will push to lower the taxes paid by the decisive voter, in order to win that voter's support. A simple application of the law of demand implies that, when the decisive voter's tax price is lowered, the quantity of government demanded by the decisive voter will rise, resulting in larger-than-optimal government expenditures. Democracy contains an inherent bias toward inefficiently large government.

Wicksell and Lindahl attempted to counter this bias in two ways, but ways that are really two sides of the same coin. Wicksell is remembered for his idea that a substantial consensus should be reached on matters of public expenditure. Seeing the problems with simple majority rule, he advocated an approximate unanimity rule. Lindahl is remembered for Lindahl pricing, in which everyone's marginal tax price equals the value they place at the margin on the public good. These ideas are two sides of the same coin because taxpayers will agree on the level of public expenditures only when they face Lindahl tax prices.

While it may not be practical to design a tax system that produces Lindahl pricing exactly, it is possible to keep the principles of Wicksell and Lindahl in mind so that there is some correspondence between tax prices and the benefits of public expenditures. A number of states have moved in this direction by requiring supermajority approval for taxes and expenditures in their legislatures, or in some cases direct voter approval, implementing the Wicksellian principle of consensus. User charges are an obvious mechanism for moving toward Lindahl pricing, and earmarked taxes levied on items associated with the resulting expenditure, such as the gas tax to finance roads and the federal excise tax on airline tickets to finance air traffic control and airport improvement, are but two examples. When Lindahl pricing can be approximated, it creates a consensus regarding the level of public expenditures, and is a mechanism for leading the political process toward the optimal level and mix of public expenditures. The benefit principle is much more than just a principle of tax equity.

FEDERALISM

One method of applying the benefit principle is to adopt a system of fiscal federalism and undertake all public sector expenditures at the lowest possible level of government. Following Tiebout's (1956) model, this can result in an efficient sorting of individuals with different preferences for government expenditures and can provide a revealed preference mechanism for public expenditures. It also means that there will be less opportunity for interests in one geographic area to receive location-specific government benefits paid for by taxpayers in other areas. As Buchanan (1967) notes, the budgetary process works better when the government output benefits the population in general, rather than a subgroup of the population, and federalism helps achieve this goal. Without accounting

for political costs, a public finance analysis might argue for taxation at a higher level of government to internalize fiscal externalities and to prevent taxpayers in one taxing district from free riding on the government production of other districts. This free riding will lead to inefficiency only if the public choice mechanism in local districts does not account for the benefits produced for those outside their districts. It is possible for districts to negotiate among themselves to internalize externalities, so intergovernmental spillovers do not necessarily imply a role for a higher level government on efficiency grounds. [10]

When politics enters the picture, one must balance the potential inefficiencies of intergovernmental spillovers against the potential for inefficiently redistributive programs if a higher level government is employed, as Holcombe (1994) notes. McKenzie and Staaf (1978) have argued that tax collection at higher levels of government to finance expenditures at lower levels of government acts to cartelize lower levels of government, reducing the benefits of intergovernmental competition. This line of reasoning might be applied to tax harmonization in the European Union, for example. One can think of good reasons for having a high degree of uniformity in tax structures across districts, but uniformity imposed from above reduces intergovernmental competition and may produce a uniformly undesirable tax structure. Thus, the benefits of enforced uniformity must be weighed against the benefits of intergovernmental competition, keeping in mind that the process of intergovernmental competition itself might lead to more uniformity in tax systems. From a public choice standpoint, a federal system with much local autonomy has much to recommend it.

Public choice analysis also suggests some problems with federalism. Sobel (1997) shows that, when two levels of government tax the same base, there is a tendency for the combined tax rates to be inefficiently large. This happens because when one government chooses its level of taxation, it takes the other government's tax rate as given. Thus, a rate increase by one government reduces the tax base of the other, but governments have no incentive to take these fiscal externalities into account. This obviously applies to federal and state taxation of income and lends a different perspective to the debate on a possible national sales tax. More generally, the political dynamics among different levels of governments need to be taken into account in an analysis of taxation in federal systems.

THE MOTIVATIONS OF PEOPLE IN GOVERNMENT

In the same way that neoclassical microeconomics has characterized firms as profit maximizers, Niskanen (1971) has characterized government bureaucracies as budget maximizers. Niskanen's idea has crept into the analysis of fiscal systems to a limited degree, but most models of taxation, even when undertaken from a public choice perspective, paint the public sector as a type of market in which the competing demands of various interests are balanced against each other to determine public policy. McKenzie and Staaf (1978), as just noted, build upon Niskanen's ideas to describe the efforts of local governments to cartelize and reduce intergovernmental competition. More ominously, Brennan and Buchanan (1980) examine the concept of optimal taxation under the assumption that the government's motivation is revenue maximization to show the welfare-enhancing properties of a fiscal constitu-

tion to constrain the power of government. Holcombe (1994) argues that it is in the government's interest, even if it wants to maximize revenues, to impose constitutional constraints on its own actions. Usher (1992) combines public choice analysis with a public finance foundation to show both the role of government and the benefits of constraints on government.

All of these studies are suggestive, but at the same time, public choice analysis has done little to examine the effects of the motivations of legislators who pass tax law, and of the bureaucrats who interpret and enforce tax law, on the tax system. The public choice foundation is there, but the application to taxation is not, suggesting an avenue for further research.

Conclusions

No analysis of tax policy is complete unless it includes an explicit recognition of the public choice environment within which tax policy is made. The related areas of public expenditures and redistribution policy have already been analyzed much more extensively from a public choice perspective, and tax policy would benefit from the same attention to public choice issues. Not only is there a substantial opportunity for academic research applying public choice ideas to taxation, any analysis of tax policy that does not consider the political environment must be viewed as incomplete.

While this essay has suggested one possible direction for incorporating public choice analysis into the study of taxation, the companion paper in this issue by Winer and Hettich takes a different tack by depicting the tax structure as a political equilibrium, where the legislature weighs the demands of interests on all sides of an issue and acts as a political marketplace. In the Chicago tradition, Becker (1983) and Wittman (1989) suggest that this type of political process results in an efficient outcome, and Winer and Hettich echo this idea by arguing that, once the political process is taken into account, provisions of the tax code, including special interest provisions, can be seen as efficient responses to political interests. In contrast, the present paper advocates a broad-based and uniform tax system that constitutionally prevents special interest tax benefits.

This difference between the papers is an example of the difference between what Lott (1997) and others have called the Chicago and Virginia approaches to public choice. Within the context of the Coase theorem, the Chicago approach depicts transactions costs as low enough that political markets respond to political demands relatively efficiently. The outcome of political exchange, including special interest tax provisions, tends to be efficient. The Virginia approach views transactions costs as more significant, preventing political markets from allocating resources efficiently. Parties to the political bargain may be better off, but high transactions costs prevent most people from participating in the political exchange process, and the costs imposed on those outside the bargaining group exceed the benefits generated for special interests. There may not even be any net benefits to the interest groups themselves, as the rent-seeking literature begun by Tullock (1967) and Kreuger (1974) has demonstrated, and when one recognizes that political costs are incurred by those who only want to preserve the status quo, this conclusion is reinforced.

In the Chicago approach, negotiating for special interest provisions in the tax code is efficiency enhancing, while the Virginia approach argues against special interest provisions and, more significantly, argues against allowing them to be negotiated through the political process. For efficiency, any special interest provisions in the tax code should be part of the fiscal constitution. This contrast between approaches shows that public choice is more a method of analysis than a set of conclusions, and that, even when public choice factors are taken into account, there are a number of open questions with regard to tax policy. Despite some points of disagreement, both papers are largely consistent with each other and show the additional insights that can be gained by incorporating public choice into the study of taxation.

While these essays suggest a number of ways that public choice analysis could be applied to the study of taxation, relatively little has been done in this area. Empirical studies of political costs would shed light on their magnitude and might indicate institutional changes that could be made to limit political costs. This avenue of inquiry would make a contribution to the understanding of tax policy and also to the understanding of rent seeking more generally. Models of the policymaking process that better capture the motivations of policymakers might lend more insight into the way the tax structure actually evolves, as Winer and Hettich indicate, and also might suggest desirable features for the fiscal constitution. The tax system is a creation of a political decision-making process, and the idea that it is worthwhile to take a public choice approach to the study of tax policy says nothing more than that we would understand more about taxation if we understood more about the process by which taxes are designed.

ENDNOTES

The author gratefully acknowledges helpful comments on an earlier draft from James Buchanan, Thomas McCaleb, Joel Slemrod, and Stanley Winer.

[1] Public finance textbooks have been taking more account of public choice, but usually public choice analysis is confined to one chapter. Rosen (1995), the market leader, devotes one chapter specifically to public choice, but does not discuss public choice considerations much outside of that chapter. Holcombe (1996), my public finance textbook, has more chapters devoted to public choice and also tries to integrate public choice ideas throughout the book, but I will leave it to readers to decide if I am any more successful than other textbook authors.

[2] This theme has run through much of Buchanan's work on taxation. Brennan and Buchanan (1985) present a more general argument in favor of constitutional rules.

[3] Administrative costs are mainly a budgetary item, so they are relatively easy to estimate. Compliance costs are spread among all taxpayers and take the form of time, storage costs for records, and monetary payments for tax collections. Slemrod and Sorum (1984) estimated that taxpayer compliance costs for the U.S. individual income tax were about five to seven percent of the revenues collected. Recent estimates by the IRS indicate that compliance costs for all federal taxes are 8.7 percent of total tax collections, exceeding the Slemrod and Sorum estimates, and that administrative costs are about 0.5 percent of collections.

[4] For example, when the Tax Reform Act of 1986 was being written, realtors lobbied hard to retain the home mortgage interest deduction. The result was to retain the status quo, and substantial political costs were incurred without raising any revenue.

[5] Of course, people may favor using the public sector to transfer income from them to others, as Hochman and Rogers (1969) noted.

[6] For a public choice argument going in the other direction, see Buchanan (1967), who argues, "under certain conditions progressive income taxation may be rationally preferred by the individual, and, at least to some extent, these conditions embody features of real-world institutional choice" (p. 237).

[7] Note, however, that Buchanan (1987) correctly predicted that, after the reform, both tax rates and government expenditures would rise.

[8] This can occur because, under majority rule, voters realize they are unlikely to cast the decisive vote, so their vote will not determine the election outcome. However, their vote always determines whether they are in the majority or minority coalition. If there are advantages to voting with the majority, this can produce a situation where everybody votes for an outcome that makes everyone worse-off. A voter who defects from the majority coalition loses the advantages of being in the majority, but the election outcome remains the same.

[9] Meltzer and Richard (1981) argue that more income inequality increases the amount of redistribution, whereas Peltzman (1980) argues the opposite.

[10] Foldvary (1994) discusses ways in which communities can work together without the intervention of higher level governments to internalize intergovernmental spillovers.

REFERENCES

Atkinson, Anthony B. *Public Economics in Action: The Basic Income/Flat Tax Proposal.* Oxford: Clarendon Press, 1995.

Ballentine, J. Gregory. "The Structure of Tax System Versus the Level of Taxation: An Evaluation of the 1986 Act." *Journal of Economic Perspectives* 6 No. 1 (Winter, 1992): 59–68.

Becker, Gary. "A Theory of Competition among Pressure Groups for Political Influence." *Quarterly Journal of Economics* 98 No. 3 (August, 1983): 371–400.

Brennan, Geoffrey, and James M. Buchanan. *The Power to Tax: Analytical Foundations of a Fiscal Constitution.* Cambridge: Cambridge University Press, 1980.

Brennan, Geoffrey, and James M. Buchanan. *The Reason of Rules: Constitutional Political Economy.* Cambridge: Cambridge University Press, 1985.

Buchanan, James M. "The Economics of Earmarked Taxes." *Journal of Political Economy* 71 No. 5 (October, 1963): 457–69.

Buchanan, James M. *Public Finance in Democratic Process.* Chapel Hill: University of North Carolina Press, 1967.

Buchanan, James M. "Taxation in Fiscal Exchange." *Journal of Public Economics* 6 No. 1-2 (July/August, 1976): 17–29.

Buchanan, James M. "Tax Reform as Political Choice." *Journal of Economic Perspectives* 1 No. 1 (Summer, 1987): 29–35.

Buchanan, James M. "The Political Efficiency of General Taxation." *National Tax Journal* 46 No. 4 (December, 1993): 401–10.

Buchanan, James M., and Gordon Tullock. *The Calculus of Consent.* Ann Arbor: University of Michigan Press, 1962.

Foldvary, Fred. *Public Goods and Private Communities: The Market Provision of Social Services.* Brookfield, VT: Edward Elgar, 1994.

Hall, Robert E., and Alvin Rabushka. *The Flat Tax.* Stanford: Hoover Institution Press, 1985.

Hayek, Friedrich A. *The Constitution of Liberty.* Chicago: University of Chicago Press, 1960.

Hettich, Walter, and Stanley L. Winer. "Economic and Political Foundations of Tax Structure." *American Economic Review* 78 No. 4 (September, 1988): 701–12.

Hochman, Harold M., and James D. Rogers. "Pareto Optimal Redistribution." *American Economic Review* 59 No. 4 Part 1 (September, 1969): 542–57.

Holcombe, Randall G. "Public Choice and Public Spending." *National Tax Journal* 31 No. 4 (December, 1978): 373–83.

Holcombe, Randall G. "Non-optimal Unanimous Agreement." *Public Choice* 48 No. 3 (1986): 229–44.

Holcombe, Randall G. *The Economic Foundations of Government.* New York: New York University Press, 1994.

Holcombe, Randall G. *Public Finance: Government Revenues and Expenditures in the United States Economy.* Minneapolis/St. Paul: West Publishing Company, 1996.

Holcombe, Randall G. "Selective Excise Taxation from an Interest Group Perspective." In *Taxing Choice: The Predatory Politics of Fiscal Discrimination*, edited by William F. Shughart II. New Brunswick: Transaction Publishers, 1997.

Kreuger, Anne O. "The Political Economy of the Rent-Seeking Society." *American Economic Review* 64 No. 3 (June, 1974): 291–303.

Lindahl, Erik. "Just Taxation—A Positive Solution" (orig. 1919). In *Classics in the Theory of Public Finance*, edited by Richard A. Musgrave and Alan T. Peacock. New York: St. Martin's Press, 1967.

Lott, John R. "Does Political Reform Increase Wealth? Or, Why the Difference Between the Chicago and Virginia Schools is Really an Elasticity Question." *Public Choice* 91 No. 3-4 (June, 1997): 219–27.

McKenzie, Richard B., and Robert J. Staaf. "Revenue Sharing and Monopoly Government." *Public Choice* 33 No. 3 (1978): 93–7.

Meltzer, Allan H., and Scott F. Richard "A Rational Theory of the Size of Government." *Journal of Political Economy* 89 No. 5 (October, 1981): 914–27.

Mirrlees, James A. "An Exploration in the Theory of Optimum Income Taxation." *Review of Economic Studies* 38 No. 114 (April, 1971): 175–208.

Mirlees, James A. "Optimal Tax Theory—A Synthesis." *Journal of Public Economics* 6 No. 4 (November, 1976): 327–58.

Niskanan, William A. *Bureaucracy and Representative Government.* Chicago: Aldine–Atherton, 1971.

Peltzman, Sam. "The Growth of Government." *Journal of Law and Economics* 23 No. 2 (October, 1980): 209–87.

Ramsey, Frank P. "A Contribution to the Theory of Taxation." *Economic Journal* 37 (March, 1927): 47–61.

Rosen, Harvey S. *Public Finance.* 4th ed. Chicago: Irwin, 1995.

Samuelson, Paul A. "The Pure Theory of Public Expenditure." *Review of Economics and Statistics* 36 No. 4 (November, 1954): 387–9.

Slemrod, Joel. "Optimal Taxation and Optimal Tax Systems." *Journal of Economic Perspectives* 4 No. 1 (Winter, 1990): 157–78.

Slemrod, Joel, and Nikki Sorum. "The Compliance Cost of the U.S. Individual Income Tax System." *National Tax Journal* 37 No. 4 (December, 1984): 461–74.

Sobel, Russell S. "Optimal Taxation in a Federal System of Governments." *Southern Economic Journal* 64 No. 2 (October, 1997): 468–85.

Stigler, George J. "Director's Law of Public Income Redistribution." *Journal of Law and Economics* 13 No. 1 (April, 1970): 1–10.

Tiebout, Charles M. "A Pure Theory of Local Expenditures." *Journal of Political Economy* 64 No. 5 (October, 1956): 416–24.

Tullock, Gordon. "The Welfare Cost of Tariffs, Monopolies, and Theft." *Western Economic Journal* 5 No. 3 (June, 1967): 224–32.

Usher, Dan. *The Welfare Economics of Markets, Voting, and Predation.* Ann Arbor: University of Michigan Press, 1992.

Weingast, Barry R., Kenneth A. Shepsle, and Christopher Johnsen. "The Political Economy of Benefits and Costs: A Neoclassical Approach to Distributive Politics." *Journal of Political Economy* 89 No. 4 (August, 1981): 642–64.

Wicksell, Knut. "A New Principle of Just Taxation" (orig. 1896). In *Classics in the Theory of Public Finance*, edited by Richard A. Musgrave and Alan T. Peacock. New York: St. Martin's Press, 1967.

Wittman, Donald. "Why Democracies Produce Efficient Results." *Journal of Political Economy* 97 No. 6 (December, 1989): 1395–1424.

WHAT IS MISSED IF WE LEAVE OUT COLLECTIVE CHOICE IN THE ANALYSIS OF TAXATION

STANLEY L. WINER* & WALTER HETTICH**

Abstract - *Omission of collective choice prevents the analyst from understanding the central role of political equilibrium. To create a framework that places tax policies in a broader equilibrium context, we must model the underlying collective allocation mechanism and use it as a starting point, whether we do empirical work explaining observed features of tax systems or whether we engage in research on tax efficiency. A broader perspective of this nature also forces us to re-examine well-known concepts, such as tax expenditures, flat taxation, and the marginal efficiency cost of public funds, and to question and reinterpret some of the conclusions that have been reached in the literature related to these concepts.*

INTRODUCTION

Omission of collective choice analysis causes us to miss a concept that is fundamental to the understanding of taxation, namely, political equilibrium. Outcomes in the public sector are a consequence of the balancing of political forces taking place in the context of resource use in both the private and the public economy. If this is acknowledged, we must create an explicit link between collective choice mechanisms describing political equilibrium and the determination of tax policies.

We show in this paper how the perspective on tax research is changed if such a broader approach is adopted. We start by considering collective allocation mechanisms that can serve as a basis for positive tax analysis. This is followed by a discussion of how an explicit acknowledgment of political equilibrium affects the normative evaluation of tax systems and tax policy proposals. At various points in the paper, we draw out the implications for the use of several major policy concepts or issues, such as tax expenditures, the flat tax, and the marginal efficiency cost of a tax source.

In keeping with the purpose of the symposium, references to the literature are kept to a minimum and are intended to be illustrative in nature. [1]

*School of Public Administration, Carleton University, Ottawa, Canada K1S5B6.
**Department of Economics, California State University, Fullerton, CA 92834.

411

ALLOCATION MECHANISMS AND THE ANALYSIS OF EQUILIBRIUM IN THE PUBLIC SECTOR

The concept of an allocation mechanism plays a crucial role in economics. Markets provide the most familiar example. Buyers and sellers transact with each other according to a given set of rules. Outcomes depend on the motivation of the participants, on their numbers, and on the framework of rules, as well as on available information. Depending on the number of those acting as sellers and/or buyers, and on the nature of interaction, we get different market structures and quite different prices and quantities in equilibrium.

Economists approach the analysis of allocation mechanisms, such as markets, by asking four basic questions: (1) How does the mechanism work? (2) Does it result in an equilibrium allocation and what are the values of the major variables in equilibrium? (3) Is the equilibrium allocation stable? (4) Is it efficient?[2]

In the public sector, the role of markets is assumed by voting mechanisms of various sorts. While the resulting decisions are collective rather than purely individual, they nevertheless serve the same overall purpose, namely, to determine output levels and, by implication, factor use for the production of public output. Collective choices also determine who pays for the provision of public output and who receives the benefits.

Because voting mechanisms serve a purpose analogous to that provided by markets, it is appropriate to ask similar questions for both. Such questions are at the heart of analyzing the use of scarce resources and, therefore, must

have relevance to both sectors. In the same way that it is necessary to understand the functioning of markets in the private economy, it is necessary to understand the operation of voting mechanisms in the public sector. Different collective choice arrangements lead to different outcomes, have different stability properties, and have different implications for the normative assessment of public policy.

Modeling Collective Choices

An analysis, be it positive or normative, that disregards public choice, nevertheless, must posit a decision-making framework to describe the behavior of politicians and public servants. This may involve someone who chooses policies to maximize the welfare of a mythical representative citizen or a planner who maximizes a welfare function determined outside of the model. As has been pointed out by other writers, such an approach imputes motives to public decision makers that differ radically from those specified for their private counterparts, who are assumed to maximize their own utility. It also disregards the essential nature of the public decision mechanism, which has as a primary role the aggregation of diverse and generally conflicting objectives of different citizens into an overall outcome.

Brennan and Buchanan (1980) and others have drawn attention to the importance of the motivation of public officials in the analysis of taxation. Prescriptions for tax policy formulated for a neutral planner may have unforeseen consequences, for example, if they are implemented by a government that attempts to maximize revenue from the private sector rather than to maximize welfare. Optimal tax rules that allow revenues to be increased while suppressing economic activity as little as possible can become rules for exploiting citizens and for enlarging the public sector (Brennan and Buchanan 1980: 80–82).

On the other hand, it is important to note that not all collective choice models give a full description of the implied allocation mechanism. While the Leviathan model has served the useful function of drawing attention to the appetite of public decision makers for private resources, it does not model a process where citizens participate in a meaningful manner and where public decision makers are constrained by voters. Nor is it clear whether the dictatorial elite in a Leviathan world would be stable and whether a unique equilibrium would exist if entry and exit into the government elite were allowed.

This suggests that the question in the title of the paper should be extended somewhat. We may not only want to ask what is missed if public choice is disregarded, but also what may be missed if we allow for collective choice but choose a model that is too restrictive to give a full description of the allocation mechanism that actually applies.

There are several available frameworks in the public choice literature that can be used to analyze taxation and other public sector choices. Because of space constraints, we shall mention only three here. The most familiar one is the median voter model. In addition, there is work based on the concept of structure-induced equilibrium and analysis based on probabilistic voting. All these approaches imply somewhat different answers to the four basic questions posed above and result in different predicted outcomes.

The difficulties raised by the median voter approach relate primarily to the

stability of outcomes. As is well-known, outcomes in a median voter framework are stable only under very restrictive conditions—choices can occur only in one dimension and preferences of voters must be single peaked. These conditions rarely apply in the real world. Tax choices made by legislators, for example, are inherently multidimensional, since budgetary procedures generally involve adjustments of a multitude of revenue instruments. Analysts who use this framework are forced to place severe restrictions on the process of choice—decisions on different tax parameters must be made sequentially and be independent in the minds of those involved. In addition, it must be assumed that there is no agenda setting that restricts the alternatives over which voting is allowed. Otherwise, the median voter's most preferred outcome will not be the winner.

Work based on structure-induced equilibrium analysis introduces specific institutional features of legislatures and committees ("the structure") to explain how the choices facing elected officials are limited, and shows why such institutional arrangements result in an equilibrium rather than vote cycling in a multidimensional issue space. [3] This approach thus extends the median voter model by placing it in a more realistic institutional context. It opens the possibility of studying the influence on equilibrium tax choices of committee structure and other specific features of congressional or parliamentary systems of government. One should note, however, that the institutional framework itself is not explained and that the deeper question of why there is no cycling over institutional features is not addressed directly.

Probabilistic voting starts from somewhat different premises. Parties are unsure about how voters will cast their vote in the next election. They view all voters as potential supporters, with each having a different probability of voting for the party. Parties structure their platforms and policy mix so as to maximize expected support and keep adjusting policies continually toward this goal. Voters, in turn, evaluate different policies according to the utility that they will derive from them and cast their vote accordingly. The framework predicts stable equilibrium outcomes for choices in multiple dimensions. On the other hand, it lacks specific institutional features and specific references to actual governing arrangements.

The brief review of models indicates that analysis of public sector outcomes raises many interesting methodological questions, which require the attention of economists in the field. If we disregard collective choice, we miss the understanding of how allocation mechanisms influence public and private outcomes. But beyond that, we also fail to address the more specific questions of how to model equilibrium allocation in some detail and how to link it to observed institutional features.

Implications for the Positive Analysis of Taxation

The broader way of looking at the public sector puts a direct focus on equilibrium. Political equilibrium is as important as the balance of forces in the marketplace. In addition, we become more aware of the substitution of policies—governments can achieve the same aim by using different means. If their main aim is re-election, they will use all available policy instruments to pursue this goal, and there will be political as well as economic trade-offs in the use of instruments. This will apply,

for example, to the joint use of various taxes. Since each tax has a different political cost function associated with it, reflecting factors such as the costs of organizing political opposition and the economic adjustments to taxation associated with a particular base, governments will aim for a tax mix that equalizes the marginal political costs of raising another dollar of revenues from various sources.[4] They will readjust this mix if outside factors change that affect particular political cost functions. For this reason, we may expect frequent changes in tax laws. Often, these changes will be presented as tax reform, yet they may not arise from any normative concerns, as the term "reform" seems to imply. Governments merely readjust revenue mix in order to respond to different economic or political realities.

Furthermore, policy instruments themselves may arise as a consequence of the pursuit of political objectives. Hettich and Winer (1988, 1998) and Warskett et al. (1998) argue that tax bases, rate structures, and special provisions can be explained in this manner. Governments group related activities into composite tax bases to lower transaction costs for themselves— the costs of becoming informed about taxpayers, of designing tax structures, and of enforcing tax laws. In a similar manner, they combine taxpayers into rate bands, rather than taxing each individual at a unique rate. However, such grouping creates a loss in expected support, since differentiated treatment of heterogeneous taxpayers would maximize expected political support in a frictionless world.[5] Governments must balance this loss against the gain in support from spending fewer resources for administrative activities and more resources for the provision of public goods.

By extension, similar arguments can also be used to explain the existence of special provisions. If there is a group that offers effective opposition to the inclusion of a specific economic activity in a particular base, it may be cheaper to placate it with a special provision, rather than with the creation of a separate base for the disputed item. Thus, capital gains may become part of a fairly broadly defined income tax, while being taxed at a rate that differs from the rate applied to other types of income.

The focus on the equilibrium mix of policies has important implications for tax analysis. To take an example, it casts doubt on the separate treatment of tariffs in a context where they are a significant source of revenues. This was the case at earlier stages of economic development for both Canada and the United States and may still be true today for some developing countries. In 19th century Canada, for example, tariffs were the major source of revenue, together with borrowing in foreign capital markets and excises on commodities such as tobacco and liquor. Setting of tariffs therefore involved a trade-off among these three revenue sources, as well as questions of protection for domestic production.

In a more modern context, differences in the size and nature of available tax sources, as well as in the tastes of, and constraints faced by different groups in the electorate can help to explain the considerable variation in fiscal policies observed among states in the United States (Chernick 1997; Hettich and Winer, 1998) and among provinces in Canada, as well as variations in national policies among developed countries, such as the members of OECD (Goodspeed, 1997). In such empirical research, it is important to consider the choice of the collective allocation mechanism and to forge an explicit link to the voting framework that the researcher uses as a basis for his work.

The possibility of an endogenous explanation for special provisions also has implications for the understanding of other policies. In particular, it throws doubt on the concept of tax expenditures, which has been widely used in recent years. From this perspective, special provisions are seen as a rational response by governments who compete with opposition parties in future elections. They cannot be interpreted as deviations from some ideal tax base designed to satisfy particular normative criteria, which may have limited or little support among voters. Nor are they introduced primarily as a hidden substitute for direct subsidies, as is so often argued in the tax expenditure literature. Special tax provisions would exist even in a world where no attempt is made to give direct subsidies to encourage particular activities. We shall return to this point below, where the use of the tax expenditure concept in normative analysis is considered.

One should also note that calculations of tax expenditures become quite suspect. Although those who refer to such figures often are aware of the limitations that arise because the economic consequences of removing the provisions are not taken into account, they rarely, if ever, point out that the existing size of the budget represents a political equilibrium. It is hard to imagine that the balancing of political forces would ever allow a government to raise the "revenues foregone" that are determined in such calculations. In fact, one may suspect that abolition of all so-called loopholes would result in a lower overall budget, since removal of available policy instruments increases the political costs of raising a particular budget. [6] A meaningful discussion of alternatives must thus consider political as well as economic equilibrium.

A final application concerns the flat tax. Those who have followed the discussion of recent proposals that are labeled with this name will realize that the term is applied loosely in public discussion, since the comprehensiveness of the proposed tax bases varies widely. Nevertheless, it is possible to comment on the topic in general. If special provisions are indeed a means of making the tax system politically more efficient, it will be unlikely that a policy can succeed that removes this type of policy instrument completely. We may expect democratic tax systems to be complex tax systems. While "reforms" can occur that lower complexity to some extent, if this becomes a politically popular aim, the result will probably be a tax system that retains a considerable amount of complexity.

In addition, one should note the implications for the use of other policy instruments. If the personal income tax, for example, were made into a "flat" levy, governments may well react by introducing more special provisions into other tax instruments. Furthermore, substitution may also be possible with other, somewhat less directly related policies, such as regulation. Special interest groups that lose favored tax treatment may succeed in obtaining relief through new regulatory measures. Forced simplicity in one policy area may thus lead to greater complexity elsewhere.

NORMATIVE ANALYSIS WHEN TAX STRUCTURE IS AN INTEGRAL PART OF A POLITICAL EQUILIBRIUM

The fourth question relating to an allocation mechanism concerns economic efficiency. It takes us into normative analysis, where we judge equilibrium outcomes according to some predefined standard. Such analysis for allocation mechanisms operating in the private sector usually refers to the concept of Pareto optimality, and the demonstration that one mechanism—the competitive market—yields an equilibrium allocation that is optimal in this sense plays a key role. Normative analysis for the public sector can be carried out in the same general manner. We can evaluate the nature of political outcomes, as that of private markets, in relation to Pareto efficiency, and we can inquire into the conditions under which a political equilibrium is efficient.

Because of the wide use of the median voter model, some analysts feel that allocations representing a political equilibrium cannot be optimal except under highly unrealistic conditions. While it is true that the preferred choice of the median voter is rarely Pareto efficient (see, for example, Bergstrom (1979)), the same conclusion does not hold for the outcomes of all collective allocation mechanisms.

In addition to assessing the nature of a political equilibrium in a manner similar to that used in private sector analysis, we can evaluate the impact of specific policy proposals. However, an additional question must be answered in this context, namely, whether our recommendations are consistent with the operation of the collective choice mechanism.

The most widely used type of formal normative analysis, the theory of optimal taxation (see, for example, Mirrlees (1976)), disregards collective choice and postulates a planner who maximizes a social welfare function. While this work is theoretically sophisticated, it suffers from a serious shortcoming that we have already hinted at: It remains unclear why evaluations flowing from this approach should be consistent with the democratic approach to solving public sector problems that society has chosen. [7]

In the remainder of this section, we shall illustrate some of the implications for normative tax analysis when the nature of equilibrium in both public and private sectors counts. A more general discussion doing justice to all the available literature would take more space than is available for this article. The discussion presented below draws mainly on our own work making use of the probabilistic voting model.

Three Steps in Welfare Analysis

An examination of the foundations of normative theory in economics points to three analytical steps needed to construct an appropriate framework in the presence of collective choice. To begin, an analysis is required that plays the role of the first theorem of welfare economics (the "invisible hand" theorem) in the context of political economy. Put differently, a set of ideal conditions must be formulated that serves as a counterfactual, and a proof must be provided that, under these conditions, equilibrium tax policies will be efficient. The second necessary step is development of an analogue to the analysis of private market failure. Cases where the basic theorem does not hold must be identified and an examination of such cases developed to give guidance to policy analysts. Third, measurement is required to make the analysis complete. It is necessary to formulate ways of assessing the consequences for welfare, or other specified social objectives, of any suggested policy changes, so that comparisons across alternative proposals become feasible.

We shall offer brief comments on steps 1 and 2, and then turn to a more extensive examination of issues associated with step 3, which thus far has received the least attention in the literature. As a way of illustrating some of the issues that arise in taking the third step, we focus on work evaluating the marginal efficiency costs of different tax sources and on the concepts of tax expenditures and broadly based taxation.

The standard of reference and the analysis of political market failure

In can be shown that, under certain conditions (including the concavity conditions required for existence of an equilibrium), the resulting allocation in a probabilistic voting model is Pareto efficient. The intuition is the following: Assuming that voters cast their ballots strictly on the basis of how policy outcomes affect their utility, adoption of a fiscal platform that makes some voters better-off without making any other voter worse-off must increase overall expected support. Competition for office ensures that, in a political equilibrium, no such Pareto-superior policy platforms remain to be adopted. This result, which is sketched somewhat more fully below, has been shown formally by Coughlin and Nitzan (1981), Ledyard (1984), and others. We shall label the tax structure that emerges in such a perfectly functioning representative democracy an optimal representative tax (ORT) system.

Many applied tax policy analyses (for example, Jorgenson and Yun (1991)) use an equal yield, lump sum tax system as their point of departure for judging proposed policies. As a way of linking our discussion to current methods of tax policy evaluation, it is of interest to ask how an ORT system compares to this often used standard of reference. [8]

In a normative public choice analysis, lump sum taxation cannot serve as the standard of reference since it cannot be assumed that such taxation represents the outcome of a competitive political process. As explained above, tax structure represents a compromise between attempts to discriminate among voters in order to increase support and attempts to save on transaction costs. The resulting tax system is likely to be complex and to include arrangements that result in some separation of spending and taxing in the minds of citizens, even when the political system is perfectly competitive. Such separation will arise whenever individuals are not able to link marginal adjustments in the level of public goods to marginal changes in the taxes that they pay. Allocation under an ORT standard thus will differ from allocation in a system with lump sum taxes of equal yield. In fact, we may expect an ORT system, even though it represents an ideal standard, to show positive welfare costs if it is compared to a system of lump sum taxation.

Of course many things can go wrong with collective choice processes, and actual political equilibria may not be Pareto efficient. Consideration of these problems takes us to the second step in welfare analysis, one that has received much attention in the public choice literature. While a concern with imperfections of the political marketplace will be evident in our discussion below, we shall limit ourselves to only two points here. First, in order to link the existing literature on government failure to tax analysis, it is necessary to make specific connections between principal-agent problems, rent seeking by interest groups, and other problems that may prevent the attainment of an efficient equilibrium, on the one hand, and specific features of a tax structure, on

the other. With some exceptions, this link is generally missing in the literature. [9]

Second, to provide a basis for normative prescription, the analysis of political market failure must be conducted within a framework where the standard of reference used to define "failure" can be shown to be an equilibrium outcome of a collective choice process. When this is not done, an analysis based on identification of political market failures is not persuasive, a point we illustrate in the next section.

Policy evaluation and measurement

The marginal efficiency costs of alternative tax sources: Measures of the welfare costs associated with alternative tax sources are often used as a basis for the design of tax reform. It is argued that a tax system should be designed so as to equalize the marginal excess burden of taxation per unit change in revenue across tax sources, because, only in this case, will the total unweighted sum of excess burdens for a budget of given size be minimized.

An example is given by the work of Jorgenson and Yun (1991), who calculate the change in excess burden per dollar change in revenue, or marginal efficiency cost (MEC), associated with each major part of the U.S. tax system. [10] They do this by using a general equilibrium model to compute the reduction in the unweighted sum of excess burdens across individuals that would occur if each distorting tax were lowered and the lost revenue replaced with a nondistorting, lump sum tax. Jorgenson and Yun conclude that the U.S. system could be improved by reducing reliance on income taxes, which have a relatively high MEC, and by increasing reliance on sales and property taxes, where the MECs are lower.

As already noted, one problem with such studies is their use of an equal yield, lump sum tax system as the basis for comparison. Two further problems arise when tax policy is regarded as part of a political equilibrium. The first of these is the following:

In a representative democracy in which political influence differs across voters, a political equilibrium will exhibit MECs (as usually calculated) which vary across tax sources, and this situation may be consistent with Pareto efficiency. Thus, a proposal to equalize MECs will generally be inconsistent with political equilibrium in a representative democracy, and may not involve a Pareto improvement.

The criticism requires that we characterize the nature of political equilibria in a representative democracy. While there are several ways to accomplish this, we shall continue to rely on the probabilistic voting framework in our discussion. In this view, tax policy outcomes reflect a balancing of opposing forces, a feature shared with many other models of political pluralism. The argument below may thus carry over to other frameworks in which the equilibrium also represents a balancing of the interests of different parts of the electorate.

In a probabilistic voting model, as pointed out above, political competition tends to force parties to adopt Pareto-efficient policies. Otherwise the possibility remains that the opposition can propose a Pareto-improving policy platform and thereby increase its electoral support. This does not imply, however, that MECs will be equalized. Voters differ in their effective political influence as seen by the parties, even when the franchise is universal. Thus, in seeking to optimize political support from voters who care primarily about their own economic welfare, and in directing resources toward politically influential voters, an incumbent will accept an increase in the MEC of a particular tax source (as usually calculated), above that of other taxes, if that is the price of maximizing the chances for re-election.

Some algebra is useful in clarifying this point. To simplify, we limit the discussion to a situation with two political parties, two tax bases, two tax rates, and one public good. To acknowledge tax administration and information costs implicitly, we assume that the number of tax rates is less than the number of voters and that taxation is proportional rather than lump sum. Indirect utility for voter h is $v_h(t_1, t_2, G)$, and, after substitution of the general equilibrium structure of the private economy, the government budget restraint can be written as

$$G = R_1(t_1, t_2, G) + R_2(t_1, t_2, G).$$

Each party chooses tax rates and the size of public expenditure to maximize its total expected vote. The probability that voter h supports the incumbent as perceived by the party (f_{hi}) depends on the difference in the voter's evaluation of her welfare under the incumbent's policies and those of the opposition (o):

$$f_{hi} = f_h(v_{hi} - v_{ho}).$$

The expected vote for the incumbent government then is

$$EV_i = \Sigma_h f_h(v_{hi} - v_{ho})$$

and the vote for the opposition may be defined analogously.[11] In addition, we assume that knowledge of the probability density functions describing voting behavior and of the structure of the private economy is common to the competing parties.

Given the platform of the opposition, first-order conditions for the choice of tax rates that maximize EV_i subject to the budget restraint are of the form

$$\frac{\Sigma_h \partial f_h/\partial v_h \cdot \partial v_h/\partial t_1}{\partial(R_1 + R_2)/\partial t_1} = \frac{\Sigma_h \partial f_h/\partial v_h \cdot \partial v_h/\partial t_2}{\partial(R_1 + R_2)/\partial t_2}$$

from which it can be seen that the platform chosen by the incumbent equalizes the marginal effect of tax policies on expected votes per dollar of revenue across tax sources. [12] Since the fiscal policies of the opposition are determined by essentially the same conditions, it is evident that party platforms will converge in an equilibrium, if one exists. [13]

After substitution of equilibrium values of the partial derivatives in equation 1, these conditions can also be used to characterize the tax system that emerges in a Nash equilibrium of the electoral game, and can be used to illustrate the result referred to earlier that the outcome in such a model may be Pareto efficient. Let θ_h be the particular values taken by the partial derivative $\partial f_h/\partial v_h$ at a Nash equilibrium of the electoral contest, assuming that one exists, and let the other partial derivatives also be evaluated at the same equilibrium. Then the first-order conditions for politically optimal (equilibrium) strategies take the form

$$\frac{\Sigma_h \theta_h \cdot \partial v_h/\partial t_1}{\partial(R_1 + R_2)/\partial t_1} = \frac{\Sigma_h \theta_h \cdot \partial v_h/\partial t_2}{\partial(R_1 + R_2)/\partial t_2}.$$

To see that policy choices characterized by condition 2 are consistent with

Pareto efficiency, it suffices to note that this condition also represents a solution to the problem of choosing a fiscal system to maximize a political support function, $S = \Sigma_h \theta_h v_h$, subject to the government budget restraint. [14] It is also useful to point out that, since this particular function is maximized, it makes sense to think of the weights θ_h appearing in it, which represent the perceived responsiveness of voting behavior to a change in individual welfare at a Nash equilibrium, as measures of the effective influence exerted by different voters on policy outcomes.

Using condition 2 as a representation of political equilibrium, we can proceed with the main argument about MECs. In the special case where the θ's for all voters are equal, we can substitute the definition $W_k = \Sigma_h \partial v_h/\partial t_k$ into condition 2, subtract 1 from each side, and simplify to get

$$\frac{W_1 - \partial(R_1 + R_2)/\partial t_1}{\partial(R_1 + R_2)/\partial t_1} = \frac{W_2 - \partial(R_1 + R_2)/\partial t_2}{\partial(R_1 + R_2)/\partial t_2}$$

where W_k is the sum of individual losses in utility due to an increase in tax k (measured, for example, as the unweighted sum of equivalent variations in income); the numerator on each side of the equation is the excess burden of the corresponding tax change; and the quotient on each side represents the marginal efficiency cost of each tax source.

Thus, we see that, if the θ's are all equal, the tax system equalizes the MECs of all tax sources and minimizes the total excess burden of taxation, measured by the sum of unweighted welfare losses. On the other hand, if political influence is distributed unequally as in condition 2, unweighted marginal welfare losses for different tax sources may vary significantly as parties trade off the welfare of and support from different voters, even though Pareto efficiency is being achieved. In that case, a proposal to equalize the MECs of the two tax sources (as usually measured) may lead only to a movement along the Pareto utility frontier, or, quite possibly, to a less efficient allocation.

To put this another way, in weighting welfare changes for different people equally, existing welfare analysis of the public sector imputes all observed inequality of MECs to the inefficiency of public policy. This is odd in view of the role that competition between parties for the support of self-interested voters plays in democratic countries. In the simple model outlined above, all of the inequality in MECs stems from inequalities in effective political influence, and no economic inefficiency is implied. However, one need not believe that actual political equilibria are fully efficient to agree that some part of the inequality in the unweighted sum of welfare changes may be due to reallocation that is conducted as costlessly as possible in the pursuit of political power. [15]

A normative analysis that uses weights from an ORT system to aggregate welfare changes would be of much interest, though determining what weights should be used is not an easy matter. Equality of the franchise is not the same thing as equality of effective influence, and it is far from clear that, in a perfectly competitive political system, all the θ_h in condition 2 must be equal. The problem of the choice of welfare weights has also been addressed in the

literature on benefit-cost analysis, where an attempt has been made to infer from choices across different projects a set of "distributional" weights that may be used in aggregating individual welfare gains. One should note, however, that such empirically derived weights do not only reflect ideas about equity, since the public projects used in calculating so-called distributional weights are in fact equilibrium outcomes of an existing political system. Thus, it may not be appropriate to use these distributional weights to aggregate welfare losses for the purpose of a normative evaluation.

In the absence of a suitable set of political weights, it may be reasonable for tax policy advisers to proceed on the assumption that the Hicks–Kaldor criterion based on equal weighting is appropriate for judging the direction of tax reform. When this is done, though, it is not clear what more can be said by the tax policy analyst when his proposal to equalize the MECs of tax sources is rejected. In particular, it cannot be argued on the basis of such a rejection alone that politics has corrupted tax policy.

Whatever weights are used to aggregate individual welfare changes, a further problem with the use of MECs arises when it is acknowledged that an evaluation based only on the excess burdens of alternative tax sources does not allow for the substitution of governing instruments that will occur in any political equilibrium:

> The tax system is part of a broader set of equilibrium policy outcomes, and tax measures cannot be evaluated in isolation from related policies.

Changes in tax structure that are made in response to shocks in other policy fields cannot be judged independently of what happens in those other areas, even if MECs associated with taxation become more unequal as a result. Such a change in MECs may in fact be Pareto improving if tax policy is compensating for the effects of policy in other areas.

As a case in point, it is interesting to consider the actions by the U.S. Congress in connection with recent minimum wage legislation. The increase in the minimum wage was passed together with a package of tax breaks designed to soften the impact on small business. If these tax breaks make MECs across tax sources less equal, can it be concluded that social welfare has been reduced as a result?

Broadly based taxation and tax expenditures: To complete the discussion of applied tax analysis, we consider normative assessments that rely on the concepts of broadly based taxation and tax expenditures.

The understanding of political equilibrium presented in earlier sections is unlikely to fit well with the arguments for broadly based taxation advanced by Simons (1938) and used by Surrey (1973) to support the tax expenditure concept. In a competitive political system, governments create special provisions as a way of taking differing economic and political responses to taxation into account, while economizing on administration costs. This suggests that those special provisions that were introduced to make the tax system administratively or politically more efficient should be preserved rather than eliminated.

Following Simons, one may argue that the political power to create special provisions can be misused and that limitations on this power are desirable. Simons, like some proponents of a broadly based consumption tax (see, for example, the Meade Report, IFS 1978, 44), believed that broadly based taxation would minimize the inefficiency resulting from manipulation of tax breaks in the course of the democratic process. [16]

Since these analyses are not formally cognizant of how tax structure actually emerges in a democratic system, it is not clear on what basis the proposed reforms are being made. In a framework that accounts for transactions costs, it is necessary to trade off the welfare gains from special provisions introduced to increase efficiency against the losses from tax breaks that reflect the misuse of political power. It will not be clear what the appropriate trade-off should be until it is better understood how political market failure affects tax policy outcomes. In our view, it is unlikely that an analysis that trades off the good and bad aspects of special provisions in a fully specified model would suggest substantial limitations on the power to open and close special provisions in the course of the democratic process. In any event, the issue, like those discussed earlier, cannot be resolved without recourse to a normative analysis that explicitly acknowledges the existence of collective choice and that links specific political market failures to structural features of equilibrium tax systems. [17]

Concluding Remarks

A valuable part of a symposium of this nature is the opportunity to exchange views and to respond to the conclusions of other participants. Although Holcombe (1998) starts his analysis with the same basic questions, and although he takes a collective choice approach, his recommendations concerning the role of special provisions in the tax system differ markedly from ours. The same applies to his treatment of the related topic of flat taxation as a policy option.

In some ways, this difference is more apparent than real. While we hold that some special provisions are an efficient response to the existence of transaction costs and to the need of self-interested political decision makers to differentiate effectively among taxpayers in a democratic system, we do not argue that all observed "tax breaks" are efficient or desirable. In our view, the challenge is to analyze particular provisions in relation to the operation of political markets in order to determine if they arise as a justified response, or whether they represent the result of imperfections in the operation of political markets.

Our conclusion flows from the methodological position underlying our approach. We believe that welfare analysis for the public sector should include the same basic steps that are used when such analysis is carried out for the private sector. We must define a standard or reference allocation of resources; conduct an examination of market failure in relation to this standard, and provide for the measurement of deviations from the optimum.

In an earlier part of the paper, we argue that the reference allocation has to be defined with regard to an allocation mechanism that represents collective choices explicitly and for which the existence and stability of equilibrium can be established. We use the probabilistic voting model, when there is effective competition among parties, to illustrate such a standard. Our approach differs from the constitutional literature, referred to by Holcombe, since work in that tradition does not show how ideal constitutions arise in the context of a

political mechanism for which existence and stability can be demonstrated.

Our approach in no way obviates the need for an analysis of political market failure. While we have not emphasized this step, we believe that it is an essential ingredient in the understanding of observed tax systems and in the evaluation of special provisions. To make an assessment of tax efficiency, it is necessary to link specific features of the tax system directly to the functioning (or malfunctioning) of political markets and the definition of political equilibrium. While there is some research on this topic, economists so far have not devoted sufficient attention to this task. As a result, the implications of imperfect political markets for tax structure and tax policy are not well understood.

One may perhaps object that such an analysis raises many difficulties that cannot easily be overcome. It should be realized, however, that the research questions that arise in this context are very similar to those in many areas of the private sector, once the existence of transaction costs is admitted. There is an extensive literature relating to industrial organization that asks whether particular aspects of firm or market organization represent an efficient response to transaction costs that are faced by participants, or whether we deal with phenomena that are noncompetitive and require public intervention. Once we adopt a parallel approach to efficiency in the public sector, it becomes clear that questions of this nature must also be answered with regard to policy structures and outcomes in the public economy (Hettich and Winer, 1995).

Although we have high regard for the work of the economists associated with the University of Chicago, who have made major contributions to the literature on transaction costs and to the understanding of collective choice (Coase, 1960; Becker, 1983; Wittman, 1995), we do not believe that advocacy of the three basic steps of welfare economics in tax analysis qualifies us for inclusion in the so-called Chicago School, as Holcombe suggests. We rather feel that we occupy a part of the substantial middle ground between Chicago and Virginia. We make no claim that either the private or the public economy, as observed, is necessarily competitive or efficient in every instance, or even in most aspects. At the same time, we would argue that competition exists and is a viable force in both sectors.

In closing, we would like to return to the main emphasis in our paper. Omission of collective choice prevents the analyst from understanding the central role of political equilibrium in the analysis of taxation. This applies to work of a positive nature, as well as to the examination of tax efficiency.

To create a framework that places tax policies in a broader equilibrium context, we must model the underlying collective allocation mechanism and use it as a starting point, whether we do empirical work explaining observed features of tax systems or whether we engage in research with a normative emphasis. A broader perspective of this nature also forces us to re-examine well-known concepts in tax analysis, such as tax expenditures, flat taxation, and the marginal efficiency cost of public funds, and to question and reinterpret some of the conclusions that have been reached in the literature related to these concepts. Only in the context of political equilibrium can we gain a full understanding of how tax systems arise, function, and should be evaluated in democratic societies.

ENDNOTES

We are indebted to Calum Carmichael, Randall Holcombe, Jim Poterba, and Joel Slemrod for their helpful comments. Hettich wishes to acknowledge a summer stipend from the State Special Fund for Research, Scholarship and Creative Activity.

[1] For comprehensive surveys, see, for example, Head (1997), and Hettich and Winer (1997, 1998).

[2] A fifth question may relate to the distributional effects of the allocation mechanism.

[3] For an introduction to and application of the structure-induced equilibrium approach, see, for example, Shepsle and Weingast (1981), Inman and Fitts (1990), and Stewart (1991).

[4] In the context of this discussion, political costs represent the loss in electoral support for the government from levying taxation. Administration costs enter the framework as a wedge between the collection of tax revenues and the provision of public services, and affect the political costs associated with raising a given net amount of revenue (net of administration costs) from the various tax sources. To the extent that rent seeking affects the welfare of voters and thereby their voting behavior, its consequences also will be taken into account in the formulation of policy platforms.

[5] It should be noted that government is not allowed in this model to selectively punish taxpayers who are singled out by name—the rule of law applies, albeit implicitly. On the other hand, criteria related to the distribution of income are taken into account only to the extent that they further the government's objective.

[6] Imagine, for example, that a budget is raised from several tax bases and that reliance on each base has associated with it an increasing marginal political cost (or marginal loss of expected support) function. Moreover, assume that special provisions that reduce tax payments for people who engage in specific, favored activities are present in each base. Now, if special provisions are eliminated, raising the same revenue as before from each base will imply that the total and the marginal political cost associated with each base will rise, since the effective rate of tax on each base faced by at least some taxpayers must have increased. As a result, the total marginal political cost of taxation will now be greater than the marginal political benefit of another dollar of public services. To restore equality of total marginal political costs and benefits, the size of government must decline.

One should note that this argument assumes that the marginal political benefit derived from public spending is not affected by the elimination of tax loopholes. It is possible that removal of some special provisions may result in an increase in the price of private substitutes for particular public services. A final judgment about the effect of eliminating particular special provisions on the size of government thus depends on the effect of these provisions on the relative, after-tax price of public and private goods.

[7] Buchanan (1976) provides further discussion of this point.

[8] It might be argued that it is possible to avoid the complexities of using a first best standard defined by a lump sum tax of equal yield or by an ORT system by comparing the status quo to an alternative tax blueprint. While this procedure is useful, it should be kept in mind that, without an ideal standard and the corresponding measure of the total loss of welfare relative to it, there is always the danger that a proposed policy will lead away from, rather than closer to, the first best.

[9] For a recent contribution that explores the link between principal-agent problems and the structure of taxation, see Gordon and Wilson (1997).

[10] The MEC is equal to the loss of consumer surplus from increasing reliance on a particular tax source less the additional tax revenue collected (the marginal excess burden of the tax), all divided by the change in tax revenue. If a tax does not generate an excess burden, its MEC is equal to 0. The marginal cost of funds associated with a tax source, another often used measure of the welfare loss due to taxation, is equal to 1 plus the MEC.

[11] If H is the number of voters, $EV_o = H - EV_r$.

[12] To derive condition 1, one may use the Lagrangian $l = EV_i - \lambda (R_1 + R_2 - G)$ to derive the separate first-order conditions for the optimal choices of t_1, t_2 and G. For tax rates, these separate conditions are of the form $\Sigma_h(\partial f_h/\partial v_h \cdot \partial v_h/\partial t_k) - \lambda \cdot \{\partial(R_1 + R_2)/\partial t_k\} = 0$, $k = 1,2$. In words, such conditions state that each tax instrument must be adjusted until the marginal loss of expected votes from a further tax increase is equal to the gain in votes from using the additional revenue to supply more public services. Condition 1 then follows as a result of manipulating the first-order conditions above so that only λ is on the right-hand side of each.

[13] Recall that parties have common knowledge of probability densities describing voting behavior, as well as common knowledge of the economy. Enelow and Hinich (1989) discuss the conditions required for existence of the equilibrium in a probabilistic voting model and provide a formal proof of policy convergence. One may note that neither the existence of an equilibrium nor the convergence of platforms is guaranteed under all conditions. Usher (1994), for example, has shown that the equilibrium is unlikely to exist when preferences of the electorate are highly polarized.

[14] To see this result, maximize the Lagrangian $l = S - \mu(R_1 + R_2 - G)$ with respect to t_1, t_2, and G while treating the weights in S (the θ_h's, which are each set equal to $\partial f_h/\partial v_h$ at the equilibrium) as constants, and follow the same steps as described in note 12. Note that second-order conditions for

this "Representation Theorem" also apply. See Coughlin (1992) and Warskett et al. (1998) for further discussion.

[15] For a complementary but different treatment of the meaning of efficiency in representative democracy, see Besley and Coate (1998).

[16] Simons was also, and perhaps primarily, concerned with equity. One should also note that there are other arguments for a broad definition of tax bases, notably that a good tax should be neutral with respect to the incentives it creates for taxpayers to shift among activities. This is a rule of thumb for the application of the idea that MECs should be equalized across tax sources and, as such, is subject to the same problems.

[17] At present, the literature does not provide analyses that can be used to illustrate the point. An interesting case to study is the treatment of income from capital gains. At the outset, the question arises as to why this type of income is usually treated as part of a personal income tax base rather than constituting a separate tax source. In a full welfare analysis of the sort we are suggesting, one would have to determine to what extent this treatment is a response to transactions costs, and whether it has anything to do with particular sources of political market failure.

As a first hypothesis, we would suggest that the absence of a separate base is due to transactions costs. Preferential treatment in some specific cases may more likely be due to political market failure. A case in point concerns the actions of the newly elected Conservative government in Canada in the mid 1980s, which introduced a five hundred thousand dollar lifetime exemption for income from capital gains shortly after being elected. The exemption was reduced after a few years to one hundred thousand dollars, and then abolished by the next government. This episode may be due to the lack of continual political pressure in a parliamentary democracy with periodic elections. In a perfectly competitive system, the government would be forced to continually adjust tax structure to maximize expected votes.

REFERENCES

Becker, Gary. "A Theory of Competition among Pressure Groups for Political Influence." *Quarterly Journal of Economics* 98 No. 3 (August, 1983): 371–400.

Bergstrom, Ted C. "When Does Majority Rule Supply Public Goods Efficiently?" *Scandinavian Journal of Economics* 81 No. 2 (1979): 216–26.

Besley, Timothy, and Stephen Coate. "Sources of Inefficiency in a Representative Democracy: A Dynamic Analysis." *American Economic Review* 88 No. 1 (March, 1998): 139–56.

Brennan Geoffrey, and James M. Buchanan. *The Power to Tax: Analytical Foundations of a Fiscal Constitution.* Cambridge: Cambridge University Press, 1980.

Breton, Albert. *Competitive Governments: An Economic Theory of Politics and Public Finance.* Cambridge: Cambridge University Press, 1996.

Buchanan, James M. "Taxation in Fiscal Exchange." *Journal of Public Economics* 6 No. 1-2 (July/August, 1976): 17–29.

Chernick, Howard. "The Choice of Tax Base and Government Behavior: On the Determinants of Tax Progressivity in Sub-National Jurisdictions." Unpublished paper delivered at the International Seminar in Public Economics Conference, Oxford, U.K., December, 1997.

Coase, Ronald H. "The Problem of Social Cost." *Journal of Law and Economics* 3 (1960): 1–44.

Coughlin, Peter J. *Probabilistic Voting Theory.* Cambridge: Cambridge University Press, 1992.

Coughlin, Peter J., and Shmuel Nitzan. "Electoral Outcomes with Probabilistic Voting and Nash Social Welfare Maxima." *Journal of Public Economics* 15 No. 1 (February, 1981): 113–21.

Enelow, James M., and Melvin J. Hinich. "A General Probabilistic Spatial Theory of Elections." *Public Choice* 61 No. 2 (May, 1989): 101–13.

Goodspeed, Timothy. "Redistributive Tax Structure in Open Federal Economies: Theory and Evidence from Local Governments in OECD Countries." Unpublished paper delivered at the International Seminar in Public Economics Conference, Oxford, U.K., December, 1997.

Gordon, Roger H., and John D. Wilson. "Tax Structure and Government Behavior: A Principal-Agent Model of Government." Unpublished paper delivered at the International Seminar in Public Economics Conference, Oxford, U.K., December, 1997.

Head, John. "Prolegomena to Fundamental Tax Reform." In *Tax Conversations: A Guide to the Key Issues in the Tax Reform Debate. Essays in Honour of John G. Head,* edited by Rick Krever, 19–48. London: Kluwer Law International, 1997.

Hettich, Walter, and Stanley L. Winer. "Economic and Political Foundations of Tax Structure." *American Economic Review* 78 No. 4 (September, 1988): 701–12.

Hettich, Walter, and Stanley L. Winer. "Decision Externalities, Economic Efficiency and Institutional Response." *Canadian Public Policy* 21 No. 3 (September, 1995): 344–61.

Hettich, Walter, and Stanley L. Winer. "The Political Economy of Taxation." In *Perspectives on Public Choice,* edited by Dennis Mueller, 481–505. Cambridge: Cambridge University Press, 1997.

Hettich, Walter, and Stanley L. Winer. *Democratic Choice and Taxation: A Theoretical and Empirical Analysis.* Cambridge: Cambridge University Press, 1998, (forthcoming).

Holcombe, Randall. "Tax Policy from a Public Choice Perspective." *National Tax Journal* 51 No. 2 (June, 1998): 359–71.

Inman, Robert P., and Michael A. Fitts. "Political Institutions and Fiscal Policy: Evidence from the U.S. Historical Record." *Journal of Law, Economics and Organization* 6 (Special Issue, 1990): 79–132.

Institute for Fiscal Studies. *The Structure and Reform of Direct Taxation.* Report of a Committee Chaired by Professor J.E. Meade. London: Allen & Unwin, 1978.

Jorgenson, Dale W., and Kun-Young Yun. "The Excess Burden of Taxation in the United States." *Journal of Accounting, Auditing and Finance* 6 No. 4 (Fall, 1991): 487–508.

Ledyard, John O. "The Pure Theory of Large Two-Candidate Elections." *Public Choice* 44 No.1 (1984): 7–41.

Mirrlees, James A. "Optimal Tax Theory—A Synthesis." *Journal of Public Economics* 6 No. 4 (November, 1976): 327–58.

Mueller, Dennis C. *Public Choice II.* Cambridge: Cambridge University Press, 1989.

Shepsle, Kenneth A., and Barry R. Weingast. "Structure-Induced Equilibrium and Legislative Choice." *Public Choice* 37 No. 3 (1981): 503–19.

Simons, Henry C. *Personal Income Taxation: The Definition of Income as a Problem of Fiscal Policy.* Chicago: University of Chicago Press, 1938.

Stewart, Charles H. "The Politics of Tax Reform in the 1980's." In *Politics and Economics in the Eighties,* edited by Alberto Alesina and Geoffrey Carliner. Chicago: University of Chicago Press, 1991.

Surrey, Stanley S. *Pathways to Tax Reform: The Concept of Tax Expenditures.* Cambridge, MA: Harvard University Press, 1973.

Usher, Dan. "The Significance of the Probabilistic Voting Theorem." *Canadian Journal of Economics* 27 No. 2 (May, 1994): 433–45.

Warskett, George, Stanley L. Winer, and Walter Hettich. "The Complexity of Tax Structure in Competitive Political Systems." *International Tax and Public Finance* 5 No. 2 (May, 1998): 127–55.

Wittman, Donald. *The Myth of Democratic Failure: Why Political Institutions are Efficient.* Chicago: University of Chicago Press, 1995.

PUBLIC FINANCE AND PUBLIC CHOICE

JAMES M. POTERBA[*]

Abstract - *This paper explores the contribution that public choice models can make to the traditional efficiency and distributional analyses of tax policy. It notes the relative lack of attention to political economy issues in public finance, at least in comparison with other policy-oriented subfields in economics. It then discusses two key insights that emerge from public choice models of taxation. The first is the notion that different tax systems may be associated with different opportunities for political rent seeking, and the second is the possibility that actual tax systems equate the marginal political cost of raising revenue from different tax instruments, rather than the marginal efficiency cost. The paper concludes with a brief discussion of the role of traditional efficiency and distributional analyses in contributing to tax policymaking, even in a political world.*

Most applied tax policy research addresses the efficiency costs of different tax rules, the behavioral effects

of taxation, or the distribution of gains and losses associated with a switch from one tax policy to another. There is usually little accompanying discussion of how and why various tax policies are adopted. While most researchers would readily admit that political factors are a fundamental determinant of the tax system, and some with policymaking experience might say "it's all politics," the implications of this insight receive relatively little attention. Brennan (1984) argues that this derives in large part from the intellectual origins of applied tax policy research in the work of Smith, Ricardo, and Marshall, rather than in work of continental "public goods" scholars such as Wicksell and Lindahl.

In contrast to the limited emphasis on policy formation in public finance, other subfields of applied economics are more concerned with the political economy of policy. Regulatory economics is a prime example. Almost three decades ago, Stigler (1971) galvanized regulatory economists to move beyond analyzing the efficiency cost of regulations and to model the political factors that generated regulatory policy. Joskow and Noll (1981) note that, prior to Stigler's work, much of the research in regulatory economics implicitly assumed normative analysis as a positive model. This framework presumes that efficient

[*]Department of Economics, Massachusetts Institute of Technology, Cambridge, MA 02142-1347 and National Bureau of Economic Research, Cambridge, MA 02138.

policies are the ones that policymakers will adopt.

One of the key factors that contributed to the success of Stigler's message was the substantial body of empirical evidence suggesting that observed regulatory policies did not enhance economic efficiency. Stigler and others in the "Chicago School" developed models in which self-interested regulators chose policies on the basis of rent transfers offered by special interest groups. They argued that well-organized and well-financed industry groups could divert regulators from efficient policies and toward policies that generated rents for such groups. This approach has proven useful in describing the structure of regulatory policy. Peltzman (1989) surveys the successes and failures of this "economic theory of regulation" in explaining the rise and decline of industrial regulation over the last half century. A key effect of Stigler's work was to reduce the research emphasis on documenting economic inefficiencies in government regulations, which are unsurprising in this setting, and to increase the attention devoted to measuring the gains or losses that regulation imposed on various interest groups.

Regulatory economics is not the only field that has recognized the importance of policy formation. In international economics, a rapidly expanding literature explores the origins of tariff policy. Grossman and Helpman (1994) relate the tariffs on different goods to the degree of political organization in, and potential campaign contributions from, the industry producing the good, as well as to the potential costs that the tariff may impose on the broader economy. Their model has immediate application in the tax policy process. Members of the tax-writing committees in the House

and the Senate are traditionally among the top Congressional fund-raisers in campaign years. The narrow tax provisions that generate many tax expenditures are conceptually similar to tariffs on particular goods, in that they have potentially large effects on a small set of economic agents.

The situation in public finance today is in many ways similar to that in regulatory economics in the early 1970s. While computable general equilibrium studies find that the marginal deadweight burdens differ across tax instruments, much applied research on tax policy maintains the assumption that efficiency considerations alone are the driving factor in policy design. Discussions ranging from fundamental tax reform to the modification of detailed tax provisions are carried out in a framework that focuses on efficiency, but neglects the political factors that may bear on policy reform.

Some would argue that this state of affairs is as it should be. In this worldview, the role of economic analysis should be to identify and describe efficiency-enhancing policy options, while leaving policy choices to the political process. Yet at least two factors suggest that it is important to consider positive models of tax policymaking. First, understanding why tax rules change can affect empirical research on the behavioral effects of taxation. If political factors, such as who chairs key committees in Congress or which party controls the White House, have an important effect on policy outcomes, then from an economic perspective changes in policy may be "quasi-experimental." (In contrast, if tax policy only changes when the change will raise economic efficiency, conditional on revenue needs, empirical work needs to incorporate this constraint.) Second, the political system is one of the ways resources are allocated in modern market economies. The link between the political process and the structure of taxation therefore is directly relevant to the central question of economics.

The two papers in this symposium provide a welcome antidote to the usual neglect of political economy issues in public finance. They emphasize different but important issues that are easily overlooked when tax policy research does not consider the broader political context in which tax policies are framed. The papers are complementary in many ways, and I will focus on two of the insights that they develop.

Equal Marginal Deadweight Loss, or Equal Marginal Political Cost? Winer and Hettich (1998) explore the impact of political considerations on the nature of tax systems that might emerge in representative democracies. They modify the neoclassical optimal tax model by replacing the benevolent social planner with a self-interested politician. Such a policymaker will equate the marginal political cost per dollar of revenue raised from different policy instruments, rather than the marginal efficiency cost as in the standard Ramsey tax analysis. This model implies that departures from an economically efficient tax system may be the result of rational political calculations by elected officials. It expands the traditional public finance dialogue regarding tax efficiency to allow for the possibility that "political market failures" result in politically inefficient tax policies.

Once we recognize the role of politics in the determination of tax policy, results like those described by Winer and Hettich (1998) seem inevitable. Unfortunately, in many cases, results of this type

are sufficiently general to lack empirically falsifiable predictions. One of the historical impediments to refining the set of accepted models in positive political economy has been the lack of well-defined and potentially refutable empirical predictions from these models. Determining whether a particular tax provision is part of an efficient political bargain is extremely difficult. It requires a metric for evaluating the political power of various special interest groups, as well as detailed measures of the gains or losses that different groups receive from particular policies. Because both of these measurement tasks are difficult, there has been relatively little empirical work directed at testing these models of policy choice. Hettich and Winer (1996) provide a detailed summary of the existing literature. Confronted with a tax code provision that appears to have particularly high efficiency costs, we are not currently able to determine whether the policy rule is the result of a political bargain, or simply a poorly crafted policy that was intended to be efficient.

This limitation aside, the "politico-economic equilibrium" approach described by Winer and Hettich (1998) has important implications for discussions of tax reform. If the current tax code is part of a grand political balance that determines the allocation of resources to different political interest groups, then it is difficult if not impossible to discuss tax reform without considering the changes in other redistributive programs that it might stimulate. Consider, for example, replacing the current income tax with a consumption tax. This tax would raise the tax burdens on those later in life, who rely on consumption financed by asset decumulation, relative to their burdens under an income tax. Yet the elderly are politically powerful, so the political bargains that might be needed to enact fundamental tax reform could involve some redistribution (higher Social Security benefits?) toward this group. A realistic discussion of policy alternatives should recognize this need for side payments to interest groups and the resulting reduction in potential efficiency gains associated with tax reform.

Rules of the Game Matter. While Holcombe's (1998) paper also discusses the link between the political system and tax policy outcomes, it emphasizes the impact of tax structure on the nature of political activity such as lobbying. Different tax systems provide interest groups with different opportunities to lobby, or otherwise expend resources, in order to affect the tax-affected allocation of resources. Neoclassical optimal tax theory, which starts from the premise that a benevolent social planner is trying to choose a set of taxes to minimize the efficiency cost of revenue raising, does not assign any particular merit to an equal-rate tax system. (If the standard model is expanded to recognize the greater potential compliance costs associated with multiple-rate systems, a simple flat-rate tax might in fact attract some preference.) Holcombe, building on Buchanan (1993), argues that a tax system that treats different activities differently opens the door to lobbying efforts by various interest groups. Because lobbying is costly, this insight creates a presumption for taxing all types of income, and all individuals, according to simple and universal rules. In this framework, proportional income taxation, or sales taxes levied at the same rate on all goods, would reduce the opportunity for lobbying.

Anyone who has read about or witnessed the lobbying frenzies that can be associated with tax reform debates will find some sympathy for this point. It can be made even more powerful by noting, as Deaton (1987) does, that the empirical basis for differentiating taxes, on efficiency grounds, is limited. Yet just as the observation that political factors affect tax policy does not imply that taxes are set to equate the marginal political cost of raising revenue from different sources, the observation that equal or proportional taxes reduce opportunities for lobbying does not imply that these tax systems are efficient. Supporting that claim requires evidence on the resource cost of lobbying under different tax regimes. This resource cost must be compared with the potential efficiency gains that proponents of differentiated taxes would associate with such policies.

Even if the empirical case for a fiscal constitution with equal-rate or proportional taxes remains unproven, the important insight that emerges from this discussion is that the nature of the tax system can affect behavior through more than just traditional taxpayer behavior channels. Effects on political behavior may be important to consider, along with effects on economic behavior such as labor supply or consumption, in choosing a tax system. This is a neglected insight in the current policy debate on "the flat tax" and related proposals.

Holcombe's (1998) discussion of tax design, and the potential merits of a simple and flat-rate structure, focuses on efficiency issues. Yet many advocates of progressive taxation would view distributional concerns, rather than efficiency factors, as the primary motivation for departing from a proportional system. Arguments for particular tax rules based on redistribution lack the "value-free" appeal of arguments based on efficiency. Redistributive considerations nevertheless are important in determining at least some share of voters' views on the nature of desirable tax policy, and it is possible that the loss in redistribution associated with a single-rate tax would outweigh the gains from reduced lobbying activities for many observers. Of course, a crucial insight of the public choice approach is that the degree of redistribution through the tax system is the outcome of a political process. This implies that discussions of economically efficient redistributive policies that do not consider what is politically feasible may provide limited guidance for actual tax policy.

What Role for Economic Analysis? There is no doubt that political factors, notably the political power of various interest groups, play a key role in the determination of tax policy. One might consequently ask, if tax policy is largely about equating the marginal political costs of different taxes, whether economic analysis has any ultimate impact on the tax-writing process. Fortunately for practitioners of "neoclassical tax policy analysis," the answer is yes, for at least two reasons.

First, well-crafted economic analysis can quantify the net burdens of current policies and alert policymakers to unintended consequences of actual or prospective tax policies. Economic analysis that shows widely different marginal efficiency costs of raising revenue with different policy instruments can provide an important input to the political analysis of tax systems. If politicians are not receiving greater political benefits from the special interest groups that benefit from high efficiency cost taxes, or if they do value the welfare of groups that are adversely affected, this may lead to changes in the tax system.

The importance of such analysis is illustrated by the recent experience with the excise tax on excess distributions from retirement saving plans. When this tax was enacted in 1986, primarily as a device to raise revenue, most policymakers were unaware that it could interact with the income and estate taxes and place some taxpayers in an 85+ percent tax bracket with respect to accumulated assets. Shoven and Wise (1996) described the economic effects of this tax, and their work attracted substantial attention in the tax policy community as well as in the popular press. This resulted in a strong sentiment for repeal of the tax, which led to inclusion of a repeal provision in the Taxpayer Relief Act of 1997.

Second, efficiency-based tax policy analyses can provide a crucial input to the policy process by identifying aspects of the current or prospective tax code that impose substantial efficiency costs. In the hands of "political entrepreneurs," who are prepared to argue for efficiency-based reform of the tax system, these findings can influence policy outcomes. Noll (1989) notes that, in studying the history of regulatory reform, it appears that the political impact of economic research depends on the presence of a catalytic political actor who can bring the research implications to a broad audience. Senator Edward Kennedy was the political entrepreneur who played this role with respect to trucking deregulation in the late 1970s; Ronald Reagan played a similar role in sparking the policy shift toward lower marginal income tax rates in the early 1980s.

The Tax Reform Act of 1986 is a particularly encouraging example for those who study the efficiency aspects of tax rules. Research findings by King and Fullerton (1983) and others suggested that the efficiency costs of interasset differences in marginal effective tax rates were much larger than had been previously suspected. These findings were an important stimulus to the "level playing field" approach that characterized the Tax Reform Act of 1986, in spite of the political opposition of interest groups that had previously benefited from low effective tax rates.

Explaining the Timing and Direction of Reform. Reference to the Tax Reform Act of 1986, or other major changes in the tax code, raises several important challenges to positive political economy models of tax policy. These include explaining why major tax reforms occur, why they occur when they occur, and why they take the forms that they do. Positive political economy models typically take the relative political influence of different interest groups as given. In such models, tax reforms should result from changes in the interest group balance of power, the structure of the economy and the associated relative costs or distributional effects of different taxes, or the institutional setting that affects the set of political actors who determine tax policy. Such empirical predictions are beyond most of the current positive models of taxation, but they need to be developed. Virtually every Congress considers a set of tax reform proposals, and in many cases, the same proposal is considered by several consecutive Congresses. Tax policymaking therefore should provide a valuable opportunity to test and refine positive political models of policy determination.

ENDNOTES

I am grateful to Peter Diamond, Randall Holcombe, Nancy Rose, Andrei Shleifer, James Snyder, and Stanley Winer, for helpful comments, and to the National Science Foundation for research support.

REFERENCES

Brennan, Geoffrey. "Elements of a Fiscal Politics: Public Choice and Public Finance." *Australian Economic Review* No. 67 (3d Quarter, 1984): 62–72.

Buchanan, James A. "The Political Efficiency of General Taxation." *National Tax Journal* 46 No. 4 (December, 1993): 401–10.

Deaton, Angus. "Econometric Issues for Tax Design in Developing Countries." In *Theory of Taxation for Developing Countries*, edited by David Newbery and Nicholas Stern, 92–113. Oxford: Oxford University Press, 1987.

Grossman, Gene, and Elhanan Helpman. "Protection for Sale." *American Economic Review* 84 No. 4 (September, 1994): 833–50.

Hettich, Walter, and Stanley L. Winer. "The Political Economy of Taxation." In *Perspectives on Public Choice: A Handbook*, edited by Dennis Mueller, 481–505. Cambridge: Cambridge University Press, 1996.

Holcombe, Randall G. "Tax Policy from a Public Choice Perspective." *National Tax Journal* 51 No. 2 (June, 1998): 359–71.

Joskow, Paul L., and Roger G. Noll. "Regulation in Theory and Practice: An Overview." In *Studies in Public Regulation*, edited by Gary Fromm, 1–65. Cambridge, MA: MIT Press, 1981.

King, Mervyn A., and Don Fullerton. *The Taxation of Income from Capital*. Chicago: University of Chicago Press, 1983.

Noll, Roger G. "Comment." *Brookings Papers on Economic Activity: Micreconomics* (1989): 48–58.

Peltzman, Sam. "The Economic Theory of Regulation after a Decade of Deregulation." *Brookings Papers on Economic Activity: Microeconomics* (1989): 1–41.

Shoven, John B., and David A. Wise. "The Taxation of Pensions: A Shelter Can Become a Trap." NBER Working Paper No. 5815. Cambridge, MA: National Bureau of Economic Research, 1996.

Stigler, George. "The Theory of Economic Regulation." *Bell Journal of Economics and Management Science* 2 (1971): 3–21.

Winer, Stanley L., and Walter Hettich. "What Is Missed If We Leave Out Collective Choice in the Analysis of Taxation?" *National Tax Journal* 51 No. 2 (June, 1998): 373–89.

PROFESSIONAL OPINIONS ABOUT TAX POLICY: 1994 AND 1934

JOEL SLEMROD*

INTRODUCTION

Tax professionals are not inclined to replace the graduated income tax as the backbone of the federal tax system or abandon the property tax and sales tax as important features of the local and state revenue systems. They do, though, on average favor some significant reforms of the federal tax system, such as integration of the corporate and individual income tax, comprehensive inflation indexing, and elimination of the mortgage interest deduction. With regard to state and local taxes, a majority favor extending the sales tax to services, increasing reliance on user fees, and eliminating homestead exemptions from the property tax.

These are a few of the results of a tax policy opinion survey sent out on April 28, 1994 to the 1309 American and Canadian individual members of the National Tax Association (NTA). Of the 1309, 521 were academics, 406 were employed by a government or international agency, and 382 were in the private sector. There were 503 responses received before the cutoff date, representing an overall response rate of 38

*School of Business Administration and Department of Economics, The University of Michigan, Ann Arbor, MI 48109.

percent, which is on the high side for mail surveys, especially ones for which there was no follow-up notice sent to those who did not respond promptly. The response rate was 45, 32, and 28 percent, respectively for academics, government, and the private sector.[1] Although the response rate was relatively high, the nonresponse rate is certainly high enough to leave open the possibility that those who responded are not representative of the NTA membership.

A unique aspect of this survey is that it repeats *verbatim* a subset of survey questions given to senior American public finance professors 60 years ago. In 1934, Mabel Walker, then executive secretary of the Tax Policy League, administered a survey of the senior professors in public finance in 52 of the country's 100 largest colleges or universities. The responses were summarized in the 1935 edition of the Tax Research Foundation publication, *Tax Systems of the World.* Fifty-four questions found in the 1934 survey are repeated verbatim in the 1994 survey, enabling a comparison of how views have changed in that 60-year period.

The 1994 survey data contain an enormous amount of information. After a review of previous surveys, the third section discusses as much of it as seems possible to digest.[2] In this section, I also make some broad generalizations about the findings and how they compare with the responses in 1934. The fourth section returns to the 1994 results and investigates differences in response patterns by occupation, level of education, and age. It also examines differences in opinion between public finance specialists and economists as a whole and between the opinions of each of these groups and the opinions of politicians. In the fifth section, I analyze to what extent variation in policy opinions can be explained by differences in values and economic model assumptions.

PREVIOUS SURVEYS

I have discovered only one survey, other than the 1934 one referred to above, that targeted tax economists. Behrens (1973) asked the 450 registrants to the 1972 NTA conference the same seven questions asked in a May 1972 survey of the general public conducted by the Advisory Commission on Governmental Relations (ACIR). Three of the questions have been part of the ACIR's annual surveys almost every year since 1972. The tax professionals ranked the local level of government as the one from which they get most from their money, while the general public in 1972 chose the federal government. To the question of which tax is the fairest, tax professionals overwhelmingly chose the federal income tax, while the general public favored that tax only barely over the state sales tax. Both groups in 1972 agreed that the local property tax was "the worst tax, that is, the least fair."

There have been several surveys of the opinions of economists generally, in both the United States and other countries. Kearl et al. (1979) surveyed 600 United States–based economists selected from the 1974 Directory of Members of the American Economics Association.

They concluded that, contrary to the widespread perception that there was little agreement among economists on matters of theory or policy, there was in fact significant consensus on a wide range of questions. The consensus was stronger on microeconomic than on macroeconomic propositions and was stronger on positive than on normative questions.

Alston, Kearl, and Vaughn (1992b) report on a similar survey of 1350 economists conducted in 1990. Because 21 of the questions were common to the 1976 and 1990 surveys, a comparison of the distribution of responses provides a natural test of whether economists' opinions had altered over time. They found that they could reject the hypothesis of no change in opinion for ten of these 21 questions. Of particular relevance for public finance, they found significantly less agreement in 1990 compared to 1976 with the statement that "the government should restructure the welfare system along the lines of a 'negative income tax.'" Alston et al. (1992b) also investigated whether responses differ by the vintage of the respondents' degree and found that the hypothesis that degree vintage does not matter can be rejected for 16 out of 40 propositions, two of which are relevant to taxation questions. Older vintage respondents were less likely to agree that "lower marginal tax rates reduce leisure and increase work effort" and that "reducing the tax rate on income from capital gains would encourage investment and promote economic growth." Those who received their highest degree prior to 1970 showed a greater tendency to disagree with the notion of a self-correcting economy and to agree that fiscal policy has a significant stimulative impact on a less-than-fully-employed economy. Interestingly, for the subset of economists working in the top ten universities, there was no vintage effect at all and greater consensus than for the other groups, results which Alston *et al.* remark to be "consistent with the view that involvement in research does serve to change the perceptions of researchers and to keep them abreast of the field" (p. 208).

Frey, *et al.* (1983, 1992, 1993) discuss the responses to the same set of questions posed in 1980 and 1981 to economists in Belgium, France, Germany, and Switzerland. They concluded that although there is a considerable amount of consensus among European economists, there is less so than in the United States. There also exist substantial differences in opinion between countries and ideological views. On public finance issues, economists from each European country were much less likely to favor restructuring the welfare system along the lines of a negative income tax. Belgian and French economists looked more favorably than Americans on indexing the income tax rate structure for inflation, but German and Swiss economists were less favorably disposed than Americans.

Similar surveys have been carried out in ten East Asian Nations (Anderson, Blandy, and Carne, 1993); Canada (Block and Walker, 1988); South Africa (Geach and Reekie, 1991); New Zealand (Coleman, 1992); Australia (Anderson and Blandy, 1992, 1993); and for the United Kingdom (Brittan, 1973, and Ricketts and Shoesmith, 1990, 1992).

The paper by Ricketts and Shoesmith (1992) also examined to what extent attitudes toward policies are conditioned by (1) views about the desirability of the objectives and the ethical acceptability of the means or (2) predictions about the consequences of policies. This recalls the debate between Milton Friedman (1953, p. 5), who argued that policy differences

"derive predominantly from different predictions . . . rather than from fundamental differences in basic values," and Paul Samuelson (1959), among others, who stressed ethical views as the cause of disagreement. Ricketts and Shoesmith found support for both normative and positive influences on policy attitudes—attitudes toward government intervention in income distribution and attitudes toward the effectiveness of markets incentives to influence behavior both were significantly correlated with policy stances.

Fuller, Alston, and Vaughan (undated) compare the views of economists with those expressed by delegates to the 1992 Republican and Democratic National Conventions. They found that the views of both parties' delegates showed large divergence from those of economists. On average, Republican delegates disagreed with the general support economists expressed for the desirability of a more equal distribution of income and active government involvement in the redistribution of income. Democratic delegates were more likely to disagree with the preference economists reveal for market-oriented investments such as marketable pollution permits and to see less economic cost from programs designed for lower-income individuals such as rent control and minimum wages.

PROFESSIONAL OPINIONS IN 1994 AND 1934

The breakdown of responses to all 96 questions is provided in Table 1. In what follows, I try to characterize some noteworthy aspects of the responses. The percentages used to characterize the distribution of responses refer to the percentage saying yes of those who answered either yes or no. There was a third category in cases where the respondent was "unsure or (could not) provide an unqualified answer." Over all

TABLE 1
RESPONSES TO TAX POLICY QUESTIONS: OVERALL AND BY DEMOGRAPHIC CATEGORY
(FIGURES REFER TO THE PERCENTAGE ANSWERING YES OUT OF THOSE WHO GAVE A YES OR NO ANSWER)

Question	All	1934 Survey	Sector			Age					Highest Degree Obtained				Government		Academic	
			Academic	Govern	Private	20 to 30	31 to 40	41 to 50	51 to 60	Over 60	PhD	MA MS MSc	BA BS	Law	Fed Govt	State/Local	Econ Prof	Other Acad
1 In general, should there be a high protective tariff on agricultural products?	4	2	3	2	7	6	8	3	3	1	2	6	16	0	0	4	0	4
2 In general, should there be a high protective tariff on manufactured products?	3	0	2	3	6	6	6	3	4	0	1	3	18	0	0	5	0	2
3 Should there be a tariff to equalize the difference in cost of production at home and abroad?	10	17	6	12	14	24	9	8	11	10	6	9	29	10	3	17	4	7
4 Should there be a tariff at uniform rate on all imports?	12	0	9	16	14	24	11	14	9	9	10	11	25	10	13	18	7	10
5 In general, should there be a tariff for revenue only?	19	62	22	19	13	8	22	18	17	22	21	14	17	17	29	18	21	23
6 In general, should there be free trade with only incidental tariffs?	91	64	94	85	92	94	87	89	94	96	94	89	80	95	85	84	97	93
7 Should there be retention of property tax as a major source of local revenue?	85	86	85	86	83	76	85	84	88	87	86	85	87	75	91	81	93	82
8 Should the general property tax include intangibles?	17	8	17	23	13	6	18	20	21	7	18	14	21	23	22	27	15	18
9 Should the general property tax include tangible personalty?	35	47	35	36	33	13	40	40	29	30	35	27	48	33	34	40	33	36
10 Should the general property tax be restricted to realty?	57	57	56	51	68	81	54	51	65	61	55	62	55	63	53	49	54	57

Question																		
11 Should improvements be taxed at a lower rate than land?	38	54	44	26	34	67	36	34	32	51	44	27	34	24	27	24	54	40
12 Should improvements be exempted?	10	2	14	5	8	43	15	5	11	8	11	13	8	2	3	6	10	16
13 Should there be a special tax on unearned increment of land values?	22	62	28	18	14	38	16	19	23	34	27	22	12	15	13	18	24	29
14 Should there be homestead exemptions?	42	21	40	38	51	43	42	43	43	38	32	51	61	50	9	52	32	43
15 Should local property taxes be at the same rate for business and residents?	64	n.a.	61	65	73	50	51	65	68	77	63	59	64	73	63	63	60	61
16 Should business be taxed at a higher rate than residents?	26	n.a.	25	30	23	21	35	27	24	19	24	34	29	27	30	34	19	28
17 Should residents be taxed at a higher rate than business?	6	n.a.	9	3	2	21	9	6	4	1	9	3	2	0	7	1	12	7
18 Should inheritances be taxed by the federal government?	72	92	81	73	53	71	68	72	75	77	83	62	42	72	86	68	84	79
19 Should gifts, whether or not in contemplation of death, be taxed in order to avoid evasion of the inheritance tax?	71	90	79	74	51	67	72	68	74	75	81	59	33	79	89	68	84	77
20 Should there be a graduated personal income tax?	80	100	75	91	72	53	80	80	75	91	80	81	79	78	100	86	73	76
21 Should there be a flat-rate income tax, with personal exemptions and a standard deduction?	28	n.a.	32	17	32	56	26	29	30	18	27	31	29	22	3	23	39	29
22 Should the top federal marginal tax on income be 50% or higher?	13	n.a.	16	8	9	0	12	9	12	28	14	13	2	14	6	7	13	17
23 Could a poll tax be so fitted into our general tax scheme (under the income tax) as to make it a desirable element thereof?	9	33	10	4	12	23	12	8	8	6	11	5	9	5	3	4	12	9

TABLE 1
CONTINUED

Question	All	1934 Survey	Sector			Age					Highest Degree Obtained				Government		Academic	
			Academic	Govern	Private	20 to 30	31 to 40	41 to 50	51 to 60	Over 60	PhD	MA MS MSc	BA BS	Law	Fed Govt	State/Local	Econ Prof	Other Acad
24 Should realized nominal capital gains be taxed as ordinary income?	34	n.a.	31	45	23	6	41	36	30	32	31	38	34	36	29	55	24	34
25 Should realized inflation-adjusted capital gains be taxed as ordinary income?	65	n.a.	71	68	50	65	61	67	72	59	70	63	53	62	75	66	78	68
26 Should accrued real capital gains be taxed as ordinary income?	30	n.a.	38	24	18	50	31	28	33	27	35	21	23	27	19	26	46	34
27 Should capital gains be taxed at a lower rate than ordinary income?	32	n.a.	23	26	61	38	24	27	41	45	22	38	61	46	19	30	19	24
28 Should there be higher income tax rates for unearned (i.e., capital) income?	7	66	9	6	6	13	7	8	3	11	8	7	10	5	0	8	4	10
29 Should all future federal, state and local government securities that are issued be fully taxable as to income?	61	96	71	57	46	27	65	57	69	64	73	43	36	53	73	47	84	65
30 Should cash dividends be taxed to the stockholder if there is a corporate income tax?	44	68	45	54	32	18	48	42	42	54	45	42	40	47	67	51	50	42
31 Should stock dividends be taxed?	43	35	45	62	22	53	48	48	39	27	47	49	40	21	62	64	48	43
32 Should social security and unemployment benefits be fully taxable?	62	n.a.	71	61	45	64	66	65	58	51	70	48	50	52	74	54	72	71
33 Should the definition of capital income be fully corrected for inflation?	70	n.a.	76	63	66	80	70	69	81	52	71	67	73	69	63	61	84	72

Question																		
34 Should mortgage interest be deductible?	47	n.a.	37	50	60	41	41	48	53	44	38	45	81	51	34	59	36	38
35 Should imputed rent of owner-occupied housing be taxable?	25	n.a.	34	17	15	20	11	26	32	34	32	9	16	23	12	15	55	25
36 Should there be net income tax on corporations?	70	98	58	82	77	53	73	71	64	78	62	76	87	84	88	79	50	62
37 Should there be a graduated rate?	37	23	32	42	38	25	44	39	32	29	29	49	56	30	23	54	25	34
38 Should there be a flat rate?	49	77	48	50	48	56	42	49	53	50	52	36	45	63	68	40	57	44
39 Should there be a gross tax on business incomes?	14	12	12	17	13	7	20	14	10	14	13	19	12	14	0	25	15	11
40 Should banking business be taxed in a different way than general incorporated business?	27	54	28	24	29	6	34	23	29	29	26	28	33	23	26	24	32	26
41 Should insurance business be taxed in a different way than general incorporated business?	28	73	27	27	35	6	33	22	31	38	27	27	38	31	35	22	31	25
42 Should railway and public utility business be taxed in a different way than general incorporated business?	24	55	21	28	27	18	29	21	22	29	19	28	38	27	23	31	19	22
43 Should the personal and corporate income taxes be integrated?	72	n.a.	82	64	64	94	69	72	74	68	81	64	52	71	82	55	87	80
44 Should the alternative minimum tax on corporations be abolished?	53	n.a.	56	35	69	75	46	51	56	58	52	50	47	67	47	28	56	56
45 Should Congress legislate to create uniformity of state income apportionment formulas?	73	n.a.	74	64	77	54	64	74	73	83	76	56	76	81	71	59	77	73
46 Should there be a tax on motor vehicles as such with exemption from general property tax?	52	67	49	51	53	33	44	53	49	65	52	47	60	49	57	50	50	49

TABLE 1
CONTINUED

Question	All	1934 Survey	Sector			Age					Highest Degree Obtained				Government		Academic	
			Academic	Govern	Private	20 to 30	31 to 40	41 to 50	51 to 60	Over 60	PhD	MA MS MSc	BA BS	Law	Fed Govt	State/Local	Econ Prof	Other Acad
47 Should there be a gasoline tax to pay for all highway construction and maintenance?	86	48	85	83	93	71	81	88	91	86	84	84	91	97	85	86	84	85
48 Should any highway cost be paid by levies on property?	31	66	35	35	17	20	33	29	24	43	39	24	20	15	50	25	48	30
49 Should it be mandatory that all proceeds from gasoline and motor vehicle taxes be devoted to highways (including streets and bridges)?	43	59	37	38	57	56	48	39	38	46	34	52	60	46	23	44	21	44
50 Should there be a general retail sales tax at the federal level?	33	13	35	28	39	44	32	37	36	18	34	30	32	36	30	29	32	36
51 Should there be a general retail sales tax at the state level?	91	12	89	97	91	88	84	93	95	92	90	91	94	93	91	99	97	85
52 Should there be a general retail sales tax at the local level?	56	0	54	67	55	40	54	59	66	42	56	60	63	46	67	66	61	51
53 Should there be a tobacco tax?	95	95	96	97	88	94	94	95	92	97	96	91	95	91	97	96	99	94
54 Should there be a high tax on tobacco?	87	70	89	87	81	73	86	88	83	90	89	78	83	88	89	84	94	87
55 Should there be a special tax on oleomargarine?	3	11	2	3	0	0	2	2	5	1	2	6	2	0	0	4	0	3
56 Should there be a tax on billboards?	47	88	47	51	34	56	48	46	44	53	47	49	40	46	43	53	50	46
57 Should retail sales tax be extended to sales of services?	77	n.a.	79	90	56	65	74	80	75	81	84	75	69	67	91	91	94	73

Question																		
58 Should social security benefits be financed out of general revenues instead of the payroll tax?	30	n.a.	34	29	29	57	30	35	23	22	35	22	18	32	21	36	37	33
59 Should the caps on the social security tax base be eliminated?	50	n.a.	58	57	27	54	58	55	36	46	55	51	38	33	52	61	62	56
60 Should the state supervise local assessment of real estate?	79	96	77	93	69	79	66	81	85	86	82	74	83	74	90	93	93	70
61 Should the state constitutions contain tax limit provisions?	38	6	29	31	60	46	30	43	40	30	30	40	60	47	10	31	32	28
62 Should constitutional uniformity clauses be abolished?	16	91	17	16	10	50	20	12	18	16	20	10	14	10	25	13	22	15
63 Should education be a part of and subject to the fiscal control of the regular local government?	54	47	46	60	58	54	48	53	60	54	52	54	61	53	62	59	40	49
64 Should education be independent of the regular local government?	43	39	48	32	42	54	41	45	41	39	42	45	38	44	18	36	47	49
65 Should states raise all taxes for and administer the entire system of public education?	29	34	29	25	32	33	26	34	24	24	26	26	33	31	19	26	22	32
66 Should state and federal aids be distributed on the basis of need?	79	81	80	88	64	80	77	81	77	79	82	76	75	71	88	86	83	79
67 Should states limit debt incurring powers of local governments?	69	95	66	73	67	64	61	69	76	71	67	67	83	67	70	74	77	61
68 Should there be an abolishing of all except federal personal income taxes with distribution of part of the proceeds to states?	12	45	14	9	13	43	8	14	9	13	12	12	12	14	3	11	10	15

TABLE 1
CONTINUED

Question	All	1934 Survey	Sector			Age					Highest Degree Obtained				Government		Academic	
			Academic	Govern	Private	20 to 30	31 to 40	41 to 50	51 to 60	Over 60	PhD	MA MS MSc	BA BS	Law	Fed Govt	State/Local	Econ Prof	Other Acad
69 Should there be an abolishing of all except federal corporate income taxes with distribution of part of the proceeds to states?	16	51	17	16	14	27	9	17	18	18	20	12	10	12	18	14	29	12
70 Should state and local governments use tax abatements and other incentives to attract business?	30	n.a.	29	22	41	47	41	24	34	21	22	39	43	37	19	19	17	33
71 Should the entire cost of the next war be financed by current taxation?	22	42	21	19	30	17	17	23	25	23	15	33	28	31	10	25	12	25
72 Should the entire cost of the next war be financed largely by bonds?	37	11	42	36	28	54	47	39	28	25	44	30	30	18	29	36	53	38
73 Should the cost of the next war be financed largely by tax on profits of munition makers?	16	79	20	15	14	25	27	16	10	6	15	20	19	12	9	17	10	24
74 In general, should there be a severance tax on various commodities, such as oil, coal, ore, and timber?	80	94	79	90	69	38	74	84	81	83	83	79	73	76	81	93	84	77
75 Should there be a value-added tax to replace much or all of the current income tax?	36	n.a.	33	33	49	85	29	38	42	27	33	37	53	44	19	37	27	35
76 Should localities impose income taxes on those who work but do not live locally?	61	n.a.	67	58	51	53	62	58	60	70	66	52	42	67	59	58	74	64

Question																		
77 Should governments increase their reliance on revenue from user fees?	74	n.a.	76	78	62	67	72	77	73	72	77	70	71	70	85	75	81	74
78 Should wealth be taxable?	59	n.a.	62	66	42	29	52	63	67	51	66	46	52	49	55	73	71	58
79 Should the distribution of income in the United States be more equal?	64	n.a.	73	68	40	59	62	61	60	81	74	53	40	60	83	59	83	69
80 Is the redistribution of income within the United States a legitimate role for government?	68	n.a.	79	73	39	47	68	69	65	72	83	60	29	55	97	62	94	72
81 Should the government restructure the welfare system along the lines of a "negative income tax?"	71	n.a.	78	67	60	75	70	69	72	72	78	66	49	64	69	63	86	75
82 Do lower marginal income tax rates reduce leisure and increase work efforts?	57	n.a.	60	49	59	67	64	56	58	47	63	52	48	51	60	42	71	56
83 Do lower taxes on the return to saving increase private saving?	71	n.a.	66	66	82	87	72	67	78	62	68	76	70	73	44	74	67	66
84 Does reducing the tax rate on income from capital gains encourage investment and promote economic growth?	54	n.a.	45	48	76	73	59	50	58	49	46	68	67	51	32	56	36	49
85 Should the level of government spending relative to GNP be reduced (disregarding expenditures for stabilization)?	62	n.a.	54	60	82	86	65	63	60	55	53	70	77	71	30	74	45	58
86 Does a large federal budget deficit have an adverse effect on the economy?	89	n.a.	84	94	91	93	88	91	90	82	87	91	92	91	93	93	87	83
87 Are sales taxes regressive?	77	n.a.	76	83	69	67	85	75	72	78	79	76	70	73	90	84	67	80
88 Are corporate income taxes largely passed on to workers and consumers?	75	n.a.	72	77	79	80	78	76	75	68	68	86	91	73	53	90	56	78

TABLE 1
CONTINUED

Question	All	1934 Survey	Sector Academic	Sector Govern	Sector Private	Age 20 to 30	Age 31 to 40	Age 41 to 50	Age 51 to 60	Age Over 60	Highest Degree Obtained PhD	Highest Degree Obtained MA MS MSc	Highest Degree Obtained BA BS	Highest Degree Obtained Law	Government Fed Govt	Government State/Local	Academic Econ Prof	Academic Other Acad
89 Are taxes an important determinant of business location?	59	n.a.	64	32	77	87	70	56	52	57	57	60	66	62	46	23	43	72
90 Should there be a balanced budget amendment to the U.S. Constitution?	30	n.a.	23	26	49	44	34	31	34	16	19	42	59	32	3	36	14	26
91 Should administrative and compliance concerns play an important role in designing tax policy?	98	n.a.	98	99	98	94	97	99	99	97	99	99	96	100	100	99	99	98
92 Should capital income be exempt from taxation?	12	n.a.	9	3	28	29	11	10	18	5	10	14	15	14	0	5	11	9
93 Should the fraction of individual tax returns that are audited be substantially increased?	62	n.a.	59	69	60	27	58	56	66	83	63	58	60	70	76	66	66	56
94 Should the penalties for tax evasion be substantially increased?	60	n.a.	67	57	48	40	62	62	55	64	65	61	53	44	55	57	71	65
95 Should the foreign-source income of U.S. residents individuals be taxed by the United States?	82	n.a.	87	89	60	77	74	87	76	91	86	73	85	78	97	88	91	86
96 Should the foreign-source income of U.S. corporations be taxed by the United States?	74	n.a.	79	82	50	62	70	79	69	75	77	65	77	72	96	80	78	79

96 questions, the average percentage that either checked the third category or checked no box at all was 9.1 percent.

Tariffs

The respondents are overwhelmingly free traders. Only four percent favored high protective tariffs on either agricultural or manufactured products, and only 12 percent favored a uniform rate on all imports. As many as 19 percent favored a tariff for revenue only. However, 91 percent thought there should be "free trade with only incidental tariffs."

Opposition to protective tariffs was even more pervasive in 1934.[3] Only one respondent of 48 at that time supported a high protective tariff on agricultural products; there was no support for high tariffs on manufactured products or a uniform rate on all imports. Somewhat surprisingly, though, 62 percent of respondents in 1934 favored a tariff for revenue only. Although there was near unanimous opposition to protectionist tariffs, only 64 percent were willing to support free trade with only incidental tariffs. This may indicate that even "incidental" tariffs were unacceptable, or may suggest that more-than-incidental tariffs for revenue were acceptable. Recall that in 1934, customs duties comprised 10.4 percent of federal receipts and had comprised 45.0 percent as recently as 1912. In contrast, customs duties and fees made up only 1.6 percent of federal revenues in 1993, and that figure will drop further if and when the Uruguay Round of GATT modifications comes into effect.

Property Taxation

Of the respondents to the 1994 survey, 85 percent favor retaining the property tax as a major source of local revenue; 86 percent felt the same way in 1934. A slight majority (57 percent) believe that the property tax base should be restricted to realty; only 17 percent favor including intangible assets, and 35 percent believe it should be extended to tangible personalty. Similar opinions prevailed in 1934.

Only 10 percent of respondents in 1994 favor exempting the value of improvements from the property tax base, although 38 percent would allow improvements to be taxed at a lower rate than land. Public finance economists in 1934 were more favorably disposed to the latter policy, which 54 percent favored; however, only two percent in 1934 favored complete exemption of the value of improvements.

One notable change in attitude between 1934 and 1994 concerns whether there should be a special tax on "unearned increment of land values," presumably interpreted as capital gains not due to improvements. While only 22 percent favor this in 1994, 62 percent favored it in 1934. This change is one example of the greater tendency in 1934 to favor higher taxes on capital income compared to labor income. Public finance professionals in 1994 are split but slightly against (42 percent support) homestead exemptions; only 21 percent supported them in 1934.

A set of three questions on the 1994 survey addressed whether local property taxes should differentiate between business and residences.[4] Of the respondents, 64 percent support an equal property tax rate for businesses and residences. Of those who favor differentiation, slightly over 80 percent would impose higher rates on business.

Inheritance and Gift Taxes

Of those responding, 72 percent support federal taxation of inheritances, and a slightly lower fraction (71 percent) also favor taxing gifts in order to avoid evasion of the inheritance tax. There was even stronger support for these taxes in 1934, with 92 percent and 90 percent support, respectively.

Personal Income Taxes

In 1994, there is strong (80 percent) support for retaining a graduated personal income tax. Only a small minority (28 percent) favors moving to flat-rate income tax, and an even smaller minority (13 percent) would substantially increase the current progressivity by re-establishing a top federal marginal tax on income of 50 percent or higher. In 1934, there was unanimous support for a graduated income tax.[5] The flat-rate and 50 percent rate alternatives were not posed in the earlier survey, but 33 percent of respondents in 1934 did allow that a poll tax should be part of the income tax; in 1994, only nine percent of respondents thought this was desirable.

In the 1994 survey, four alternative tax treatments of capital gains were offered for evaluation. The only one supported by a majority (65 percent) is to fully tax inflation-adjusted realized gains. Taxing nominal gains as ordinary income receives only 34 percent support, taxing fully accrued real gains receives only 30 percent support, and taxing capital gains at a lower rate (with nominal or real unspecified) receives only 32 percent support.

Many, but not all, tax changes that would move toward a more comprehensive definition of income are supported by a majority of respondents in 1994; 61 percent favor subjecting interest of state and local securities to tax, and 62 percent favor full taxation of social security and unemployment benefits. A slight majority (53 percent) oppose the deductibility of mortgage interest. Seventy percent favor a full inflation indexing of the definition of capital income, a percentage slightly higher than that favoring full

taxation of inflation-indexed realized capital gains. Some moves toward comprehensive taxation are not supported by the majority. Seventy-five percent oppose taxing the imputed rent of owner-occupied housing; as noted above, a similar fraction oppose taxing accrued, rather than realized, real capital gains. Of the base-broadening questions, only the one relating to taxation of state and local bond interest was asked in 1934. At that time, it received overwhelming support; 96 percent supported it, compared to 61 percent in 1994.

The 1994 survey featured several questions related to whether there ought to be a shift of emphasis from income taxes to consumption taxes. The majority of respondents does not favor such a policy shift. Only 12 percent of the respondents favor exempting capital income from taxation (Question #92). Thirty-six percent favor replacing "much or all" of the current income tax with a value-added tax (Question #75). Because replacing all of the income tax with a value-added tax would in essence exempt capital income from tax, it is reasonable to conclude that 36 percent favor a move from income taxes toward consumption taxes, but only 12 percent would entirely eliminate the income tax element.

Neither of these two questions was asked in 1934, although the responses to other questions make it clear that there was then even less acceptance of replacing much or all of the income tax with a consumption tax alternative. First of all, as already noted, in 1934 there was unanimous support for a graduated income tax. Even more convincing, 66 percent of respondents favored *higher* income tax rates for unearned income compared to earned income, thus supporting a move in the opposite direction from a consumption tax. In 1994, only seven percent of the respondents favor such a policy.[6]

Another element of many comprehensive income tax reform proposals is an integration of the corporate and personal income tax system, so as to avoid two layers of tax on dividend income. Integration is favored by 72 percent of the respondents in 1994 (Question #43). A predisposition toward integration is also evident in that less than a majority of respondents (43 percent) favor taxing cash or stock dividends if there is a corporate income tax. No question about integration was asked in 1934. However, in 1934 there was considerable support (68 percent) for taxing cash dividends even in the presence of a corporate income tax, although much less support (35 percent) for taxing stock dividends. The 1994 respondents do not draw a distinction between cash and stock dividends as the 1934 respondents did.

Business Taxes

In 1994, 70 percent of the respondents support a net income tax on corporations; of those expressing a preference, 57 percent favor a flat rather than a graduated rate. The 70 percent approval in 1994 represents less consensus than in 1934, when all but one (98 percent) of the respondents favored a net income tax; at that time, 77 percent preferred a flat to a graduated rate. Neither in 1934 nor in 1994 was there much support for a gross tax on business income. Support for taxing banking, insurance, and public utilities, including railroads, differently from other business has fallen since 1934. In 1994, special treatment is favored by about a quarter of all respondents; in 1934, a majority favored special treatment for all three sectors, with the most support for insurance.

A slight majority (53 percent) favor abolishing the alternative minimum tax on corporations. Finally, 73 percent favor Congressional legislation to create uniformity of state income tax apportionment formulas.

Gasoline and Motor Vehicle Taxes

Respondents to the 1994 survey overwhelmingly support (86 percent) the use of gasoline tax to pay for all highway construction and maintenance and generally do not favor (31 percent support) levies on property being used for highways. However, the majority stop short of support (43 percent approval) for making it mandatory that all proceeds from taxes on gasoline and motor vehicles be devoted to highways, streets, and bridges.

Opinions on these issues differed markedly in 1934. Only 48 percent supported a gasoline tax for highway expenditures, while 66 percent preferred levies on property for this purpose. Yet, 59 percent of the respondents supported the mandatory earmarking of gasoline and motor vehicle taxes for highway expenditures.

Sales and Excise Taxes

Respondents to the 1994 survey are overwhelmingly (92 percent) in favor of state-level retail sales taxes (RST), generally favor local-level retail sales taxes (56 percent), while a majority of 67 percent oppose a federal-level retail sales tax. These responses are in sharp contrast to 1934, when general retail sales taxes at any level of government received scant support; only 13 percent supported a federal RST, 12 percent supported a state RST, and there was no support at all for a local RST. Arguably, the opposition in 1934 reflects the much lower reliance on sales taxes at that time; only 16 states had a general sales tax by the end of 1934, and in all but one of the cases, the tax had been adopted in 1933 or 1934.

Respondents to both surveys expressed near-unanimous support for an excise tax on tobacco: 95 percent in both 1994 and 1934. Support dropped somewhat to 87 percent in 1994 and 70 percent in 1934 when a "high" tax on tobacco was the issue. There was little support in either year for an excise tax on oleomargarine, although 1934 respondents largely (88 percent) favored an excise tax on billboards; 47 percent favor this in 1994.

One of the most controversial sales tax issues in 1994 is whether its base should be extended to include services. Seventy-seven percent of respondents favor this in 1994; the question was not asked in the 1934 survey.

Payroll Taxes

Two questions in the 1994 survey addressed aspects of the social security payroll tax. Because they were first introduced by the Social Security Act of 1935, there are no comparable questions in the 1934 survey. Of the respondents, 70 percent favor the current system of financing social security benefits from the payroll tax, as opposed to financing them out of general revenues. Respondents are evenly split over another significant reform of the payroll tax structure, that of eliminating the caps on the tax base.

Relationship of Federal, State, and Local Jurisdictions

Of the 1994 respondents, 79 percent support state supervision of local real estate assessment, and 69 percent support states limiting debt incurring powers of local government. Both of the measures received near unanimous support in 1934.

In 1994, a majority, but by no means an overwhelming one (54 percent), support a system under which education was part of and subject to the fiscal control of the regular local government; a significant minority of 29 percent of the respondents favor having state governments be responsible for public education.

Respondents generally support (79 percent) distributing federal and state aids on the basis of need. But they are clearly not willing to cede revenue gathering authority to the federal government and rely on distribution of the proceeds to the states; only 12 percent support this system for personal income tax and 16 percent for the corporate income tax. Respondents in 1934 were much more favorable toward this idea; 45 percent supported it for personal income taxes and 51 percent for corporate income taxes.

The final question in this section of the survey concerned the controversial issue of whether state and local governments ought to use tax abatements and other incentives to attract business. Overall, only 30 percent of respondents support this policy.

War Costs

Respondents to the 1994 survey believe that the costs of the next war should be financed by a combination of tax and debt finance. I infer this because a substantial majority rejects financing it entirely by current taxation (78 percent) or largely by debt (63 percent); only 16 percent would finance it largely by taxing the profits of munitions makers.

The 1934 respondents held sharply different views. Taxing munitions makers was favored by a majority of the respondents, followed by current taxation and debt finance last. This is a reverse ranking to that of 1994.

Other Taxes

This section asked about an assortment of taxes. Respondents generally favor

(80 percent) severance taxes, local income taxes on inbound commuters (61 percent), increased reliance on user fees (74 percent), and taxing wealth (59 percent). The majority support for wealth taxes is of interest, because the federal government presently does not levy such a tax, although it is fairly common in European countries.

Other Tax Issues

The last section also solicited views on some miscellaneous tax issues. The question that attracted the most support of any in the survey was "Should administrative and compliance issues play an important role in designing tax policy?" with 98 percent of respondents answering yes. This may reflect nothing more than a motherhood and apple pie phenomenon—how can one disagree with this?[7] But it may also reflect a pervasive belief in this criterion for evaluating tax policy.

A majority of respondents support strengthening the enforcement of the income tax. Sixty-two percent favor substantially increasing the fraction of returns that is audited, and 60 percent favor substantially increasing the penalties for tax evasion.

The final two questions concerned whether to continue the current system of taxing the foreign-source income of United States resident individuals and corporations, the alternative being to adopt a "territorial" system, under which only United States source income is taxable. There is widespread support for continuing the current system, 82 percent for individuals and 74 percent for corporations.

Inputs to Opinion Formation: Values and Models

One's opinions on tax policy questions will be in part determined by one's values concerning income distribution and

by one's beliefs about how the economy operates. Values matter because most tax policy changes will benefit some set of individuals and hurt others, so that favoring a policy implicitly or explicitly involves evaluating the gains against the losses. One's beliefs about how the economy operates matter because they will determine what one believes is the impact of a particular policy.

Two questions in the 1994 survey concerned the distribution of income. Sixty-four percent of the respondents believe that the distribution of income should be more equal, while 68 percent believe that redistribution of income is a legitimate role of government.

Fifty-seven percent of respondents believe that lower marginal income tax rates increase work effort, while an even larger 71 percent believe that taxes on the return to saving depress private saving. Fifty-nine percent believe that taxes are an important determinant of business location, and 54 percent believe that reducing the tax on capital gains encourages investment and economic growth.

Thus, for all four of these questions, more than a majority of respondents believe that there is a behavioral response to taxation. However, no magnitude of behavioral response is specified; thus, one interpretation of these results is that a significant minority is unconvinced that there is any response at all to taxes on labor supply, saving, or business location.[8]

Two questions pertained to the incidence of taxes for which the incidence is thought to be controversial. Seventy-seven percent believe that sales taxes are regressive, while 75 percent believe that corporate income taxes are largely passed on to workers and consumers. Finally, 89 percent of respondents believe that the federal budget deficit has an adverse effect on the economy.

POLICY OPINION DIFFERENCES BY JOB, DEGREE, AGE, AND SPECIALIZATION

Below I discuss notable differences in the distribution of responses by the characteristics of respondents as to what sector they work in, what discipline they are in, what final degree they hold, and what age group they are in. In evaluating these results, it is important to keep in mind that the personal characteristics are not independent. For example, while overall 35 percent of the respondents were age 50 or over, 52 percent of private sector economists, 53 percent of those with law degrees, and 55 percent of economics professors are 50 or older. Not surprisingly, the most pervasive relationship is between job held and highest degree attained. This is the Ph.D. for 86 percent of academics (and 100 percent of economics professors), 38 percent for those in government, and only 18 percent for those in the private sector. Law degrees are much more prevalent among those in the private sector, representing 31 percent of that group, but only 8 percent of government and 5 percent of academics.

Because of these patterns, the associations discussed in the following sections do not necessarily identify, for example, the relationship between opinions and sector, holding age constant. This requires a multivariate statistical analysis. However, multivariate probit analyses of the policy responses, with dummy variables for sector, age, and highest degree attained, reveal essentially the same patterns as those discussed below.

Differences among Academic, Government, and the Private Sector

There are clear differences in opinion among academics, government officials,

and private sector respondents. The biggest divergence is between private sector respondents and either academics or government, who tend to have more similar responses. One measure of similarity is the average absolute difference in the percentage of yes responses.[9] Over all 96 questions, this came to 7.3 percent between academic and government, but 12.1 percent between academics and the private sector and 12.5 percent between government and the private sector.[10] Table 1 lists the percentage answering yes for each question and each category.

The pervasive policy inclination of private sector economists is clear—they favor lower taxes. With few exceptions, whenever a question involves choosing a level of taxes or deductions, private sector tax professionals on average favor lower taxes and higher deductions. This applies to the property tax, where they are less likely to want an extensive definition of property subject to tax, and more likely to favor preferential taxation of improvements and homestead exemptions. They are more likely to favor abolishing inheritance and gift taxes.

As noted above, there is a large amount of similarity between the views expressed by academics and those in the government sector. Some interesting differences do, though, emerge. My own characterization of these differences is that the academics are more likely to favor fundamental changes from the *status quo*. Consider, for example, the academics' significantly greater support for a flat-rate income tax, taxing accrued real capital gains and the imputed rent from owner-occupied housing, eliminating the federal tax exemption of state and local bond interest and deductibility of mortgage interest payments, integration of the personal and corporate tax systems, and abolishing the alternative minimum tax for corporations. On average, the academics favor a more orthodox approach to a comprehensive Haig–Simons income tax base. With respect to state and local issues, academics are more likely to support a lower property tax rate on improvements and to increase the independence of education from local governments.

Greater support for a comprehensive tax base could be due to more concern about the efficiency costs of deviating from it, to the horizontal or vertical inequities that result from deviating from it, or to some other concern. Which is most important is not clear from the survey. Academics are slightly more likely than government employees to prefer a more equal distribution of income, and support a government role in achieving this, but the difference in support is not very large (73 percent versus 68 percent). Perhaps the key lies in the government respondents' significantly lower level of agreement (45 percent versus 60 percent) that lower taxes increase work effort, or are an important determinant of business location (32 percent versus 63 percent); if this is indicative of a view that the behavioral consequences are not significant, then the efficiency arguments for a comprehensive tax base are muted. However, there is essentially no difference in the fraction of each group that believes that lower taxes on the return to saving increase private saving, or that believes that lower capital gains taxes encourage investment.

There are also some noteworthy differences between the responses of those who work for the federal government and those who work for state and local governments (of this latter group, 74 of 82 work for a state government). Most of the large differences do not relate to the policies themselves, but rather to the

values and economic parameters. For example, those who work for the federal government are much more likely than state and local workers to think that the distribution of income should be more equal (83 percent versus 59 percent) and that redistribution of income is a legitimate role for government (97 percent versus 62 percent). One possible explanation for the latter result is that the government respondents are referring to their own level of government, so that state workers believe that redistribution is not a legitimate role for *state* governments, although it may be for the federal government.

There are several differences regarding the impact of taxes on private decisions, but there is no clear pattern to these differences. Those working for the federal government are more inclined to think that taxes affect labor supply and business location, but less likely to think that taxes affect saving or that lower capital gains taxes encourage investment and promote economic growth. Finally, the federal government workers are much less likely to favor a balanced budget amendment (3 percent versus 36 percent), or to favor a much lower level of government spending (30 percent versus 74 percent).

Somewhat surprisingly, these differences in values and economics do not translate into a lot of differences on specific policy issues. Those working for the federal government are more likely to support a graduated (100 percent versus 86 percent) tax on a comprehensive definition of income, taxing the interest on state and local securities (73 percent versus 47 percent), taxing social security and unemployment benefits (74 percent versus 54 percent), and eliminating the deductibility of mortgage interest (66 percent versus 41 percent). Federal officials are less likely to support moving toward a value-added tax (19 percent versus 38 percent).

Differences by Degree

How does an advanced degree affect one's views on policy? If this is assessed by comparing the views of those whose highest degree is a Ph.D. to those whose highest degree is a bachelor's degree, several noticeable differences are evident.

First of all, those with a B.A. or B.S. as their final degree are much more likely to favor protectionist measures, although the fraction in favor still falls far short of a majority. For example, 18 percent of this group favor a high protective tariff on manufactured goods, compared to 1 percent of Ph.Ds.

Other than on tariffs, there are more than 15 questions on which the fraction saying yes differed by more than 20 percentage points between those with a Ph.D. and those for whom the B.A. or B.S. is the final degree. With only one exception, all of the significant divergences fit into one pattern—those with a terminal bachelor's degree are more likely to favor tax breaks, exemptions, and less government spending. They are more likely to favor homestead exemptions, property tax abatements to attract business, mortgage interest deductions, and preferential tax rates for capital gains. They are less likely to support taxes on inheritances, gifts, or state and local bond interest.

The origin of these policy opinions can be traced back to beliefs about the proper role of government. On average, those with Ph.D.s favor a more activist and interventionist role. The Ph.D.s are overwhelmingly more likely (83 percent versus 29 percent) to support a legitimate role for government in redistribution, and much less likely (53 percent versus 77 percent) to favor reducing

government spending or a balanced budget amendment (19 percent versus 59 percent). The difference in policy opinions is not apparently due to differences in opinions about the impact of tax policies on private behavior; there is no significant difference in opinion about how taxes affect labor supply, saving, or business location.

Respondents with law degrees are much more likely to favor a tax on corporations (40 percent versus 10 percent overall). They are also more likely to favor a flat-rate corporate tax (63 percent versus 49 percent) unencumbered by an alternative minimum tax (67 percent versus 53 percent). Their views on integration of the personal and corporate tax systems do not diverge from the average. They are less likely to support lower property tax rates on improvements (24 percent versus 38 percent) or extending the retail sales tax to services (67 percent versus 77 percent), but more likely to support lower taxes on capital gains (46 percent versus 32 percent) and to exempt stock dividends from taxation (79 percent versus 57 percent).

Age Effects

There are many examples of a significant difference in policy opinions by age category. Because only 17 respondents were in the 20 to 30 age category, I will not discuss how their responses differ from the other age groups. Among the other four age groups, it is the over 60 group whose responses differ most from the others, and the biggest average absolute percentage difference of 8.8 percent is between the over 60 group and the 31 to 40 group; the smallest difference of 4.9 percent is between the 41 to 50 group and the 51 to 60 group. In what follows, I focus on those questions for which the 30 to 40 group and the over 60 group diverge significantly; I'll refer to these groups as the "young" and "old," respectively.

With respect to property taxes, the old are more likely to favor taxing improvements at a lower rate than land, and levying a special tax on the unearned increment of land values. These views are reminiscent of the attitudes expressed in 1934, when both of these positions were supported by a majority of respondents. In 1994, the former policy was supported by a slight majority (51 percent) of the old, but the latter received only 34 percent support from that group.

The old are more likely to favor a graduated income tax, and look less favorably on a flat-rate tax, than the young; furthermore, the old are more likely to prefer a top rate of 50 percent or higher. Somewhat surprisingly in view of their tendency toward more progressivity, the old are more likely to support lower tax rates on capital gains.

The old are more likely to believe that the distribution of income should be more equal, but are not much more likely to support an active role for government in redistribution. They are generally less convinced of the importance of taxes in affecting labor supply, saving, and business location. They are much more likely than any other age category to support a substantial increase in the fraction of individual income tax returns that are audited.

Comparing the Views of Tax Professionals to Economists Generally and to Politicians

Seven of the 1994 survey questions were identical to questions asked in 1990 by Alston, Kearl, and Vaughan (1992b) of economists. There is some ambiguity in comparing responses across surveys, because in the Alston et al. survey, respondents were given the response alternatives of "generally agree," "agree with provisos," or "generally disagree." It is impossible to say how those who agreed with provisos to a proposition would answer if forced to choose, as in the NTA surveys, between "yes," "no," or "not sure or cannot provide unqualified answer." Table 2 compares the results of the 1994 NTA survey with the Alston et al. results using two alternative methods of dealing with the "agree with provisos" responses. In Method A, these are ignored, and in Method B, they are presumed to be "yes" responses.

The pattern of responses for the two questions about the distribution of income and about the negative income tax are broadly consistent across the two groups of professionals. However, the tax professionals are apparently slightly more likely than economists to believe that tax rates affect labor supply and that lower capital gains taxes encourage investment. Furthermore, they are more likely to believe that the level of government spending should be reduced and, perhaps related, that a large federal deficit has an adverse effect on the economy. Keep in mind that the surveys were not done concurrently—the NTA survey was carried out in 1994, five years after the Alston et al. survey.

The right-hand panel of Table 2 lists the distribution of responses to six of these seven questions for delegates to the 1992 Republican and Democratic National Conventions, as reported by Fuller, Alston, and Vaughn (undated). There are striking differences between the Republican and Democratic responses on five of the six questions, much larger divergences than between any subset of the NTA respondent group; there is, though, near unanimous agreement in both parties that a large federal budget deficit has an adverse effect on the economy.

TABLE 2
COMPARISON OF SURVEY RESPONSES AMONG TAX PROFESSIONALS, ALL ECONOMISTS,
AND POLITICIANS

| | | Professionals | | | Politicians | | | |
| | | | All Econo-mists | | Rep. | | Dem. | |
		Tax Only	A	B	A	B	A	B
79. Should the distribution of in-	All	64	65	73	13	30	90	91
come in the United States be	Academics only	73	73	81				
more equal?	Gov't only	68	55	76				
	Bus. only	40	44	57				
80. Is the redistribution of income	All	68	77	83	4	12	69	74
within the United States a le-	Academics only	79	85	89				
gitimate role for government?	Gov't only	73	75	84				
	Bus. only	39	55	70				
81. Should the government re-	All	71	70	81	n.a.	n.a.	n.a.	n.a.
structure the welfare system	Academics only	78	70	82				
along the lines of a "negative	Gov't only	67	56	66				
income tax?"	Bus. only	60	68	79				
82. Do lower marginal income tax	All	57	34	56	49	64	13	35
rates reduce leisure and in-	Academics only	60	33	58				
crease work effort?	Gov't. only	49	32	52				
	Bus. only	59	38	57				
84. Does reducing the tax rate on	All	54	30	50	99	99	31	46
income from capital gains en-	Academics only	45	24	47				
courage investment?	Gov't only	48	23	39				
	Bus. only	76	50	69				
85. Should the level of government	All	62	44	55	95	96	67	77
spending relative to GNP be re-	Academics only	54	31	43				
duced (disregarding expendi-	Gov't only	60	45	59				
tures for stabilization)?	Bus. only	82	69	73				
86. Does a large federal budget	All	89	69	84	97	97	92	93
deficit have an adverse effect	Academics only	84	67	82				
on the economy?	Gov't only	94	79	89				
	Bus. only	91	72	83				

Notes: "Tax only" results are from NTA survey, as reported in Table 1. "All economists" results are from Alston et al. (1992b). Academics include 80 AEA members from the top 10 leading graduate programs plus 80 other academic AEA members, government includes members of the Society of Government Economists; business includes members of the National Assocation of Business Economists; all includes these categories plus a sample of economists who teach principles courses and a sample of members of the Association for Evolutionary Economics. "Politicians" results are from Fuller, Alston, and Vaughn (undated). Figures under column A calculate the percentage answering yes by ignoring responses of "agree with provisos"; figures under column B presume these to be yes answers. In all cases, nonresponses are ignored.

Regarding the distribution of income, the NTA respondents resemble the Democratic delegates much more than the Republican delegates, although the NTA respondents from the business sector are approximately in between the two groups of delegates. The same is true for evaluating the level of government spending; the NTA respondents do not exhibit the near unanimous support for

reduction that the Republican delegates do.

However, the tax professionals resemble Republicans when it comes to assessing whether taxes decrease labor supply; only among the Democrats do significantly more than half disagree with this proposition. On capital gains taxes, the tax professionals lie in between the

Democrats and Republicans, though much closer to the Democrats and far from the near unanimous Republican belief in the investment-enhancing properties of capital gains tax reductions.

DETERMINANTS OF POLICY OPINIONS: VALUES AND ECONOMIC MODEL ASSUMPTIONS

To what extent are policy opinions influenced by a person's values? To what extent are they influenced by beliefs about how the economy operates, in particular how tax policy affects the economy? In order to answer these questions, I report below on a series of multivariate probit analyses that explain the answers given to each of the policy questions as a function of the demographic indicator variables discussed above, plus dummy variables for the answers to a set of questions concerning attitudes toward distribution of income and certain aspects of how taxes affect the economy.

Values

The two questions related to values concerned the distribution of income. Question #79 asked "Should the distribution of income in the United States be more equal?"; Question #80 asked "Is the redistribution of income within the United States a legitimate role for government?" The answers to the questions were highly positively correlated ($\rho = 0.61$), raising the possibility that multicollinearity will increase the standard error on each coefficient, even though the sum of the coefficients on the two variables might be significantly different from zero. In what follows, I report on cases for which either estimated coefficient, or the sum of the two, is significantly different from zero with 95 percent confidence.

The answer to Question #80 is much more likely to be associated with policy responses than the answer to Question #79, and is more likely than any other question about values or economic behavior to be a statistically significant correlate with policy preference. A tax professional who answers yes to Question #80, whom I will label a "leveler," favors retaining the property tax as a major source of local revenue. A leveler also favors taxing inheritances and *inter vivos* gifts. With regard to the income tax, the leveler favors a top rate of 50 percent or higher, eliminating the federal tax exemption for state and local bond interest and taxing real capital gains as ordinary income. Levelers are more likely to favor taxing wealth. They are against the use of abatements and other incentives to attract business. Levelers oppose exempting capital income from taxation but do not favor taxing capital income at a higher rate than labor income. Levelers also have distinct opinions about the expenditure side of the budget. They oppose reducing the share of government spending relative to GNP and oppose a balanced budget amendment.

As already mentioned, for the most part when both answers concerning values are entered into the probit equation, Question #80 is more likely to be a significant determinant than Question #79. There are, though, two exceptions worthy of note. It is a belief that the distribution of income should be more equal, rather than a belief that government has a legitimate role in redistribution, which is associated with favoring having education be independent of local government. The same pattern applies to explaining who is more likely to oppose a flat-rate income tax and favor taxing real accrued capital gains as ordinary income.

There are two cases of interest for which the coefficient on the answer to neither Question #79 nor Question #80 were significant, but the sum of the coefficients was significantly different from zero. Those who are generally more concerned about redistribution are more likely to support a graduated personal income tax and substantially increased penalties for tax evasion.

Economic Model Assumptions

Questions about the respondents' economic assumptions fall into three categories: those about how responsive behavior is to tax parameters, those about the incidence of various taxes, and one about whether deficits have an adverse effect on the economy.

There are four questions about behavioral responsiveness, concerning the effect of taxes on labor supply, on saving, on business location, and of capital gains taxes on investment and economic growth. With only one uninteresting exception, respondents' views regarding saving responsiveness to taxation never has a significant partial association with a policy preference. For example, it has virtually no partial effect on whether one favors exempting capital from taxation, or whether the United States should replace some or all of the income tax with a VAT.

Beliefs about the other three behavioral response magnitudes do often affect policy opinions. Those who believe there is a negative labor supply response to marginal tax rates are, not surprisingly, more likely to favor a flat-rate income tax and less likely to favor a graduated income tax and less likely to favor a top tax rate of 50 percent or higher; they also would like to see a federal retail sales tax, presumably (although this was not explicitly asked) as a substitute for income taxes. These respondents also tend to believe that the property tax should be restricted to realty and should exempt improvements; because the economic issues surrounding these policy questions do not directly depend on labor supply elasticities, the partial correla-

tions in this case presumably reflect a generalized belief in the inefficiency of relating tax liability to productive economic activity. As one would expect, those who believe that taxes play an important role in business location decisions are less likely to support property taxes as a major source of local revenue, and, conditional on there being a property tax, are more likely to favor a preferential rate on business property.

A belief that low capital gains taxes have beneficial economic effects has predictable associations with policy opinions. These respondents favor preferential taxes on capital gains and oppose taxing accrued real gains or nominal realized gains as ordinary income; there was, however, no significant association with opinions regarding taxing inflation-adjusted realized gains as ordinary income. These respondents also have distinct views on the taxation of owner-occupied housing, favoring mortgage interest deductibility and opposing the taxation of imputed rent. They are, *ceteris paribus*, likely to favor the complete exemption of capital income from taxation.

The two incidence questions referred to the sales tax and the corporation income tax. One's views about whether the sales tax is regressive often affected policy opinion, but not concerning sales tax issues! No discernible pattern was evident. Question #88 asked whether corporation income taxes were largely passed on to workers and consumers. The answer to this question rarely had a significant partial effect on policy opinions, with one notable exception. Those who thought that the corporation tax is passed on were more likely to be in favor of retaining the alternative minimum tax on corporations. The logical connection is unclear, because the goal of the alternative minimum tax is to impose one measure of equity across corporations, which is an especially slippery concept if the tax is shifted to workers and consumers.

Summary and Conclusions

The majority of tax professionals does not favor abandoning the income tax as the backbone of the federal tax system. They would not favor moving substantially from an income tax to a VAT or to a federal retail sales tax, or otherwise exempting capital income from the tax base. Nor would they favor moving from a graduated to a flat-rate tax. Neither would a majority favor increasing the graduation to a pre-1986 level by reimposing a top federal income tax rate of 50 percent or above.

A majority does, though, favor certain important changes in the income tax system. On the list of reforms is to tax inflation-adjusted, rather than nominal, capital gains at realization; to eliminate the corporate alternative minimum tax; and to tax fully the interest on state and local bonds. More controversial and radical reforms that are favored are integrating the corporate and individual income taxes, fully indexing the measure of capital income and eliminating the deductibility of mortgage interest payments. In addition, a slight majority (59 percent) of respondents favor making wealth taxable.

Nor is radical reform of the state and local tax system preferred by a majority. A majority favor retaining the property tax, at the same rate for business and residences, as a major source of revenue; a slight majority would, though, eliminate homestead exemptions. Most favor a general retail sales tax at the state and local level, but not at the federal level. Some important changes are recommended, though, including eliminating homestead exemptions, extending the sales tax to cover services, and increasing reliance on user fees.

Although a major shift from income tax to consumption tax is not supported by a majority of tax professionals in 1994, it has apparently gained in support since 1934. This shift can be inferred from the fact that in 1934, nearly two-thirds of respondents favored higher income tax rates on capital, versus labor, income, a move in the opposite direction from consumption taxes; in 1994, only seven percent supported that. Other notable changes from 1934 are the drop off in support for distinguishing land and improvements in the property tax base and basing war finance on taxation of munitions makers.

A tax policy supported by tax professionals is not necessarily an appropriate one. The results of this survey are not offered as a guide to action. I am not so optimistic about the influence of tax professionals to state, as Mabel Walker did in 1935, that "every responsible tax administrator or legislator desires to know the opinions of such matured students of taxation, and particularly how unanimous are the opinions of such authorities on live questions." It is my hope, though, that these results will be of interest to both tax professionals and policymakers, and will stimulate a discussion of the policies themselves.

ENDNOTES

I would like to thank Mary Ceccanese and the National Tax Association office staff for helping to carry out the survey described in this paper and Joseph Hyde and Young Lee for excellent research assistance. Helpful comments on an earlier draft were provided by John Bowman, Paul Courant, William F. Fox, Jane Gravelle, Fritz Stocker, and Emil Sunley. Partial financial support for the project was provided by AT&T and General Mills.

[1] These disaggregated response rates do not include 32 respondents who either did not indicate any current position, or else selected more than one of the three possible fields.

[2] The survey response data, on diskette, is available upon request.

[3] Note that here, and in the rest of the paper,

the 1994 summary statistics refer to all respondents, while the 1934 survey included only academics. The reader interested in comparing the 1934 responses to the 1994 responses of academics is referred to Table 1. Some of the differences in 1994 between the academic and nonacademic responses will be discussed in a later section.

4 The survey inadvertently referred to "residents" rather than "residences." I suspect that most respondents were not confused by this error.

5 Recall that, until World War II, the federal income tax applied to only a small fraction of the population. In the 1930s as a whole, it covered only four percent of the total population.

6 Note that, for clarity, the word "capital" was placed in parentheses after "unearned" for the 1994 survey. This is the only case where there was any alteration of the wording of a question that was reported from the 1934 survey.

7 In retrospect, it would have been desirable to ask similar questions about the role of equity and efficiency in taxation, so as to compare the level of support chosen.

8 For labor supply and saving, no change in behavior could be due to offsetting income and substitution effects. Thus, no observed response does not necessarily imply the absence of efficiency costs due to distorted behavior.

9 Another indicator of the relative similarity of academic and government views is the number of questions on which the extent of private support lies between the academic and government level of support—only 15 out of 96 questions. The academics had the middle ground for 38 questions, and the government respondents for 41 questions.

10 One could also perform formal statistical tests of whether differences in the percentage of respondents answering yes are significant. The minimum significant difference is difficult to summarize, as it depends on the two sample means and the two sample sizes. For example, a difference between the academics percentage yes and the government percentage yes would be significant at the 95 percent confidence level if it exceeded ten points if the two sample means were not at the extremes, and seven points if the sample means are near 0 or 100.

REFERENCES

Alston, Richard M., J. R. Kearl, and Michael B. Vaughan. "Agreement and Disagreement Among Economists: A Decade of Change?" Unpublished manuscript. Ogden, Utah: Weber State University, 1992a.

Alston, Richard M., Kearl J. R., and Vaughan, Michael B. "Is There a Consensus Among Economists in the 1990s?" *American Economic Review* 82 No. 2 (May, 1992b): 202–9.

Alston, Richard, J. R. Kearl, and Michael B. Vaughan. "Consensus Among Economists: The Role of Employment Affiliation." Unpublished paper presented at the Empirical Studies on Economic Consensus session, Western Economics Association, San Francisco, CA, July, 1992c.

Anderson, Malcolm and Richard Blandy. "What Australian Economics Professors Think." *Australian Economic Reviews* (4th quarter, 1992): 17–40.

Anderson, Malcolm and Richard Blandy. "Academic Economists on Trial: The Value of Economists' Opinions." *Australian Quarterly* 65 No. 1 (1993): 482–97.

Anderson, Malcolm, Richard Blandy, and Sarah Carne. "Academic Economic Opinion in East Asia." *The Australian Economic Review* (Third Quarter, 1993): 5–19.

Behrens, John O. "The Public and the Publicans Talk Taxes." *National Tax Journal* 36 No. 2 (June, 1993): 221–32.

Block, Walther and Michael Walker. "Entropy in the Canadian Economics Profession: Sampling Consensus on the Major Issues." *Canadian Public Policy* 14 No. 2 (1988): 137–50.

Brittan, S. *Is there an Economic Consensus: An Attitude Survey.* London: Macmillan, 1973.

Coleman, W. "Concord and Discord Among New Zealand Economists: The Results of An Opinion Survey." *New Zealand Economics Papers* 26 No. 1 (1992): 47–81.

Frey, Bruno S., Victor Ginsburgh, Pierre Pestieau, Werner W. Pommerehne, and Friedrich Schneider. "Consensus, Dissension and Ideology Among Economists in Various European Countries and in the United States." *European Economic Review* 23 (1983): 59–69.

Frey, Bruno S., Werner W. Pommerehne, Friedrich Schneider, and Guy Gilber. "Consensus and Dissention Among Economists: An Empirical Inquiry." *American Economic Review* 74 No. 5 (1984): 986–94.

Frey, Bruno S. and Reiner Eichenberger. "Economics and Economists: A European Perspective." *American Economic Review* 82 No. 2 (May, 1992): 216–20.

Frey, Bruno S. and Reiner Eichenberger. "American and European Economics and Economists." *Journal of Economic Perspectives* 7 No. 4 (1993): 185–93.

Friedman, Milton. "The Methodology of Positive Economics." In *Essays in Positive Economics*, 3–43. Chicago: University of Chicago Press, 1953.

Fuller, Dan A., Richard M. Alston, and Michael B. Vaughan. "Political Economy: Views of Economists and Politicians." Undated manuscript. Ogden, Utah: Weber State University.

Geach, S. and W. D. Reekie. "Entropy in South African Economics: A Survey of Consensus and Dissent." *South African Journal of Economics and Management Studies 6* (1991): 63–86.

Kearl, J. R., Clayne L. Pope, Gordon C. Whiting, and Larry T. Wimmer. "A Confusion of Economists?" *American Economic Review 69* No. 2 (May, 1993): 28–37.

Ricketts, Martin and Edward Shoesmith. *British Economic Opinion: A Survey of a Thousand Economists.* London: Institute of Economic Affairs, 1990.

Ricketts, Martin and Edward Shoesmith. British Economic Opinion: Positive Science or Normative Judgment? *American Economic Review 82* No. 2 (May, 1992): 210–5.

Samuelson, Paul. "What Economists Know." In *The Human Meaning of the Social Sciences* edited by D. Lerner. New York: Meridian, 1959.

Walker, Mabel L. "Opinion of American Professors of Public Finance on Important Tax Questions as of January 1, 1935." In *Tax Systems of the World.* Tax Research Foundation, 1935.

WHAT CAN AMERICA LEARN FROM THE BRITISH TAX SYSTEM?

WILLIAM G. GALE*

***Abstract** - This paper examines elements of British tax policy and discusses their implications for the United States, where several recent proposals would mirror aspects of the British system. These include reducing filing requirements under the individual income tax, indexing capital gains for inflation, cutting mortgage interest deductions, enacting a value-added tax, and integrating the corporate and personal income taxes. The paper also discusses implications of the poll tax for tax reform. Britain and America have made different choices involving equity, efficiency, simplicity, and other goals. These choices offer the chance to help identify the impact of tax policy.*

Tax policy debates in the United States are noteworthy for their frequency, intensity, and largely inward-looking focus. Very seldom is reference made to the experiences of other countries, and the references that are made are often seriously misleading. Yet many of the

major reform ideas put forth in recent years in the United States are closely related to programs that already exist in other countries.

This paper examines selected elements of British tax policy and experience and discusses their implications for United States tax policy. Britain is an instructive choice for this purpose because the British tax system is fundamentally like the American system in many respects, but contains many features that relate directly to changes currently or recently proposed in the United States.

The systems are most obviously similar in that they rely on income and payroll (social security) taxes for the bulk of their revenue. Both countries experienced, indeed led, the drive in the 1980s to reduce tax rates and broaden tax bases that caught on around the world and was encapsulated in a series of changes made in the 1980s by Conservative governments in the United Kingdom and in the United States Tax Reform Act of 1986.

But many features of the British system differ significantly from that in the United States. For example, the personal income tax is based on individual rather than family income, and only about ten

*The Brookings Institution, Washington, D.C. 20036.

percent of taxpayers have been required to file returns in recent years. Capital gains are indexed for inflation, while deductions for mortgage interest and other items are much more limited than in the United States. In general, relative to its American counterpart, the British income tax emphasizes simplicity, downplays the role of social policy, and limits attempts to obtain finely tuned measures of income. These differences date to the origins of the income tax in each country.

The British corporate income tax is partially integrated. Excise taxes and a value-added tax (VAT) raise a significant amount of revenue. The United Kingdom recently lived through an unsuccessful attempt to replace local government property taxes with poll taxes.

Analysis of each of these differences may contain important lessons for academics and policymakers alike. However, it should be clear at the outset that Britain has not found any way to "solve" the various trade-offs among equity, efficiency, simplicity, and other goals. Rather, the lessons stem from the fact that the United Kingdom has chosen different points (hopefully, but probably not) on the frontiers of these trade-offs. Thus, the lessons to be drawn here are not in generating conclusions about what is right or wrong about tax policy, but in providing evidence on the costs and benefits of different policies and in locating the biggest gaps between "textbook" analyses and the real world. Another set of issues involves assessing the political and other factors that have led to the differences in policy in the first place. For one such discussion, see Keen (1997).

The next section provides a very brief overview of the current status and recent evolution of British taxes, along with some comparisons to the United States. The following sections discuss what I view as some of the major differences between the systems, as noted above.

The final section offers some concluding thoughts, but all of the issues discussed below leave plenty of scope for new cross-country and within-country analyses that could sharpen the conclusions. Such analyses—for example, of the impact of alternative forms of capital gains taxation on investment and entrepreneurship—need to consider the interaction of several tax policies as well as other existing regulations or economic conditions. Thus, many of the conclusions are, of necessity, of a limited or tentative nature.

OVERVIEW OF THE BRITISH SYSTEM[1]

Total government tax revenues were 37.6 percent of gross domestic product (GDP) in Britain in 1995, compared to 31.3 percent in the United States. This difference has fluctuated over time and stood at 7.7 percent in 1970, 6.0 percent in 1980, and 7.2 percent in 1990.

Table 1 describes the composition of tax revenues in Britain for 1993–94 and the United States for 1993. The taxes in the table are grouped by United States convention. (British tables typically classify capital gains as a separate tax from the individual income tax.) Both countries obtain the most revenue from their individual income tax and social insurance payroll taxes, though the United States collects more from each than the United Kingdom does. The countries collect about the same proportion of their revenue from corporate income taxes, though the

TABLE 1
THE COMPOSITION OF TAXES IN THE UNITED KINGDOM AND THE UNITED STATES

| | United Kingdom, 1993–4 | | United States, 1993 | |
	Percent of Taxes	Percent of GDP	Percent of Taxes	Percent of GDP
Income tax	25.6	8.6	36.0	9.7
Individual income tax	25.2	8.4	—	—
Capital gains	0.4	0.1	—	—
Corporate income tax	6.4	2.1	8.2	2.2
Social insurance	17.0	5.7	23.2	6.3
National insurance	17.0	5.7	—	—
Social security and Medicare	—	—	23.2	6.3
Broad-based consumption taxes	16.8	5.6	7.9	2.1
VAT	16.8	5.6	—	—
General sales tax	—	—	7.9	2.1
Specific consumption taxes	10.9	3.6	2.6	0.7
Alcohol	2.3	0.8	0.6	0.2
Tobacco	3.0	1.0	0.6	0.2
Transportation fuel	5.6	1.9	1.4	0.4
Property taxes	9.0	3.0	10.8	2.9
National nondomestic rates	5.5	1.8	—	—
Council taxes	3.5	1.2	—	—
Estate and gift taxes	0.6	0.2	1.0	0.3
All other taxes	13.7	4.6	10.3	2.8
Total	100.0	33.4	100.0	27.0

Sources: OECD Revenue Statistics, 1965–95; Dilnot and Stears (1997); Fleener (1997); and Budget of the U.S. Government, Fiscal Year 1998.

annual figures vary over time. Property taxes and estate and gift taxes account for a somewhat smaller share of revenues in the United Kingdom than in the United States.

The major difference shown in Table 1 is the importance of consumption taxes. The VAT raises about one-sixth of all tax revenues in Britain, more than double the proportion of revenue raised by general sales taxes in the United States. Taxes on specific consumption items also differ. Taxes on alcohol, tobacco, and gasoline totaled 10.9 percent of tax revenues in Britain compared to only 2.6 percent in the United States.

Given these differences, effective tax rates on different types of economic activity may be expected to vary in the two countries. Quick and Neubig (1994) present data on measures of average tax rates. They estimate that, in 1991, consumption tax revenues totaled about 19.4 percent of aggregate consumption in the United Kingdom compared to 6.2 percent in the United States. Economy-wide average tax rates for payroll taxes and combined individual and corporate income taxes were similar in the two countries. The average total tax rate on labor income—including income, payroll, and consumption taxes—was estimated to be 36.5 percent in the United Kingdom compared to 29.3 percent in the United States. While such information is instructive, data on effective marginal tax rates would be more useful in understanding the tax incentives faced by firms and households. However, obtaining systematic, comparable, and current data is difficult.

There is a general sense in both Britain and the United States that the British system, especially the income tax, has fewer deductions or loopholes. It would be interesting to quantify this difference, but is quite difficult to do so.[2]

Table 2 reports estimates of the distribution of the burdens of taxation in the two countries. Most striking, the British tax system provides virtually no net redistribution of income on an annual basis. This is in part due to the presence of taxes that appear to be regressive with respect to annual income, such as the VAT and excise taxes. In addition, substantial redistribution occurs through government spending in the United Kingdom. In the United States, most redistribution occurs through the spending system, but the tax system also redistributes resources from higher-income to lower-income households.[3]

A series of tax acts has significantly altered the British tax system since the late 1970s. One major theme has been to reduce the income tax and raise consumption taxes—the VAT and excise

taxes. The basic VAT rate was raised from 8 percent to 15 percent in 1979 and to 17.5 percent in the early 1990s. Taxes on alcohol, tobacco, and gasoline have also increased substantially. The reduction in income taxes has been tilted toward the high end of the income distribution, while the increase in consumption taxes has been borne by all income groups (Hills, 1988).

Within the income tax, rates have fallen dramatically. The top rate on wage income fell from 83 percent in the late 1970s to 40 percent by 1988. An additional surcharge of up to 15 percent on investment income, which raised the top rate to 98 percent, was eliminated. The "basic" rate faced by most taxpayers fell from 33 percent in tax year 1978–79 to 24 percent by 1996–7, and is now 23 percent.

The base changed in several ways. Deductions for mortgage interest have been curtailed. At the same time, however, thresholds for the income tax brackets were raised substantially in real terms, the treatment of capital gains was liberalized significantly, and several new saving incentives were introduced.

Income tax rates for large corporations fell from 52 percent in 1980 to 33 percent by 1996–7; tax rates on small corporations fell from 40 percent in 1980 to 24 percent by 1996–7. At the same time, expensing of some types of corporate investment was swept away in 1984 and replaced with a significantly less generous set of depreciation schedules that helped equalize the present value of depreciation allowances across assets. The extent of integration between personal and corporate taxes has been reduced.

In the estate tax, the exemption has grown dramatically, but remains lower

TABLE 2
EFFECTIVE TAX RATES BY INCOME QUINTILE,
UNITED KINGDOM AND UNITED STATES 1994

Quintile	United Kingdom	United States
First	39.4	5.0
Second	33.9	14.9
Third	36.5	19.5
Fourth	35.8	22.3
Fifth	34.2	27.9

Sources: Calculations based on data from CSO Economic Trends (1994), as reported in Dilnot and Stears (1997, Table 17) and U.S. Congressional Budget Office (1994).

than the U.S. exemption. The large number of estate tax rates that applied earlier have been collapsed to a flat 40 percent. National insurance (social security) taxes have increased by several percentage points, the employer ceiling for contributions has been abolished, and the base has been broadened to cover some fringe benefits.

At the local level, in 1989, residential property taxes were replaced with a "community charge," or poll tax, which was abandoned in two years and replaced with a new tax that is based on property value and number of adults living in a household.

The new Labour government elected in the Spring of 1997 has proposed additional changes that would further reduce corporate tax rates and the extent of integration between corporate and personal taxes, cut mortgage tax relief by one-third, provide targeted investment incentives, and change other items. Other recent developments in British taxation look decidedly American. There has been recent speculation about adding additional tax brackets, moving to a two-tier capital gains tax— depending on how long the asset is held—and introducing tax incentives modeled after United States individual retirement accounts and earned income tax credits. The new Labour government even has its own "no new taxes" pledge—Chancellor of the Exchequer Gordon Brown promised in the campaign at one point not to raise income tax rates for five years and at another not to raise income tax rates on those with income below £40,000.

The Individual Income Tax

The unit of taxation is the individual, although a system of joint filing was used before 1990. The tax base includes wages, interest, dividends, some capital gains, pension benefits, unemployment benefits, royalties, property income, business income and other items.

The personal allowance (the equivalent of a United States exemption) was £3,765 in tax year 1996–7 (which ended in April 1997).[4] Married couples receive an additional allowance of £1,790 that can be allocated arbitrarily across spouses. Taxpayers who are blind, recent widows, or elderly receive additional allowances. There are no child allowances, but there is a child benefit spending program.

After subtracting the exemption and any allowances, the marginal tax rate in 1996–7 was 20 percent on the first £3,900 of taxable income, 24 percent— the basic rate–on additional income up to £25,500, and 40 percent on higher levels of income. The basic rate has since been reduced to 23 percent. It is estimated that in 1996–7 about 25 percent of taxpayers faced the lower rate, 67 percent of taxpayers faced the basic rate, and the remaining 8 percent faced the top rate. Allowances and tax brackets are indexed for inflation.

Filing

From an American perspective, probably the most interesting aspect of the British income tax is that very few citizens actually have to file tax forms. Filing is usually unnecessary because the tax structure is sufficiently simple and because withholding regulations generate, in principle at least, exactly the right amount of withheld taxes at source on wages and other income.

The main instrument of exact withholding is the "pay as you earn" (PAYE) system. The PAYE system is a cumulative withholding scheme that applies to wage income. Workers provide their employers certain basic information, including marital status and age, that is used to calculate withholding allowances. Employers then withhold taxes as directed by these formulas. The key to exact withholding is that the process is cumulative. At each paycheck, the taxes withheld equal the difference between cumulative taxes owed (on cumulative earnings to date) and cumulative taxes paid until then. Thus, employees that stop working in the middle of the year nonetheless have the correct amount withheld. When an employee changes jobs, information on his or her cumulative wages and taxes is provided to the new employer, and the calculations continue. In contrast, in the United States, taxes on wages are withheld, but withholding is neither cumulative nor intended to be exact.

Withholding wages at source is a necessary but by no means sufficient method of ensuring that most people do not have to file tax returns. Coupled with PAYE, a number of features of the British tax system enhance the feasibility of a nonfiling system. First, exact withholding is facilitated by requiring that taxpayers file individual, rather than joint, returns and setting the tax brackets so that a majority of taxpayers face the same basic rate.

Second, taxes on capital income are structured in a way that reduces filing requirements. Taxes on interest are withheld at a 20 percent rate. Personal-level taxes on dividends are in effect also withheld at a 20 percent, as discussed in a subsequent section. Capital gains on owner-occupied housing are completely exempt from taxes. On other assets, only inflation-adjusted capital gains in excess of £6,300 per person per year are subject to taxation. Indexing, however, cannot be used to turn a gain into a loss or to increase a loss. The effect is that

very few households pay capital gains taxes. The first £3,250 of net rental income on rooms in the owner's home is exempted from taxation. Tax-preferred saving is incorporated via payroll deductions for pensions. Taxpayers may also contribute to saving incentive plans, but these contributions are limited and are "back-loaded"—the contributions are not deductible but earnings and withdrawals are not taxed. Thus, moving funds in and out of such accounts does not generate tax consequences.

Third, expenditures that would qualify as itemized deductions in the United States receive much less generous treatment in the United Kingdom. Subsidies for mortgage interest are provided, but not through tax filing and not, in fact, in a way that is at all related to taxes. Limited interest relief is provided at source. In 1996–7, the subsidy was a 15 percent rate, regardless of the taxpayer's marginal rate. For example, a household with a 10 percent mortgage would pay 8.5 percent interest on the first £30,000 of the loan, while the lender would collect the remaining 1.5 percent interest on that amount from the government. The full amount of interest on the remaining balance is charged to the household.

A limited amount of charitable contributions can be made through a payroll deduction plan, and taxpayers can also "covenant" income—earmarking the income to charity for four years or more. The contribution generates a deduction at the basic rate of tax. The charity recovers this amount (the basic rate times the contribution) from Inland Revenue (the British tax agency). Single contributions between £600 and £5 million may also be deducted.

Deductions for employee business expenses are generally very strict and allowed only for items that are "wholly, exclusively and necessarily" related to business. Medical expense deductions have been extremely limited. (Of course, the structure of health expenditures is quite different in the United Kingdom than in the United States). There are no general deductions for personal interest payments, casualty losses, or local taxes.

Each of these features—individual filing, exact withholding of taxes on wages, a wide tax bracket applying to the basic rate, the treatment of capital income, and the treatment of deductions—reduces the need for individuals to file tax forms in order to reconcile tax liability with taxes withheld. Despite all of these features, however, about ten percent or more of British taxpayers have to file tax returns in any given year. These are largely high-income taxpayers with asset income (taxes on which have been withheld at a lower rate), those with capital gains above the exempted amount, and those with self-employment income.[5]

What can be learned from these policies? First, although filing requirements are clearly an administrative issue, they appear to have important effects on the structure of tax policy. The British income tax is marked by systematically different choices than its United States counterpart. The system has fewer rates, fewer deductions, and more withholding. There are (currently) no dependent allowances, earned income tax credits, alternative minimum taxes, income-based phaseout of allowances, income-based cap on deductions, child tax credits, or education tax credits. In general, then, the British income tax features more compromises in favor of simplicity and in opposition to measuring income or ability-to-pay exactly. There are also fewer attempts to enact social policy through the tax code. This

should not be read as British indifference to such social concerns; many such programs are enacted through the spending side instead.

It seems plausible that at least some of these structural differences are due to differences in withholding patterns and the administrative features of the tax code. In particular, once withholding and nonfiling become important aspects of the tax code, many special tax subsidies or loopholes may become more difficult to design and enforce.

For example, there is a long tradition of withholding at source under the British income tax. In 1799, Pitt imposed a ten percent tax on all incomes above £200. The tax raised £5–7 million annually for three years, which was much less than had been predicted by the revenue estimators of the time. The revenue shortfall was due at least in part to "gentle" administration of the tax law by local commissioners and to widespread evasion. In 1802, the tax was repealed, but in 1803, Addington restored the income tax (apparently under the name of a property tax) and included withholding at source. By 1806, the tax raised about £20 million, even though the tax rate was only half as large as under Pitt's income tax. The income tax was repealed again in 1816, but since the tax was restored in 1842, withholding at source has remained a prominent feature (Sabine, 1980). Exact withholding of wage income was established in the 1940s, when the financing requirements of World War II led to a 150 percent increase in the number of taxpayers over a two-year period. The immediate goal of exact withholding was to reduce the number of mistakes and ease the computational burdens imposed on the large number of inexperienced taxpayers.

In contrast, the United States income tax has always contained a variety of special deductions. Even the original 1913 version of the modern income tax included deductions for mortgage interest, state and local income and property taxes, casualty and theft losses, and life insurance investment income, and excluded interest income from state and local bonds. Deductions for employer-provided health care and charity, as well as special treatment of capital gains, were introduced within ten years. Of the estimated $403 billion in tax expenditures in the 1993 United States tax code, over two-thirds were due to provisions enacted before 1929 (U.S. General Accounting Office, 1994). Although the United States did initiate withholding in the 1940s when the income tax was expanded greatly to finance the war, withholding was never intended to be exact and households were still required to file returns. This not only made it possible to enact social policy through the tax code, but made the tax code a highly visible way to enact such programs.

If nonfiling is expected to generate large administrative and compliance savings, the British experience may be somewhat surprising. The total administrative and compliance costs of a tax system include those faced by individuals, firms, and government. Since so few individual forms are filed in Britain, individuals' compliance costs seem much more likely to be higher in the United States (see, for example, Blumenthal and Slemrod, 1992). But costs imposed on government and firms are likely to be higher in Britain. Kay and King (1990) cite Inland Revenue administrative costs of about two percent of revenue collected. This is between three and four times the comparable figure for the IRS relative to total United States revenues. Comparable estimates of costs borne by firms

in the two countries are difficult to obtain.

In any case, complaints about the complexity and administrability of the British tax system cannot be ignored. Kay and King (1990) argue forcefully that the compliance and administrative costs are significant. Recent events suggest that the British are moving toward a self-assessment system more like the United States (Johnston, 1996). The interaction of more self-employment, more contract work, and problems with the exact withholding system has pushed the system in this direction. Up to one-third of British taxpayers are expected to be required to fill out forms in the near future. A new system of self-assessment—where taxpayers report all of their own income, claim deductions, and calculate their own tax bill—apparently has broad support from both political parties, even amid criticisms that the forms appear to be quite complex.

Recently, Senator Dole and Representative Gephardt have independently proposed no-return systems for a substantial portion of United States taxpayers. In 1994, about 40 percent of taxpayers filed the simplified 1040A and 1040EZ forms, and about 78 percent of all returns faced a marginal rate of 0 or 15 percent. This suggests that a substantial portion of the population could be integrated into a no-return system. But current withholding formulas are not designed to be exact for any but the simplest situations, and so would need to be amended.

A tax agency reconciliation (TAR) system is an alternative approach to eliminating tax filing. In a TAR, withholding is typically as close to exact as possible, but the tax agency calculates each household's tax at the end of the year and sends a bill or refund.[6]

Gale and Holtzblatt (1997) estimate that, with minimal changes in the structure of tax policy, but with significant changes in tax administration, withholding at source could be established for wages, the earned income tax credit, interest, dividends, pensions, individual retirement account distributions, and unemployment insurance benefits. If so, then up to 56 million, or almost half, of all United States taxpayers could be placed on a tax-agency reconciliation system. These are households who have income only from the sources mentioned above and do not claim itemized deductions.

The saving in compliance costs may not prove significant, however. Of the 56 million households, 44 million currently file the relatively simple 1040A and 1040EZ returns and probably spend very little time filling out forms to begin with. For example, Blumenthal and Slemrod (1992) provide survey evidence that 30 percent of households spent zero to five hours complying with the income tax (including keeping records, learning about the tax rules, filling out the tax form and other items) and an additional 15 percent spent less than ten hours. Almost half made no financial expenditure on tax preparation and an additional 17 percent paid less than $50.

Adding large numbers of additional taxpayers to a TAR may prove more difficult, and at the very least would require changes either in the structure of policy and/or in how policies are administered. Even if taxpayers with the forms of income mentioned above and who had itemized deductions and capital gains were brought into the system, which would be difficult, only six million more taxpayers would be covered.

No-return systems raise several additional considerations. Many taxpayers may experience significant psychic or emotional costs when filing any income tax return. Thus, even if the vast majority of affected taxpayers already face relatively simple tax situations in an objective sense, a no-return system could still provide significant benefits to certain households. However, in the United States, unless state income taxes were also shifted to a no-return system, the reduction in filing and psychic costs would likely be minimal. Notably, there are no local income taxes in the United Kingdom.

Second, United States taxpayers clearly like receiving refunds, perhaps as a form of forced saving or for some other reason. A cumulative withholding system would likely eliminate refunds, but could in principle be designed to overwithhold systematically. In a TAR, however, refunds could still be obtained.

Third, under either type of no-return system, citizens would likely want to examine the agency-provided forms carefully and would have to keep records to do so. It is unclear whether taxpayers would be willing to trust the IRS to calculate their taxes for them. This might be compounded by the notion that a no-return system is likely to leave people less aware of the tax system they face and hence of the tax consequence of their actions. Indeed, numerous commentators note what they view as the typical British citizen's ignorance of the tax system (see, for example, Kay and King, 1990). In contrast, a recent proposal by Richard Armey would have done away with withholding and required people to file tax payments every month. The idea behind the proposal was to make people more aware of the tax system in general and the tax burdens they face.

Fourth, a TAR system would place much more stringent requirements on payers to file forms with the IRS and on the IRS to process the forms promptly. Whether each of these tasks could be accomplished in a timely and accurate manner is unclear.

Marriage

An income tax can embody at most two of the following three principles: marginal tax rates should rise with income; families with equal income should pay equal taxes; and the tax system should be neutral with respect to marriage.

The British system, like the American, violates the third principle. But, whereas the American system contains a complicated pattern of marriage taxes and marriage subsidies, the British income tax contains only marriage subsidies. This is accomplished directly via individual filing and the additional allowance that married couples can allocate across their respective returns. An additional benefit to married couples stems from the ability, in an individual filing system, to allocate capital income to the family member with the lowest marginal tax rate. The British system violates the second principle as well. Individual filing with rising tax rates implies that, controlling for total income, married couples with unequal income will in general pay more tax than married couples whose income is distributed equally.

Housing

Since housing is both a consumption and investment good and generates income, it is potentially exposed to a wide variety of taxes. The treatment of housing under the VAT and the property tax is discussed in other sections below.

Under the income tax, imputed rent from housing, net of interest and maintenance costs, was taxed in years prior to 1962. Imputed rental values were determined based on periodic government valuations of property. By 1962, however, the imputed rents were still at prewar levels, and the government decided to abandon the tax on imputed rent rather than update the rental amounts.

The British system has never taxed capital gains on an individual's main residence, but some sort of mortgage interest relief has always been provided. When tax subsidies for most forms of borrowing were eliminated in 1974–5, subsidies for interest on the principal private residence were retained, subject to a loan limit of £25,000. No subsidies were provided for mortgages on second homes. This limit was raised to £30,000 in 1983–4 and has stayed fixed ever since. The limit applies to the sum of loans against each property.[7] Tax relief in earlier years was provided at the taxpayer's marginal income tax rate. More recently, the subsidy has been provided only up to a fixed rate, which was set at 25 percent, then reduced to 20 percent, and, in 1995, was reduced to 15 percent for new loans. The new Labour government has proposed cutting the rate to ten percent.

These policies raise several interest issues. First, mortgage interest relief has been effectively divorced from the tax system. The statutory rate of subsidy and the loan limit are independent of marginal tax rates. Second, because £30,000 is well below the average new mortgage loan, mortgage subsidies provide almost no incentive on the margin for most taxpayers. Third, the decline in the value of mortgage interest subsidies has been gradual but gigantic.

By 1996, the price level in Britain was 5.5 times its 1974 level. Over the same period, the loan amount that could be subsidized rose by 20 percent (to £30,000), so that the real loan limit fell by 78 percent. Over the same period, interest rates have also fallen dramatically, and, as noted above, the rate of subsidy is much lower currently than in the past. These factors have combined to reduce the subsidy to a tiny fraction of its former value.[8]

It is very difficult, however, to find any trace of these changes in aggregate U.K. data. Homeownership rates in the United Kingdom *rose* from 52.7 percent in 1974 to 66.8 percent in 1994. By comparison, U.S. homeownership rates were stagnant at about 64 percent during this period. The ratio of mortgage debt to GDP also rose in the United Kingdom, from 25 percent in 1974 to 56 percent in 1994. This exceeds the increase in the United States, where the ratio rose from 47 percent to 64 percent over the same period. Both mortgage debt as a percentage of the housing stock and the housing stock as a percentage of private fixed capital stock rose more in the United Kingdom than in the United States over this period. These trends, of course, are due to many other factors besides the reduction in the value of the mortgage interest subsidies. For example, privatization of public housing in the 1980s undoubtedly raised homeownership rates in the United Kingdom, and liberalization of financial markets accelerated the rise in mortgage debt (Attanasio and Banks, 1997).

Subsidizing mortgage interest at a fixed, low rate, rather than allowing mortgage interest deductions, could have significant appeal for the United States. Suppose the deduction were converted to a credit at a 15 percent rate, the lowest marginal tax rate. This would significantly reduce the cost of mortgage interest subsidies and reduce the overall level of subsidies to housing, which are quite generous in the United States. It would also be a very progressive tax shift, as it would have minimal impact on the taxpayers in the 15 percent marginal tax brackets and, if it were refundable, would assist those in the zero percent tax bracket. Estimates suggest that reducing the subsidies would be unlikely to hurt homeownership rates significantly, if at all (Green and Reschovsky, 1997; Capozza, Green, and Hendershott, 1996).[9]

A major constraint on such proposals in the United States is the alleged firestorm of protest that would occur were policymakers to touch such a sacred cow. In that light, it is interesting to note that the reduction in mortgage subsidies in Britain has been gradual and has been supported by ruling parties on the right and the left.

Capital Gains

Capital gains taxes were introduced in 1965. Only real capital gains that have accrued since 1982 are taxable now, and the first £6,300 per person is exempt from taxation in each year. Real gains less the exempt amount are added to the individual's income and taxed at ordinary income tax rates.[10]

Both indexing and the exemption level raise several interesting issues. Opponents of indexing in the United States have argued that such a change would not be feasible. The British experience, at first glance at least, refutes that claim, but any refutation should be highly qualified. First, it is notable that indexing cannot be used to convert a gain into a loss, or to raise the value of a loss, and that interest payments are not tax deductible at the personal level in Britain. Each of these features diminishes the opportunity to use indexing to engage in tax sheltering activities, and none of them is commonly raised when indexing is proposed in the United States. Second, indexing does not achieve the goal of taxing real income. For most taxpayers with capital gains in Britain, the gains are fully exempt from taxation either because of the large exemption level or because assets such as housing, which comprise a large portion of most households' wealth, are exempt from capital gains taxation. Third, it is unclear how well the system of capital gains taxes operates. Data on the evasion rates and compliance and administrative costs associated with indexing are difficult to obtain.

The large exemption is interesting in its own right. Suppose the United States exempted the first $20,000 in capital gains for joint filers and the first $10,000 for all other filers. Calculations from the 1994 IRS public use file indicate that the exemption would reduce the number of taxpayers with taxable capital gains by 89 percent, so that only about one percent of taxpayers paid capital gains taxes, but would reduce taxable capital gains by only 29 percent. Thus, in the absence of changes in realization patterns, such an exemption would greatly reduce the number of taxpayers facing capital gains taxes but would reduce capital gains revenues by a smaller amount. These figures indicate the simplification potential of an exemption.

In practice, however, people would change their behavioral patterns to take advantage of the exemption. Formal evidence suggests that the elasticity of

the timing of capital gains realizations with respect to taxes is quite high (Burman and Randolph, 1994), and casual evidence suggests that much activity of this sort occurs in Britain currently. Such behavior would reduce both the number of people who had to pay capital gains taxes and the revenue yield. Indexing gains for inflation would reduce both items further.

The net result of the treatment of capital gains is that very few people pay capital gains tax in Britain, and the tax raises almost no revenue, accounting for only 0.4 percent of all taxes and 1.6 percent of taxes raised by the income tax plus the capital gains tax (see Table 1). In the United States, in contrast, federal capital gains taxes alone account for about 2.5 percent of all tax revenue and 7 percent of federal income taxes (Burman and Ricoy, 1997).[11] Thus, capital gains tax revenues are roughly five to six times larger as a percentage of GDP in the United States than in the United Kingdom.

It is unclear, however, which country treats capital gains more generously at the margin, for taxable investors. Indexing and preferential rates of taxation are alternative methods of reducing the tax rate on nominal gains. In principle, the relative generosity should vary by asset and time period. For example, since 1982, the S&P 500 has risen in the United States by about 660 percent, while the price level has increased by only 66 percent. Hence, a 29 percent exclusion, as has been provided in the United States for high-income taxpayers in recent years,[12] would have been much more valuable on the margin than the British system of indexing combined with taxing real gains at the ordinary income rate. The latter would have provided an effective exclusion of about ten percent for nominal gains at the margin. Clearly, results for other assets and other time periods will vary.

While the notion that the income tax should tax real income is a sound one in principle, the British experience suggests that indexing of capital gains for inflation should be considered in the broader context that includes the tax rates on capital gains, the tax treatment of interest payments, the exemption level for capital gains, and rules about when indexing may not be used. To a large extent, the British system of taxing capital gains appears to be an abolition of gains taxes for almost all households, plus positive taxation of large gains on the margin, in order to reduce large-scale tax arbitrage. The lack of visibility may be one reason why the taxation of capital gains barely appears on the radar screen of major issues in British tax policy, whereas capital gains taxes are hotly contested in the United States.

Saving Incentives and Pensions

Personal saving rates for the United States and United Kingdom have followed different trends. The U.S. rate fell about four percentage points from the early 1980s through 1987 and has remained low. The British rate fell by over 8 percentage points from 1980 to 1988 and then rebounded in almost as dramatic a fashion, rising 5.6 percentage points in four years before leveling off. These trends, of course, are affected by many factors other than tax policy. For example, financial liberalization appears to have been an important part of the saving decline in the 1980s in both countries, with Britain experiencing a dramatic rise in personal liabilities relative to personal income, even relative to the increase that occurred in the United States. The run-up in equity values, social security reform, budget

deficits, and other factors may also have played an important role in saving trends.

Tax policy toward saving offers another potential source of the differential trends. The bulk of personal saving in both countries is directed toward assets with generous tax treatment (Banks and Blundell, 1994). Private pensions and housing receive treatment more favorable than just not taxing the return on saving. Like the United States, Britain has also experimented with a variety of other tax incentives for saving. These schemes—TESSAs, PEPs, and PPPs, described below—provide an effective tax rate of zero on the return to saving.

Tax-Exempt Special Savings Accounts (TESSAs) were introduced in 1990. Any individual aged 18 or over was eligible to open a TESSA in an approved financial institution. Contributions could total £3,000 in the first year, and up to £1,800 in each of the next four years, subject to a total of £9,000 overall. Contributions were not deductible, but interest was entirely free of income tax if the principal was left in the account for five years. Withdrawal of the principal would trigger tax payments, but not penalties, so a TESSA, even under the worst circumstances, had at least as generous a tax treatment as ordinary saving. The net-of-tax interest could be withdrawn as it arose without losing the tax preference.

By 1992, there were 3.5 million TESSA accounts (out of about 22 million households in the United Kingdom). Thus, about 15 percent of households took out TESSAs, roughly equivalent to IRA take-up rates in the United States after two years of universal eligibility.

It should be clear that TESSAs are very close substitutes for taxable interest-bearing accounts. Notably, about 95 percent of households with TESSAs also held other interest-bearing accounts. These households also tended to hold larger TESSA balances than others. Like IRAs, TESSAs tended to be held by wealthier, older households, who could more easily substitute existing funds into these accounts. Banks, Blundell, and Dilnot (1994) present preliminary evidence consistent with the view that increases in TESSA balances were offset to a very large degree by reductions in other interest-bearing accounts. Given the revenue costs of TESSAs (from the foregone tax on interest), they conclude that TESSAs probably did not raise private saving much, if at all, and may well have reduced national saving.

Personal Equity Plans (PEPs) were introduced in 1986 and expanded in subsequent years.[13] Contributions are not deductible, but investments that are retained for one year, with reinvested dividends, are untaxed. The tax benefits of PEPs, however, were initially almost nonexistent for small investors because of the high exemption on capital gains and because, as explained below, dividends were already effectively not taxed at the individual level, at least for taxpayers in the lowest tax bracket. Expansion of the contribution limits led to bigger take up in subsequent years, but PEP ownership remains highest among older and high-income house-holds. The PEPs are likely to be very good substitutes for equity holdings for such households, and most PEP holders had other direct equity holdings. Banks, Blundell, and Dilnot (1994) find evidence of significant substitution between PEPs and other equity hold-ings.

Britain has also moved toward replacing its unfunded public pension at the margin with a prefunded private alternative; this may have contributed to an increase in the saving rate as well.[14] Britain has a three-tier pension system. The first tier (the basic benefit) is a state-supported minimum annuity payment that is financed out of progressive national insurance contributions made by workers and employers. Basic benefits are about 15 percent of average male earnings and are indexed to the price level, and so are expected to fall to 7 to 8 percent by 2030. The third tier consists of conventional private pensions and other saving.

The second tier is more complex, consisting of a State Earnings Related Pension Scheme (SERPS) and private alternatives. In 1978, the SERPS was introduced to provide a benefit of one-quarter of average wages in the highest 20 years of earnings, subject to earnings limits. Accrual formulas for SERPS entitlements were cut in 1986 and again in 1995. Combined with SERPS being indexed to retail prices rather than wages, these cuts suggest a large reduction in replacement ratios in the future.

Most workers, however, have exercised their option to contract out of SERPS, with 50 percent of workers now in occupational pensions (employer-provided defined benefit plans) and an additional 28 percent in Private Personal Pensions (PPPs). When the personal pension option was initiated in 1988, workers were allowed to contract out to an IRA or employer-provided defined contribution plan. The government provided that workers who chose this option would have 5.8 percentage points of their national insurance contributions redirected to the private pension. Also, an additional rebate of two percent of covered earnings was offered for those who had not already contracted out. In addition, the rebate was grossed up to take account of the income tax relief on an individual's pension contributions—yielding a total contribution of 8.46 percent of eligible earnings. Given the generosity of the program and the large accompanying volume of advertising, the option turned out to be very popular.[15]

Workers also have the option of contributing additional amounts to their personal pension. Total contribution limits are a function of salary and age and rise from 17.5 percent of covered earnings for those aged 17 to 35 to 40 percent for those 61 and over.

It is unclear how these tax-incentive plans have affected national saving. Estimates in Disney and Whitehouse (1992) indicate that, for about 80 percent of workers, a government contribution of less than 8.46 percent of salary would have been sufficient to induce them to contract out. This suggests that the option created substantial positive income effects that could have raised consumption and thereby reduced private saving.

About 60 percent of workers with PPPs make no contribution to their PPP above the contracted out rebate, incentive payment, and income tax relief. For this group, current disposable income is the same as if they were still in SERPS, but their wealth is higher. This suggests that, if anything, they would increase their consumption. For the other 40 percent, who do contribute beyond their national insurance payment, some of the *extra* contribution may be new saving.

As an illustrative calculation, suppose that the 40 percent of workers who contributed additional amounts contributed twice as much as the ones who only contributed their national insurance

contribution, and that all of such additional contributions were new saving. Then 2/7 of all contributions to PPPs would represent net additions to national saving. This seems to be an upper bound for the proportion of contributions that would be new saving (under the assumption that workers who contributed above their national insurance contribution gave double what other workers contributed). However, the additional contributions were tax deductible and thus reduced public saving, all workers may have saved less in other forms because of the income effects of PPPs, and workers who contributed more than their national insurance contribution may have financed part or all of their additional contributions from existing assets or funds they would have saved anyway. Thus, the net effect is unclear.

The VAT

The presence of a significant VAT is the single largest structural difference between the U.S. and U.K. tax systems. Although the United States imposes sales taxes at the state and local level, these generate only about half as much revenue as the VAT does in Britain.

The standard VAT rate is 17.5 percent, with a rate of 5 percent applied to domestic fuel. The VAT system provides special treatment of various goods and services in different ways. Zero-rated goods do not have net VAT levied on the final good or upon the inputs used in its creation. That is, the seller of a zero-rated good owes no VAT, but may claim credits for the VAT paid on inputs. Exempt goods do not have VAT levied on the final good sold to the consumer, but firms cannot reclaim the VAT paid on inputs, so they face effective VAT rates between zero and the standard rate, depending on the fraction of value added at the retail level. About 25 percent of consumer expenditure in the United Kingdom is on zero-rated goods. These items include most food, new dwellings, passenger transport, books, newspapers and magazines, prescription medicine, and children's clothing. About 15 percent of consumer expenditure is exempt. This category includes rents, private education, health services, postal services, finance and insurance, and burial and cremation. Broadening the base of the VAT has proven very difficult in recent years.

Perhaps the most notable feature of the VAT, and certainly the least examined in the United States, is the extent to which the provisions of the VAT are dictated by international convention. European countries have jointly set certain parameters of the VAT in a series of "directives" over the last several decades. Prior to 1992, VAT rates were unrestricted by the directives. Currently, the standard VAT rate is not less than 15 percent, but reduced rates could apply to certain targeted goods, as noted above.

The elimination of border controls in 1993—part of a larger European agenda that includes removing domestic preferences in public purchases, exchange controls, and restrictions on intercountry mergers—causes additional problems for the VAT and creates the possibility of fraudulent claims since the VAT on exports is rebated.[16]

It is unclear how important the limited autonomy over VAT really is. To some extent, conservative governments in the 1980s may have used the European dictates as externally imposed reasons to do what they wanted to do anyway—raise the importance of the VAT and reduce the income tax. It is also unclear how important such problems

might be for the United States were it to adopt a VAT. Presumably, one of the benefits of doing so would be the ability to coordinate if possible with other countries, but a destination-based VAT would not be difficult to enforce internationally as long as the United States did not maintain completely open borders.

The textbook view of the VAT is that it is simple, cheap to administer, and self-enforcing. These attributes apply to the British VAT only with important qualifications, if at all. As noted above, the VAT base exempts or zero-rates a significant amount of consumption. Note also that most health care is provided publicly in Britain and is not subject to VAT. In applying the VAT in the United States, there may be pressure to exempt or zero-rate health care. The VAT base, however, is narrower in Britain than in many other European countries, which raises hope that an American VAT could be relatively broad based.

The United Kingdom employs a credit-invoice VAT—firms calculate their sales, calculate the VAT due on the sales, and then take a tax credit for VAT that has been paid by others on the items the firm purchased.[17] In principle, an enforcement advantage of a credit-invoice VAT is the ability to match invoices from sellers and receipts of buyers. The basic idea is that, since the buyer of a good is going to report the transaction to the tax authorities in order to claim a VAT refund, the seller, knowing that the buyer will report, chooses also to report, so as not to be caught evading the tax. The paper trail also assists authorities in audits.

In practice, the British VAT authorities do not match invoices as an enforcement mechanism, due in part to the belief that doing so would generate only tiny gains in revenue and compliance. The authorities instead use other methods to estimate revenue, such as total sales, input purchases, etc. This is obviously an indirect approach that relies on incomplete information and, if enforced aggressively, could lead to an intrusive and frequently incorrect tax authority insisting on inappropriate levels of tax payments.

One of the inevitable problems with taxing different goods at different rates is that there are no hard and fast definitions for particular good categories. One famous case involved Jaffa "cakes." The VAT authorities claimed that the product was a biscuit, while the Jaffa company claimed it was a cake, which would face a lower VAT rate.[18] Similar problems arise in the taxation of many other goods. Another problem is the taxation of services, where the absence of a physical inventory makes auditing and enforcement more difficult.

The VAT can also be complex in other ways. For example, many small businesses are exempt from the VAT. Thus, the number of firms in the VAT system exceeds the number of firms paying VAT, because the former want to receive rebates on their purchases. In addition, businesses in the VAT system need to keep track not only of the value of their purchases, but the composition as well.

Compliance and administrative costs average about five percent of VAT revenues. This is about half as high as estimates for the U.S. income tax (Slemrod, 1996) but about the same as the income tax, capital gains tax, and national insurance scheme in the United Kingdom (Sandford, Godwin, and Hardwick, 1989). Compliance costs are heavily weighted toward small firms that pay VAT, and are a very high proportion

of VAT payments for such firms. One reason compliance costs are high is that the VAT is not integrated with business income taxes for auditing and control purposes.

Evasion rates also appear to be fairly low, around five percent, and evasion appears to be concentrated in a few sectors, notably small businesses that are just large enough to have to pay VAT but do not. One likely reason for higher evasion in this sector is the higher compliance costs. Another is that declaration of sales not only creates VAT liabilities, but also often creates income tax and national insurance contribution liabilities for the business owner. Thus, the effective return to evasion may be much higher for small businesses than that indicated by the VAT rate alone.

Although almost no one advocates that the United States completely scrap the income tax and replace it with a VAT, many experts note the viability of reducing the size and scope of the income tax and replacing the lost revenue with a VAT (Slemrod and Bakija, 1996; Graetz, 1997). The British experience with the VAT, however, is probably not as satisfactory as one would hope for before signing on to a similar plan. In particular, a VAT that did not zero-rate or exempt so many goods, that was integrated with other business taxes in administration, and that handled exports more effectively would represent a better model for the United States to build on.

Corporate Income Tax

The corporate income tax is levied against the profits of United Kingdom resident companies, public corporations, and unincorporated associations. Deductions are allowed for interest payments, a limited amount of research and development expenditures, wages, and pension contributions. Depreciation deductions vary by assets. For equipment and machinery, 25 percent of the unused basis may be deducted in each year. Hotels and industrial buildings may be deducted at a four percent straight-line rate. Unused depreciation deductions and losses may be carried back for three years and carried forward indefinitely.

In 1996–7 taxable income faced a marginal tax rate of 24 percent on the first £300,000 of profit and 35.25 percent on profits between £300,000 and £1.5 million. Both the average and the marginal tax rate are 33 percent on profits above £1.5 million.

The British corporate tax is partially integrated with the individual income tax. When a company pays a dividend, it pays an additional 25 percent of the amount in "advance corporate tax" (ACT). For tax purposes, shareholders are deemed to have received both the dividend and the tax payment and to have remitted payments in the amount of the ACT to Inland Revenue. The tax payment is also credited against the corporation's income tax. The net effect is that, for dividends paid to certain taxpayers, there is no change in net tax revenues.

For example, consider a firm that pays £100 in dividends. Under current law, it is required to send a check to Inland Revenue for an additional £25, as the ACT. (This is considered a 20 percent ACT rate, because £25 is 20 percent of the "grossed-up dividend" of £100 + £25.) The firm credits this payment against its corporate income tax, so that the dividend does not change the firm's total tax payments. (The ACT can be carried back six years and forward indefinitely.)

The shareholder receives dividends of £100, and is deemed to have received £125 in income and to have paid £25 in taxes. Thus, if the investor is in the 20 percent tax bracket, there are no further tax consequences. The deemed £25 in tax payments exactly offsets the deemed £125 in income, so that the dividend does not change tax payments for the shareholder. However, a shareholder in the 24 percent bracket would owe an additional £5, and a shareholder in the 40 percent bracket would owe an additional £25.[19]

The ACT credit is a major feature of corporate taxation. In 1995–6, the corporate tax raised £24.7 billion. By way of comparison, the ACT totaled £9.9 billion, 40 percent of corporate tax revenue and 3.6 percent of all tax revenue.

Historically, pension funds, which are tax exempt, could receive refundable ACT credits on their dividend receipts. Because dividends paid to taxpayers in the 20 percent tax bracket have no net revenue consequences, credits given to pension funds *reduce* overall tax revenue. That is, if the dividend had not been paid, tax revenue would have been higher. Thus, the payment to pensions represents not just a tax exemption, but a partial refund of corporate taxes.

The extent of integration has declined in recent years. The Conservative government cut the ACT rate from 25 percent to its current 20 percent in 1993. The new Labour government proposed in July 1997 to eliminate ACT refunds for pension funds immediately and for other zero-rate taxpayers in 1999. Another Labour proposal would reduce the rate of tax credit to ten percent starting in 1999. At the same time, Labour has proposed reducing the top corporate tax rate to 31 percent from 33 percent.

The stated intent of these changes is to encourage investment by reducing the tax rate on corporate profits and encouraging retained earnings. But while raising the tax on dividends might encourage firms to reinvest earnings, it would also raise the overall taxation on corporate earnings. It is thus not obvious that the proposed policy would encourage investment in the long run.

Caution is required in translating these patterns into lessons for the United States. Partial corporate integration is feasible and does not appear to have created a political firestorm, but it could be quite expensive. The effects of partial integration on corporate investment and dividend policy in Britain are of particular interest, but are difficult issues. Since 1985, both investment and the ratio of dividend payments to GDP have soared in Britain relative to the United States. It is not obvious that such trends are largely attributable to tax policy, though.

The Poll Tax[20]

The British experience with the community charge, or poll tax, is a fascinating chapter in recent tax history. Before the poll tax, local government in Britain was financed by a combination of grants from central government and local business and residential property taxes. The latter are referred to as "the rates," because the tax liability was determined by multiplying the notional rental value by a tax rate set annually by the local authorities. The central government grants were often called block grants, but had important matching elements.

This system of local finance was criticized on several grounds, some seemingly more reasonable than others. Rental values were not always adjusted appropriately. Because of the matching elements of central government grants, local governments and their residents did not bear the full marginal costs of decisions to raise local spending. Property taxes varied substantially across localities, which, according to Smith (1991), gave rise to apparent inequities across regions. Finally, because only the head of household was legally liable for property tax, there appears to have been a (mistaken) notion that very few people had to bear the burden of local property taxes, making the general public less accountable for the costs of local decisions and placing unfair burdens on those who paid property tax.

The Thatcher government wanted, in general, to introduce more local accountability for local spending and, in particular, to reduce the level and improve the efficiency of local spending. This was to be accomplished, across localities, by requiring each locality as a whole to internalize the entire cost of its marginal increases in expenditures and, within localities, by requiring the increased costs to be spread over all voters.

Toward this end, a new system of local finance was implemented in Scotland in 1989 and in England and Wales in 1990. The business property tax was altered; business property was revalued, and rates were to be set by the national, rather than local, government. The residential property tax was abolished and replaced with a community charge, an equal tax on each adult in a locality. There were a limited number of exemptions, and rebates of up to 80 percent for the poorest individuals. The central government grant was set so that, if a locality spent funds at its assessed needs level, the local community charge would equal a national standard level. Each dollar by which local spending exceeded its assessed needs had to be financed from the poll tax. The poll tax was intended to represent about one-quarter of local government revenues. Thus, raising local spending above assessed needs level by, say, 15 percent would require a 60 percent increase in the local community charge.[21]

Both the conceptual basis and the implementation of the poll tax were severely lacking. On the implementation side, central government gave little thought to enforceability, transition, or intergovernmental issues. Unlike property, residents are mobile. Annual population turnover rates were as high as 36 percent in some rural areas and up to 55 percent in inner London. This made it quite difficult to ensure that people registered for the tax. Local governments recognized the compliance problems immediately and opposed the legislation on those grounds.

Smith (1991) notes that, in response to their opposition to the tax, local governments may have set the tax higher than it needed to be. That is, they may have used the change in regimes as a way to increase their own spending, gambling that the concomitant increase in taxes would be blamed on the central government and would increase the unpopularity of the tax. Recall that even small increases in local spending would generate large percentage increases in the required poll tax. The average poll tax ended up being 30 percent higher than predicted and more than double what was proposed in 1987.

The tax change redistributed resources across regions and across families within regions. The major regional winners were areas with high property values in southeast England, an area with strong conservative support. Within regions, multiadult households lost relative to single-adult households. In response to the losses created by redistribution, the national government set up a safety net of compensating payments from "winning" regions to "losing" regions, to be phased out over several years. This system proved inadequate in several dimensions. It raised costs and reduced support for the poll tax in the winning regions, it did nothing to address within-region redistribution across families, and it only redistributed local burdens—it did not reduce the overall local burden, on average.

On the conceptual side, the tax change replaced a set of taxes based loosely on ability-to-pay with one based loosely on the benefit principle. Smith (1991), however, argues that a poll tax is an inappropriate application even of the benefit principle. While it is certainly true that not all taxes need to be progressive to make the overall tax system progressive, it seems clear that voters rejected the idea that, for example, Buckingham palace staff should have to remit more in community charges than the royals themselves.

Moreover, while the poll tax clearly raised the local marginal costs of increasing expenditures, Smith (1991) argues further that it may have done little to improve accountability, since voting mechanisms, in general, are not efficient and local choices, in particular, are often constrained by national parties. Thus, localities received the burden of higher marginal costs without much in the way of increased autonomy.

For all of these reasons, the poll tax came to be regarded as extraordinarily unfair and ultimately unmanageable. Nonpayment campaigns developed, and estimated nonpayment rates reached 50 percent in some areas. A member of parliament was arrested for not paying the tax. More than 20 percent of taxpayers required a summons before paying the poll tax, 7 times higher than the proportion requiring a summons under the old property tax. Noncompliance was not due primarily to unfamiliarity with the tax, since noncompliance rates rose over time (Besley, Preston, and Ridge, 1997). The administrative costs of local taxes tripled in the first year of the poll tax. Disapproval rates reached 90 percent.

In the second year, the central government provided some overall transition relief in the form of reducing the burden of the poll tax, but the die had been cast. The poll tax was abandoned shortly thereafter, by the Conservative party that proposed it in the first place, on grounds that it was uncollectible.

The new council tax, initiated in 1993, is a function of property value and the number of adults in the households and raised about 20 percent of local revenue in 1995–6. Properties are placed in certain classes based on their value in April, 1991. The rate structure applied to the classes is determined by the national government,[22] but the rate levels are determined by local government. This system allows the national government to control the progressivity of the tax burden, but lets the local government determine the overall level of the tax burden (and spending).

There is obviously much to learn from these events. Smith (1991) lists some appropriate conclusions: the importance of adminstrability and equity in determining whether a tax can remain in place, and the need for transition relief if significant tax restructurings are to be politically palatable. Besley, Preston, and Ridge, (1997) note emerging compliance problems in the council tax, and

suggest that this may be an effect of the poll tax. Hence, the longer-run effects on compliance may also be important. They also note that compliance can present problems even in countries with a well-developed tax and monitoring system.

One odd aspect of the entire episode, from an American perspective, is the extent to which central government can dictate local tax policy. This raises obvious issues of autonomy as well as principal/agent problems. The central government wanted to change the behavior of local governments in a way that the locals resisted. To accomplish this goal, the central government needed and expected the cooperation of local governments. There is some evidence to suggest that such co-operation did not occur. The agency problems that arise when one government is expected to enforce another government's taxes is a little explored area of public finance. The issue relates directly, however, to proposals that would establish a national retail sales tax in the United States that would be collected by the states.

A final set of observations falls under the general category "an old tax is a good tax." The property tax clearly suffered from technical complexities in determining rental values and political difficulties in adjusting values. But Besley, Preston, and Ridge, (1997) describe the property tax as a 600-year-old system that faced little non-compliance and was based, at least loosely, on ability-to-pay. Smith (1991) notes that the property tax was easy to administer. This is not to say that all taxes should stay the way they are, just that major changes in taxes should take careful account of the costs and benefits of the existing and new systems, as well as the transition costs of establishing the new system. Moreover, the fairness, or perceived fairness, of new taxes that are quite different from the ones they replace appears to be an important constraint on policy options. In short, the poll tax episode is, among other things, a case in point about the dangers of overselling the theoretical and empirical advantages of tax reform and about ignoring fairness, transition, and administrative considerations in developing new tax proposals.

Conclusions

The British and American tax systems have much in common, several important differences and experiences, and much to learn from each other.

One major theme is that the structure and administration of the British income tax are much simpler than those of its American counterpart. It seems quite plausible that differences in administrative arrangements led to important differences in the structure of income taxes in the two countries. This could have happened directly, in that some tax subsidies are simply too difficult to handle in a no-return system. Or it could have happened indirectly, in the sense that, when people do not file tax returns very often, they do not immediately look to the tax code as the natural way to subsidize various activities.

In any case, the British example shows that the United States income tax could be much simpler if Americans were willing to reduce the extent to which the income tax attempted to tax all income or tried to administer social policy through the tax code. A larger issue, unexamined here, is whether the resulting tax/transfer system would end up being more efficient and equitable.

A second major difference is the importance of consumption taxes in the United Kingdom relative to the United States. The experience of Britain and other countries shows that a VAT could be established in the United States to replace a substantial component of income tax revenues, but that VATs are neither as simple, nor as much of an elixir for growth, as is sometimes claimed. Also, the willingness of the population to accept the VAT, in the United Kingdom and in other countries, may be conditioned heavily on social spending programs that are more generous than those found in the United States.

It would be of great interest to pursue the behavioral effects of these differences in tax policy: that is, do taxes matter? Detailed investigations along these lines are beyond the scope of the paper, but it is interesting to note that, despite the virtual elimination of mortgage interest subsidies and of capital gains taxes, Britain is neither suffering from a collapse in housing nor benefiting from an extraordinary boom in investment and entrepreneurship. As these are two of the most controversial sets of issues in America, further investigation is clearly warranted.

It would be interesting also to pursue further the role of differing political systems and institutions on the conduct of tax policy (see also Keen, 1997). In the British parliamentary system, the party in control often has much more power than the majority party in Congress. Thus, one might imagine that parties with such extensive authority could push through tax breaks for whatever favored constituency they chose. Yet the British system seems, at least at a distance, to be remarkably devoid of such loopholes, at least relative to the American system. Why that is the case would be an interesting further "lesson" for America. One possibility is the differing role of campaign contributions in the two countries (Keen, 1997; Graetz, 1997).

Recent changes in the income tax and the corporate tax suggest that Britain may be moving in the direction of the American tax system in certain ways. It is difficult to know what to make of this development. It seems unlikely to be due to any inherent superiority of the American approach to taxation. Rather, the change may be best interpreted as part of the cyclical variation one would naturally expect as taxpayers and political leaders continue to make trade-offs among policies that support the conflicting goals of equity, efficiency, simplicity, and revenue requirements.

ENDNOTES

I have received very helpful advice and comments from Orazio Attanasio, Gerry Auten, James Banks, Richard Blundell, Edie Brashares, Len Burman, Richard Disney, Howard Glennerster, Rachel Griffith, Janet Holtzblatt, John Hills, Michael Keen, Joel Slemrod, Stephen Smith, and Eric Toder. I thank Jasper Hoek and Stacie Carney for research assistance, and am particularly grateful to Joel Slemrod for suggesting the project, the National Tax Association for funding, and scholars at the Institute for Fiscal Studies and the London School of Economics for their hospitality and insights. All errors remain my own.

[1] Unless otherwise noted, factual information on the British tax system was taken from Dilnot and Stears (1997), Kay and King (1990), King and Robson (1993), Inland Revenue (1996), and HMSO (1996).

[2] Several conceptual problems arise. The value of a tax expenditure depends in part on which taxes are considered part of the "normal" tax structure and what is considered a normal design for each of those taxes, as well as the level of tax rates. The level of tax expenditures will depend on a country's willingness to provide resources via spending programs versus tax preferences.

[3] The United States data in Table 2 apply only to federal taxes, but similar qualitative findings occur when state and local taxes are included as well (Gale, Houser, and Scholz, 1996).

[4] For readers interested in converting the figures to dollars, the British pound was worth about $1.63 as of the writing of this paper. In the past ten years, the value has fluctuated between $1.50 and $1.80.

[5] Taxes on self-employment income are outside the PAYE system, because there were too many disagreements between tax authorities and taxpayers to make the system work well. Kay and King (1990) describe the taxation of self-employment income as follows: "It is impossible to provide a brief and intelligible—or indeed lengthy and intelligible—description of the rules."

[6] Under either a TAR or an exact withholding system, households need to file information to allow withholding to occur. Worldwide, about 30 countries practice some form of TAR, while only the United Kingdom and the Russian Federation use exact withholding systems.

[7] Applying the limit to each property, rather than to all properties owned by a taxpayer, prevents two single people living together from each receiving tax benefits on separate loans of up to £30,000, which would represent an implicit marriage tax.

[8] For example, if the interest rate fell by one-third, the tax rate against which the deduction occurs fell by half, and the real loan limit fell by four-fifths, the current subsidy would be worth less than ten percent of the subsidy in 1974.

[9] The debate largely centers around the effects on the price of housing. See Capozza, Green, and Hendershott (1996) and Holtz-Eakin (1996) for divergent views.

[10] Capital gains tax relief is also available for entrepreneurs who sell their assets upon retirement. As in the United States, the death of the owner does not trigger capital gains tax payments under the income tax.

[11] These estimates are based on "stacking" capital gains income last. That is, the estimates calculate income and taxes due without capital gains, and then add capital gains to income and calculate the increase in taxes.

[12] As of 1996, taxpayers in the highest tax bracket faced rates of 39.6 percent on ordinary income and 28 percent on capital gains. This is equivalent to a 29 percent exclusion of capital gains income for those taxpayers.

[13] Originally, PEP funds had to be invested in equity in United Kingdom firms, but that requirement has been dropped.

[14] See Disney and Johnson (1997), Disney and Whitehouse (1992), and Banks, Blundell, and Dilnot (1994).

[15] The rebate has been cut back and is now structured more generously toward older workers than toward younger workers.

[16] The current set of proposals would change the parameters of the VAT to conform with the

absence of border controls. The specific components include abolition of zero-rating exports in exchange for extending the VAT "chain" to include cross-border transactions; uniform VAT rates and bases across countries; allocation of VAT revenues across European countries in relation to aggregate consumption rather than to derivation of revenues; establishing a single "location" for each business; and cross-country cooperation and supervision of VAT administration. These provisions raise a host of concerns about tax administration, equity, and incentives. See Smith (1997).

[17] Under the alternative approach—a subtraction-method VAT—firms add up their sales, subtract their purchases, and pay VAT on the difference. Both methods give the same tax payments when all goods and services are included in the VAT and are taxed at the same rate. The credit-invoice method facilitates special treatment of different goods and services.

[18] The company won the case, but a little real-time empirical research revealed that the Jaffa cake looks, feels, and tastes like what the British call a biscuit and, in a sample of one shop, is even sold on the biscuit shelf.

[19] The shareholder in the 24 percent bracket would owe total taxes of £30 (=0.24 × 125), but would have been deemed to have paid £25 already. The shareholder in the 40 percent bracket would owe total taxes of £50 (=0.40 × 125), but would have been deemed to have paid £25 already.

[20] Smith (1991) and Besley, Preston, and Ridge (1997) provide detailed and informative studies of the poll tax.

[21] For example, if the poll tax raised £25 out of £100, raising spending to £115 would require raising poll tax revenues to £40, a 60 percent increase.

[22] For example, property in one value class is assigned a rate of one, and policies in other classes are assigned rates ranging from 2/3 to 2.

REFERENCES

Attanasio, Orazio, and James Banks. *Trends in Household Saving: A Tale of Two Countries.* London: Institute for Fiscal Studies, 1997.

Banks, James, and Richard Blundell. "Taxation and Personal Saving Incentives in the United Kingdom." In *Public Policies and Household Saving*, edited by James M. Poterba, 57–80. Chicago: University of Chicago Press and NBER, 1994.

Banks, James, Richard Blundell, and Andrew Dilnot. *Tax-Based Saving Incentives in the UK.* Mimeo. Paris, OECD, 1994.

Besley, Timothy, Ian Preston, and Michael Ridge. "Fiscal Anarchy in the U.K.: Modelling Poll Tax Noncompliance." *Journal of Public Economics* 64 (, 1997).

Blumenthal, Marsha, and Joel Slemrod. "The Compliance Costs of the U.S. Individual Income Tax System: A Second Look After Tax Reform." *National Tax Journal* 45 No. 2 (June, 1992): 185–202.

Burman, Leonard E., and William Randolph. "Measuring Permanent Response to Capital Gains Tax Changes in Panel Data." *American Economic Review* 84 No. 4 (September, 1994): 794–809.

Burman, Leonard E., and Peter D. Ricoy. "Capital Gains and the People Who Realize Them." *National Tax Journal* 50 No.4 (September, 1997): 427–51.

Capozza, Dennis R., Richard K. Green, and Patric H. Hendershott. "Taxes, Mortgage Borrowing, and Residential Land Prices." In *Economic Effects of Fundamental Tax Reform*, edited by Henry J. Aaron and William G. Gale, 171–210. Washington, D.C.: Brookings Institution Press, 1996

Dilnot, Andrew, and Gary Stears. *A Short Survey of the British Tax System.* London: Institute for Fiscal Studies, 1997.

Disney, Richard, and Paul Johnson. *The United Kingdom: A Working System of Minimum Pensions?* Institute for Fiscal Studies. Mimeo, 1997.

Disney, Richard, and Edward Whitehouse. *The Personal Pensions Stampede.* London: Institute for Fiscal Studies, 1992.

Financial Statement and Budget Report 1997–8. London: HMSO, 1996.

Fleener, Patrick, ed. *Facts and Figures on Government Finance.* Washington, D.C.: Tax Foundation, 1997.

Gale, William G., and Janet Holtzblatt. "On the Possibility of a No-Return Tax System." *National Tax Journal* 50 No. 3 (September, 1997): 475–86.

Gale, William G., Scott Houser, and John Karl Scholz. "Distributional Effects of Fundamental Tax Reform." In *Economic Effects of Fundamental Tax Reform*, edited by Henry J. Aaron and William G. Gale, 281–354. Washington, D.C.: Brookings Institution Press, 1996.

Graetz, Michael. *The Decline (and Fall?) of the Income Tax.* New York: W. W. Norton & Co., 1997.

Green, Richard K., and Andrew Reschovsky. "The Design of a Mortgage Interest Tax Credit." National Housing Institute. University of Wisconsin. Mimeo, 1997.

Hills, John. "Comment on United Kingdom." In *World Tax Reform: A Progress Report,* edited by Joseph A. Pechman, 236–43. Washington D.C.: Brookings Institution Press, 1988.

Holtz-Eakin, Douglas. "Comment." In *Economic Effects of Fundamental Tax Reform,* edited by Henry J. Aaron and William G. Gale, 198–210. Washington, D.C.: Brookings Institution Press, 1996.

Inland Revenue. *Inland Revenue Statistics, 1996.* London: HMSO, 1996.

Johnston, David Cay. "British to Adopt American-Style Tax Filing." *New York Times* (February 15, 1996): D6.

Kay, John A., and Mervyn A. King. *The British Tax System.* Oxford: Oxford University Press, 1990.

Keen, Michael. "Peculiar Institutions: A British Perspective on Tax Policy in the United States." *National Tax Journal* 50 No. 4 (December, 1997): 779–802.

King, Mervyn A., and Mark H. Robson. "United Kingdom." In *Tax Reform and the Cost of Capital: An International Comparison,* edited by Dale W. Jorgenson and Ralph Landau, 300–32. Washington, D.C.: Brookings Institution Press, 1993.

Quick, Perry D., and Thomas Neubig. "Tax Burden Comparison: U.S. vs. The Rest of the G-7." *Tax Notes* 65 No. 11 (December 12, 1994): 1409–24.

Sabine, Basil E. V. *A Short History of Taxation.* London: Butterworths, 1980.

Sandford, Cedric, Michael Godwin, and Peter Hardwick. *Administrative and Compliance Costs of Taxation.* Bath: Fiscal Publications, 1989.

Slemrod, Joel. "Which is the Simplest Tax System of Them All?" In *Economic Effects of Fundamental Tax Reform,* edited by Henry J. Aaron and William G. Gale. Washington D.C.: Brookings Institution Press, 1996.

Slemrod, Joel, and Jon Bakija. *Taxing Ourselves: A Citizen's Guide to the Great Debate over Tax Reform.* Cambridge, MA: MIT Press, 1996.

Smith, Peter. "Lessons from the British Poll Tax Disaster." *National Tax Journal* 44 No. 4 Part 2 (December, 1991): 421–36.

Smith, Stephen. "The Definitive Regime of VAT: An Assessment of the European Commission's Proposals." Institute for Fiscal Studies. Mimeo, January, 1997.

U.S. Congressional Budget Office. *An Economic Analysis of the Revenue Provisions of OBRA-93.* Washington, D.C.: 1994.

U.S. General Accounting Office. *Tax Policy: Tax Expenditures Deserve More Scrutiny.* GAO/GGD/AIMD-94-122, Washington, D.C., June, 1994.

PECULIAR INSTITUTIONS: A BRITISH PERSPECTIVE ON TAX POLICY IN THE UNITED STATES

MICHAEL KEEN*

Abstract - *By both effect and example, tax policy in the United States has a huge impact on the rest of the world. This paper explores five features of the American tax system that seem, from a British and European perspective, to be both especially peculiar and potentially instructive. These are the remarkably low overall level of taxation; the absence of a value-added tax (or any other major general national tax on consumption); the absence of any explicit interstate equalization; the marginal subsidization of low earnings under the earned income tax credit; and the fragmentation of power in policymaking, an important aspect of which is the role played by the Constitution.*

INTRODUCTION

The tax policy pursued by the United States has powerful effects far beyond its borders. It has a direct impact on

*University of Essex, Colchester, and Institute for Fiscal Studies, London.

economic activity and well-being in other countries: changes in the tax treatment of savings or investment in the United States, for example, can induce significant capital flows,[1] while ensuring and exploiting the availability to U.S. multinationals of the foreign tax credit on their repatriated profits is a major concern for many countries in designing their corporate taxes. The U.S. tax system is also widely looked to— rightly or wrongly—as an embodiment of best practice. This is true both of the broadest elements of tax strategy—as is evident in the widespread emulation of the base-broadening, rate-cutting strategy of the 1986 Tax Reform Act[2]— and in the most detailed matters of tax design. Many American practitioners clearly regard important features of the U.S. tax system as undesirable or, at any rate, not necessarily to be universally recommended. Nevertheless, any country reviewing its tax structures or administration is sure to ask: How do they do it in America?

Now is an especially good time for British observers to ponder the U.S. tax system, for the new Labour government elected in May 1997 shows signs of being strongly influenced by U.S. tax policy. The first budget of the new Chancellor of the Exchequer had as its centerpiece a "welfare to work" program, with both label and spirit borrowed from the United States. It also foreshadowed a new savings incentive, to be called the Individual Savings Account; the reference to IRAs is clear, though the acronym will have to be changed! The budget speech also referred explicitly to the possibility of introducing a scheme modeled on the Earned Income Tax Credit (EITC). And, not least, the possibility has also been raised of introducing a distinction between short- and long-term capital gains of the kind that was made in the United States until 1986 and reintroduced there in 1990, but which has not been seen in the United Kingdom since 1971.

The American tax policy experience is also of increasing importance from a wider European perspective. For as the European Union evolves toward some as yet unknown form of federalism, the forms and features of federalism elsewhere acquire increasing importance as potential exemplars. The United States is not the only model of federalism, of course, but it is a uniquely successful one and is widely referred to in Europe. Experience with the states' sales taxes, to give one small example, has strongly influenced discussion of the appropriate degree of indirect tax harmonization in Europe. As European integration proceeds further, more fundamental lessons from the United States will be looked for.

This paper explores a few key aspects of American tax policy. No attempt is made to describe the U.S. system,[3] nor is the purpose to draw lessons from one side of the Atlantic to carry over to the other (though there will be some of that). Rather, the object is to explore a handful

of aspects of the American tax experience that, to British and European eyes, are liable to seem distinctly strange. To many American eyes, of course, they will look perfectly normal, and the oddity will be that anyone should find them strange. Of course, it is not oddity that ultimately matters, but whether these features reflect any useful diversity of experience.

There is no shortage to choose from in constructing a list of features of U.S. tax policy that are liable to intrigue British observers: it would include, for example, the use of a classical system of corporation tax, the attempt to tax U.S. citizens wherever in the world they reside, formula apportionment, the alternative minimum taxes, the universality of tax returns, and what seems now to be the almost ubiquitous practice of phasing out the benefit of exemptions through high marginal rates over some interval. The focus here, however, is on just five peculiarities. These are not necessarily the most important; we do not discuss, in particular, key issues in the treatment of savings and investment, which are treated in the companion paper by Gale (1997). Their selection is entirely eclectic: they are interesting, and perhaps instructive.

The five, dealt with in turn, are the very low level of taxes in the United States; the absence of a value-added tax (VAT) (or any other general national tax on consumption); the absence of explicit interstate equalization; the marginal subsidization of low earnings under the EITC; and the peculiarities of tax policymaking, not least the role of the Constitution.

WHY ARE TAXES IN THE UNITED STATES SO LOW?

Many outside observers will have been shocked by President Clinton's announcement, in his 1996 State of the Union address, that "The era of big government is over." Shocked because, by the standards of most advanced economies, the United States has never had big government.

In 1995, taxes (at all levels of government and including social security payments) accounted for about 28 percent of gross domestic product (GDP) in the United States.[4] The average in European OECD countries was nearly 15 points higher, at 42.5 percent of GDP; for the United Kingdom, the ratio was 34 percent. Indeed, on this measure— which, for familiar reasons, is a very imperfect indicator of the extent of government activity (not capturing for example, the extent of regulatory activities)—among all OECD countries only Mexico and Turkey have smaller governments than does the United States. While much of U.S. politics apparently revolves around a perception that taxes are too high, the interesting question is surely the exact opposite: How come taxes in the United States are so low?

A first hypothesis that might occur to the outsider, dimly aware of continual agonizing over the seemingly perennial federal budget crisis, is that perhaps the United States maintains public expenditures at levels comparable to those elsewhere by massive borrowing. But, in fact, the federal deficit[5] is now relatively modest; in 1996; a year of essentially full employment, it ran at 1.4 percent of GDP.[6] This is well within the guidelines for fiscal probity in the Maastricht criteria for participation in the single European currency—the benchmark by which Europeans now instinctively gauge such numbers— which requires a deficit of no more than three percent of GDP. Indeed, in July 1997, agreement was reached on

a package to balance the federal budget by 2002. Deficits have certainly been run at higher levels than these since the early 1980s, resulting in a ratio of federal debt to GDP of 69 percent in 1996. This is above the Maastricht figure of 60 percent, and in that sense looks rather high. But it is by no means unprecedented even in the fiscal history of the United States; the federal debt/GDP ratio is now at roughly the same level as in the mid-1950s.

Nevertheless, work on generational accounting tends to confirm that low taxes in the United States reflect a marked propensity to postpone tax payments. It suggests that irrespective of the current pattern of receipts and expenditures—open, to some degree, to manipulation by judicious relabeling of items—a comparison of the present values of taxes and benefits anticipated under current rules indicates that those currently alive in the United States have made themselves promises—in terms, especially, of pension and health care— that can ultimately be met only by substantial future tax increases. Auerbach, Gokhale, and Kotlikoff (1994), for example, estimate that the lifetime tax rate—the present value of taxes divided by the present value of lifetime incomes—on those born in 1991 was around 34 percent on the rules then in place; but that the lifetime rate required on those born thereafter —in order to balance the books—was 71.1 percent. Thus, the low tax ratio in the United States may well reflect a deferral of higher rates to the future. What is not so clear, however, is whether this deferral is any greater in the United States than in other economies, many of which—not least Japan, with an equally low ratio of taxes to GDP—face even more marked demographic challenges.

A second potential explanation of small government in the United States is by assertion of an American exceptionalism: Americans traditionally dislike government. This is a nation, after all, whose dominant citizens were for centuries virtually self-selected by a deep-rooted fear of oppressive government and in which the only significant home-grown terrorist movement is aimed at the federal government per se. There are traditions here from which both the Chicago and Virginia schools of economic analysis grew, and now in themselves feed—schools which, for all their differences, share a profound mistrust of government. And there is indeed, it seems, some survey evidence that Americans tend to be more hostile to government than other nations.[7] But, historic exceptionalism of this kind, however appealing, will not entirely do as an explanation of low taxes in the United States, for the divergence of tax levels in the United States from those in most of its natural comparator countries is relatively recent. In 1900, the ratio of government spending to GDP in the United States was about eight percent, midway between the levels for the United Kingdom (ten percent) and Germany (six percent).[8] As late as 1970, the tax ratio in the United States (29.2 percent)—though lower than that in the United Kingdom (36.9 percent)—was almost exactly the same as in the European OECD (30.7 percent). Since then, the United States and the United Kingdom have been almost unique among OECD member countries in maintaining broadly constant tax ratios, while in others—including such old industrial nations as France and Germany, and even Japan—taxes have very substantially increased. Much of the most interesting divergence has thus occurred in the last 25 years.

But, although the notion of a generalized distrust of government cannot in itself provide an entirely satisfactory explanation of small government in the United States, there are persistent differences between the United States and its natural comparators in the role perceived for government. Perhaps the most fundamental of these is the relatively low expenditure on social transfers (meaning pensions, welfare, unemployment, and health). This is deep seated: Lindert (1994, Table 1A) reports that throughout the 50 years from 1880 the United States spent a significantly smaller proportion of GDP on social transfers than did either Germany or the United Kingdom, and indeed finds a tendency for such transfers to have grown less in the United States over the period than one would predict on the basis of demographic and other considerations: some sign, that is, of American exceptionalism in this regard. By 1990, social transfers stood at 12.2 percent of GDP in the United States compared to 16.2 percent in the United Kingdom and well over 20 percent in other European countries.[9] Indeed the divergence between tax/GDP ratios that we seek to understand arises very largely because the United States did not participate in the further growth of social transfers over the last thirty years or so. Broadly then, to explain low taxes in the United States, one has to explain relatively low programmatic redistribution there—or high redistribution elsewhere—especially since about 1970.

This though leads to a puzzle. One would expect one of the primary determinants of the extent of redistribution to be the extent of pretax inequality, with simple models predicting that greater inequality will lead to more redistribution. In an optimal tax context, greater inequality is likely to increase the weight placed on the equity gain from redistribution relative to the efficiency losses. In a voting context, greater inequality is usually expected to increase the gap between median and mean incomes, leading to more redistribution (because the loss to the median voter from an increase in the tax rate, which depends on her own income, is now reduced relative to her gain from the increased amount available for redistribution, which depends on mean income).[10] Since the United States is characterized by relatively high interpersonal income inequality, one might on both counts expect to observe more redistribution in the United States than elsewhere: exactly the opposite, that is, of what we actually do seem to observe.

In fact, this is but one instance of a more general puzzle. For it seems to an empirical regularity—first noted by Peltzman (1980) and recently confirmed by Persson (1995)—that greater inequality actually seems to lead to *less* redistribution and *smaller* governments. Why this might be remains unclear. Lindert (1996), building on Peltzman's argument, explains it in terms of social affinity: greater inequality means less commonality of identity between middle and lower classes, weakening their ability and inclination to win redistribution toward themselves. Persson (1995) builds an alternative explanation on the notion that people care not only about the level of their own incomes but also about their incomes relative to those of others. This creates an externality that leads people to work too hard—because they neglect the envy their earnings cause others—so that introducing a linear income tax in an economy with relatively little pretax inequality can make everyone better off: it mitigates the externality by discourag-

ing effort, an effect which may lead even those who lose (a little) from the direct effect of redistribution to support it. This explanation is not entirely compelling: such preferences imply, for example, that the nonpoor would actually gain by taking resources away from the poor and simply throwing them away. Thus, the regularity, if such it is, remains mysterious. There may be other and more particular factors also at work in the U.S. context. For instance, snapshot measures of income inequality may significantly overstate the inequality in lifetime incomes relative to other countries; and the ease and willingness with which labor moves across the United States may reduce the need for social insurance.

This brings us to a third potential explanation of low taxes in the United States, which is one of special interest in the nascent federal context of the European Union: perhaps the low tax ratio reflects the constraints imposed by interstate tax competition. There is of course a strong vein in American federalism—dating back to the *Federalist Papers* and powerfully articulated by Brennan and Buchanan (1980)—which sees competition between the states as a key weapon in the armory of checks on tyranny: through the mobility of people, capital and commodities, and the scope for yardstick competition in evaluating politicians, competition between the states places downward pressure on tax rates that provides the citizenry with some protection from grasping governments.

There is a sizable empirical literature, stimulated by Oates (1985), addressed to the question of whether greater centralization of tax powers is associated with larger government. This remains broadly inconclusive, but it is the case that, within the OECD countries, and conditional on both the level of national income and the ratio of central to total taxes, the ratio of tax to GDP is significantly lower in federal countries.[11] But the effect is slight: less than one percentage point of GDP. Moreover, both Canada and Switzerland have participated in the general increase in tax/GDP ratios since 1970, so that federalism itself does not seem to account for U.S. experience.

Indeed, the conventional presumption that federalism is conducive to low tax rates is itself open to question. For although horizontal tax competition between the states may be expected to exert downward pressure on tax rates, recent work has emphasized that co-occupation of the same tax base by both federal and state levels of government may create a vertical tax externality that points in exactly the opposite direction.[12] An increase in the tax rate levied by either level of government reduces the common tax base and so adversely affects the revenues of the other level. If this effect is not fully internalized—and it seems plausible to suppose, for example, that many states will neglect the loss that they impose on other states by raising their own tax rates and consequently reducing federal revenues and, hence, expenditures—the combined (federal plus state) tax rate on the shared tax base will wind up excessively high. How real an issue this is for the United States is unclear. On one hand, the extent of co-occupation is clearly considerable: over 97 percent of the federal tax base is shared with the states.[13] On the other, it is also clear that the combined tax rates on many shared bases, such as cigarettes, are far from high by international standards.

It is conceivable, of course, that the operation of such vertical externalities means that taxes are higher than they should be in the United States, even though they are at the same time relatively low by international standards. That would be consistent indeed with much of the tenor of U.S. politics.

TAXING CONSUMPTION (OR NOT)

Probably the single most peculiar feature of the American tax system is the absence of a VAT.[14] All other major countries apart from Australia (which is thinking of introducing one)—and pretty well all minor countries too—now have a VAT (in substance, if not always in name). Indeed, indirect taxes in general are extraordinarily low in the United States. There are general sales taxes at state and local levels,[15] of course, but these are light: the average statutory rate is about 5 percent, and sales tax revenues took only about 2.2 percent of GDP in 1992, compared to 7.4 percent in the European OECD. Excises too are very low, taking 2.1 percent of GDP rather than 4.7. Low indirect taxes clearly go a very long way toward accounting for the relatively low tax ratio in the United States.

It is thus no surprise that the possibility of a greater role for consumption taxes has been widely discussed in the United States. What is surprising is the normal context of such discussions. Surely the obvious way of dealing with the long-term budget crisis was—is—by introducing a general federal consumption tax of some form. Indeed, an early response to the emerging deficits of the Depression era was to propose a national sales tax. But all such proposals have failed. Instead, the context in which radical movements toward consumption taxation are most usually discussed—which, as Auerbach and Slemrod (1997) observe, has remained strikingly disjoint from the budget crisis discussions—is that of fundamental tax reform. Indeed, the very term "fundamental tax reform," as used in the United States, seems now to be virtually synonymous with the question of whether it would be desirable to shift toward some form of general consumption tax.

Ten years after the 1986 Tax Reform Act (TRA 86), it seems that fundamental tax reform is returning to the political agenda (an excellent account of the issues and options is provided in Aaron and Gale (1996a)). It is striking, indeed, how rapidly many of the central features of the TRA 86 began to unravel. The TRA 86 was the paradigmatic move toward comprehensive income taxation, with capital gains (albeit only nominal) taxed as other income and significant measures of base broadening and rate reduction. Yet, preferential tax treatment of capital gains did not take long to re-emerge—the top rates of personal tax on income and capital gains are now 39.6 and 20 percent—nor did the special pleading for such breaks as the tuition credits. Perhaps even more striking is that the response to these difficulties has been to return to essentially the same policy agenda as in the 1980s, with the alternative strategy most widely canvased again being the replacement of (personal and corporate) income taxes by some form of consumption tax: the class of options, that is, which so spectacularly lost the political battle (though perhaps not the intellectual one) against the comprehensive income tax.

Consumption taxes come in many forms, and the U.S. tax policy debate has thrown up an impressive array of proposals: a VAT of some form, a retail sales tax, a flat tax, the USA tax. Of the many issues that they raise—a compre-

hensive account being provided by the contributions in Aaron and Gale (1996b)—we focus on just two.

The first is implicit in what has already been said: How is it that the United States has resisted the charms of a VAT, which have so beguiled tax policy-makers in almost every other country in the world?

The barroom explanation most commonly given seems to be that, simply put, Republicans oppose a VAT because they think it would prove a money machine for inherently untrustworthy governments and Democrats oppose it because they think it would prove regressive. Neither view is compelling.

Compared in the usual way—with people ranked by their current incomes—a uniform VAT certainly looks regressive compared to the present income tax.[16] But, of course, that is not the only comparison of interest, either conceptually or as a guide to practical policy. Conceptually, it is well-known that, when viewed from a perspective of lifetime welfare, a proportional tax on consumption may be more equitable—both horizontally (taking the same present value of revenue from those with the same lifetime opportunities) and vertically—than one on income. Movement to a VAT might also have broadly progressive asset price effects.[17] In practice, however, it is surely hard to conceive of a wholesale replacement of the current income tax by a sales tax applied at a uniform rate to all commodities. There would doubtless be pressures for rate differentiation—which, of course, has its cost in terms of simplicity and, perhaps, efficiency—of the kind that have led in the United Kingdom to the zero rating and exempting of many sensitive items (amounting to well over 40 percent of consumer expenditure). A VAT might also be accompanied by compensating income transfers, as in the Canadian Goods and Services Tax: Feenberg et al. (1997) show that such measures can also substantially affect the progressivity effects of shifting to a general sales tax.

The money machine concern seems even less well-placed. One can perhaps concoct an argument for restricting untrustworthy politicians to inefficient instruments as a way of increasing the political cost to them of increasing taxes. But surely it would be better to impose constitutional limitations—of a kind that, as discussed later, U.S. policy-makers put such faith in—on overall levels of expenditure, while enabling this to be financed in the most efficient way.

Even taken on its own terms, moreover, there is a sense in which the money-machine fear is ultimately unconvincing, for a uniform VAT is equivalent, to anyone born after its introduction, to the combination of a wage tax and an inheritance tax,[18] and the federal government already has both of those instruments at its disposal. In the long run, a uniform VAT thus adds nothing to the federal government's power to tax. In the shorter term, things are different. For those alive at the time of its intro-duction, a uniform VAT is equivalent to a tax on their future and current earnings—again, an instrument already available—plus one on the financial assets they have built up under the previous tax regime. The federal government already has devices by which it might, in principle, impose capital levies, but nothing quite as powerful as this. Perhaps then, the money-machine concern is best seen as another aspect of the standard transi-tion problem that arises in moving to any form of consumption tax, not just a

VAT: concern at the prospect of substan-tial intergenerational redistribution through an implicit levy on the initial wealth of current generations. At which point, of course, the argument is again essentially one of equity.

A quite different but perhaps no less fundamental obstacle to the adoption of a federal VAT, emphasized by McLure (1987), is the issue of how this would relate to the pre-existing retail sales taxes (RSTs) of the states. This has two aspects. One is the political issue of states' rights, general sales taxation having previously been preserved—de facto, not as a constitutional right—to the states. The other is technical: how does one best combine a federal VAT with continuing state sales taxation?

On this latter, one possibility is to superimpose a federal VAT on existing state RSTs. The bases and administration of the two taxes would likely be so different, however (services, for ex-ample, would be within the VAT net but are effectively excluded from the state RSTs), that this would be a very cumber-some structure. And converting the states to VATs, which are then simply piggybacked on the federal VAT, has its own problems. The key issue here is the treatment of interstate sales, the difficulty being to eliminate any risk of strategic tax setting by the states— seeking to advantage themselves at the expense of others—while securing the VAT chain (and maintaining the identical administrative treatment of inter- and intrastate sales) by avoiding, if possible, the zero rating of out-of state sales. These same issues currently arise in several federal contexts, not least in the European Union; for the traditional VAT, whose appeal is very largely the ease with which it handles international transactions, has difficulty reconciling the aspirations to both a preservation of sovereignty at lower levels of government and seamless economic integration between them, which is a hallmark of federal systems.

There is, though, one form of VAT that goes a long way toward reconciling these objectives. This is the "VIVAT," proposed in a European context by Keen and Smith (1996). Though the problems in Europe are very different, this scheme also seems to provide a natural structure for the United States. Its key feature is that there would be two distinct rates of tax for any item: one for purchases by VAT-registered traders (at, say, 10 percent) and the other on final sales (at, say, 13 percent).[19] This, in turn, is equivalent to the combination of a VAT of the usual kind levied at ten percent (on all transactions) and an RST (albeit with a broader—better—base than state RSTs at present) of three percent. The obvious strategy in the U.S. setting then is to allocate the former component to the federal government and the latter to the states. The state RSTs would thus be replaced by a tax charged by all VAT-registered traders on all sales to those not so registered. They are thus integrated into a coherent national VAT structure, with no need for restrictions on states' sovereignty in tax setting or for any reallocation of tax revenues across states. In this way, existing state RSTs can be combined with a federal VAT in such a way that the only structural changes required of the states look like improvements.

A second set of questions is prompted by the observation that the principal item on the menu of fundamental tax reform—offered in various dishes—is exactly the same as 20 years ago: consumption taxation. What have we—or should we have—learned since the time of the U.S. Treasury's *Blueprints*[20] and the Meade (1978) report?

The balance of the arguments made for consumption taxation has certainly changed. One of the merits especially emphasized in the 1970s was the ease of dealing with inflation. This is no longer to the fore. Now the emphasis is much more on simplification—the TRA 86 strategy being seen as less than a complete success in this regard[21]—and, especially for academic writers, the desire to exclude from tax the return to savings. Of course in many respects—such as the IRAs—the U.S. system already offers consumption tax treatment. The question is whether to move to such a system thoroughly and explicitly.

On this issue, it seems to bear emphasizing, again, that the theoretical case for a pure consumption tax is not overwhelming. The limitations are familiar to many of those most active in the U.S. debate (many of whom have indeed helped develop them), but seem all too often to be at risk of being forgotten. One thing we should surely have learned over the last 20 years is that the optimal rate of tax on capital income in an economy like the United States is almost certainly not zero. The well-known results of Chamley (1986) and Lucas (1990), with optimally zero rates, may seem to say otherwise. But these rely on a dynastic view of intergenerational relationships that is increasingly mistrusted as a useful approximation of reality—and outside of which the optimal tax treatment of capital turns sensitively on issues of preference structure and debt policy (see, for example, King (1980))—and sidestep a profound time consistency issue by supposing governments are able to commit credibly to zero taxation of capital. Nor, contrary to an impression sometimes given, is the optimality of a zero rate on capital income a corollary of the Diamond–Mirrlees (1971) theorem on production efficiency.[22] For a small economy that is unable to monitor its residents' income from investments abroad, it may indeed be optimal not to tax the return to saving; but that hardly seems to be the position of the United States.

While sole reliance on consumption taxation is thus unlikely to be fully optimal for the United States, the same is also true of a comprehensive income tax; indeed, there seem to be no known circumstances in which—as a matter of principle rather than a requirement to control avoidance—it is optimal to tax labor and capital income at the same rate. But rather than focus on the two extremes of consumption and comprehensive income taxation—or indeed on the uneasy hybrids of the two that have emerged in the U.S. and elsewhere— perhaps one should explicitly consider the possibility that these two kinds of income might optimally be taxed at different nonzero rates.

One such scheme—arguably the most important innovation in tax policy since the TRA 86—is that developed in the Nordic countries since the start of the 1990s (and very nicely described in Sørensen (1994, 1997)). The archetypal Nordic scheme comprises a flat (and low) personal rate on capital income (at the same rate as that on corporate income) plus a progressive tax on labor income. Put differently, this is essentially the Hall–Rabushka (1983) tax, except that the tax on wage income may take a general nonlinear form and a flat tax is levied on even the normal return to capital. Here then is a scheme that provides a third alternative to the consumption and comprehensive income tax options that have so dominated the fundamental tax reform debate in the United States and elsewhere for the last 20 years. Such a system could have helped deal with

many of the concerns that the TRA 86 attempted to address, such as the inter-asset variation in effective marginal tax rates and—something a pure Nordic system would eliminate but a progressive income tax intrinsically invites—the arbitrage possibilities and distortions arising from interpersonal variation in marginal tax rates on capital income.[23] Whether the approach has much to offer the United States now is not immediately clear; obviously, the Nordic system reflects the particular experience of being a small player in increasingly globalized world markets. But perhaps the United States is evolving toward some such system, with a differential opening up between the progressive taxation of labor income and the taxation of capital income—assuming one can choose to take it as capital gains, when preferable—at a lower and fairly flat rate. Perhaps an explicit recognition of this, along Nordic lines, would help the task of simplification.

One last observation on the consumption tax debate. In pondering a wholesale move to consumption taxation, it is natural for the United States to look for examples to follow elsewhere in the world, and to be discouraged by their absence. It may then be worth bearing in mind that one of the principal reasons others have rejected the consumption tax route is their view that the U.S. Treasury would not regard a cash flow tax as eligible for foreign tax credits. A country that adopted the Hall–Rabushka tax, for example, would find that U.S. multinationals might well be unable to claim foreign tax credits on repatriating their profits to the United States. For many countries, indeed, this is enough to immediately preclude movement to cash flow taxation.[24] It would be a shame if the world were to find itself locked into an inefficient equilibrium, with the United States discouraged by an absence of successful experiments in consumption taxation elsewhere that, in itself, reflects U.S. policy.

FEDERALISM WITHOUT EQUALIZATION

All men may be created equal, but the states of the Union have surely been very differently endowed by their creator. The same is true, of course, of very many federations. Others, however, respond to these differences in a way that the United States does not: by arranging explicitly equalizing transfers between the states. In Canada—the most obvious comparator for the United States—the principle of inter-state equalization is written into the Constitution, and such payments amount to about 15 percent of the recipient provinces' revenues from their own sources. Switzerland, too, implements explicit equalization across the cantons. This is on a somewhat smaller scale, but still substantial: about 13 percent of federal tax revenues is redistributed across the cantons in accordance with population and fiscal capacity. Australia, India and Germany also operate explicit equalization across the second-tier jurisdictions. The United States stands alone among the federations of the advanced economies[25] in its failure to equalize across the states.[26] For a Europe that appears to be advancing toward some form of federal structure, and in which the prospect of monetary union has raised questions as to the potential for a new and enhanced role for inter-jurisdictional transfers, this further peculiarity of the American experience is of special interest. How is this absence of equalization to be explained?

There are broadly three purposes that might be served by an equalization system (by which we mean one of unconditional horizontal transfers across the states): horizontal redistribution, insurance in the face of state-specific shocks, and the correction of market distortions. Does none of these call for explicit equalization in the United States?

The immediately relevant dimension of redistribution here is not between persons—national views on this are presumably dealt with through the federal tax-transfer system—but between state governments. And the rationale for this is presumably a view that irrespective, to some degree, of their own resources, states should be able to afford similar levels of public provision of key goods and services. This is made explicit in Section 36 of the Canadian Constitution, which envisages equalization payments sufficient ". . . to ensure that provincial governments have sufficient revenues to provide reasonably comparable levels of public service at reasonably comparable levels of taxation." Viewed in this light, equalization is essentially a matter of ensuring horizontal equity across the nation, with a belief in the legitimacy of this seen as key part—to some, almost a definition—of nationhood. Note, too, that this view of equalization as facilitating the public provision of some key goods comes very close to a rationale for conditional grants, so that the line between equalizing payments and conditional grants can become blurred. Interestingly, litigation in a number of states—following the decision of the California Supreme Court in the *Serrano* case in 1976—has enjoined some equalization of spending on education *within* states. No such imperative has emerged for equalization across the states themselves.

Is there then any less need for interstate redistribution of this kind in the United

States than elsewhere? Certainly interstate income inequality seems to be somewhat lower in the United States than in some natural comparator federations, though not dramatically so;[27] in 1991, the coefficient of variation of gross state product per capita was about 0.22 in the United States, compared to 0.28 in Canada and 0.24 in Switzerland. Australia, however, implements an equalization system despite apparently much lower interstate inequality (with a coefficient of variation in 1995–96 of around 0.12).[28]

Or perhaps significant redistribution does, in fact, occur between the states of the United States, but it is simply not labeled equalization.[29]

The question this raises is whether, in fact if not in name, federal transfers to the states tend to favor the poorer among them. From their purposes and structure, one might suspect that they would. Well over half of all federal grants to the states in 1994, for example, were for Medicaid and family benefits, and so might be expected to benefit most the most distressed states; moreover, the rates at which the federal government matches these state expenditures decrease with the state's per capita income. Other items supported by grants—highway improvements, for instance—can presumably also be targeted, de facto, to poorer regions. Is it then the case that states whose gross state product per capita is low tend to receive more federal aid per capita? The answer is a firm "No": in 1993, states' receipts of federal grants-in-aid per capita—taken in the widest sense, including payments related to Medicaid, Aid for Families with Dependent Children (AFDC), roads, education, and so on—were essentially unrelated to their GSP per capita.[30] Part of the explanation may lie in the importance of

matching grants: poorer states can afford only lower target levels of expenditure—lower benefit levels for AFDC, for example—and so may end up attracting no more federal support despite, perhaps, facing a more generous matching rate.

One might take a wider view of the potential role of the federal government in redistributing across the states by also taking account of both federal taxes and benefits (such as social security) that the federal government pays directly to individuals. The progressivity of these will mean that average state incomes are more equal after its operation than before. This does not directly redistribute between state governments, of course, but it does, in a broad sense, equalize their tax bases. Looking at the combined effects of taxes, transfers, and grants, Bayoumi and Masson (1995) find the net impact of the federal government to be progressive: a $1 increase in average state income leads to a reduction of about 22 cents in net receipts from the federal government. Somewhat higher figures have been found (using slightly different methodologies) by Sala-i-Martin and Sachs (1992) and MacDougall (1977): 35–44 and 25 cents on the dollar. This implicit equalization does look rather low compared to that found in other federations: the analogous figure has been put at 30–39 percent for Canada[31] and at 35 cents for the United Kingdom and Germany.

Though the reconciliation of these various results is not entirely clear, it seems that there is very little (if any) interstate redistribution through the full set of grants-in-aid, but that—in terms of the interstate distribution of net incomes—the progressivity of federal taxes and transfers more than compensates. The full extent of implicit interstate redistribution in the United States, though not high, is far from zero.

The second potential role of equalization is as a source of insurance for the states. Of course, the kind of interstate redistribution just discussed can itself be thought of, to some degree, as a form of social insurance—behind the veil of ignorance as to how the states will be endowed, all might wish to mutually insure each other—but here we have in mind a role in stabilizing shorter-term macroeconomic disturbances. The focus thus shifts from equalization across the cross section of states to the smoothing of each state's income or consumption over time. Asdrubali et al. (1996) estimate that the extent of federal smoothing is fairly substantial (around 13 cents on the dollar) and perhaps even greater than in Canada,[32] but that other devices—investing in or borrowing from other states—are qualitatively more significant. Moreover, although smoothing of state consumption remains incomplete, it seems that there is little scope for a beneficial expansion of the federal insurance role, much of this remaining risk being undiversifiable within the United States. It may also be that the considerable mobility of workers across the states provides a means of insurance that reduces the need for financial transfers.

This brings us to the third argument for equalization payments: as a response to inefficiencies in location decisions. These arise from the likely fiscal externalities that migrants will impose on pre-existing residents through, in particular, congestion effects that drive up the per capita cost of providing public services. Judicious transfers to (so discouraging emigration from) states offering relatively low net fiscal benefits—which one would expect to be the poorer ones —may for this reason prove beneficial to both recipient and donor. But despite significant and systematic internal migration in the United States, this efficiency consideration has received far less attention in the United States than it has, most notably, in Canada. Why?

Three potential explanations come particularly to mind. First, it may simply be that the efficiency gains to be had are small, as Watson (1986) argues to have been the case for Canada. Second, while the potential for Pareto improvement suggests that beneficial transfers might emerge voluntarily,[33] perhaps the constitutional prohibition on states making agreements among themselves without Congressional approval has prevented the emergence of the agreements between subsets of states that would be required; it is hard, however, to detect signs of any very great suppressed pressures. Third, perhaps the United States recognized earlier than others that equalization schemes can also create efficiency losses by encouraging game playing by the states. Smart and Bird (1996) provide an intriguing account of this in the Canadian context. The equalization formula used there partially insulates each province against the main revenue cost of raising its tax rate, since any induced contraction in its tax base—an increase in tobacco taxes reducing expenditure on cigarettes, say—is in effect regarded as increasing its neediness and so entitling it to greater equalization receipts. The consequence is clear: receiving provinces are encouraged to set excessively high tax rates. It may be that such efficiency losses from equalization are sufficiently high that it is best not attempted.

American federalism is strong, at least in the sense—perhaps the only one that matters—of there being no significant regional separatist movement. It would be too much to conclude that this is because of, rather than despite, the absence of explicit equalization: not least, the experience of a Civil War fought to rule out secession doubtless still leaves its mark. Certainly, though, equalization has not gone hand in hand with national unity in, for example, Canada or Yugoslavia: the resentment of the "haves" has been all too clear. One can, it seems, go a long way toward explaining the absence of an interstate equalization system without invoking any American exceptionalism.

WHAT ROLE FOR THE EARNED INCOME TAX CREDIT?

The EITC seems to be widely reckoned a success. Certainly, it has grown substantially since its birth in 1975, to the point at which in 1997 it is expected to cost the federal government about $27 billion (which is about two percent of total federal receipts).[34] The EITC has been described as the "cornerstone of the Clinton administration's welfare reform agenda,"[35] with its growth projected to continue. This perceived success has not been lost on the new British Chancellor, whose budget speech in July 1997 indicated that the government would "consider at an early stage the advantages of introducing a new in-work tax credit for low-paid workers. [This] would draw upon the successful experience of the Earned Income Tax Credit, which helps reduce in-work poverty and now helps 19 million low paid workers."[36] The U.S. experience with the EITC is thus currently of special interest to British observers.

The EITC is a refundable credit against the federal income tax. An interesting and distinctive feature is that at low levels of earnings the amount of the credit increases with income, so that the scheme acts as a marginal earnings subsidy; that is, the effective marginal rate of tax on earned income is *negative* at low earnings. In 1996, for example, the credit rate for a taxpayer with two children was 40 percent, up to an annual earnings level of $8,425; within this "phase in" range, earning an additional dollar actually brought $1.40 into the house.[37] Above this earnings ceiling, the amount payable ($3,370 in the running example) remains constant until another ceiling is reached and the benefit starts to be phased out (at a rate of 21.06 percent).

It is not the idea of a refundable tax credit that is novel from the British perspective—a scheme of this kind was indeed discussed in a 1972 Green paper—but rather the notion of a marginal subsidy on earnings.[38] Thus, our concern here will not be to judge the success or failure of the EITC—which requires placing it in the wider context of a complex tax-transfer system (of which more later) and evaluating, *inter alia*, its labor supply effects and the potential for fraud that has been a continuing concern[39]—but with a question of deeper principle that it raises: what role, if any, do marginal earnings subsidies have in optimal tax-transfer schemes?

The answer is not as simple as it might seem. Consider the lowest earning individual in the United States, and suppose this person's earnings lie in a range over which a marginal earnings subsidy applies. Imagine now a reform that reduces the marginal subsidy rate on this person while leaving her net income unchanged at her initial level of earnings. This reform will certainly leave this lowest earner no less happy. She can achieve exactly the same combination of leisure and consumption as before simply by working exactly as hard as before, so that, if she chooses to change her behavior, it can only be because doing so makes her even happier. Moreover, the government will find that its net revenue rises. Since the individual faces a higher marginal tax rate than before, any change in her effort will be in the direction of working less; and, since her earnings are being subsidized, this will reduce the government's outlays. Starting from any situation in which the earnings of the poorest are subsidized at the margin, one can thus reduce that subsidy in such a way that both the welfare of the poorest earner and the government's revenues are increased. The conclusion to which this argument points—that marginal earnings subsidies cannot possibly be optimal—is a direct implication of the seemingly innocuous and little-remarked result in Mirrlees (1971) that the optimal marginal tax rate is always somewhere between zero and one.

Does this then mean that there is no good argument for a marginal earnings subsidy?

One potential rationale comes from supposing that policymakers care not about the welfare of the poor—which will reflect, among other things, the number of hours they work—but only about their disposable incomes. In practice, discussions of poverty do indeed focus on incomes rather than, for example, the possibility that the poor may be holding multiple jobs to secure those incomes. If no significance is attached to the number of hours worked, then reducing a preexisting marginal earnings subsidy in the way described above is no longer an unambiguously sensible thing to do: recall that one of the consequences of such a reduction is to induce the poorest worker to work less hard, and so to earn a lower income. With such a nonwelfarist emphasis on income,

encouraging the poorest to earn more by subsidizing their earnings is indeed optimal.[40]

A very different line of argument[41] rests on the existence of involuntary unemployment, which is assumed away in the (standard) conceptual frameworks used above. By subsidizing wages, one may hope to both expand employment and increase the net wage of those in work. Moreover, if the employment response is sufficiently great, the revenue cost of the wage subsidy may be more than offset by the reduced cost of supporting the unemployed; even the unemployed could then be made better off by increasing the level of benefit paid to them. And firms, too, should surely be better off, since one would expect them to be able to share in the financial benefit of the subsidy. In a context of involuntary unemployment, subsidizing earnings thus holds some prospect of a Pareto improvement, with all—unemployed, employed, employers, and the Treasury—benefiting.

The precise impact of an earnings subsidy will depend on the cause of unemployment. The working paper version of this paper considers the case in which unemployment emerges from efficient bargaining between unions (who care about both wages and employment) and profit-maximizing firms. The analysis confirms the possibility of a Pareto improvement, but emphasizes that this is by no means assured. An earnings subsidy in this model certainly reduces unemployment and increases profits. The government's revenues increase, as one would expect, only if the expansion of employment is sufficiently large and/or the unemployment benefit saved on each person moved into work is sufficiently high. Perhaps surprisingly, however, it emerges that the net wage received by the employed (inclusive of the subsidy) may quite plausibly actually *fall* as the earnings subsidy is increased; the intuition, it seems, is that a subsidy makes it more attractive for the union—acting in the interests of all its members, not just the employed—to accept offers involving low gross wages (and high employment), because these no longer imply such low consumption for those in work.

Though clearly model-specific, this result serves to draw attention to one key aspect of the EITC that seems to have been little studied: the extent to which it reduces the gross wage paid by employers rather than increases the net wage received by employees. The conventional assumption on this incidence issue—in both the theoretical optimal taxation literature referred to above and such empirical studies of the effects of the EITC on labor supply as that of Dickert et al. (1995)—is that the net wage to the worker rises by the full amount of the subsidy. In practice, of course, one would typically expect—as the result above emphasizes—that at least part of the benefit will be taken by employers. Indeed, such a reduction in the gross wage has a key role to play in generating the expansionary effect on employment that seems to be a central part of the subsidy's rationale. Any assessment of the impact of an EITC must take some view on this incidence issue. Theory indicates some of the factors likely to be important: in the efficient bargaining framework mentioned above, for example, the increase in the net wage brought about by an increase in the subsidy rate is greater the higher is the replacement ratio (workers then having a more attractive outside option) and the less elastic is the demand for labor[42] (employers then being willing to pay more to prevent workers taking the option of unemploy-ment).[43] Here, as in many other areas of tax policy, our empirical knowledge on key questions of incidence lags far behind both theory and the empirical study of lesser but more tractable problems.

Unemployment may thus create a role for the marginal subsidization of earnings that is precluded in the classic optimal tax setting. In practice, however, the effect, and hence potential rationale for the EITC, is further and profoundly affected by its likely interaction with other instruments of policy. Two such linkages stand out.

The first is that with the minimum wage. Unlike the United States, the United Kingdom has never had a national minimum wage. The incoming Labour government, however, has a manifesto commitment to introduce one. And there may then be merit in seeking to mitigate the potentially adverse employment effects of a minimum wage by an accompanying earnings subsidy. Or, put differently, the presence of a minimum wage may limit the extent to which the benefits of an earnings subsidy can be reaped by employers in the form of a reduced wage.

The second set of interactions are those with other taxes and means-tested benefits, which tend to raise marginal tax rates on the poor. Holtzblatt et al. (1994) report that, in 1993, the mar-ginal subsidy received by those in the "phase-in" range of the EITC—about 3.5 million filers—was large enough to offset income and payroll taxes, the average marginal rate for this group being –21.3 percent. But, those also receiving foodstamps and AFDC[44] would be very likely to face positive marginal rates overall.[45] Moreover, most recipients of EITC—about 90 percent[46]—are not in the phase-in range. In practice, the main effect of the EITC seems to be to imply low effective marginal rates at the lower reaches of the earnings distribution, not negative ones. The observation is simple, but fundamental, and perhaps has lessons for the United Kingdom: if the important structural feature of the EITC in practice is not the negative marginal rate that it carries, in itself, but rather the effect it has in reducing the effective wedge between net and gross real wages of the poorest workers, perhaps it would not be as radical an addition to the armory of instruments currently deployed in the United Kingdom as it might at first seem. The real issue that it highlights, it seems, is the choice between delivering benefits through the tax or welfare systems.

SECRETS, LOBBIES, AND CONSTITUTIONS

Some of the most striking differences between tax policy in the United States and United Kingdom are in the way in which it is made.

To the outsider, the most obvious contrast is in the degree of consultation in the formation of tax policy. In the United States, major tax policy initiatives are developed, marketed, analyzed, and negotiated at great and doubtless often tedious length. In the United Kingdom, they are commonly announced in the annual budget speech of the Chancellor of the Exchequer as, in effect, *fait accompli*. The classic example of this is the 1984 corporation tax reform. Though there had been a Green paper —that is, an official consultative document—on the topic a couple of years previously, this did not consider the option actually adopted and nor, indeed, was there any expectation when the Chancellor rose to make his speech that he would have anything much to say about corporation tax. This contin-

ued budget secrecy—which now results in the Chancellor going into a silent purdah for two months before the budget in the fear that he might say something interesting—is, of course, widely criticized. There have been some signs of greater openness in recent years (Higson, 1995). And, certainly, many major structural reforms are discussed in advance. The windfall tax that the new Labour government has imposed on privatized utilities, for example, was a manifesto commitment and had been widely discussed; and the reference to the EITC in the 1997 budget speech will doubtless stimulate analysis. Less happy —for the openness, if not the effectiveness with which policy is conducted—is the apparent practice of occasionally leaking measures under consideration to the media, allowing the government to market test its ideas without having to enter into any intellectual debate and while also distancing itself from any adverse political reaction. This was the case, for example, of the decision in the 1997 budget to withdraw imputation credits from nontaxpaying pension funds; this was widely anticipated in the financial press, but, of course, could not be discussed by any in authority because of budget secrecy. When in opposition the Labour party promised to ". . . open up the secretive budget process."[47] In office, their first budget contained significant surprises—a cut in the rate of corporation tax, for instance, and an increase in investment allowances—that smacked of furtive business as usual. More promising is the new government's commitment to set out its options in a 'Green budget' to be issued in advance of the annual budget.

The ability of British governments to proceed as they have reflects the vast power that the executive enjoys relative to the legislative and judiciary branches. A government with a majority in the

House of Commons can do pretty much what it wants in terms of tax policy. Thus, it is that, with rare exceptions—usually on quite technical issues, such as the troublesome matter of the tax treatment of dividends paid from overseas income—the measures announced in the Chancellor's budget speech find their way into the Finance Act. In the United States, in contrast, taxing powers are fragmented between the executive (equipped with a Presidential veto), the legislative (home of the tax-writing committees), and the judiciary (guardian of the Constitution) branches. This fragmentation underpins the widespread consultation on tax matters in the United States just discussed. It also has other consequences.

One is the apparently greater vulnerability of tax policymaking in America to lobbying by special interest groups. Making campaign contributions to key figures on Congressional committees is a very direct way of exerting influence on tax policy in the United States. There are no such natural targets in the United Kingdom. This is partly because of tighter rules on campaign financing, though there are other means of rewarding helpful politicians: contributing to their party, for instance, or holding out the prospect of future employment. But the great concentration of tax-making power in the United Kingdom means that there are rather few politicians worth influencing; and those that are have so much power in setting tax policy that the political damage they would suffer from appearing to have been influenced would be much greater. Perhaps, too, the greater ability of parties in power to deliver tax favors (or disfavors) in the United Kingdom enables them to extract their rents in return for fewer favors. In any event, the apparently

greater vulnerability of the U.S. tax system to lobbying is evident in the notoriously wide range of provisions favoring special groups that have typically characterized the U.S. tax code and which have been the particular target of reformers: Aaron and Gale (1996) report that deductions, allowances, and credits in the United States reduce the personal income tax base by about 50 percent. The U.K. tax code is cleaner, with the Treasury, in particular, having traditionally fought hard against special provisions. But British tax policy is not immune to special pleading; the 1997 budget brought special tax breaks for the film industry, for example, just a few paragraphs after the Chancellor had stressed that "[t]he route to success is not for the government to pick winners . . ."[48] A second consequence of fragmentation in the United States—clearly related to the lobbying issue just raised—is the greater complexity of the U.S. system. This is true both on the tax side, as just discussed, and on the spending side; Barfield (1981) quotes the example of there being four different federal water and sewer grant programs, corresponding to the four separate committees of Congress. Joe Pechman, in contrast, once asked a senior U.K. Treasury Official why tax bills in the United Kingdom are so much less complicated than in the United States, to be told it is because "we are bullying Parliament."[49]

A third consequence is a greater difficulty of bringing about significant tax reform in the United States, there being more constituencies to carry along. Perhaps the ease with which a British government—indeed a few people within it—can bring about major tax reform will be looked on with envy by would-be tax reformers in the United States, all too aware of the thin line between checks and balances, on the one hand, and gridlock, on the other. But, consider the poll tax.

A final and fundamental aspect of fragmentation is the pivotal role played by the Constitution, which has shaped U.S. tax policy throughout the nation's history and continues to be a focal point for discussion; in April 1997, for example, a balanced budget amendment failed in Senate by one vote. The United Kingdom, of course, has no written constitution. While the case is sometimes made for acquiring one, this is rarely, if ever, with issues of tax policy in mind.

In the United States, the notion of gaining credibility by writing restrictions into the Constitution is deeply ingrained. From the U.K. perspective, there does seems scope for some skepticism on the ultimate effectiveness of constitutional restrictions. The Canadian Constitution, for instance, restricts the provinces to the use of direct taxation; but this has not stopped them from deploying provincial sales taxes that look, to all but a few smart lawyers, pretty indirect. It is clear too that ill-judged, outdated, or unclear constitutional restrictions can prove extremely costly. Fiscal structures in Australia, for example, currently face upheaval at the prospect of a court decision that may interpret the phrase "duties of excise" in the Constitution in such a way that the states become empowered to levy a general sales tax, which it previously had been assumed they could not do. And was it really worth waiting nearly 20 years for the Sixteenth Amendment to permit federal income taxation? Nor do constitutional restrictions seem necessary for governments to build strong reputations for responsibility in a tax setting. British governments have implemented retrospective "windfall" taxes on capital income twice in 16 years[50] without, it seems, encountering serious credibility problems.

Constitutional restrictions have thus played little role in British national tax policymaking, but the potential reshaping of intergovernmental relations in the coming years—both relative to the European Union and also, perhaps, in terms of devolution within the United Kingdom—means that this may change. The European Union currently places few restrictions on member states' tax policies. There are minimum rates of indirect taxation, but these were very largely nonbinding at the time of their introduction. In any event, the likelihood of tight constraints being imposed by the Union is powerfully limited by the veto that each government currently enjoys over all European tax proposals. Probably, the most important constraint yet imposed by membership of the Union is that the necessary conditions for membership include implementation of a VAT; this was certainly the proximate reason for its adoption in the United Kingdom. Over the coming years, however, it may be that tighter rules will come to be written to deal with a perceived risk of tax competition, and, as the Union expands, the requirement of unanimity on tax matters is likely to come under increasing strain. Within the United Kingdom, too, it is interesting that the Scottish parliament (forthcoming) has been endowed with tax powers that are strictly proscribed: it may raise or lower the basic rate of income tax applied by up to three percentage points. But the still more significant constitutional innovation would come if the United Kingdom were to join the single currency. For this would entail commitment to maintaining a budget deficit of no more than three percent of GDP, with fines levied, under the terms of the stability pact, if this target is missed. It may be that the United Kingdom will have something approaching a balanced budget amendment before the United States does.

Concluding remarks

The U.S. tax system is a construct of awesome power and complexity. This discussion has done scant justice to either attribute (or to the daunting volume of research in the area). The peculiarities considered here have not been fully explained nor have their implications been fully understood. The closer one looks, the more clearly there emerge unresolved issues of politics and federalism. As Gale (1997) remarks, for example, it is not entirely clear why the tax base seems to be so much cleaner in the United Kingdom than in the United States. Nor do we fully understand how vertical relationships in federal structures are likely to affect tax levels and structures. What is certain is that the United Kingdom and other European countries will continue to look to the United States for guidance on the organization of federal structures, and that—in this and other areas—U.S. experience will continue to stimulate and puzzle outsiders. (One immediate puzzle, for example, is why fiscal federalism has not been a much more central issue for American tax economists.) History teaches us, of course, that Britons who take an interest in American tax affairs are liable to end unhappily; but both sides, one hopes, can acquire some wisdom in the process.

ENDNOTES

I am grateful to Richard Bird, Robin Boadway, Bill Gale, Christos Kotsogiannis, Charles McLure, Jr., Jeff Petchey, Peter Short, Janet Stotsky, and David Wildasin for helpful discussions and advice. Mike Devereux and Joel Slemrod provided invaluable guidance and encouragement. Errors, views, and additional peculiarities are my own.

[1] Sinn (1985) estimates, for example, that the encouragement to domestic investment in the Accelerated Cost Recovery System induced capital inflows to the United States on the order of $1 trillion (about seven times the current account deficit of the time).

[2] Few British observers could resist remarking, however, that this strategy was anticipated in the 1984 reform of corporation tax in the United Kingdom.

[3] An excellent account is in Stotsky and Sunley (1994).

[4] Revenue statistics are from OECD (1996), except where indicated.

[5] All states other than Vermont have balanced budget rules, of some form, intended to ensure that current expenditures are not financed by borrowing. Thus, we focus here on federal borrowing. (Including state borrowing, the ratios of deficit and debt to GDP in 1993 were around 5.3 and 84 percent respectively.)

[6] *Economic Report of the President, 1997.*

[7] Steinmo (1993) refers to such evidence.

[8] Peltzman (1980, Table 1).

[9] Lindert (1996, Table 1).

[10] A classic treatment of this is in Meltzer and Richard (1981), and a recent variant is given in Persson and Tabellini (1994).

[11] This result is in Keen (1996). The federal countries are taken in this exercise to be Australia, Canada, Switzerland, and the United States; the centralization of tax powers in Austria and Germany is so great that these countries are regarded for this purpose as unitary.

[12] See, for example, Dahlby (1996), Flowers (1988), and Keen and Kotsogiannis (1996).

[13] Keen (1996).

[14] The lonely exception being the business transfer tax in Michigan, which is essentially a subtraction form of a VAT.

[15] Sales taxes are deployed by 45 states, the District of Columbia, and 6,000 local governments.

[16] Gale et al. (1996).

[17] Gentry and Hubbard (1997).

[18] For simplicity, the arguments in this paragraph abstract from capital market imperfections, intergenerational linkages, and administrative issues.

[19] VIVAT works best on an invoice basis, it being necessary to distinguish sales by the identity of the purchaser.

[20] Bradford et al. (1984), originally published 1977.

[21] See Auerbach and Slemrod (1997).

[22] Production efficiency requires, in a competitive world, that there be no tax wedge between the producer prices faced by different enterprises.

Capital income taxes operate on a quite different wedge, between consumer and producer prices (of deferred consumption).

23 See Gordon and Slemrod (1988).

24 McLure (1997), for example, cites this as a sufficient reason for Kazakhstan not to have adopted cash-flow taxation.

25 There is no explicit equalization in Russia or (though not formally a Federation) China either, though, of course, one does not usually think of these as natural comparators for the United States.

26 President Nixon did propose a thoroughgoing system of revenue-sharing that would have had a strong equalizing component. In the event, however, only relatively minor schemes of this kind were introduced. There is now no general revenue-sharing at the federal level.

27 A fuller comparison, of course, would need to allow for possible interstate differences in the cost of service provision.

28 Figures are calculated from U.S. Bureau of the Census (1995), Tables 27 and 703, CANSIM of Statistics Canada, and Ruding (1992, Table 9B.2). The Swiss figure is for 1989. Australian data are from the Australian Bureau of Statistics Time Series Service (gopher://gopher.statistics.gov.au).

29 Indeed, there is no entirely clear economic distinction between equalization payments—in the sense of unconditional horizontal transfers—and conditional grants. That is, the same pattern of transfers may be represented in many different ways, with different "equalization" components. This reflects the familiar point that a conditional block grant, which is smaller than the amount that the recipient state would otherwise spend on the item concerned, is, in principle, equivalent to an unconditional grant of the same amount. The "flypaper effect"—the feature that grants do not seem as fungible in practice as this argument implies (for reasons that remain unclear; see Hines and Thaler (1995))—diminishes the force of the argument, but the point remains: the concept of an equalization payment is not well-defined.

30 One finds, for instance, the regression line

$$\frac{G}{POP} = 0.53 + 12.31 \left(\frac{GSP}{POP}\right) - 0.063\ POP;$$
$$\quad\quad (0.24)\quad (14.57)\quad\quad\quad\quad\quad (0.56)$$

$$R^2 = 0.07,\ N = 49$$

where G denotes federal grants-in-aid in 1993 ($mn), GSP gross state product in 1991 (the most recent year available ($bn)), POP population in 1993 (mn), and the figures in parentheses are White standard errors. Alaska is excluded, being a clear outlier; inclusion results in a strongly significant positive coefficient on per capita GSP—that is, in a strongly perverse distributional effect.

The data are from U.S. Bureau of the Census (1995), Tables 27 (POP being column 10), 418 (G being column 6), and 703 (GSP being column 10).

31 Bayoumi and Masson (1995) and MacDougall (1977).

32 Bayoumi and Masson (1995), who look instead at the stabilization of state incomes net of federal taxes and transfers, also find a more significant effect than in Canada.

33 As shown by Myers (1990).

34 Analytical Perspectives: The Budget of the United States Government Fiscal Year 1997, Tables 3-1 and 5-6.

35 Dickert et al. (1995), p. 42.

36 Budget Speech, line 133.

37 The scheme was initially restricted to taxpayers with children, but was extended to those without in 1993.

38 The closest U.K. relative to the EITC, Family Credit, operates by bringing earned income up toward some target level that depends on family composition, and thus implies a strictly positive marginal tax rate.

39 On these, see, in particular, Dickert et al. (1995), Scholz (1994, 1996), and—for a direct comparison with Family Credit in the United Kingdom—Whitehouse (1996).

40 This result, established by Kanbur, Keen, and Tuomala (1994), requires that it be optimal for all to work. Altruism defined over the consumption of the poor has similar implications, as is shown by Oswald (1983): it is optimal to subsidize earnings, and hence consumption, because, when making their labor supply decisions, the poor neglect the benefit that their consumption conveys on others.

41 There are others that, for brevity, we do not develop here. Complementarities between skilled and unskilled labor, for example, may create a case for subsidizing the earnings of the unskilled: see Allen (1982). In an efficiency wage setting, to give another example, it may be better to support the low paid by means of a wage subsidy than by a lump sum transfer; for, while the effect of the latter is to reduce the net income of the poor (Ravallion, 1984), the effect of the former, it can be shown, is to increase it.

42 Or rather, the reciprocal of the elasticity of the marginal product of labor, which is the elasticity of labor demand in the competitive case.

43 An overall assessment of the incidence of the EITC would also need to take account of the effect of the ranges in which the subsidy is constant and then phased out; this lends a progressivity to the tax structure that one might expect to encourage employment and depress net wages (there then being some advantage to having several low-paid workers rather than a few high-paid ones). See Koskela and Vilmunen (1996).

44 The eligibility links between these and the EITC are complex.

[45] See Dickert et al. (1995).
[46] Holtzblatt et al. (1994, Table 1).
[47] Andrew Smith M.P., then Shadow Chief Secretary to the Treasury. I owe this quotation to Michael Devereux and Malcolm Gammie.
[48] Budget speech, line 81.
[49] Quoted in Steinmo (1993, p. 145).
[50] On banks in 1981, and now on utilities.

REFERENCES

Aaron, Henry J., and William G. Gale. *Economic Effects of Fundamental Tax Reform.* Washington, D.C.: Brookings Institution Press, 1996a.

Aaron, Henry J., and William G. Gale. "Introduction." In *Economic Effects of Fundamental Tax Reform*, edited by Henry J. Aaron and William G. Gale, 1–25. Washington, D.C.: Brookings Institution Press, 1996b.

Allen, Franklin. "Optimal Linear Income Taxation with General Equilibrium Effects on Wages." *Journal of Public Economics* 17 No. 2 (March, 1982): 135–43.

Asdrubali, Pierfederico, Bent E. Sørensen, and Oved Yosha. "Channels of Interstate Risk Sharing: United States 1963–1990." *Quarterly Journal of Economics* 111 No. 4 (November, 1996): 1081–110.

Auerbach, Alan, Jagadeesh Gokhale, and Laurence J. Kotlikoff. "Generational Accounting: A Meaningful Way to Evaluate Fiscal Policy." *Journal of Economics Perspectives* 8 No. 1 (Winter, 1994): 73–94.

Auerbach, Alan J., and Joel Slemrod. "The Economic Effects of the Tax Reform Act of 1986." *Journal of Economic Literature* 35 No. 2 (June, 1997): 589–632.

Barfield, Claude E. *Rethinking Federalism: Block Grants and Federal, State, and Local Responsibilities.* Washington, D.C.: American Enterprise Institute, 1981.

Bayoumi, Tamim, and Paul R. Masson. "Fiscal Flows in the United States and Canada: Lessons for Monetary Union in Europe." *European Economic Review* 39 No. 2 (February, 1995): 253–74.

Bradford, David F., and the U.S. Treasury Tax Policy Staff. *Blueprints for Basic Tax Reform.* 2d ed. Arlington: Tax Analysts, 1984.

Brennan, H. Geoffrey, and James Buchanan. *The Power to Tax: Analytical Foundations of a Fiscal Constitution.* Cambridge: Cambridge University Press, 1980.

Chamley, Christophe. "Optimal Taxation of Capital Income in General Equilibrium with Infinite Lives." *Econometrica* 54 No. 3 (May, 1986): 607–22.

Dahlby, Bev. "Fiscal Externalities and the Design of Intergovernmental Grants." *International Tax and Public Finance* 3 No. 3 (July, 1996): 397–412.

Diamond, Peter, and James Mirrlees. "Optimal Taxation and Public Production I: Production Efficiency." *American Economic Review* 61 No. 1 (March, 1971): 8–27.

Diamond, Peter, and James Mirrlees. "Optimal Taxation and Public Production II: Tax Rules." *American Economic Review* 61 No. 3 (June, 1971): 261–78.

Dickert, Stacy, Scott Houser, and John Karl Scholz. "The Earned Income Tax Credit and Transfer Programs: A Study of Labor Market and Program Participation." In *Tax Policy and the Economy* 9, edited by James Poterba, 1–50. Cambridge, MA: MIT Press, 1995.

Feenberg, Daniel, Andrew W. Mitrusi, and James M. Poterba. "Distributional Effects of Adopting a National Retail Sales Tax." In *Tax Policy and the Economy* 11, edited by James Poterba. Cambridge, MA: MIT Press, 1997.

Flowers, Marilyn. "Shared Tax Sources in a Leviathan Model of Federalism." *Public Finance Quarterly* 16 No. 1 (January, 1988): 67–77.

Gale, William G. "What Can America Learn from the British Tax System?" *National Tax Journal* 50 No. 4 (December, 1997): 753–778.

Gale, William G., Scott Houser, and John K. Scholz. "Distributional Effects of Fundamental Tax Reform." In *Economic Effects of Fundamental Tax Reform*, edited by Henry J. Aaron and William G. Gale, 281–315, 318–20. Washington, D.C.: Brookings Institution Press, 1996.

Gentry, William M., and R. Glenn Hubbard. "Distributional Implications of Introducing a Broad-Based Consumption Tax." In *Tax Policy and the Economy* 11, edited by James Poterba. Cambridge, MA: MIT Press, 1997.

Gordon, Roger, and Joel Slemrod. "Do We Collect Any Revenue from Taxing Capital Income?" In *Tax Policy and the Economy* 2, edited by Lawrence Summers, 89–130. Cambridge, MA: MIT Press, 1988.

Hall, Robert, and Alvin Rabushka. *Low Tax, Simple Tax, Flat Tax.* New York: McGraw-Hill, 1983.

Higson, Chris. "The Effectiveness of the Tax Reform Process in the UK." London Business School. Mimeo, 1995.

Hines, James R. Jr., and Richard H. Thaler. "The Flypaper Effect." *Journal of Economic Perspectives* 9 No. 4 (Fall, 1995): 217–26.

Holtzblatt, Janet, Janet McCubbin, and Robert Gillette. "Promoting Work Through the EITC." *National Tax Journal* 47 No. 3 (September, 1994): 591–607.

Kanbur, Ravi, Michael J. Keen, and Matti Tuomala. "Optimal Non-Linear Income Taxation for the Alleviation of Income-Poverty." *European Economic Review* 38 No. 8 (October, 1994): 1613–32.

Keen, Michael J. "Vertical Tax Externalities in the Theory of Fiscal Federalism." International Monetary Fund. Mimeo, 1996.

Keen, Michael J. "Peculiar Institutions: A British Perspective on American Tax Policy." University of Essex. Mimeo, 1997.

Keen, Michael J., and Christos Kotsogiannis. "Federalism and Tax Competition." University of Essex. Mimeo, 1996.

Keen, Michael J., and Stephen Smith. "The Future of Value-Added Tax in the European Union." *Economic Policy: A European Forum* No. 23 (October, 1996): 373–411, 419–20.

King, Mervyn. "Savings and Taxation." In *Public Policy and the Tax System*, edited by Geoffrey M. Heal and Gordon A. Hughes. London: Allen and Unwin, 1980.

Koskela, Erkki, and Jouko Vilmunen. "Tax Progression is Good for Employment in Popular Models of Trade Union Behaviour." *Labour Economics* 3 No. 1 (August, 1996): 65–80.

Lindert, Peter. "The Rise of Social Spending, 1880–1930." *Explorations in Economic History* 31 No. 1 (January, 1994): 1–37.

Lindert, Peter. "What Limits Social Spending?" *Explorations in Economic History* 33 No. 1 (January, 1996): 1–34.

Lucas, Robert E., Jr. "Supply-Side Economics: An Analytical Review." *Oxford Economic Papers* 42 No. 2 (April, 1990): 293–316.

MacDougall, D., and others. *Report of the Study Group on the Role of Public Finance in European Integration.* Brussels: Office for Official Publications of the European Communities, 1977.

McLure, Charles E., Jr. *The Value-Added Tax: Key to Deficit Reduction?* Washington, D.C.: American Enterprise Institute for Public Policy Research, 1987.

McLure, Charles E., Jr. "Tax Reform in Kazakhstan." Stanford University. Mimeo, 1997.

Meade, James E., and others. *The Structure and Reform of Direct Taxation.* London: Allen and Unwin, 1978.

Meltzer, Allan H., and Scott F. Richard. "A Rational Theory of the Size of Government." *Journal of Political Economy* 89 No. 5 (October, 1981): 914–27.

Mirrlees, James A. "An Exploration in the Theory of Optimum Income Taxation." *Review of Economic Studies* 38 No. 114 (April, 1971): 175–208.

Myers, Gordon. "Optimality, Free Mobility and the Regional Authority in a Federation." *Journal of Public Economics* 43 No. 1 (October, 1990): 107–21.

Oates, Wallace E. "Searching for Leviathan." *American Economic Review* 75 No. 4 (September, 1985): 748–57.

OECD. *Revenue Statistics of OECD Member Countries, 1965–1995.* Paris: OECD, 1996.

Oswald, Andrew J. "Altruism, Jealousy and the Theory of Optimal Non-Linear Taxation." *Journal of Public Economics* 20 No. 1 (February, 1983): 77–87.

Peltzman, Sam. "The Growth of Government." *Journal of Law and Economics* 23 No. 2 (October, 1980): 209–87.

Persson, Mats. "Why Are Taxes So High in Egalitarian Societies?" *Scandinavian Journal of Economics* 97 No. 4 (December, 1995): 569–80.

Persson, Torsten, and Guido Tabellini. "Is Inequality Harmful for Growth?" *American Economic Review* 84 No. 3 (June, 1994): 600–21.

Ravallion, Martin. "How Much is a Transfer Payment Worth to a Rural Worker?" *Oxford Economic Papers* 36 No. 3 (November, 1984): 478–89.

Ruding, Onno, and others. *Report of the Committee of Independent Experts on Company Taxation.* Brussels: Commission of the European Communities, 1992.

Sala-i-Martin, Xavier, and Jeffrey Sachs. "Fiscal Federalism and Optimum Currency Areas: Evidence for Europe from the United States." In *Establishing a Central Bank: Issues in Europe and Lessons from the U.S.*, edited by M. Canzoneri, V. Grilli, and P.R. Masson. Cambridge: Cambridge University Press, 1992.

Scholz, John K. "The Earned Income Tax Credit: Participation, Compliance, and Antipoverty Effectiveness." *National Tax Journal* 47 No. 1 (March, 1994): 63–87.

Scholz, John K. "In-Work Benefits in the United States: The Earned Income Tax Credit."

Economic Journal 106 No. 434 (January, 1996): 156–69.

Sinn, Hans-Werner. "Why Taxes Matter: Reagan's Accelerated Cost Recovery System and the U.S. Trade Deficit." *Economic Policy* No. 1 (November, 1985): 240–50.

Smart, Michael, and Richard Bird. "Federal Fiscal Arrangements in Canada: An Analysis of Incentives." University of Toronto Working Paper No. 8. Toronto: International Centre for Tax Studies, 1996.

Sørensen, Bert E., and Oved Yosha. "Income and Consumption Smoothing Among U.S. States: Regions or Clubs?" CEPR Discussion Paper No. 1670. London: Centre for Economic Policy Research, 1997.

Sørensen, Peter B. "From the Global Income Tax to the Dual Income Tax: Recent Tax Reforms in the Nordic Countries." *International Tax and Public Finance* 1 No. 1 (May, 1994): 57–79.

Sørensen, Peter B., ed. *Tax Policy in the Nordic Countries*. London: Macmillan Press (forthcoming), 1997.

Steinmo, Sven. *Taxation and Democracy: Swedish, British, and American Approaches to Financing the Modern State*. New Haven: Yale University Press, 1993.

Stotsky, Janet G., and Emil M. Sunley. "The Tax System of the United States." *Tax Notes International* 9 (December 5, 1994): 1755–83.

U.S. Bureau of the Census. *Statistical Abstract of the United States: 1995*. 115th ed. Lanham, MD: Bernan Press, 1995.

Watson, William G. "An Estimate of the Welfare Gain from Fiscal Equalization." *Canadian Journal of Economics* 19 No. 2 (May, 1986): 298–308.

Whitehouse, Edward. "Designing and Implementing In-Work Benefits." *Economic Journal* 106 No. 434 (January, 1996): 130–41.

INDEX